Born to

Born to Run
The Story of Hector & Jason

C. J. Hill

YouCaxton Publications
Oxford & Shrewsbury

Published by YouCaxton Publications 2020
YCBN: 01

YouCaxton Publications
enquiries@youcaxton.co.uk

DEDICATION

For sublime spirits: Victor; Hector & Jason

'*Thus, from the war of nature, from famine and death, the most exalted object which we are capable of conceiving, namely, the production of the higher animals, directly follows. There is grandeur in this view of life, with its several powers, having been originally breathed into a few forms or into one; and that, whilst this planet has gone cycling on according to the fixed laws of gravity, from so simple a beginning endless forms most beautiful and most wonderful have been, and are being, evolved.*'

On the Origin of Species - Charles Darwin

'*Let Hercules himself do what he may,*
The cat will mew, and dog will have his day.'

Hamlet - William Shakespeare

FOREWORD

1 December 1998 was, for most people, just another day on planet Earth. Another day to be spent working, eating, loving, shopping, surviving. This first day of Winter in *anno domini* 1998 happened to fall on a Tuesday. There were no major global events to mark the day, or portents of great happenings to come, as there might have been in ancient Athens or Rome. It is true that Aston Villa were headed for the top of the Premier League, but even that seemed less than miraculous at the time.

The Gods themselves missed their cue: a spectacular solar eclipse slipped into the following August. Even the weather that December day was unremarkable. For my wife, June, and me, too, no doubt, just another day. We were, as it happens, increasingly anxious about the sudden, frail health of our beloved Golden Retriever, Victor. Even so; just another day.

And just another day, too, in rural Staffordshire. Except, in a straw filled barn, in nowhere in particular, new life stirred - in fact, six new lives stirred - and were *here*.

The happy events of 1 December 1998, then unknown to me, ensured that the years arcing into the new Millennium became the Golden Age of my life; more exuberant and intense, and more full of promise, and earthly pleasure, than I could ever have imagined. These halcyon years spent in the company of Hector & Jason - they were always Hector & Jason, never the other way around - and this earthly pleasure, was never a coincidence, but cause and effect. Hector & Jason were always at the centre of my life, always influencing the mood and tone, always an influence for good, an inspiration, a deep well of joy.

There is very little in this tome about the great political events of the day; no tales of conquest or man's - often violent - struggles; no dredging up of political scandal or human outrage. Little, too, in the way of culture, music or fashion; no economic crises - though goodness knows how many have punctured the serenity of these times - and no commentary on the rise or fall of empires, or the roll-call of changing regimes. Shelley's *Ozymandias* may serve as a warning:

'And on the pedestal these words appear:
"My name is Ozymandias, king of kings:
Look on my works ye mighty, and despair!"
Nothing beside remains. Round the decay
Of this colossal wreck, boundless and bare,
The lone and level sands stretch far away.'

I have, I hope, been alive to most of the significant political and economic events of the last two decades; but, in the end, what affects us, what moves us most, are the memorable or extraordinary things that happen in our own homes, on our own hearths; and in those daily adventures in our own circumscribed universe. Though given a time and space by the great wash of news, events, and flickering pictures that dominate our media-obsessed society, it is the exquisite little tableau in the living memory that *really* count: these are priceless, and immortal.

It is often said that some individuals are 'characters' that stand out from the crowd; they may be lovable rogues, or one of the boys. Hector was one of those guys - bright, crafty, extrovert, brimming with personality and mischief. Always with his own take on the world, and his own highly-calibrated agenda.

It is also said that a very few, ultra-rare individuals have the gift of lighting up a room when they enter, through sheer personal magnetism. James Byron Dean was one of those people. And Elvis Aaron Presley. And Ava Gardner. So, too, Bardot. You will know who thrills you, who *does it,* unutterably, for you. Though not a performer like his brother, his ravishing presence and the matchless warmth of his welcome rendered Jason one of those charismatic personalities - a bringer of unadulterated delight.

The word 'genius' can be ascribed to only a handful of supremely gifted poets, painters and composers - to Shakespeare, Leonardo da Vinci, or to Mozart. And to scientists such as Newton or Einstein. Even to astonishing sportsmen such as Pelé, Muhammed Ali, or Roger Federer. We don't usually describe animals as possessing genius. A peregrine falcon is the fastest flyer in the world, and cheetahs are the quickest land mammal. Other species have better vision than human beings, or better hearing, or have extraordinary abilities that are quite beyond our capacity. Even so, those powers are an aspect or a quality of their nature; part of their evolution and function.

So, when one comes across a Golden Retriever, or a *pair* of Golden Retrievers - usually a breed that comprises solid all-rounders - who are quite extraordinarily different, in a special sense, then the word genius may well apply. During the course of this book, dear reader, you may draw your own conclusions.

Certainly, Hector & Jason became full-on, larger-than-life, super-phenomena, straight out of *Boys Own - Hotspur* or *Wizard*; impossibly dashing and derring-do. They were, for me, the most outrageously alive guys on the face of the planet. As daring, dashing and dynamic a duo as any recorded in the annals of dogdom.

Their almost supernatural gifts ensured that Hector & Jason, as an inseparable band of brothers, rendered life magical. With them I entered the realms of the moon, stars and planets. Anything seemed possible; the world and its mysteries unfurled before us every day, as we explored our expanding universe at exhilarating speed.

This is a tale of two extraordinary 'boys', and their two human carers, over an eventful span of years. Nothing more, nothing less. To share such experience was an absolute joy, and a unique privilege. This book is a record, and a celebration, of two wonderful lives.

This book is also a memoir of love - about love, and written with love - while the memories are still fresh and vibrant. I have tried to make it a beautiful book, as befits two beautiful boys. And as I write, little flutes of memory keep breaking on the surface of the mind...

Kierkegaard said that life is lived forwards, but can only be viewed, and perhaps understood, backwards. I hope that you read *Born to Run: The Story of Hector & Jason* with pleasure: it has been written with deep affection, and deep gratitude. Hector & Jason lit up my life; and that light continues to shine into the future. I hope that - if just for a day - they light up your life, too.

Let us, then, re-discover the magic that is Hector & Jason.

PART 1: SEIZE THE DAY

1: New Birth, New Beginning

We are alone, absolutely alone on this chance planet; amid all the forms of life that surround us, not one, excepting the dog, has made an alliance with us.

Maurice Maeterlinck

No one can fully understand the meaning of love unless he's owned a dog. A dog can show you more honest affection with a flick of his tail than a man can gather through a lifetime of handshakes.

Gene Hill

"*I hope you don't mind, but I've just bought a forest*", I announced, as nonchalantly as I could. Silence. "*It really didn't cost very much. It just came up. I've not even seen it, yet.*"

More silence, but the mood remained up-beat. We were speeding back home - in our trusty, a little rusty, Ford Sierra - returning from a tiny hamlet near Uttoxeter, Staffordshire. We had just re-entered the Black Country, like astronauts re-entering the Earth's atmosphere. Sandwell had never seemed so attractive.

Nothing would daunt us that day. My wife, June, accepted the idea of our new woodland as readily as if I had just indulged in a - nice but naughty - bag of chips. We were excited; elated, even. The last few months had been truly horrible. We had lost our nearest and dearest, our wonderful, irreplaceable, Victor. And now we had just seen two 'boys' who would become our pride and joy. The emotional roller-coaster had been almost too much too bear. We could still hardly believe the almost out-of-body experience that the last few hours had presented.

A few days earlier, seeking consolation and comfort from numbing, visceral grief, June had seen a photograph of a Golden Retriever on the cover of *Dogs Monthly* in a local newsagent, and had bought the magazine, to read and reminisce. Flicking through the pages, she came across an advert, for Golden Retriever pups - near Uttoxeter. "*What do you think?*" she asked, in hesitant tones. "*Let's think about it*", I replied, uncertainly. Overcome and numbed by loss, I had not given much thought to the future. And was it too soon to embark on another adventure...?

The thinking process lasted less than 24 hours. "*Shall we 'phone, and see whether any are still available?*" I suggested. Without further ado, June rang the number given in the magazine. There had been six pups; only two remained - both male. "*Can we arrange to visit and see them, please, with no obligation?*". (After all, the owners/breeders might not find us suitable owner material, and of course we might not gel with the young dogs; or conclude that, after all, this was just a bit too soon). The pups, we learned, were just eight weeks old, and very recently weaned.

The 'phone conversation - with Mr and Mrs Vernon - took place on a Thursday. We were invited to visit their Farm, 'Hall Farm', in the little rural hamlet of Fradswell, the following Saturday morning. We tried hard not to build up our hopes. There was so much that could go wrong, that might not feel *quite* right. Our emotions were raw with recent grief and profound loss, and this might not be the 'right' time for us. Or the visit might present a heaven-sent opportunity. We would find out, one way or another, very shortly.

This particular Saturday - 6 February, 1999 - could have been like any other Winter Saturday: a few grey, unmemorable hours, soon blanked in the memory. Yet that day turned out to be one of the happiest days of our lives. It was on that day that June and I first set eyes on two brothers, who would shortly, and for all time, become known as Hector & Jason.

By the strangest coincidence, the Farm we were due to visit was located in a hamlet - in a remote, rural area of north Staffordshire - where June's own story began. As we discovered, Fradswell is a delightful little village, with over 1,000 years of history. It was a Saxon village before the Normans, and is recorded in the Domesday Book. Was this some strange presentiment, or just one of those peculiar coincidences that life throws up more often than we like to admit? Time would tell.

We set off for the Farm that Saturday morning, trying hard to keep our emotions, and expectations, in check. Then, suddenly, we were there: the Ford Sierra entered an ancient gateway, and rattled up the stony drive. As if waiting to greet us, a young Golden Retriever, standing atop a battered Land Rover, noted the new arrivals. Alerted to our presence, she let out a deep, distinguished bark. It was a voice, strong and resonant, that I would come to know, and love, as gifted to a singular son. This was Jess, the four-year-old mother of six; a working farm-dog, and excellent mother. As we would soon learn, the-boy-who-would-be-Jason had inherited her beautiful pale coat - and that rich, resonant voice. Jess was the model, physically, of Jason, though smaller and more compact - blonde and lovely, and with that soon-to-be-familiar bark. That was the only time I ever saw her. Though twenty years ago, now, I still remember the moment perfectly.

The Farm, as it emerged before our eyes, was a delight to the senses. Old and rambling, its ancient stone walls seemed to have grown naturally out of the earth. The building had an air of permanence, of solidity, but also of mystery. A wood-pile occupied a corner of the yard, a massive axe embedded in a giant oak log. The whole scene reminded me, then, and now, of the huge stone-built edifices that add character and warmth to the Normandy landscape that we already knew so well.

We introduced ourselves to Mr and Mrs Vernon. Mrs Vernon was warm and welcoming. Her husband was a genial, ruddy faced farmer, with a ready smile. The farmer was so at one with his surroundings, so much a part of the place, he could have been carved from the piled oak himself. Mr Vernon led us to an old stone out-building, set a little distance from the Farm house. At the centre of the dark space was a newly constructed miniature 'house', built from sawn timber. It was lit with a large lamp from above, that shone into the body of the little nursery, providing both light and a little warmth. Inside, sitting on a thick bed of straw, were two pups, who wagged their tails in greeting. They were the only puppies not yet to depart the scene of their birth, from the original litter of six. And they were barely eight weeks old.

At the farmer's invitation, we repaired to the Farm itself, carefully carrying the pups, and setting them down in the large, flag-floored living room. Despite the unfamiliarity of this new environment, the pups were unutterably charming as they fussed around us, muzzles nudging, tails wagging. The one lad was a pure, even blonde, which contrasted superbly with his dark eyes and even darker nose. His brother's coat was a bright, glossy chestnut. Even at this stage, it was clear to see that this pup had a small, raised quiff on the crown of his head. This difference in coloration - and perhaps character - between the young lads would continue to excite comment and query whoever we met, and wherever we roamed.

Set down on the floor, the brothers were lively, playful, curious; adorable...

Immediately, we knew that we wanted them - wanted them *both*. They *had* to be ours. How greedy was that? But we just knew. They belonged together, and to us. And they would be superb company for each other - become great friends, as well as brothers. Maybe, for me, there was just the trace of a thought that the gap left by Victor would take a great deal of filling, and this was our attempt to fill it. Two boys would truly extend us. We would throw ourselves into their total care. That instinctive response - to gather them both up into our arms - turned out to be one of the happiest, most joyous decisions we had ever made.

Mr and Mrs Vernon explained that the blonde pup was destined for the Earl of Fradswell, but that the said Earl had not confirmed his interest...sigh of intense relief. It may be that the good Earl had had a dream...and had been forewarned that this dog might take his life in a different, unexpected, and perhaps unwelcome direction. Whatever the reason, it was our huge good fortune. The whole experience at Hall Farm was warm, lovely and intimate, and I knew at once that, from our perspective, it could lead to only one delightful outcome.

But first, there was a bridge to cross, or maybe a hurdle to surmount. Mr and Mrs V probed us gently, but firmly, about our circumstances. *Why did we we want a dog? Where, and how, did we live? How would we look after, care for, our new young charges?*. Carefully, we answered their questions. It reminded me a little of my courtship days, and of the natural solicitude of June's parents. We were glad that Mr and Mrs Vernon took nothing for granted; that we were required to establish our 'dog credentials', good intentions, and personal integrity.

Our responses must have satisfied for, after this rite of passage, we settled terms very easily. In all honesty, I think that June and I would have agreed to anything, that day. Pedigree dogs are not 'cheap'; nor should they be. Moreover, they cost a fortune to care for properly - good food, vets bills, with all manner of extra costs - beds, toys, and a variety of equipment such as collars, leads and feeding bowls. We knew all that, but we didn't mind in the least: we cared only for these superb young lads.

Mr Vernon warned us, with a smile, that these boys would be *"great time wasters"*. Time wasters, maybe; but life-enhancers, for sure. It was our mission to raise, and care for these guys - really care. A sacred pact. And that, as we know, is that - a living, breathing, glowing experience, to dwell on with satisfaction and pride; a team effort, involving the four of us in equal measure. And so, on that day, our destiny was decided. These were brothers who would remain together, and with us; whom no-one, and nothing, could ever tear apart.

Not on that day, surely, since the boys were so young, and we had only just met; nor in that week, or in the month or so that followed; but at some indeterminate point I became truly, utterly smitten. I could *believe* Hector, and quickly became familiar with his ways - not that they were always straightforward, or predictable. He was indeed a deep one, and a life-long surprise. But Jason was pure, delightful enigma. From nowhere, it seemed, I was possessed by an unutterably exquisite thrill. The pulse of paradise passed through me. And I was somewhat awed by him - a feeling that only grew on acquaintance. I was so utterly proud; it was a privilege to call him mine, to be able to say, and know, that he was to be my constant, my truest companion. So it became my almost sacred duty to care for this lad, to protect him, to do him due honour.

But to be able to care for both these brothers, who were so complementary, and who would form such a strong bond, with each other, and with June and me, was a rare privilege indeed.

I remember feeling nervous when we left the pups at the Farm, as we needed to do: the boys were still young, and (though now on their own) perhaps not quite ready to leave mum. And we had arranged a short break in Normandy, after which we would prepare to receive the young boys - preparing our home, their new home, as best we could. We took the precaution, not of leaving a deposit, but of writing a cheque for the whole amount requested by their owners and breeders. They were decent, honourable people; but we were taking no chances.

Little did I realise at the time the deep interconnections between the boys' birthplace, and their breeders, with Norman history. The town of Vernon is historically important within the Eure Department of Normandy. Richard of Vernon, as he became known, was one of the Conqueror's chief lieutenants, and for his invaluable support was named after the town. As well as being awarded Vernon itself, Richard was also granted large estates in England. The Vernon family therefore have a strong Norman connection. So it was fitting that the fine dogs they had bred should be destined to be going 'home' - not merely to suburban Stourbridge, but also to lovely, rural Normandy.

Whilst on our short Winter visit to Normandy, June confided that she had thought of names for the two young lads, who had hitherto been nameless: Hector; and Jason. I thought these were inspired; the boys could not possibly be called anything else. Their names were not only perfect, but perfectly fitting. And we both already knew, without further discussion, which was Hector, and which was Jason. Hector, Prince of Troy and heroic defender of the City, could not have had a more noble canine incarnation than his name-sake. Jason, fearless seeker of the Golden Fleece in romantic adventures across the high seas and dangerous lands, could not have desired a more sublime canine equivalent than his name-sake. And, strange to tell, in all our adventures still to come, we would never meet another Hector, nor yet another Jason.

That handful of Winter days in France were full of excited thought about the future: preparations for the boys, how we would best care for them, and the various arrangements that needed to be made. And anxiety that, despite our careful plans and commitment, something might go awry at the last moment. There was a natural concern that our hopes might, somehow, and for whatever reason, be dashed. I spent this time in Normandy in a kind of agitated anticipation that was at once delicious and yet fraught - like the anticipation of a first evening with a girl one has just met. The mind is in a whirl: all that adrenalin and high hopes. Would she turn up? Would it work? Would she like me? Might it become serious?

The following week, after feverish anxiety, and anticipation - and no unpleasant surprises - (and with me stuck, in a welter of expectation, in the office) June raced up to Hall Farm in the Sierra to collect the young Hector & Jason. It was a big wrench for the pups and, not surprisingly, they were car-sick on the journey 'home'. Perhaps Jason's dislike of cars can be dated from this time. Whilst, from a tender age, Hector would leap into the back of a car with both relish and athletic ease, Jason would not budge from *terra firma* and always had to be lifted into the car: first his front legs, and then the back. And so it remained. Many a passer-by would enquire whether Jason had a physical problem of some sort. I always laughed; this was the most athletic dog on the planet; but he had firm views of his own!

I rushed home from work that singular afternoon, eager and wondrous: *there* they were, as I will always remember them; the brothers, a little fazed, but beginning to explore and settle into their strange new home - replete with carpets, cats, and two homo sapiens who had become their anxious, but so-proud, new carers.

We knew that raising Hector & Jason, looking after them properly, and making them happy, would be a life's mission, but also a 'stretch'. They would quickly become large dogs, with a variety of needs and, as we know, a dog is for life.

Fortunately, money was not a particular problem. Though not wealthy by the world's standards, we both had regular jobs, and reasonable incomes. Also, there were no children: Hector & Jason would be our over-riding pre-occupation. The biggest challenge would be time - time to care for them, time to enjoy them. Until now, June and I had both 'enjoyed' full time careers, and we decided to change all that. I had already accomplished more than a quarter of a century of nose-to-the-grindstone activity, and we concluded that this was the ideal time to pare down my working commitments, and reduce my working week to three days.

Luckily, I had a sympathetic employer. Even so, I was informed in grave tones that, in addition to losing 40% of my salary, 'going part-time' would inevitably impact upon my eventual pension income. In my mid-40s and at the height of my earning power, these factors might have been expected to weigh heavily on my decision. They didn't. Strangely, for one steeped in financial wisdom, and studying to become a financial adviser, I had decided that different priorities should apply.

Since not all the riches of King Midas could re-create time - not even a day - and since no-one has yet found a way to take their wealth on to their next journey, I chose to politely ignore all advice. For once, financial planning was kicked into touch. The future could take care of itself. Heart had triumphed over head. This was our time.

I never did return to full time work: three days per week would henceforth become my normal working routine. It was one of my wisest, sanest decisions - ever.

When, a couple of years later, I was head-hunted for a new, full-time role, I insisted on an arrangement that allowed me to work at home on two days per week. Though not perfect, this weekly pattern enabled me to share more time with Hector & Jason. For four years I was a happy member of staff, and H&J were happier boys for each of those super years. Every year thereafter followed a similar, three-day, working pattern.

In addition, we already had an excellent support system in place, with good, dog-loving neighbours, happy to walk H&J at lunchtime on the three days that I was obliged to attend the office.

It was an auspicious, pregnant beginning. We somehow knew, from the conjoining of stars bringing us delightfully together, that we were destined for great things.

And there was a further auspicious connexion. The Vernon's were not the only grand family to accompany William in 1066. From their Château of Monfreville in what is now the world-famous butter-producing village of Isigny-sur-Mer, near Bayeux, Hugues d'Isigny and his son Robert rode and sailed to England with their inspirational leader. The family eventually settled in Lincolnshire, and the name d'Isigny eventually became Anglicised to Disney. The first of the illustrious clan to move to America was Will Disney, who landed in Maryland in 1677. If there is a single association that best exemplifies the many links between Hector, Jason and Normandy, it is surely that conveyed by the single word 'Disney': the heroic fantasy, the feel-good quality, the flights-of-fancy, and the overwhelming *joie de vivre* that would illuminate every aspect of our daily lives.

Like those ancient Normans on the high seas, we were all set to begin a startling new adventure, and to unleash a new phenomenon on the world.

Together, they were Hector & Jason. A special destiny awaited both them - and us.

This is their story.

2: First Stirrings

I think dogs are the most amazing creatures; they give unconditional love. For me they are the role model for being alive.

Gilda Radner

No matter how little money and how few possessions you own, having a dog makes you rich.

Louis Sabin

My first memories of dogs are my first memories. These memories, clear but now long ago, are of our family pet dog, Judy, when I was barely three years old.

These first memories are sepia-toned: Judy, a border collie, was expecting puppies, and duly gave birth to - I think - six healthy pups, in a half-buried old Anderson shelter near the bottom of our long garden. In truth, our Victorian house, and orchard-garden, was home to a menagerie of dogs, cats, rabbits, guinea pigs, mice, canaries - and chickens, plump Rhode Island Reds that produced the most sumptuous eggs. But, together with Ginger the cat, it is the dogs that I remember most vividly.

Judy's young progeny were quickly dispersed to neighbours, family and friends. Two of the pups stayed close to home: Tim, who moved in with neighbours in our street, and Jack, who was acquired - I use the term loosely - by my father's parents, who lived just a few streets away.

I grew up on the cusp of the Stour Valley; Stour Valley, Black Country, that is, in the English West Midlands - not the more glamorous Stour Valley in rural Dorset. This Stour Valley is a small oasis of green, dotted with clumps of hawthorn and ash; the modest, brackish river and undulating fields hemmed in and encircled by an invading urban congestion, and an industrial sprawl that, even then, threatened to spill over the Valley's banks.

We are shaped, at least to a degree, by our environment. 'Made in the Black Country' is what I was, and am, even if Dudley, and the Black Country were, by the 1950s, markedly different places to the nail-making, chain-making, coal-producing era of the almost unremittingly bleak 1850s - or, indeed, the 1750s. The pressure of unrelenting hard and heavy work - digging coal, working metal - made the people what they are. A brutal industrialisation fashioned the community's culture, with a factory-hardened new culture moulded from the colliery, foundry and chain works. I admire the grit of the area's down-to-earth people, while I deplore the conditions in which they were condemned to work and live. And, most of all, I admire the almost miraculous art that emanated from the hands and minds of the area's greatest sons, and in particular from the glass makers, such as the cameo glass artists John Northwood and George Woodall.

Although born a good 50 years after the demise of the 'Great White Queen', I was, I believe, the last Victorian child. I was expected to be seen and not heard, to do as I was bid, and to observe my parents strictures as though they were scripture. Perhaps because of this uncompromising upbringing, I became a child who listened, and watched. I was full of wonder. Very quickly, my early memories transmuted into 3-D, technicolour.

A full 250 years after Dudley's emergence as the centre of the new, industrialised world, this world still displayed the scars and wounds of an epoch-changing cataclysm. In this adult world, smoke and fire still belched from chimney, furnace and factory, and grime, soot and 'pea-soup' fogs choked the earth and air. Every neighbours' washing - white sheets, white vests, white pants - was strung out in serried ranks each Monday morning, more in hope than belief that it would actually stay white. Britain's 'post-Industrial Revolution' was still decades away. There were corner shops on every street corner, but there was still no Tesco on every street corner. The Black Country is proud and insular in equal measure. Together with its neighbour, Birmingham, the Black Country was the anchor-chain to Britain's boast to being 'the workshop of the world'. The area derived its name from a description by the American Consul to Birmingham, Elihu Burrett, who in 1863 described it as "*black by day and red by night*". In *The Old Curiosity Shop* (1841), Dickens describes how the area's factory chimneys "*poured out their plague of smoke, obscured the light, and made foul the melancholy air."*

There are many who have not forgiven Jane Austen's caustic reference to this region, in her masterpiece, *Emma*, where Mrs Elton observes, with casual callousness: *"They came from Birmingham, which is not a place to promise much, you know, Mr Weston. I always say there is something direful in the sound."* Since *Emma* is a work of fiction, and Mrs Elton one of Austen's most gloriously insufferable creations, it would be unwise to attach too much significance to this description as representing Austen's own views. Even so, since my visit to Austen's home at Chawton, a gnawing thought lingers that genius often enriches us, through the grit in the oyster shell.

In September 1826, a decade or so after the publication of *Emma*, William Cobbett passed this way, praising the nearby rural idyll of Worcestershire in his *Rural Rides*. After describing the Cathedral as *'indeed, a poor thing, compared with any of the others, except that of Hereford'*, (oh dear) Cobbett goes on to call Worcester (City) itself *'the very best I ever saw'* and *'in character with the beautiful and rich country in the midst of which it lies.'*

However, that is as close to the Black Country as the great man ventures, before retreating to beatific Hampshire. A little later, Manchester and Leeds are described as *'Hell-Holes'*. Perhaps the Black Country was also in Cobbett's thoughts, as a poisoned cauldron of filth and slavery.

It cuts both ways. In *A Rough Ride to the Future*, Professor James Lovelock declares that Newcomen's invention of the steam engine was perhaps the most significant event in the history of the planet since the evolution of photosynthesis, two billion years earlier. Newcomen's invention kick-started the Industrial Revolution - the global phenomenon that continues to shape and re-shape our world. Lovelock says: *'It was the cause of our glory and our predicament. It may have changed the Earth for ever.'* Newcomen's revolutionary steam engine was first employed at a coal pit, in 1712 - in Dudley.

The Stourbridge Lion, built by Foster, Rastrick & Co in 1829, was the first locomotive to operate commercially in the United States. And Black Country factories were also responsible for the iron skeleton that holds up the Palace of Westminster, and for the very substance -

glass and iron - of Paxton's famous Crystal Palace, home of the Great Exhibition in 1851.

In 1832, around the same time as Cobbett and Dickens were venting their spleen on the Black Country's transformation, the inimitable JMW Turner's painting, *Dudley* reveals a landscape gorged with furnace, fire and fury: as though newly erupted from a molten underworld. An unstoppable, Promethean energy is unleashed on an unsuspecting world. The fearful image proclaims: "I am the future".

If Cobbett - like Turner - had visited the Black Country of the 1820s, and been able to return, time-traveller steed-style, in the 1950s, he would have found that it had retained its essential character, like lettering through rock. The lettering may have grown fainter, but the adult world in which I grew up was still one of belching chimney-stacks, soot-smeared faces and beer gulped gratefully in smoke-rich rooms.

My childhood here was an age and time that saw Captain, the shire-horse, drawing Mr Dawes's cart to our little street, and offering a menagerie of house-hold staples to a community which still lived largely without the luxury of the motor-car. Captain was a magnificent chestnut, with white socks and a white blaze down his muzzle; we children would reward the gentle beast with our stale bread crusts, and he would nod his noble head in appreciation.

Another abiding memory is that of Prime Minister Harold Macmillan's ebullient speech, when he declared: "*Let us be frank about it. Most of our people have never had it so good.*" The speech was made on 20 July 1957 - the day after my 5th birthday. Super Mac's hubristic peroration gave rise to one of my father's infamous rants. Dad had only recently returned from Canada, where he had searched for a new life for his family. It was *new* all right, but this brave new life turned out to be less appealing than the one available in the Old World. We were to stay 'put' in our little corner of the Black Country; no Rockies or Niagara for us.

Even so, the Stour Valley was a little magic space, and a perfect, enchanted playground for energetic boys: rattling down tracks on home-made 'trolleys', climbing gnarled trees, tobogganing down the grassy banks, and riding the chained horses, bareback. This secret child's world was one of Tarzan-like swings, woodland camps, sledges, flying arrows, fishing for sticklebacks, newts and tadpoles, and slurping sherbets and *Lucky Bags* with unrestrained enjoyment. And, on Summer evenings, we would gather under the gas-light, marvelling at the iridescence of tiger moths, and the ghostly glistening of chestnut gourds. It was a time when bright-eyed schoolboys delighted in dark, musty, corner shops such as Kendall's and Annie Kyers, where we would fill our flannel pockets with sweet delicacies, chocolate bars, trick novelties and 'stink bombs'. And it was a time when dogs roamed the unreformed streets like furry dinosaurs.

This was still a 'cup of sugar, doors left unlocked' culture, though, inevitably, there was a darker side. Notably, the gulag, entered through the school gates, where sadism was tempered by a thin spread of learning. A school-friend once proclaimed, rather airily, that Jesus was 'a teacher'. "*Not at our school*", I replied, with some feeling. Bullying, however, was not confined to the classroom. Vicious fist-and-foot fights, urged on by cheering crowds, were a regular feature of the after-hours curriculum. These fights would continue until, at last, one of the protagonists lay sprawled in a bloody heap. Since I stood out as being a little different - a shy and bookish lad - I was lucky to avoid being goaded into one of these grisly, gladiatorial encounters. Little did I realise at the time, but such public entertainments perhaps betrayed signs of a stuttering progress - since no animals were hurt during these pugilistic performances. A mere hundred years earlier, cock-fights - or dog fights - were a favoured means of settling scores and deciding who became King of the Dung-heap.

In wider society, the film of civility was often sheared by rough currents beneath. A brutalised community's simmering resentment, and myopic outlook on life, saw casual violence as the answer to every problem. A menacing Cold War chasm between Man and Child frustrated understanding and festered alienation. These worlds - of a narrow-disciplined, and abusive 'school', which corrupted every relationship within it, and that of the 'grown ups', and their stultifying oppression - joined and over-lapped. Even my errant footballs, trespassing on to a neighbour's garden, would be returned, slashed angrily with a knife. We were quite unaware - and would have been astonished to learn - that the bungalow's modest frontage, with its single-glazed window panes, harboured a world-class collection of antique glass crystal.

Rare acts of kindness penetrated the gloom. The spotlight of fame shone briefly on Dunn's Bank when a neighbour, Mr Folkes, won the football pools. At the party held to celebrate this, literally, good fortune, each of the children in the street was presented with a £1 note (perhaps £50 today). Such generosity of spirit stood out like a beacon - a pound was a veritable fortune to a small boy. For me, it was an object lesson in disinterested generosity– of the kindness of strangers, and the importance of giving - that I would never forget; such lessons would prove invaluable in the adult world-to-come. A short time later, the Folkes's sold up and moved on - no doubt to a more salubrious neighbourhood. I would never see them again.

There are, perhaps, two titanic forces unifying these distant worlds; the distinct worlds of the Man and Child, and those separating the '50s and the present. One of these forces is benign, joyful, even; the other, less so. That less benign unifying force is our near obsession with economic 'progress', 'development' and 'growth', that spread their dark shadow over the 1950s as they did the Nineties and the Noughties - and onwards still. At its most benign, this force has helped transform an archaic, dangerously outmoded, carbon-hungry economy into a cleaner, perhaps greener, means to greater prosperity. At its worst such progress has involved trashing the livelihoods and hope of a generation, and burying alive every wild flower, pond and copse beneath concrete and asphalt.

As a ten or twelve year old boy, I had probably never heard of Gerard Manley Hopkins. However, the yearning of my heart was always thus:

> *'What would the world be, once bereft*
> *Of wet and of wildness? Let them be left,*
> *O let them be left, wildness and wet;*
> *Long live the weeds and the wilderness yet.'*

My natural instincts responded to the reality of 300 years of stultifying industrialisation on lives and landscape - but they responded *in extremis*, in reaching out to the remaining butterflies and birds. So, in that sense I am with Austen, Cobbett and Dickens - but I stayed, to make my own modest contribution to the natural world. And, as adults, from June's and my little house on the edge of the Black Country, we worked, and planned, and brought our lives, and the lives of those we cared for, to fruition.

Remarkably, the Stour Valley itself has hardly changed; the river itself, and its steep valley sides, providing unpromising material for development. But the worlds we then knew - those of the Adult and the Child - have now disappeared, utterly. The Black Country is no longer black - merely grey. Those worlds can be recalled only through memory, and in still-familiar walks with one's dogs. These can conjure memory, and connect the old, strange and forgotten worlds, with a new world in a still-familiar landscape.

The other unifying force was - is - music: first Elvis, and then the minor miracle of *The Beatles* – and *The Beach Boys* - sprinkling gold dust over a new generation - my generation - and glistening and gladdening our senses then, and now; and glimmering and glittering into the future. Even in recent years, Hector & Jason in tow, I would play *Pet Sounds*, and play *Rubber Soul*, whilst hacking around in local traffic - perhaps shopping, or an excursion to visit my parents. These albums remain transformational, joyful - young men's fizz and optimism - still lighting our everyday lives and charging our hearts.

In these far-off days, the '50s and early '60s, many dogs lived quite different lives to the canines of today. These pets were distinctive and characterful: the result of happen-stance and chance meetings - and matings - and mongrels through and through. Many were 'shown the door' in the morning, and allowed to roam at will among the streets, rough ground and parks that made up the local neighbourhood. They were not expected back at any particular hour, but would dutifully report home when fatigue, boredom or hunger had got the better of them. They were not picked up by diligent dog wardens, and were not regarded as strays. Neighbours knew their local dogs, and were content to watch them sniff, roam and defecate at will, and all day long. The culture that formed me now seems as alien as our contemporary, more neurotic doggy ways would be to 1950s Britain.

One or two exceptions to this picture of beatific *laissez faire* must rather painfully prove the rule. An early memory, shocking and sad, is of a neighbour's brutalised German Shepherds ('Alsatians' to us) breaking out of their steel stockade and embarking on a terrifying rampage - attacking and causing appalling injuries to poor, gentle Judy. She never recovered from this vicious attack, and was soon lost to us for ever.

Roll forward a handful of years, and another neighbour's young, rangy, hound inveigled his way through our ramshackle fence, and into our looking-glass garden, where he terrorised and traumatised our flock of free-range chickens, leaving a trail of utter carnage in his wake. For me, these were early, shocking, lessons. *Canis lupus familiaris*, it seemed, could be a mixed blessing.

There remained a continuity, of sorts. All through the mid and late '50s, and well into the shining '60s, while Elvis, and then *The Beatles*, were dominating popular culture, Judy's son, Tim, reigned supreme. In this quiet backwater there were precious few vehicles passing along our little road - the modest thoroughfare had only recently been metalled - and it was still something of an event for a car to pass by our house. Tim was doggedly determined to keep it that way. From the time of Elvis's pulsating *Hound Dog* through to The Fab Four's *'Got to get you* (for Tim - *out of) my life'*, Tim patrolled his patch, intent on 'escorting' every interloper to the very edge of his known universe.

For a decade or more, Tim performed his heroic, solo mission to chase away as many motorbikes and cars as possible - chase them to the end of the street, and out beyond his ken. Since Tim lived at the end of a road that led to nowhere, the cars and bikes simply had to travel around a bend, and up the hill, at last veering away, and disappearing from view. Tim surely thought that he was uniquely successful in chasing these iron monsters out of his own little patch of Heaven, and must have brought a quiet satisfaction to his calmer moments.

We always knew when a car was passing - the doughty defender would bark incessantly whilst chasing the metal monsters. Tim reminds me of Churchill's quip about his dog, Rufus: *"Our dog chases people on a bike. We've had to take it off him."* Amazingly, as far as I know, there were no complaints, and no mishaps; Tim was an essential part of the local landscape. And there was a desperate courage in all this, like preventing loggers from entering virgin rainforest. Partly because of the (merely) once-hourly event of a car passing by, and partly because he was so adroit, Tim lived to a ripe old age. Dogs such as Tim were very streetwise; the less streetwise 'brothers' had short lives, and un-remarked deaths.

I recall walking - mostly, running with - Jack, to help out my elderly grandparents. In those days, everyone over 60 years of age was regarded as old, and regarded themselves as old. Jack was generally confined to his house and garden, so I enjoyed walking this friendly, happy lad as often as possible. My grandparents lived in a war-built, white-washed 'pre-fab', a bare half-mile from our own home. My clearest memory of Jack is of running with him, as fast as we both could go, along the grass verges, and up and down the local pavement near our homes. I was young, energetic and very fit; luckily, so was Jack, and he seemed to find these walks - possibly the only ones he ever had - as exhilarating as I did. Running to-and-fro encompassed Jack's small but happy world.

Indeed, I was always running, with or without Jack: running to school, running back from school, running to and around our local Lye woods. While running, I felt an exhilaration, a power and a freedom that was almost intoxicating. Every Wednesday I would eagerly await my 'comic' - in my case, *Victor*. My favourite character was the working-class athlete, Alf Tupper, the *Tough of the Track* who, inspired by his daily diet of fish & chips, would compete manfully, and against the odds, with toffee-nosed, glass-accented opponents. I may have seen a little of Alf in myself. Fish & chips has always been a favourite. As an adult, I have dined at Michelin-starred restaurants, but the fish & chips I was served as a boy - wrapped in newspaper, steaming hot, and smelling of vaporised vinegar - I would happily consume as my own last supper.

Perhaps the inhospitable world that I inhabited - a strange, raw mix of the familiar and the hostile - inspired this love of running. I loved, always loved, running - usually with a favourite song in my heart - along the ragged coppice, and through the crooked, Victorian terraces, to school - and back. Running freed me, if only for a moment, from a regimented, oppressive, dreary, pea-soup and jelly world. Running gave me escape, and released me into a different world, a world of wonder, and delight in the realm of nature.

And my love of running became a life-long passion. From this time onwards I watched my favourite athletes on our small, black-and-white TV - the bare-footed Bruce Tulloh, Derek Ibbotson, and Chris Brasher. They were the first of many athlete 'heroes'. This was a sport that did not seem to need an exclusive education, or expensive equipment, in order to succeed. One needed only talent, training, and the will to win. Pure *Chariots of Fire*. There was irony here, if I could have seen it, since many of the athletes I doted on were from the very backgrounds represented by Alf Tupper's opponents.

Wind forward a year or so - I was about eleven years of age - and we spent one of our rare family holidays in a tiny, ramshackle caravan in the middle of a huge hill-farm in North Wales - Talsarnau. Two adults and three young boys, squeezed and tucked into an optimistically styled 'four berth' caravan in the middle of nowhere. The farm consisted of 10,000 acres of that distinctive, close-cropped Welsh mountain-side, bordering the North Wales coast. I could walk, and run, along these majestic hills, seemingly forever. The rolling hills eventually merged on to a beach, popular not with bathers but with night fishermen, fishing for sea bass, by the light of a glittering moon.

That anyone could actually own 10,000 acres was totally outside my knowledge or comprehension. But I loved it. I loved hunting for sea bass and flounder trapped by snares on the retreating tide. I loved helping the crusty, but kindly, old farmer, Mr Jones, with his chickens - feeding the flock, and rounding them up at dusk - to frustrate the waiting foxes. For this, I would be rewarded with a banana or two - not the empty gesture one might now imagine. I think, also, this is where I first came into contact with death: limp, lifeless chickens, hidden in a barrel in the barn, plucked and left to gain flavour. And milking, too - with milk fresh from the cows - in a way that is now unthinkable in our sanitised, homogenised world.

But most of all I recall Mr Jones's border collie dogs - amazingly agile, bright and obedient - responding with alacrity to every command. One day, I resolved, I would own one, or more, of these quite brilliant, responsive creatures. Before we left at the end of the week - whisked home by kindly neighbours, since we had no car of our own - I left a note, stuck in a crevice in the ancient barn, expressing my ever-lasting devotion to my favourite among these superb dogs. Of course, I never saw him again, and never returned to Talsarnau. Even so, the emotional intensity of these experiences has helped to shape my own story: our woodland at Tafolog is a mere ten miles from Talsarnau; and Hector & Jason's first extended trip, at five months of age, would be to visit Tafolog for the very first time.

Although any year that contains a 13-year-old boy is momentous, 1966 was doubly so. Such epochs happen only very rarely, as Wordsworth observed of the 1789 French Revolution: *'to be young was very Heaven'*. While, in the global dog-fight, Britannia's fortunes were fast slipping beneath the waves, in terms of music, fashion - and football - she was suddenly, unexpectedly, glamorous, and sitting astride the world.

A country that had resembled a crusty old grandpa was transformed by the images and heroic antics of, amongst others, the Fab Four, Twiggy, and Georgie Best. It was as if, along with its greatest symbol, Churchill, an old way of life was passing, and a new, more confident, more extrovert age was rising in its place. If Quarry Bank was hardly gay, carefree or 'swinging', we fed on the flickering images, and danced to the echoes that emanated from Liverpool and London. Saturday after Saturday after Saturday found me in nearby Cradley Heath, at the *Music Box,* a tiny emporium that supplied an eclectic range of music, from the latest 'sounds' to the great masters. I would buy and play these liquorice treasures on my trusty, if rather tinny, little BSR record player: Bach, *The Beatles*, Sinatra, Schubert. Our living room pulsed with a new spirit, and a new 'me' began to emerge from the erstwhile boy.

Though barely a teenager (itself a newly minted term), my eyes became wide open, and my senses alive, to the dawn of an exciting, expansive and altogether more forward-looking world. Suddenly, all was vivid, technicolour, multi-dimensional, and intoxicating. It is often said that, if you remember the '60s, you weren't there. I was there all right, even though on the outermost edge, rather than at the epicentre. That edge was quite near enough to be mind-blown, without the availability of, or the need for, drugs, alcohol or any other artificial stimulant or substance.

The *Music Box's* centrepiece was of course a dog - HMV's (His Master's Voice) little pooch, his head cocked to the phonograph. And dogs made headlines in the newly-populist news, when the dog Pickles discovered the missing Jules Rimet trophy in a south Norwood garden, just prior to the 1966 World Cup Finals. This was the titillating *hors d'oeuvre* for a mouth-watering feast, that would power our hearts - and expectations - for decades to come.

Around this heady time I was be-friended by, and be-friended, an eccentric, I suppose, but exceedingly kindly, elderly lady, who ran what we euphemistically referred to as 'The Farm'. Known locally as Rod Mill Farm, and in reality a nineteenth century, brick built, rambling edifice with rows of rickety outbuildings, the site was set in its own splendid isolation, near to the end of a dirt-track (to us, 'the lane') in the middle of the Stour Valley. The Farm had, hitherto, been home to a genuine farmer-type, since I recall a few cows in the old barns. But now, under the stewardship of Mrs Henslow (as I later discovered), the whole establishment was given over to the care and breeding of dogs.

Mrs Henslow was a remarkable character. Perhaps 60 years old - and perhaps always 60 years old - she dressed in a military-type blue jumper, and dungarees; her grey hair cropped short, unfussy, in the no-nonsense man's style of the time. Although quite a large woman, in height and girth, there was no obvious evidence of female attributes; she spoke deeply, brusquely, like a man, walked like a man, and, in her labours, worked like a man. Still, she was far more interesting, and kindly, than most men of my acquaintance.

For some time, I was not really sure whether my new friend was indeed a woman or a man, since she was quite unlike any woman I had ever met. This was not the result of complete ignorance on my part: there were many young women at my College, and this was the Age, if not of Aquarius, then of the Mini-Skirt. The corridors, the classrooms, and the cafés at College were crammed with beautiful girls in dizzying array. But with her military-style haircut, her no-nonsense working attire, and somewhat brusque manner, Mrs H remained a puzzle to a young mind absorbed - despite the dizzying array - with the mysteries of Shakespeare and the French Revolution.

When, finally, I arrived at a firm conclusion - woman, of course - I decided that I was not in the least interested in the matter. I was only interested in companionship, what Mrs Henslow could teach me about dogs, and my being with the dogs. Whatever my friend's history, and reason for her unconventional lifestyle, my mentor was an expert in all matters canine.

There were perhaps twenty or so dogs on the premises - mainly Elk-hounds, Dobermans and German Shepherds. The ostensible reason for their being there was to breed puppies. These days we might describe the operation as a 'puppy farm'. Yet this notion was in fact risible: whilst the dogs were well cared for, and their pens cleaned out regularly, I could detect little sign of a systematic breeding programme. Although puppies did result from various matings, it all seemed rather random and haphazard. One of the dogs' staple dishes was sheep heads, which now sounds rather macabre. I would gaily throw these grisly offerings to the salivating and appreciative dogs.

Although I helped with feeding the inmates, my main role was to take the dogs into the nearby field and to exercise them, on or off-lead, depending on the nature of each boy or girl. My favourite animal was a male Doberman, very strong and lithe, and who ran exceedingly fast - with me holding on for grim death, since I dared not allow him to escape. Despite what seemed, to my untrained eye, the fairly chaotic management of the place, the dogs, certainly by the standards of the time, were well cared for, and treated with proper respect. They were real dogs, in a no-nonsense, doggy environment. They behaved - and barked - accordingly.

On a certain Sunday, having been invited by Mrs Henslow to lunch (perhaps to reward me for my modest efforts) I was treated to a splendid Sunday roast. It was a memorable afternoon: all manner of dogs and cats inhabited and surrounded the scene, keeping us entertained as they dived over and under the furniture, in the respectably distressed Victorian-style, earthen-tiled living room.

A short time time passed, and sadly, I fear, without a happy ending. I approached The Farm one Sunday morning, to find feverish activity. The lady, I was told by another familiar of the place, had died suddenly in her sleep. Best to keep away, I was darkly advised. Later that day, all the dogs were removed, I knew not where. Had I been an adult, and able to wield a little influence, things may have worked out differently. But I was a 16 or 17 years old college boy, and my views of no account. In those days, still, boys were expected to be quiet, and not question their 'elders and betters'.

With almost indecent haste, 'The Farm' was bulldozed by contractors working for the local Council, and all trace of it removed. Where the Farm once stood, only rank grasses remain.

At least the weeds grow undisturbed.

3: Victor the Valiant

My goal in life is to be as good a person as my dog already thinks I am.

Unknown

Nothing but love has made the dog lose his wild freedom, to become the servant of man.

D.H. Lawrence

Games People Play

Properly trained, a man can be dog's best friend.

Corey Ford

Victor was our first dog; and our first love. He fills a chapter in our lives that is big, bold and boundless. Without the profound impact of Victor, there would have been no Hector & Jason. They would have been someone else's story.

Victor was a Golden Retriever, too, and in a very different mould to H&J. But I jump ahead: when we 'acquired' Victor in March, 1985, Hector & Jason's grandparents, even, were probably not yet a glint in their daddy's eye.

The direction of one's life can be changed utterly by a single thread; a glance, a gesture - a casual remark. In early 1985, June was about to change roles. We thought this was 'the big deal' for the year, setting our life's course. Shortly before the due leaving date, two cheekily irreverent, life-enhancing chappies approached June in the office, and grinned: "*They're planning to get you a cut-glass vase: would you like that? Or would you like a puppy?*". Our lives were about to change utterly - but immeasurably for the better.

3: Victor the Valiant

That casual remark, or suggestion, was all the catalyst that we needed; the seed that transformed into a luxurious plant. For at this critical moment June and I - in our early thirties and in our adult prime, which is also a crossroads - decided that if we were *ever* to welcome a dog into our family, then this was the ideal time. I had been a runner, or 'jogger', for many years, and felt that, in the inevitable (physical) winding down that begins to take place in one's 30's, a dog would prove a welcome companion to my various wanderings, and a genial enhancement to our home and social lives.

By supreme good fortune, we decided that a Golden Retriever would be the perfect companion. The decision made, June's work colleagues - to whom we will always owe a debt of gratitude - helped to locate a suitable family, with puppies available. There was a link with Crufts in terms of family and breeding connections. As if by magic, Victor was secured for us.

Born locally, in nearby Lye, Victor was eagerly received by us as a seven week-old pup. From the outset, he was a bundle of fun and mischief. We still have the first - Polaroid - pictures taken of him, and us, together for the very first time. June and I happen to have deep suntans, having just returned from a late-Winter holiday in Lanzarote. We look very young on these photos, and our delight is evident. The pictures were taken over 30 years ago, now, and the world has changed greatly since then. But nothing can change or replace the many happy years we shared with this unique, characterful, boy. Victor will always have a special place at the heart of our history, memory, and affections.

I had a pretty good idea about the general care and needs of dogs before Victor, although it is fair to say that Vic moulded my view of the Golden Retriever. He was, and remains, for me, the archetypal Retriever: handsome, strong, deeply loyal, profoundly affectionate, and great fun to be around. Vic had a big, big heart. He was an unforgettable personality, inspiring great affection in all our friends, since he also became their friend. His very first outing - he was no older than nine or ten weeks old - was to Bridgnorth, when he was proudly carried around the busy streets by June. Since his vaccinations were not yet complete, it was important not to expose him to other dogs. Nevertheless, this little tour was his gentle introduction into society. We have many fine pictures of Victor, growing up. One of my favourites, taken when he was around four months old, shows him looking proudly towards me, from his vantage point on the sofa. It is quintessential Victor - supremely self-aware, even then, and supremely confident.

Vic became a magnificent figure of a Golden Retriever; as handsome as handsome could be; a large dog, but superbly made; muscular, without a trace of surplus flesh, and a rich glossy coat. He was imperious, imposing, and super intelligent. Though without rosettes or awards of any kind - not our bag - he was the essential Golden Retriever, and a great advertisement for the breed. Had another Noah's Ark been necessary, Victor should have constituted one half of the GR contingent. That would have pleased him enormously; the elephants and giraffes would have had to have made way.

Victor was a presence: big, bold and impressive, with a look that told one: 'I am here!'. There was a gravitas, an air of authority about him, that was truly remarkable. He was a genuine alpha dog - in charge, and possessive of his home. On one occasion, so upset was he with the visiting postman, he burst through a glass door-panel; though fiercely protective of his property, he posed no danger at all to the postie. I also recall a day when we had a new fireplace fitted - the year, 1987. Vic loved visitors, but this 'brickie' was here all day: I had to hold Victor on his lead, murmuring reassurance, to allow the said artisan to complete his excellent work. It was all a little enervating, but a small price to pay for a relaxed boy - and a grand new fireplace.

Some time before June and I welcomed Victor into the bosom of our family, we had acquired an almost life-sized teddy-bear. The bear occupied pride of place on our bed, at least during daylight hours. And so it remained for a few years - bear, bed, snug and smug. Vic, who from an early age slept in our bedroom, quickly decided that it was either the bear, or him: there was no place for both. There was no contest. Victor, as his name might suggest, was victorious. We arrived home from work one day to find a scene of shocking carnage in the bedroom. The bear had been reduced to its constituent parts: shredded into thousands of tiny pieces, and scattered like confetti throughout the room. In effect, it was an ex-bear. The clean-up operation took several hours, and for weeks to come we would continue to unearth the little cubes of foam that had formed the innards of the former bear.

A similar fate awaited 'Margaret Thatcher'. The popular satirical show *Spitting Image* spawned a range of merchandise, including a rubberised dog-toy based on Mrs T. The dummy squealed when chewed, and became a firm favourite of Vic's. The toy could be heard squeaking day and night in house or garden - a noise that became a little wearing over time. But Vic would not be satisfied until, at last, the dummy was reduced to shards of plastic, that littered his domain. At least it outlived its contemporary, Ronald Reagan, who fell an early victim to the determined Vic, and his fearsome jaws. We had been warned: a new, Victor era, had begun.

Our cats - Sherpa, the Burmese, and Dougal, a huge, cob-faced British White - shared Vic's home. Although, in an early fit of pique, the haughty Sherpa had attacked the young Vic, and sent us scurrying to the vets, the storm soon passed, and an uneasy truce put into place. Vic gradually asserted his rights, and became the dominant force. It was Victor's world; the rest of us merely shared it.

Vic loved to play, and his favourite playmate - was me. In the early evening, following his dinner, he loved to indulge in a little wrestling. Whether it was my idea, or Victor's, I cannot now recall, but wrestling, on the hearth - no holds barred - was his favourite pastime. It helped him relax after his repast. Who could pin the other to the floor? Vic was an immensely strong, though gentle, boy, and we played this game - in the friendliest of spirits, and the best of humour - throughout his life. He often gained the upper hand and, when he did so, I would suddenly go limp, and pretend to have expired from exhaustion as the result of his powerful assault. It may seem a mean trick, but I sometimes needed to curb his over-enthusiasm. In any event, it worked: Vic immediately became concerned and solicitous, and our game ended, as I miraculously 'revived', with a flourish of (metaphorical) back-slapping, and mutual congratulation. Though only Victor had a tail to wag. Innocent, happy days.

We also invented another little game, that always gave me great amusement. When June and I were out on walks with Vic, I would sidle away and hide somewhere. Victor knew the game, and what was expected of him. With a few words of encouragement, June would release him from his lead. Seconds later, and without fail, I was tracked down: Vic was proud and amused in equal measure; I always gave him a big fuss to reward his cleverness. Of course, dogs have an amazing sense of smell, and my scent print must have been second nature to Vic, but the game remained great fun, since it was a family game that gave mutual pleasure.

Much, much, later, Hector & Jason also knew how to have fun, how to interact and beam a smile on me - and loved a hug and a fuss - but would have been horrified if I had tried to grapple them to the floor. That was what *they* did best - with each other. Similarly, H&J would have been oblivious to the purpose of the hide-and-seek game: I could have remained in my hideaway for an inordinate time before they returned from their mission to collect me, and take me home.

When Vic was specially pleased with me, or sometimes when he was a little anxious or unsure, he would rear up on his hind legs, place his paws on my chest, and look straight into my face. This was difficult to ignore, since we were practically eyeball to eyeball. Having gained him the notice that he required, he would only relinquish this position following the requisite number of assurances as to how good a boy he was, and how much I loved him. I trust there were no platitudes there, since I did love him to distraction.

Just once or twice, to vary our - and his - routine, Vic accompanied June to the office. Just once or twice, because Vic soon vented his boredom and frustration on the contents of the waste paper bins - scattering their contents far and wide - and quickly, impatiently, barked his way to freedom.

With Victor, we established our regime of three walks a day, morning, lunchtime and evening, and this maintained his health and fitness - and mine. We strode out purposefully and manfully, taking an unfeigned interest in all around us. My running was much reduced: brisk walks in the countryside with Victor as my companion seemed much more gratifying, much more fun. Because I bonded to him, and he to me, our walks were quite delightful. Our ventures were an effusion of mutual pleasure, mutual back-slapping, and 'sunburnt mirth'. Even from his early adolescence, Victor and I walked almost as one, with little need for a lead once we were clear of roads. There was a genuine connection between us, which only deepened over time. Vic strode with me, beside me, almost glued to my side - certainly, without wishing to drag me along in pursuit of some real or imagined goal.

If one of Vic's daily walks was to his beloved woods, another would be to the local Park, which he relished with equal zest. Most of these visits passed off without incident or mishap, or indeed excitement, with only the odd brush with a surly dog, surly owner, or otherwise surly encounter. I do recall one particular Summer evening: we were meandering back to our car when I spotted a chap in a fluorescent vest about to lock the heavy double gates that secured the Park's entrance. Puzzled, I exclaimed something along the lines of: *"Excuse me, my good man, but could you lock the gates after we've left?"*. The 'good man' 'hollered' back, in deepest, purest Black Country, *"I-aya-goona-miss-ma-buz-cos-ayo!"*. Roughly translated, this means that this heart-of-gold needed to catch his bus, and was quite unconcerned for my convenience, or welfare. Presumably, my car could languish until the morning, when the Park was re-opened. However, we quickly negotiated a settlement - there was no war or international incident - and Vic and I were soon motoring to a peaceful home.

Outside, on our walks, (despite the occasional distraction) there was no finer companion than Vic - alert, dignified, confident, and clearly and openly enjoying my company, or June's company, or our company. If June returned from work before me, she would often take Vic for a short drive to Highgate Common, where he would stroll happily by her side. However, Vic would exhibit a certain despondency on beholding a lone walker, as though unfit for purpose. *'Where is your dog?'*. *'Why have you been let out on your own?'*. Sadly, the more I've seen of human nature, the more I share his misgivings.

Our friends and neighbours, who had two wonderful dogs of their own, Emma and Holly, generously agreed to walk Victor for us at lunchtimes during the week, and they carried out this sterling task, come rain or come shine, throughout Victor's long life. Emma was a beautiful and soft-hearted English Setter; Holly, an equally lovely, gentle, English pointer. The lunch-time walking arrangement was ideal for us - and for Victor. He would stride out manfully with these gorgeous girls, with a strong sense of possession. When the 'girls' were in season, Victor was walked separately, in order to prevent distraction, annoyance, or worse, to his female friends. But most of the time he was an attentive, affectionate and protective companion.

Vic did, however, have an eye - and a nose - for the ladies. There is a scene in *Don Giovanni* where the Don sniffs the air and proclaims: *"I smell woman!"*. The words quoted are those of Mozart's brilliantly versatile (and colourful) collaborator on the opera, the librettist, Lorenzo da Ponte. Certainly, he should know. A friend of Casanova - who attended the opera's première - da Ponte tells us in his *Memoirs* how he wrote the libretto whilst, at the same time, engaged in writing libretti for two other composers:

'I went to the Emperor, laid my idea before him, and explained that my intention was to write the three operas contemporaneously.

"You will not succeed", he replied.

"Perhaps not", I replied, "but I am going to try. I shall write evenings for Mozart, imagining I am reading the Inferno; mornings I shall work for Martini, and pretend I am studying Petrarch; my afternoons will be for Salieri; He is my Tasso!"...I returned home and went to work. I sat down at my table and did not leave it for twelve hours continuous - a bottle of Tokay to my right, a box of Seville (tobacco) to my left, in the middle an ink-well. A beautiful girl of sixteen - I should have preferred to love her only as a daughter, but alas...! - was living in the house with her mother, who took care of the family, and would come to my room at the sound of the bell. To tell the truth, the bell rang rather frequently...'

The sight or scent of a female (dog) in season presented an irresistible temptation to the dashing Victor. In this respect, he was an unashamed, and fully paid-up member of the real-dog club. Having spotted a likely paramour, Vic was prone to gallop after her, with me trailing in his wake. As with Jason, many years later, there were people who asked, querulously, why I couldn't keep up. Well, Victor was a pretty good athlete, with the wind in his sails - or his nostrils. Although I was a pretty fair runner at the time, 20-25mph was just a notch above my top speed. Despite his best efforts, however, no harm (not his take, assuredly) ever befell his intended paramours.

Vic's exploits in this regard have seared on my memory and on that of our dog-walking friends. On one occasion (I can readily imagine) Vic dashed from the woodland path, having espied a lucky lady some way off: he was only prevented from achieving his ultimate goal by the lady (owner) barring his way resolutely whilst shouting: *"No! No! No!"* Even Vic was sufficiently discomforted by the tirade for his animal spirits to dissipate. On another occasion a certain gent - no doubt suspecting the intentions of our Vic - lifted his dog into the safety of his arms, only to find the frustrated Victor clamped fast to *his* leg.

My own experiences were of a similar bent. Victor's strong swimming stroke would see him cross from river bank to bank, to be near to his paramour - a little awkward when his 'owner' was stranded on the opposite bank. And I have painful recollections of a grim November morning - now more than 25 years ago - when he scented or espied a 'damsel', and ran gallantly after her, storming through the local woods. Hampered by a bad cold, I scampered after him, only to fall heavily into glutinous mud. I eventually retrieved him - I was most worried about Vic leaving the safety of the woods, in his hot pursuit - but returned home with a painfully throbbing thumb. A long, uncomfortable day at work - embroiled in endless meetings - ended with a visit to A&E. The x-rayed thumb was found to be unbroken, but very badly bruised - a permanently damaged reminder of Vic's youthful - and not so youthful - escapades.

Nor was that all. On one - painfully memorable - morning, when I was 'twixt bathroom and bedroom, Vic lunged at me and grabbed my genitals. I was too shocked - nay, mortified - to seek an explanation, but never again exposed myself to such rude intercourse. Vic had never bitten me before, or since, even in play, and even now I hesitate to offer an explanation. Yet, as I have said before, he was always the alpha dog.

There were also sexual encounters of a different type, in Vic's favourite haunt, our local woods. Walking, strolling, rambling, whatever the term, exposes one to new experiences of many types; exciting, surprising, unexpected, occasionally unpleasant. On one occasion, strolling along the woodland path, we came across a young woman leaning upright, her back against a tree; a man in a suit leaning upright, against her. Seeing us, they panicked, and fled, somewhat dishevelled. It reminded me of lines from John Keats' *Eve of St Agnes:*

> *'And they are gone: aye, ages long ago*
> *These lovers fled away into the storm'*

I was sorry to have been the cause of a coitus interruptus that must have been as painful as it was unexpected.

When not seeking amorous encounters, Victor was an enthusiastic and inveterate chewer of sticks found in the woods. He would invariably pause by a favourite tree, an ancient beech on the crest of a hill, and explore its latest tasty offerings. He never tired of this particular spot, where he would sit, chew, and contemplate life. That hallowed ground, on the brow of a familiar hill, is forever part of his memory. All these years on, this scene has hardly altered. I never pass that place without thinking fondly of him. His shade is there.

In the natural slope, or depression, just below Vic's favourite spot, a treasure-trove of leaves gathered each Autumn; piled into rich, golden heaps by the brisk wind that amused itself in creating delicious, molten shapes between the trees. Vic loved dashing into these downy, wavy heaps, rolling around in something approaching ecstasy, his eyes and mouth betraying an intense enjoyment. Such simple pleasures, so innocently enjoyed!

A boy with a strong and passionate nature, Vic's final, irresistible, passion was, undoubtedly, the humble tennis ball. He was continuously on the look-out for these furry little round objects, patrolling the Park, and rooting around in hedges, to add to his burgeoning collection. Vic's ball collection dominated our modest garden. He never had enough tennis balls, and was always on the look-out to add to his impressive haul.

One might almost say that Vic had a fetish for these small, yellow, spherical objects. Together we collected hundreds of them over the years. Most often, he found the little trophies through endless searching in the hedges and undergrowth that framed the local tennis courts, but he was equally happy to snaffle a misdirected ball from a budding Wimbledon star. These were usually returned - most reluctantly, in Victor's case - although, to the dismay of the owner, suitably mauled and wet with saliva.

If ball collection was an obsession in itself, it was not an end in itself. For Vic was an expert at ball games. He delighted in playing with his acquisitions in the garden, with me as his partner. My role was to throw the thing - and his role was to catch. Indeed, we would spend many hours so occupied - me in throwing, he in catching - these furry prizes. He never tired of ball games, and showed great dexterity in catching the in-flight balls. Fascinating rhythm, indeed. Vic's face displayed his pleasure at this success in catching a ball. Yet more good, clean, innocent fun.

In 1987 I was admitted into hospital for minor (dental) surgery, (not to be recommended) and languished away from home for a few days. During this time, of course, June assumed responsibility for walking Vic - not too onerous a task, since he was devotedly loyal and obedient. However, on one occasion, having just returned home in the car, Victor jumped from his seat - and disappeared! June searched for him for an hour, with increasing desperation. At last she found him, wandering the streets, and they were happily reunited. Of course, I was oblivious of this escapade until my return. On reflection, Vic was clearly upset and unnerved by my unusual absence, and had perhaps gone on a reconnoitre, hoping to find me. Fortunately, we were *all* re-united a few days later, when I returned with much relief from my hospital experience. I fondly recall Dougal, magnificent and magical, giving me almost as warm a welcome home as Victor himself.

Victor and I had our 'moments' meeting other dogs. I took my care responsibilities very seriously, and on the few, memorably unpleasant occasions when we were attacked - the owners usually as guilty, and as brazen, as their supposed charges - I stood shoulder-to-shoulder with my boy. And Vic stood his ground nobly, always defending himself. But, despite his physical prowess, Vic never went on the offensive against any dog. He was a man's dog, and (aside from these errant, mercifully few, examples), a dog's dog.

The above incidents were sufficiently rare so as not to deter either our neighbours, or June and myself, from allowing Victor freedom from his lead. Incidents were relatively rare, and could generally be nipped in the bud. Much later, our dog-walking neighbours took a similar sanguine view of Hector & Jason. I think they maintained this view just once - or maybe twice - before concluding that these boys were made from a *very* different cloth. Thereafter, wherever they went, H&J remained firmly on their leads - one walker, to one very enthusiastic dog.

With a single exception, Victor showed a supreme disinterest in native wildlife, whether squirrels, rabbits or foxes. And he harboured strong suspicions about any cows or bulls that he encountered - clearly, very wise. Certainly, chasing squirrels was beneath his dignity. Vic did, however, show a decided interest in wildfowl, and would often slip into a lake or canal on this account. I recall one unfortunate incident at Bourton-on-the-Water, in the lovely Cotswolds. Butterscotch Bourton - the limpid River Windrush wandering through its heart - is a glutinous, gorgeous confection. Yet Victor only had eyes for the birds: the geriatric gentility of Bourton was shattered as Vic lunged noisily into the Windrush in pursuit of a small flock of mallards.

Seeing Vic splashing excitedly in the river, an elderly gentleman, elegantly coiffed, puffed himself up into a rage. Frothing at the mouth, he exploded: "*I suppose you think that's funny!*". The gent had a point, but only that of benign neglect. The incident was really my fault, for not keeping a closer eye on my boy, as generally he was proud to be trusted without a lead. On this occasion - certainly not the only one - Vic's natural instincts exerted their inexorable sway. I quickly recalled a clearly reluctant Victor. I imagined this gentleman later, in complacent repose, feasting on *duck a l'orange*. I do hope I was right.

Long afterwards, a fellow dog walker explained the water-phobia of her pet: *"He used to love water, but was attacked by a duck. Since then, he's been too been frightened to go in."* Vic would have smiled at the prospect of a free lunch.

I was scolded on yet another occasion when we visited a local beauty spot, Himley Park, one bitterly cold Boxing Day afternoon. There is a large lake at Himley, the ancestral home and former haunt of the Earls of Dudley. On this particular afternoon the surface of the lake was frozen as far as the eye could see. Without any bidding or encouragement from me, Victor plunged through the ice, and swam in the water beneath. Since he was near the edge, I quickly hauled him out. Though Vic gave himself a good shake, the water in his fur froze at once. A gentleman who had witnessed this act of bravado - or folly - took me to task. *C'est la vie.* Needless to say, a brisk towelling down and Victor was absolutely fine. He was his own dog on these occasions; if I had a role, it was to protect him from his over-exuberance.

In fact, Victor simply adored snow and ice, and had a real talent for the stuff; whether walking or running in it, rolling around in it, or retrieving snowballs lobbed by yours truly. And then, suddenly, he would dive into a snow drift, for sheer sensual enjoyment. His thick coat and strong physique made him ideally suited for these conditions. One bitter Winter's day, snow fell very thickly, and was blown into deep drifts by a tremendous blizzard. We found ourselves in the local Park, with snow drifts three and four feet deep, and the sharp wind flinging snow horizontally into our faces. Victor stood four square and proud, shielding his eyes with his fine eye lashes; he looked magnificent in, and against, the swirling snow. How I recall that look, that pose, as if it was yesterday! The photographic image is lodged in my mind for all time: the young dog, in his element, in his time.

Victor also adored cars, and travelling. Invariably, he enjoyed the destination, but also enjoyed the thrill of the journey. In the Spring of 1983, a friend-of-a-friend visited us to quote for some minor building work, arriving in his almost new, white, Ford Escort 1600 Sports. For some reason - I am the very opposite of a petrol head - I remarked that I admired the car. *"Would you like to buy it?"* he responded immediately. Within days, our shining new acquisition was proudly parked in our garage. This car would - as well as conveying June and me all over Europe - become Victor's favourite. He experienced his very first trips in this two-door sporty car, and loved adventures in it throughout his life.

Whilst Vic enjoyed other vehicles - another, more homely, Ford Escort, and later our Ford Sierra - his favourite continued to be the Escort Sport, which remains fiercely in my possession. He was a great 'front seat driver'. From a very young age, he would sit magisterially on the front passenger seat, looking ahead, and to each side, at people, dogs, and the passing scenes, as they flashed quickly by. Vic was incredibly well-balanced, and would adjust automatically for corners and roundabouts, as though his legs contained hydraulic suspension. Much, much later, I naively introduced the young Hector and Jason to this favourite vehicle. They recoiled in obvious horror. *"You want us to do what?"* their faces enquired. Victor would have regarded the (later) Volvo as providing unimaginable luxury, but he retained his fondness for the Escort. Perhaps it kindled his spirit of adventure, as indeed it did mine.

Victor liked to know just *where* he was going, by car. Short trip, or long trip? Tell him *"shops!"* and he would prepare for a short - but interesting - local trip, observing all around him, and taking a keen interest in people and events whilst 'stationed' on the car park. Longer trips required preparation, and he was aware - and was always up for - the adventure to come. As a fully adult boy, he was quite happy to leap on to the rear seat, which offered greater comfort. He was the most versatile and easy travelling dog, whether visiting my parents - his favourites - or touring Scotland, Dorset or Cornwall. Indeed, our visit to Pitlochry was accomplished in the said Escort. Victor was welcomed with great warmth and hospitality by the hotel's staff and guests; a welcome which he responded to with due decorum, and an easy grace; he was the perfect young gentleman, and the perfect country dog.

Animal or human, we all have our little idiosyncrasies, and Victor was no exception. A brave, bold lad, he could not abide bridges - particularly bridges that you could *see* through - for example, those made of wooden planks or pre-fabricated steel - to the river beneath. On one occasion we were walking over an impressively long, narrow bridge that gracefully spans the river at Pitlochry: Victor suddenly stopped - suddenly aware - and refused to budge, sticking like a limpet to the 'floor' of the bridge. This floor consisted of a kind of steel mesh - very sturdy, but see-through. There was nothing for it but to carry Victor over the bridge to the other side - no mean feat since he weighed around seven stones. Victor repeated this trait when crossing smaller bridges, though of course we made every effort to avoid such structures wherever possible. What caused this anxiety I can't be sure, though I have noticed - in myself, and others - an increasing trauma, with age, in confronting heights - particularly man-made heights.

Thus, my parents, when we were about to negotiate the mighty *Pont de Normandie*, suddenly, violently exclaimed that they wanted to stop the car and get out - now! But the car was speeding inexorably towards the bridge, and there was no way back. Perhaps there's an innate suspicion that these man-made structures, unlike *terra firma*, can't be guaranteed to be safe - and that Victor's fears were yet another sign of a most intelligent and discriminating lad.

And yet, in all other respects Victor was fearless. Fireworks, in particular, held no worries for him. No precautions necessary. Every year we held a community Bonfire Party, in the service road that links two small streets. Here, we would light our bonfire, contained within a large oil drum. A barbecue, complemented by a drinks bar, kept everyone fortified against the cold. The fireworks display would continue all through the long, dark evening, puncturing the blackness with multi-coloured bursts of light; these would be 'answered', like ricochets, by similar bursts, exploding all over the night sky.

Throughout these excruciatingly loud, powerful, spectacular eruptions, Victor would doggedly remain, wagging his tail - while waiting for stray burgers and hot-dogs from the barbecue to come his way. This became one of his favourite nights of the year, and he became a celebrity - famous for his appearances on such an inauspicious occasion for a dog. He appeared like a Hotspur: oblivious to the din and dust and smoke, enjoying the high spirits, and in thrall to barbecued meats, Victor cut a handsome and impressive figure; the only dog amongst the excited throng of adults and children, and partying well into the night.

When the BBQ eventually exhausted its delights, Victor retired to his warm bed, no doubt dreaming of burgers and buns.

On Sunday lunchtimes Vic established a tradition of joining June and me for cheese and biscuits, following our roast lunch. Sadly, as we know, one cannot eat one's cheese and still have it. After his snack, Vic would continue to focus on me with eager eyes. Then I would show him my empty palms. Instantly, he absorbed the message, and turned to one of his many other interests, such as eating Brazil nuts. He displayed an astonishing facility for breaking the shells - *just* the shells - of these nuts, in his strong but delicate jaws, before devouring his prize - the juicy seed within.

Victor dominated the house, and insisted on meeting, and greeting, every visitor and guest, sometimes continuing his solicitations beyond what might be considered courteous. He was ever the entertainer, but also keen to demonstrate his proprietorial gift. A regular party trick took place when we had guests to dinner. Vic would creep - if a large dog can creep - under the table and remove the guests' serviettes, one by silent one, before tearing them to shreds. If he did this to gain attention, it certainly worked: he was determined to be the focus for everyone's interest, and everyone seemed to think that his antics were not only clever, but hilarious.

And, visiting my parents, Vic made a bee-line to a space in the kitchen where socks and dusters were kept: he would remove these triumphantly, laughing and wagging his tail. '*Ha ha!*' he seemed to say - found you again! Similarly, he took delight at the postman's daily visits; we would regularly return home to find the mail efficiently shredded. Fortunately, there were few cheques amongst the flotsam and jetsam littering the hall floor.

However, Vic did have his limits. One Christmas Day afternoon, when we were endeavouring to entertain our guests, my parents, Victor disappeared. Such was the stress of the occasion that we didn't notice his absence for some time; by the time reality dawned Vic must have been missing for a whole hour. June went out in search, and found him shut in a garden in a nearby street - barking his head off. Apparently, he had been placed there by a well-meaning, if tipsy, neighbour who mistook Vic for another Retriever. This small misadventure was a complete one-off: our view is that he voted with his feet - for whatever reason, he did not find the occasion to his taste. I hasten to add that Vic loved visiting my parents on their own territory, and was always greeted with marked affection. But his squeezing through the tiny spaces in our wrought iron gate is testament to a desperation that I can only, ruefully, recognise.

Whilst Vic was generally agreeable about June and me both going out to work each day, and greeted us effusively on our return home, the wrench back to work following holidays, and particularly after Christmas, clearly irked him. Now, chocolate is poisonous to dogs; it was a pity nobody advised Victor of this fact, since he loved the seductive stuff. On our return to work after the Christmas break the piqued Vic would help himself to all the seasonal left-overs - including entire boxes of luxury chocolates - and consume these with a resentful relish. He never experienced any ill-effects from such indulgence, exhibiting only a grim satisfaction. Yet Vic never showed the slightest interest in chocolates at any other time - leave them lying around as we might.

In those days, I normally arrived home at around 6.00pm, give or take a minute or two. My friend would be alerted to my return by the 'Bong! Bong! Bong!' of Big Ben on Radio 4. Vic became excited on hearing this announcement of my imminent arrival: and there I was, in the doorway. And there we were - re-united.

Grand Days Out - Over Hill and Dale

Such deeds as madmen do, with courage in the fight;
Such things as madmen do, will we do with delight!

Colin Hill

One of the drawbacks to living in the English West Midlands is that the distance from the coast - any coast - is around 100 miles. This did not deter us - indeed it incentivised us - since we longed to be close to the sea. But the awkward fact of distance did circumscribe the possibilities. Day-long excursions were limited to North Wales, North Somerset and Lancashire. We embraced all three with enthusiasm each Summer, as did Vic.

So, Aberdovey, Barmouth and Llandudno; Weston-super-Mare; and Southport and Lytham-St Annes were our regular triumvirate of day-long, Summer excursions. Lovely Barmouth, framed by the Welsh mountains, was a real favourite. As was beautiful Aberdovey, where we caught crabs from the harbour wall, and ran wildly along the soft-sand beach. Happily, in those days, dogs were not excluded from beaches, so Vic was able to scamper with us on the golden sands.

Weston is a familiar 'English playground', with its vast, empty beach. The site was still a small village until the 19th century when it became a seaside resort, and was connected with local towns and cities by a railway; two piers were also built, one of which remains. Owing to the large tidal range in the Bristol Channel, the low tide mark in Weston Bay is about a mile from the seafront. Although the beach itself is sandy, low tide uncovers areas of thick, glutinous stuff - hence the colloquial name, Weston-super-Mud. It remains, however, a charming resort, and Vic enjoyed vigorous walks along the long, broad promenade.

Southport, with its bracing air, impressive fairground, and lively promenade, was another regular rendezvous. We always enjoyed the fish and chips at Southport. Perhaps it's the sea-breeze, but they always seem to make 'em better, 'up North'. Wherever we went, Vic was energised, and enjoyed the ride - and a run along the beaches, where dogs were still welcome. And I recall scampering with Vic along the soft, deep sands of Lytham, on a deserted, breezy Saturday afternoon.

Vic just loved beaches, and the sea. One memorable Sunday we wove our way through the mountainous scenery of mid-Wales, near to Plynlimon, plummeting through a glorious valley, winding steeply and dramatically to the sea at Ynyslas. It happened to be a scorching day in July, and the beach, thronged with happy sun-worshippers, was seductively inviting. We parked the car near to the sea wall. Vic had, admittedly, been looking round excitedly - from his seat in the car. But before I had any chance to set him on his lead, Vic hurtled like a missile in an unerring line to the sea. I cringed with embarrassment as he galloped - not past, but over - startled sun-seekers lying prone on the sand. Luckily, Vic's victims hardly knew what had occurred, so fleeting was the impact, with Victor's backside disappearing into the distance, where his front-end burst into the surf. I followed him, with apologetic nods towards clumps of people, settling back into sun-bliss after their rude awakening. Even so, sand-blasted sun-tan oil is hardly a marriage made in heaven.

Happily, Victor, as well as being a passionate traveller, was mesmerised by water of all types. Sea, lakes, rivers, canals - each held a special allure, and he was excited by every variety. He was a strong, expert swimmer - certainly the most accomplished and strongest (dog) swimmer I have seen; reminiscent of an otter, it was a pleasure to observe his skilful exploits in water. Vic loved the River Severn at Arley: once he had negotiated the rickety wooden bridge, we were in perfect bliss. The sandy shore resembled a beach, and Vic would chase my skimming pebbles into the shallow, calm river. He never tired of this 'retrieving' game, and we had many long afternoons of this innocent, enjoyable pastime. The icy torrents around the Elan Valley, and cool limpid waters of Lake Vyrnwy, provided yet more favourite locations for Vic's swim-fests.

And, in deepest Summer, we loved to walk along the placid River Severn at Shrewsbury: pristine oarsmen glided past, and kingfishers darted along the riverbank. The perfume from wild-flowers and the intoxication of courting couples somehow mingled as we made our way, briskly but open-minded, open-hearted, towards the next foot-bridge, the next expanse of majestic river.

Carding Mill Valley, near Church Stretton, was another sought-for weekend destination; an amble through the valley, with its cascading stream, was a Sunday afternoon delight. I marvelled at how the rowan ash trees could cling on to rock faces, without any visible means of support or soil to sustain them. And I was always perplexed by the serried ranks of cars at the valley opening - their occupants busily drinking coffee and poring over newspapers. These day-trippers seemed to be congealed in their steel boxes so that, as we ascended through the valley, the human presence diminished to a veritable dribble, like the stream itself, and we were left, two ramblers and our loyal boy, alone amidst the silent majesty of these ancient hills.

At Carding Mill, as elsewhere, we carefully avoiding wandering sheep. Once, however, in the remote valley, we came face-to-face with a lone sheep: Vic hesitated for just long enough for me to collect him on to his lead; a brief encounter that seemed to fascinate both of the protagonists. Nearby lies the beautiful Long Mynd, *the blue remember'd hills*' of Houseman's Shropshire - perfect walking country for a couple and their faithful friend.

Sunday afternoons also found us in the romantic, lovely, Malvern Hills, beloved of artists such as Sir Edward Elgar. Even in Summer, we often battled against fierce gusts of wind on our little pilgrimages towards Hereford Beacon or Worcester Beacon. On the smooth, steep hill, Vic was buffeted and battered by forces that sculpted his shape, and revealed his *joie de vivre*. Vic is 'captured' in heavenly motion as he braves the blasts in a favourite photograph:

Buffeted, battered, on Malvern Hill -
Bravely battling the storm blasts, still.

Cannock Chase, as the name suggests, was formerly the hunting ground of medieval kings, and remains a vast expanse of forest and moorland in rural Staffordshire. The Chase was used for military training during the First World War, and also has a Memorial to the Polish elite murdered by Stalin's forces at Katin. Despite these tragic reminders of human sacrifice and cruelty, the scale and tranquillity of the Chase provided many hours of happy wanderings for Vic, June and me over numberless quiet afternoons. Although the Chase remains a haven for wild deer, Vic showed little interest in their presence, and none in chasing them. Ponds and water-courses were his chief delight. Fresh air and wild landscapes inspired us all.

Our Summers were punctuated by visits to my brother's new home near Amersham: Victor would travel in the rear of the Sierra for the two-hour journey. It was an exciting time, filled with the hustle and bustle of frenetic family life, and an air of change, transience, and the brightness and laughter of growing children. I was often reminded of Hardy's evocative *During Wind and Rain*:

'They change to a high new house,
He, she, all of them - aye,
Clocks and carpets and chairs
On the lawn all day,
And brightest things that are theirs...'

On one such occasion, driving to Amersham, and with my parents occupying the rear seats, Vic was ominously quiet in his place in the hatch-back. We arrived to find that Vic had munched his way, silently but surely, through the contents of our packed lunch, which included a huge pork pie. On that same afternoon, we - my brother, his wife, five year old James, June, Victor and me - embarked on a stroll to the local woodland - recently blasted by the 1987 'Great Storm'. We reached a cricket ground on the woodland edge, and young James pleaded to hold Victor's lead. We hesitated: Vic was a very strong dog, and was used to walking at a certain, brisk pace. Finally, not wishing to sound at all churlish, we agreed: young James was hooked up to Victor.

In a matter of seconds, the said James, yanked off his feet, was being dragged along on his tummy, while clinging desperately to Victor's lead. After what seemed like an age, and fifty yards of scurrying to catch up with said Vic, frantic attempts at rescue retrieved both boy and dog. James coped manfully with the dirt and scratches of the misadventure; Victor was quietly puzzled by the commotion.

Only minutes later, Victor strolled ahead into the woodland, and was lost to sight. After a pause, we heard cries of anguish, not unlike those of Zerlina at the end of Act 1 of *Don Giovanni*. The mention of *Don Giovanni* and Victor in the same breath is, as we know, not entirely coincidental: but on this occasion Victor had merely attacked a picnic, helping himself to the largesse of a family's pastoral idyll. Finder's Keeper's, and all that. Again we retrieved him, with profuse apologies to the injured parties. It is a simple, if regrettable, fact that dogs cannot resist food laid upon the ground; they really do believe that it is 'fair game', a present from heaven, and not to be abjured. Temptation; Oscar Wilde, all over again.

The Peak District, famed for centuries for its picturesque and romantic scenery, became a favourite destination. In *Pride and Prejudice*, Jane Austen writes of *'the celebrated beauties of Matlock, Chatsworth, Dovedale, or the Peak'*. Though the heroine, Lizzie Bennett, sees hardly more of the area than Pemberley - and Mr Darcy - she nevertheless relishes the landscape that encloses the mansion: *'Every disposition of the ground was good; and she looked on the whole scene, the river, the trees scattered on its banks, and the winding of the valley, as far as she could trace it.'*

How could we refuse such an invitation? The Peak District deserves special mention: throughout the 1980s and into the '90s, the Derbyshire Dales were the scene for our myriad sorties and secret weekend excursions. With Vic such a natural traveller, and the Dales so close and inviting, our excursions were irresistible. The Dales were sufficiently 'other' to the West Midlands - with wild crags and rivers, turbulent streams, desolate moorland and, in Autumn, great vistas of heather - to make it a an area of physical and spiritual renewal. Though only ninety minutes or so from home, the very air seemed different, vivacious and alive.

Dovedale, Matlock, Chatsworth, and the Peak (Kinder Scout) were all within our ken. We would often stop in the characterful, popular resort of Ashbourne, where we bought paintings of flowers - peonies and roses - to adorn the walls of our home. And Vic loved to visit nearby Bakewell where, in addition to the obligatory - and delicious - pastries, we would amble alongside the River Dove, restraining Vic's urgent attentions to the flotillas of ducks that patrolled the pretty river.

Whether Winter or Summer, we drove to Dovedale, or Froggatt Edge, or Miller's Dale, wherever our mood and muse led. Dovedale, crowded but romantically beautiful, was at the heart of our wanderings; the stepping stones over the River Dove were no challenge to Vic. He would often veer off the path for a quick dip into the inviting waters, perhaps having spied a mallard or two from the corner of his eye. One needed to keep a good distance when he re-emerged, since his energetic shaking produced an enormous shower of spray.

This Dale was a real favourite, with its beautiful river winding through a magnificent landscape. After crossing the stepping stones, Vic and I would climb the steep, scree-lined contours of Thorpe Cloud, a mere 1,060' high, before returning to continue our ramble along the valley bottom, towards and past Ilam Rock. Vic, of course, would enjoy numerous plunges into the pure, cool waters, before a leisurely return to base.

Among my most vivid images are Miller's Dale, and the Monsal Trail which commences at a deserted old railway station (closed in 1968) that is so atmospheric and reminiscent of a film set: *Brief Encounter* might have been filmed here. And the walk itself - along the line of the old railway track - is fascinating, both for its topography and its history. Vic loved it, and he loved the river (Wye) flowing past. And, of course, he would take the occasional dip into the sparkling, fast-flowing waters.

The railway itself, opening in 1863, was controversial from the first, since the route blasted its way through the Peaks. John Ruskin fumed: *"every fool in Buxton can be at Bakewell in half-an-hour, and every fool in Bakewell at Buxton."* The derelict railway - and the huge railway tunnels - though incredibly impressive in their own way, are also a testament to money, vanity and the ultimate transience of human ambition. Even so, they now seem to add a frisson of excitement, and a kind of juxtaposition, to the natural beauty of the trail. It is hard not to admire the Herculean labours of the 'navies' - many of whom lost their lives in this gigantic enterprise. Their titanic labours meant that Victorians could now travel direct from St Pancras, all the way to Manchester, which they continued to do along this route for over 100 years. Travelling by four-feet drive rather than by train, Vic was in his element - whether dipping in the river, eye-balling the local sheep, or clambering over rocks, stepping stones and scree.

Victor also accompanied me to the town of Derby itself, by train. In a highly successful one-off, Vic showed no worry or trepidation at this novel form of transport; he was confident when riding on all types of wheeled machines. The taxi driver at the station was a little nonplussed, as it happened, to be ferrying a dog to his onward destination: but Victor was perfectly happy with the arrangement, and took the whole experience in his stride, being perfectly calm, dignified and relaxed throughout the journey.

On the station platform itself Vic was the subject of almost over-whelming interest, since passengers saw few travelling dogs, other than guide dogs. Indeed, Vic was the epicentre of attention, from travellers determined to find something - anything - of interest to relieve the tedium of commuting. Needless to say, Vic lapped up the smallest to the grandest gesture of attention; it was his birthright, and he accepted it all with manful dignity.

One Saturday, when Victor was just five years old, and in his majestic prime, we travelled to Twycross Zoo, in Leicestershire. I had a meeting with a member off the Zoo's staff, to discuss wildlife conservation in the tropics - another passion. Whilst I was thus absorbed, June and Victor embarked on a trip to the site of the Battle of Bosworth Field where, in 1485, Richard III lost a definitive, bloody contest that brought Henry VII to the throne. 'A horse, a horse..' and all that.

In the meantime, I was being cordially invited to meet the Zoo's chimpanzees, behind the scenes. I was guided passed the adult chimps, and warned not to touch them: a misguided attempt to shake their hand could result in an arm being ripped off (and who can blame them?). Instead, I was introduced to a two-year-old girl chimpanzee. It was a powerful meeting of minds. She looked straight into my eyes; I looked straight into hers. There was the electricity of instant connection, on a human level, that I have not experienced in any other 'non-human' being. Human beings share over 99% of their DNA with these primates - they are our closest relatives. It was a singular and moving experience: even thirty years later, I recall that frisson of direct and complete recognition.

Minutes later, still in a reverie, I re-joined the returned June and Victor. Suddenly, I saw Victor in a quite different light. He was a great dog, my dog, and I loved him passionately. Still, my relationship with Vic was different, very different, to what I had just experienced with the young chimp. The latter was on another level, another world of understanding, with different dimensions and parameters. With Victor, I enjoyed one of the deepest non-human relationships I have ever experienced. Yet what I had just seen and felt was extraordinary, and unforgettable.

We are often told that 'the big question' - for which we do not yet have the answer - is *Are we alone in the Universe?'* The answer, surely, is 'No! No! No!' No, because there are trillions of planets in the Universe, vast numbers of which must have conditions suitable for life. No, because we all share the genes of two species (don't ask) within our very core: homo sapiens, and Neanderthal. And No, because we are surrounded by all manner of life on Earth; with millions of species sharing a single, fascinating planet. And foremost among these species is the said chimpanzee, and pygmy chimpanzee, together with four sub-species of gorilla, four sub-species of orang utan, and all nine sub-species of gibbon. As homo sapiens, we share around 99% of our DNA with these magnificent hominids. There is simply no need to explore the heavens for little green men - they're probably there, but the Earth is quite crowded and gloriously diverse enough, thank you.

To return to Vic: we captured some powerful, enduring images during these memorable excursions, showing Victor at his magnificent best. Standing proudly in the Royal National Rose Society show-grounds at St Albans. Relaxing with my brother's young family, in their Summer garden, at Amersham. And in the midst of bluebell woods, looking lovingly towards me. And, near Lake Vyrnwy, Vic is majestic, the soul of nobility, while standing beside Rhiwargor waterfall.

We have splendid photos of Victor, too, astride cliffs, in the most verdurous woodland, and on broad, empty beaches. And breasting a river: confident, resplendent in his pride and prime.

And pictures remembered in the mind's eye: Vic, noble and majestic, facing the raging snow-storm. So, too, at Dovedale, shaking himself in front of a setting sun, the water droplets spraying from his coat like white diamonds.

Vic was always himself, and always unique. We have so many superb pictures of Victor, reflecting his life's story: growing up, and as a mature, magnificent lad, in a myriad splendid locations. They are all to savour; all to remember him, with immense, undying affection. In fact, imperishable.

Grand UK Tours

Dogs are not our whole life, but they make our lives whole.

Roger Caras.

Victor was such an enthusiastic and courageous traveller! Where we were, he was happy to be. He loved being in the car, observing all around him as we travelled. He did not seem to find travel enervating, but rather fascinating, even inspiring. From an early age he would travel happily on the front seat of our Ford Escort, re-adjusting his balance as the car turned corners or veered around islands. All he needed was a pair of goggles and a leather cap to appear the complete motor enthusiast. Later on, transferring to the relative luxury of the Ford Sierra, he would occupy either front or rear seats, or indeed the 'boot' section. Vic - Mr Versatile.

During these years, we toured the UK extensively, seeking out new places, or re-visiting favourite haunts: Devon, Cornwall, Wales, and Scotland were our playgrounds. Sometimes we camped; at other times we stayed in dog-friendly hotels. I fondly remember hotel holidays in Devon, the Isle of Wight, the Yorkshire Dales, and Northumberland, as well as distant Scotland. It still amazes me that Victor had the stamina, and the desire, to travel such distances, in search of new adventures. Had Vic not been 'up for it', it is unlikely that we would have travelled quite so far. Vic's confidence and love of travel meant that we - and he - saw far more of the United Kingdom than most people - and certainly most dogs - and he enjoyed a vast array of stimulating experiences and environments: from rugged countryside, lochs and lakes, to beaches on every coastline, throughout England, Scotland and Wales.

Favourite destinations included characterful hotels at Hope Cove, in Devon; Malham in the Yorkshire Dales; Teesside in Durham, and Pitlochry in Scotland. Though, sadly, pet travel to the Continent was not yet permitted, and still some years away, Victor experienced - and enhanced - walks in some of the country's finest landscapes. His very first trip of this kind - when he was barely five months old - was to Malham, in the Yorkshire Dales. We rambled around such magnificent sites as Gordale Scar, Malham Cove and mysterious Janet's Fosse. This latter, in its pulsating life, and sense of intimacy combined with danger, gave birth to a poem. The opening stanza runs:

Gold and green is Janet's Fosse,
Rich with goblins, rolled in moss;
Shadows haunt the valley floor,
Eagle-eyed for tail or paw...

The weekend was Spring-showery, but we little realised at the time - the 'fall-out' reached us faster than the news - that the seemingly reviving rain that fell on us had been polluted by the fall-out from the Chernobyl nuclear disaster.

The Malham trip took place in May, 1986. A few months later - September - saw us in the New Forest, Hampshire, for a week of woodland walks and strolls along the beaches near to Bournemouth. Young Victor - a mere 10 months old - was already a seasoned traveller. On this trip, we visited the bustling Dorchester Fair; still, in the mid-80s, retaining an echo of its medieval origins. The stainless steel drinking bowl we bought there - for Vic - has retained its place of merit ever since.

Holidays around St Ives and Land's End, Boscastle, Tintagel, the Peak District, the Lake District, County Durham, Northumberland and Perthshire followed in seasonal progression. Victor was happy to stay in a fine hotel, a modest guest house, or the family tent; he was remarkably at home wherever *we* were. 'Loyalty' could have been his middle name, and we probably thought that all Golden Retrievers shared these characteristics, if not to the same elevated degree. Victor was calm and courteous when staying in hotels and, following an evening walk, slept soundly near to our bed, for the duration of the night.

I recall one brilliant Summer evening, spent on the Dorset coast above the dramatic and justly renowned limestone arch called Durdle Door. In the calm blue waters far below, the Royal Navy were engaged in an 'exercise': twelve warships firing at each other, in a mock battle. It was terrific stuff, and a superb spectacle, as the guns boomed their thunder. Victor sat on the cliffs' grassy slopes with us, absorbing the panorama and splendid performance below, while not in the least perturbed.

It was here, also, in a calm sea at Durdle Door, that the adolescent Victor first learned to swim - or at least discovered a natural ability, that he continued to delight in for the rest of his life. Sea, river or lake - he loved them all - and simply could not resist their magnetic lure.

In the social club on our camp-site, while we were supping 'Thomas Hardy ale', a young Captain in the British Army, relaxing with his men, made a tremendous fuss of the young Victor. He received this as his aristocratic due. We do not deign superiority; but we are who we are.

This little stretch of coast, part of the 'Jurassic Coast' carries historic and romantic resonance. On 28 September 1820, John Keats, his ship becalmed, landed near here, and delighted in showing his friend Joseph Severn his previously-discovered delights of Durdle Door and Lulworth Cove.

Tragically, Keats was on a final journey - to Italy, and to death. But, says Severn, *'he became like his former self. He was in a part that he already knew, and showed me the splendid caverns and grottoes with a poet's pride, as though they had been his birthright.'* On board ship that same evening Keats borrowed the copy of Shakespeare's Poems that he had given Severn a few days before, and composed, (or perhaps wrote out) on the blank page opposite *A Lover's Complaint*, one of the most beautiful and poignant sonnets in the English language:

> *'Bright Star, would I were steadfast as thou art -*
> *Not in lone splendour hung aloft the night,*
> *And watching, with eternal lids apart,*
> *Like nature's patient sleepless Eremite...'*

I have always been fascinated by landscapes that have inspired great art, so that we experience such a scene with a certain recollection of emotion and memory, as through a prism. A hundred years after Keats' visit, Thomas Hardy envisaged the scene in his poem, *At Lulworth Cove a Century Back*. We - and the young Victor - breathed in the magical air.

We had camped at the site above Durdle Door; on other trips we camped above the cliffs at Tintagel, and at a small family site near to St Ives. Victor was happy sharing these experiences with us - cliffs, coast, beaches - since he was confident and relaxed in practically any environment.

It was in August 1980, in an isolated pub near near Land's End, that June and I had witnessed an appalling scene that could have come straight out of a Western, saloon-bar brawl; fortunately, it was pre-Victor. The memory is enshrined in this verse:

Just a dozen bristling bikers
Descend on the fine 'First and Last'-
Destroy like demented Vikings,
Leaving just blood, and glass, and waste.

Fortunately, the memory did not deter our return to those lovely Cornish shores, and we often camped around St Ives and Sennen Cove. One evening in the Summer of '86, on a homely, family-run Cornish camp-site, our 'neighbours' - four teenage lads - returned noisily, with four young ladies in tow. How they had squeezed themselves, and the young women, into a regular Ford Escort I will never know. I can only conclude that they were galvanised, nay inspired, by the prospect of pleasures soon to come. And perhaps their tent, a very modest affair, doubled as the Tardis, since somehow they all proceeded to enter and wedge into the tiny, bulging canvas. The term 'enter' is perhaps apposite, since the rest of the night was spent in an orgy of fulfilment.

Our tents were all *too* close, and the noise levels emitted resembled those of jet aircraft screaming up the runway. The frolics continued without interruption, and with regular changes of personnel, all-night-long. They concluded at first light; *I* was exhausted. I had enjoyed the same amount of sleep - zilch - as the happy troop, but with none of the pleasure. History does not recall Victor's verdict, but his instincts would have been alert to the nature of events. That morning, he left a hopeful calling card or two close to the deserted but still evocative, pungent scene of passion. It was a Turner Prize in the making.

The roads to, and from, Cornwall, were notorious for their congestion in those pre-(South-West) motorway days of the 1980s. I remember one baking hot July or August morning, trying to drive the long, hard road back home from St Ives. We had reached the romantically named 'Indian Queens' and were crawling along more slowly than Sid the Snail. In frustration, Victor and I decided to abandon the car (to June) and walk alongside for a mile or two. We not only stretched our legs, but rapidly out-paced the car itself. But there were no tantrums; no *"Are we there yet?"*. Vic was as good as gold, as responsive and loyal as boy could possibly be, on those 8-hour-long odysseys.

More serenely, I recall a week-long tour of the Isle of Wight - Autumn 1987 - sandwiched between the 'Great Storm' and the forthcoming stock market hurricane. We stayed at a small, family hotel near to Freshwater. Vic distinguished himself on the Ferry. Unlike the ferries to France, where dogs are confined strictly within their owners' vehicles, Victor was allowed to travel with us, and enjoy the sea and breeze on deck. However, on arrival, and with the ferry secured on its berth, Vic could contain his excitement no longer: he dashed over the ship's side and into the sea, ahead of the first passengers. This was a happy augury of an enjoyable holiday. The most exhilarating of many super cliff walks was along the famous Needles on the island's rugged north coast - as memorable as Tintagel, or Dorset's Durdle Door.

One evening we were watching TV with the hotel's proprietor when the picture became fuzzy, and the sound crackled. "*Quick!*" he shouted, "*outside!*". We hurriedly ran out - Victor included: the animated landlord pointed excitedly to the bay below: there, like a floating, sparkling town, the QE II was sailing majestically by, bound for New York. I'm not sure what Victor made of it, but he revelled in every new experience. We have never returned to the island, but I think of this trip every time we pass the coast of the Isle of Wight, aboard the *Normandie* or *Mont St. Michel*.

Our Pitlochry holiday was spent, memorably, at a superb hotel - at Killiecrankie - popular with the hunting set. It was a golden, Autumnal week in late September. Though we were not a part of the (glass-accented) hunting fraternity, they all - to Vic's great delight - made a great fuss of Victor, who was of course a Retriever, around three years old and in his youthful prime. Given the opportunity, Victor would have performed royally 'in the field'. As it was, we enjoyed breathtaking walks in the wooded gorge called the Pass of Killiecrankie, criss-crossing the magnificent torrent that is the River Garry.

Here, in 1689, the bloody Battle of Killiecrankie took place, between the Jacobite supporters of James VI of Scotland, and the forces of William of Orange. Here, also, is the 'Soldiers Leap', where one of the protagonists made a death-defying jump to escape the fray. The day belonged to the Jacobites, although their forces were so depleted that the rebellion was quickly crushed. Three hundred years on, infused within the beauty and tranquillity of the scene, something of the spirit of this conflagration remains.

And, before leaving this superb corner of Tayside, we gazed on the glorious 'Queen's View' over Loch Tummel. From Killiecrankie, we were directed to another hotel, which resembled a small castle. Whilst we indulged in a splendid breakfast, facing the broad garden, the hotelier himself - the local laird - entertained us. There he strode on his manicured gravel drive, be-kilted in his finest tartan, serenading us with his bagpipes. Poignant and stirring, we enjoyed the spectacle immensely as, I believe, did Vic. As we departed, the landlord genially advised us to tour nearby Glen Lyon. The Glen was remote, lonely, lovely, and panoramic as only Scotland can be, within these Isles. My senses thrilled to the lure of the Glen, echoing John Clare's sensually-charged lines:

> 'Meet me by the sweetbrier,
> By the mole-hill swelling there;
> When the west glows like a fire
> God's crimson bed is there.
> Meet me in the green glen.'

Another daring trip undertaken in Vic's favourite transport - his resplendent, throbbing Escort Sports.

It is heartening to recall now, how Vic would relish these long trips to Cornwall, or Scotland. Clearly, there were comfort stops for all of us, but he seemed to know intuitively that there were good times ahead. Much later, when Victor was a senior boy of ten years of age, we travelled to North Yorkshire, believing that our (special offer) hotel was located there; in Otterburn, a village that we had visited a few years earlier. It is a small, compact village and we felt we could hardly go wrong. However, after a turn or two round the main street, and despite our best efforts. the hotel could not, would not be found. But why not? I asked an elderly farmer and his wife - mounted on a passing tractor - for directions. They replied confidently, in a pure Yorkshire dialect, that, to the best of their knowledge, no such hotel existed thereabouts. And they had lived in the village for more than 50 years!

A frantic 'phone call revealed, to our horror, that the hotel was actually in a village of the same name - but in Northumberland, almost on the Scottish border. Only another 100 miles, then! Victor was far less frayed than June and I, when we eventually arrived. He was happy, and relaxed, wherever we were. On arrival, I rewarded Vic with a walk around the immediate area, in the semi-dark; and then we all enjoyed our respective meals before retiring - and sweet oblivion.

There followed memorable days of rural idyll, in and around the enormous, remote Kielder Forest. Sadly, days spent bumping along forest roads - the scene of the RAC Rally - completely knackered the Sierra's universal joint, which required urgent and expensive repair. Thirty or so years later, I recall the adventure as though it was yesterday. Northumberland is one of the few regions of the UK that feels truly remote, with views over vast, undulating fells, and big, empty skies. This trip prepared us, psychologically, for adventures that lay on the far horizon.

For these were also the years when we were discovering France: from Arras in the North, to Angers in the West; from Strasbourg in the East, to St Tropez in the South. Whilst Victor travelled with us to the four corners of the UK, we always deeply regretted that he could not accompany us on our tours exploring the breadth and depth of La Belle France. How he would have adored those adventures! Occasionally, then, Vic was boarded at a kennels in the Staffordshire countryside, where he enjoyed loving care, and the freedom of a large paddock to exercise and play. I hated boarding him, but there was little choice if we were to make these early forays into France.

It was my chief delight on returning home to go-get-him. I can still recall the peculiar thrill that I experienced, on rushing to greet him, and giving and receiving a celebratory hug. Our first walk on re-acquaintance was always to nearby Highgate Common, where we would run around together in the sweeps of long grass and heather. How these tiny, apparently insignificant drops of pleasure still magnify in the memory, as though created yesterday.

On one occasion our Vic-caring neighbours received a call from the kennels. The kennel-maid had detected a swelling in Vic's ear, which required urgent surgery. After hasty consultation, a small operation was duly carried out by a local veterinary surgeon. The next day, our neighbours visited the patient to fuss and re-assure him, and check on his condition. The operation - for a common complaint amongst Retrievers - had been successful. However, Victor sported a bandage around his head and ears that made him look like a cartoon character. I do wish I had a photo of that moment. Needless to say, the recovering boy soon removed said bandage, and reverted to his cheerful, but dignified, self.

The Summer of 1990 found June and me enjoying the heady, mysterious Black Forest, near Rudesheim. As it happened, England were playing West Germany in the semi-final of the World Cup. We repaired to a local bar to watch the action. Every possible space was occupied by enthusiastic German supporters. There was much shouting and flag-waving, as the match ebbed to-and-fro. We were the only non-partisans in the place; the atmosphere was super-charged, but totally good-humoured. All eyes were fixed like lasers, on June and me, to observe our response to the game's high points.

Despite a splendid performance from Bobby Robson's men, England lost on penalties, (as usual), after extra time. Our new friends could not have been more hospitable, offering us drinks galore, no doubt to drown our sorrows. *"Don't worry, it's only a game"*, we were told, consolingly. A real pity Vic couldn't be there - he would have soaked up the atmosphere - and, no doubt, the attention. Germany went on to beat Argentina in the final. 1966 seemed an awfully long-way away.

Even so, we were grateful, and happy, that we achieved so much; and that Victor toured so many wonderful corners of the United Kingdom with us. He gazed on the magnificence of the Bowes Lyon Museum, the awesome north Cornish coast, and the sublimity of Durham Cathedral. And, for good measure, he looked out on the long, glorious mountain vistas of the Scottish Highlands. Again, strolling along the upper Tees Valley, he experienced the equally majestic 'Low Force', a terrific torrent, with an almost perpetual halo - a rainbow that arcs over these stunning falls. What Victor made of these wonderful places - and of Tintagel, Queen's View at Pitlochry, and Lulworth Cove - is not recorded. But we did note his pleasure at the time, and the photographic evidence is testimony to a boy who was enjoying himself immensely.

In October 1998 - whilst gardening in France - I suffered a 'slipped disc'. A stiff and sore back had provided one or two intimations of mortality but, like most good advice, it had been promptly ignored. My reward had been - agony. On the return sea-crossing to the UK we experienced a terrific storm: I sat grimly, welded to my chair in the dining room, determined not to let the tumultuous seas and jolting, shuddering ship ruin either my spine or my steak and chips. The said dining room, however, resembled the *Marie Celeste*: abandoned *steak frites,* and *poisson frites* lay everywhere, their owners heaving pitifully into their *sac de mers.*

My unexpected and acute disability resulted in a prolonged convalescence at home. It was a blessing in disguise, since it enabled me to share irreplaceable quality time with Vic. Together, we watched the wind chasing leaves across the fields, and enjoyed gentle, delicate walks around familiar haunts.

I simply doted on him. Victor was a powerfully built boy; with his strength came not only confidence, but gentleness. And he was such an impressive character: sleek and muscular, intrepid, profoundly affectionate, bright as a button - and ferociously loyal. Though he was also fiercely proud, I cannot recall a single aggressive act towards another dog. He was a fundamental, inseparable part of our family, and we treasure pictures of him throughout our home. He remains, for me, the quintessential Golden Retriever: an aristocrat at home - our alpha and omega boy; as magnificent as can be, as game, as bright, as loving.

Vic was also a terrifically healthy dog, barely experiencing any ill health, until his final months. And then, despite my desperation, not all the magic I could muster, nor all the spirits I could summon, in supplication, could long prevail against the powers of darkness and dissolution. When we finally lost our beloved Victor, aged 14 years, my world fell in. I had never known grief of this depth, and struggled to cope. There was no comfort. There was no escape. There was no respite. Our little house had become an empty, gaping space; empty hearth, empty home. The youthful Victor's teeth-marks - as fresh as ever - upon bookcase and table leg, only added to the desolation.

A loving family sealed around me, and I threw myself into a maelstrom of work: it helped me to somehow get through the days. June and I visited Ludlow, glad for the distraction to our dispirited, dejected minds. Yet it was many, many months before the iron grip around the heart began to loosen - and that was some time after we had welcomed Hector & Jason into our lives.

Victor: in so many respects, the model Golden Retriever, and *uber* personality; a true pet, the truest of companions. My larger-than-life, special friend. My blood-brother. My secret sharer. Vic was such a wonderful companion, complete in himself. There was no need for a further chapter, or a sequel. When we lost him, despite the inevitable questions, we had no thought of acquiring another dog, never mind *dogs.* Victor was a star; an immortal diamond. I know that we will be re-united in death.

Little did I think, dream, or imagine, that our future companions had already been born, and were snuggling in their bed of straw, beginning their life's journey. But so it was. Had I known this on 22 January 1999, I may have smiled incredulously, through my tears. And I might also have reasoned: *"I know dogs, and the best Golden Retriever in the world has taught me everything I need to know about this superb breed".* Our experience of Victor, not unnaturally, informed our knowledge of the inherent nature of the Golden Retriever. I was confident - perhaps over confident - that I knew this superb breed through and through.

But I was wrong. Perhaps it's like marriage: 14 years experience may provide a good deal of insight and understanding of the institution, and one's partner, but not insight and understanding of a new partner; their personality, traits and foibles. Hector & Jason were as different to Victor in as many essentials as it was possible for dogs, or at any rate Golden Retrievers, to be. Any complacency that I might have felt was immediately - and very rudely - shattered. Life is full of the most unexpected surprises, and I had just embarked on a lifetime's worth of sudden and unimagined surprises. Contrary to all my expectations, Hector & Jason turned out to be very different to Victor - very different indeed.

Unjustly, but inevitably, I at first judged our new companions by a very strict and probably unique standard. I was actively looking for signs of Victor, in Hector & Jason. While a few points of similarity did emerge over time - Hector shared Victor's love of swimming, and his keen interest in tennis balls - this was pretty superficial stuff. And besides, Jason...well, Jason was Jason. And these similarities, or nuances suggesting similarities, took time to develop or emerge, and often flattered to deceive. Even within the same breed - or the same family - dogs, it turns out, are as individual as we are, and do not conform either to our expectations or our pre-conceptions.

Victor's image continued to shine ahead, and his loss continued to weigh on my spirit, even though I was now the proud carer of two gorgeous new boys. Although this unseen presence was a heartfelt tribute to Victor's memory and the love that he inspired, at first I struggled to adjust to new realities. The crippling pain of loss could not be wholly assuaged, even by the tumultuous impact of two 'new kids on the block'. An unwelcome truth asserts itself: arriving with 'new' pets comes a resurgence of intense grief, like a blast of cold air out of a clearing sky. It is certainly not the case that one dog in any real sense replaces, or can replace, another.

One must learn to love again.

4: Puppy Love versus Growing Pains

There is no psychiatrist in the world like a puppy licking your face.

Bern Williams

And you are come: unbidden, unalloyed;
Mad miracles of gold, and love, and joy,
With stunning eyes and smiles, great hearts, sweet noise -
Bundles of warmth, and hope, and life; such boys!

Colin Hill

Hector and Jason grew up rapidly, boisterously, noisily, uproariously. It was as though life was being lived fast-forward, in glorious, almost hallucinogenic, technicolour.

At first, the house was a mass - and mess - of thick newspaper and muddy foot-prints. Growing, rampant, mad-cap puppies are not for the faint-hearted, even less for the hygienically-obsessed or morbidly house-proud. Augean stables the house was not but, no doubt, lurking amidst the piles of newspaper and bedding, there were pungent, hopefully temporary, 'litter odours'. The lounge was similarly customised by two boys eager to play, and exercise their growing powers.

The modest back garden, too, mostly lawn, and now trampled by the happy duo, soon bore the scars of puppy-dom. The garden became a chaotic playground, was dug up at will, and very quickly resembled an unkempt heap of mud.

And the boys absorbed, indeed demanded, copious amounts of time - just as we had been warned. We accepted all this with a smile, sometimes a shrug: these were our boys - and that was that.

We - and H&J - were surrounded by a babble of local interest that seemed to share in our delight. Our friends and neighbours bought gifts for the newly-arrived little-ones. A pet-loving neighbour, Anne, was among the first to greet and fuss the new arrivals, generously bringing - chewable - gifts.

H&J quickly recognised their toys, and played with them - and with each other - all the time. It is sound advice not to allow your young dog to chew your shoes - even old shoes - since this gives them the wrong signals. They will make no distinction between chewing your old slipper and chewing your Jimmy Choo's. Fortunately, expensive footwear is not one of our priorities, and H&J performed little damage on this front. A small mercy...

Our local newsagent provided us with great swathes of the local newspaper, which were put to very effective use. And, if one harbours negative thoughts of a certain politician, celebrity or sports star, it can always be arranged for their photo to be prominently displayed, for your puppy to target. However, H&J rapidly became semi, and then fully, house trained. When reaching this point, at around 16 weeks of age, there is huge relief - no pun intended - in finally getting rid of all the (necessary) paraphernalia of 'toilet' newspaper, plastic sheets and the veritable arsenal of cleaning substances.

When they were not 'bombing around' the living room, the two pups fizzed around the garden like rockets on speed: chasing balls, chasing tails, chasing each other. It was crazy, madcap stuff. Jason also delighted in pulling the washing from the clothes line - he quickly displayed a love of clothes, in particular towels and tea-towels, that never left him. The young Jason would also chase his tail, circling round and round, for sheer joy and exhilaration; he stopped only when, presumably, giddiness over-took him.

The whole world believes that puppies are little cuties, and so they are - while asleep. Awake, and seeking adventure, they can be little wild-eyed monsters - with teeth like sharks, and a desire to muscle in and frustrate every human activity. The young lad, or girl, will usually arrive at their new home in the midst of teething. I can personally verify that a ten-week old Retriever's milk teeth are devilishly sharp, like little shark's teeth. Their new carers are seen as their natural ally in this respect - hands and fingers provide a warm, writhing and welcome teething ring. Toys - whether 'rabbits', or shoes, or artificial bones - are definitely second best. Certainly, the young Victor regarded me as his special play-mate, and I (and my fingers) responded as best they could.

Yet Hector, and especially Jason, hardly touched me: responsive and loving as they were, their teething tussles were confined pretty much to each other, and they conducted these activities successfully, but invisibly, since they were always engaged in combat, wrestling and chasing each other around their home. It is hard, in any case, to think of the so-delicate Jason touching my skin, other than to lick or nuzzle me. In different circumstances the same could probably not be said of Hector.

The intensity of H&J's exercise was matched by the intensity of sleep. Puppies sleep a great deal - to recover, to digest, to grow, and to prepare for the next slice of being alive. Despite the mud, smell and chaos, life was burgeoning again, and I was glad - very, very glad.

Only too quickly, aided by four large, special meals a day, (two of them involving weetabix and milk) H&J put away forever their puppyish things. The newspaper toilet, teething, and toys and 'bones', were abandoned with some relief. As early as late Spring, the boys had transformed into excited teenagers - sometimes unruly, sometimes responsive - as they continued to absorb learning, advice, instruction, experience.

And transformed, as well, physically, into the most handsome adolescents. This happens as if by magic, and if you blink - yet again re-arranging or repairing the garden, or making the house habitable - you miss it. The growing process really is akin to magic: from birth to maturity, a young dog grows by an incredible ninety times - in a mere 18 months. Fortunately, I remembered to take some pictures of this brief but unforgettable episode in H&J's lives - so we have a cute Hector, asleep in his little bed, and Jason, asleep on his back - his pink belly revealing his glorious puppy-hood. The boys were much easier to photograph when asleep - awake, they were restless, non-stop little furies.

Each day, as the young lads continued their amazing transformation - a *sea change, into something rich and strange*, I asked myself the question: *"which of the boys is Victor?"* before answering - emphatically, if a touch sadly - *"neither: they're totally different"*. It was an answer delivered with a tinge of regret, but with conviction. They shared a heritage, and Hector would later reveal a few curious similarities to his distant uncle; but in essence they were as different as whisky from wine, or champagne from sparkling water. No value judgements here - just genuine, head-scratching diversity, within a single, super breed.

Quickly, startlingly, Hector & Jason became powerful, adolescent dogs, and dominated the house and household with their mad-cap antics and play-fighting. June affectionately named them '*mad, and madder*', Jason being the real loony-toon. In their burgeoning strength, grace and confidence they were invincible, and immortal; like knights of old, glinting and shining in the sun, and eager for adventure.

But, unlike knights of old, they were also incorrigible. We were not to know at this point, but Hector & Jason had the longest adolescence in history. Though, physically, they grew to majestic maturity in their first 12 to 18 months, in their mentality, outlook, and approach to life, Hector & Jason remained young at heart for an almost indecent length of time - well into what might be regarded as middle age. This vigorous, fresh, youthful approach to life was to stretch through the years, ensuring that their company remained a delight - occasionally an exasperation - to us, and to each other, so that our own lives, and indeed outlook on life, entered a different trajectory.

Viewed in isolation, there was only bliss. But this was the real world - the one of consequences. The continuing casualty of their growing powers remained the garden. H&J would tear round at break-neck speed in all weathers, pulverising the 'lawn' as they did so. The erstwhile patch of grass would never fully recover, and would need to be completely replaced every two or three years - the toughest lawn seed being no match for H&Js running, digging, and of course the odd pee. Two large dogs in one medium-sized garden does not equate to an Alan Titchmarsh-like result. Quite simply, the garden was their playground, and we ruefully accepted this reality.

The second casualty remained the house - the curtains ripped down, carpet torn up, and furniture chewed. It was not pretty, but it was expected; leave two over-grown puppies to their own devices for a couple of hours, and they will soon become restive, and customise what they regard as a large kennel, to their complete satisfaction: it is their den, their playhouse, their home, to adapt as they see fit. It was a crazy time, but we were happy to live with our decision; fortunately, this next stage in their development was also mercifully short.

Dogs are physically mature at around 18 months of age, so you have only one shot at raising them to peak health and fitness. As puppies and young dogs, Hector & Jason were given the best of everything, and consumed enormous amounts of cereal, specially formulated high protein biscuit, mince and chicken. Both boys had keen, healthy appetites, and it was a delight to witness their burgeoning growth and development, day after hectic day. H&J grew rapidly into something special, prodigious, even. Their physical potential was fulfilled, oh how it was fulfilled! But the full implications of this physical development, in terms of our experience of living together, only became clear over time.

Time seemed to gallop forward - raising two young dogs makes one pretty oblivious of time - and suddenly Hec and Jas had 'arrived' as superb young adults. They were pretty much the same in stature - tall, trim, muscular, but not heavy set or ponderous Retrievers. The ugly duckling analogy doesn't apply in this case: Hector grew into himself - an impressively handsome, confident and out-going young boy. Jason, meanwhile, became, and remained, breathtakingly beautiful. They were startlingly attractive: light, fast, eager, and full of, and demanding, fun.

Hector became not only handsome, but physically and mentally strong, tough, resilient, and craftily intelligent: loving and loyal, but always with an eye to the main chance. Hector also had a distinguishing characteristic - a little fur quiff on the top of his head that set him apart from other Retrievers, but which we thought was rather charming and distinctive.

Hec was built and crafted like his dad. Hector also had the most indomitable will; lunging into the most impenetrable of thickets, or plunging into lakes, rivers or sea to keenly pursue whatever bee was in his bonnet. He had a proud independence, sometimes bordering on the sly, so that he sometimes simply disappeared on his walks; one second beside you, the next second gone: only to return - quite unconcerned - half an hour later. Hector was as bright as his sun-flecked fur, full-on, savvy, spirited, and independent. Quite simply, he was the cleverest, and smartest, and *deepest* dog I had ever met.

And he developed into a formidable, brave, loyal companion, with a passion for footballs, and a mission to tackle errant local wildlife. Hector was the animated life of the party, gregarious and full of fun. He became a totally distinctive character.

A rich, dense, chestnut coat - and the glossy, golden mane that adorned his broad shoulders - distinguished Hector from his brother.

Jason, however, was entirely, and evenly, blonde. Yet their coats were the least that set them apart. While, even at home, Hector was exuberant, excitable, intelligent, cunning, demonstrative and always fun to be around, Jason was quiet, reserved, responsive and deeply, deeply, affectionate. In fact, Jason developed into the most loving, and lovable - and crazy - boy: with breathtaking agility, and an unquenchable lust for life. And heart-achingly beautiful.

Jason would become a Greek God. And run like the wind. From the first - or almost from the first - I adored him. His face was lovely - verging on the feminine, and so like his mother; the finest eye-lashes framing deep-set blue-brown eyes, a shiny black nose, and black-rimmed mouth. And a gorgeous, luxuriantly soft, rich, blonde coat, which feathered on his strong, long legs; the coat quite flat on the body, but thick at the neck and the hind quarters, and completed by a wonderfully wafted tail. And faultless features. His body was perfectly proportioned, with the most handsome limbs - a deep sprung chest, and superb, shapely legs. Even Jason's pads were black, contrasting with his coat. To complete the picture: if Jason was not the most cerebral of boys, (his intelligence was on a different level entirely), he had a depth of character, and generosity of spirit, that were truly touching. Jason was affectionate, and the very soul of gentleness: there was not a bad brain cell, or bad bone, in his nature.

Jason's early promise blossomed into something quite sensational. He was every inch the matinee idol. A regular Rudolf Valentino among dogs. Animal, vegetable or mineral, Jas was the most beautiful spirit - inside and out - that I have ever known. A veritable Adonis. Yet I often think of him as Ariel, or Mercury; almost as a spirit, without true bodily form. Or a shooting star, flaming through the heavens. Of course, this is fanciful, since he had a perfect physical presence; but in movement he was so light and ethereal, appearing almost as an apparition.

And Jason became a glorious free spirit. He was brave, bold, blonde, beautiful - and barmy. Jason, outwardly reserved, but the absolute light of one's life, joyous at seeing you, only wanting to be near you.

Though Jason was of course every inch a boy, I was always reminded of Caliban's awed description of Miranda, in Shakespeare's *The Tempest*:

> *'...I never saw a woman,*
> *But only Sycorax my dam and she;*

*But she as far surpatheth Sycorax
As great'st doth least'.*

For me, Jason was the canine equivalent of a Sumatran tiger, or a snow leopard. His features were as delicate and lovely as fine porcelain. And his tail was like a wand - which complemented every other aspect of his nature. Jas was always the dashing prince, the prince of hearts; his twin brother - nearly - always at his side. And he was, unashamedly, *mine.*

I felt awed by his aura. Jason was just pure love. Just as you can't really reduce love, or pure gold, or diamond, so with Jason. Perfection. From the tip of his shiny black nose, to the tip of his superb tail, Jas was simply, utterly magnificent. So physically spectacular, he was an innocent abroad: enigmatic, luminous, but within a sea of tranquillity. He was like a jewel-box that is full of exotic and unexpected delights and surprises; every facet and nuance shone, not with a reflected light, but with a deep, inner glow. Yet at home he was calm, devoted, whole-hearted - his alter-ego took over only when he was set free, and his genius unleashed at white heat. Outside, in the big, wide world, Jason was outside the box - every box.

I have always thought that cats are the most beautiful creatures. I still think so - their feline grace and physical perfection is a cause of wonder, and they often have characters to match. June and I share a home with three magnificent Burmese cats, so I have had plenty of time to study and admire their beauty. But, dog, cat or human, I have never *felt* beauty as I felt it with Jason. He was simply awesome. Michelangelo, with loving eye and aching heart, might have carved him from Carrara marble. As John Donne swoons in *The Good-morrow*:

*'If ever any beauty I did see,
Which I desir'd, and got, 'twas but a dream of thee.'*

This is not to denigrate Hector in any sense: he was a most handsome dog in his own right, and an incredible character. This was a case of Mr Perfect and Mr Personality. H&J were complementary; not only brothers, but the very closest of friends, with an instinctive understanding and desire to love and protect each other. But just to touch Jason, to stroke his head and fur, gave me a thrill, a sense of pride, a lump in the throat. I never grew out of it, never got over it; it was quite marvellous.

Of course, like most dogs, Hector & Jason wagged their tails when excited or happy. Hector wagged his strong tail at the least sign of encouragement: a kind word, a biscuit, the sight of his lead. Jason's slightly longer, fan-like tail wagged less frequently and, when it did, moved more slowly, and in a broader arc. One learned that that slow, broad arc spelt pure love.

The two brothers, though different 'characters', became inseparable. Indeed, they were hardly ever separate. All their walks were taken together. Their meals - they competed to see who could clear their plate first - together. They slept - together. Together, also, they were rays of sunshine - inspiration, solace, affection - in a world sorely in want of such qualities.

Except to the eye that loved them, H&J seemed, to the majority of people who met them, to be somewhat less than brothers, let alone twins. I revelled in their differences, their uniqueness, as much as in their points of similarity of physique and character. There was so much to observe, marvel at, delight in, remark on, reflect on. Where to begin? On some things, they exhibited a unity of spirit. When departing for our walks, they were of one mind: I cannot recall a single occasion when they desired or suggested we traverse in different directions, but would pull me enthusiastically, and with one mind, towards the chosen place. And, to me, they were certainly brothers, but very, very far from being clones. As I have said elsewhere, like two sides of the same coin, but still so very, thrillingly different...

I need to recognise these differences as best I can. If Jason's beauty was dazzling, the same could not quite be said of Hector. Yet he *was* majestically handsome and, yes, had great depth of character. If Hector was 'earth', with all that that implies in richness and resonance, Jason was air - quicksilver, mercurial, tantalisingly enigmatic.

In Hector's 'earth', and Jason's 'air', they represented two poles of the fundamental elements that make up this planet's constitution. Hector: warm, deep, fertile, with rich seams of precious minerals rippling beneath the surface, pure hidden springs, and submerged caverns that led to uncharted regions. Jason, quite different: magical and mysterious, he was a zephyr soaring unseen through the fresh new leaves of a Spring morning. And yet, their relationship was as close and strong as any I have known; they were spiritually and physically inseparable, spending only a few days apart throughout their lives. They were the essence of effervescence: Hector, hot, fiery, and furious as Henry IV's Hotspur; while Jason's passions ran as deep and pure as a mountain torrent.

The scene was set for a lifetime of adventure, where every single day in their exalted company became a fun-filled, magic day.

******

The infant Hector & Jason were not parachuted into an 'empty nest'. Our household comprised - in addition to June and me - two redoubtable Burmese cats, Oscar and Charlie. These guys had grown up and lived cheek-by-jowl with the equally redoubtable Victor and, in their physical prime, were not to be messed with by the two new boys on the block.

Oscar and Charlie were friendly lads, but believed in a policy of 'live and let live'. They had their own, hectic, schedules, and played only bit-parts in Hector and Jason's lives - and indeed, vice versa. The two Burmese guys were not to be 'dissed' by the two young Retrievers. It was an important lesson, since they could easily have become a tasty morsel for the growing, and always hungry, young titans.

Oscar and Charlie were a formidable hunting team, and might have provided a role model for the young Hector, who would, however, have bridled at the suggestion. The magical Oscar seemed to charm mice, squirrels, goldfish and even snakes on to his paws, like iron filings on to a magnet; while the fierce but loyal Charlie became a splendid and indefatigable partner, with a penchant for sleeping in motor cars. Tragically, we were to lose Charlie at all too young an age to a freak motor accident; Oscar lived alongside the boys, in a kind of splendid but amicable isolation, for many years thereafter. Oliver and Louis would later join a household containing Oscar, as senior partner, but a household by then dominated by the youthful Hector & Jason.

5: First Walks, First Larks

Rarely, rarely, comest thou,
Spirit of Delight!

Song: Rarely, Rarely, Comest Thou - Percy Bysshe Shelley

O, you are young and crazy, son -
True offspring of the racing sun:
And truly, will we make him run!

Colin Hill

With huge relief that we had successfully got through - or overcome - that brief, joyous but demanding period of puppy-hood, we prepared for our first trips out, first on foot, and then by car. These first car trips were to the local beauty-spots of Kinver, and Highgate Common, both popular dog-walking haunts a mere five or so miles from home, and ideal for an inauguration into the mysteries of the big wide world that lay on our doorstep.

Young dogs have a very steep learning curve. They must pack into months the life-skills that humans take perhaps ten years to develop. They must learn about people - strangers, as well as friends; about their home and neighbourhood; about the roads, and risks from traffic. They must learn to become accustomed to, adjust to, cars, buses and lorries thundering past within a few feet. They must learn commands - or at least guidance - from their 'master', in order to remain safe, and to behave in accordance with modern society's rules and expectations. They must learn to cross the road safely, not 'foul' other people's gardens, and to behave with reasonable decorum. If learning is fun, it can also be stressful.

So, at just four months old, Hector & Jason were young, immature dogs with much to learn. As soon as they were old enough, and had had their inoculations, the young boys began their first forays into this strange new world beyond our closeted home. We were relieved to start this introduction to the outside world: at four months of age, H&J had far too much energy to be confined to the house and garden. They were ready for the tantalising horizons that lay beyond the back gate. And their body language expressed a fierce pride in their place in the world, and the sheer joy of being alive: they were immortal, and invincible.

The very first walks from the home, and on to the unfamiliar, alien streets, can be anxious times, and the boys needed encouragement and protection on these short, hesitant walks. At first, and on their leads, H&J appeared to be willing learners, quickly absorbing the basic lessons. Jason, admittedly, took his time; he seemed fazed by anything that was not a natural phenomenon: a crisp packet blowing on the breeze, or a street sign clanking under the strain of wind and rain. But learn they did - it was a journey we embarked on together, with me as mentor, and it helped cement our bond, our dizzyingly intense relationship.

However, I should have realised, from the experience of familiarising the boys with their home environment, that these guys were, to say the least, different. The canine familiarisation process takes place in distinct stages. First, getting to know the house and garden; then, following vaccination, short walks around the local neighbourhood, avoiding as much traffic as possible. After that, longer walks, combined with trips in the car to areas of woodland and common, where the young boys will also encounter and become familiar with other people - and other dogs. Generally speaking, this process becomes more difficult as it progresses, and widens out - the first trips beyond the garden being quite traumatic for the young dog.

We would soon learn, with Hector & Jason, to expect the unexpected; convention, expectations, norms, all went out of the window. And so it was with these first walks - the opposite of most dog behaviour. H&J never felt entirely comfortable with the house; they disliked the vinyl floor of the kitchen, (but which had to be put-up-with for the sake of food-glorious-food); and they were none-too-keen, either, on the wall-to-wall fitted carpets. On the whole, the house probably compared unfavourably with their kindergarten barn, plus straw. The garden was fine, though - and outside the garden was even better.

And so, to the next phase - *off piste* or, in our case, off leads. Rather than a further tour of the housing estate - where Jason in particular had shown a slightly febrile anxiety - and since they were country dogs, we decided to take H&J into the countryside for their first proper walk. Since the young H&J were quite unfamiliar with anywhere outside their immediate neighbourhood, I had fondly imagined that, let off their leads, the boys would walk, or run, close to us, and obey commands - albeit reluctantly. They were, after all, already accustomed to their names, and had proved responsive in short walks on their leads. However, our expectations could not have been further from the truth. All complacency, all fond imagining, was rudely shattered. Even a lecture by Wittgenstein could not have prepared me for what was to come.

These first outings turned out to be the canine equivalent of a wild ride at a theme park. The beautiful area of Common that we took H&J to - nearby Highgate Common - is a popular destination for walkers and dog owners. This Common - flat and clear - seemed ideal for those first walks. However, for Hector & Jason - for months confined to house and garden, and walks around our Estate - it must have seemed like paradise on speed.

In their mutually-inspired confidence H&J set about this aspect of the learning process with apparently scant reference to me. Released - with words of caution and advice - from their leads, H&J responded like the proverbial bulls in a china shop - or perhaps like young dogs in a toyshop. It quickly became clear that, to say the least, neither boy was the traditional Retriever who, well, retrieves, and looks to its 'master' for direction. Neither could these guys be bribed with ball or biscuit: running, exploring, chasing, digging and generally setting the place on fire was H&J's way of executing their intended walks.

In a state of youthful, ecstatic exuberance, H&J simply went wild, in crazy, early-adolescent frenzy. This was a journey of discovery, inspired by an immediate and innate love of freedom and countryside: other dogs; fox holes; ponds; copses. This was a wild, wacky, world and they explored everywhere and everything, with all the optimism and joy of new love. June and I were at first, amused, then exasperated, then finally frantic, at our inability to control H&J's headlong, maniacal exploration of nature's bounty. Urgent 'commands' to return went unheeded as, instincts ignited, each boy strove to seize the intensity and variety of opportunity, and to revel in every millisecond of pleasure. And, when he did - eventually - return, Jason expressed his delight by crashing into the back of my legs with the impact of a missile. Thankfully, he grew out of this particular trait though, as time went on, I would have preferred this particular surprise to the anxiety of seeking my flying boy over hill and down dale.

Hector & Jason were, clearly, country dogs through and through - from the tips of their shiny noses to the tips of their swishing, sumptuous tails. The world, as suddenly and gloriously revealed, was infinitely exciting: where to run first, explore first, dive into first? There were burrows to explore and dig into, ponds to jump into, thickets to dive into. The apparently unending countryside was a phantasmagoria of sights, scents, spirit-revving things to do and delight in, all in sharp 3D technicolour.

Even the transport to such earthly pleasures was a big issue. On being ushered towards my trusty Escort Sport, H&J recoiled in horror; no way, Jose. So I learned a very quick lesson, and re-introduced them to the car that brought them to us - the Sierra. This had a hatchback that was flat, and that they could either jump into, or (in Jason's case) be placed into. But, whilst the boys acquiesced with Sierra travel, they were happier by far with the Volvo 940 Estate that we acquired that September; the rear was spacious, flat and provided a great all-round view. Hector loved this car, and its successor, a Volvo V70, with a passion. Jason, as we shall see, gritted his teeth and joined his brother for the ride, thanks to my helping hand.

Yet the big wide world itself they took to like the proverbial 'ducks to water'. It was as if they were born to be released, to be set free. Hills, woodland, commons, parks, even residential streets, were H&J's passport to adventure and excitement. From their very first trips out, they loved this big outdoors; it attuned with their passionate nature. As young boys they disliked the imposition of a collar and lead; these were devilish devices that restrained their freedom and controlled their movement - as indeed they were designed to do. But H&J were at one with the elements, and embraced the world with their instincts and their hearts. We had been warned. They are not only immortal and invincible - they are incorrigible.

And already, at this very early stage, it was clear that we had two exceptional, if unconventional, Golden Retrievers in our care. This was more than youthful high-jinks or wilful mis-behaviour. In their excitement, H&J were covering the - often uneven - ground of

Common or Park at an exceptional rate; the young Jason in particular being mesmeric in his speed. In our small garden, these characteristics had been disguised, or blunted, since the enclosed, grassy space gave scope for only a brief, if electric, circuit.

It quickly became apparent that we had contained two rockets in a shoe box. I could almost feel the electricity crackling among the boughs, as H&J coursed excitedly in all directions. It was a kind of alchemy: my life transformed, not from lead into gold, but from one state of being to another: from cool, calm and collected, to heady, enervating, and ecstatic.

It was also abundantly clear to June and I that we faced a challenge: how to allow these boys their freedom, at least in managed, relative terms, without jeopardising their safety, or the safety of others. This was a challenge that we grew to accept, and attempted to meet, on a daily basis, and which stretched us continually; it is the theme of this book.

I very quickly concluded that, such were their physical demands, these were young men's dogs; and I could no longer regard myself as young. But I was shocked back into youth, at least in spirit, and shocked back to fitness, as I chased the boys along the woodland's winding ways. Adrenaline coursed through their veins - and through mine. The crumbling tower that was my body quickly acquired stronger, and more supple, foundations. It was simply *necessaire*.

Many, many times, whilst walking, apparently on my own, I would be asked by fellow dog-walkers *"where are your dogs?"* to which I would reply - sometimes through gritted teeth - *"I really don't know"*, or *"somewhere ahead"*. But, almost invariably, I would find them or, more accurately, they would unerringly find me. Unless he was hormone-crazed by 'lady magic', Victor would be a constant at my side; unerring, reliable. While not remotely seduced by the lady-lure, H&J were as different to Vic in this respect as chalk from cheese.

Highgate Common continued to play host to some of our earliest sorties; it is rich in memories. Some of these may serve to illustrate the quick-silver nature of Jason. When H&J were maybe a year or so old, we were striding across the Common when a hot air balloon was suddenly spotted - straight above, and at a low altitude - at a height of maybe 200'. We looked up, as one does, to get a closer look. Two seconds later we looked down: Jason was nowhere to be seen. Clearly, he had been spooked by such an unnatural object, and had fled. Despite the fact that we had clear views in all directions, Jason had simply disappeared. Thirty minutes of anxious calling and searching ensued before, just as suddenly, he re-appeared. For this relief, much thanks.

One of my clearest memories of Highgate, however, still causes me some consternation. Every Saturday we visited the Common, and the boys came to know the large expanse of down and woodland extremely well. H&J always ran ahead of us, but within sight - they knew every path and walk intimately. Then, suddenly, Jason would depart from the well-trodden path, and disappear. After what seemed like an age - but actually around twenty minutes later - he returned from whence he had been, panting hard but otherwise fine. We had no idea where he went, or why, or how he found his way back. Almost certainly, he had left the Common itself, since the flying boy would have covered several miles in his absence.

Jason repeated this performance many times, always returning to the same spot, and to us (and the equally mystified Hector), following his secret mission. I was astonished at his athleticism, and his natural intelligence. After a year or so of this apparently miraculous activity I think I lost my nerve, either keeping poor Jas on his lead, or changing our route. I loved Jason's free spirit but, in a complex and often dangerous environment, strived to find some kind of balance. After all, only a short time before, on land adjoining the Common, we had been accosted with - "*I'll shoot those dogs if they come on my land again!*". We needed to protect the boys from themselves - and from the quick and easy anger of others - as far as we possibly could.

It was Jason, also, who came foul of a fox's den. Both boys loved searching around fox holes, and digging excitedly and with real intent. No matter how we discouraged this practice, the boys always regarded fox earths as a source of deep interest. In one instance, (I was absent, apparently nursing an injured ankle) Jason - running ahead of June - disappeared yet again. Un-beknown to June, the young Turk had found a fox hole, and buried himself within. Foxes are of course smaller and slimmer than the typical Golden Retriever. Twenty minutes later, to June's intense relief, Jas extricated himself - through furious back-peddling and perhaps with the help of the 'home-owner'. He re-emerged, *sans* collar, and *sans* blonde face for, from the neck upwards, he was covered in the bright, sandstone soil of the Common. Luckily, his nose was still intact. Yet he was un-harmed, boyishly ecstatic, even.

Late one afternoon, in the midst of the commuter rush-hour, we were returning from said Common when, without warning, the Sierra jarred to a halt on the cusp of a busy traffic island; a terminal case of clutch failure. A kindly motorist or two helped me push the stricken car on to the kerb, and I called the AA for assistance. Since it would be the best part of an hour until help arrived, I decided to walk H&J home, and then return to the scene. The boys jumped from the vehicle with an almost feline grace, and we practically shot the two miles or so home, along sun-flecked, hedge-trimmed lanes. My cares already seemed to be behind me, as we powered along the pavement abutting the highway. Hector & Jason transformed even the most annoying, frustrating experiences into the liquid gold of pure optimism and *joie de vivre*.

A little further from home, and more salubriously, we began H&J's early instruction into England's medieval history. Ludlow was one of our very first trips with the adolescent Hector & Jason. This town, as everyone now knows, is a fascinating, bustling market town in rural Shropshire. There is a distinctive old world charm, an ancient and lively market, and an impressive medieval castle. We have always been drawn to castles, and cathedrals; however, with H&J in attendance we were now de-barred from cathedrals, though still welcomed to most castles.

Ludlow was no exception. The superbly well-preserved Castle was built around 1086 - one of the first great wave of Norman castle building - in this case designed to guard against the dreaded Welsh. In fact, Ludlow was charged with oversight over most of what we now call Wales.

Ludlow Castle's most famous claim is as the site of 'the most controversial wedding night in history', when Prince Arthur and Catherine of Aragon celebrated their wedding there. Only to think that this Castle was the home of Prince Arthur and his new bride! And how the (supposed) pestilential air of Ludlow - in 1502 - caused the demise of the young king-to-be. The outcome, of course, was the eventual accession of Henry VIII, and his own marriage to Catherine - leading to a chain of events with profound historical consequences: England becoming a Protestant state, the reign of Elizabeth I, the

Spanish Armada, the eventual accession of a new, Stuart, dynasty...one could go on. And it all started at Ludlow.

Ludlow was also the key power base for the powerful, dangerous, Roger Mortimer. The Castle passed to him in 1306. Mortimer had a colourful, not to say sinister, career, later taking Edward II's consort, Isabella, as his mistress, and helping to depose the King. In 1328, Edward was murdered, in Berkeley Castle, (more of which, later) and Mortimer become *de facto* king. Mortimer was himself overthrown in 1330, and met his end at Tyburn.

And here were H&J, showing a keen interest in the various walls, baileys and towers where the ghosts of princes and courtiers still strutted and dissembled. I remember H&J's entrance into the Castle with pride: the ladies selling tickets welcomed them warmly, and with (metaphorical) open arms. The pictures show the young lads, attentive and lively, with the Castle as a backdrop. As they paused and posed in front of the massive castle walls for a photo, taking in all that their young minds could assimilate, the adolescent, beaming Hector & Jason could of course know nothing of these historic events, which had shaped the present - their present. Never mind; this was *their* time.

Another trip, early in the new Millennium, was to Chatsworth Country Fair, described as *'one of the most spectacular in England'*. The Fair is a wonderful celebration of country life, with all kinds of massed pipe and military bands, demonstrations and parades; all quality jollity and colourful display. H&J loved the sense of occasion and visual and sensory stimulation. We steered the young Hector & Jason around the thronged, pulsing arenas and processions. We dallied for fish and chips: quite superb - guess who snaffled most of mine? We also briefly met the famous, then newly retired racehorse, *Desert Orchid*, who was putting in a guest appearance at the Show. I had a thrilling thought: my boy, the magnificent athlete, thundering alongside another magnificent athlete, and equine legend. Dreams placed firmly back inside their box, in a highly excited (Hector & Jason) and enervated (me) return to the car, Hector performed a 'dump' beneath the perfumed portal of Chatsworth itself; the first of many such moments.

In these early days, too, I recall a heady afternoon spent at Cannock Chase - a vast area of ancient common and forest, and famous for its wild deer. Jason careered away from us at great speed along the crest of a high, long ridge and, though I could see him for most of this time as a fast-moving dot on the horizon - albeit a very fast moving dot - I was still relieved at his mercurial return, without incident, half an hour later. To watch Jason's maverick spirit was quite marvellous, but it was equally wonderful to see him safely returned, glad in his spirit, fresh from his mighty endeavours.

On one exhilarating - for them - early walk at Highgate, H&J emerged from the dense undergrowth, a bra between their teeth. They ran rejoicing along the path, both ends of the *soutien gorge* clamped fast between the jaws of each lad. Fortunately for her, the gyrating undergarment was no longer attached to the young lady owner.

Shortly after this episode, Hector brought home a pair of knickers in evident triumph, swinging them from side to side. Oh, well, better than the squirrels that formed his regular booty. The incident provoked a dream:

Knock at the door. Open: Girl. Young. Pretty. Brunette.
"I believe that you've found a...garment that belongs to me..."
"Well, my boys - that is, my dogs - have found a pair of er...knickers..."
Awkward pause.
"How...?"
"Do I know they're mine? They'll be black, naturally".
"Naturally. And...?"
"The size? Size medium, of course."
"Of course. And where...?"
"Did I lose them? In the local woods, not far from the main drag."
"I see. Well, (producing small plastic bag) *"everything seems to be in order, Miss. I wonder, is..."*
"There a reward?" (Smiles) "Just my thanks."
"Well, enjoy - that is, goodbye..."

This was a portent of far worse embarrassment to come. We were keenly aware that these were two, still very young, boys, and were anxious to protect them from others, and from themselves. While we were taken aback - myself, visibly shaken - by the experience of these first trips out, there was the consolation of preparing *us* for a brave new world. Forewarned is, or at least should be, forearmed. Time would tell.

Thus were our early walks: exciting, challenging, stomach-churning. A template for the journey yet to come.

Young Vic: already the superstar!

Vic with my father

Vic with June, at Rhiwargor Falls

Victor, enjoying the moment

Vic relaxing, with Oscar

Majestic...at Malvern

Puppy Hector: in rare repose

Puppy Jason: amid the carnage

Your carriage awaits!

Going for a ride!

An early trip: Ludlow Castle

With Richard and David - atop Malvern Hills

Relaxing at home

The perfect profile

Young Hector… seeking mischief

Young Jason… seeking mayhem

6: The Hunter Gatherers

*The day has passed delightfully. Delight, however, is a weak term
to express the feelings of a naturalist who, for the first time, has
wandered by himself in a Brazilian forest.*

Voyage of the Beagle - Charles Darwin

*Let Hercules himself do what he may,
The cat will mew, and dog will have his day.*

Hamlet - William Shakespeare

The woodland near to our home rises as an ancient green oasis on the
edge of vast suburban sprawl. It's like a full-stop; a blob of medieval
greenery, separating that which is Man's - twenty miles of one of the
United Kingdom's most densely urbanised conurbations - from that
which is still, just about, Nature's.

In Summer, the canopy appears to rear above the surrounding
landscape, as vibrant and exotic as a tropical rainforest. A deceptively
modest 53 acres in extent, this Midlands forest is surrounded by fields
on three sides, and massed boundaries on the other, where serried rows
of back gardens terminate in gates, walls and fences.

June and I are incredibly fortunate in that, living on the extreme
western edge of the West Midlands conurbation, we have this ancient
and beautiful woodland within 250 yards of our home. To add to our
blessings, a large municipal Park lies barely half a mile in the opposite
direction. These fair and friendly places formed our default options,
and were the main focus of our daily walks with H&J. Because the
woodland itself boasts so many paths and routes, which the boys quickly
learned, we had a wide variety of options to choose for walks, on a daily
basis. This variety proved invaluable because, with some trepidation, I
could let the boys off their leads to run around - or run amok - once we

were safely embedded into the body of the woods - or Park - and at a safe remove from local roads.

The woodland itself boasts fine avenues of English and sessile oak, lovely glades of beech and, to add to its lustre, gnarled and ancient, but still stately, sweet chestnut trees. Dense thickets of holly, a sprinkling of rowan ash, and a century-old conifer plantation complete the woodland picture. A perimeter path extends all the way round the verdant glade. This impressive green lung also provides a breeding ground and refuge for a variety of wildlife, but most commonly grey squirrels, foxes, and the most frequently seen birds such as wood pigeon, robin, blackbird, and squalling crows, with a few rarities thrown in - the occasional jay, nuthatch, woodpecker, a buzzard gliding overhead and, on a solitary occasion, a magnificent peregrine falcon, sitting astride a (dead) pigeon.

This happy shade provided the ideal setting for our early morning walks, and the potential for relaxation, exercise and delight in nature. H&J, however, had not read the script.

Following Darwin's famous observation (quoted above) in *The Voyage of the Beagle,* the great man went on, a little later, to write that *'In England any person fond of natural history enjoys in his walks a great advantage: by always having something to attract his attention; but in these fertile climates, teeming with life, the attractions are so numerous, that he is scarcely able to walk at all'.*

Such luxurious description leaves me slightly envious. Our local, native woodland had perforce to serve as our own patch of tropical forest. In late Summer, particularly, the lushness of the foliage and canopy, and occasionally the heat, allowed me to imagine that I was exploring my own small but singular patch of a sylvan Eden. Fanciful, I know; but, in the absence of H&J, I would often observe, and record, the species present in this blessed little plot: twenty-three species of tree and shrub, a dozen species of wild flower, ten or so species of bird - with perhaps half a dozen species of butterfly - were the best that I could muster. Not even a bloody tick. So, not exactly Brazil, but very Black Country.

Yet the landscape that now appears to be so stable and familiar has been shaped and forged by gigantic forces, over aeons. The sandstone escarpment itself was formed over 200 million years ago during the Triassic period, its sea-smoothed pebbles testament to its mind-stretching past. The current landscape has been sea-bed, glacial ice-sheet and, yes, tropical forest. Sixty million years ago, dinosaurs roamed through these dense tropical forests, and vaporous swamps.

As recently as 14,000 years ago - a mere blink of an eye in geological time - this landscape, now so domesticated, homogenised, even, was prowled over by super-size lions, and trampled by mammoth and woolly rhino. In 1986, mammoth bones were discovered in nearby Shropshire. The historical record suggests that our ancestors first arrived in the area around this time, emboldened by the retreating ice-sheet. Whether their arrival, and the disappearance of mammoth and other great mammals was coincidence, or cause and effect, can only be speculative.

In medieval times, Ridgehill would have formed part of the vastly more extensive Kinver Forest, itself recorded in the Domesday Book. Unlike the forests of today, with their emphasis on rambling and recreation, medieval forests were regarded as a source of wealth: of timber, firewood and game, and this forest was no exception. In fact, these were royal hunting forests: William II and Henry II are both recorded as having stayed and hunted here. A little later, King John visited the royal hunting grounds of Kinver in 1200, 1206 and 1207, and nearby Stourton - a mere stone's throw from Ridgehill - in 1207 and 1215. King John had a royal hunting lodge erected at Stourton in 1195-96, at a cost of £24 18s 9d. The forest would have been teeming with game, especially deer: in 1257 alone, the (then) king ordered 50 stags from the forest.

Over centuries, if not decades, a rising human population and timber-thirsty industry ensured that the demands on the forest became unsustainable, and signs of ecological stress became apparent. Wild boar, for example, were hunted to extinction by the end of the 13th century. By 1626, it was reported that Kinver Forest had neither deer nor timber. Despite unremitting persecution, however, the grey wolf clung on, and wolves were not finally extinct in England until around 1500, in the reign of Henry VII.

Sans mammoth, rhino and lion - and wolf - only a supreme effort of will can take one back to a world that is almost beyond our imagination. Even so, these epochs existed as surely as the present age. These days, certainly in the West Midlands, woodland cover is patchy and fragmented, and the richness of its fauna and flora much depleted; the only monsters to be found are the juggernauts that ply along the A449, close by, on-route to the flesh-pots of Wolverhampton or

Kidderminster. In the heady, crazy, 'Noughties', where the only natural danger was posed by homo sapiens, it was the mission of Hector & Jason to re-wild this ancient place, re-energising its passion and otherness, re-connecting it with speed, risk and danger.

For Hector & Jason approached these humdrum, humble woods with an orgiastic anticipation. Even now, 'Into the woods!' is a phrase redolent with expectation and wonder. How much fun can be extracted from the coming hour? What will we find? What can we do today? What wonders will be revealed? Hector & Jason had already decided that retrieving was not for them: running and chasing was Jason's passion; hunting and gathering was Hector's delight. I did all I could to discourage, prevent, and avoid these daily skirmishes and encounters with wildlife that was merely attempting to eke out an existence on its own terms. Hector, however, had other ideas. For H&J, this was Serengeti, not Stourbridge.

The verdant woods were not only inviting and exciting, there were residual dangers. And not only the risks from human beings and perhaps other dogs. I knew there were adders among the bracken and brambles, since I had once come across a (dead) young specimen. A bite could prove fatal since, clearly, I would be ignorant of the fact until the doleful effects of the poison became apparent. So, the hunter could become the hunted. I had to trust to Providence and my boys' sound instincts; the lure of the wild was simply too powerful to resist.

In early Summer we would brush through sun-dappled 'beechen green', the woodland drenched in shades of green and gold. In Autumn we would ramble along a path that glinted with gold leaf, as though gold sovereigns had rained from a giant's pocket. In Winter, we would pick our way along a path silvered by a sumptuous moon. If happiness is an accretion of small pleasures, then my happiness, throughout this time, reached a pitch of perfection.

Whatever the season, with confidence and guile, Hector would go his own way in searching for prized opportunities - which might include a ball in someone's garden, a hole in a bank (no doubt home to an animal) or chickens - luckily - confined by a mesh fence. He was completely un-fazed and unembarrassed by these leanings. Returning home swinging a squirrel in his jaws was his recognition, to himself, and the world, that he was a dog amongst dogs.

This behaviour came as a complete shock to me. I had fondly imagined that Golden Retrievers did not indulge in hunting with the focus of an Exocet missile (the clue was in the word 'retriever'). I quickly concluded, however, that it was essential to their nature, and should only be prevented on a case-by-case basis: the behaviour seemed vital to Hector's well-being. Many people seem to think that dogs are essentially domestic creatures, with the wildness bred out of them - sheepdogs are often cited as proof of this. Not so - dogs remain wolves in sheep's clothing, even if they have acquired a 'human face'. As for the sheepdogs, their instincts have been sublimated, and re-directed, not fundamentally altered; hence the opening scene of Hardy's *Far from the Madding Crowd* when Gabriel Oaks' two sheepdogs chase their flock of sheep over a cliff, their hunting-chasing instincts re-igniting, and their 'madness' causing mayhem.

While Jason's incredible athleticism seemed to have no end but itself, Hector's forays had two closer-to-home motives. The first was footballs or, failing these, tennis balls. Goodness knows where he found them in these woods, but find them he did, in copious numbers. Where he obtained these items from is still a source of mystery, but I suspect that he raided people's gardens for them. And how did Hector get into these gardens? I never knew, since I never actually saw him in action. But gates, fences and barriers meant little to Hec, except as an opportunity or a challenge. There must have been an awful lot of footballs lying in dozens of gardens - or one garden that horded them like buried treasure. What I do know is that our own garden became a repository for these prizes, joyfully brought back, like looted treasure, by a Hector puffed up with pride. We could - gladly - have supplied Manchester United.

Hector amassed a collection of footballs and tennis balls that was amazing in its profusion and diversity; small, medium, large, white, black, red, yellow. If they were not innumerable, they were beyond my counting; well into three figures, with more added every week. When he was not observing me, I sneakily relegated the ripped and tatty to the waste bin; but most would sit proudly in the garden, awaiting Hector's fickle favour. When Hector lost interest in them, they were deposited freely around our patch of *velde,* adding only structural interest.

Hec's second great passion was hunting - a hunting intimately connected with food. Dogs, very much like us, are supremely interested in food. We do tend to think of the human race as somehow superior in this, as in most other respects; but I have seen very well-heeled and sniffy citizens eating utter crap with relish when they have been deprived of even one meal - or when it is free, or when there is an opportunity to eat as much as possible for a set price. A preposterously slim young lady scoffing all ten available desserts in the Brittany Ferries restaurant took the biscuit, literally, along with the gentleman who returned to the breakfast buffet three times to re-load his plate with yet more eggs and bacon.

Hector's attitude to food was very much that of the hunter-gatherer - for him, a fundamental purpose of walks was to find food: bread put down for the birds, left over chips, or a discarded hamburger. Failing that, a squirrel or pigeon would do nicely. Revelling in these baser instincts, Hec was surely reverting to history's urgings - eat what you can, now, for you don't know where your next meal is coming from, or when. And the humble squirrel is both gamey, and tasty, and commendably low in cholesterol.

I severely discouraged these marauding habits, mainly out of concern for Hector's health and well-being, but to little avail. Jason was far less interested in marauding for food - he was usually too busy just running: even the need to relieve himself seemed to inconvenience his missions. However, even Jason could not resist the temptation provided by the great chunks of bread left in our local Park in Winter to feed (mainly) pigeons and seagulls. He would descend like a meteor on this familiar patch of breadcrumbs, causing dozens of startled sea-gulls to ascend in a raucous cloud, squawking for all they were worth.

Hector's was a far more deadly purpose. As Jason was born to run, so Hector was born to hunt. The clue lay in their jaws: while Jason's teeth were beautiful - regular and white, Hector's were super-sized, almost wolf-like. These canines seemed to announce his destiny. It was this instinct for wildlife that really set Hector apart. A prize greater even than a football was a tasty snack - a grey squirrel. Hector was skilfully adept at catching these tree-living rodents. Despite heroic efforts that would have won plaudits from those pioneering aviators, Hector quickly concluded that he could not fly; indeed, he could not even climb a tree. Terra firma was his element, his path to glory. As fast as they move along the ground, the nimble grey rodents were no match for the crafty Hector, on his chosen territory. In the blink of an eye, Hector would calculate the distance, speed and trajectory of his target with mathematical precision. His success was the result not just of impressive speed over a short distance, but focus, determination - and razor-sharp cunning.

Hector's success rate was phenomenal, given the natural guile of squirrels - and the inevitable proximity of a tree, and safety. Hec caught, and despatched, hundreds of these fast and nimble creatures. Unfortunately, that was not the end of the story. When Hec felt peckish, I'm sorry to say that he crunched up and ate these surprisingly substantial tailed rodents. He would devour the still-warm beast as one gargantuan mouthful, rather like a kingfisher eats a fish. I never failed to find this revolting, but was reluctant to interfere. Indeed, I was frightened to intervene, lest some harm came to Hec in trying to eat his prize, since he would feel impelled to ingest the animal even more quickly. Fortunately, Hector's instincts in this respect never did him any harm. In the USA - where grey squirrels originate - they're well known as wild food. Elvis, too, ate squirrels, as a kid; they taste like pork, apparently:

> *Run squirrel, run squirrel, run, run, run,*
> *Or you'll end up in Hec's rum, tum, tum:*
> *A tasty meal, with mustard and a bun,*
> *So run squirrel, please squirrel, run, run, run.*

Grey squirrels, it must be said, are hardly an endangered species, and are regarded by many as a foreign and invasive pest. Hector seemed to have little problem catching them, and despatching them with immediate effect. Hec's skill - and will - in this department lasted throughout his long life. Sometimes - depending on his whim - rather than consuming his fast-food morsel on the spot, he would carry the critter home with a certain swagger - the limp body swinging proudly from his jaws. During the journey home, and depending upon his fancy, Hec would often place the squirrel upon the ground, the better to gaze upon his prize, and savour the gilded moment.

I squirmed with embarrassment as we walked back along the pavement towards home. Some passers by - waiting for a bus, or school-girls walking to school - variously smiled, or recoiled in horror or dismay. *C'est la vie.* So many times, gloriously or ingloriously, depending on one's point of view, the *'hunter came home from the hill'*, complete with his spoils. Once home, and the excitement of the chase already fading from memory, the sad little bodies were always left - thank goodness - at the front door. It fell to me to dispose of the (surprisingly substantial) remains.

No harm ever became the knowing Hector as a result of his squirrel obsession. No bites from the cunning little critters; no infections or digestive upsets. Almost uniquely among domestic dogs, I honestly believe that Hector could have survived all on his own, had the need arisen. Two squirrels a day would have sufficed - supplemented by the occasional wood pigeon or two, let down by their dull complacency. And a bowl of rainwater to wash them down.

I never counted the number of squirrel kills - but they ran into many hundreds. Hector was a dog with a mission. Many other dog owners were amazed at his facility - their own dogs had often chased squirrels, excited by these scampering, furry little bundles - but had never caught one. Good - Hector had none to spare.

Unfortunately, Hector did not stop at squirrels. He really was the *crème de la crème* of hunting dogs, extraordinary in a non-hunting (as distinct from retrieving) breed. Amazingly, wood-pigeons, crows, foxes and badgers were all grist to his particular mill. Any creature, in fact, that crossed his path was putting itself in harm's way. Apart from, that is, human beings and other dogs, to whom he was invariably, graciously, chivalrous.

Despite Hector's 'body count', he never injured so much as a hair of the creatures we encountered in Normandy; with Hec on his lead, red squirrels, deer and hares were able to stay clear of danger. In a neighbour's garden, he once feasted on the leg of a deer, but the leg had long been detached from its unfortunate owner.

Strangely, I never ever saw Jason with anything unedifying in his mouth. His love of the chase seemed to be combined with the lack of a killing instinct, for which I was eternally grateful. One hunter in the family was quite enough.

Schubert's *Wanderer Fantasy* might best describe Hector's outlook on his walks. His approach spoke volumes on his innate curiosity and lively interest in all aspects of his environment, including people, topography, and especially local fauna. This helps explain Hec's keen interest in visiting new places - a canal, a lakeside, a forest with strange and exciting smells, sights and sounds: all offered the promise of alluring, mouthwatering contraband.

So many times - gloriously, riotously, and also stressfully - Hector & Jason would give me the slip and dash off together into the unknown. On one occasion we had just arrived at the Severn Valley Country Park, and opened the rear of the car: in a flash, leads still attached, H&J launched themselves down the hill and into the green blur beyond our sight. They returned a full ten minutes later, still excited and elated. Again, dropping their leads for a second in unfamiliar territory - possibly to tie a shoe-lace - they dashed off at full pelt, this time (I think) to explore the local river. They returned, like nuclear-fuelled boomerangs, to where I stood, plaintively calling. It was a delight to watch them heaving back into view, approaching at the speed of sound, great grins upon their faces. *"See, we are back! What larks!"*. And what larks they were!

Hector, it must be said, was very deep, but in a markedly different way to Jason. Not a dreamy, swash-buckling romantic, but practical and focused, bright as a button in exploring any opportunity for profit and satisfaction. Even in grand old age Hector had an indomitable will - what to call it at three or five years of age! One second he was by your side; the next, there was an absence, a gap where he had been. He would simply vanish. I'm as sure as I can be that this was not day-dreaming on my part, but crafty opportunism on Hector's. Not fathomless speed, but pure guile. In admiration, and no little frustration, I called him 'the shadow', and I would often have to search him out in the deep woods, or even send out search parties made up of the local dog-walking fraternity. Whenever found, he could never understand my wagging finger, as if to say: *"What's the problem? - I've been here all the time!"*.

On yet another notable occasion, when we had been admiring a Severn Valley locomotive strutting its steam and speed near Trimpley Reservoir, and were heading back to the car, Hector decided to double back; he had seen ducks on the river, and that was as good a reason as any. Luckily, his absence was soon noticed, and he was reeled in. If the 'reeling in' sometimes involved a heroic intensity, it always gave huge relief, and the newly reeled-in Hector - or Jason - bright and eager - were always a supreme joy.

Hector's appetite for hunting knew no bounds. One cloudless morn, I was strolling in the woods - both boys out of sight - a circumstance so not unusual that I hardly gave it a second thought. Then I heard a commotion in dense under-growth just a small distance away. Leaves and branches were shaking violently; grunts and growls filled the air. Dashing over to investigate - and to my horror - I witnessed two animals, each standing bolt upright, engaged in mortal, toe-to-toe combat: there was my boy, my Hector, fighting - with an adult badger!

I launched myself between the combatants, grabbing Hector with both hands and, exerting all the power I could summon, forcing him away from his intended victim. Badgers have fearsome weapons, and can commit severe damage to a dog, but I had no doubt exactly who had started this particular fracas, and little doubt, either, of the outcome, in the tragic event of my not having chanced upon the *melée*.

The badger, disengaged, scuttled away to safety, hopefully unharmed - but not before giving me a rueful, perhaps reproachful, backwards glance.

I was, and am, aware of my civic responsibilities. In my defence, I had never before seen any evidence of badgers in these particular woods. And I love badgers, as I love dogs; the incident upset and shook me. Hector remained firmly attached to his lead until we reached home that morning, and I watched him particularly carefully for many mornings thereafter. Thankfully, there were no more badger incidents...

This little story may serve as a metaphor for Hec's incorrigible behaviour:

A dog comes in from the garden, his tail wagging: a (slightly) dead cat between his teeth.

She screams: *"O my God! It's the neighbours cat!"*

He soothes: *"Don't worry. I'll go round and explain."*

"Hello. I'm so very sorry about your cat..."

"Oh, that's very kind of you. 'Shandy' died, quite unexpectedly, yesterday." She smiles. *"We buried him in the garden."*

"Ah..."

So delicious, one almost hopes it might be true. And how very, very, Hector!

And so, so often, returning from the scene of adventure, H&J would retrace their fleeting steps along the woodland path, in order to find their (disappointingly slow) companion. The first sight of them would always gladden - and quieten - my fast beating heart. And then we would return home, to the prospect - and certainty - of peace, love and content.

7: THE GENIUS GENE

Genius does what it must, and Talent does what it can.

Edward Robert Bulwer, Earl of Lytton

Do not go where the path may lead; go instead where there is no path, and leave a trail.

Ralph Waldo Emerson

I will keep returning to the mysteries of genes, and genetics. Dogs have 39 pairs of chromosomes - but these give rise to almost endless, astonishing, possibilities, even within the Golden Retriever itself. If it's true - as I'm assured - that a pack of cards, being dealt, has never before revealed cards in that particular order, or that there are more possibilities on a chessboard than there are stars in the universe, (and there are trillions of those) then the potential inherent in genes is explosively mind-boggling. But, for me, it took Hector & Jason to drive home the reality of genetics 'magic'.

The vast majority of homo sapiens are, let's be frank, quite conventional, quite ordinary: we live our little lives, make a ripple, and are gone. In J.K. Rowling's wonderfully conceived world, we are the *muggles*. This does not mean, of course, that we cannot lead good lives, and carry out sterling public service, breathing our last with some satisfaction, and a *soupçon* of regret.

But a tiny number of people - far fewer than 0.1% of us - are quite exceptional, and make a big, memorable, splash. These might be stupendous artists such as Michelangelo, Mozart or Shakespeare; scientists with the vision of Galileo, Darwin or Einstein; formidable philosophers such as Kant or Wittgenstein; fearless life-changers, like Wilberforce or Mandela; or even iconic sportsmen, of the calibre of Muhammed Ali or Roger Federer. These extraordinary talents may not always be forces for unalloyed good, nor unambiguously positive moral forces - but in what they are, and what they have achieved, they stand like colossi in the human firmament.

It is my unshakeable belief that, in their own way, in their own sphere, there are animals that share these extraordinary qualities. Since they can't speak, write or use an i-phone, it may be more difficult to demonstrate this, or at least to prove to the indifferent crowd. However, as far as self-absorbed, self-important humanity is concerned, animals are rarely impressive. It is human beings who are infinitely superior; created and designed by God for a higher purpose. 'We' can do everything an animal can - and a great deal more. Homo sapiens, only, are special and unique.

My belief is that this view is far too simplistic, and utterly patronising. Reflecting on (our) own micro level, June and I have be-friended many super cats over 40 years. Of these, three were what I call 'magic cats': the mysterious Dougal, the amazing Oscar, and the crazy Lenny. To describe their special traits, qualities - and adventures - would probably require a volume of its own.

Examine closely the Kennel Club's description of the Golden Retriever, however, and the emphasis is on adaptability and versatility, within a defined framework. Retrievers may be working dogs, guide dogs, narcotics and explosives detecting dogs, tracker dogs, and obedience competitors - even therapy dogs. In addition, of course, to their universal gift for being superb companions and affectionate members of any (human) family.

That's a pretty impressive and varied skill set, as well as heart-warming stuff. Yet of course one of the advantages, or benefits, of a 'pedigree' dog is that their characteristics are well-defined, generally as a result of careful breeding and selection programmes. In other words, the skill sets, whilst impressive, are a given, a known. And we can be relaxed, complacent, even, in knowing exactly what qualities and attributes to expect from a particular breed.

So I have not, in truth, met many - any - dog, nor indeed heard of any Golden Retriever, that has this magical quality - except Jason. Possibly he is not alone, but he is in very exalted company. This does not mean that he was always easy to live with, or shape around our lives - such beings rarely are. They have their own spark, set their own standards, have their own agenda. They can be mercurial, difficult, uniquely trying at times. But also awe-inspiring, emotion-tugging, unforgettable. Jason's genius, as we shall see, lay in his extraordinary athleticism, a quality only equalled by his breath-taking beauty, and his unquenchable affection.

Hector, too, had his own special talent. Hector's genius, to borrow a famous phrase, lay in the content of his character. There were more facets to his personality, an unrivalled richness and depth, than any dog had a right to. All his life I remained fascinated by his behaviour: he was unpredictable, funny, bold, brave, crafty, deeply intelligent, always with a plan in hand - often unannounced to me, or even to his brother. Yet even Hector, Jason's twin, seemed to be awed by his brother's gifts. Yet there was no arrogance in this case: Jason was the most loving of siblings, always caring for and protecting his brother, and deeply affectionate towards June and myself.

Great artists are surely the best of us; humanity's highest offering to the gods. They serve to placate the deities for our many sins, and our otherwise miserable, mean existence. Once upon a time, at Dudley Town Hall, I heard the delicious strains of Bach's *Concerto for Two Violins*, played by Yehudi Menuhin and a star pupil. I had to pinch myself that I was actually there –for Bach was certainly there. My mind, ears and eyes were entranced by such divine sensation. The Stradivari, the music...the musicians...the spirit of Bach himself seemed to soar into the heavens. And I suddenly saw him, not as an ill-humoured gent in an ill-fitting wig, as seen in the lithograph portraits, but as an artist with a divine spark.

On another occasion, we were privileged to see and hear the Welsh National Opera's performance of *Cosi fan Tutte*. Act 1 of *Cosi* ends - more aptly, climaxes - with the Sextet *'Dammi un bacio, o mio tesoro'*, (*'Give me a kiss, my treasure'*). It's a miraculous synthesis of voices, emotions, and melodies. When I heard this music, I was overcome. The effect was as mesmerising as the *scena* itself, where mesmerism is employed in the - delicious and hilarious - action. Could a mere mortal have created such a work, have produced such a stupendous effect upon the senses: transcending structures and musical conventions, and transforming such an unpromising theme into the sublime? Heavenly alchemy, indeed!

So I wrote a little ditty: the attempt at humour should not disguise the awe and reverence at its heart:

> *For scintillating Cosi, God sweats, sighs, opines;*
> *While, in the 'Crowned Hope' Lodge, Mozart gaily dines.*

And I saw *him* - fabulous, fathomless Mozart - as an artist possessed of a divine spark.

The moral ambivalence of *Cosi fan Tutte* is redeemed by the most exquisite music ever to emerge, gossamer-spun, from the mind of Man. Even now, each time I hear this extraordinary music - an aria, a bar, a note, even - it is redolent with the spirit of Jason.

I once hurried off the bustling, rain-drenched street - more accurately, Trafalgar Square - and straight into the National Gallery, as one does. Within seconds I was staring, gob-smacked, at the most exquisitely beautiful image: a cartoon for *Virgin, Child and St Anne,* by Leonardo. I could not tear myself away. It was a knee-trembling moment, as I was overwhelmed by an image of breathtaking, intense loveliness. Again, on a recent visit to Birmingham's superb Art Gallery, amongst an array of work by renowned artists, I was brought up short by a portrait - *Mrs Luther* - by Sir Joshua Reynolds. The canvas was quite miraculous; painted with such love, the lady seemed - more than 200 years after the event - so vivacious and alive.

My initiation into the realm of 'Literature' was somewhat different. I had journeyed through the State education system untroubled by, and unacquainted with, any serious works by critically acclaimed writers. This was curious since, from the age of five, I had been a voracious if uncritical reader. Indeed, my first and truest passion was reading: I took to the printed page like the proverbial duck to water. Reading became my life-long friend, and eternal joy.

I simply needed a little guidance, a little direction. The direction duly arrived. At the age of 15, and at (Dudley) College, I was introduced to Shakespeare, and *Macbeth*. It was not just the penny that dropped, but the whole cash register, over-loaded with gold. I never looked back; it was a life-changing moment. Another genie had 'scaped the bottle.

Many years later, we visited the RSC at Stratford-upon-Avon to experience a performance of *Hamlet*. The booming bass of Brian Blessed's Claudius rang out, while his great eye fixed me, riveted to my front-row seat. His Gertrude, Virginia McKenna, responded with intense, sulphurous sensuality. Their demonic energy could have lit up not just Elsinore but the 'rotten state' itself.

To be touched by true genius is a truly uplifting experience. In the somewhat unlikely figure of Jason, I was to be exposed to genius of a very different kind. Jason, indeed, has shown me the way.

The Runner Extraordinaire

To realise one's nature perfectly - that is what each of us is made for.

The Picture of Dorian Gray - Oscar Wilde

Hector and Jason's personalities were very different, but they added up to something special, and complementary. Hector was spirited, independent, proud, bright, always looking for the main chance, whilst unfailingly loyal and affectionate. He was a surprise around every corner.

Jason was the most gentle and generous spirit; the most open-hearted and loving boy imaginable. And, as Hector was handsome, Jason was simply beautiful. Truly, that would have been enough. Few would have imagined, unless they observed his physical attributes acutely, that he had a secret gift: the desire, and ability, to run like the wind.

Hector & Jason were of almost identical dimensions - in height, length and girth. They were as big, physically, as the majority of male retrievers, though standing taller than most. However, despite their stature, and their rippling muscle tone, they were around two or, in Jason's case, three kilos lighter than other Retrievers of the equivalent size and scale. There was no spare flesh; all was taut, honed, formed for function. They looked, and performed, like prime athletes.

When we chose to acquire - when we were smitten - by the infant Hector & Jason, our very last thought or intention was to acquire a dog, or dogs, for speed, for running. That is not what Golden Retrievers do. No, if I had wanted speed, I would have sought a greyhound, a whippet, even a borzoi - and trawled their pedigree for exceptional dogs, exceptional achievers. Needless to say, I had no such intention, or expectation.

When one creates a child, or merely acquires a cat or dog, there is a certain leap into the unknown - a leap of faith, and hope. Clearly, we were hoping to acquire loyal, loving boys - and H&J gave that in spades. But there are always other, unexpected characteristics, and one has to live with these - and shape and guide them - as best as one can. These traits can be good, bad, or indifferent. The boys were both highly individual, and characterful. But in Jason's case, in particular, the unexpected reached extravagant heights. An extravaganza of the surreal.

Jason's extravagant gift gave him the electric acceleration of a cheetah, the grace of a gazelle, the thrill of a mustang. He was a runner, both by temperament and physique. Jason just ran - all the time, everywhere. Even when he slept, he made running movements - so powerfully, he should have been linked to the National Grid.

It was his soul's nature. Hector himself was a fast, even runner and, by himself, would have appeared an impressive athlete, and the quickest Retriever I had known. But as I once said, (from pride, but still a little foolishly and unfairly), comparing their respective speeds was like comparing a Ford Escort with a Ferrari.

To employ an old Black Country phrase, Jason ran 'like a thing possessed', and his brother ran in his slipstream. In the cold-water-slap-on-face that was our early morning constitutional, I would walk, perhaps jog, sometimes run, maybe two and a half miles, depending on the necessary response to H&J's trajectory, while Hector & Jason themselves would speed through five or six miles. It was as exhausting as it was exhilarating.

As I thrilled to his power, and gloried in his passion, the fabulous lines from William Blake's *The Tyger* would surge through my mind over and over again:

> *'When the stars threw down their spears*
> *And water'd Heav'n with their tears,*
> *Did he smile his work to see;*
> *Did he who made the lamb, make thee?'*

Such was Jason's headlong propulsion, regardless of obstacles, that on at least two occasions he returned to me minus his leather collar, but otherwise unharmed: the force of his charge having snapped the collar, or at the least yanked it over his head. His buccaneering spirit was revealed when, at regular intervals, we needed to check his microchip at the ferry terminals: Hector's chip remained where it was originally placed - by his right shoulder. Jason's, on the other hand, was a moveable feast, since his maniacal manoeuvres had dislodged it, and sent it wandering erratically down his leg.

What caused Jason to be so extraordinary, that to watch him took the breath away? In his autobiography *Running my Life*, Sebastian Coe says that the elements that determine ultimate speed are: length of stride, the power that one can push into that stride, and the rate of one's stride - how fast the legs can be made to pump. That seems to sum up the matter perfectly. Jason had a phenomenal 'engine', with powerful heart and capacious lungs, encased within a strong, athletic body, that was somehow a little lighter than it appeared. The superhuman heart and lungs were complemented by legs of unusual muscularity and extraordinary flexibility - so that, after extreme exercise, Jas would lie panting with his back legs splayed out, at full length, in a straight line behind his body.

This almost unique combination of characteristics meant that Jason had both a quickness of action and extraordinary stride length, giving him the arching propulsion that one also sees in film of cheetahs in extreme motion, when chasing prey. It was as if, in addition to the various elements that together make up the modern Golden Retriever, some mad or inspired scientist had mixed in spirit of greyhound, and essence of cheetah. Finally, perhaps, was his *will:* Jason loved running, was addicted to it, like human beings love - what? - food, sex, cars, money, music? It was his passion, the goal of his life, and this added a final ingredient to an explosive and exciting mix - exciting for him, awe-inspiring (sometimes stomach churning) for me.

Quite simply, in terms of design, articulation, power, and inclination, Jason was endowed with every conceivable facility for grace and speed of movement; rather like the Formula 1 super-cars that scream around the circuit. But he was rather deceptively cast in the mould - in his case, a particularly attractive mould - of pure, pedigree Golden Retriever. From his keen black nose, to his dark, shining eyes, to his superbly balanced posture, to his shapely but largish paws, and to the tip of his powerful tail, Jason was the most perfectly fluid athlete that I have ever witnessed. How does one catch lightning in a jar?

Whether Jason was charging over a short distance (say a hundred yards, towards me), a half mile or so, or longer distances - two or three miles - hardly seemed to make any difference. He simply ran like the wind. If it was a long distance, he would return, lie and pant heavily, suggesting that he had been running anaerobically - that is, faster than even he could replace oxygen. Yet he never seemed to pace himself - it was always glorious full tilt, with an explosive kick action and amazing forward thrust.

When I declare that Jason was fast, I still sense you smile: *"you mean, fast for a Golden Retriever?"*. No - I mean blisteringly *fast*, period. As fast as Frankel; far faster (with respect) than Usain Bolt. As it happens, I've not seen Mr Bolt run 'in the flesh' - or, for that matter, Frankel. And I know that TV has the effect of neutralising speed by panning. But I have seen great sprinters, such as Colin Jackson, in action, and watched the highest-rated thoroughbreds sprint, at Royal Ascot. So I have witnessed exceptional human and equine speed. No: Jason was not only the fastest Golden Retriever I had ever seen, or even the fastest dog I had ever seen. Man, woman, child or animal, he was the fastest mammal I have ever seen. Jason's magnificent sprints across his planet - a planet itself travelling at 18.5 miles per second around its sun - touched the sublime.

Now, if I had indeed owned a champion greyhound, (most of whom, by the way, are exercised on their leads, and for very good reason) such a talent would be, (perhaps) unexceptionable. But for a Golden Retriever to possess such powers is, it can be said, uncommon in the extreme. It was a kind of genius; Ariel re-cast as canine. It is as though, on his 'outings' - really, his lightning charges - he lived to run, as fast and as far as possible, only returning when he had achieved his objective - which was...only he could tell. Running was, in many ways, his *raison d'etre*, what made him who or what he was. He was, to all intents and purposes, '*born to run*'.

If there was a problem, it was my problem: how to respond; how to give free rein to his spontaneity, whilst protecting him, keeping him safe, either from his own exuberance, or more usually from the narrowness of others. At one point, John Bradshaw (in *In Defence of Dogs*) states that *'we take it for granted that we can exercise them off-lead...'*. However, in the modern world, that 'for granted' faces many obstacles - from roads, gardens, livestock and a whole multitude of risks and dangers.

Lucille Sawtrell, in her excellent *All about the Golden Retriever,* also stresses that, wherever possible these dogs *'should have some freedom to run... Unfortunately, far too many dogs do not get enough exercise to stretch their legs and harden their muscles... I do not think that the average person can walk fast enough to really do a lot of good without some free ranging as well'.* I have to agree. However, she later states *'Nothing can be more embarrassing than for the dog to become suddenly deaf'* - a feeling I know only too well. All too frequently, when on walks I was asked: *"Where are your dogs?"* Quite simply, if I could have kept up, I would have been selected immediately to represent the UK at athletics at the next Olympic Games - and won a gold medal with daylight to spare.

Jason's explosive talent filled me with wonder, and was a joy to behold, as I followed in what I hoped were his paw-steps. Every walk was an experience, and sometimes I longed for a little tranquillity, not to say the normality seen in other dog owners and their charges. Where was he? What was he doing?

I hardly feared that Jason was posing a threat, or danger, to anyone, or their pets, or to wildlife within the woods; my overriding concern was for his safety, from our own dear fellow homo sapiens.

With Hector & Jason, a precarious balance had to be maintained; a balance challenged on a daily basis. It is true that, whenever I lost Hector & Jason, a sense of terror came over me. Yet our life together was an adventure, never comfortable, but re-affirmed with passion each and every day. Despite the anxieties and little human problems that we encountered along the way, I am glad in my heart that we tried, and proud that we succeeded. In following Jason's star, it never ceased to surprise me how many of our fellow citizens apparently harbour firearms. I know this because, on so many occasions I was angrily informed that *"if that dog comes on my land again I'll shoot it!"*. Since Jas perpetrated no harm to other dogs, cats, plants, lawns or whatever, I was always mystified by the violence of the reaction. Jason was a meteor passing through, and would be away, very shortly; in the meantime, please let him brighten your miserable little life for a few special moments.

The risks of freedom were daunting. Our regular woodland is formed of a hilly ridge, with a track all around, as well as tracks through and over the ridge. The boys might get lost - or, more likely, lose me. Once out of sight, it was difficult to know quite where the duo actually were, and where they would re-emerge. Merely heading in their last known, general direction risked compounding the folly of Grouchy, at Waterloo - following Blucher's army, rather than cutting it off. The boys would be back at the stile long before me - and then what would they do?

There were so many possible dangers. A collar might get snared on a low hanging branch. One or both boys might become entangled in one of many thickets - always harder to exit, than to enter. They might push past an unfastened gate, and into a garden, only to find the gate swing shut behind them. Either Hector or Jason might be apprehended by a stranger, and led away - out of kindly, or more sinister, motives. They might be attacked by a violent dog, of whom we had seen quite a few. Or, God forbid, they might actually be harmed by some nutter...or they might pick up poison, either deliberately put down, or negligently left lying around. Or even, running out of the woods, one boy or other might be involved in a road traffic accident, with horrific consequences...

I am sure Hec was, like me, in some consternation at the extravagant athleticism of his brother. It was clear to me that Jason exulted in his own acute powers. Not surprisingly, this daily onslaught of extreme activity, at 7 o'clock each morning, did create in me an acute nervous anxiety. Although the network of dog owners were generally well aware of my deviant boys, there was always the prospect of someone - innocently or otherwise - finding Jason running loose and taking him home. Fortunately, this never happened, though there were one or two scares. I was certainly often asked whether my dogs were lost, to which I always gave the same answer, with as much good humour as I could muster: "*No, they know where they are - it's just that I don't always know where they are!*". And that was the case - they knew every inch of the woodland, every path, every prospect. Then again - while the woods were a fair distance from local roads - Jason's very speed and verve could quickly carry him into harm's way. To my eternal relief, this eventuality never happened.

In addition, there was the very real prospect of Hector & Jason (and me) getting into hot water with the owners of adjacent properties - such as paddocks that lay next to the woods - given the boys' headlong, unconstrained flight. Finally, there was the wear and tear on my nerves, as I struggled to locate them, and entice them back. Sometimes H&J were out of sight - and effectively out of my control - for half an hour or more. I knew - or thought I knew - that they were in the woods, but not exactly where, and finding them was worse than finding a needle in a haystack, since this was a dynamic situation. At the same time, I could take some comfort in the simple fact that they did always return, in their own time, and at their own unworldly pace.

Of course, H&J would have had no idea that they were the cause of any concern as they majestically powered around: they were young dogs, enjoying their youth, freedom and power; they were invincible. And they stayed young dogs for many, many years. Only too well aware of my responsibilities as a citizen and dog owner, I was less quiescent. Certainly, H&J were committing no harm, and knew every nook and cranny of their local haunts; but the uncertainty of their whereabouts, and the timing of their return, always remained a worry to me. I mulled over a number of strategies, and implemented some of the more pragmatic ones. The first was to keep Jason, in particular, on his lead for rather longer, until we were deep into the woods and I had at least established his trajectory, and his likely route of return, before unleashing his rocket. Another was to increase the number of walks in the local Park, where there was greater visibility, and certainty of movement (Jason always bounded around the perimeter, although often becoming side-tracked by an open gate, or the Council workmen's compound).

We - I, and the boys - faced all these challenges. In the end, I was obliged to trust to their instincts, their loyalty, their good sense...and to review our progress on an almost daily basis. If there had been a specific incident, a mind-gnawing moment, in recent times, I would be more cautious over the following few days. But I would always relent...

In the early days, the young Jason arrived home on two occasions without Hector and me. And, on a further occasion, Hector arrived home without Jason and me. These were potentially fatal incidents, but Providence spared us. On many, many occasions I stood rooted to the entrance stile, calling and calling. Where was Jason? Where was Hector? If they were still in the woods, they would eventually return to this spot. But what if they had already gone home? What if they were trapped, or injured, or even kidnapped? There were very many critical moments, with the boys missing for long periods, and I will be eternally grateful to dog-owning colleagues who, on many occasions, helped me to locate and re-unite with the errant duo - who were in blissful tune with their mojo.

At various times I mulled over the possibility of dog training - it seems so obvious now - but I felt intuitively that this would have limited impact. When the boys were confined to the house or garden, they were pretty perfectly behaved. I doubted the ability of dog training to curb their natural instincts when out in the natural world. Maybe I was wrong; or maybe I sensed that their respective gifts, and exuberance, would or should not be curbed. In any event, we never tested the theory. Certainly, when on more adventurous walks at weekends, in less familiar territory, the boys seemed happy to pull me along on their leads - though always in their inimitable, headstrong style.

In those early days, I tried carrying tit-bits, tennis balls, and for a while one of those silent whistles that only dogs can hear, in a futile attempt to exert a touch of discipline. None of these attempts at exerting a little control seemed to work; the alternative temptations were always too strong - the squirrel just ahead, the smell of a fox, the overwhelming desire to exert a majestic power. Happy - and mightily relieved - as I was to witness the boys' return, often by the entrance stile, maybe there was a secret part of me that exulted in their freedom, and their own joy in that freedom. As the years wore on, I could also gauge - not always accurately - where the boys were headed, and the likely trajectory of their return. Other dog owners would also provide me with intelligence reports on the last sightings. It might have been a safari in the Serengeti: "*seen the cheetahs?*".

There will be people who question why I persevered with allowing the boys such freedom. "*Where are they?*" I was so often asked by fellow dog walkers who, I wondered anxiously, should have seen them. But I knew - certainly in Jason's case - that this was his great mission in life. I needed to respect his genius, and his evident joy in exercising this genius, his expression of an almighty gift. And I loved to watch him, to marvel at his powers. A febrile anxiety lessened with familiarity, and on almost every occasion the boys came back - belatedly, or on a different route - but they came back.

For a while, my nerves shattered by enduring endless hours of H&J's absence on their forays into the unknown - and having seen a notice several miles from home announcing 'Paddocks for Sale' - I flirted with the idea of purchasing a fenced paddock. I made earnest enquiries: if only I could exercise Jason in a secure environment, letting him run freely over several acres of pasture, we could all enjoy our walks without the daily heart-in-mouth experience. This would have been an expensive option, but I would have persevered if the right property had been available. Sadly, perhaps, I could only find paddocks to rent, at sky-high prices. This option had little appeal, given the interminable years of rental that would lie ahead, and the idea progressed no further. In one sense, this was a pity, since it would have been fun to see H&J running around in the sunshine, without the daily worry as to where they were, or quite when they would return.

Yet any disappointment was fleeting: I remained free to enjoy my boys - enjoying their freedom. My anxiety was always on their behalf, since I was acutely aware of lurking dangers. But the point to stress - and stress was ever present - is that, though H&J were often on different trajectories, separate missions - they always did return, and (with the exception of one disgraceful incident) always safely.

On reflection, there was a further factor at play. In entering the woods, we were entering a new realm of experience. The boys sensed this right away. It was different. It was exciting. It was 'other'. H&J became dogs in the fullest sense, exercising every ability and faculty available to them. If it was dangerous, it was dangerous magic, and intoxicating; to me vicariously. And, while there were 'hairy' moments, the experience, and the excitement, of their mad-cap adventures was irresistible, and unforgettable.

Over the years, of course, things settled down a little as the boys matured, but they were well into middle age - for them, their second decade - before they trotted around the woods a little more sedately; and Jason was more than ten years old before I allowed him to walk freely on his Normandy walks. A dog with that kind of speed - and on a mission - can cover several miles - in any direction - and be effectively lost before you can curse your own stupidity. True, they were micro-chipped, but that fact could not guarantee their safety, or their safe return.

Yet to see Jason suddenly appear - from goodness knows where - now on the horizon, now hurtling towards me - in belated recognition of my calls - his breath steaming in the mist as he ran, was just pure delight. I see it now, re-playing in my mind's eye, and will re-live such magical moments forever.

I have many photographs of Jason running, but little in the way of video film - he would, in any case, have been away, long before the camera could have been encouraged to roll into action. So - when you see greyhounds chasing the 'hare', or the thundering hooves of thoroughbreds at Epsom - you may have some vague impression of the effect of Jason. Except, of course, that the greyhounds or thoroughbred horses are not running free, or wild, so these comparisons are themselves anaemic. A Jason 'charge' was, to me, infinitely more thrilling, and its outcome far less predictable.

I have long said - when I glimpsed Jason over the fields perhaps half a mile away, and called him excitedly - that the sight of him flashing towards me, like the God of Speed, rendered me ecstatic and misty eyed. There has been no finer or more beautiful sight for me, before or since. Some lyrical lines from Dylan Thomas's *Fern Hill* often sprang to my enchanted mind:

> *'In the sun that is young once only,*
> *Time let me play and be*
> *Golden in the mercy of his means....*
> *All the sun long it was running, it was lovely....'*

On one such woodland idyll, when we were safely, deeply within the verdant forest, I slipped Jason's leash, and he was off, careering through the trees in a sublime arc. An elderly gent, witnessing this, removed his cap, scratched his head and said, looking towards the now distant Jas: "*I've never sid (sic) a dog run that fast!*". Exactly, my man.

O so many, many times I had a bird's eye view as, heart in my mouth, Jason ran out of the woods and shot along the hedgerow at breathtaking speed, after 300 metres turning 90 degrees to continue alongside the perimeter of the field, parallel to the road; then turning a further 90 degrees at blistering pace to head up the far side, and back into the woods - and to me. He repeated this awesome spectacle - awesome in its speed and control - many, many, times. As far as I can tell, he had no other purpose or objective than the pure expression of his power, the thrill and exhilaration of his immense athleticism. Hector watched with me, metaphorically speaking, scratching his head.

Jason ran every time, and all the time, he was freed, though it did cause us many heart-stopping moments. For me, running with your dog along a deserted shore, intoxicated by the tide, salt spray and sea-breeze is one of the great pleasures of life. I did enjoy this pleasure with Hector & Jason - Hector loved chasing stones into the sea - but just as often they created their own script. Between the resorts of St Bernieres-sur-mer and Courselles-sur-mer on Normandy's Côte de Nacre is a long, flat, broad expanse of beach, which feels blissfully remote: the breeze ruffles the grasses and flowers on the sand dunes, and the breakers spume. There are few facilities, or people, along the deserted coast. The beach provided an ideal stop for a picnic lunch, during our multi-foray day trips around Normandy. This is, in fact, Juno beach, made famous by the historic, heroic role it played on D Day, 1944.

Generally, as the years progressed, Jason used his beach experiences to run around excitedly with Hector, searching for cuttle-fish or other smelly prizes, and simply having fun. On this beach, however, he had other ideas. Immediately he was off-lead Jason powered along the strand at breakneck speed, and was soon a dot on the horizon. I ran along the headland with Hector, but obviously made no impression on the fast-disappearing Jason.

I could just see the outline of Courselles-sur-mer - perhaps a mile and a half away in the distance - but no Jason. Then, another dot on the horizon - it was Jason, as though on the finishing straight at Epsom - running headlong towards us. It was a gladdening sight, for many reasons. He was welcomed with great gladness, and with much relief. He had been absent for only a few minutes - minutes that had seemed like hours - and had reached the outskirts of Courselles, before flying back to our arms.

Some years later - in fact, in early October 2011 - on a sublimely beautiful day that reached more than 30' centigrade - we found ourselves back on this beach, enjoying another picnic. Following our repast, I thought the boys deserved a run along the golden sward. What was it about this beach - its wildness, its loneliness, the bracing air? To all our astonishment, Jason - the almost 13 year-old Jason - was sprinting off again, far, far faster than I - or any human being - could ever hope to catch him. Hector looked on, with senior disapproval, I thought. As on the previous occasion, and after a similar interval, Jason returned once more. I could not begrudge his freedom, and exulted with him in his glory. *Carpe diem.*

Jason made the question 'why' almost irrelevant. God bless him.

Storm, Steam, and Speed

Before the doomsters abound
Before the sharkies surround
Our lives, and ground our hearts into dust,
Let's paint the city, or bust.

Colin Hill

Mammals, mainly land animals, are equipped by nature for their specific purpose. The big cats and dogs of the African savannah, that hunt other mammals - themselves equipped for speedy getaway - are therefore amongst the fastest land animals on Earth. The cheetah, the fastest, is reputed to be capable of speeds of up to 70mph over short distances. Less well known is that a hunting lion (usually lion*ess*) can reach speeds of up to 50mph.

Extraordinary sums of money are invested in the breeding of thoroughbred race horses, just to acquire that extra edge of speed and acceleration - to win the Derby, or the Arc de Triomphe. Thoroughbred horses have been recorded at speeds of up to 47mph, over short-based races. In terms of top speeds, dogs are not far behind: the Wild Cape Dog, at 45mph, is as fast as the fastest greyhounds.

I strongly suspect, however, that the speeds quoted are far from typical, and that they represent the peak speeds of a few super individuals over very short distances - in the same way that, in examining human achievement, we look at the great sprinters, at their physical peak, rather than Mr Joe Average, or even the mean average of competitive athletes.

So, by way of comparison, the greatest sprinter ever (in terms of fastest times recorded), Usain Bolt, has set a world record for the 100 metres of 9.58 seconds; the top speed recorded in setting that time was 27.45 miles per hour. Now, that's pretty fast. But if Mr Bolt had broken 5 seconds, at a speed of 45 mph, he would just about equal the fastest dogs and horses. So, despite all the palava over the greatest human sprinters, these super-honed athletes can muster only a relatively modest, plodding even, effort compared to their four-legged counterparts.

Not surprisingly, there has been very little research into the speed of the humble Golden Retriever, since speed is not their thing. Yet it is thought that some young, healthy specimens can achieve around 20/25mph at full tilt. Even at those speeds, they are certainly way out of the top ten quickest dog breeds. Retrievers are simply not bred, or built, with speed in mind. Which made the young - and not so young - Jason, quite a phenomenon. Neither the Kennel Club nor the Golden Retriever Club lists speed, or turn of foot, or any other similar skill as a characteristic of the Golden Retriever. Jason's gift came like a googly, from a parallel universe.

My conviction is that Jason was - at least - twice as quick as the typical, energetic young Golden Retriever. Which brings us back to Mr Bolt, and those 5 seconds, if he is to exercise similar dominance over his own species, rivals and competitors. Well, that ain't gonna happen any time soon. So that sets Jason apart as a very special dog, inhabiting his own special universe. Now, of course there's no particular reason why you should believe any of this; then again, there's no particular reason why you should not. I crave the reader's indulgence, since the simple fact of Jason's enormous athleticism is the central dynamic that shapes our story, and its headlong gallop.

If we had not owned the ultimate speed machine, Hector would have been the fastest Retriever that I had ever known. He was certainly a match for any Olympic sprinter - as hundreds of nifty squirrels might ruefully testify. There was no chance, even in my athletic prime, such as it was, that I could be anywhere but flailing in the dust of his paw-steps. Hector's powerful rhythmic clip came just within the bounds of convention. Indeed, he could probably travel at around 30mph - stretching God's spectrum for this breed. Still, more than once, I noted his look of disbelief as he saw his brother take-off on another blistering tour of a woodland or beach.

Hector's quick pace, just on the edge of Retriever-land normalcy, provided a useful comparison, and kept me rooted in reality, while I closely observed his brother. Jason's sheer speed of movement, and ethereal grace, was a joy to behold. One moment he was hurtling along the woodland path, careering between the trees, before disappearing out of sight; then he was over the hill at the rear end of the woods, again disappearing from view; then he was pluming through an adjacent cornfield, invisible but for the ripples of the corn, opening before, and closing behind him; then again hurtling along a nearby field, following the rectangular contour of the hedges. I watched him with something approaching awe, sometimes bewilderment.

Unleashing the straining Jason was akin to releasing a bow-string: the arrow flew straight and true. The only difference was that Jason, Mr Perpetual Motion, never stopped. Hector would often be running behind, but following in Jason's slipstream, or at other times on his own journey of discovery - especially if he had unearthed a cache of footballs - or sometimes even remaining close to me.

The daily pattern of our walks was similar, irrespective of weather or seasons: H&J's joyous exultation was oblivious to rain, wind or snow, to Summer and Winter. My own perspective changed with the seasons: for me, the pleasure of the walks increased exponentially as Spring and Summer curved into view, and the sights, sounds and scents of returning life and beauty excited the senses, and delighted the heart. Summer, however, in its lushness, meant that the boys were quickly lost to me in the leafy body of the woods; I detected them from their excited barking, before their eventual, climactic, return. In the depth of Winter, however, with its spectral intensity, I could follow the boys' giddy progress along the slopes of the woodland, until the curvature of their trajectory took the galloping duo out of sight.

H&J were always magnificent in their power and, when I could actually see them, I marvelled at their prowess. They did seem to especially enjoy Spring and Autumn, no doubt because of the extra scents and sights on offer. My heart surged as the boys swished through the leaves blown into huge piles by the Autumn winds; or as the first rays of the Spring sun burst above the woodland edge, and burnished with gold the boys' chosen path.

Jason was the unquenchable spirit. He was the essence of life; just to be with him, was to be thrilled to the core. Hector, meanwhile, was the soul of intrigue and mischief. They both responded to the wild, to its surprises and unknowns - transforming a little patch of woodland into a daily cauldron of adventure. So many times, I would return to the stile, anxious and alone; I would often be hoarse, and sick with worry. I wore my voice out with frequent Tarzan-like cries of: "HECTORR!!'...JASSONNN!!" But, almost always, there they were, coming at last across my line of sight: then they came thundering towards me, enveloped in a cloud of spume. The spectacle sent a thrill along my heart, and resonated with a passage from *Macbeth*:

> 'As hounds and greyhounds , mongrels, spaniels, curs,
> Sloughs, water-rugs and demi-wolves are clept.
> All by the name of dogs: the valued file
> Distinguishes the swift, the slow, the subtle,
> The housekeeper, the hunter, every one
> According to the gift which bounteous nature
> Hath in him closed, whereby he does receive
> Particular addition, from the bill
> That writes them all alike...'

In 'the swift', and 'the subtle', Shakespeare identified Jason, and Hector. 'The slow' must have been someone else's dog.

Cosford Capers: Apprenticeship of an Athletics Aficionado

*If you can fill the unforgiving minute
With sixty seconds' worth of distance run,
Yours is the Earth and everything that's in it,
And - which is more - you'll be a Man, my son!*

Rudyard Kipling

I hope that I have the experience, and a little insight, to place Jason's talent into some kind of context. I've been a life-long fan of athletics, following and admiring the achievements of Britain's - and the world's - greatest athletes with huge respect and admiration.

Though it is hard to imagine now, until quite recently RAF Cosford was the country's only indoor athletics venue, and therefore the focus for major indoor athletics events and championships in the UK. In the intimate little arena, with its raised and banked wooden track, spectators were almost viscerally close to the action, and to the athletes themselves.

Unlike the experience of watching athletics on TV, or even in a mega-stadium such as the setting for the London Olympics, at Cosford one saw - practically smelled - athletes in their glorious primal state, and witnessed at close hand the struggle, the exertion, the adrenalin, the sweat, the strength, the sheer speed.

As a keen runner and follower of athletics, I attended the British Indoor Amateur Athletics Championships at Cosford for many years. These events were, invariably, enormously entertaining; there was always an almost bewildering amount of action taking place, with a packed schedule of track and field to get through in a single, exciting afternoon. There was a real buzz to the place - and it was near at hand, being a mere hour's drive away.

The 1979 '3As' (Amateur Athletics Association) Indoor Championship sticks firmly in my mind. The event took place on 27 January, and I recall it well. We did not quite know it then, but the British were on the cusp of greatness: the young Sebastian Coe, Daley Thomson, and Geoff Capes were all competing at these Championships. Only Steve Ovett was missing - it being some kind of policy, or pact, to keep the aspiring Coe and Ovett from competing against each other - until the following year's Moscow Olympics.

I watched Sebastian Coe win his race - the 3,000 metres - with stylish ease. I'm grateful to Lord Coe's autobiography for reminding me that the winning time was 7:59.8, a personal best. I still have the photograph of the winner crossing the line! Minutes later - athletics was different back then - Seb slumped beside me, in a spare seat. On my other (left-hand) side sat Geoff Capes, the great shot-putter, and later celebrated as the world's strongest man. Even then, it seemed amazing; Seb Coe was already a star in the athletics firmament. I certainly didn't ask for autographs or anything that might appear intrusive - and neither did anyone else. It just seemed very normal, very blokey.

A mere handful of months later, the said Seb Coe had broken the world athletics records at 800 metres, 1000 metres, 1500 metres, and mile. In fact, in that extraordinary Summer for middle-distance athletics, Seb Coe set three new world records in 41 days. As he relates in *Running My Life*: *'I had left England unknown outside the small world of middle distance running, but I returned home a hero.'*

In that same Summer of '79, I was competing in the West Midlands Civil Service Athletics Championships. In my third race of the day - the 800 metres - I achieved a hard-won third place. God knows the time, but it would certainly have been well outside two minutes. I still, proudly, have the medal that I was presented with at the time. The 800 metres is perhaps the toughest race on the track: for 80% of the distance, one is running anaerobically - that is, without the body's being able to replace the oxygen it is expending. Seasoned athletes of this distance are, of course, well used to this phenomenon, and judge their speed to run the best possible race, and time, before their body burns up completely. For me, it's horrible; these athletes have my complete admiration.

I would later compete in a number of marathon and half-marathon events, (much better suited to my modest talents), but the Summer of '79 marked the apogee of my obscure athletics 'career'. I was pretty much the other end of the spectrum, from a competitive athletics perspective, from the amazing Mr Coe, but felt that I understood the essence of running; the exhilaration - the pain - and the sense of achievement.

A few years later, on a tour of the iconic sites of ancient Greece, I had sprinted along the millennia-old race track at Olympia, with my new buddy, 14 year old Holland, who hailed from Houston, Texas. I relished running in the sizzling heat of the day on the most famous and inspiring race track in the world; I finished a close but chastened second to my new friend. Jas would have loved the thrill of running on this - or any other - track, but at the time the only Jason I had heard of was he of Argonaut fame.

Through my 20s and into my 30s, I would run, or 'train', four or five times a week, setting out from my own front door, and following my nose. My favourite memories are of slipping off on warm Saturday afternoons, heading for the nearby countryside, and running just within my capacity - sometimes right on that capacity - for 15 miles or so - in a glorious two-hour session. It is hard to explain the exhilaration one feels, the speed in one's own body, that sense of strength and power. This experience gave a perspective that, much later, I could bring to bear on a certain Jason Hill...

To return to Mr Coe. Over the next few years I, like everyone else, watched mesmerised as Seb Coe and Steve Ovett competed on a titanic scale, against each other, against the world and against the clock and record books, smashing - again and again - world records for 800 metres, 1500 metres and mile. British athletics - British sport - had seen nothing like it. In the 1980 Moscow Olympics Seb Coe and Steve Ovett both won gold - Coe in the 1500 metres, Ovett in the 800 metres. Oh, and Daley Thomson also won his first gold in the Decathlon. These athletes were on top of the world and, just a few years older, with my own small well of experience and knowledge, I relished every moment.

On 10 June 1981 I watched a 'meet' in Florence - on TV this time - as Seb Coe glided to a fantastic new world record time for the 800 metres. I still recall the time - 1.41.73. The record was so so good that it stood until 1997.

It is abundantly clear from Seb Coe's *Running My Life* that thorough preparation, and a scientifically-based, innovative training regime - for which his father Peter must take immense credit - put the gilding on Seb Coe's natural talent. And, whatever the talent, it would be silly to suppose that success in any global sport can be achieved without utter dedication and determination. '*Raw talent*', he writes, '*will only take you so far, and moving beyond it is never going to be comfortable.*' But again and again, in his autobiography, (Lord) Coe draws attention to the joy, and the exhilaration, that he derived from this natural talent, long before the prospect of an athletics career presented itself.

While watching the extraordinary (Florence) race - more accurately, a formal attempt on the world record - it occurred to me for the first time that there is, or can be, a genius in sport, and sports people, as well as in artistic and intellectual pursuits. It is rarely seen, but does exist. We have no problem referring to Mozart as a genius - or Leonardo, or Shakespeare. And we do not think this the less because they have been taught, or received formal tuition or training, or have studied their art assiduously. *The Marriage of Figaro* or *King Lear*, or *Madonna, Child and St Anne* are - while clearly arising from their contemporary artistic and social contexts - just so beyond and above the contemporary and expected as to appear on another, more elevated, plane.

And so I believe is, or can be, in athletics and sport: performance that is lifted beyond the expected, beyond the probable, towards the extraordinary and barely believable. What I observed in Seb Coe seemed to be somehow beyond the physical, and beyond the mental; it was sort of metaphysical, as though every atom that made up human existence was being directed towards a supreme end - to run faster than a human being had ever run before. There was something God-like about this, something inexplicably great.

The clear objection to the above is that records will always be broken: that athletes will always run faster, and put the achievements of the past into perspective; make them relative and remove their gloss of immortality. In its way, quite true. But genius can be the inspiration of the moment, a searing glory etched on to existence in a millisecond, a triumph of spirit, will, and flesh, united in achieving a hitherto undreamed of level of performance. Sure, this performance may be 'bettered' one day, but only by someone equally extraordinary - not one in a million, but one in a billion.

At first sight it is odd that human beings still run around tracks trying to become faster and faster. After all, we have motor cars, trains and planes that can travel from a-to-b much more quickly (and with less effort) than even the greatest athlete can, self-propelled. Yet we remain captivated by humans travelling at speed, under their own propulsion, and doing so faster than has ever been done before. That is why the 100 metres is the blue riband event, and why Mr Bolt is such a super-star. It is to experience the entirely new; entering a brave, uncharted world. Maybe it has something to do with the God in man - or so we like to believe.

Mountaineering Moments

The more one gets to know of men, the more one values dogs.

Alphonse Toussenel

From the mid 1970s, and well into the 1980s, June and I were enthusiastic mountaineers - that is, we enjoyed hill walking, combined with some scrambling and, in my case, a dabble in pure rock-climbing. I had enjoyed long walks in the Scottish Highlands - climbing Ben Nevis, in John Keats's (August 1818) foot-steps, together with a wonderful ascent of Ben Lawers on Tayside, with its magical views over a sparkling sea, towards the island of Eigg.

I was also an experienced runner, having competed in a number of marathons, and, as we have seen, was well used to running 15 miles or more in an afternoon. The strength and endurance I had developed at this time through my running came into their own in my mountain walking. With friends, we toured North Wales, the Lake District, North Staffordshire, Derbyshire and Yorkshire National Parks. Many of our trips were organised walks, in small groups. No dogs were involved, from our point of view; this was all pre-dog. I recall many such trips and excursions - including a gruelling 17-hour Lyke Wake Walk across the Yorkshire Moors.

I had also - twice - attempted the equally gruelling feat of ascending all fourteen 3,000' peaks in Snowdonia within 24 hours. Despite being, by my standards, supremely fit and well-prepared, my best effort 'bagged' ten peaks. Though both of these attempts, separated by a year or two, were noble failures, they were memorable, for all that, for the majestic scenery, and for the challenge of stretching oneself almost to the limit. It was all heady stuff and, had I known it, invaluable training for my future life with Hector & Jason.

Sadly, I would often arrive at the most remote and lovely destination to find that I shared the sacred spot with a crisp packet and a Coke can. The assembled detritus were similarly mute in admiration of the view. My experiences of these wild and wonderful landscapes - crisp packets aside - strengthened my determination to, one day, own my own little patch of heaven.

I say there were no dogs involved in our Snowdonia expeditions but, in a single case, there was. Three young couples embarked on a trip to North Wales one glorious weekend in May. One of these couples consisted of June and me; another was a lovely, gentle couple with a beautiful (girl) Irish Setter. We camped on a hill farm with the barest of facilities, and hens clucking at the walls of our tent. The Setter took the expedition in her elegant stride. This was to be yet another attempt at the 14 Peaks, but we awoke at 5.00am on Saturday morning to find the landscape covered in a blanket of thick snow. Certainly, a landscape to admire, to photograph, but not one in which to risk life and limb, that day. We were young; there would be time enough. The attempt was halted in its tracks.

The purpose of the trip being nullified, the three couples went their separate ways - June and I drove to Conway, for an English breakfast and to admire the Castle. Some years later, the young couple with the Setter left their former lives and became missionaries, and their mission took them to Tibet. Returning home, their plane crashed, with the loss of everyone on board.

The tragedy only came to my attention when I looked at a copy of *The Times* a day or two later. There they were, in a photograph taken on board the plane, looking straight ahead, and purposefully, positively alive. They were the best of us; Heaven would be richly deserved.

Another such walk in North Wales, around 1980, entailed a coach that disgorged its well-prepared party of thirty or so ramblers in Llanberis for an 'attempt' on Carnedd Lewellyn, at 3,400' the second highest peak in the Snowdonia range. This was a long, arduous but exhilarating climb, on a scintillating Winter's day. There was no competition as such, no juvenile race to the top. Still, I was a very strong walker, and quickly became part of the leading group. With only a few hundred metres to go, and the Summit in sight, my enthusiasm rather got the better of me, and I strode proudly, alone, to the summit cairn. A few yards behind, walking strongly but nonchalantly, was a lean, quiet gent, with receding ginger hair and full beard, who I confess I had kind-of noticed.

We were soon joined by the rest of the party, admired the wonderful panorama, took a few photos, and began to head back down, conscious of the shortness of the day. On the way back, someone pulled me aside. "*Do you know who that is?*" he asked, nodding towards the red-headed gentleman. "*No, should I?*" I responded. "*That's Basil Heatley.*" He must have seen the look of ignorance on my face. "*He competed in the Tokyo*

Olympics - Marathon. Silver, behind Abebe Bikila". I gulped. What a chump.

Despite such *faux pas*, it was as if I was being prepared: developed and strengthened, in readiness to be tested by phenomena that were, as yet, beyond my ken.

8: Bond of Blood, Band of Brothers

Bond of Blood

Hector & Jason were brothers, but very different in their personalities, and very different boys. They were vulnerable - and valuable. And they were *dangerous*, on the edge; certainly not violent, but dangerous in their passionate, uncompromising, Byronesque appetite for life.

On our travels, Hector would be variously accused, by passers by, of being Jason's father, mother, older brother, or other relative, while it was quite plain to see that he was Jason's brother or, as I would prefer, his biological twin.

Hector was the ultimate cheeky chappie, full of guile and mischief - mischief delivered with a knowing smile. Hector had an acute, cerebral intelligence that was as bright as a new pin. His antennae were alert to his world every minute of every day. By way of contrast, Jason possessed a rich, emotional intelligence that embraced everyone in his world with deep care and love.

Hector was earth - powerful, life-bringing earth; Jason was air - the air that is a caressing zephyr of Spring. As Jason was luminous, and lovely, Hector was larger than life; a character among characters. But there was such chemistry between them, that they were not quite entire by themselves, and somehow more complete together - greater even than the sum of their parts. They were soul-mates before the term entered common parlance.

Two dogs, in their crackling energy, their sparring and playing, their need for fuss and affection, somehow equate to more than two dogs; there are two bodies and a large, uniting and dividing, spirit, that enlarges the whole. It is hard to put this into words, simply because it is indefinable. Hector & Jason thrived and grew in each other's company, seeming to spark extra nuances of personality and activity. They loved being together; loathed being separated; licked and fussed one another; revelled in each other's company. They were, in every sense, inseparable, whether at home, abroad, or 'in the field'.

Although they were not overtly similar in appearance, colour or character, as with all siblings, there was a deeper connection. The interplay between their unique features and their underlying family characteristics shaped their - and our - daily lives. Jason had his aura; Hector had his character - and his inimitable quiff.

Lord Byron was reputed to be *'mad, bad and dangerous to know'*. Hector & Jason were certainly neither bad, nor dangerous to know, but June proclaimed them *'mad and madder'*. It was clear from the outset who was merely *'mad'* - and who was *'madder'*.

Jason loved his brother to distraction. His love was returned in full measure by Hector. They were each other's world. Their bond was stronger than steel; stronger than silk. Hector never regarded himself as 'just a dog'. He was of high birth; an aristocrat; noble and proud. Jason adored his brother's spirit, and wanted only to love and protect him. I often felt that, despite his bravura, Hector was also a little in awe of his majestic, almost mystical, brother.

The bond was forged very early. When we made our first, tentative, enquiries with the Vernon's, the two boys were already a force of two, their brothers and sisters having found new homes. Then of course June and I went to meet them, and then departed for a few days pre-arranged holiday. This meant that the two boys, at an early and formative stage, were already forging a deep bond. At this stage, also, their mother's attention was becoming less intense; they were weaned, and she was probably relieved at the opportunity to revert to her accustomed role around the Farm. So, whilst they were impeccably cared for, they were left more to their own devices in their little house, where they were always together.

I believe that the force of their bond was already stronger than spiders' silk when we assumed responsibility for their care. As it began, so it continued: throughout their lives, they hardly spent a day, a minute, without being in each other's loving company. That is what they so clearly wanted, and that, ultimately, is the greatest gift that we conferred.

Hector and Jason's attachment and devotion to each other was quite profound. They cared for each other, looked after one another, and doted one upon another. Everywhere we went, it was together; there was never any possibility that they should take it in turns for the most tedious of local trips - to the shops or other such errand. We really were all in it together, even if Jason did not care to be in the car, or to be driven anywhere. He *must* go with Hector and I, no question.

Whenever we visited the vets - or anywhere else - H&J both had to attend the surgery. There was absolutely *no way* that one boy was going anywhere without his brother. And so, time after time, we could be found waiting patiently (at least in my case) in the vet's waiting room, and then in the consulting room, though only one boy needed advice or treatment. When either Hector or Jason was being examined by a vet, the other would become edgy, in wanting to protect his twin, and I would soothe the ruffled feathers. Yet the brother's presence added confidence and reduced anxiety. It may sound strange, but was just the way we were; the calming influence certainly worked for us.

There never seemed to be any jealousy concerning me. Whatever H&J thought of me - and they both gave endless tides of love - it did not affect their own, intense relationship. They just did everything together, and were always together, from birth onwards. Perhaps Jason worried about Hector rather more; he certainly fretted about him if they were visiting the vets, and was frantic with worry on the single, unique occasion when Hector was away, following the infamous stone-eating incident. But then, there never was any reason to fret about Jason; he was a force of nature.

If there was any competitive edge, it existed only at mealtimes - always 6.00pm, wherever we were - when H&J seemed to compete for first-to-produce-a-clean plate. Mealtimes were always a serious business. Almost invariably, happy, smiling boys became earnest at feeding time; their faces focused on the demolition of their one hearty meal in 24 hours. The conclusion was always neck and neck, but the winner - usually joint first place - earned the right to muscle in on the other's (of course empty) bowl. So they swapped bowls, with vigorous but good-natured eagerness. When H&J waited for snacks - invariably sharing my meals - perhaps a bit of bacon or toast - they knew that each boy would get his separately packaged share, and waited patiently for the spoils. I never knew them to get cross with one another. As I reflect now, it's as though they were two halves of a living sculpture, complete when together.

Many people think that a dog's greeting is always the same - not so. Both Hector and Jason had many types of greeting depending on personage and circumstances. These greetings, to friends and relatives, were always warm and affectionate. They would each locate a special item - a stick, a toy, a towel - and offer this to their honoured guest - taking care, at the same time, to keep control of this treasured item.

H&J also knew many dozens - even hundreds - of words and phrases, and this helped me a great deal, particularly when we were out and about. 'Stay', 'sit' and 'come' were the obvious, and well understood commands (if more honoured in the breach than the observance). They also knew phrases such as 'over the road' and 'careful', for instance when we were traversing obstacles, or the inevitable barbed wire that surrounded local fields and, in responding to these, showed a lively intelligence.

Admittedly, H&J did not always appear to take much notice of my 'calling' phrase, when away on a mission. Only my assiduous and repeated calling their names - expressed at some volume when they had been away for some time, and sometimes through gritted teeth - ultimately had the desired effect. Often it was the 'right' psychological moment that delivered success - with Hector, and or Jason - hurtling towards me out of the forest undergrowth, or along one of the myriad paths. Though I would have paid good money to be spared the anxiety of the daily wait, (and spared the head shaking of fellow dog walkers) my heart always leapt on seeing them; I was always amazed by the sheer vitality and verve of their re-appearance.

Jason often employed a favourite game that left both me - and Hector - awe-struck. This game occurred regularly, but only within our local Park, or in the garden in Normandy. Jason would be standing ten or twenty yards from Hector, and adopt a certain pose - or poise. Hector sensed what was coming, and positioned himself to avoid the onslaught as best he could. It never made the slightest difference.

With a speed that was quite unfathomable - bat out of hell springs to mind - Jason pounced, sweeping Hector off his feet with a skill that was just breathtaking: Hector was never injured, merely removed instantly, silently, from his feet to his back. I never quite worked out how Jason achieved this trick of 'throwing' a strong, six-stones dog; so adroit was he, so quick, at attacking the 'right' point. And I never even understood *why*, since Jas was never a dominant or aggressive character. Some instinct deep in his dog brain was no doubt responsible - I have seen footage of hunting wolves, and it's not dissimilar to Jas's technique: but he never caused injury to Hector, or offence to any other dog, to whom he was the soul of gentleness.

Hector & Jason presented a good-humoured, friendly face to the community and diversity of local dogs. This never changed with Jason: even if attacked, as he was on a few unfortunate occasions, he never responded in kind, but adopted a stoical attitude. It was his quick-fire acceleration - along with the thick fur around his neck and throat - that ensured that he was never injured by another dog. Hector, on the other hand, whilst never, ever, aggressive, defended himself staunchly, and proudly, whenever threatened or attacked.

Though H&J respected, and were on nodding terms with, a number of familiar dogs, they took no particular, certainly no sexual, interest in any, including the girls; this was not Miss Ogyny, simply that they were complete in themselves. Their relationships with other dogs were cordial, friendly, sociable, but perhaps a little distant. They had each other, and June, and me; their lives were complete.

Over the span of years, dangerous or difficult incidents with other dogs were remarkably rare. The boys had their aura; they were princes among dogs, and first among equals.

The Band of Brothers

He is your friend, your partner, your defender, your dog. You are his life, his love, his leader. He will be yours, faithful and true, to the last beat of his heart. You owe it to him to be worthy of such devotion.

Unknown

My early years with Hector & Jason were, professionally, an intense, pressure-cooker of a time, in what may loosely be termed the 'regeneration' business. To echo Bill Shankly, it wasn't as important as life and death, but it often seemed to be. It was a time of sharp suits, sharp tongues and sharp knives, metaphorically speaking, and I would not have missed it for the world.

One short story must exemplify a decade of strife and struggle to improve the prospects of our green and pleasant land. There was a rather prickly colleague, let us call her Mrs Nettle, and an equally combative business partner, let us call her Mrs (slightly prickly) Pear. In order to squeeze the Pear, so to speak, Mrs Nettle decided to take a rather strict and uncompromising line with Mrs Pear and her organisation; all for the public good. Cut and thrust was met with parry and riposte. Eventually, withdrawing temporarily from the field of battle, Mrs Nettle repaired on maternity leave. Some weeks later, Mrs N found herself in the Delivery Room, trussed up like a basting turkey, and as helpless. Who should march in but Mrs Pear, attired for her day-job of midwife, but wearing mainly a thin smile. *"Good morning Mrs Nettle; you're in my hands, now".*

So, one must choose one's battles carefully, even if passionate about the cause. This world ended abruptly - though another very similar regime took its place, aka *Animal Farm.* A hostile voice hissed down the telephone: *"We just want your money, and to be rid of you".* And they were - like tossing left-overs to a dog.

The year was 2000 AD. When I was a young boy - perhaps aged 12 - I shuddered to think ahead to the year 2000, when I would be 48 years of age. I would be 'old', and life, for me, pretty well over. There is a child's naivety in this, of course. We often regard ourselves at 48 years as in the prime of our lives: in mid-career, with a mortgage, family, and putting the kids through University. We have never been busier, or more at the centre of an expanding universe of connection and need. But the child can be father to the man. By the age of 48, the course of our lives is set; and our ambitions vaguely realised. We are beyond 'maturity', and on the cusp of decline. We have probably achieved most, even all, that we are going to achieve. Achievement lies behind. A blank wall - the future - lies ahead.

I can say without exaggeration that H&J checked this trajectory for me, and helped to re-set it. Life took a different course. Not 'career wise', but even my career would henceforth take a different road. Henceforth, I would take more risks, and show less regard for continuity and stability. This may appear reckless, but the stars were conjoined; the time was right. Hector & Jason were not responsible for this change in me, in the sense of being culpable, but my relationship with them did help create a new mental outlook that enlarged my life's horizons. The boys released something in me - something which had never before been realised. The momentous year 2000 came and went, but I never saw '48'. Thanks to Hector & Jason, I remained a sprightly 47. Suddenly, we had everything to look forward to. Every day became a sun-flecked, fun-filled, champagne aria day, almost unblemished with wearisome concerns. I have so much to thank them for, in addition to their being their always seductive selves.

Hector & Jason provided sanity, humanity, bucket-loads of affection, and the sheer joy of their love and being. They provided a parallel, more real world, with more solid values. Sharing one's life with one dog with the energy output of a power station was life changing; sharing it with two was truly transformative.

I quickly found that caring for H&J was a full-time occupation. Though not unexpected, this *was* rather stretching, given my (and our) other responsibilities - which included demanding jobs, maintaining the house and garden, tending an allotment, keeping up a variety of family-and-friend relationships, generally attending to all the flotsam and jetsam that life throws at one - and enjoying little slivers of relaxation from time to time.

How is the scarcely achievable accomplished? H&J's breeder had famously warned us that they would be great '*time wasters*', and indeed they did absorb as much time as we could possibly devote. If there's a secret to coping, I think it comes down to teamwork, hard graft, and a focused approach. We just rose earlier, and worked harder, faster and longer than most folks we knew. Our having no children might have helped - though children of a certain age can be useful, or at least cease to be totally dependent. That can never be said of dogs, who have to be fed, walked, fussed, groomed - and whose daily depredations in the house and garden will erode yet further the carer's time and energy.

Yet in the end one does it because one *wants* to - because one cares. June and I had volunteered for this journey, applied for this privilege, and entered into it with 100% commitment from day one. If there was labour, it was a labour of love. We never questioned each other, and rarely complained. There was an implicit understanding that H&J were - indeed had to be - the primary focus of our lives. Because they were part of the family, involved in so much of our daily activity - work excepted - it rarely seemed that there was an additional burden. This was our life - as we had planned and chosen it. And the *charge* that H&J gave - physical, emotional, psychological - generated huge rewards that were beyond monetary value.

So, the relationship with Hector & Jason was very quickly established: they were not 'part of' our family; they *were* our family. As they were our family, so we were theirs. There was also an extended family: my parents, our natural family, and our friends became H&J's family, too, and they loved meeting the people they knew, and greeting new people. H&J's infectious enthusiasm at the mere sight of their friends was deeply touching. No mere play-acting, or show, or slavish instinct, or self-serving subservience, but genuine, heart-felt affection.

H&J loved life like few individuals I have ever known. They also adored their family and circle of friends, and to feel that love gave a glow of deep inner pleasure. The mere mention of the words 'Granny and Grandad' (my parents), or 'Uncle Ray', or 'Alan and June' or 'Margaret and Trevor' would have them whooping with joy, and whirling around the garden, performing (metaphorical) cart-wheels. They would be ecstatic at the mere prospect of greeting; doubly so when the rendezvous actually occurred.

I found it touching then; I still do. What is life, if it is not about love, and the mutual pleasure to be derived from love? H&J were the bringers of unalloyed delight - at once, to their friends, to me, even to themselves. Of what individuals, from what other species, could one say as much? Certainly not from our own gene pool, of whom such rare, iconic individuals are generally categorised as saints.

Domestic bliss. Our boys were a foci of domestic activity and attention, inseparable from the daily and weekly routine. There was, of course, dog food and dog biscuit 'mixer' to buy (H&J enjoyed any high quality canned food - and enjoyed it even more if fresh meat was mixed with it). There were also visits to the local farm shop, to buy 'treats' for reward *after* walks: (H&J never responded to treats during walks - there was far too much going on). And there were *accoutrements* to purchase and maintain - their collars and leads, upholstered dog beds, a range of brushes, and towels for drying the boys - much-needed after rain drenched walks.

We therefore built a happy, if intense, lifestyle, centred around Hector & Jason, that was integrated in the maelstrom of activity that revolved around work, home and garden, and social interests. Indeed, H&J were an important aspect of these other lifestyles - through conversation with colleagues and friends, an interested physical presence in observing practically everything that I did, or accompanying us to shops, friends and relatives. H&J were as much a part of my life as, speaking personally, the nose on my face. If life didn't revolve around them, they were involved, as well as deeply interested, in every aspect of our complex lives.

And the boys developed a delightful relationship with our family of Burmese cats - first, Oscar and Charlie; succeeded by (half-brothers) Oliver, and Louis, and finally the incorrigible Lenny. The confidence of Louis - the supreme instinctive knowledge of his species - knew that the boys held no risk to him. More remarkable, a bond of real affection developed, particularly from the (otherwise) fierce Louis, whose heart melted when he fussed round H&J - though he could be tigerish to his brother and nephew.

I *loved* sharing my food with Hec and Jas. Of course, one had to discriminate - they would have eaten everything, given the chance, and it was not for me to spoil them with chocolate, or sweet and fatty foods. But I knew what they liked best - chunks of meat, a share of a bacon sandwich, chips, toast, and of course cheese, which they enjoyed every Sunday lunchtime. Hector would take no prisoners in his excitement, and I learned to make my fingers as small as possible in offering him food. Jason had the softest mouth imaginable; I honestly think that, if he had carried a live duck, he would have put it down uninjured.

When at rest in the evening, Hector - or Jason - or both - would often lie on their back, smiling up at us, tails wagging. At these times they would love to be fussed and tickled. This must sound cheesy and sentimental to non-dog lovers, but such small, intimate moments are the gold standard for anyone who has enjoyed the privilege of a loving relationship with a being from a different species.

Though I never enjoyed separation from H&J, even to go to the office, I returned home with keen anticipation. The warmth of their welcome was simply un-matched; always spontaneous, and almost over-whelming. I never quite overcame my daily delight at their special show of excitement and overwhelming joy each and every time I returned from office, or the odd lone shopping or other trip. Every day - sometimes several times a day - Hector & Jason accorded me the special, intense welcome they would had I been the Emperor of Europa, or the Sultan of Samarkand, bearing riches beyond their wildest dreams.

Hector & Jason were the perfect antidote to an over-active, stressful day life. Whatever depression the working day had effected in my spirits or my humour, they would offer a welcome that restored my better self. Energetic, eternally affectionate, and with a mind-set at once predictable but always a million miles from petty human concerns and ambitions, they took me out of my fretted, humdrum world, and enabled me to embrace their special, self-contained universe.

There was no sadness in their lives, unless when left alone for a little while; for the most part, all was breathtaking optimism, vivacity, content, and happiness, depending on time and circumstance. Life in their company was all pretty infectious - there was no time to be bored: there was fuss, and play, and the prospect of food, and the forthcoming walk. Whatever the vicissitudes of work, or weather, or personal or family anxieties, H&J shone through it all, providing perspective, stability, a source of need and a source of strength; and a great well of affection. The welcome home was always pure, unalloyed gold.

Apart from those time-punctuations necessitated by work - which, for me, was a mere fifteen minutes drive away - we were together practically all the time, and travelled everywhere together - whether on trips, on walks or merely on the supermarket run. We found that even a shopping trip was better for H&J than the relative tedium of the house, since it entailed the stimulation of a short journey, and the opportunity to scour the supermarket car park, watching a lively, colourful, Dickensian world go by.

I often felt that I was regarded as a third brother - certainly not owner, master or even coach. Through our constant walks, our close companionship, and the experiences that we shared, we became a band of brothers, an unbreakable team. I exulted in my status; hopefully, without vanity or arrogance, but certainly with a lively pride. I felt that my life was enhanced by the presence and intoxicating experience conferred on me, and brought to me, by these magnificent lads. They trusted me, licked me, communicated with me on a variety of levels, sometimes even agreed to take advice and return to me. Generally, I was placed in the position of lead brother - but the one who couldn't keep up. Even when H&J were 'doing their thing' in woods or park, I was certainly not forgotten; they may have been pushing the envelope, but there was always an envelope. We were united by a powerful sense of belonging, and H&J would invariably return from every mission into my waiting arms.

During the remarkably long, golden years of H&J's maturity and prime, I felt like one of the luckiest and happiest men alive; I was walking on air. There were the usual vexations of worry over work, money, family headaches, and a host of daily concerns, irritants, and incidents, all resulting from our common humanity and struggle to get through life. But nothing could dent or deny the dimension of exuberance and excitement, the deep knowledge that H&J were waiting for me, rooting for me. It was a defence against everything, and buoyed me up through all kinds of challenges and frustrations. With that kind of loyalty and commitment, 'troubles' were reduced to their proper dimensions. Even H&J's needs - for walks, attention, fuss, food - took me out of myself, and my petty cares. They transported me to another, warm but non-human world, with different values and ideas - and I hope enabled me to put some distance between myself and the pettiness and frustrations that infect modern life.

I find this all pretty impressive, since neither Hector or Jason could speak English - though they could comprehend a good deal - or had access to money. Neither could they change a light bulb, drive a car, or give advice on work, family or finance. But, unconsciously, subliminally, H&J have been there, rooting for us, all the while. What are the highest points of life, after all, but love; rich, shared experience; friendship; giving; joy in togetherness?

Indeed, H&J were my constant companions, on whom I lavished, I hope, every care and compassion. But this could never be an adequate return for the emotional riches they showered on me. At the most basic and on the most profound levels, Hector & Jason were passionate devotees of 'life'. They were the most positive role models - for life itself - that I have ever known.

Even when not physically by my side, Hector & Jason were *there*: whether I was at work, or shopping, eating, or sleeping - whatever humans do - they were in my heart and mind, a constant energy, pride, source of strength, anticipation, expectation, thought, presence. H&J provided an extra dimension to my conscious and even unconscious life; a thread of being that was extra-ordinarily thrilling and fulfilling.

The relationship I shared with H&J was deeper, more intense, more complete and less conditional than practically any I have ever known. Though caring attentively to dogs is enormously time-consuming, I was rewarded a million times over with boundless love, generosity and devotion. All that shared love; all that shared experience.

I was their hero: I was their Lancelot, I was their D'artagnan. This was intoxicating, since this was not the result of slavish obedience, but of deep affection, freely bestowed. The pride I felt was never excelled by Edmund Hilary, on top of Everest, or Felix Baumgartner, returning jubilantly to Earth from outer space.

The boys were, for me, at once a beacon, a herald, and a sanctuary. A beacon because they were devotion and goodness itself in a faithless, careless world. A herald, because they were the epitome of loyalty, love, and 'the real' in a society increasingly devoid of true values. And a sanctuary - against the vicious money-go-round of commercial exploitation that is the modern economy. That may seem a lot of expectation to place on one's canine friends, but hopefully they were oblivious to most of the flotsam and jetsam, the superficial, trite and nastier aspects of contemporary life. What Hector & Jason gave was uniquely precious, real and rare.

It is hard indeed to describe their effect on me, personally. A few, very rare, human beings - and a few other beings - have a gift for enhancing the lives of everyone they touch. Others are drawn to them as if by a magnet, and feel as if they are enveloped in a shower of gold-dust, or in the rainbow beside a waterfall. Jason, in particular, was imbued with that gift in glorious abundance: the what? - act, process, of admiring him, communing with him, or responding to his pleasure, was accompanied by a frisson of excitement that thrilled, and lifted the spirit. This effect is hard to describe: yet we all know that moment when we experience the presence of someone, or something, truly, utterly remarkable.

Comparisons are tepid but, hopefully, meaningful. Listening to the minor miracle of The Beach Boys *Pet Sounds,* or the searing sincerity of Sinatra's *Only the Lonely*, or Strauss's exquisite, unbearably poignant *Four Last Songs* evokes a response that lifts our being. Similarly, Vermeer's *Girl with a Pearl Earring*, or van Gogh's *The Night Café*, uplift the soul, as the most fabulous art, only, can do. Or, in literature, Byron's inspired and inspirational *She Walks in Beauty*, or Shakespeare's *Shall I compare thee to a Summer's Day,* evokes an emotional response that seems as pure and rare as the thought that inspired such wonders.

In the film *High Society* Frank Sinatra sings *You're Sensational* to, who else, Grace Kelly. It's a moment that is so tender, so thrilling, that it always sends a shiver down the spine. The phrase, the delicate lyric, perfectly captures my feeling for Jason: sensational, and life enhancing.

'*Shall I compare thee to a summer's day, Thou art more lovely and more temperate*' are lines that just dance with beauty. They also express the essence of Jason's effect on my being and psyche. With him, I felt as though I was experiencing a kind of enhanced, super-charged, overwhelming sense of being alive, and joyfully. Just to touch him, to be with him, sent a thrill along the heart. To know him was to love him. But, of course, he had an excuse: not fashioned by human hand - just nurtured by one: he was a force of nature, and a gift from God.

Surprisingly, perhaps, not everyone is dazzled by the Pyramids at Gizza, the Acropolis at Athens, or France's Mont St Michel. They may merely recall the crammed cafés, the eye-watering prices (of ices), the trashy trinkets. Each person is entitled to their own view, their own take on things. And yet; and yet... Let us fondly imagine that these worthy citizens were suddenly transported, to their evident surprise - that is, at dying - to the radiance of Heaven. After a day or two listening to harp-plucking angels, and catching up on '*Corrie*', they turn to their fellow saved-souls and sulkily confide: "*To be honest, I'm a little disappointed...I thought Jesus would be taller than that*".

Hector & Jason were *never* disappointed: the world was full of wonder, and endless tasty treats. A colourful French market, a lush forest, the broad sweep of a beach - were yet more wonderful still.

And *they* never disappointed.

In *On First Looking Into Chapman's Homer* John Keats writes:

'*Much have I travell'd in the realms of gold*
And many goodly states and kingdoms seen'.

Most of Keats' travels were in the realms of his imagination; I have been fortunate in seeing many goodly kingdoms, as they have opened their gates and welcomed me in. I have marvelled at the grandeur of the Alps and Scottish Highlands. I have been awed by the glories of the Parthenon, enchanted by exquisite Sainte Chapelle, almost overwhelmed by the Musee d'Orsay, and struck dumb by the Tapestry of the Apocalypse. I have gazed on the glamour of Royal Ascot and St Tropez. But I will search the world in vain for the greatness of spirit that is Jason.

His temperament was simply delicious: at home, with other humans, with other dogs, he was the prince of gentleness, one's soul's delight. Hector regarded his outdoor life very seriously. To Jason, it was a great adventure, a delicious game. In 'the field' he displayed the boldness, courage and élan of Lancelot du Lac, Michel Ney or Joachim Murat. He was beyond compare. But one must compare: Hector was deep, guileful, full of zest and playfulness: he could plan, and execute his plan. If Jason was the essence of exuberance, of *joie de vivre*, Hector was the epitome of desire, in his need to execute his daily mission. Hector had a spirit and sensibility that was almost human in its depth and subtlety.

Together, Hector & Jason were sunbeams in a world that, both figuratively and literally, is often '*rack'd by basest clouds*'. I never plumbed the depths of their affection. I simply came to realise that, the more love you give, the more will be returned.

It is my passionate hope that, in return, in response, to the overwhelming affection bestowed on me by H&J, that I gave Hector & Jason the affection that they truly deserved, and that they *felt* my love.

Our relationship was a simple, beautiful, equation: they adored each other; they adored me; I adored them.

Indeed, H&J bought a smile to everyone's face, and a tingling effervescence to my whole being, whenever we were abroad in the world. It is only now that I can summarise my feelings: I came to love Jason with all my heart and all my soul; I came to love Hector with all my heart - and all my mind. Hector was simply the cleverest, and smartest, and *deepest* dog I had ever met. My love for him deepened, and deepened again, through our years together. Together, our love reached a pitch of perfection.

Together, H&J gave a purpose to life - an extra purpose to life - that made the glass full to brimming. There is a sort of warmth that dogs bestow on a family; an intimacy and a closeness that brings one back to the root of being, and is reminiscent of days long past: a bond of need and loyalty; an alliance based on mutual interest and shared affection. If the lust for life exhibited by Hector & Jason was occasionally frustrating - and beyond most dog carers desire for a quiet, balanced life - this was more than offset by the immense rewards of watching - and following - their giddy gallop across their world.

Ultimately, it's all about love. Madison Smartt Bell's short story, *Barking Man,* ends with the dog-hero, Alfie, being treated by a hypnotist. With the dog in a trance, the hypnotist questions Alfie as to what is missing in his life. After all, he enjoys a warm home, good food; he has no worries or responsibilities:

"What is it Alf? What is it that you lack?"...The hypnotist leaned a little closer to him. *"Dogs don't love"*, the hypnotist whispered. *"They haven't got the capability. They feel, yes, but they don't love."*
"That", said *Alf*, *"is a debatable point."*

In Tobias Wolff's *Her Dog,* the hero, Victor (it had to be a Victor!) enjoys a family consisting of a married couple, Grace and John. But it is Grace who he bonds with; Grace who takes him for his best walks. And Grace who dies. Victor, now an old dog, has a frank conversation with John. Victor bristles:
"Did I ever want another mistress?"
"No."
"You did. You looked at them in the park, on the beach, in other cars as we drove around."
"Men do that. It doesn't mean I wanted anyone but Grace."

"Yes you did."

"Maybe for an hour. A night. No longer."

"Then I loved her more than you. I loved her with all my heart."

From (inspired) dog-fiction to dog-fact. John Bradshaw's *In Defence of Dogs* has confirmed me in the views and feelings I developed while sharing my life with H&J. Bradshaw explains that *'dogs...have very unusual brains, which allow them to construct several social milieu simultaneously.'* Certainly, that rings true to experience. And he points out that *'the need for a human attachment figure seems to be unusually strong in the domestic dog.'* Again, on the basis of real-time experience, who could suggest otherwise?

Our emotional lives, too, turn out to be similar - but not identical. As species, however, we both show our emotions openly. Finally - my favourite finding: dogs may experience joy and love more intensely, and in more nuanced ways, than human beings.

So there are sound biological reasons for believing that the answer to the vexed question of *'does you dog love you?'* is a most definite *'yes!'*

I truly never doubted.

9: On the Home Front

Tis sweet to hear the watch dog's honest bark
Bay deep-mouthed welcome as we draw near home;
Tis sweet to know there is an eye will mark
Our coming, and look brighter when we come.

Don Juan - Lord Byron

There is no faith which has never yet been broken, except that of a
truly faithful dog.

Konrad Lorenz

June and I live on the extreme western edge of The Black Country, and this patch of black and green provided the framework for our daily lives. This is a peculiar (in the best sense) part of the world. The area is famed for its industrial past, and its distinct culture, as hard and brittle as the coal and iron that shaped and moulded the landscape. While the mines and foundries are now long gone, our view to the east is filled with their indelible legacy: row upon row of houses, shops, factories, warehouses, and roads flanked by serried ranks of street lights, stretching to the horizon. Towards the west, our view is of green fields, hedges, trees, and the woodland of Ridgehill. At night, in one direction, we have a blaze of - thousands - of garish, sulphurous street lamps, blotting out the night sky; in the other direction, only darkness, pierced by stars.

While our work lay eastward, our play, and vision, was westward - towards the green fields of South Staffordshire, Worcestershire and Shropshire, which surround the Black Country with a ring of green and unfulfilled promise. For many decades these 'green lungs' have provided the respite, solace and freedom, if only on Sundays, to the huddled masses fleeing the oppression of mine, factory and mill. We needed no urging: H&J were country dogs, and westward lay our destiny.

Let me guide you around these nearby woods, Ridgehill Wood, since they have a central place in our story. Given their elevation, the woods dominate the local landscape, and can be viewed from far afield. They are characterised by a steepish, sandstone ridge, studded with a superfluity of trees. A pathway or track, oval in shape, passes all around the woodland perimeter. The path is thus verging on two miles of earthy, undulating track, with further paths interlacing and picking through the wood, and along the 'plateau' formed by the ridge.

Given their precarious position on the fringe of the intensely urbanised Black Country, the woodland's very existence is quite extraordinary. The woods are hemmed in along one side by houses, whose fences and gates act as a common border. Along the other, long, perimeter edge, the woods give way to cultivated fields, and paddocks, replete with horses.

These are ancient woods, carpeting a dominant sandstone ridge. They are composed mainly of stands of oak, beech, and sweet chestnut, but also with large numbers of sycamore, and interspersed with thickets of holly. At one end, too, there is a mature plantation of pines. Apparently destined for pit props, these now century-old trees have survived the local collieries, which became silent in the '60s and '70s.

It's often said that, if you need a job to be done, give it to a busy person. June and I were busy people, balancing work, home, and family, with responsibility for our boys. We were pretty squeezed, but the boys were warped and wefted through our lives, integral to our daily routines. Somehow, working within it, we stretched time, and bent it to our will. The zest for life, and the urgency for it, was automatic, and axiomatic: H&J were a profoundly important element in our thinking and planning, and when not *with* them, I was thinking *about* them.

Each day began with H&J, all smiles and sunshine, crowding around our bed, and greeting us to the new morning. In a matter of minutes we would be out in the fresh air. 'Majestic' would not sum up how, I think, we all felt, striding out into the brand new day. Within minutes, we were in 'our' woods, where we passed - me in an early morning reverie, H&J on the wings of Mercury - elegant beech trees, dripped in green-wash; slender sessile oaks, gracefully unfurling their long limbs; hoary old English oaks, rearing their stags heads to the heavens, and ancient, fragrant sweet chestnuts, like Petra, '*half as old as time*'.

While Jason ran and ran through and among these woods, Hector was often loitering with intent. A neighbour living at the extreme end of the woods kept chickens, which were poised invitingly near to the border fence. Hector found the glimpses of plump birds, clucking contentedly, quite irresistible, and often ducked below my radar, speeding onwards towards his goal. The border fence, thankfully, was impenetrable. Hector drooled on, his acute senses fully alerted, enjoying the anticipation of warm, moist chicken.

While I set off in pursuit of beauty - always, beauty - H&J set-off in response to their own muse - their nature's passionate spirit. It often felt that, on their 'walks' - a polite euphemism - H&J were linked to a line of elastic, very long, and very strong, which would eventually return them to me; and this was almost invariably the case. However, I can recall one occasion when Hector - two or three when Jason - (presumably thinking that I had left the woods) ran home, alone. This was worrying - mainly because it was dangerous - and, thankfully, soon ceased. Generally, H&J were so busy in the woods on various pre-occupations that they would have happily stayed all day; only my incessant calling, combined with their deep attachment to me, eventually brought them back. I recall two occasions - one in what I call the 'lower woods', which has a small river nearby, the other a country park - where the boys, still united to their leads, leapt off to savour the delights of hill and stream, returning breathless and muddy ten or fifteen minutes later.

Roaming the countryside, and particularly these local woods was, for me, a release: an opportunity to day-dream, to think on life, to allow thought, even poetry, to float into my head. So:

Did Shakespeare pen a play, while his wife baked bread,
And badgered him to tend the geese, draw water from the well?
"If writing's waned today, and winning words won't gel,
Then kindly black the fire, or make our feather bed."

"I own, this tale, of Hamlet, is proving quite a slog."
She smiled: "in these brief lives of ours, choice is rarely free:
So, I'll finish this brave piece of yours, "To be..."
Sweet William, while you bravely walk the dog."

My day-dreaming might lead me to ponder on the state of the world, or just the state of 'the markets'. Or I might muse, for example, as to who had contributed more to the sum of human happiness: artists, or scientists? Shakespeare himself, or the brilliant polymath, Francis Bacon? Lord Byron, or his daughter, Ada, Lady Lovelace? - a mathematical genius, who helped lay the foundations for modern computing, and the Internet. The poet, prophet and visionary William Blake, or Sir Isaac Newton? whose reductive, rationalist-materialist explanation of the Universe Blake detested. Jane Austen, or Sir Edward Jenner, her contemporary, and the discoverer of the smallpox vaccine? The 19th century scientists who discovered the make-up of the rainbow, or John Keats who - despite his own scientific training - complained of the *unweaving of the rainbow*? And so on: the Brontë sisters, or Brunel? Bizet or Bazalgette? Brahms or Benz? And, in recent times - Britten, or Berners-Lee?

Leonardo, of course - painter, inventor, engineer, architect, musician - would not have recognised any distinction between art and science, and there are clear underlying links - for instance, between music and mathematics. But I never arrived at a conclusion to these, no doubt, simple musings. And, after all, modern man appears to be so fortunate in enjoying the fruits of both art and science. Yet, can we continue to eat our cake and still have it? More urgently, more practically, my need to tear myself from thought, and re-connect with the absent H&J, usually frustrated any deeper or more fertile conclusions.

And there were other distractions. Each morning, on our daily, frenetic, walk, we would encounter an array of other dogs: perhaps four Border Collies, two Staffies, a Boxer, a German Shepherd and a Bearded Collie, besides a smattering of 'defined indefinables'. In addition, say ten flowering plants, twenty-odd species of tree, and seven or so species of bird. Oh, and brief, snatched conversations with our dog-caring chums and passers-by, people passing singly or in small, chatty clusters. Not a bad return for sixty or so minutes of hard walking! My finest hour came when, in a small clearing, I came across a peregrine falcon, no less, sitting astride a warm-but-dead, recumbent pigeon. It was a one-off, magnificent sight - but for my dog-walking I would not have witnessed this, or enjoyed many other *piquant* little experiences.

Instinctively, H&J were clean dogs: they did not go in search of mud and squelch, but their rapid movement did result, in wet weather, in a coating of mud on what I called their 'under-carriage'. They were easily, if reluctantly, towelled down. And they were certainly not difficult dogs in the sense of chasing the female of the species. Whatever my anxiety concerning their absences, and whatever antics I imagined them to be engaged in, I knew for certain that they were not 'chatting-up' any female admirers. They were focused exclusively on doing their own, inimitable, 'thing'.

Golden Retrievers are generally allowed to be 'handsome', an epithet that does them positive justice. Even so, sometimes, on our travels, we would meet exceptional looking dogs - a husky, a German Shepherd, perhaps another Golden Retriever.

Always, always, I would smile to myself and whisper, through clenched teeth: *"yes, you're handsome; you're lovely: but you're not as beautiful as my Jason."*

Home Comforts

Don't accept your dog's admiration as conclusive evidence that you are wonderful.

Ann Landers

Despite my day-dreaming, our timetable was - had to be - highly disciplined: both June's and my work schedules, and our home life, demanded that kind of traction. So H&J enjoyed their first walk of the day between 6.50am and 7.00am. We all needed to be back home by 8.00am at the latest, since June and I needed to leave home for work at around 8.40am. This gave me a (leisurely) 20 minutes to enjoy breakfast, kindly prepared by June, (and shared by H&J) and 20 minutes to perform the three 'S's' - s—t, shower, shave - to shed the caveman image, and emerge as a modern day professional. The routine was always intense and frenetic, but somehow hugely enjoyable.

The only pang of regret was the actual point of departure for work, leaving a quizzical H&J wondering just *why* I was leaving - and for whom. By the time I arrived at work to begin a new day I had already, it seemed, been awake and alive for half a day. But each day brought memories of our most recent walk, always with different, often unique experiences, and the warm glow of a life lived to capacity. In a different, 'dogless' life, I could have settled for an extra hour in bed. There will be enough time for sleep, anon.

Indeed, sleep can be a way of getting through life without actually living. H&J slept hardly at all - a habit that inevitably embraced me, though I quickly became accustomed to the disturbed sleep, early starts and late-to-beds. One quickly habituates to a new sleeping pattern - essentially, to manage on less sleep, and broken sleep. But at least one knows that one is alive, active and *doing*.

When I left home for work, I was on a cloud of love; when I returned, I returned to love. This made travelling, and everything in between, a joy. It was as though I was suspended, carried along on this cloud of reverie. I looked forward to my return almost as much as did H&J; it was a return to sanity; time to reflect on life's ups and downs, and to clear, and re-energise, the mind.

Living with a force of nature and his extrovert brother was remarkably easy. At home, H&J were a delight: gentle, attentive, obedient and affectionate. They loved each other - and they loved us. They were simply ecstatic at meeting guests - particularly friends or relatives who they regarded as close friends. The boys revelled at carrying around t-towels, oven gloves, balls and bits of wood or coal in rapturous greeting. When 'chillin' in our own company they were quiet and charming, though mealtimes always sparked intense interest.

Even from a young age, Jason would eat his tit-bits with the utmost grace, a real gentleman - with the softest mouth. Hector on the other hand took no prisoners; my fingers might disappear along with the ham sandwich unless I took great care. And not just the fingers - family meals had to be protected from Hector, at least during the early years. I recall one Saturday lunch of chicken salad that turned out to be merely salad when, just for a moment, our backs were turned. One Golden Retriever was left licking his lips in appreciation, but without a trace of guilt. Hector, of course. *'Your dinner is in the dog'* could have been his life's ambition.

Even so, their mealtimes were a joy - watching the two boys enjoying their food, lasciviously, as though it was the best thing they had ever tasted! How we take food for granted, as a necessary bit of filler before the next slice of activity or experience. As George Orwell reveals of his Parisian experiences in *Down and Out in Paris and London, 'we were too hungry even to try and think of anything except food.'*

Early each evening, the boys' furious assault on their long-awaited dinner was a wonder to behold. Demolition of dinner took a mere handful of seconds. H&J ate every single scrap - and then, without fail, each boy inspected the brother's dish, to see whether there were any morsels still lurking in a corner. There never was. A few hopeful licks - but nothing. After all - if you are a dog - you can never be entirely sure where the next meal is coming from. Or as the financial adverts have it, *'the past is not necessarily a guide to the future'.*

Following their meal, mutual satisfaction, and vigorous wagging of tails, there followed in Jason's case a celebratory cleaning of his muzzle on the three-piece suite. This was followed by an equally enthusiastic run around the lounge, and the garden, in a state of almost overwhelming happiness. And then... quiet, and rest, and a little sleep, with undisguised content. When not running in his sleep, Jason's back legs would often be crossed, as though making a conscious effort *not* to run. At such times, a big smile would light up his face, even whilst recumbent on his back.

H&J shared our humble home and everything in it: they lived with us, ate with us, and slept in our bedroom - on their own bed. And they travelled everywhere with us. The boys have always shared our - their - home with Burmese cats - usually three in number. Dogs and cats have always proved friendly, even affectionate, partners and co-habitees. In one instance, the partnership proved strong and enduring. Young Louis, (aka Louis Quatorze, the Sun King) and cream Burmese, was 12 weeks old when he was parachuted into our household. He had been brought by car from Stourport, his childhood home, to our own home 15 miles away. He has always hated cars, then and since, and howled the whole way back.

Unavoidably, and understandably, Louis was an anxious little boy. We carefully placed Louis in the house, only too conscious that he was about to meet - or confront - two excited, giant dogs, in their physical prime. We knew that the boys did not constitute a danger, as such, since they were already living with Louis' young half-brother, Oliver, and a mature Burmese lad, the unique Oscar. Even so, we were quite anxious on behalf of young Louis, who had already undergone a pretty upsetting experience. What happened surprised and delighted us both: without fuss or ado, the tiny Louis strode up to each huge, panting boy in turn, and wrapped himself around first Hector, and then Jason. The boys accepted this affectionate welcome with good grace; a partnership of (almost) equals ensued.

As at first, so it continued. Louis, Hector and Jason became the firmest of friends, sharing genuine affection and warmth. It was a miracle of instant bonding, like love at first sight, even more remarkable in that Louis had never before met a dog. And so began a lifelong bond of enduring power: Louis slept with the boys, fussed them, licked them, almost regarding himself, at those times, as an honorary dog. The irony is that Louis was the most fearsome cat we have ever known, treating his fellow felines with utter disdain, and bullying them with haughty nonchalance. But with H&J he was a real pussycat - kind, gentle and patient - and never displaying the slightest impatience or aggression. He had decided, from the outset, to make them his friends. And so it remained - friends for life.

In fact this was the beginning of a decade - the 'Noughties' and beyond - of a pretty constant, unchanging cast of characters in our household, with June and I balancing the varied but constant needs of two super boys, in Hector & Jason, and three super Burmese boys, all eager to play the fullest roles in our - and their - daily lives. Our Weekend schedule reflected these myriad demands and responsibilities, and was never less than extraordinarily full and active. Saturday mornings was shopping day, and one regular stop on our shopping expedition would be to the local farm shop, where we would load up with goodies for the boys - little treats such as bonios, miniature bonios, chews and toys. This was always a pleasure; the choosing, and the giving, to the delighted H&J (and their cat chums). Sometimes, the best things in life are the simple pleasures, quietly enjoyed.

Everyone knew H&J in the dog-walker community, in the community as a whole, and in our local vets, which seldom saw them, in view of their rude health. As we know, when we did visit the vets, both boys - Hector Hill, and Jason Hill - had to be there, even if only one lad required treatment; it was an absolute necessity. H&J were a terrific presence in the waiting room, a unity of grace and a supreme life-force. And, when we were called by the vet and I rose to my feet, the boys' reaction never varied: they headed for the exit! So, we were not a familiar sight - but we were a noted and much-enjoyed 'item'.

One bright Summer evening we were together - we were always together - at the said vets. Hector & Jason were alive with anticipation, monitoring every move and nuance of activity. Suddenly, a young, blonde, veterinary nurse, brimming with beauty, bounced across the threshold from the busy street outside. As she saw H&J, her pleasure all too evident, her face lit up in a lovely smile: *"Hello boys!"* she beamed. All three of us returned her greeting, grinning and gurning our broadest smiles.

Walk for Life

Walking with a dog - or dogs - provides physical, social, psychological and even spiritual enrichment. Of what other activities can that be said?

Colin Hill

Hector, Jason and I walked - and walked, and walked. We seemed to be known by everyone, everywhere. Why do we walk dogs? There are many reasons. 'Toileting' may not be the most glamorous reason, but ensuring one's charges are properly toileted gives a certain relief, and satisfaction; job well done, as it were. Better out than in.

Then there's the exercise, and the fitness that results. The fresh air, the passing through and experiencing a diversity of countryside. The sights, sounds and smells of the changing seasons; the distraction, and relief from stress; the cheer of occasional company; the sunshine and the rain; the chance meetings with wildlife. And, sometimes, thought, ideas, even poetry, sprang new-born into my mind, as though out of the intoxicating air. Yet above all else - the sheer, glorious pleasure of one's boys enjoying themselves, *being* themselves: your joy in their joy; the physical and mental exhilaration of witnessing, and sharing in, their power, strength and discovery.

So what's in it for the dog? The opportunity to meet old (dog) friends, and their carers; the opportunity to meet new dog friends, and their carers. The chance to explore countryside - familiar and new - and the prospect of encounters with wildlife. The chance to visit territory, and to claim some sort of dominion over it: '*Hector is here!*'. The thrill of adventure - morning, noon and night. This proved a heady cocktail for Hector & Jason; and they drank deeply from it.

The Walking Ritual. For every dog walker, there is something about walking with one's dog companions that is a little mysterious; a kind of throw-back to the long-forgotten days when ancient Britons, and their wolf-like companions, roamed the moors and woodlands in search of game. It is a true antidote to modern life, with its incessant, 24/7 pace, and its blinkered pursuit of material and - elusive - personal happiness.

One is walking with one's dog, in places few others seem to know or care about; and one's pre-occupations revolve around fur, and earth, and panting, and falling leaves, and unexpected surprises - a fox, a badger, a suicidal squirrel, another (hostile) canine, a cat running for cover, a suited man with his lover, an outcrop of wild flowers. So many tiny, almost microscopic events and secret pleasures that one experiences with one's dogs; that build up, layer upon layer, into a rich tapestry. Normal, prosaic activities were enhanced by the presence, the company, of H&J, and often transformed by their seizing possibility and opportunity, as they dragged me - literally and figuratively - out of my comfort zone.

The three-a-day walking ritual is time-consuming for sure, but deeply satisfying on the most human level. And what else would you be doing over those two hours? Watching TV? (Can anyone remember what anodyne drivel they watched the night before last?). Or shopping? Jogging? Reading a newspaper? No, walking one's dogs is one of those terrifically feel-good activities, along with playing with one's children, helping elderly relatives or neighbours, cultivating vegetables or cooking a 'scratch' meal. It's worth doing for its own sake, and has splendid by-products - exercise, the wind in one's face, renewed exposure to nature, the satisfaction of healthy, happy dogs. Each and every walk was intense, exciting, challenging, often nerve-wracking (for yours truly) - enjoy the ride!

Again, H&J would lead me to Park or woods, depending on their mood and their previous walks that day - variety being the spice of life. In the Summer, under a cloudless sky, this was pure delight. If it was Winter, we might still enjoy a quick dash to our favourite haunts, or just as often tour the local streets, still looking for adventure - new people, new dogs, food left unwanted, a cat scurrying away, strange scents in the hedgerow.

Unless it was a non-working day for me, in which case the Park or woods would beckon around midday (H&J generally preferred the Park at lunchtimes) the next walk took place immediately upon returning home from work, and sandwiched between, appropriately enough, the boys' main, evening, meal.

We now know just *why* President Kennedy seemed imbued with a permanent smile. Hector & Jason's smiles - stretching from ear to ear, and along the body to the tail - were just as permanent: another walk was always omni-present, with all its promise of good things - people, dogs, countryside, wildlife. Picking up a lead was the equivalent of waving a magic wand. The enchanted garden was about to be revealed.

Our walks were not optional, or pedestrian, but the centre of our lives. Sometimes, the flesh - my flesh - might weaken, but never that of Hector & Jason. They loved every second, and anticipated every new walk with a kind of timeless, tireless enthusiasm. A greater zest for life was never seen, and I exulted in their exultation.

Passers by would often pass comment, exuding admiration: "*They walk so beautifully!*" ."*How I love the way they move!*". Such praise, coming as it did without invitation, was music to my ears, and gladdened my heart; sheer bliss. When out-and-about, Hector always wore a black leather collar, that set off his handsome, rich, golden fur. Jason - *vive la différence* - always wore a red collar, which contrasted superbly with his blonde mane.

Every day, on the literally pedestrian walks, we had to dodge frogs and snails, poo, snot and grot. There was never a moment's complacency, or lapse of concentration. It was as if H&J - and therefore, me - were participating in a major sporting event. We were always on top form, at the peak of our powers. The boys were not 'better than', or 'improved upon' but *different to...*

But for Hector & Jason, the pavement was never pedestrian, but paved with gold - vital nuggets of stuff: an enticing wonderland, an orgasmic profusion of exotic scents. Just as in the *Don Giovanni* scena where the Don proclaims: "*I smell woman!*" (as we have seen, quite literally for Victor) so Hector & Jason explored a rich palette of scents and perfumes each and every day. To me, the 'book' they deciphered was closed, a perfect enigma: they of course understood every code, every nuance of meaning. It was a world as exciting and seductive as any from the Arabian Nights: perfumes lingered, and the impression of hot hands on scabbards. Calling cards were left, subtly, or thrown down - H&J left theirs, too, in goodly greeting.

My own observations were in a more boringly human dimension. Our street walks remind me of Lennon and McCartney's *Penny Lane*. There was the man in the garden from morn till evening, and I thought he loved gardening - until I met his wife. There was the guy whose vans advertised his running two businesses - a greasy spoon, and a fitness centre (thus able to eat his cake and still have it). There were twitching curtains, dogs heard but never seen, hostile signage, every conceivable style of frontage: loved, smart, handsome, eccentric, scorched-earth, concrete, variously 'open' or surrounded by thick hedges. Hector &

Jason knew that their trail lay on the pavements and roadside verges, and we never wavered from these, merely observing 'all human life' and its material excrescences as we passed - always *very* quickly.

'Walking the streets', if I may use such a term, was not without its fascination. Most - if not all - human life is exposed (I use the term advisedly) to the constant, curious dog-walker. So often, according to the TV 'News', bodies are found *'by a man walking his dog'*. On several occasions H&J and I were fortunate not to be in this position, human bodies being found by others a mere minute or two ahead of us. Even so, passing hundreds of homes in the course of a typical walk, one cannot be unaware of people's lives and interests. The condition of homes and gardens, the types of vehicles, the twitching curtains, the skips over-flowing with discarded 'stuff', revealed so much about local lives, and even the local economy, as I sped by with my thrillingly energetic charges.

Street walking, however, could be hazardous, especially at night, owing to the profusion of structures, known collectively by the euphemism of 'street furniture'. Street lights, telegraph poles, post boxes, one expects; but there is an ever-growing army of grey, red, green and yellow boxes, or 'cabinets', clogging the footpaths and asserting their steely right to be there. These devilish contraptions - all mounted on pavements - can easily clatter and up-end the unwary wayfarer, like muggers in a dark alley. H&J knew only the 'as the crow flies' or 'Roman road' method of walking - straight as an arrow, or a dye. So it fell to me to negotiate these hazards. Whenever the Red Sea parted (Hector shaving one side, Jason the other), I had to dribble around said object or objects (there is rarely only one) and pass on to the sunny uplands beyond.

I suppose I was the pack leader, though H&J had a pretty fluid, flexible notion of this arrangement. Certainly, I was a familiar sight in our neighbourhood, and I'm sure provided amusement to many: being pulled up hill and down dale, like a man on a dog-led sled - but without the sled. Maybe I could have curbed H&J's enthusiasm over time by restraint - by employing a collar that tightens as the dog pulls. But, whatever the merits of these devices, this was not our way; it was not necessary. Quite simply, if I had gone down that path, been that breed of carer, my memories would be very different, and I would not be writing this book.

Amazingly, not only did H&J know exactly where they wanted to walk, but they were always in agreement. And Hector & Jason often decided our walks - and were always unanimous - pulling in a particular direction towards woods, different woods or Park. Their preference could usually be guessed at since, if we had visited the woods in the morning, the Park would be their preferred destination at lunchtime. And vice versa. The boys wanted change, the maximum excitement, the biggest thrills - so we launched on at least three quite varied walks each day, to optimise the potential that might be extracted.

Not many dog owners *enjoy* the sensation of being pulled along with or by their charges. My views were irrelevant. Always, and on every walk, I was pulled along by eleven stones of muscle, keen to get to the next phase of excitement. Though I tried - often in vain - to exercise some control, some management, some discipline, even, as we chose and executed our walks, the spirit of excitement and adventure always reigned supreme.

I was propelled along, a lead in each hand, at a prodigious speed by H&J. If a mile normally takes a brisk 20 minutes on foot, it took us threesome - with me as brake man - maybe 14 minutes. H&J were always energised, and exuberant, at the prospect of adventure before them. It was all dash, brio, exhilaration. These longer 'lead walks' were generally the mad-dash hard pavement walks in the evening. Since most walks were to woodland or Park, we often had only five minutes of H&J propulsion before I was able to hiss, "*halt, enough!*" and slip them from their leads, then watch as they plummeted along the path or into the undergrowth. Every day I was thankful for 25 years' experience of running and mountaineering, which gave me the stamina and the fine balance needed to, somehow, make a stumbling semblance of a partner for my extraordinary duo.

Oddly, perhaps, but in all honesty, I grew to enjoy the boys' energetic forward thrust. I was part of Hector's and Jason's team, and they were part of mine. The exhilaration, and the adrenalin rush, were unforgettable. There was a unity of purpose, of common endeavour, and I thrilled to their strength and sense of excitement - how different from the public's general ennui and lack of interest in life's, and nature's, colourful and complex tapestry. The journey was always the object, never the destination. Mr Perpetual Motion, and his partner in joy, were always out on the town - and always having fun.

I remain rather proud of this arrangement. This was a partnership, and I wanted to make it as fair and responsive as possible. People exert great control over the lives of their pets - where they go, what they do, even what they eat. I always wanted to ensure that *we* were in some kind of agreement, so that our outings became real, memorable adventures. By giving H&J control, I knew they were expressing a preference which also promised me the frisson of surprise. Provided the route was safe, I followed where they led.

Our 'core' walks were undoubtedly our two sets of local woods, plus local Park, plus our residential Estate. The network of walks extended during the working week to, for example, the old railway walk near to Himley, and to Himley itself, the former seat of the Earl of Dudley, and to neighbouring Baggeridge Country Park, with its picturesque lakes. When visiting my parents, the boys also enjoyed my own boyhood haunts, along the Stour Valley. Then there are the canals, famous in the area, that we would frequent around the Stewpony canal basin, and close to our own Wordsley Woods. Hector would always be on the lookout for local ducks, moorhens and coots, which bobbed about the reeds and moored narrow boats.

Certainly, when darkness had descended - as it so often had for our evening walk in Winter - our walks would often entail a trawl around our Estate, with H&J charging ahead of me, (on their leads) with great excitement. They would choose one of a variety of walks through the housing estate, many of which had welcome splodges of greenery which might permit a little wander - or gallop - off the lead. In this guise we quickly achieved a sort of fame, or perhaps notoriety. A friend who lived along one of these walks often said: "*I saw you being taken for a walk again the other night!*". He was quite right, since his home lay along one of our intrepid Winter evening gallops.

Since this particular road was very steep, and we were travelling down-hill, I had to be very careful not to lose my balance and tumble forward, such was the force of our motion. There is no doubt that, equipped with a sled, we would have galloped along at a mighty pace; it would have been quite a sight. As it was, these local walks would generate a good deal of amusement for local people, who often noted this strange guy, whooshed along by two excited boys. "*Who's walking who?*" was a favourite, if not very original, expression, as we swept past on our mission. I usually managed a faint grin, but the joke wore very thin.

How fizzing with energy we were! The more experiences we encountered, the more we enjoyed. Each day unfurled, a new-born miracle of life and love. Every walk was breathlessly exciting - a wild, break-neck roller-coaster ride. We were on a high, an adrenalin rush, a giddy, unpredictable, mystery tour.

Life with Hector & Jason was dangerous, unpredictable, and on the edge; life had never been so...so unexpected, so full of promise. H&J are always seeking, striving, searching, for the next adventure, the next slice of action; their gusto and appetite for life was as inexhaustible as life itself.

Each and every walk was imbued with a sense of excitement, wonder, and unfolding drama. Sometimes, after a visit to Highgate, or even Tafolog, with H&J, with all their transformative energy and passion, I've returned home and said to myself: *"Life just doesn't get any better than this."* I meant it.

Truly, it doesn't.

Walks on the Wild Side

There was a time when meadow, grove and stream,
The earth, and every common sight,
To me did seem
Apparelled in celestial light
The glory and the freshness of a dream.

Ode on Intimations of Immortality - William Wordsworth

So many, many walks! Hector & Jason re-defined the concept of a 'walk' - for them, a storming, super-charged affair. Wherever we ventured, the quest for adventure could never be quelled.

The presence of H&J would transform even the most banal 'affair' into a tempting gambol. Collecting a car from the garage following service or repair can be logistically awkward, since one normally *needs* a car to collect the car, as well as another driver for the returning vehicle. Hector & Jason were a great help in this respect. No, they couldn't drive, but they could march me the two-and-a-half miles to the local garage, along narrow footpaths flanking a busy road. Once there, I would bundle the excited duo into the rear of the vehicle, whilst I paid for the work done. Then it was off home - and their reward - a lazy meander without any further effort, and enjoyment of the view. Happy, innocent excursions, and a satisfying jaunt.

Yet H&J also travelled by car to all manner of places, to give variety and a fizz of pleasure to our daily lives. Even visiting the local shops was an excuse to give the boys the stimulation of fresh sights in less familiar locations. When I returned to the car, shopping in tow, my first glance was towards H&J: the boys were exquisitely attentive, patrolling the whole area with their eyes for any sign of my presence. And then the frisson of recognition, and the deep connection.

Then, there were walks around local beauty spots where, for the cost of a short drive, we were spoilt for choice: Kinver, Highgate, the Wyre Forest, the old railway cutting near Himley, the sandstone cliffs of Habberley Valley, the mysterious Bunker's Hill Wood, and Hartlebury Common - strolling on the heath amidst an array of butterflies.

And so much history: heady, social, economic and political history. Ludlow, with its association with Prince Arthur; the splendidly evocative Witley Court, a favourite of the Prince of Wales - later Edward VII; and Himley, with its own royal associations - another Prince of Wales, (later, Edward VIII), who visited chiefly for the charms of Freda Dudley Ward. And we travelled much further back in time: our stamping grounds around the canal tow paths at nearby Stourton had once performed duty as the medieval hunting estate of King John (son of Henry II, and brother of Richard the Lionheart). By a strange twist, the Norman town of Domfront, which was to become well known to H&J, was also a favourite of the Plantagenet dynasty.

It is often said that Birmingham and the Black Country have more miles of canal than Venice. If so, it must also be said that their character and ambience are somewhat different from that of the Italian city so beloved of artists and writers. But, for the boys and me, the local canals formed an important part of our near-to-home wanderings. Though determinedly commercial in character when they were built, in the late 18th century, the canals' primary use today is for leisure: messing around in narrow boats, fishing, cycling and walking. These days, the 'cuts' that link and surround the Black Country have a deliciously other-worldly feel, teeming with ghosts, and reverting to nature; quiet, and dripping with melancholy.

H&J loved gambolling along the Stourbridge Canal in Summer. There were always ducks, and moorhens, to liven up the walk and, in Hector's case, to lust after. There were bridges to navigate for me since, though I'm of only moderate height, the bridges' arched brick roofs are menacingly low. There are also cyclists and other walkers, travelling in both directions, to watch for and manoeuvre around. Apart from Hector's occasional plunging in the waters and heading for an armada of ducks - which sensibly flew away - there were not too many 'incidents'; if I occasionally released Hector from his lead, I could not risk Jason's 'doing a runner'. So these walks, as always, were brisk, energetic affairs beside these waterways, our onward propulsion only interrupted by gentle ripples from passing boats, or encounters with lovers and laconic fishermen. A few miles covered at prodigious speed - admiring the intense colours and reflections of the boats, bridges and over-hanging trees - then return happily to the waiting car.

Close by, too, a short drive away, were favourite walks around Highgate Common; we have already viewed the young H&J's early adventures there. H&J always enjoyed the extensive areas of open heath, together with old woodland and some decent-sized pools which they would find with alacrity - Hector invariably diving in the fresh, cool water. The boys became intimately familiar with every area we frequented; it surprised me how they retained the topography of all their walks and explorations in some internal satnav.

Hector & Jason zoomed around the Severn Country Park, dissected by the majestic River Severn itself, like wild boys in a sweet shop. The Severn Valley Railway, funnel steaming, hooter hooting, runs excitedly along-side the river. One fine Saturday afternoon, the young Hector ran on to the railway line itself, and lay down, admiring the view. The whistle of a train was suddenly heard. A frantic call, and Hector ran back, to be fastened to his lead. Until that point, he had never seen a train - never mind this very special, Severn Valley steam loco of yesteryear, chugging and belching its steam and smoke. This was the first of many encounters - respectful encounters - that H&J had with the railway, in the Valley of the Severn; but from that day on, we always kept the boys at a respectable, and respectful, distance from the track.

Hawkbatch Wood, part of Wyre Forest, near Bewdley, offers magnificent views of the Severn Valley from Seckley viewpoint. Far below, the loco can be seen, pulling its line of carriages, and chugging, steaming and whistling on its way through Arley, and heading for Bridgnorth or Bewdley. On a cold, blurry day, how reminiscent it seems of Turner's *Rain, Steam and Speed*! There we stood, thrilled, so many times as, from the depths of the river valley far below, the engines of the Severn Valley Railway fumed bravely along their appointed route, like a scene from a 1920s movie. And, near Trimpley Reservoir, we enjoyed an up-close view of trains and carriages as they pounded across the lines. I recall Hector doubling back on one of these excursions, unseen by us, so that he could enjoy a dip in the nearby River Severn.

Another favourite excursion was to the historic market town of Bridgnorth, a town with a history stretching back to Norman times. Following the Norman Conquest, the manor of Bridgnorth was granted to Roger de Montgomerie. The town itself was not created until 1101, when Robert, son of Roger, constructed a castle and church on the site of the modern-day town.

King Charles I, visiting the town in 1642, remarked that the view is "*the finest in my domain*". However, by that date, only Bridgnorth and Ludlow remained Royalist strongholds in Shropshire. In March 1646 the town - and the Royalist forces holed up within it - was attacked by Roundhead forces. The subsequent battle for Bridgnorth saw much of the town reduced to ashes in the 'Great Fire', caused by incendiary bombs fired from the Castle; this led to the explosion of munitions stored in St Leonard's Church. The town's 16th century Gatehouse gave shelter to the Royalist commander, Prince Rupert, who was evading capture by Cromwell's soldiers. On 26 April 1646 the Castle surrendered to Roundhead troops, and during the next year it was virtually destroyed; the shattered but now peaceful remains are a picturesque, and poignant, site.

Had the dreaded World War II invasion taken place, Bridgnorth was the German's intended HQ. Of all the town's claims to fame, this must be the most bizarre. One can only imagine that this cunning plan was based on the site's quiet rural setting, allied to its strategic proximity to the major industrial concentrations of the West Midlands. Each time we visited the medieval town to pore over the Saturday market, and drool (in my case) over fine wines and cheeses, I thought about this curious fact. As they padded along the narrow pavements, H&J - like most people - were gloriously unaware of one of the 'what-ifs' of modern history.

Bridgnorth boasts fine river walks along the banks of the River Severn. H&J were keen frequenters of the quiet, broad river banks, with their splendid views over the town, delighting in every nuance the river had to offer. In terms of human interest, there is a plaque here to commemorate Hazeldine's Foundry, which in 1808 built the very first operational steam locomotive, designed by Richard Trevithick. The site marks, for better or worse, the beginning of a revolution that was to transform the world. Similarly, we would venture to an impressive river (Blackrock) walk near Bewdley, with high cliffs framing the Severn through a dramatic sandstone gorge.

Stourport-on-Severn is the only town in Britain built solely as a consequence of the coming of the canals. Before the growth of the town there existed a small hamlet called Lower Mitton. The famous Stourport Basin is a network of canal basins built in 1776 to accommodate the newly developed Worcestershire and Staffordshire canal complex, that terminated at Stourport. The canal opened to Stourport in 1771, and by 1812 five canal basins had been built. The town quickly became the busiest inland port in the Midlands.

On Summer afternoons, and with H&J at the forefront, we would then embark on an - always vigorous - stroll along the tree-lined Severn, our promenade culminating in the vicinity of a huge, ancient, shapely oak tree, that must have witnessed England's story since, at least, Elizabethan times. This noble tree might have greeted King Charles and Prince Rupert, riding by; it certainly greeted Hector & Jason, racing by.

There were also excursions to some of the delightful nature reserves belonging to Worcestershire Wildlife Trust, such as the impressive Tiddesley Wood, near Pershore, brimming with bluebells in Spring, and Monks Wood, near Worcester itself. These were definitely 'lead walks', both in view of the possibility of losing one or other of the boys, and the eventuality of their finding and harassing wildlife that has a perfect right to live peacefully within what are, after all, nature reserves.

There was a further delightful walk near Pershore - along the banks, and golden water meadows, of the River Avon. Here, we could even allow the boys to range free, whilst ensuring that Hector kept away from the river's edge. On our most recent visit, while June took in a little retail therapy, I sat with the boys in the car: listening to *Stairway to Heaven* I watched the sun going down aslant the river, gilding the still waters, whilst silver swans flew magically across my view. H&J sat contentedly watching, as I sat mesmerised.

Sometimes, returning a little late from work, I would find an empty house; no June, no boys. A resounding silence. June had taken H&J for their early evening walk. I set off in pursuit. I knew their likely trajectory, and was seldom wrong. I would invariably chance upon the party a little way off: Hector & Jason always looked quintessentially alive, vibrant, urgent. Then they would *see me,* and the expression on their faces transformed: from that of general alertness to one of rapt attention.

It was like switching on an electric light. At that moment, June would drop their leads and H&J would leap into my arms, their hearts full to bursting. As was mine. Shivers of deliciousness would consume my being, as though I had been pierced by a celestial spear. That, indeed, was how I felt, every evening, and that is how I best remember the sheer joy of reunion.

The Grand Day Out

Full many a glorious morning have I seen,
Flatter the mountain tops with sovereign eye,
Kissing with golden face the meadows green,
Gilding pale streams with heavenly alchemy.

Sonnet 33 - William Shakespeare

We all loved 'The Grand Day Out'. Sometimes, it seemed that I was the ringleader, and H&J the two guys on a jolly boys' outing.

One memorable Summer we gorged on the beautiful Cotswolds. All around, the countryside was rich and glorious - gold, green and purple. And the Cotswold villages, picture perfect, revealed their unctuous, buttery shapes and shades.

We visited Broadway, Chipping Camden, and Winchcombe, with their golden contours and inviting, sometimes eccentric, shops. I glanced longingly through the windows of the antique emporiums that adorn these villages as, in tow to H&J, we sped gracefully, gratefully, by.

The extraordinary tower near Broadway is delightful, while the views from its ramparts are quite stunning. Broadway Tower is a gothic folly, created by the 6th Earl of Coventry for his Countess, Lady

Coventry. Designed by James Wyatt, the crenellated tower was built in 1798/99, and stands 20 metres high. The tower is magnificently sited, on Broadway Hill; at 312 metres, it is the second highest point in the Cotswolds. From the tower, on a clear day, a panoramic view stretches over 16 counties. The Earl - and his Countess - could admire their view of the tower from their magnificent seat at Croome Court, 22 miles away. Here, I took yet more iconic pictures of H&J, in the warm, honeyed sunshine.

In the exquisite market town of Chipping Camden, June bought a charming wicker basket from the medieval market. I picked up a tome of a price list from an excellent, traditional wine merchant, who clearly knew his claret from his *clairette*. In the meantime, H&J whizzed me along the main thoroughfare, so I could only glance at the treasures displayed in the myriad of antique shops and specialist emporia.

Winchcombe, situated on the River Isbourne, is a picturesque old town, with impossibly photogenic little streets, the cotswold stone beaming buttery in the afternoon sunshine. The lovely, 15th century, parish church at Winchcombe portrays 40 gargoyles around its exterior. Called the 'Winchcombe Worthies', they are said to portray the town's medieval abbey's most unpopular monks. The abbey itself was dissolved in 1559, and little of its fabric remains; the Worthies, however, have achieved a certain immortality. The church also contains a fragment of embroidery attributed in part to Catherine of Aragon. While I took copious photos, H&J lapped up the ambiance. Then home, Jeeves.

A trip to Ironbridge, the very cradle of the Industrial Revolution, and a mere hour away, was an absolute must. The single-arched structure crossing the Severn Gorge at the town now called Ironbridge was begun in 1777, and, as one might suspect, was the world's first bridge made entirely from iron. The bridge was funded largely by Abraham Darby III, and built by John 'Iron Mad' Wilkinson (whose coffin would later be made of iron). The site is, quite rightly, one of the UK's 26 World Heritage Sites. I can only report that H&J walked - with energetic resolution - over the bridge, (and back) with me hanging on for grim death. There was no question of their crossing entirely under their own steam, though it was noteworthy that they never suffered the same 'bridge syndrome' that so affected Victor. Visitors now flock to Ironbridge from all over the Globe to marvel at the iconic structure that has come to symbolise the beginning of the modern, industrial, world.

The Stiper Stones, in deepest Shropshire, is another fabulously evocative experience. This was a memorable one-off for us, sufficiently remote and incredibly different to excite us all - with H&J propelling me along even more vigorously than usual. A mysterious lunar landscape enveloped in swirling mists, The Stiper Stones ensured a memorably madcap walk along its length for the excited duo. The site is now in the care of Shropshire Wildlife Trust - ensuring that this exhilarating, unique place is protected for all time.

We visited the romantic river valley, and soaring cliffs, of Symonds Yat on a couple of occasions. It was clear from their body language that H&J loved this place, since it contained everything they loved: deep countryside, including a fascinating former railway line, long river walks, and cliffs and gorges, where peregrines nest. I remember one bright Sunday afternoon at the Yat, when we were tempted to call in at a welcoming Hotel for Sunday lunch. June and I had a direct view of the car from our restaurant table. And of course H&J had a direct view of us. All through our three course repast, we had what appeared to be an engaged and envious audience. I think - I hope - that I rewarded the boys with some tit-bits from the table. And we did reward them for their patience with a further walk along the nearby river, before venturing happily home.

Another absorbing day out led us to Eastnor Castle in Shropshire. A brief 'pit stop' at Malvern, before heading for the Castle (sorry, closed). It reminded me of an old Sinatra joke: *"Recently, we've run into a spell of bad luck. Last Sunday, we visited the Grand Canyon...and it was closed"*. So, we journeyed onwards, to the charming, but bustling, historic market town of Ledbury. Narrow pavements and busy streets meant danger for the ever-enthusiastic H&J, who just loved the excitement of new places, but who were unused to the twists, turns and thunder of heavy traffic running through the town. I quickly brought the boys back to the car park, and June and I paid separate visits to the town centre, with its tempting, art-filled shops.

But the Malvern Hills were the boys' real delight as, on our return that day, I released Hector from his lead as a special treat. Hec shot off in front, following the path - and then disappeared, as the path wound steeply down a hillside. Not running, but trotting quickly and aided by momentum - Hec continued until I eventually reeled him in. He was non-plussed, but I am sure that the lead-bound Jason was secretly quite envious. Strange - those little explosions of joy, or anxiety, or surprise - from walks that have made an asymmetrical mark in one's mind.

On the high-days of Summer we often spent days in the Herefordshire countryside, coupled with walks in the lovely, petite City of Hereford, and a visit to the great Cathedral itself. The City has a Norman feel, so it was no surprise to learn that the market place was laid-out shortly after the Norman Conquest by William Fitz Osbern, a close ally of William the Conqueror. On a memorable occasion, and despite a long meander beforehand through the quiet, green heart of the City, Hector decided to 'do a dump' right outside the entrance to the Cathedral itself. The bronze statue of Sir Edward Elgar, leaning against his bicycle, looked on benignly. It was in Hereford's old quarter, with H&J in tow, that we bought a favourite version of *Cosi fan Tutte,* featuring the glorious Cecilia Bartoli, from one of those emporia that is rich in earthly delights.

We visited the Welsh Food Festival on a lovely late Summer day in September, at Glan Severn House, near Welshpool, in central Wales. Glan Severn House is a beautifully restored manor house, with impressive, Victorian walled gardens, and a tranquil air. H&J were transfixed by the hundreds of displays overflowing with choice meats, cheeses and exotic offerings. Despite the crowds, there was an air of ease and enjoyment, and even H&J relaxed into the atmosphere. We returned, as usual, with a wide selection of preserves, cheeses - and specialist beers.

How the seasons rush by! A bright, early Spring afternoon found us at Upton-upon-Severn. We glanced at the many antique shops primed with art and artefacts gleaned from across the world. My eyes chanced upon a signed photograph of Rudolph Valentino (who incidentally owned an Irish Wolfhound called Centaur Pendragon*)*. In a calmer moment I would have bought the picture, but my concentration was, as always, divided between my searching out interesting artefacts whilst propelled by the boys' headlong momentum. The photo was 'one that got away'; a perfect image of a Hollywood 'star' who was perhaps the human equivalent of Jason.

Upton is a little jewel of a town, with a rich history. It's famous for its lovely location on the River Severn, for the 'pepperpot' cupola, and also celebrated for the climactic (in several senses of the word) inn-scene in Fielding's *Tom Jones*. Tom and Mrs Waters repair to an inn that '*presented the fairest appearance to the street*'. The Inn, believed to be the 16th century *White Lion* (which was frequented by troops of both sides before the Battle of Worcester), is described by Fielding (perhaps ironically) as '*a house of exceeding good repute*'. Very soon, all is confusion and muddled circumstance. Here, in '*violent uproar*'. Tom seduces Mrs Waters, and is chased by the odious Squire Weston, searching for Jones and his beautiful, errant daughter, Sophia: '*He.... laid hold of Jones, crying, "We have got the dog fox, the bitch is not far off*".' I took a photo, and imagined the epic confusion as Squire Weston rampaged through the Inn in search of his runaway offspring.

Westonbirt, in Gloucestershire, is perhaps the diamond in the crown of the country's arboretums. Cheek-by-jowl with Highgrove, Westonbirt boasts 16,000 trees - and 2,500 tree species - gathered from across the world, and set in 600 acres of rolling parkland. Perhaps a little too much artifice for my tastes, but a magnificent spectacle, nonetheless. We were speed-walked around by H&J at the top of their form, almost bumping into a startled work colleague of mine, jolted from her reverie in the midst of one of the myriad of leaf-strewn paths. My photos, though, are mostly of ancient English oaks, '*half as old as time*'.

At the village of Twyning, we enjoyed superb walks along the valley of the River Avon; wandering towards Tewkesbury, the calm, blue river was edged with golden rushes. Tewkesbury Abbey shimmers hauntingly out of the river mists like a Turner canvas. The Abbey was commissioned by Robert Fitzhamon, one of William the Conqueror's most influential barons. The majestic edifice was constructed between 1102-1121 from stone bought from Normandy, and transported by barge along the River Severn.

June suggested to me that the boys were always particularly spirited along the shores of the Avon, the endless riverbank exciting their passionate natures. Afterwards (rather like the cigarette following sex) I recall us all relaxing happily, a sweet sojourn in the riverside gardens of *The Fleet* public house; a moment of perfectly realised repose, after a tempestuous outing. H&J remained on the river bank, enjoying water, sunshine and tranquillity - and of course the wildfowl.

With H&J, with June: complete English Summer perfection.

Barking at Baggeridge

From coal, and soot, and ash, transformed to blue and green -
And now to black ice glaze, we slide, and dance, unseen.

Colin Hill

Whether in England or in France, we always enjoyed those cold, bright, post-Christmas walks, in the inimitable company of H&J. One of these walks was to Baggeridge Country Park - formerly the site of one of the world's largest coal mines, in its early-20th century heyday. The Country Park is conveniently situated adjacent to the Himley Estate.

Back in the 1970s, following the end of coal production, the site had been transformed into an extremely picturesque country park, with reed-fringed lakes, resurgent woodland, and myriad walks criss-crossing a hundred acres of undulating, re-claimed countryside.

There had been copious snow around Christmas Day but, in the days following, a gradual thaw had melted the white blanket, so that only a few grey shreds of icy slush remained. My wisdom decreed that an afternoon walk at Baggeridge would be ideal, in helping to clear away those festive-induced cobwebs.

As soon as we entered the sunny, enticing site we sensed a problem: it was abundantly clear that a river of ice had replaced the main path. The ice was glazed and smooth, but with a liquid sheen that made for a slippery, treacherous surface. Walkers returning along the path warned that the route became even more difficult further on, and that the atrocious conditions had caused them to retreat from whence they came. Wisely, June decided to return to the car but, since H&J were *so* expectant - and had their own four-feet drive with built-in crampons - I decided to press on, on a 'suck it and see' basis. It turned out to be a foolish decision.

I skirted and skidded along, my sure-footed companions dragging me ever-onward across a bleak, freezing landscape. I recall scrambling up, and then down, a steep embankment, desperately keeping H&J safely on their leads. If they had broken free, my chances of catching up with them were less than zero, and this was unfamiliar territory for them.

After an hour and a half of struggling to keep my balance whilst skating on ice and pulled along by my fiery 'pack', we managed to re-gain the car. For this relief, much thanks. The painful outcome of this foolhardy adventure was a flare up of arthritis - which had lain dormant for years - in both my knees. The predictable result of jarring, skidding, and desperate balancing required x-rays and pain-killers. It would be a couple of weeks before I was tolerably mobile again.

Now, more than a decade later, I have had no recurrence of this painful and immobilising condition. On the other hand, we have not attempted to reconnoitre Baggeridge again in the icy depths of Winter.

I should add, maybe unnecessarily, that H&J ended their intrepid expedition as fresh and spirited as they had begun, and enlivened by their many sightings of people, dogs and wildfowl.

Beasts of Bodenham

Though lovely, languid, liquid, we fractured that serene
When wild-eyed Hec & Jas came bursting on the scene!

Colin Hill

One fateful Summer afternoon, we decided that a visit to a local arboretum - Bodenham - was long overdue. After all, I was a tree lover, the site was only five miles from home, and we really needed to doff our hats to the herculean determination of the local family who - from virtually nothing - had created this marvel of diversity and tranquillity. So off we went.

The arboretum was indeed superb - with thousands of specimen trees established across hundreds of acres of rolling countryside. However, we had not expected, or planned for, exotic species of chickens, and ducks, strutting and clucking around the walks, and puffed up by their inalienable right to roam.

As they surveyed the scene, H&J must have thought that all their birthdays had come at once. Super-charged, they dragged me around as though I was the proverbial rag doll. Not only did their excitement know no bounds - the chickens, in particular - Chanticleers all - responded, if they responded at all - with a nonchalance bordering on the foolhardy. So the fowl did not - as one might have expected - give the boys a wide berth, but continued their promenading and preening, as before. This was, after all, their patch. So, to avoid mayhem - or, to give Hector's take - Christmas without the cranberry sauce, I was impelled, desperately, to contain the boys' enthusiasm.

Half an hour of pure farce - two minutes of calmish strolling, interspersed with two minutes of desperate lunging, and so forth - led us to a premature return to the car - and voyage home. The Arboretum contains 3,000 natural specimens, but the only specimens I was able to focus on were Hector & Jason! Slightly disappointing, but no-one's 'fault'; in fact, 'just one of those things'. Discipline among dogs is a fine thing, but it is impossible to totally over-ride the instincts developed over millennia. Incarcerate the most perfectly behaved 18 year-old young man with a dozen adoring women, and the result is hardly in doubt. Dear Oscar Wilde; temptation, all over again.

A similar Saturday visit, to Witley Court, was far more successful - because less eventful. When June and I first visited Witley, perhaps around 1980, the entire site was an impossibly romantic but overgrown and unprotected ruin; it is now firmly under the care and protection of English Heritage.

This imposing mansion was the seat of the Earls of Dudley; the 1st Earl bought the property in 1837, and loaned it to Queen Adelaide (William IV's widow) in 1843. The Dudley's moved to Witley, from Himley, later in the century, allegedly because the family was distressed by the nearness of Himley to the out-pourings from the Black Country - and the pits at nearby Baggeridge. The family had, of course, played a leading role in developing the local coal, iron and steel industry; pursuits that had generated their vast wealth. As someone once said, you couldn't make it up.

The boys enjoyed strolling - perhaps more energetically - in the footsteps of the rather portly Prince of Wales (later, Edward VII) - who, with his hosts, shot prodigious numbers of pheasant and grouse. The numbers involved - thousands per shoot - I find quite stomach-churning. However, it goes without saying, on the evidence of Bodenham that - whooshing back to 1900 - H&J would have enjoyed an orgiastic day in the field.

The Earl of Dudley sold Witley in 1920, and in 1937 the building was engulfed by fire. Witley is now an impressive, picturesque, hollowed-out edifice. A magnificent baroque fountain, representing Perpheus and Andromeda, dominates the superb gardens. At scheduled intervals, the fountain erupts with quite brilliant, diaphanous effect. H&J observed the spectacle with barely disguised glee.

Clearly unable to satisfy our aristocratic leanings, shortly afterwards we re-visited magnificent Chatsworth House, in order to admire the splendour of this most imposing pile, and gaze wistfully on its stunning vistas. The delights of the Farm Shop also beckoned, as did the tasteful range of goodies in the Estate's Gift Shop. (We succumbed to a very up-market bird-box). However, alive to the recent nightmare of Bodenham, the free-range chickens, strutting around their impeccably appointed hen-houses, were given a very wide berth. For H&J this was a very low-key visit: no chasing chickens, or running with the deer. Obliged to maintain an aristocratic mien, their good manners would surely have impressed the new Duke and Duchess. I recall remarking on the elegance of the 'facilities' as, our appetites and curiosity sated, we departed this heady, blue-blooded world and meandered back to the local smoke.

But birds, and game birds, were not yet off the H&J radar. In July 2006 - actually Friday the 13th - we paid an overdue visit to Tafolog, (of which, more anon) to review the development of the woodland. One of the magical aspects of woodland is that, without any particular involvement from humans, it continues to develop, all by itself. The trees grow, and the area changes, both organically and in response to the changing seasons, quite independently and oblivious to human cares and concerns. And so it proved: only a cursory inspection was needed to tell me that all was indeed well.

Miraculously, the 50,000 trees that had been planted were not only all *still there*, but were continuing to thrive, despite (or perhaps because of) all that the North Wales weather could throw at them. I noticed, too, a few incursions by sheep. Given our adventure of the previous year, when H&J had reached the 1300' summit of Tafolog, I had no appetite to repeat this particular, over-strenuous, feat, or to risk further face-to-face confrontations with our woolly friends.

As an alternative, I pointed H&J towards and along a decrepit bridge, and a narrow path which flanks the eastern border of Tafolog, adjacent to a gushing stream. Almost immediately, we were confronted by hordes of young pheasants - clearly being raised on a neighbouring property. H&J responded predictably to this unexpected bonanza. The pheasants dashed to and fro, like crazed road-runners, when their obvious response might helpfully have been to have taken wing. As we lunged on, more and more pheasants blocked our path, until it became clear that - from my perspective, if not H&Js - the planned 'inspection' had become impossible.

So, not without difficulty - since Eldorado beckoned - we turned round the good ship H&J, and made fast to our harbour. The boys safely - if disconsolately - on board, I crawled along, desperately dodging the crowds of waggling pheasants that crowded our 'vessel'. With some relief on my part, we left this beautiful, remote place behind. I steered towards home, and the fleshpots of the West Midlands.

Sunday Sensibility, Sunday Serendipity

We savour Sundays' soft-centred sentiment: deep,
Silent satisfaction; the boys all fast asleep.

Colin Hill

Sunday has always been my least favourite day of the week. As an adult, the knot that appears in the pit of the stomach on Sunday evening, as one contemplates the new working week ahead, is no doubt partly responsible for the cloud hanging over Sundays in general.

Yet on reflection, I fear my ambivalence towards Sunday harks back to childhood, when a deadness seemed to descend on everything and everybody, as though enveloped in volcanic ash. Sundays were redolent of steamy kitchens, jelly and condensed milk, and church bells. And boredom, since the hand of history demanded real constraints to our freedom of action.

Though Sundays are nowadays lived differently, for me there are still echoes of the strangely subdued Sundays of my youth. Although I have now ceased the trauma of the daily grind, my mind refuses to accept the new reality. I am still subject to a certain disquiet with every seventh revolution of the Earth.

But H&J - and Victor before them - helped to transform Sunday into a special day for us, where the atmosphere and pace is different, but positively different. We still always rise early, especially so in Spring and Summer, when the morning light is so magical, and the air is fresh and still.

Sundays were, and are, calmer, softer, more reflective. Our day would begin - very early - with a circumnavigation of the woods by Hec, Jas and myself. June would meet us in the 'carriage', just above a flight of stone steps that led directly from the woodland. The boys would wait patiently for the car to arrive, back up, and then - in Hector's case - leap into the rear of the car. In Jason's case, as we know, it was perforce a gentle lift into the vehicle.

This invigorating start to the day, particularly in Spring and Summer, provided an appetite for breakfast and the day ahead. We encountered few people, or dogs, on these early Sunday walks; 7.00am is a touch too early for most folk on this day, if not on others, so I could day-dream, whilst keeping a beady eye on the progress of the boys.

As the boys matured, these walks became an unmitigated pleasure. H&J's vitality and energy, and their quickness of movement, were always apparent, and nearly always delightful: they explored the hedges and spaces, sniffed the forest floor, and ultimately returned, happy and satisfied, to the entrance stile. Then our complete party returned for breakfast and the morning's relaxed Radio 4 broadcasts. Following our early morning constitutional, I gorged on the feast of fast-food that is the Sunday newspapers. Mid-morning may have required a trip to the allotment, or perhaps a visit to 'Granny & Grandad'. In all, a completely relaxing contrast to the frantic activity and stress-filled hours of the office, and its manically-demanding computer screen.

Later in the day, around lunchtime, a further H&J walk was called for - this time around the Park, giving a wide berth to the teams of intrepid footballers performing their mud-spattered Sunday ritual. H&J were always genuinely respectful of this 'other' space, and rarely trespassed on to the field of play. Or maybe they were just intimidated by the football fury, which often looked and sounded like a field of battle.

We would all - all - gladly return home for one of June's superb Sunday roasts, and a treat of which H&J never tired: cheese and biscuits. Following a post-meal nap, it was time for a final walk, usually on the pavements and green spaces around our housing estate. The boys knew this to be the final staging post before the yearned-for dinner, followed by contentment, sleep and, in June's and my case, an evening in front of the telly. The routine was maybe common-place, but also somehow special and extraordinary, in the depths of satisfaction and content - call it happiness, if you will - that were plumbed. Life can be a great deal more exciting, I know; whether it can be better, or more satisfying, is another matter.

Yet Sundays, whilst starting quiet and dreamy, could often, despite my best efforts, become lumpy and difficult. It seems that many people only go out for walks on a Sunday; when they do so, they choose somewhere a little distant from their usual abode - a special Sunday walk; and they often bring with them a dog or two last exercised, at best, the Sunday before, and therefore disposed to be ill-mannered or downright hostile. So, nearly all the scrapes that we had over the years, as the victims of crazy people and crazy dogs, occurred on Sundays. There are perhaps too many to mention; but suffice to say that the only times that Hector, Jason, or I, were attacked, assaulted, or abused, happened to be on Sundays. The feeling was akin to going out to sea in a thunderstorm - one knew that there was an above average risk of something unpleasant happening. But, unlike the said thunderstorm, we had little alternative but to brave the risks, such as they were; as we know, worse things happen at sea.

One incident may suffice to represent many others. A fierce gentleman accosted me in the woods: *"get those dogs on their leads - they're frightening my son!"* he fumed. Beg pardon? The dogs and the son were as far from one another as it was possible to be, whilst remaining within sight. The said gent then threatened me with the Police. If he had *owned* the woods, and H&J had been tormenting his - very quiet - child - (which would have required a change of mind, body and soul) the gent could not have been more unpleasant. What can one do when confronted by a nut-case? Certainly not reason with him - withdraw, quietly, with a heart-felt sigh.

Despite every irritating, enervating experience, and despite grievous provocation, Jason would never growl at, confront or show aggression towards any other creature. He was the canine equivalent of Sir Bobby Charlton who, throughout an illustrious career, never received a booking. My ever gracious friend.

10: The Four Seasons

When the hounds of spring are on winter's traces,
The mother of months in meadow or plain
Fills the shadows and windy places
With lisp of leaves and ripple of rain.

Atalanta in Calydon - Algernon Charles Swinburne

O, Wind, If Winter comes, can Spring be far behind?

Ode to the West Wind - Percy Bysshe Shelley

Our ever-busy walking regime - not nearly busy enough for H&J - enabled us to witness at first hand the changing of the seasons, and the relentless speed with which they melded into each other.

There are seasons, and there is weather. The dedicated dog walker will enjoy all four seasons, but will always have to endure whatever the weather inflicts at any time of the year. At times of extreme weather there is a universal response: "*We must be mad!*". Invariably, I grin and nod. We *are* all in this together. A steely resolve in the face of adversity binds us. The rain, sleet, wind and mud should not blind us to the rewards of walking with our dogs: the delights of the ever changing seasons, the sweetness of the Spring's grass and flowers, the flame and brilliance of Autumn.

I think of the seasons as green, blue, gold, and black and white. Spring, green, is for me - and the boys - the most exciting of them all. Still, we would plunge into our local woods whatever the season, and whatever the weather. So often, at least in the West Midlands, a leaden sky flattens the landscape, dulling the shine of foliage, smudging the otherwise brightness of birds, flowers and bees. Yet, there was never any dullness for H&J; every situation, every occasion, every walk, was for them a virgin adventure into the unknown.

Together we sped through glutinous mud, ice, hail, and sheeting rain, almost irrespective of the season. Often we would return home needing to be wrung out, or caked with thick, sticky clay. And me, joyfully, if through gritted teeth, playing Feste, the Fool from *Twelfth Night:*

> *'When and I was and a little tiny boy*
> *With hey hoe the wind and the rain;*
> *A foolish thing was but a toy,*
> *For the rain it raineth every day.'*

Or, quite naturally, singing along to Gene Kelly's inspired splash-dance in *Singin' in the Rain.* Or perhaps whistling Gershwin's charming Promenade *Walking the Dog* from *Shall we Dance.*

We like to imagine Spring and Summer as repositories of warmth and fragrance. Yet, in reality, in Britain, even Summer is often a cold, grey, endless squall. And so much rain! H&J seemed not to mind; they were always mercurial, intent upon their respective missions. I needed to be prepared for anything, and was wrapped up against wind, cold and wet, as I scoured the woods, sometimes for far longer than expected - or was conducive to one's health - in pursuit of my passionate boys.

Cold, pulverising rain, sluicing and soaking - and sucking the air from your lungs - is not everyone's cup of tea at 7 o'clock in the morning. But I knew that a hot cup of tea awaited; and a hot shower, too; and a vigorous rub-down - for Hector & Jason.

So often the elements seemed to be mischievous. Setting out merrily on a dry and cloudless day, we would be hit by a cloudburst mid-walk, and thoroughly soaked through, only to return home, dripping wet, and feeling faintly foolish, as the sun beamed down once more. Yet, sometimes at least, we bathed in glorious sunshine, when the woodland scene was transformed into gold, burnishing the boughs and canopy with *'heav'nly alchemy'.*

Whatever the season, whether I was following, or waiting for, Hector & Jason, I would be half-absorbed in watching for birds, searching for wild flowers, and observing and counting the diversity of trees that comprise 'the woods'. Every day brought something new to discover, different flowers coming into season, new perspectives and changing landscapes, as the shades and varieties of greens that make up the natural world of Spring and Summer emerged and evolved. The lives of the ancient beeches, oaks and sweet chestnuts unfold daily, and fascinate the careful observer with their nuanced changes.

And, whether January or July, we would always return home happy, and eager for biscuits (in H&J's case), and breakfast (in mine). On the approach to home, H&J would invariably power to our front door, happy and expectant, tails wagging furiously.

Spring Sensation

This is the weather the cuckoo likes,
And so do I;
When showers betumble the chestnut spikes,
And nestlings fly:
And the little brown nightingale bills his best,
And they sit outside at 'The Travellers' Rest',
And the maids come forth sprig-muslin drest,
And citizens dream of the south and west,
And so do I.

Thomas Hardy

My favourite season was always - always - Spring: I looked for signs of Spring from mid-February onwards - and found them. In early February, the Winter landscape is at its most spare and skeletal; every living thing seems reduced to its bare essentials. It is then that we begin to seek, anxiously, for the first flickers of fresh life. There are some common signs: snowdrops, and a blaze of catkins, of course. A new liveliness among the garden birds. A fresh vivacity among the grasses; the first glossy leaves announcing the awakening of bluebells; a sheen on the bark of trees. The brave trill of a robin. The vivid re-awakening of native plants. The expanding daylight - the silent miracle of the turning Earth. England's greatest poet-naturalist, John Clare, wrote eloquently on this theme: 'signs of Spring' clearly exercised his keen observation; harbingers of the delights about to unfold.

I was mesmerised at how what seemed like death, and the end of things, was quietly transformed into a glory of green; first tiny flickerings; then life rejoined with riotous abandon. The first bursting of buds, the unfurling of leaves, is exciting, magical, even. The young sun breasts the woodland ridge, gloriously scattering sparks across the firmament; early sunbeams cascade through young beech leaves; bluebells and violets burgeon into intoxicating new life. In ritual and prayer, our forebears fervently sought the return of the sun - the harbinger of new life, warmth, and plenty.

Spring, for me, is always spectacular. To experience Spring was like little sight-and-scent bombs exploding in my head but, instead of causing pain, providing exquisite pleasure. The freshly emerged leaves of beech and oak and ash look almost psychedelic in their new-mintedness. And whilst I revelled in the majesty and minutiae of all this, H&J were also deeply excited; their exultation was evident in their ever-increasing energy and renewed zest for life. Then, perhaps, and only then, is it time to hum the glorious melody from Richard Strauss's ecstatic *Fruhling*.

'Being close to nature' may seem pretentious and far-fetched - all that 21st century baggage - but I believe that we can come close; and the effort is always worthwhile.

The arrival of Spring was symbolised by my discarding my Winter raiment. Off came my ancient, but snug, Winter jacket - almost like wearing a quilt - together with my comforting woolly hat. On came my T-shirt, and a new, more smiley, persona.

Running through the newly-sprung verdure during April and May, H&J were simply marvellous; perfect. They were part of nature, and revelled in the sense of occasion, and their keen sense of life being renewed. As the season progressed into Summer, I would lose the boys in the spread of glossy foliage that closed around them as they ran, though I could often sense their whereabouts from the excited barking that ricocheted among the trees.

Soon, through experience, patience (mine) and intent on all sides, we would be joyously, ecstatically, re-united.

Summer Swoons

Shall I compare thee to a Summer's day?
Thou art more lovely and more temperate:
Rough winds do shake the darling buds of May,
And Summer's lease hath all too short a date...

Sonnet 18 - William Shakespeare

We place a burden of expectation on the three months of Summer that is almost unbearable. For Summer is the repository for our hopes, our dreams, our accumulated longings. The season's brief passport seems to offer freedom, romance, excitement. Light and warmth seem to provide a passport to anywhere and anything; we have never been so alive. There is a heady sense of optimism, and opportunity, that we know we have to seize, since it is so fleeting. We are achingly aware of each passing day and, in being so, are at our most intense, and most expectant. And so it was with us - June, me and the boys. At home, abroad, on land, on sea: Summer was the scene and setting for our most epic and memorable adventures.

24 June is my favourite day of the year. The day falls around the time of the Summer Solstice, when the days are almost endless, and the sun high and bright in the sky. This day became my favourite when, one fine and lovely 24 June, Hector, Jason and I enjoyed the perfect walk, in the familiar setting of our local woods. The sun shone overhead out of a clear sky, with the woodland in its majestic prime: a full canopy, fresh, sensual, luxuriant:

> *My heart o'erwhelms me as, with perfect pride, we fly;*
> *Sleek missionaries of mirth, gliding, gaily, by*
> *Fields of flax and flowers, 'til in sweet glade we lie:*
> *Beneath a concave vault, beneath a cobalt sky.*

Hector & Jason always loved Summer, and were happy and passionate in its midst. The days were so inviting - whatever the weather - and H&J were always eager, and ready, for yet another walk, in woodland, Park, or in one of our many favoured haunts. The Summer heat (when present) was never a deterrent - always a blessing, always sweet invitation.

H&J were for ever brave pioneers of the here-and-now, exploiting every conceivable opportunity. New horizons always beckoned - new walks, fresh places, new experiences. And there was France, and the preparations for France; the anticipation almost as heady as the arrival, in the mystery of the gloaming. Hector leaping into the car, ages before our departure, eager for the the moment of departure; Jason cavorting in the stillness of the Normandy garden, venting his joy in life, his love for life.

Yet this was also the most anxious of times. Summer's lure so energised the boys, and the woodland canopy was so luxuriant, that H&J were often missing from my sight and sound for a veritable eternity. I would run and call frantically before they re-emerged - as they always did - flying along the path, along the crest of the ridge, or through the scattered trees. No matter: this was their time, their glory.

Almost before we knew it, August was wearing thin; dry, dusty, and tired, as seemed the sun itself. The Summer had run its course, had excited and exhausted itself, and us; but we had run with it. We had freshly-coined memories to cherish, to contemplate, to savour. And an eternity of longing, before the Earth's voyage around its sun returned glorious Summer to us once more.

Autumn Auguries

Season of mists and mellow fruitfulness,
Close bosom friend of the maturing sun...

Ode to Autumn - John Keats

Like parents returning home to the scene of their teenage son's party, Autumn always comes too soon. In my mind I always pushed it back, whilst anxiously looking for tell-tale signs: leaves 'turning' or beginning to fall; wild fruits beginning to ripen; swallows and martins departing for their long migration. By 22 September, of course, I had to bow to the inevitable, and perhaps start whistling - ruefully - whilst we walked, the deliciously melancholic melody from Strauss's *September*.

Yet, as I relaxed into and acknowledged the changing season, Autumn could often surprise and delight. In our woods, the season could be stunning, thanks to the ancient stands of oak, beech and sweet chestnut that lined our walks: gold, red, yellow, amber and ochre leaves still clinging to the trees, and scattered thickly along the paths. The boys would rustle noisily, greedily, through the dense leaf-litter that enlivened their every step.

It was in Autumn that the beauty of the woodland paths became most apparent. Sometimes, the slanting sun would sparkle along the forest floor, strewing gold nuggets liberally along our path. The very trees seemed to be decorated and bejewelled, dripping precious bounty all around.

I often mused as to who had planted - yes, planted - these graceful avenues of - now majestic - sessile oaks, perhaps when Jane Austen was a girl, circa 1780. Near these soaring trees I once found an old penny, dated 1806; minted the year following the Battle of Trafalgar. I wondered if the landowner who planted the young saplings had had in mind the needs of the naval fleet, decades hence. After all, around 2,000 mature oaks were needed to build an English Man o'War.

As we now know (as captured in Turner's poignant, *The Fighting Temeraire*), marine technology was soon to change forever, and thankfully this magnificent avenue of oaks has survived into the 21st century - to witness the lives and times of Hector & Jason. And so has my favourite tree, an enormous, wise old sweet chestnut, that has seen the coming and going of kings and empires, wars, cataclysms, and the fury and sweetness of the ever changing seasons.

Directly below the Normandy garden a giant oak, known to be over 500 years old, would have been a mere sapling when Henry VIII and his French rival, Francis I, met on the Field of the Cloth of Gold. I would watch this huge organism through the seasons; as its first leaves appeared late in April, as its wonderful canopy rose and spread in the blue of mid-Summer, and as it burned gold and ochre in Autumn's misty mornings. In Winter, its boughs reared to the sky, naked and proud, fearlessly awaiting the tempests yet to come.

What must such ancient trees have witnessed, of wars, revolutions and human progress: wagons and carriages become cars, horse-drawn ploughs become tractors? This magnificent being was already a majestic, mature fellow when Napoleon seized power. Hector & Jason gambolled below its spreading boughs like two excited young colts, a small frisson in the tree's kaleidoscopic vein of memory.

Autumn is, most tellingly, the graceful harbinger of sleep, of loss and death; of death followed by renewal:

> *We are the lonely, ranting loonies; left*
> *To smile at seasons' sighs, time's on-long theft.*

When so often immersed in their midst, each one of the turning seasons reminded me palpably, poignantly, of the swift passage of time. Unforgettable, memorable time, spent, with my boys, at the highest heights.

Winter Walks and Christmas Cheer

> *I, singularly moved*
> *To love the lovely that are not be-loved,*
> *Of all the seasons, most*
> *Love Winter.*

> *The Unknown Eros* - Coventry Patmore

So, so suddenly, the *'maturing sun'* departed, distant and estranged; plunging the world into dark, cold and dread. Whilst Winter brought its own cadence, with its bleak, aborted days and seemingly endless dreariness, we established fresh routines, and became, necessarily, more inventive, with H&J at the centre of a new resolve.

While we tried hard to maintain our walking routine during the short, dark Winter months, it was often through (my) gritted teeth. Yet, even in the depths of Winter, we were drawn by a longing that would not be denied: we would step into the cold, the dark, the storm-tossed, and become part of the wholeness. Again and again, setting out for our early morning walk, we would enter a landscape that seemed smothered in almost perpetual darkness, and that drew us into its midst.

I longed for dawn, for the light to return. Even in the deepest recesses of Winter, the darkness would - grudgingly, reluctantly - begin to lift during the course of our morning walk, revealing the mighty shapes of slumbering trees. Sometimes, also, amid the gloom, we would see a startling splash of crimson, from hawthorn and holly berries, and rose hips dripping like rubies from the hedgerows.

The cover of darkness presented no problem for H&J, who would speed inexorably along the paths and through the trees; but many a time my progress would be hampered by a tree root, or in navigating a mud slick, or pan of ice. If I peered hard through the grey, I could just see the boys, spectrally, as the darkness dissipated in the coming day. On some mornings, majestically, the woods would be illuminated by an enormous moon, spreading its ghostly green light along the path and through the bare branches.

Although enveloped in darkness, and often gloomy, these early-morning Winter walks were no more anxiety-stricken than their Summer equivalents. Indeed, Winter, for all its grimness, was often more benign in this respect: I could even - just - espy Jason as he ran along the woodland ridge, through the bare, skeletal trees. And, if there had been snowfall, I could see him, highlighted in the reflected light, somehow even more galvanised by clear air and the soft white carpet underfoot. With eyes adjusting to the half-light, or aided by a beam of moonlight, I could usually make out the shape of the boys, as they stood out against the semi-dark. The naked trees, too, afforded me brief glimpses of the spectral H&J as they flashed along.

Nothing seemed to deflect or deter Jason's headlong flight: I would observe him, open mouthed (me, that is) as he cut a silent, speeding figure through the bare trees. There seemed to be no lessening in his electrifying speed, his onward propulsion. My fantasy, that Jason was an 'SAS dog', was further fuelled by his ability to run at full tilt in the Winter gloom. It was cutting-edge proof, if any were needed, that the boys' night-vision was 500% better than my own.

I would often lose sight of both H&J for long minutes at a time, often detecting their whereabouts by a furious - and, to me at least, welcome - excited barking. In the still Winter air, sound carried with extra sharpness, and I could pin-point the boys' whereabouts more accurately. And almost always, as I turned for home at the far end of the woods, H&J were either waiting for me, or else responded to my calls, and we would return - if not together, then at least travelling in a common direction. By the time we reached home a febrile, half-light had emerged, and the world had awoken.

On so many walks we confronted dark, cold, wet, mud, ice and wind; in the boys case the conditions were confronted unflinchingly. This was what they were here for, made for. In releasing them from their leads, I had to hope and trust to their innate good sense, since, tramping through glutinous mud or harsh frost, I could follow them only with some difficulty. But the trust was rewarded, and we always returned home together, happy and fulfilled.

On these Winter mornings, only the hardiest of dog walkers ventured into the waiting woods. I enjoyed the silence, the loneness; but also the companionship of the odd walker and their dogs. It is rare these days, especially near to our congested urban centres, to find oneself in places that offer such quiet, and stillness - perhaps punctuated by a dog bark, or an owl calling. Spiritual fulfilment, a mere walk away. And we knew that, mere minutes away, lay a warm welcome home, nourishing food, and (for me) tons of hot coffee.

Sometimes the Winter evening walk would take place in the familiar setting of the Park. But in the darkest months of December and January, when the Park gates were shut at dusk against all-comers, we would pretty much be confined to exploring the empty streets. We would criss-cross these on our myriad of routes, determined to extract the maximum of interest from the least promising of options and scenarios.

O, the streets! These, too, were dark, quiet, cold, often wet, often deserted. We had planned so many routes, with so many variations. H&J grew accustomed to two very different festive seasons during these bleak months. The first of these was 'Bonfire Night' - a festival that seemed to begin in early October, and eventually climax in the first mad week of November.

Most pet owners regard Bonfire night, or rather firework displays, with some trepidation. H&J always hated fireworks - the unpredictability of the noise, the sheer loudness and closeness of the bangs. On our walks over the extended fireworks season we would be treated to a nightly spectacle of colour, light and ferocious whizz-bangs. I often felt that we had wandered, innocently, onto a battle-field at night, a war zone without people. There was only the crash and boom of a barrage of artillery, followed by another, then another, furious fusillade.

I re-assured H&J each time one of these unpredictable explosions occurred. We kept to the pavements, but the boys pulled me even more assertively each time these assaults on our senses took place. I held on tight - no way was I letting go. These were extraordinary, surreal walks. I could have pinched myself - was all this frenzied activity, so colourful, so powerful, really happening all around us? And with no-one, apart from the hidden activists, to watch, admire, wonder? As we walked down the main drag, Hector, Jason and myself probably had the best possible views of these exploding munitions, and we had paid not a penny piece for the privilege. Nevertheless, the boys were always particularly pleased at this season to get back to their warm, quite noiseless, home.

On Bonfire Night weekends themselves, we would most definitely be at home with H&J: curtains drawn, TV and radio turned up, talking loudly, re-assuring the boys - probably too much so, because they were never quite convinced. Some good friends threw the most wonderful, traditional Bonfire parties each year, replete with hot, tasty dishes, and gaggles of excited children marvelling at the luminous effervescence of the unfolding display. June and I would attend these parties singly, as if we were taking shifts, in order not to leave H&J home-alone. I would usually join the festivities following June's return, mid-way through the proceedings. Hopefully, we all enjoyed the spirit and sparkle of a special evening, with H&J cocooned in the comfort and security of their home. This was the one and only occasion on which their spirit of adventure was sorely tested, though their courage never deserted them. The loudness and unpredictability of the noise was almost too much; I saw my role as supporting H&J through what they regarded as an ordeal, albeit an impressionable one.

The second memorable season was of course Christmas. H&J enjoyed Christmas for itself - and for the same reasons we humans enjoy this special season: good food and drink, gifts, toys and decorations, the cheer and companionship of friends and family. H&J participated fully, and excitedly, in these festivities. Carrying on a tradition begun with Victor, we would fashion tinsel collars for H&J: green and gold, and red and gold, enhancing their already splendid shoulders. And, every year, they would enjoy presents - edible gifts, as well as toys and chewable treats. Frankly, the boys *made* Christmas for us - lighting and gracing the season with the special warmth and charm of their personalities.

Yet what H&J seemed to enjoy most about Christmas - apart from friends and family - were extraordinarily long walks through the maze of linked streets that made up our vast residential estate, admiring the Christmas decorations that illuminated homes, gardens and whole avenues: miles and miles of mesmerising light shows, nativity scenes, sleighs and reindeer, and Santas climbing suggestively into bedroom windows.

Every year we made a ritual of these walks - wrapping up snugly and setting off each evening in the quietly restorative week following Christmas Day. Stepping out briskly into the cold, my lips warbling warm seasonal melodies from Sinatra, Schwarzkopf or the divine Anne Sofie von Otter, we quickly entered a sort of long gallery of light. The community-wide response to seasonal drabness and gloom made an incandescent impression, seeming almost heroic in its defiance of 'the long dark'. I enjoyed the variety, never quite knowing what inventive sights would greet us around the next corner; the effect produced an excited, extra spring in the momentum of H&J themselves.

Sometimes, it seemed that we were the only beings admiring and enjoying these festive scenes; indeed, that they had been created especially for us. Certainly, we never tarried, but would walk miles, lured on by the lights, like ancient sailors mesmerised by the Lorelei - but with a happier outcome. Together, we would consider such matters as: which was the best-dressed house? Which was the most colourful street? - and provide marks out of ten. At long last we would meander home, cold-of-face but happy, to a welcome drink - beer, or water, depending on taste.

Yet, for all this gaiety, Winter was the only season that seemed to outstay its welcome: whole days together were dark, cold, wet and muddy. Our first walk took place around 7.00am, and from November until February, I, certainly, was feeling my way along the main woodland path, avoiding tree roots and obstacles; H&J seemed oblivious of these difficulties as they galloped ahead. Still, despite the darkness, rain and mud, there were always points of interest: a late tawny owl, entertaining me with its calls, or a buzzard, floating mysteriously overhead. Or another dog walker, and the chance to exchange a few cheery words in the desperate dullness.

Returning home each morning - more often than not soggy and mud-be-splattered - I would release H&J as we entered our little cul-de-sac: they would run like fury - and usually in a straight line - to the front door, barking excitedly, but cheerfully, if kept waiting to be let in for more than a moment.

A few, precious, seconds later, H&J were rewarded with their breakfast treats. More treats were to follow, as a portion of Colin's breakfast was served up to the (sometimes) embarrassingly drooling lads, who had, betimes, been eyeing me with lazer-like attention.

And there is a supremely overriding impression. How many walks, through so many years, and each and every one imbued with a unique energy and passion! It was in their mercurial walks that Hector and Jason were at their most authentic, and able to express their full and proper nature. There was mischief, anxiety on occasion, madness galore. But what gladness and what joy in their self expression, and in my letting go!

With Hector & Jason by my side, I could truly say:

With thee my truest guide -
Whatever time and tide unfurl -
I'll tarry by thy side
To the rim of the world.

All is memorable: but it is Spring and early Summer that I will remember most fondly, with my fine, agile boys leaping along amidst the intense, glossy greens of their woodland, eager and expectant. As keen, happy and fulfilled as any dogs ever were.

11: A WALK IN THE PARK

I like to hike with my dog, Webster. It helps clear my mind.

Calista Flockhart

Money will buy a pretty good dog, but it won't buy the wag of his tail.

Josh Billings

Somewhat to my dismay, H&J loved the humble local Park. For me, this was a pretty bare, characterless, expanse of grass - flat, relatively featureless, and not particularly interesting. The Park represented, at best, a little green oasis in the midst of a dense, urban desert of brick, concrete and tarmac.

Despite such misgivings, the Park did offer a modest, secure, and pleasant alternative venue for walks - and it was close to home. A row of ancient beeches, magnificent in Spring and Autumn, and a superbly graceful English oak, provided a *soupçon* of interest against a rather boring, bland backdrop.

For Hector & Jason, however, this was love at first sight. For H&J, the phrase 'walk in the park' held a very special meaning. To the boys, it meant, not a sedate and civilised saunter, but adventure, excitement, unalloyed enjoyment. There were a myriad, a multitude of exciting opportunities - a flat expanse of meadow, or tundra, where there were birds, other dogs, (foxes, even), people eating, people playing tennis and people playing football. And, rather unexpectedly, the Park proved to be the unlikely scene for some of our - or rather H&Js - most memorable adventures.

Crucially, the ability to *see* and exploit possibilities over half a mile, and the prospect of running unencumbered around a perimeter that probably stretched for a mile or more, was not to be sniffed at. And there were endless gardens, and doors to gardens, all along one aspect of the Park. When these doors blew open, or were left open, there were even more chances for fun and profit - balls, cats, food and frolics in prohibited expanses of territory; for H&J, this must have seemed like unexpected vistas of tropical beaches, or rampant rainforests, opening to the view.

The Park kept us in touch with humanity in all its variety - footballers, dog-walkers, people jogging or promenading, children playing, young mothers proudly presenting and pushing their babies in buggies around the green and pleasant undulations. And memories are often intertwined. We were travelling to the Park by car on 11 September 2001, when all hell broke loose on the radio. The mayhem sounded like a play - *War of the Worlds* sprang to mind. Sadly, it was all too real and horrific. In the Park, all was weirdly normal, quiet, gentle, whilst, half a world away, appalling atrocities were traumatising a nation. H&J ran around as usual, oblivious to the international and universal explosion, shock and condemnation.

But most days were cheeringly normal, if any excursion with H&J might be called 'normal'. On week-day mornings, H&J's dismount from the car would be greeted by young children from the adjacent school, clapping their hands with glee, and leaping into the air at the sight of the galloping duo. The innocent response made me smile, every time. The said duo rarely paused - unless Hector spied an errant tennis ball, creeping beneath the school fence - that would claim his immediate attention.

The boys' behaviour on entering this favourite space was extraordinary. Their leads removed, they would at once bound away, generally in the same direction. The Park is oblong in shape, with quite sharp corners at each end, and Jason would follow the perimeter closely, charging around this boundary as though following an imaginary hare. For most of the time, I could follow his progress, though he was generally on his second lap, and overtaking me, before I had completed the first circuit.

I learned to cut across the Park in order to intercept Jas, usually towards the end of his second lap. Sometimes, Jason would take time out in order to tussle with his brother, stalking him in the most exceptional way. Hector, when not being stalked, was pursuing his own interests - footballs, tennis balls, and the possibility of food - dropped, or even draped, from bushes. My biggest fear was that one or both of the boys, seeing a garden gate leaning open (rows of garden fences forming the perimeter of one complete side of the Park) would disappear into a long, rambling garden, never to be seen again. The boys could never resist the temptation of an even half-opened gate - perhaps loosened by a stiff wind - and would push ecstatically into the newly revealed garden, as though it were the entrance to Paradise.

This disappearing act happened on so many hundreds of occasions that I was always on the lookout for this potentially dangerous situation. When I spied the trespass, I would pursue the errant boy and call him back, as sharply as I dared. Somehow, H&J knew they were on thin ice, and would noisily return, still over-excited. When I missed the trespass - it all happened with inveterate speed - my only recourse was to look for open gates, which by then may have swung shut, and possibly re-found their fastenings, or to await the familiar bark of one or other boy. There are 28 such properties along this straight boundary, each with a gate that opens on to the Park. Some of these gates formed formidable defences, protecting deep, practically impenetrable gardens.

On a few, very anxious, occasions, boy or boys remained missing for some little time, perhaps stuck in a garden and unable to return. But which garden? I could only proceed by a process of elimination. Jason's motive was pure fun; virgin exploration. Hector's desires were food and football. The boys were always - in the end - safely retrieved, or retrieved themselves, thankfully returning without the family cat, rabbit or ferret.

Variety is the spice of life, and if Hector discovered the treasure of a tennis ball or football - which he often did - this interrupted his progress and made him a happy boy. He was equally happy to let me throw the ball for him, and even happier to run after the object, and regain it. Jason, meanwhile, looked upon these goings-on with a doubtful, deep disdain.

The Park has five exits around its perimeter, all giving access to and from football pitches, paths and highways. Wherever H&J were - and I did not always know where they were - they (almost) never ventured beyond the limits of the large, green rectangular space. Despite their wild careering, some inner sense kept the boys within the walled, fenced safety of the Park itself.

When we exited the Park, by design - and on foot - it was just too easy to take the long, straight route towards home. However, H&J insisted on a tour of the Estate, to squeeze the last sweet drops of excitement from their walk. The exact route varied with each walk, just to make sure that no opportunity, sight or smell would be overlooked.

Most memories coalesce over time through the blur of repetition, though a number stand out. I vividly remember seeing - couldn't help seeing - the most stunningly beautiful girl, leaning elegantly, languorously, against a brick wall, her long blonde hair caressed by a gentle breeze. She wore the ubiquitous white top and jeans, but beauty is transformative, and the girl's clothes only served to delineate an exquisite figure. She seemed impossibly glamorous, in an incongruous setting.

I wondered why on earth this young woman was standing there, so carelessly, nonchalantly, on a bright but chilly Sunday morning in Spring. It soon became clear that she was watching, with casual interest, a football match being played by young men with all the usual sound and fury. I looked again in her direction - one eye checking the location and direction of H&J: she was simply glorious. Seconds later, the climactic whistle blew, and a young man, caked in mud from head to toe, as though returning from raging battle, marched up to her. "*Ow'm the maggots?*" he demanded. O, the joys of football and fishing! Whatever *could* surpass them? With a smile stretching from ear to ear, I bounded after my boys.

One Sunday lunchtime in high Summer, a young family spread a tablecloth on the green sward, and laid it elaborately with cutlery, plates and, most importantly, a range of tasty fare. It was a charming scene. Out of the corner of one eye, from my viewpoint fifty or so yards away, I watched the father and his two young daughters making their careful preparations for a delightful picnic. H&J were near to me, and apparently oblivious of the feast about to commence. Aware, however, of present and future danger, I had the whole situation covered. Then, as we neared the scene - since this was our normal trajectory - both father and daughters left their assembled treasures, and returned to their car, no doubt to collect yet further goodies.

It was at this point - alerted by the movement - that H&J's antennas were activated, and they galloped unerringly towards the un-defended feast. The boys had just reached the picnic, trampling the tablecloth, when both I, and the returning party, converged on the spot. There was a good deal of "*What the..? Can you control your..?*". The evident disaster had all happened so quickly, there was hardly time to react.

In their defence, I should say that H&J would not have 'attacked' a picnic that was properly protected by its owners. It was an Oscar Wilde moment - again. Free food is a temptation that no dog can resist. No - or not much - damage done, apart from my embarrassment and profuse apologies.

This was all too reminiscent of Victor's foray at Amersham. Hector & Jason had experienced many people enjoying picnics in our French adventures, and had often been treated to tit-bits by the friendly revellers. They may well have thought, then, that this lovely 'spread' had been specially left for them by the picnic fairy.

However, the municipal Park could be an alien and even dangerous place, darkened by hostile people attracted from far and wide, and marauding gangs, otherwise known as teenagers. Over the years, I developed defence mechanisms for dealing with the unwelcome attention that we seemed to attract from time to time, from personal abuse to not-too-veiled threats of actual violence. On one occasion, passing a band of teenagers 'ensnared in grass' (possibly several types) I heard a sneering: *"Emma, that old bloke can see your arse!"*. Until that moment, my eyes had not visited the proffered derrière. Even so, it was the 'old' that upset me.

On another occasion - I was simply accompanying H&J one Sunday lunchtime - a mother called out to her daughter - who was half a league distant from me - *"Skye, get away from that man, now!"*. At least I was spared the 'old'. On yet another chastening occasion two young lads zoomed past us on their bikes, homing in on two pre-pubescent girls playing in the middle of the Park. I couldn't help overhearing the exchange which, in its decorum - the one gentleman's representative courteously addressing the companion of the lady of desire - might have been taken from a chivalric romance. Archly announced the one: *"My friend would like to **** your friend."*. Though the asterisks do not quite represent what you may infer - these were, after all, 12-year-olds - I was nevertheless staggered. Still shocked, I listened for the - no doubt scandalised - reply. *"You're too late - she already has a boyfriend!"*. O, such decorum, such delicacy!

Despite all its potential for unpleasant interference, the Park made life fairly easy for me: I simply had to watch, and to follow, unless H&J decided to raid a defenceless garden, perhaps getting trapped behind a swinging gate. Their general routine was to charge along the Park's perimeter, then charge again, completing a double circuit in more than double-quick time. Despite the five different access/exit points, with a single exception (they were very young, and had seen another dog) H&J never strayed out of the Park gates. Jason nearly always headed for a rough area where I suspect foxes lurked, or into the Council Gardeners' compound, where he would fling himself into a large stockpile of manure and other smelly stuff. On hearing my calls, Jas would excitedly re-trace his steps, and speed around or under the steel gate that allegedly protected the site.

I was often asked where H&J were - I was the lone dog-walker - and would point to a spot several hundred yards away, where there were two dots skimming along, full of super-charged, electric energy. After the completion of two circuits, which often became three, it was a case of encouraging the reluctant H&J back to the car, and home. Overall, the Park played host to perhaps one in three or four of all our walks. These walks could be made exciting and eventful by the boys madcap adventures, but blissfully the whirling dervishes generally 'did their thing' without getting us into too much trouble.

On a special occasion I channelled the boys' energies in a way that gratified us all. The Park formed the venue for the Wordsley Festival Fun Run, an annual event that inaugurates the Festival itself. The Fun Run, over a two-and-a-half mile course, beginning and ending in the Park, attracts several hundred runners each year. In 2004 I participated with H&J, who breezed around the course, somewhat constrained by their ponderous charge. Nevertheless, we completed the circuit in pretty impressive time - perhaps 18 minutes, and half-way down the field. We collected our medals with a genuine sense of pride. Had H&J been able to run free, they would have had a massage and shower, and been sipping orange juice in the refreshment tent, long before the first human athlete appeared on the horizon. This was, however, their only experience of competitive running; they were fun loving boys, and I had no thought of racing them - even had the opportunity been available - against people, or other dogs.

So often, too, the Park did sterling service as our last 'pit-stop' on the long journey home from France. We would reach the golden gates at 5.00pm or 6.00pm, usually in bright Summer sunshine; and the excited boys would leap out of the car and alight on to familiar territory - figuratively speaking, dancing and skipping along the sun-lit grass.

H&J knew they were home at last, and their high spirits were spent in re-discovering, with acute pleasure, a much-enjoyed playground.

For June and me, also, much relief, and an opportunity for reflection and a light stroll, before directing the car the short distance to home, with its weight of expectation.

Festival and Fright

Dogs have given us their absolute all. We are the centre of their universe. We are the focus of their love and faith and trust. They serve us in return for scraps. It is without a doubt the best deal man has ever made.

Roger Caras

Hector & Jason had many sightings of owls on our daily walks, especially during the Winter months, when tawny owls would continue to hunt through those interminable dark mornings; and also in Normandy, when we were inching our way along our little road, often by the light of the moon, at three or four o'clock in the morning. The tawny owls seen - or more often heard - in Normandy were a constant, ghostly presence: flying on silent wings, and emitting haunting calls, while on their deadly missions. How often would we find eviscerated mice along our path, which Hector would inspect, in grudging admiration!

But this next owl story is a bit different, and requires a little context. The story begins, again, in the Park. Every year, around mid-Summer, the suburban village of Wordsley holds its annual Festival. These are colourful events, with marching bands, a Carnival Princess, pageants, a frenetic fair ground, serious entertainment such as jousting knights, musical extravaganzas, all kinds of displays, and a plethora of charity stalls, tombolas and vendors.

I always enjoy this time of year - days of almost perpetual light: so fresh, so green, so full of expectancy. The Festival always seems to be a climactic occasion, marking the high point of the year. The event is always held on a Saturday afternoon, and attracts large crowds intent on an old-fashioned and thoroughly fun-filled afternoon. The air is alive with the smell of burgers, chips, candyfloss - and not a little nostalgia.

My very favourite time has always been the evening before Festival Day, when the various displays - consisting variously of army cadets, a pig-roast, fire engines, and a host of tents and marquees - are being assembled ready for the following day. There is so much positive energy, excitement, anticipation, activity, and good humour in evidence. Amongst the diversity of entertainment, for many years, was an elderly gentleman who specialised in rescuing birds of prey, while at the same time educating the great British public about the healthcare, special needs and threats faced by these iconic raptors. Appropriately enough, this gentleman was known as 'The Birdman' and he seemed to be held in affection by the general public. The owls and falcons, certainly, were always a magnet for adults and children alike.

Early one mid-June evening, (it was a Friday) Hector, Jason and I entered the Park with some relish, to take our walk and admire the attractions that were being so energetically and enthusiastically assembled. The whole scene bore a passing resemblance to a medieval pageant, and there was an air of gaiety and anticipation. Later that evening, a number of brave souls would sleep in the tents, providing security against any attempted theft or vandalism. But at this moment, all was abuzz with activity and energy, as a small canvas town newly emerged before our eyes. I prepared for a pleasant walk as I slipped H&J off their leads. However, this evening, their reaction seemed even more focused than usual. While Hector ran smartly and purposefully away, Jason's trajectory was as swift and straight as an arrow.

Suddenly, perhaps four hundred yards from where I stood, there was a commotion, a blur of movement, angry shouts and animated kerfuffle. As quickly as my legs could carry me, I ran towards the scene: there was my gentle Jason - Jason! - lunging frantically at a tethered snowy owl, while the incensed, puffed-up creature lunged defiantly back at him, hissing for all he was worth.

I grabbed my excited and errant dog, fixing him to his lead, and apologised to all and sundry. To my profound relief, no damage had been done, other than wounded pride and a sense of what might-have-been. It was yet another lesson learned: I did not stop attending these pre-Festival occasions, but was far more careful to keep the boys - who I am sure regarded all this as a good natured romp - under closer control.

I've been told since that this particular snowy owl was the very same (or one such) that appeared in the Harry Potter films. If that is true, he was very nearly an-ex owl, and Harry would have needed to deploy his magic to create a replacement bird. Snowy owls are truly magical creatures, as was Jason - he could well have appeared in a Harry Potter film himself - *as* himself. This may have been the only occasion when snowy owl and Golden Retriever came face-to-face in such intimate and dangerous proximity.

The good news is that The Birdman continued to display his hawks and owls - including Snowy - for some years to come, to the enjoyment and hopefully enlightenment of many hundreds of people. But also that Jason, almost Snowy's nemesis, was never again given the same careless freedom to enjoy such an unusual early dinner.

We did, in fact, continue to stroll around the Festival in subsequent years, enjoying many more sun-lit Summer evenings. And the boys were all agog, with the sights, sounds and smells - ice-creams, burgers, hot dogs, other dogs; but I took special care to avoid coming anywhere near to a particular snowy owl, and the gentle old chap who displayed these fascinating creatures.

Not long after the Snowy episode, we enjoyed a wonderful visit to a medieval pageant at Berkeley Castle. Berkeley is the perfect setting for such an event: in 1215, England's barons prepared here for their meeting with King John at Runnymede, and it was here, in 1327, that Edward II met a grisly end on the orders of Roger Mortimer. For our entertainment on this colourful occasion were hundreds of 'peasants' doing their medieval 'thing'– cooking, weaving, chopping, wood-turning, jousting, and occasionally fighting with swords. June detected French accents amongst the knights at arms.

There were exciting falconry displays, too, and the re-enactment of a Civil War battle. I've always been fascinated by these pageants, whether at Berkeley or in Normandy: the attempt to re-create the past is curious and absorbing, and is likewise entertaining and educational. Yet the attempt can never be fully realised. It is this tension between the real and present, and the heroic attempt at re-creation - the make believe - that I love. Modern culture, mind-set, even language, are all so different from the medieval. And the electronically-piped music strikes a discordant note.

I sensed a heightened zest and spring in the gait of the boys, too. Many falcons rested on their perches, in between their aerial displays. Jason, in particular, remained on his lead, and on close watch, following his adventure in Wordsley Park, still fresh in - both his and my - memory.

Hector would have his own 'moments in the sun' - arguably, far too many - and two such incidents occurred some time later. They both took place in the same Park that had witnessed the snowy owl incident. O sleepy little Park, that harbours such a capacity for surprise!

Maybe a couple of years later, strolling in said Park, I was aware of another commotion. I knew that a family of crows lived in the Park - a very pleasant home where, no doubt, they feasted on bread, left-over chips, and pigeon eggs (we all have to live). I confess that I regarded the crows as part of the background noise. But not that day: for Hector had caught and killed...a crow. How he achieved this I cannot say, but I can say that every other crow in the community went stark staring mad, dive bombing Hec and squawking with absolute fury. I was upset, since I know that crows pair for life, and one crow had just lost its better half. Hector, of course, was understandably full of himself, and trotted on regardless, ducking under the diving birds. The story does not end there. Almost to this day, a crow has followed us around, cawing and making a big nuisance of himself. Could this be the still angry partner, ten years on? I rather think so; it was Hector's 'albatross' moment.

More recently, when I fondly imagined that his hunting days might mercifully be over, I noticed Hector taking a keen interest in the Park's perimeter hedge. Another old football, I thought, kicked into touch at the end of its days. Then Hector emerged from the hedge with something orange in his mouth, that I first mistook for a discarded teddy bear. Rather, it was a discarded ferret. The animal had been threatening a blackbird's nest; no more. The petrified critter was squirming in Hector's jaws, before - with some difficulty - I released the ferret and it ran to find shelter. My timely intervention led to a bite from the terrified creature, and a precautionary visit to my GP for a tetanus jab.

The unrepentant Hector remained under close watch for some weeks thereafter.

12: Strange Sagas of the Stone, Stolen, Stabbed, Scare

My dog, my crazy dog, will be my rule
For, compared to him, all the world's a fool;
My madcap boy's a rock, a stave,
While all the world's a naughty knave.

Colin Hill

The dog is a gentleman; I hope to go to his heaven, not man's.

Mark Twain

Stone

Folk will know how large your soul is, by the way you treat a dog!

Charles F. Doran

By the time that Hector & Jason reached 18 months of age, they were physically mature and simply magnificent. They were like two young colts; individually distinctive, but glossy, lithe, and quite superb when out walking together. Hector was as handsome as could be, whilst Jason was quite the most beautiful being I had ever known. They were much admired. And they were mine.

Mentally, however, H&J were not yet *quite* the 'Full Monty'; not until the ages of three or four were they really intellectually mature, and possessing complete emotional intelligence. A paper bag blowing in the wind would startle Jason, and any slight change to his routine would have Hector registering his nervous disapproval. On several occasions whilst on our woodland walks - or runs - Jason had skipped the woods and returned home, by himself; either impatient of waiting for me to catch up, or under the impression that I had raced ahead of him (if only). There were some anxious times, and times when I determined to keep the boys on their leads. However, for the most part I was reluctant to restrain and curb their natural energy and exuberance.

H&J were also inveterate chewers of stray sticks that they found on the forest floor - a habit that I discouraged, but to no avail. One Sunday evening in early Spring, Hector declined to eat his dinner. This was an act so out of character that we immediately suspected a problem. Later that evening there was a great deal of sickness and diarrhoea, and Hector dug a huge hole at the top of the garden to lie in. That night, in our bedroom, he slept only fitfully.

Very early the next morning I took Hector, as an emergency patient, to our family vets. This was no time for making appointments. Jason was frantic as - this being a genuine emergency - I left him behind. On examination, the problem became clear immediately - Hector had something lodged in his abdomen. Though this was consistent with the symptoms, of course I had not seen him ingest any foreign body. The vet advised surgery - urgently, immediately - and I agreed at once. There was no guarantee of success, but they would do everything they could.

I remember breaking down when I returned to the car, traumatised by fear: Hector was only 18 months old, and there was a real prospect of losing him. We had a horribly anxious time ahead of us.

Mercifully, the operation was a complete success: a large stone - pebble - had been removed. The pebble was impossibly large - how, and why, had Hec swallowed it? One of the veterinary nurses sighed sagely, and muttered: *"don't ask"*. Many dogs have been known to ingest all kinds of crazy objects, equally inexplicably. But there was overwhelming relief, gratitude, and thanks, all round at the successful outcome. Hector - and pebble, in its own plastic bag - were returned to us three days later. Hec had to be gently helped into and out of the car, since a long, neat row of stitches extended along his chest. But he was alive, and would make a full recovery. Jason went berserk on his brother's return, and had to be prevented from jumping all over him in his relief and joy. However, since there would seem to be no rational explanation as to his motive, Hector's future behaviour remained a concern.

The vet suggested one more - last chance saloon - for Hec; if there was any recurrence of the stone 'incident', he would advise the adoption of a muzzle. We gave Hector that chance, and never looked back. Thank goodness. Hector returned to full health and fitness within a matter of weeks, with the usual convalescent diet of chicken and fish - light work for his stomach and colon. The stitches removed, the long scar disappeared completely over the following few months. This was to prove a unique 'one-off': Hec never 'ate' another stone.

As a rather grim memento, we still possess the pebble, which I suppose is blameless. It dates from the Triassic period, some 200 million years ago. A journey through a dog's intestines was probably one of its more unusual and memorable adventures.

Stolen

I could discern clearly, even at that early age, the essential difference between people who are kind to dogs and people who really love them.

The Confessions of a Lost Dog - Frances P. Cobbe

Not long after the 'stone' incident, one summery, Saturday afternoon, we arrived in the local Park for the usual lunchtime letting-off-steam. On the car park, a middle-aged woman with fair hair greeted us: "*What superb dogs!*" she called out, and engaged me in conversation for a moment.

Then the boys were off, on their excited tour of the landscape and its secret smells, and secret places: a favourite for Jason was the Park gardener's compound, which was closed off to all except him, as he zoomed around collecting new experiences, (certainly new smells) and disturbing perhaps the odd fox.

As always, the boys were miles ahead of me, but I knew that they would not leave the Park boundaries on their own; they would just carry on round, and round, until, eventually, I caught up. However, on this occasion, as I returned to the car park, I caught sight of said lady about to heave Jason into the back of her car. "*What's going on?*", I shouted. "*O, I thought this was a stray!*" she floundered. "*But you've just seen us!*" I blasted. "*I thought these were different dogs*", she blustered, unconvincingly. In response I muttered a few angry, dismissive words of disbelief.

Well, that was the end of that since, fortunately, no harm had actually been done, and criminal intent could not be proved. But the incident heightened my anxiety on behalf of my boys; and that H&J's habit of 'losing' me and creating their own, unsupervised, outings did involve clear and almost uncontrollable risk, through possibly innocent, possibly criminal, intervention.

There were occasions - when H&J were even madder than usual, and disappeared for worryingly long periods - when fellow dog-walkers helped me track the boys whereabouts, and return them to the fold. This was often necessary, since the woodland walk was essentially circular, and visibility quite limited, due not only due to the curvature of the perimeter walk but the height of the woodland it enclosed. Once we became separated it became almost impossible to work out which route the boys had taken. I could be heading in quite the wrong direction; or, even if in the right direction, always moments behind the flying H&J.

There were countless incidents of this kind, but H&J always returned - eventually - and to my intense relief we were always re-united. Thankfully, I never again experienced attempted theft, only help - and sympathy - from the cadre of dog-walkers who became only too familiar with the antics of my boys. I'm sure that the so-early morning walks - generally starting before 7.00am - contributed to our good fortune. And H&J were, of course, also micro-chipped, and well known locally. The *Mona Lisa* may - in theory - be stolen, but would be a tricky matter to sell at Sotheby's.

Sadly, this darker side to dog-caring has a habit of recurring. Only quite recently, while walking in the Park, an elderly chap muttered to me: "*It's startin' again...*". "*What is, my good man?*" I enquired, perplexed. "*Dognappin*", he countered. "*They see a dog apart from its owner, and bundle it in their car*". So there we are - just another risk that we dog owners face from deranged, venal and criminal elements.

If I was a little dubious about the 'dognappin' claim, any complacency was shattered when, on a routine visit to the local vets a few days later, a notice alerted pet owners to the theft of a young 'staffie' - from Wordsley Park.

Stabbed

He tells them about Bella, and they look sorry and they don't say anything stupid like, you can get another.

Wolf Hall - Hilary Mantel

Walking, strolling, rambling or running in our local woods can be an eerie business. Our ancient memories recall, like the Brothers Grimm, those dense, dark, dangerous, primeval forests. Even today, when there are no wolves or bears, there is a lurking suspicion of danger in the most benign, innocent woodland. These days, it is always a single species that one has to fear, watch for and guard against - homo sapiens.

Mercifully, incidents are few, although, tragically, there have been at least two suicides in our local woods over the years. On one occasion H&J and I were stopped by local police, who were cordoning off an area described to me as a 'crime scene'. I was truly shocked, a feeling that refused to leave me as I puzzled how to return home, when all the access routes had been blocked off. Of course, we found a way, but the feeling of being so near to - but also so distant from - an appalling human tragedy, persisted.

So it is not altogether surprising that, a little after the 'stolen' incident, further unpleasantness darkened our door. H&J were not, unfortunately, respecters of other people's gardens. Hedges, fences, gates, were to them a nuisance, or a challenge, and they followed wherever the best smell, or the last squirrel, was to be found. Paddocks, fields and gardens on the perimeter of our local woods were therefore subject to sudden invasion by my fearless boys. They caused no damage, and quickly returned, but they could be rowdy and noisy in the meantime. Many people have a very prickly approach to property ownership, and perhaps understandably resent a rampant dog on their patch even if, in H&J's case, the intrusion lasted for mere seconds.

On one occasion, a lady emerged from her large house, clad only in her nightdress, and ran into the nearby paddock, shouting and screaming at the flying Jason. It was a scene straight from the pages of *Tom Jones*. Then, still in her nightie, she began to admonish me. Only a few strips of wire separated the woods from her paddock and garden. I never ceased to be amazed at the strong reactions an innocent dog can provoke. Perhaps our lives are so narrow in their scope, and lived so much on the edge, that we are quickly tipped over into frustration and frenzy.

Then there was the beatific afternoon a nice gentleman threatened to shoot H&J if they trespassed again; and yet another old codger threatened severe action should Jason darken his (apology for a) garden again. The angry, introverted, thin-skinned underbelly of English society lurks deceptively close to the surface in Acacia Avenue; the dribble of bile and ire lies just behind the gate, or the twitching curtains. Anyway, the latter gentleman and I exchanged a few words - mine to the effect of *"sorry, but do please retain a sense of proportion"*. I suspect that this suburban mad-hatter took his revenge shortly afterwards and, if this is the case, wish him well - in Hell.

One evening, a day or two after this exchange I noticed that Jason was licking his belly, which looked sore. On closer examination, it was clear that he was cut, the wound about an inch across, and of indeterminate depth.

The very next morning, (of course), we were visiting the local vets. The vet examined Jason and, turning to me gravely, asked: *"How did this happen?"*.

"I've really no idea", I replied, truthfully but not very helpfully. *"He's been running around the local woods, and I can only think that he's cut himself on some glass or barbed wire"*.

He looked searchingly at me, again, but said nothing.

The wound needed a few stitches. Thankfully, the wound, and scar, quickly healed and disappeared. But I was left with a sense of unease that some vile mischief had occurred, and that, in all probability, some lunatic had actually stabbed my boy. My suspicions were never proven, but every time we passed that house and garden thereafter - and those passes numbered hundreds - I uttered a solemn oath:

> *Cursed be the noxious knave*
> *Caused cold calamity:*
> *Haste to thy unmade grave*
> *And rot for eternity.*

Jason, I hasten to add, was too full of the milk of canine kindness to harbour such thoughts...

Scare

Everyone needs a spiritual guide: a minister, rabbi, counsellor, wise friend, or therapist. My own wise friend is my dog.

Gary Kowalski

Health scares with H&J were mercifully rare. They were, to coin a phrase, fit as butchers' dogs. Health gleamed from every pore, and one took it a little for granted. There was just one exception - if one excepts the 'stone' incident.

These were still early days, and H&J were gadding around the local Park as though it was their virgin visit. Suddenly - really suddenly - Hector keeled over as though he'd been struck by lightning. He lay on the ground, immobile, for maybe three or four seconds - though it felt like a life-time. I trembled for his safety; my heart pounded. Then, suddenly, Hec rose to his feet, seemingly oblivious to recent events, and walked on - without expressing any concern on his own behalf (when anxious, Hector generally let us all know!). I sought the vet's view, and was advised that Hec had probably experienced an epileptic fit. He advised that this may or may not recur, and to keep a close eye on him. There was a recurrence, a year or so later - but just the once.

Hector was, though confident, also a highly strung boy, so it did not altogether surprise us that he had this condition, or tendency. It certainly raises one's blood-pressure, when such a fit or seizure occurs out of the blue.

Fortunately, this worrying tendency, or condition, quickly passed into history. Whilst I remained watchful, it gradually became apparent that my fears about a serious health issue were overdone...

For this relief, much thanks; there was already so much to think about...

13: Travails at Tafolog - Welsh Wizards and some Wild Welsh Walks

The schoolteacher asks Billy Bob: "If you have twelve sheep and one jumps over the fence, how many sheep do you have left?"
Billy Bob answers: "None."
"Well", says the teacher, "you sure don't know your subtraction."
"Maybe not", Billy Bob replies, "but I darn sure know my sheep".

(old Texas joke)

It is better to have lived two days as a tiger than two hundred years as a sheep.

Tiger of Mysore - Tipu Sultan

My boyhood dream had been to, one day, acquire a woodland. Pourquoi? - you may well ask. Quite simply, woodlands are, for me, the most sacred places. While I grew up running around woodlands and wild fields, I did so on the very cusp of an ever encroaching industrial blight, and conscious that each day might bring fresh threats to every field and flower.

Acutely aware of the dangers seemingly all around, I grew up familiar with woodlands, fields and ponds: newts, frogs and sticklebacks were my daily companions, and I delighted in the escape, the excitement and the sheer delight of *wild life* on my doorstep. All through my childhood and into my adolescence, all this natural glory seemed to come under unremitting attack from the restless, remorseless desire to 'develop', and the agitated pursuit of 'progress' at almost any cost.

Nature had no vote, no money and no power: green fields, woodland and ponds were being transformed into brick, concrete and tarmac at an alarming speed, before my eyes, until it seemed that the grim embrace of progress would leave not a blade of grass behind. If I could just hold up this inexorable advance a little, help give space to the butterflies, birds and wild flowers, then I might be glad at heart.

And I have always loved trees. Their spreading canopies; their massive trunks and variegated bark; their roots, hugging the earth. Their presence. Their beauty. Their physicality. Their venerability. Their stillness, solidity and protection. Their agelessness, their wisdom, their mystery, their other-worldliness, whilst quintessentially of this world. Their change through the seasons. The cool, dappled shade they confer; the grandeur and comfort of their girth; their changelessness. These leviathans are almost immortal. And every one is different; a unique individual.

As if that were not enough, it is trees that provide our music - and not only the kind produced by the interplay of leaves and breeze. The Stratocaster beloved of Jimmy Hendrix was fashioned from alder; without it, we would have seen only the most spectacular air guitar. And the heavenly sonorities coaxed from violins arise from instruments crafted from maple and spruce.

Few things in life have given me greater fulfilment than the simple act of planting trees, usually from seed - and watching their miraculous growth. Even as a child I had planted acorns and watched, mesmerised, as first the growing tip pushed itself above ground, and then as the first, burnished leaves unfurled. These little life-capsules were endlessly fascinating. I never tired of the seasonal miracle; and I have always delighted in Autumn's showers of 'conkers' - glistening globes of latent life.

Trees provide us with shade and shelter, and beauty which we can sit beside, and ponder, and wonder. They are sensuous creatures that give little offence. According to the journal, *Nature*, Britain contains only 47 trees per person, compared to 182 in France. And they are the very source of our air, by emitting carbon dioxide. See that tree ahead of you? That is your personal oxygen supply: guard it well.

As trees bring only joy,
So, people, only woe;
Let passions not destroy
The supple seeds I sow.

All the time that I was growing up, trees seemed to be my innocent, comforting friends. Some of them I have loved for fifty years and more;

we have grown together. Some of my favourite old friends started life when Jane Austen was a girl, and will still greet the morning sun - human action notwithstanding - for a hundred or two hundred years to come.

By Shakespeare's time, the fabled Forest of Arden was already a sad relic of its former glory, its trees plundered for fuel to drive Elizabethan industry, in the first, hesitant steps towards the Industrial 'Revolution'. Even so, one can still find trees in Shakespeare's birthplace that are old enough to have been familiar to - and to have been seen by - the young Will himself.

As a boy, I recall being absorbed by nostalgic tales of country life written by a Romany writer, the Rev. George Branwell Evans. I was also an early, eager reader of Thomas Furbanks' *I Bought a Mountain*, and found inspiration in its pages. These books struck a chord with my developing love of nature, and my fears for a natural world under relentless pressure. Maybe one day I, too, could own my own magical, mysterious patch of forest?

All that said, or dreamt, I was a little ragamuffin with a few pennies in my pockets, and prospects dragging me relentlessly towards factory, warehouse or store. My dream was exactly that - a pipe-dream. In the immortal words of my crafts teacher, Mr Brake, on being presented with yet another specimen of tortured metal, *"Industry won't accept this, laddie"*. But I had other plans for my life, and it acquired a different trajectory, different shape and, by the standards of previous generations of my tribe, kaleidoscopic opportunities. The glass ceiling, if certainly not smashed, was at least being raised to accommodate a new, better educated and less deferential generation.

The different trajectory had not come easy. As a young boy, without encouragement, or even example, I read all the time, eagerly, voraciously - novels, biographies, memoirs: from *Oliver Twist*, to the French detective, *Emile*, to Edgar Rice-Burrows' *Tarzan* stories. Through the medium of books, I was able to enter worlds both mysterious and exotic; far removed, by time, distance and culture from the gravitational pull of planet Quarry Bank.

The young Arthur Wellesley, (later, Duke of Wellington), was described by his mother, Lady Mornington, as *"food for powder"* (that is, gunpowder - a military life). In the same way, I was, undoubtedly, *'food for factory'*. At nine years of age, I was reprimanded by my teacher,

Mr Weston, for reading in class: *"Boy, stop reading when I'm talking!"*. And during a 'careers interview', asked by my Headmaster what I wanted to be, replied, *"A writer"*. *"Ah"*, he responded, clearly inspired: *"You need to look for a job in the printing industry"*. However, my delight in the written word - rather than any sliver of knowledge drummed into me by Mr Weston - was to prove my salvation. The usual factors - a little ability, a good deal of determination, and a great deal of hard work - enabled me, exceptionally for a working-class lad at that time, to progress to university, and eventually to secure a path to a 'white collar' career - in which I wrote, and wrote, to my mind's content.

By the mid-1990s (after purchasing La Haute Maison, in Normandy), and with the fruits of hard work diligently invested, I had begun to think seriously about my next project: purchasing a woodland. And I started to trawl the market in earnest. As it turned out, we acquired Tafolog in the Winter of 1998/99, at a time of extreme emotional trauma. Though, in many ways, it was an inauspicious time, at a deep level there was a connection between Tafolog and Victor. Though Vic had never travelled to Tafolog, a couple of years earlier he had visited an earlier prospective purchase, in the Brecon Beacons. I had not found any available woodland in the West Midlands - the obvious location - so had to scour further afield, and eventually to North Wales, to find a suitable property.

I was surprised that my initial, speculative, offer for Tafolog had met with success; time and experience was to put me right on this point. The property had been bought unseen, on the basis of the sales particulars, only, and a slightly cheeky offer that I feared would be too low. However, I knew where it was, and broadly what it was. A brief description, and a few photos, had been enough to tempt my offer, which was accepted with almost indecent haste.

My surprise, and pleasure, at acquiring the woodland so quickly and easily was tempered with a little apprehension. The knock-down price may have reflected the market for timber at the time, which was lacklustre, at best. But the purchase price also reflected the fact that Tafolog had, in the recent past, been subjected to a brutal 'haircut'. Perhaps 95% of the tree cover - practically every tree save those following the boundary stream - had been extracted. With the trees gone, most of the commercial value of the land had been removed.

And it would be my - onerous and expensive - task, as the new owner, to replenish, or re-stock the woodland, on terms approved by the Forestry Commission. As I was to discover, this was indeed to prove a project and a half, replete with much anxiety, and costs way beyond my early expectations. But ownership of a woodland had been *the* childhood dream, and - as the wild, swampy, boulder-strewn 60 acres was planted, grew, and developed towards maturity - that childhood dream became a wonderful reality.

As it transpired, the timing of the purchase could not have been better. The life-force of Hector & Jason was launched at the very moment that this grand project came to fruition. This 'brave new world' became their life-long playground, the soul of adventure; and the scene for one of their most memorable days.

Our very first visit to Tafolog, in the late Spring of 1999, was also a first for H&J: their very first grand outing. They were a mere five months of age. The journey would take us through Bridgnorth, Shrewsbury and Welshpool, until we entered the wild and steep winding roads of mid/north Wales: then, ultimately, passing a granite sign that read, thrillingly, 'Snowdonia National Park'. We had planned a number of car-stops along the way, for rest and comfort breaks: but this was quite an adventure, and we needed to take the utmost care for the boys. We also had to find the woodland, since it was some distance off the beaten track. The area we discovered was magical and magnificent, and I could hardly contain my excitement and delight. My anticipation was quite surpassed by the reality of the remote, steep, and wild prospect that lay before and all around us.

Though the tree-blasted property itself was pretty desolate, the location - with the rising mountains of Snowdonia surrounding like a huge cauldron - was spectacular. And, if I achieved nothing else whilst on this planet, it was my privilege to create beauty here; hopefully, everlasting beauty. I re-read my Thomas Furbanks, and felt the same sense of awe, empowerment, and responsibility: the power, scale and otherness of raw nature and its challenge struck me forcibly:

'The shepherd was impatient. He called to a wall-eyed dog with a grey-blue coat, and turned up the mountain. I plodded behind him; I waded through soaking russet bracken, jumped swift, swollen streams, carefully where turf was raised up quaking by some force of water which bubbled

through buried rocks. Presently we reached the edge of the mist. The outlines of my guide became indeterminate, and the dog a flitting ghost.'

No other human beings were anywhere to be seen but - of course - there were sheep everywhere. The five months old H&J perhaps endured rather than enjoyed the trip, though I do recall Hector's playing happily in the stream that borders Tafolog. In view of the boys' (already evident) cavalier approach to wild places and wild animals, and the turn of foot that was already approaching awesome, we took great care to keep H&J on their leads throughout the visit.

A short 'recce', (which confirmed for all time the sheer romance, and spectacle of the area, but also the inaccessibility of this place), and a few photos, and we were on our way home. I had much to dwell upon, since I had now seen at first hand the daunting scale of the re-planting task that lay before me. Any (impossibly naive) hopes that the re-planting could be accomplished on my own, with a little help from my friends, were dashed. Planting 50,000 trees, consistent with an approved plan, is a job strictly for the professionals.

H&J were car-sick on the way back - there was an emergency pit-stop at Welshpool - but they quickly recovered their poise. Perhaps, for the last time, I stopped expecting either boy to be the re-incarnation of our beloved Victor. They - and only they - were Hector & Jason. And for our fine, young boys, it was to prove the first of many memorable trips to marvel at the fast-changing face of Tafolog.

These early days, when I was seeking a contractor to help me to re-stock the land to Forestry Commission standards, were eventful: passion allied to inexperience provides a stomach-churning learning opportunity. With some apprehension, I sought a number of quotes for the cost of re-stocking the woodland in accordance with a prescribed plan.

I had quickly discovered that the terrain of Tafolog was extremely difficult to traverse, with a complete tour taking two arduous hours. Tree roots, rocks, hollows hidden by thick tussocks, steep cliffs and gashes in the hillside all contribute to a walking environment that is almost uniquely tough.

It was therefore with some trepidation that, one pleasant Saturday afternoon in the Summer of 1999 - I had wisely left the young bucks at home - I met the first contractor, by arrangement, on the small road just below the woodland. He was a tall, wiry, fair haired, genial man of about 35 years of age. After recognition and greeting, he suggested a tour of the woodland, to assess its topography and condition. I happily agreed, and we set off. Two hours later we completed our tour of the site. The athletic young man turned to me and confessed: *"I climbed Cader (Idris) last weekend, and it wasn't as tough as this!"*. I ruefully agreed, and smiled; he would be in touch regarding plans and costs, bade goodbye, and duly went on his way.

A slurp of coffee later, the second contractor pulled up and introduced himself. He was middle-height, of muscular, stocky build - no older than 30 years of age. *"I think we should have a look around - we really need to walk the site"* he suggested. I smiled weakly, and off we went. Two hours later, and me pretty weak-kneed, we returned to our cars, and said *"cheerio"*. I sighed a deep sigh, slurped some more coffee, and drove home - to exercise my over-excited boys. The walk was quickly followed by a welcome, warm, and prolonged soak. That evening, June and I enjoyed a barbecue at my brother's home. A couple of burgers and a pint of beer, and I was in never-never land.

Some of the estimates received for re-stocking Tafolog made me wince. I could have bought a very nice house indeed for the projected outlay. So, like many an innocent before me, I settled for the by-far-the-cheapest quote - and lived to regret my choice. The invoices just kept rolling in, with scant regard for the figures set-out in the exchange of letters that formed our apparent contract. On the plus side, the new woodland had been planted and was taking shape; and I had the beginnings of what could only grow and become more beautiful, year by year. My savings now almost depleted, I could breathe again. And begin to take pride in what had been achieved.

Yet I did have an exceptional piece of luck. Not only had I purchased the land at a time of depressed timber - and therefore land - prices. I had cashed in my investment chips near the top of the market, and just prior to one of the most vicious 'bear' markets in stock market history. The 'bear' (a sad euphemism) trashed everything in sight, reducing market values by 50% in its savage onslaught. My erstwhile investments were a sorry spectacle indeed. Selling when I did meant that, in effect, I had acquired Tafolog for practically nothing, since the value of my investments would, otherwise, have vanished into thin air. My life's ambition had been achieved at minimal cost, even accounting for the planting cost overrun. Such is life. The valuation henceforth could only go one way - up - as land and timber prices recovered.

Though most of the trees planted at Tafolog were sourced locally, I have taken pleasure in adding, and planting, my own trees, enhancing species and bio-diversity: native wild 'dog' roses, sycamore, the odd re-claimed Christmas tree, and a personal favourite - horse chestnut. There are horse chestnut trees growing proudly at Tafolog that started life on the Champs Elysees, and Hyde Park, as well as native trees from rural Normandy.

French children do not appear to have the same love affair with the luxurious, glossy conker so beloved of English school-boys, so I have been able to hoover them up in their droves - giving me a childlike satisfaction that lies beyond words. Horse chestnuts are now a common sight in the woodland, along with oak, birch, rowan ash and willow. These little balls of life are destined to thrive on their little patch of hillside for the next 150 years, maturing into graceful, 100' specimens, with glorious 'candle' spikes of blossom every May.

The journey to Tafolog, and wild Wales, was a delight in itself: first to Bridgnorth, and then on to Shrewsbury, and Welshpool, then taking directions towards Machynthleth. Almost the whole journey took place on one road - the A458. With every mile the landscape became wilder, more exciting, more remote, until at last we turned off, sweeping down a steep hill, past a fearsome torrent, and running on through no-man's land to our very special place. Mr Sinatra, in swingin' mood, provided the sound-track to our journey, lifting my spirits to another level: the songs of Gershwin, Cole Porter, Rogers & Hart, the giants of the 'American Songbook', were caressed anew, words and music pulsating magically in the sparkling air and along the empty roads... *You brought a new kind of love... Anything goes.. too marvellous, too marvellous for words...'*.

On one visit with a friend, to review the progress or development of the newly planted wood, we made our way up the steep hillside adjacent to Tafolog itself. Trevor walked with Hector, whilst I held firmly on to Jason's lead. It was one of only a tiny number of occasions when I walked just one of the boys, and I had imagined that that would make walking a little less crazy. Yet it hardly made any difference: Jason's excitement resulted in an immense propulsion forward, and of course I was less balanced. Jason was a powerhouse, and the equilateral force was absent. Still, it was another memorable trip for all concerned: the weather was excellent, and the trees a joy - blooming and lovely.

After a number of visits through the years, where H&J skirmished through the woodland or marched me along it's perimeter, I decided - Summer, 2005 - that it would be a life-enhancing experience for H&J and myself to hike to the 1300' summit of Tafalog. The boys were supremely fit, and if we were ever to attempt a traverse of the woodland summit, this must be *the* time.

I knew that the undertaking would be far from easy, and would present certain risks. In addition to the ferociously difficult, broken ground, there was also some trespass by sheep into the woodland. These factors had, for a long time, kept our happy troop to the undulating paths that skirted around the woodland itself.

Now, Vic and I had had a couple of near misses with sheep. When climbing the hills around Carding Mill Valley, and again at Dovedale, we had suddenly and unexpectedly come, literally, face to face with a woolly visage. And Vic was not un-moved by such close encounters. However, a sharp word, and a swift lunge to fasten his lead, and all was well. Hector & Jason were fashioned from different metal.

I weighed up these risks in my mind. In view of the possibility of encountering sheep, and facing terrain that harboured so many challenges to feet and ankles, I would need to keep H&J under control, and on their leads. This meant that the challenge of maintaining balance, and protecting the boys, was going to be compounded. Still, one fine morning, we set off on what I knew would be a severe challenge.

The route and climb were just as difficult as I had anticipated, but the boys were managing the extraordinary terrain with the consummate ease of supreme athletes. We had ascended perhaps half way, and without mishap, when disaster struck. I stumbled over one of a myriad of obstacles: with a lead in each hand, each tied to a straining dog, one of my key skills - my acute sense of balance - had been severely compromised. At that very moment, the face of a sheep loomed into view, just ten yards above us. I simply could not resist as the leads snapped out of my hands, and the boys tore away like exocets - towards the sheep.

In a trice, awful scenes flashed through my mind. I dreaded the thought of finding a mauled sheep. I dreaded, even more, the idea of finding a farmer, gun in hand, standing over said sheep. Worst of all, I dreaded finding a badly injured Hector or Jason, leg broken by the impossibly uneven and vicious broken ground. For the next ten or fifteen minutes, the boys were out of view. I could only hear the barking - at some distance - as they chased this way and that. I ran after, and towards, the barking, faster than I had ever previously dared, risking a broken ankle or worse. I was terrified that, in their maniacal speed over appalling ground, one or other dog would suffer acute injury - and then how would we get off the hillside, and to safety, a mile away?

Somehow, after what seemed like an age of worry and frantic scrambling and calling, the boys scampered back to me, flanks heaving with their effort. There was no blood on their faces or fur, and no sign of injury. Perhaps their attached leads, and the difficulty of the terrain, had hampered their eager chasing. Or perhaps the sheep were uncommonly fast or cunning. Whatever the cause, I was mightily relieved at H&J's safe return, *sans* consequences. Well, we had come this far, with boys - and sheep - miraculously unscathed. I decided to press on, since we were now nearer to the Summit than to our starting point.

The going became easier, and suddenly we arrived at our little summit - the 1300 feet feeling like five-thousand. We looked, enchanted, over magnificent panoramas towards Snowdonia to the north. I'm not sure whether delight or relief was my chief emotion, but I was certainly proud of a grand achievement. I had a small camera with me, and took some photos of my panting boys before the (thankfully) uneventful descent.

We visited Tafolog many times following this memorable trip, and H&J always relished the raw adventure found in these remote lands. It always gave me deep pleasure to see Hector swimming in the clear, crystal stream that surrounded the woodland. However, though the boys responded to the rich landscape with eagerness and majestic stride, never again did I attempt that risk-rich adventure of 2005. We had done what we had done and, like my hero Dougal Haston atop Everest, taken the snap to prove it. Sometimes, once can be enough.

Each time we visited this forest retreat thereafter, I was fascinated to witness how the young trees had developed and matured; how the woodland was becoming transformed into 'something rich and strange'. Tafolog is an enduring legacy. Hector & Jason roamed there royally, and ran supremely, amongst the living, teeming forest.

Elan in Elan Valley

The psychological and moral comfort of a presence at once humble and understanding—this is the greatest benefit that the dog has bestowed upon man.

Percy Bysshe Shelley

Tafolog was not our only destination in Wales; the spectacular Elan Valley was always a Summer favourite. A stirring walk - with the boys securely on leads - alongside the impressive sides of the dam, to the huge dam wall of Pen-y-Gareg, was always inspirational. The freezing water cascades down the sides of the edifice; atoms and ions fizz into one's face.

The vast, hugely ambitious construction project - its objective to supply water to thirsty Birmingham - had been 15 years in the making, and had transformed the area by 'drowning' many valleys. The enormous edifice was officially opened by Edward VII and Queen Alexandra on 21 July 1904.

At the visitor centre, a statue of the poet, Percy Bysshe Shelley, in dramatic pose, holds centre stage. The valley visited by the 18-year-old Shelley in July 1811 was different indeed - *sans* dam, *sans* reservoir, *sans* water towers, bridges and walls. The young poet had actually walked to Elan, all the way from his home in Surrey. Shelley stayed at Cwm Elan, a mansion owned by an uncle - and wrote ecstatically about the wonders of the local countryside:

'Rocks piled on each other to tremendous heights, rivers formed into cataracts by their projections, and valleys clothed with woods, present an appearance of enchantment.'

'This country is highly romantic; here are rocks of uncommon height and picturesque waterfalls. I am more astonished at the grandeur of the scenery than I expected...I am not wholly uninfluenced by its magic on my lonely walks.'

Shelley was a passionate lover of freedom, and lover of nature. In *The Mask of Anarchy,* a poem that heaps contempt on the venal politics of post (Napoleonic) war Britain, Shelley writes darkly of the *'seven bloodhounds'* that follow the hateful Lord Castlereagh, then Home Secretary. : The Cwm Elan mansion was itself destined to be a victim of the Elan project. It would be absorbing to seek the nature poet's views on the modern Elan, should his statue ever be transformed into life.

Blissfully unaware of these weighty historical matters, and not having encountered any blood-thirsty hounds, H&J enjoyed the thrill of the cold, ion-charged water, and the refreshing change of landscape.

Brecon Beacons' Barbecue

The SAS train here, train here, train here -
On Pen-y-Fan's steep flanks, broad flanks, big flanks;
They strive through pain and fear, with hot and heavy gear -
So we salute their ranks, strong ranks, brave ranks!

Colin Hill

For some time we had been planning an 'attempt' on the noble summit of Snowdon, with the teenage lads of close friends, to honour the memory of their dear parents.

Before tackling the - for novices - daunting peak of Snowdon itself, we clearly needed to prepare minds and bodies by tough walking, and climbing more accessible, but less arduous peaks. So, June, myself, and Hector & Jason, were accompanied by two strapping lads, Richard and David, on a series of preparatory trips towards our ultimate mission. The process of strengthening limbs and lungs began with a bracing, winding trek to the Summit of Worcestershire Beacon, in the Malvern Hills. It is a lovely area, beloved by such luminaries as Sir Edward Elgar; one can hear his music in the ever-present breeze.

We reached the Summit and its panoramic views without mishap, and with Hector & Jason, as ever, in the vanguard. This was ideal training for more strenuous walks, since sinews used only to walks on pavement need stiffening, and lungs used only to perfunctory exercise from car park to shop need to experience a little gentle stress. Mildly elated by our success - with two teenage lads - and stirred by the superb vistas that unfolded before us, we descended, satisfied, to the car park, where an excellent barbecue was soon underway. As usual, Hector & Jason, heroes of the hour, shared in the goodies prepared by June.

A month or so later, we embarked on a more strenuous and adventurous climb, an attempt to scale the sleek, handsome contours of the 886 metre high Pen-Y-Fan, 'top-dog' in the Brecon Beacons range. We were accompanied by the same sons of close friends, whose care and safety for the day rested on the shoulders of June and me. So, no heroics.

This was to be 'A Grand Day Out'. June volunteered to set up camp in the little car park below the mountain, preparing a BBQ, whilst Richard, David, Hector, Jason and I made our attempt on the majestic summit of this elegant peak.

Many years earlier, I had reached the summit of Pen-Y-Fan and, such was the ferocity of the wind, I had leaned over the precipitous edge with no fear of falling into the abyss below. On the present occasion, too, we were making steady progress up a severely steep, lung-searing track, though buffeted by powerful, swirling gusts of wind. H&J, as ever, were in the vanguard: brave, committed, eager to press ever onward.

Suddenly, as if from nowhere, severe, searing shafts struck through our bodies, and rendered the steep, lung-bursting climb infinitely harder than I had ever known. Our feet, almost torn from their footing, struggled to maintain momentum against the terrific, whooping blasts, almost devilish in their low, cunning ferocity. At last we glimpsed the summit, a tantalising few hundred feet above us, dark and brooding in the swirling mists.

I thought deeply, urgently. We were well equipped, and I knew the terrain - and the risks. My party consisted of two plucky but inexperienced mountain walkers and two amazingly brave but equally inexperienced 'boys', of course unprotected save for their thick coats. The eyes and noses of my boys continued to point forward, as ever. Still, I made the decision to call a halt. I had met such situations before, and made such decisions before: on Cader Idris, when we were ambushed by the hailstorm from Hell. On the screes of Scafell Pike, when obdurate mists reduced visibility to close to zero. And on Glyder Fach when, despite the Summer Solstice, a sinking sun had warned us that we had just 30 minutes to get off the mountain before being enclosed by darkness.

There is no shame in choosing to survive, and to safeguard life. The conditions now were treacherous, and could only get worse. Our situation admitted of only one decision. The mountains are bigger, and stronger, than we. They are not cruel, but they are unforgiving of human error.

I remembered the words of the Bard himself, that the fault lies not in our stars, but in ourselves. The summit was close, but it was a giant step too far. We started down.

We descended, cautiously, ultra carefully, given the slippery and treacherous conditions. Hector & Jason seemed to sense the danger, and - still on their leads - descended with me, working as a team. I had always referred to Jason as 'the SAS dog', in view of his élan and stoicism. The SAS themselves train on this terrain; they would have been proud of Jas, who always gave his all, as indeed did they both.

On the descent, though I was concentrating furiously, I seemed to be accompanied in spirit by my trusty companion from Glyder Fach, who had regaled me with stories as we descended the mountains through the gathering gloom. One such story involved the career of Ironic Monty who, as his name suggests, had a gift for recounting ironic stories, and turned this into a stage act. Following a long and successful career, Monty's star began to fade, as he became old and confused. One evening, a member of the audience cried out: *"That's not very ironic, Ironic Monty!"*. Monty replied, sadly: *"I know, that's the irony of it"*.

We embraced the return of the sunny, calm downlands, none the worse for our truncated adventure. Our small but exclusive party was relieved, excited and happy. We remember the fallen heroes, but they are fallen. Seasoned climbers know that there will always be other days, other opportunities, for the more calculating (in the most positive sense) ones of their kind. The sun will rise again and shine on the sensible.

Our appetites stimulated by the physical effort, the smart of the lashing wind, and the sheer relief of our safe return, the spit and steam of the barbecue promised a very welcome repast and reward. Naturally, Hector & Jason helped us to demolish the sizzling burgers and sausages that flew from the grill.

We returned home, and looked to future adventures - never far away, for H&J. Sadly, the ultimate objective, Snowdon, was never to be attempted by H&J, due purely to logistical constraints. The treacherous slopes of Tafolog, and Pen-Y-Fan, would serve as substitutes of distinction.

14: The Unembarrassables: Some very Personal Traits

For me a house or an apartment becomes a home when you add one set of four legs, a happy tail, and that indescribable measure of love that we call a dog.

Roger Caras

Dogs have given us their absolute all. We are the centre of their universe. We are the focus of their love and faith and trust. They serve us in return for scraps. It is without a doubt the best deal man has ever made.

Roger Caras

Sex and Sensibility

'Sex' is every time I look at you...
'Sense' is everything you say, and do...

Colin Hill

In the early 'Noughties', a close colleague of mine celebrated his 60th birthday. A week or two later, snug in our den in the office, he turned to me, and said under his breath, a touch conspiratorially: *"Col, I think I have a problem. I wonder if you could help me out?"*

"Well, John", (it's always a John) *"I'll do my best....",* I replied, a little distantly.

"Well, for the last year or two, so many attractive women have been very nice to me; chatty, charming, even flirty...it's never happened to me before..."

Clearly, hope burned brightly beneath his beating breast... *"That's a problem? Well, John, do you want the good news or the bad news?"*

"I'm not sure. Perhaps a bit of each?"

"Mmm...the good news is that you're now more relaxed in the company of women. You're more confident, and experienced; and maybe they're more relaxed in your company."

"And the bad news?"

"Well, to be honest, women no longer see you as a threat..."

"I see. Thanks, I think..."

"No probs. How about a bacon sarnie?"

H&J were wholesome, and whole, dogs, and quite without embarrassment. Fortunately, they did not often embarrass, sexually or otherwise, being in most respects quite sensitive souls.

Hector & Jason lived every day as a celebration of life. It might be difficult, it could be pandemonium, to be in their company and slipstream, but it was always eventful, never dull, never common-place, never 'glass-half-full'. Full-on, max pressure, 110%. As 'God' is an anagram of 'Dog' and 'Elvis' an anagram of 'Lives', H&J were Greek for, in effect, a partnership made on Mount Olympus. Their war-cry may have been: *Carpe Diem*: 'seize *the day!'*.

As we know, as adolescents bounding along on Highgate Common and elsewhere, H&J had a penchant for bras and knickers. Clearly, they were not alone in this interest. These innocent adventures were typical of H&J's mischief and love of life in the fun-loving, carefree, 'anything goes' Summer months. If it was not underwear, it was footballs, squirrels, pigeons. I was merely the accompanist, not the conductor.

Bra and knickers apart, and though 'whole', young and vigorous, Hector & Jason took very little interest in the female of their species, and never caused any problems in that direction. *"Hello, how are you?"* was their friendly greeting at every chance meeting. There was no 'Miss Ogyny', or 'Gyna-phobia'. They were supremely content with each other, and with June and me. We were complete.

Although, of course, sometimes young ladies did take a shine to one or both of these magnificent young lads...

Food and Consequences...

Food is: fuel, acknowledgement, regard, reward;
Lascivious pleasure, plunder...a smorgasbord.

Colin Hill

H&J both loved food, and their six o'clock mealtimes were always a source of amusement; they took an almost lascivious pleasure in their oversized, once-a-day meals, and competed to see who could lick the bowl clean first. Though it was nearly always a dead-heat, they would always swap bowls, ever optimistic that a stray morsel might still lurk in their brother's dish. But never a morsel could be found: the stainless steel dishes shone like they had been newly scoured. All Hector or Jason ever saw in the bottom of their bowl was a reflection of an eager, handsome face.

Meal-times were always a gas; I never lost the sense of surprise at H&J's lusty approach to demolishing their large, single meal of the day. On one occasion I proudly delivered their meal - it must have been 6.05pm - when June appeared and asked: "*What are you doing?*". "*Feeding the boys*", I replied, stupidly. "*But I've just fed them!*", she exclaimed. Oh, well, it was too late now - not only was I just placing the replenished bowls on to the kitchen floor, but serious expectations had been raised. The second meal was despatched as quickly as the first, and with no sense (from H&J) of embarrassment, no sign that anything was amiss. Needless to say, the bowls were cleared, and cleaned, again. Two satisfied boys; fortunately, no nasty repercussions.

The scene was so reminiscent of Dickens's *Martin Chuzzlewit,* where the abominable Pecksniff '*was busily engaged with the supper which, as he whispered in his fair companion's ear, was 'a contract business', and therefore the more she ate, the better the bargain was'.* On a daily basis, H&J's one moment of sad reflection came ten minutes after their evening meal, when the realisation dawned that almost 24 hours would elapse before their next repast. I've seen three (free) English breakfasts, each resembling a recumbent Mae West, voraciously consumed by a single 'gourmet'. And I've watched - with mounting incredulity - as ten desserts were consumed, equally voraciously, by a young woman who resembled a stick insect. Given the chance, H&J could have equalled such feats - also without embarrassment.

Theirs was the 'see food diet' - although chips and cheese were particular favourites. Hector took no prisoners when offered food, and I learned to shield my fingers when offering tit-bits. Jason, on the other hand, had the softest mouth, and accepted these 'presents' with the utmost delicacy.

Even so, Jason himself spent a day's sojourn at the vet's on one occasion after extracting lamb chop bones from our pedal bin. There was also an unfortunate incident when, lazily eating a *Magnum* one sunny day in Normandy, I foolishly gave Jason the last chunk of ice-cream. He swallowed it whole - complete with stick. Three days later, and to our great relief, the stick re-emerged.

Often, both June and I would accompany H&J on their early-evening walks. On our return, it was clear from their body language that the boys expected their dinner to have been pre-prepared, as though by the 'Dinner Fairy'. The priority was always to assuage their disappointment by preparing an extra-quick meal; and, following the short wait, they ate with extra-special gusto.

And they both loved picnics - either our own, or other people's. If we were enjoying a picnic - usually in France, but sometimes at places like Evesham - the boys would regard us with rapt attention, as the food entered our, no doubt greedy, mouths. And then the *dénouement* - meat, cheese, bread - quickly offered, and as quickly taken. Fair shares all round. At every bar, bistro, restaurant or picnic spot, H&J needed to be micro-managed; the reward for their impatient fretting - as they well knew - was the remains of my own lunch.

But, our own meal consumed, H&J would creep off and salute new friends - that is, anyone else who was enjoying a picnic. Amazingly, they were often rewarded - or bought off - by this (to us) embarrassing behaviour. If, as on occasion occurred, the picnic in question was spread upon the ground, then H&J would barge in without ceremony, and help the owners to sample whatever delights were on offer. I genuinely believe that their take on the matter was that the food had been prepared on a first-come, first-served basis.

Thankfully, this embarrassment only happened on a small number of occasions. Perhaps Hector was the ringleader but, as we know, nothing tempts a dog like temptation.

And that's it; they were dignified, sensitive boys: themselves unembarrassable, and with no wish to embarrass us; and an acute sense of pride, and personal dignity. Of course, being H&J, on the rare occasions when they did cause offence, the result was beyond embarrassing...

Vive la Différence...

As opposites attract - strange paradox - these boys delight
In difference - perplexing selves - as mind and paw unite.

Colin Hill

Hector & Jason - brothers, twins - had practically 100% of their genetic material in common. Yet that 'practically', that infinitely tiny percentage, made a vast difference to and between my fabulous boys.

Jason developed - or just exhibited - some very individual habits, that he retained all his life. These caused us some amusement - although some readers may find them beyond acceptable. One was his custom, following his main meal in the evening, of rubbing his head around the furniture, a three piece suite, presumably to clean his face - but unfortunately *not* cleaning the furniture. This was a very expensive habit, in terms of furniture shampoo, but Jason could not be prevailed upon to desist; his *toilette* needed to be maintained. I suppose he was also showing his satisfaction for a hearty meal.

Jas also knew that, each morning, I took a shower and left my discarded clothes outside the bathroom. Whether other men do this I do not purport to know, but it seems fairly rational to me. Jason would sneak upstairs, grab socks and underwear, and then take his booty downstairs where they would remain close to where he lay. I hope that this story does not betray too much about my own body odour, and rather more about Jason's mischief and affection for me.

Hector did not share these habits - but he did have his own. The Golden Retriever Club cautions that Golden Retrievers are excellent landscape architects - whether one requires this service, or not. So it's axiomatic that, if you do not plan and customise your garden for your dog, he will customise it for you. Throughout the year, I struggled to maintain our garden lawn in a remotely lawn-like state. The cumulative impact of pee, deposited at 11.00pm and 3.00am, and Hector's heroic digging, made my repair efforts a practically daily task. Re-seeding the lawn took place throughout the year, as the tell-tale bald patches inevitably appeared.

Hec's daily, doggy routine of digging up the back garden was fundamental to his character. Over time, and despite continual repairs, this did have the effect of giving the garden a highly customised appearance. This particular behaviour was pretty well confined to

England; perhaps the garden in Normandy was too daunting, even for Hector, although Jason did develop - and maintain - his 'redoubt', close to the *cave*.

But Hector dug with a purpose - usually, to up-root an offending shrub, to which he had taken offence. Hector seemed to take umbrage with a number of shrubs: a fine, fragrant rose bush, in particular, was his avowed enemy, and I was regularly employed in returning the soil to its roots. But all this was a necessary price, and one worth paying, for the privilege of his company.

Returning home following our Summer holidays in France was the one and only occasion when we could, albeit briefly, behold a green and pleasant land. We enjoyed it all the more, since we knew how fleeting this verdant pasture would prove to be.

Hector's 'gardening' pastime, and his habit of continually sniffing and filtering the ground, eventually led to the disappearance of the silky black membrane covering the young Retriever nose. We often called him 'digger' and, by middle-age, his digging exploits meant that he sported a duller, brownish nose. Jason, on the other hand, rarely dug, and when he did, his nose was exempt. So, Jas retained his original shiny black nose, which looked handsome against his blonde head and mane. This difference can be clearly seen in the fine portrait of H&J completed by Grace-Craig Ward in May, 2011.

However, Hector's main claim to fame - if we exempt his hunting skills - was his near obsession with searching for and collecting footballs. He always wanted to play with these trophies, and then bring them home, adding ever further to his collection. He found these - usually discarded - objects in the local Park, the local woods or, I fear, sometimes in people's gardens (though I never personally witnessed this). If the balls were too big for his mouth, they had to be burst, and then become fit for purpose. He was very proud of his ball-finding and his on-the-ball skills. Unless the ball was beyond redemption, he insisted on taking his prizes home.

Hector was not only an enthusiastic footballer; he had terrific dribbling skills, and superb ball control. He loved making the ball 'work' with his feet, whilst running. It became common-place for me to hear football coaches opine:

"I wish I had him in my team - he's the best player on the Park".

If there were no footballs available, a tennis ball would do - even if it had just emerged from a wayward shot from the tennis court. *"Can we have our ball back, please?"* was the plaintive cry of many a potential Wimbledon star. Of course the ball was returned - when I could catch up with Hec - but it was often in a fairly sorry state by then. For Hector chased, and chewed, tennis balls with real gusto, relishing the moment of success. I did not need to entertain him too often, since he created his own amusements, and conducted his own searches. As a result of Hector's forays, we accumulated many dozens of footballs and tennis balls at any one time, and could have supplied whole football leagues. And Wimbledon fortnight.

For Hector, the discovery of a football or a tennis ball had all the excitement of finding a treasure chest on some palm-fringed Elysian Island. The dirty, tired, abused balls were, to him, as precious as doubloons or pieces of eight, glittering in their old oak casket. They were prizes to be carried home in triumph, to the fanfare of trumpets and marching bands. And then forgotten: there would always be a new prize, keenly anticipated, keenly sought, on that very next trip.

Perhaps it goes without saying that this was a purely Hector enthusiasm; Jason showed absolutely no interest in footballs, tennis balls or any other round objects. Jas would look bemused at these games, beloved of most Retrievers, indeed most dogs; though not a vain or 'superior' boy, it was somehow beneath his attention, not on his radar of interest.

Hector also had a smart little routine, or game, involving the horses that graze in a nearby field. Pretending that he was absorbed in his own pursuits of pondering and sniffing, he slowly approached the horses, drawing nearer and nearer to the increasingly nervy beasts. Finally, responding to the call of a million years of repressed instincts, the spooked horses could stand it no longer, and charged at Hector. The crafty Hec, of course, has been waiting for this precise moment and, with split-second timing, showed the steeds a clean pair of heels, running to safety beyond a fence. It was a dangerous game, but was played with skill, and a full appraisal of the risks, and risk management. It's a game Hector never lost - even in comparative old age. Whilst anxious on account of my boy, I also delighted in his courage and skill.

Again, Jason showed no interest whatsoever in this game. He would, in any case, have been far too quick, even for these fast, un-nerved horses. No, he only showed interest in the perfumed poo discharged by these noble animals. Yet, it was not always thus: both Hector & Jason would nuzzle the little pony, and his mate, the donkey, when they approached their fence to greet us, as they did so often on our Normandy 'goat walk'. It was quite endearing and, in Hector's case, quite eyebrow-raising, to witness this apparent show of affection towards another species.

Both boys also enjoyed occupying the furniture - either in the daytime (if we were out of the house) or in the dead of night. So often, we would enter the lounge to find Jason spread-eagled on his back, on the sofa, or Hector curled up in an arm-chair. At least Jason had the sensitivity to look embarrassed.

Some behaviours, though not many, were shared. H&J both detested the vacuum cleaner. Since vacuuming our carpets was a daily or twice-daily necessity, they would trip happily into the garden whilst the detested noise ensued, to await peace and quiet. Floor cleaned, and peace and quiet restored, they bounced back into the house. Result - one muddy carpet: a little like the perennial painting of the Forth Rail Bridge. Old towels would be spread over the floor to help minimise the dirt bought in from outside.

H&J also hated the lawn mower and strimmer. If these tools were being deployed, they would retreat from the garden, and take refuge in the house. They simply deplored these high-pitched, unnatural sounds, and the very need for such an appalling racket. If all this could be a little trying, it was all conducted in a good cause - trying to balance the elements that make up a life, a life shared fully with two glorious boys.

As one might expect, given the English climate, on a great many occasions we returned from our walks, dripping wet, and caked in glutinous mud. Always we would pause by the front or back door, when I would give the command to "*shake!*". Immediately, Hector would shake himself vigorously, thus removing much of the surplus water from his coat. He could then be dried with a towel, indoors. Jason never seemed to understand this command - or entreaty - no matter how often he heard it. Immediately he was in the house, however, Jas would give himself a tremendous shake, flinging cascades of water droplets as far as the eye could see. We would try, with varying degrees of success, to rub Jason down before the 'shake' occurred, at least reducing the effect on the paintwork and furniture. Jas would repeat this action on every rainy occasion, and never saw the slightest problem with it. Exasperating, but how very Jason!

Jason could be equally daft at home. He often lay down across 'strategic' walk-ways in the front-room, and had the habit - or knack - of raising his head at the very point when I tried to reach over his recumbent figure; I had to be so careful not to make contact with his animated, lovely face. Jason also had the unerring ability of inserting a rear paw through the loop-handle of his lead, as soon as I had released it for any reason.

In the brief interludes when H&J were not running or, in Hector's case, hunting, they were both great chewers of sticks. Sticks can be dangerous for dogs, and I needed to be ever-vigilant. I never knew Hector have trouble with a stick - or, indeed, a squirrel - but Jason did occasionally manage to get a stick wedged in his jaws. The signs were an unusually quiet, non-barking Jason - since his jaws were glued together - and less than euphoric body language. Colin always came to the rescue, extracting said stick. Jas was a grateful boy, and all was well.

Strangely, for boys so incredibly active, H&J would never re-trace their steps. If, for example, I needed to deposit their poo in a litter bin that we had just passed - say 20 yards to the rear - they would refuse to budge. 'Forever onwards' was their unerring theme. So, I had no alternative but to drop their leads and, with a very firm imprecation of "stay!", deposit the offending matter, before returning to my ground-pawing charges.

I delighted in taking H&J with me to the car-wash. As the hoses, spray and brushes began their maniacal work, the boys looked out with unfeigned astonishment. There we were in our safe little cocoon, while the car's frame was subjected to a frenzy of activity. The boys remained interested but calm, and perhaps relieved when the frantic process was complete.

And they adored accompanying me on our shopping trips. H&J would watch intently as I left the car, following me with their eyes, until I had receded into the distance. On my return I would 'zap' the car's remote, eager to see their response: their heads would instantly bob up in the car - like the 'erotic' dolls in a famous episode of *Only Fools and Horses*. Slightly mischievously, I relished doing this - not in any way to unsettle them, but to watch the boys' bright, shining faces, as they welcomed my return, and the anticipation of a fresh walk, or simply returning home.

I observed, when H&J were still quite young that, on occasions, both boys would wrinkle their noses and lips in what, at first sight, appeared to be a snarl. It was, of course, nothing of the sort, but the very opposite - a smile, a laugh; a welcome. Either they were very happy, greeting me or, unusually, they were a little anxious or worried. When I had understood its meaning, I found this characteristic most endearing. The trait reminded me of the Kern-Fields classic, *The Way You Look Tonight,* where the lover fondly recalls his beloved's little mannerisms - like the way she wrinkles her nose whenever she laughs.

A dog wags its tail - usually - as an indication of satisfaction, or pleasure, but I have not seen this particular 'grin' in any other dog, or dogs. When H&J treated me to their special smile, I knew for certain that they were enjoying life to the full - and fully enjoying our life together. And was suitably moved.

Furniture Wars

Not dissuasion, nor heavy brow, nor coaxing o'er to win
Could stop their full-tilt charge at post, and box, and bin.

Colin Hill

Most people, going about their daily business, are probably largely unaware of 'street furniture', otherwise described as multifarious public clutter, of varied utility and aesthetic quality. Examples include lamp-posts, telegraph poles, street, road and 'place' ('Welcome to Anytown') signs, green telephone base units, post boxes, and litter/dog litter bins. These - usually metal - excrescences have proliferated in recent years. Mostly unlit, they can be a hazard to dog walkers, particularly at night. Given H&J's energy and electric pace, I needed to take special care to avoid these obstacles, since they are usually located on the very pavements whose primary purpose is for walking.

However, as most people know, lamp-posts and dogs have a particular affinity. For me the problem was not the cocked leg phenomenon, but the risk of being flattened by an on-coming vertical object. H&J seemed to think that, even with one lead in each hand, and passing a lamp-post on either side, that I could somehow dissolve through the obstacle and re-appear on the other side. My tactic on these occasions was to quickly release the lead of (usually Hector), just as quickly re-gaining same a second later. This required vigilance, sometimes a quality lacking at 6.45am on a dark Winter morning. Even so, familiarity breeds respect for the waiting hazards which, to do them justice, at least stay in the same place.

Jason also had an issue with 'kissing gate'-type entrances, which require people (and their dog/s) to walk through a steel contraption. They are, in all honesty, quite innocuous to the average human - and average dog. One of these (to Jason) infernal 'machines' was installed at the entrance to a local wood, replacing a wooden stile which had given years of sterling service. Hector quickly mastered the technique, and walked smoothly round and through. However, Jason - on the end of my other arm - regarded the whole process with a very dubious eye, as though the steel apparatus was alive and dangerous. I did, on so many occasions, encourage him through, but he never trusted this (for him) Satanic device.

Similar entrance devices were installed at one of our favourite river walks, near Pershore, and we derived much amusement from guiding my so-sensitive Jason through and past these strange barriers, and on to the paradise of river meadow beyond. This was just another example of his unique charm - a heady fusion of naivety, in its best sense, courage, devotion and lust for life.

Arriving home, after the working day, was often a return to a disaster zone: bits of broken wood - and coal - scattered over the carpet, abandoned toys, ripped-up and spattered post: the lounge generally re-designed and customised. And two excited and effusively affectionate boys to welcome whichever of us returned home first; the welcome was hardly less enthusiastic for the second tired human to emerge at the door.

A house-proud person would have died of shock at the sight of such carnage; dedicated dog-people learn to take the rough with the smooth. And one has to understand that dogs, even when they have their brother to provide company, are easily bored. And H&J were particularly easily bored. Often, the mess looks worse than it is, and is easily cleared up within a few minutes. A few more minutes with the vacuum cleaner, and all is restored to calm and a semblance of order.

None - none - of this mattered compared with the undiluted joy of homecoming and re-union. Anticipating the moment, I would hum a favourite Cole Porter song, a Sinatra standard: *You'd be so nice to come home to...*

To paraphrase Mr Darwin: 'paradise' is a weak term to describe my feelings on returning home to a warm hearth, and re-uniting with the most loving of boys.

So nice to come home to....And they were.

Water Sports

With water - wet, and winking - these boys were poles apart;
Where one brave boy wants patience, and one brave boy wants art.

Colin Hill

Retrievers - with their water spaniel breeding, and retriever instincts - are reputed to love water: paddling in it, swimming in it, retrieving from it. Hector and Jason each had his own relationship with water. They happened to be at opposite poles.

Hector just couldn't get enough of water - whether in lakes, rivers, canals or of course the sea. A river bank was, for Hec, an enticement, and an excuse to dive into the flow. The river Severn was his favourite, no doubt because most visited, although he also loved the stream that ran around Tafolog, and large lakes such as Lake Vyrnwy. He did not just want to wade, or paddle - no, he was a serious swimmer: *'throw me a ball or stick, and watch me go!'*. And he did.

Whenever on holiday in France, as soon as we had parked the car near to a beach, Hector would run to the sea, where he would happily chase stones into the waves, and attempt to retrieve them. Sneakily, I would throw them - into an incoming tide - just so far that he would have to swim to the spot where he had seen it fall. These lovely, empty beaches scattered around Normandy's coast - at Granville, or Luc sur Mer, or Coutainville - were his pride and joy. To run into the wind, along the line of the surf, and dive into the waves was to experience life at its most joyous. He loved it, and I loved him loving it.

Hector slipped into rivers and lakes like the proverbial duck to water, and as soon as one's back was turned. Hec exercised his mojo - to chase ducks, hunt among reeds, find shells and stones, or simply for the thrill of being in a different medium, and exercise a rare ability - swimming like an otter, with his tail splayed and acting as a rudder.

As much as Hector loved the element in all its forms, Jason distrusted the stuff in every way - whether it took the form of a pond, a lake, a river, a stream, or - especially - the sea. He seriously disapproved of water, whatever its guise. Not only did Jas not care for rivers or lakes, he never volunteered to set a paw in either. Jason first encountered the sea in Port en Bessin, a pretty little village and harbour on Normandy's Côte Fleurie. Here he observed with horror that the sea *moved,* and was clearly not to be trusted.

On greater acquaintance, a little later, Jas overcame this morbid dread, though he could never be persuaded to actually enter the waves. He did, however, learn to love beaches, which gave him free rein to exercise his desire to run, and on countless occasions he would career at prodigious speed along the sea-shore, fizzing along the line of the surf with a rare *joie de vivre.* The beach was always more fun - there was always a dead fish, a piece of cuttle-fish or a stick - all excellent finds, to be sampled or chewed. In this, Hector & Jason were in perfect agreement. Together with Jason's love of his Normandy home, I think his hours on its beaches provided his most exhilarating moments.

On one occasion, only, did Jason enter the sea and swim. And I'm afraid that that was my doing. One broiling afternoon we were relaxing on the beach near Carnac. There was a channel of water reaching out to the sea, which was quite shallow and still - perfect for a novice swimmer. Hector was already thoroughly wet and happy from retrieving stones, and I decided, a little mischievously, to test Jason's swimming skills. I led Jas down to the water, then gently coaxed him in. Jason walked in without fear or flinching, up to his flanks - and then, suddenly, he was swimming. I know he was swimming because his front paws - and claws - caught the back of my calves, as I held on to his lead. Swimming Jas was - but not enjoying it. I quickly led him out; a brisk shake, maybe a disapproving look - and that was that. Never again.

One tiny expanse of water, and one only, Jason loved. In Normandy we have a small wildlife pond, complete with flag irises and marsh marigolds. Whenever we arrived at the cottage, Jason would whoop with joy, dive into this pond and take in a great draught of water. No doubt after his long 'fast' he was thirsty, and he always welcomed this refreshing pool of cool. Though it was usually dark by this time, no matter: he had arrived, and was already enjoying himself.

Grooming's a Gas

Grooming's for me time, your time, our only-own time;
For be time, we time, sweet time; our little three time.

Colin Hill

The boys loved to be groomed, and sprang to attention as soon as they saw their brush in my hand. Hector always pushed to the front, insisting on being first, and would stand patiently, happily, whilst I brushed him all over. Since his coat was close and strong, not a great deal of fur came away; but his coat shone, and looked all the better for being groomed.

Jason would respond with alacrity, when it was his turn; his soft, thick coat gave up a considerable amount of fur, after which he would look even more sleek and beautiful. He would stand still and proud, until I was done. We never threw the loose fur away, but deposited it in the garden, usually in the cleft of a shrub. There must be hundreds of birds nests, over the years, that have been lined with this 'superior' soft down. I've seen the fur taken from the bushes on many occasions, by blue tits and blackbirds, so my fancy is well grounded.

H&J's enjoyment of grooming did not, sadly, extend to being shampooed and bathed. Both lads took a dim view of the whole, (unnecessary, in their view) process. Our vets advised that regular shampooing was beneficial to both coat and skin, as well as improving the boys' body odour. Since they were naturally clean, and hated the process, I resisted bathing the boys unless it was clearly necessary. However, they were both fond of fragrance of fox, which they would roll in delightedly, thus making a wash an occasional necessity.

When washing did become necessary, the routine went like this. The boys were ushered outside, and warm water sprayed over them. Special vet-supplied shampoo was then applied, and left for ten minutes. A further application of luke-warm water followed, and the process completed by drying-off with a towel. This was never enough for the boys - a vigorous shake contented them, even if it soaked me.

Finally, we embarked on a brisk walk to complete the drying process. The - perhaps quarterly - hassle was worth it, since the boys always looked - and indeed smelled - at their absolute best. But neither Hector or Jason were impressed by the unedifying ordeal.

While Hec & Jas bore the process with dignity, indeed fortitude, this occasional *toilette* suppressed - if only for a moment - their ever ebullient spirits.

15: At Home with the Parents

I could discern clearly, even at that early age, the essential difference between people who are kind to dogs and people who really love them.

The Confessions of a Lost Dog - Frances P. Cobbe

My dear old dog, most constant of all friends.

William Croswell DoaneI

Hector & Jason loved their family, and all within their circle of friends. The mere mention of the words 'Granny and Grandad' (my parents), or 'Uncle Ray', or 'Alan and June', or 'Margaret and Trevor' would have them whooping with joy, and whirling around the garden, performing (metaphorical) cart-wheels. Their rich social life, and deep affinity with family and friends, extended to neighbours, and even the milkman.

The boys would be ecstatic at the mere prospect of meeting and greeting; doubly so when the rendezvous actually occurred. I found it touching then; I still do. What is life, if it is not about love, and the mutual pleasure to be derived from love? H&J were the bringers of unalloyed delight - at once, to their friends, to me, even to themselves. Of what individuals, from what other species, could one say as much? Certainly not from our own gene pool, of whom such rare individuals are generally canonised - or crucified.

Mom and Dad had idolised Victor, and with good reason. He was a frequent and much-loved visitor to the household, and the affection was reciprocal. He was, quite simply, irreplaceable. So, at first, my parents were a touch reticent when receiving the young Hector & Jason, though the two young lads could not have been more open, friendly, and eager to please. But H&J were *so* different to Victor. My parents coolness, if such it was, was short-lived. On their own terms and on their own merits, H&J were irresistible.

Over time, H&J seemed to forge a special bond with my parents. Just like Victor, Hector & Jason relished the weekly 13-mile round trip that we would pay to Granny and Grandad, on the other far-edge of the Black Country. They always knew exactly where they were going. Dogs pick up all sorts of signs, and the boys' enthusiasm was probably enhanced, if not by the fuss that they would receive, or the prospect of a new and interesting place to explore, then certainly by the prospect of a biscuit or two. June and I never gave H&J sweet biscuits - which is probably why they liked them so much - a case of *a little bit of what you fancy...*

H&J's arrival at my parents home was the occasion for much excitement. The boys would jump from the car and rush straight to the front door, where they would bark, with unconstrained delight, to be admitted in to the house. The door being opened, they would dash around in a frenzy of energy, greeting my smiling parents. Their enthusiasm not yet curbed, the boys' would fly out of a rear door on to the terrace, down the steep steps and into the garden. It was all innocent stuff, and highly amusing, though not everyone would find 11 stones of adrenalin-fuelled Retriever a welcome prospect.

My parents always welcomed H&J effusively, even though the boys' initial over-exuberance must have been a little daunting. They did calm down eventually, but it was all good genial fun, and H&Js obvious and transparent pleasure always gladdened my heart. If the celebration continued for *too* long - it was generally a 20 minute party - I was asked to *"tell them to calm down"* - a demand that was easier made than accomplished. H&J were so excited by their arrival at my parents that it might be even half-an-hour before their animal spirits subsided. Simultaneously, they would decide that the celebrations were over, and relaxed on the carpet, awaiting further 'developments'. These developments may have included biscuit time, or a new foray into the back garden, where they would bound effortlessly up and down the steep stone staircase.

If it was a relief to see Hector & Jason - eventually - lying peacefully on the carpet, their unusual quiet usually sparked an enquiry that I found perplexing. At such long-sought-for pregnant pause my mother would quietly murmur, in her ineffable way *"They don't do much, do they?"* which was tantamount to enquiring *"what are dogs for?"*. I would smile, unsure how deep the question went. *"And what would you have them do, mother? Perhaps make a Victoria sponge sandwich? Dance a Paso Doble? Conduct a wine tasting? Translate Shakespeare into French?"*. To respond to simple commands, be themselves, love and be loved, was surely more than enough. No, they had simply exhausted current possibilities, and were as content as could be - until the next excerpt of their story, the next adventure.

Despite the boys' boundless excitement, enthusiasm and sheer energy, there was never any damage done, not even to the 1001 ornaments that squeezed into every conceivable nook and cranny of my parents' home. H&J took instinctive care not to damage or break any ornament, glass vase or other piece that had pride of place on hearth, sideboard or cabinet. Except, that is, for one occasion, when events did not go to plan; thankfully, only once....

On this visit, I knocked firmly on the front door as usual, before letting the boys through, into the lobby. On this infamous visit, the back (lobby) door being already open, instead of turning 90 degrees into the kitchen, as they almost invariably did, H&J hurtled straight through the rear lobby to the terrace, careered down the stone steps, and invaded the back garden.

I was still standing at the front door when, mere seconds later, the boys exploded forth - Hector proudly carrying a dead wood-pigeon in his jaws. *'What the...?'*. Arriving on the scene, my father - his voice shaking - explained that, moments earlier, it had indeed been a live pigeon, that he had spent weeks nursing back to health. Well, it was too late for first aid now. Oh, dear, Hector was in the dog-house, again, and I was joining him.

I apologised profusely, whilst easing the sadly deceased from Hector's reluctant jaws. I took the poor thing away with me, as the, hopefully, sensitive option. Though annoyed with myself, it was difficult to blame the boys, and hard, though I say it myself, to have anticipated my father's nursing an injured bird. The gush of sentiment was quite unexpected, and the response somewhat surprising, given the octogenarian's (hitherto) staunch protection of his treasured cherry tree - with catapult - against all-comers. And then again, when he was himself a young lad, my father's family, like so many others, had reared pigs in their back garden: there were nine hungry children to feed.

One of my father's favourite stories related to Rommel, a giant porker, (named after the wily and belligerent German general, Erwin Rommel). The Hill brood were proud of Rommel's heroic stature, and pugnacious personality. But times were hard, and Rommel's own 'time' had come. Two slaughter men, armed with long knives, confidently entered Rommel's den, in order to 'attend' to him. But, like British generals opposing his namesake in North Africa, they had not met his like before. To general consternation, noise and mayhem, the suspicious, furious porcine flew at the would-be assassins, and sent them scrambling for their lives. This was an unprecedented event, that seared deep into the family consciousness.

Eventually, and sad to say, black arts were employed to lure Rommel into a van, where he was conveyed to the local abattoir. Some time later, the manager proudly announced that Rommel had produced the largest hams he had ever seen. My father always told the story with trembling voice, though not, one suspects, from the perspective of an animal rights activist.

For good or ill, then, Hector & Jason were always, always, the centre of attention - Hector because of his ebullience and extrovert character, that *would* be noticed, and Jason because, well, he was Jason. Even at my father's 90th birthday celebrations, in May, 2011, H&J were the life and soul of the happy congregation, lending their special brand of magic to the proceedings, and undertaking a professional taste-test of the delicious fare: canapés; sandwiches; sausages.

As a child, the Stour Valley - opening beyond and below the family home - had been my playground, my little world of mystery and imagination. It had seemed much bigger, then; it is much cleaner these days, and kingfishers and buzzards now call it home, even if the water voles, sadly, have long disappeared.

Do places have a memory? I believe so but, in any event, I was touched to introduce H&J to this area, and to share the place, and my memories - walking along the winding river on a sunny morning, jumping over the ditches, wading through the long, flowery grass - just as a young, dreamy lad had done, decades before.

These early memories will now forever be intertwined with memories of endless racy walks with, and love for, my two adorable rogues.

Sin be the Poo

"Sin be the poo", sweet Nature said to me:
"Ride on my cloud; my tears will set you free."

Colin Hill

'It is an offence not to clean up after your dog' proclaims every lamp-post, as though personally affronted by the attentions of passing canines.

Someone, somewhere, must have made a fortune from the 'No Dogs' signs that adorn millions of shops, restaurants, bars, offices and schools. It is quite remarkable where dogs can't go, no doubt for very sound reasons, and one gets accustomed to this. It's different, of course, 'on the Continent' as we quaintly still call it, though it's changing there, too. One can still take a dog into most restaurants in France, and dogs can also stay with their owners in most hotels. Supermarkets, historically, have also been generally welcoming, provided that the dog remains inside the shopping trolley. Of course, this presents a problem for most Golden Retrievers...

There are also street and shop signs that command: *'No dogs allowed except guide dogs'.* How, pray, are their owners expected to know they have such access? My favourite notice is the snooty 'Do not allow your dog to foul this area'. *"Yes, OK, I'll give him a right good talking to".*

We have all seen those stickers in the rear windows of cars, usually when we are behind them in a traffic queue: *'Baby on board'* or, in France, *'Bébé a bord'.* Of course, such sign-age is designed to ensure that the driver following is more careful, more cautious, so as not to inconvenience the little prince or princess browsing the latest DVD or electronic gadget. I believe that the time is right for a new range of such stickers, proudly proclaiming (accompanied by suitable pictorial display) *'Benji on Board'*, or *'Charlie's Car'* or *'Hector's House'*, or *'Tara's Taxi'.* This may begin to redress the apparent anti-dog culture that dominates our urban signage - and policy processes.

I have always thought that, these (British) restrictions, or prohibitions, on dog access, whilst perfectly reasonable and explicable, are also symptomatic of our modern default position of saying 'no' to anything vaguely problematic; they are also deeply ironic. Neither June or I have ever suffered any kind of ailment from the fact that dogs and cats enjoy unfettered access to the house - including kitchen, bedroom and garden. We have, however, suffered gut-wrenching food poisoning as a result of lousy human (staff) hygiene in pubs and restaurants.

As one might expect, Hector & Jason were oblivious to their being unwelcome in most premises: the only premises they valued, apart from their home, was the local butcher's shop. Many a time they attempted to career into these mouth-watering emporiums, and had to be 'managed' along the street. No - they valued the Park, and their familiar woodlands. Fortunately, these facilities were not only available and accessible - but all, wonderfully, free as the air.

Now, in the UK we do have these small obsessions, and dog poo is one of these, along with sex in public (by which I mean on TV), the weather, and football. Indeed, while dog poo is almost as malodorous as that of homo sapiens itself, it gives me a strange comfort to think that the most beautiful, powerful or indeed most regal of humans must perforce spend time each day sitting upon a wc, whilst ridding themselves of the most unenviable matter. Whilst I have little knowledge of queens or corgis, the great diarist Samuel Pepys recorded that, when Charles II returned from exile in 1660 upon the aptly-named *Royal Charles,* his favourite dog 'pooed' on the deck; the incident provoked much mirth, and *"made me think that a king and all that belong to him are but just as others are".*

The letter columns of the local press, and the in-boxes of local councillors, are full of diatribes about dog poo. Not child poverty; not the global - or even local - environment, not even the local economy - but dog poo. Oddly, when walking H&J, the one glaring reality that faced us every day was the dross dropped by humans - half-eaten meals, empty cans and crisp packets, glass and plastic bottles of every description - the glass bottles often deliberately broken - and piles of vomit. On Saturday and Sunday mornings we could almost wade through this detritus, which seemed to have a genius for avoiding every litter bin in sight. Yet not a whisper about this from any of the worthy souls who were hollering from the rooftops about dog poo...

How times have changed! In the Victorian era, 'pure finding' was a useful occupation: 'pure', or dog poo, was used in the process of tanning leather. As they say, *'where there's muck there's brass'.* Even as recently as the first half of the 20th century, the application of 'night soil' was a favoured way of adding nutrition to gardens, particularly in the countryside. But there is a fine time-line between what is acceptable, even sensible, and what comes to be regarded, literally or figuratively, as offensive. I recall a story of an allotmenteer, who was much admired by his colleagues, on account of his unstinting labour, and the superb, prize-winning vegetables that he produced with unerring regularity. He almost seemed to be living on his patch. Then someone discovered that he was actually living in the garden shed that bordered his allotment. The cat out of the bag, so to speak, the gent was unceremoniously de-bagged, and sent packing from the site. Clearly, the age of night soil had passed silently into history.

The visual evidence suggests that the French are slightly more relaxed, and slightly less anally retented, about dog-poo. The increasing number of canine-hygiene machines dispensing *sachets* in towns, cities and beauty spots across France suggests, however, that even there, attitudes are changing - and hardening. We British have adopted the French word, 'pisser'; a 'pissotiere' is a French public urinal. Fortunately, in both the UK and France, it is still permissible for dogs to pee in a public place; life would be rendered very difficult, otherwise.

Even so, not everyone takes such a relaxed attitude, even to pee, even in France, where it is still a common sight to see men peeing in public places. Once, returning home from Brittany, we stopped at the usual Air at Broceliande for rest and refreshment. The site was busy with families tucking into lunchtime picnics, either at the many wooden tables provided, or merely sprawled happily upon the grass. Though our boys were secured on leads, and led away from the picnicking multitude, one of them - I think, Hector - had the temerity to cock his leg against a nearby tree. Although Hec was a good ten metres from the nearest people, this act drew a barring of teeth, and a gush of vitriol, from a male silver-back protecting his young family. An argument for dog toilets, perhaps?

Society's increasing - and largely justified - obsession with dog poo ensured that, about the same time that we embraced Hector & Jason into the bosom of our family, the little unexceptional haven of 'the Park' became a place of real menace. The powers-that-be decided to crack down on...dog poo. Though it's naturally biodegradable, nobody actually likes the stuff - whether on the pavement, in local parks, or in any public space. Perhaps, in our minds, it rather uncomfortably resembles human excreta - and our embarrassment about it is reflected in the sheer number of euphemisms that we employ to describe the noxious substance, not to mention toilet humour itself.

But let's be brutally honest: dog poo is a problem. It's estimated that the seven million dogs in the UK deposit 1,000 tons of faeces every day on to our over-crowded streets and parks. There's an old wives tale that dog poo is eaten by birds, so that leaving it lie actually confers a benefit. I'm afraid that that's one old wives tale that holds less water than a sieve. It is true, however, that the magnificent but elusive Purple Emperor butterfly, usually floating aloft oak woodlands, has a penchant for, yes, dog-poo. With this single if remarkable exception, it must be admitted that this is pretty useless and remarkably unpleasant stuff, and can cause serious health problems in the event of human contact. And, pragmatically, getting the dog-stuff on the bottom of your shoe, or worse, bringing it into your house, is deeply unpleasant. So, we're all agreed - left to fester and cause mischief - dog poo is a noxious thing. So, let's - always - clean it up.

There is no reason on Earth why non-dog owners, in particular, should have to put up with this dreadfully anti-social behaviour. It's not the dog's fault - blame the specific, careless dog owner, where possible. At the same time, let us see dog poo as one aspect of a bigger problem: the sheer - and preventable - vastness of ugly, vile litter that blights practically every town, every street and every hedgerow in the land.

No doubt in response to complaints, our local Council began to patrol the local Park, purely to catch dog poo offenders, and to fine them £75, on the spot. These worthy souls would skulk in a brick-built office on the edge of the Park, armed with binoculars that 'swept' the area for any dog walker, and dog, within range.

H&J were the most discreet of dogs, as far as their own *toilette* was concerned. Even their 'poos' were discrete, off-path affairs. Such a doggy sense of decorum. However, despite their decorum, and though I cleaned up in the local Park, as elsewhere, I felt vulnerable, since H&J ran off their leads, were never together - since they had separate agendas - and were nearly always some distance away from me when, inevitably, they would crouch to 'perform'. With Jason, particularly, such acts were always an inconvenience - no pun intended - in the midst of one of his missions. If one so much as blinked the act would be missed. But of course I persevered, and cleaned up - though it often proved remarkably difficult to find the offending poo among the piles of dead leaves and human litter that brought needles and haystacks to mind.

I was often conscious of being watched from afar, as though I was some skulking criminal, or intent on spreading the plague. This gave rise to 'poo stress', since searching for the substance among leaves and mud can be a frustrating, unrewarding experience. On a cold day one might catch a hint of steam, or sometimes the poo would be helpfully deposited on green grass or white tramlines. But often there would be a pretty exhaustive search, without the guarantee of a successful conclusion.

On one occasion a chap with a notebook approached me, and accused me (*"J'accuse!"* he might have said) of *"not clearing up after your dog"*. Now, since I *had* already cleared up after both boys, this caused me no little surprise. *"Show me"*, I demanded. He solemnly marched me across the Park, where he pointed to a pile of poo, nestling under the shade of an elder tree. *"Well"*, I said, *indignantly, "that poo is at least 24 hours old, and nothing to do with us"*. Fresh dog poo glistens - rather like a highly-glazed pot. The official offered no rejoinder to my expert analysis. Clearly, my Sherlock Holmes-like-expertise with regard to the maturity, type and consistency of dog-poo had won the day. However, given my inherent vulnerability - since the boys were rarely by my side, and since we can all make mistakes - I was probably pretty fortunate in avoiding a fine at one time or another, and forever branded as a public nuisance and social outcast.

At the same time that I was inhabiting this 1984-style universe, the detritus - bottles, cans, condoms, packets and food-wrapping - continued to accumulate, un-remarked upon, unhindered, and unpunished.

Given the unforgiving culture surrounding, as it were, dog-poo offences, whenever H&J and I stepped out, we were suitably equipped, and accompanied by a pocketful of plastic bags. Because H&J always shared mealtimes, at the same time of day, (the same food and the same amount), I could fairly accurately predict when a call of nature would occur, and be prepared accordingly. As soon as the act or acts occurred, I would be on the case: the boys would be asked to 'stay', and I would clear up. I became quite adept at this task, and quite proud to perform it. One begins to assume the moral high ground: one is carrying out one's civic duty, and I became cross when, inevitably, I came across large splodges of poo - left by offenders - in the middle of a pavement. As well as being anti-social, and a potential health risk, this behaviour gives every dog 'owner', and every dog, a bad name.

One therefore clears up the pet's poo in every public place. A (charged) poo-bag was proud, proof-positive of my confirmed status as a right-on, respectable member of civic society. Traditionally, however, many dog-walkers have not continued this practice when walking - particularly - in woodland. Increasingly, this is now becoming *de rigeur*; at the very least, the 'stick and flick' method is acceptable as a way of ensuring that unsuspecting strangers do not encounter dog poo in their path. For, if they should fail to see and skip around the poo, they will fall foul of the noxious goo - perhaps spoiling a walk, or even a pair of shoes since, no matter how wonderful the prospect ahead, the victim is henceforth accompanied, step by step, by the most unwanted of smells and substances.

Remember, this stuff will refuse to simply disappear. Either clean it up properly, or use the 'flick a stick' method if walking in woodland. Such social consideration is really quite effortless, and will avoid curses on your head, as some innocent walker steps into the foul mess you, and your charge, have left mouldering behind.

But even some 'baggers up' have odd habits. Residents, and not a few dog carers, are often incensed at the crassness of dog walkers who 'bag up' their pet's poo, only to deposit it beneath a hedge, or in the gutter. Then there's the 'tree toilet' - bags of poo suspended from the branches of trees. This is a sinister - some might say childish - act of rebellion against social conformity, and an affront - for many months - upon the eye and nose of everyone who passes:

> *'Tis shocking to believe -*
> *But I believe we must:*
> *Poo-bags hanged like traitors,*
> *So-silent, seeping dust.*

Near the entrance to our local woods is a small shoulder of earth, a bank that, for as long as I can remember, has been disfigured by the hundreds of - fully charged - poo bags deposited there. It is a disgusting, unsightly spectacle. Recently, I saw a man bravely cleaning up this foetid dung-heap. He glared at me, as I passed: "*Are you responsible for any of this s—t?*" he exclaimed. I vehemently protested my (injured) innocence. This was a reminder that such anti-social behaviour not only smears and disfigures the landscape - it smears the reputation of *every* dog owner, by association.

A message to these bearers of foul tidings, apropos the poo-fairy:

The bin's the thing,
To make the fairy sing:
Spread that foul froth,
And feel the spirit's wrath!

One acquires a certain expertise, or at least dexterity, in cleaning up dog poo - not that it will ever be recognised as an Olympic Sport. Hector & Jason made the chore far from easy, since they were never together in a single place, always in a hurry to squat and move on - and always on the way to somewhere else. This provided just another small challenge, particularly in the Park, in Autumn and Winter. If the day was cold and I was lucky, I might glimpse a spiral of steam rising from the offending spot. Mostly, though, wide swathes of ground were turned to a soggy, squishy brown under the influence of rain and rotting vegetation, and my search would be anxious, as well as guilt-ridden.

And to make matters worse, it's quite amazing just how often a plastic bag will work its way out of one's pocket so that, all too annoyingly, one is faced with a steaming pile of poo armed only with a tissue or two. One just has to 'go in' regardless.

However, for the dogs themselves, toileting is a serious (excuse the pun) business, as well as an absolute inevitability and biological necessity. Toileting has also an important social and personal dimension for the individual dog, and indeed for the dog community. And, when H&J were properly toileted, I felt an odd but personal sense of satisfaction. For this relief, much thanks, as it were.

Surprisingly, H&J also had a rather intense relationship with the poo of other mammals. They loved rolling in horse manure, when fresh and pungent, so that it scented their necks and throats with a thick, sticky goo and sweet, sickly perfume. Jason's favourite sampling place - a little rather like the back of the bike-shed - was the workmen's compound at the local Park, where a good, steaming heap of manure could reliably be found. Despite gates and every other impediment, Jason always 'homed' in to the inviting substance. The smell must have been as enticing to him as the song of the Lorelei was to sailors navigating the River Rhine.

I've been told that, for dogs, a coating of horse or similar poo is their way of disguising their smell, for the purposes of hunting - fooling their unsuspecting prey that the approaching animal is harmless. If so, this instinct must hark back to their 'woolfy' roots. However, H&J also enjoyed rolling in essence of fox - not, to my mind, the kind of smell that might be welcomed by a chicken or hedgehog.

Such habits were an irritant (for me) though H&J expressed genuine surprise at my trying to prevent their assuming the odour of other animals. The very worst of these smells, I'm afraid, was human. Before you emit a gasp, or groan, allow me to explain that most human excrement is, following processing, spread upon the land, as fertiliser. If this comes as a surprise, what did anyone imagine happened to the many millions of tons of the stuff we generate every year? Surely, an example of re-cycling at its best. Slurry is a special kind of fertiliser, applied to farmland. 'Special', because it is the sanitised, processed, treated result of what had been human excrement. 'Special' for Jason because he loved the smell - and would run to, and roll in, the stuff whenever it was available.

For a year or two - perhaps an early example of '*Buy One (ton) Get One Free*', or an irresistible subsidy offer - this fertiliser was deposited in huge piles at the side of local fields, before being spread to improve the soil. Jason in particular seemed to love this *odour de homme:* he would leap into the black stuff and roll around, as though it was a foam bath. He was, of course, miles away from me at this time, but his appearance on return, dark and earthy, and smelling somewhat the opposite of roses, was all the evidence required. I could bear horse - but human? It was horrible.

The be-rolled, slurry-caked Jason was a truly appalling sight - and smell. To Jas, no doubt, the stuff was the perfume of Heaven. But to the world at large, Jason was transformed into the Hound from Hell. Everyone we met along the woodland-way shrank with horror at the dreadful apparition; even Hector drew the line at this stuff, and his was a flexible line indeed.

If the be-caked Jason was an awful sight, even more dreadful was a mistake, when I picked up the wrong poo - that, is, from the wrong dog - and felt truly nauseous. It is cold, foreign, and truly disgusting. If someone were to invent a geiger-counter like device, for homing-in inexorably on one's own dog's poo, he or she would soon be sitting on a fortune. Where there's muck, there's brass.

However, the word most dreaded in the dog world - and indeed every other - is 'diarrhoea'. This ghastly mess is often the result of one's pet indulging in polluted water, (scavenged) contaminated food, or chewing wood. Hector & Jason were masters of all three of these hazards. Feed them the most nutritious, healthy food available, and they still looked forward to finding, and eating, unappetising extras. The dreaded 'it' happened, occasionally, but unpredictably.

Wherever and whenever diarrhoea occurred, it *was* a problem, because it's un-cleanupable. So, I devised an ingenious way of dealing with this, from which I derived no small satisfaction. Returning home, I would quickly repair to the scene of the crime, armed with a charged watering can: the offending substance would then be washed into the gutter, and down the nearest drain. Job done; social status still intact; dogs, oblivious, relaxing at home. Not the best use of time, admittedly - I could have been reading *Fifty Grades of Play.*

Whenever June and I were out of the house - whether at work or at the shops and the boys in - there was a certain, underlying anxiety, which would not be lifted until returning home - hurriedly - and finding a clean carpet. For this relief, yet again, much thanks. H&J were incredibly clean boys, but leaving dogs alone in a locked house, even for an hour or two, can be disastrous. We became adroit, dexterous, as well as philosophical, about the occasional clean-up; just get on with it.

In addition, there were a few occasions when, despite our best preparations, Hector (it was generally Hector) did a 'dump' in potentially embarrassing situations; outside Chatsworth House, as we have seen, and right outside the imposing front portal of Hereford Cathedral. Sir Edward Elgar, resting against his bicycle, looked on; hopefully not too disapprovingly. Well, of course Hector couldn't choose his moment, but there could be few less inappropriate locations. Within a year or so of the Hereford incident, Hector repeated his performance at the entrance to the Cathedral of Bayeux. The moral here is: wherever you go, always carry a ready supply of doggy bags!

In a bedroom, upstairs, in the French cottage, we still have a Chinese washed rug, that was an early victim to a Hector accident. I've washed it again and again, but a faint stain, accusingly, remains.

Eighteen years on, I've resolutely refused to discard said rug.

16: Dogs, and their Owners, in all Dimensions

The more I see of men, the more I admire dogs.

Jeanne M.

None are as fiercely loyal as dog people. In return, no doubt, for the never-ending loyalty of dogs.

Linda Shrieves

The Dog, the Owner, and The Aura

The average dog is a nicer person than the average person.

Andrew A. Rooney

Dog walkers have a proud history and tradition. The practice goes back to the Stone Age, and stirs deep memories of our hunter-gatherer beginnings; the '*hunter home from the hill*', to quote R.L. Stevenson. There is, certainly, community and *camaraderie* amongst dog-walkers, who seem to occupy a special place in society - even though, an hour later, they are transformed - into teachers, mechanics, shop assistants and librarians.

The dog owning/dog walking community is a fascinating and curious tribe; of course, I include myself in it. Dog-walkers come in all shapes, sizes, characters, and roughly equal numbers from both genders. It is dangerous to make any generalisation about this fraternity that will be universally true. They are a diverse set: young, old, friendly, chatty, taciturn, indifferent, haughty, grumpy, hostile - and frequently surprise one with their sheer 57 varieties of humanity. There is, I believe, no typical dog-walker. One develops a range of response mechanisms for dealing with hostility, unfriendliness and sheer rudeness, but far more often than not one encounters an affable bunch of people - meeting with warmth, good humour, breaking news and a constant stream of banter and anecdotes.

Dog walkers are also a fairly anonymous community; we connect for only a few brief moments of time. Often, I would be recognised only as the (un-named) carer of Hector & Jason; there, responsibility - even identity - began and ended. For ten years I was 'Roger' to one dear lady, and happily answered to the sobriquet. At 7.00am on a cold, wet morning, I would have responded to any greeting, however wide of the mark. Even so, walking-out with dogs provides a brief but actual connection with real people that is becoming only too rare in our disconnected, cyber-social world.

Yet every dog walker, by definition, needs his or her dog. Modern dogs inhabit an almost infinite variety of shapes, sizes and characters - as do their owners. And most, like their owners, are 'composites', born to parents who are themselves not a recognised breed. Sometimes, upon enquiry, a proud owner will say that their dog is a 'bitsa' - that is, a little bit of everything. Most of these dogs - pure bred or bitsa/composite - excel in any number of roles, from domestic pet, to working dog, to guide dog, to dogs trained for security and 'sniffer' duties. They are also famous - perhaps infamous - for finding 'lost' treasures, or coming across, 'finding', dead humans. How often do we hear on the news: *"the body was found by a man walking his dog"*. And Pickles, for example, became a celebrity when he found the World Cup, (or Jules Rimet Trophy) embarrassingly stolen in England, shortly before the 1966 World Cup Finals.

Just as there is no such thing as a typical human being, so there is no such animal as the typical dog, It is said that there are more moves on a chessboard than there are atoms in the Universe. Similarly, the personality of the dog. Genetics, again. He or she may be introvert, or extrovert. Happy, or morose. Affectionate, or coolly detached. Devoted, or self-possessed. Gentle, or assertive. Arrogant, or submissive. Clever, or dull. Sharp, or disinterested. Keen to please, or keen to please himself. The dog might be an optimist or pessimist, realist or dreamer, possessive or couldn't-give-a-damn, devious or innocent, sly or straightforward, relaxed or up-tight. A power, or a poop in his pants.

On their own terms, then, not all dogs are alike. Indeed, every dog is different, with its own personality and idiosyncrasies. Even among the same breed, there are more characters than might grace a Dickens' novel. And not all dogs are 'equal'. This may seem politically incorrect, but I am not thinking of the artificial 'pedigree' versus 'mongrel' divide, and am not beholden to financial criteria. The famous quotation from *Animal Farm*, '*All animals are equal but some are more equal than others*' is surely Orwell's critique of the abuse of basic human values of fairness and equality of treatment. No: like diamonds or people, some dogs have greater depths, more facets, more lustre, more brilliance, than others. To what extent this reflects the attention and love of their carers, or is an intrinsic part of their being, is open to question. I only know from experience that there are greater differences - in character, as well as in the more subjective 'appeal' - between individual dogs than between the beautiful Miranda and the 'foul witch' Hecate, in *The Tempest*.

In reality, a dog is a subtle, complex, unique blend of many different qualities and facets - some apparently inherent, some brought out and honed by their experiences, and some encouraged by the human investment in training and mentoring him or her. But dogs are not all equally good, or attractive, or faithful, or, if you like, 'special'. Experience alone will tell you when you have - as we most certainly did - the extraordinary real deal.

And I can't, hand on heart, pretend that I like all dogs any more than I can pretend that I like all human beings. Sometimes it's a matter of personalities that don't gel; in other cases it's simply a matter of abhorrent and extremely unpleasant behaviour. We need make no apologies.

There are good dogs, bad dogs, and in-between dogs - as again, there are people. Bad people create bad dogs - very, very easily. Behind every vicious dog is a deplorable human being. Conversely, it can take a good person a great deal of time and patience to transform a badly reared and consequently wild, nasty and brutish dog into a decent and sociable companion.

In fact, I view dogs with both a sympathetic and a slightly critical eye. Dogs that yap, yap, yap all day, like verbal diarrhoea, are not my kind of dogs. I really cannot abide noisy, growly, angry, snappy, bitey dogs. Aggressive, violent, vicious dogs are certainly not my type of dogs either, and I fail to comprehend why they are anybody's, unless the owner and dog - *aka* Bill Sykes - have these traits in common, and enjoy the sense of power that is this behaviour's justification.

Whether we like it or not, we live in a human-centric world, where everything is assessed in terms of human values and benefits. So the human-dog relationship is complex, and fragile. Certainly, not everyone likes dogs; some people hate them. To these folk, dogs are nasty, smelly, dirty, defecating morons - and dangerous to boot. Hateful, horrible hounds. The philosopher, Rene Descartes, (*'I think, therefore I am'*) regarded dogs as unfeeling, unthinking automatons - and treated them accordingly. Recent research by the University of Bristol, however, has revealed the astonishing adaptability and responsiveness of dogs, and the range of abilities they possess. Mr Canine can be trained for multifarious tasks that benefit and support their owners, carers and the community at large.

Over the years, and over many thousands of walks, H&J enjoyed a huge range of encounters with their canine colleagues. There's a parallel here with the 'Trinity' - Father, Son and Holy Spirit. That is, there's the Carer, the Cared-for, and the Aura. Experience taught me to look for the aura - since I then knew what to expect from any encounter. The vast proportion of these encounters passed off enjoyably, and peacefully, as we knew they would - *"good aura, Jas?"*. A casual sniff, a wag of the tail - in greeting or occasionally in warning - and we all went on our merry way.

Certainly, the majority of pets I have been fortunate to meet - many thousands of dogs, of every conceivable breed and type - have generous, friendly, open natures, though with their own distinct personalities. Very, very few dogs, in my experience, pose a risk to humans in the great outdoors. Sadly, too many - *one* would be too many - pose a danger to their fellow dogs, whether by outright aggression, or bullying and intimidation. *"He's not vicious, he's just a little excitable"*. I see. It sounds innocuous enough, but such excuses-up-front often get the warning sirens clanging.

H&J took a mild, friendly interest in their fellow creatures - friendly and polite, but on the whole preferring their own company, and pursuing their own interests. Neither 'Miss Ogyny' nor 'Master Bate' was in evidence - just a polite nod to either boy or girl. Yet when socially-impoverished dogs are unleashed on the community, how many times has a self-serving owner said to his or her bullying, growling critter - *"they don't want to play"* as if my own boys were unfriendly and stand-offish. *"If you can't be nice..."* was a common defence mechanism from someone with (usually) an over-zealous German Shepherd, or Staffie. It's a strange, surreal world, in which *"He's a bit funny"* is code for *"He's an aggressive little sod"*. Similarly, *"She's a little bit funny"* translates into: *"She's the barmiest bitch in the Black Country"*. The common-place *"He only wants to play"* translates as: *"A little bit of thuggery - and buggery - never hurt anyone"*. The tongue-in-cheek *"He's never done that before"* is really... *"Well, if we ignore the 999 other occasions"*. Or, in plural, *"well, they've never done that before"*. *"Sure, and my name is Bond; James Bond"*.

So, inevitably, there is a darker side to the delightful, innocent pastime of walking one's dog. Only too often, when one is minding one's own business, enjoying a quiet walk, one is imposed upon by two nasty, complementary, pieces of work - the dog and its owner, working in cahoots. It is amazing how inventive some dog-owners can be in defence of their errant and aggressive pets. An expression of injured surprise - that might do justice to Lawrence Olivier - generally accompanies a brute launching into attack mode. *"He's just trying to be friendly"*. No; really? *"You should control your dog"*. I could go on. But, we always took it in our stride - the boys and I - as cheerfully and with as much good humour as we could muster.

H&J were always playing, but playing their own game. One learns to shrug one's shoulders: if the boys had been interested and interfering, this would soon have drawn calls of *"call those dogs off!"* or *"put them on their leads!"*.

I generally found 'live and let live' a useful dictum. I always greeted fellow dog walkers, while knowing that, on so many occasions, my greeting would be returned by a surly silence. But this extended social experiment showed me that the glass is, as often as not, at least half full.

In addition, it's fascinating how often dogs bear an uncanny resemblance to their owners - in terms of personality, temperament, and even physical similarity. William Hogarth's self-portrait includes his pet pug, Trump, sitting by his master's side; Hogarth claimed that he increasingly came to look like Trump, and the picture appears to confirm this. As though this were not authority enough, Miranda Hart, writing in *Is It Just Me?* confirms that dogs and their owners, for whatever reason, often start to share characteristics. A smiling, chatty person is generally in possession of a happy, smiling dog. A taciturn, un-chatty person often has an aloof, uncommunicative dog. A miserable, gruff person is often accompanied by a sour, un-likeable hound. A decidedly unpleasant individual has found - or, more likely created - an unstable, even dangerous, mutt.

If all this tells me anything, it is that the personality of dog owners and, particularly, the way that they raise and treat their pets, profoundly influences, for better or worse, the characters and lives of our seven million pet dogs.

Dogs, Dangers, and Divas...

Kind sir, dear girl, how sweet you walk this way;
I trust you and your charge will smile on us this day.

Colin Hill

Golden Retrievers, as a breed, can derive from several different lines, or strains. There are the show-dog Retrievers, whose looks and progeny are central to their *raison d'etre*. There are working-dog lines, whose performance 'in the field' is what counts, and what sets them apart. And there are the pet or family Retriever strains, which may be mixes of the former two, or take a meandering line of their own.

Hector & Jason were working dogs, certainly on their mother's side, while their father had a good splash of show dog, as well as working dog, credentials. All will be pure bred Retrievers; all have their distinctive character, and other traits. While there will be a strong 'family' connection, there will always be surprising facets awaiting discovery. However, an abiding and much-loved characteristic is the innate friendliness and affability of this breed - a characteristic that H&J shared in spades.

Invariably, Hector & Jason were perfectly behaved to other people, and other dogs. I never knew Jason to become angry, or for his hackles to rise. Hector's hackles rose only very occasionally, if an attempt was made to intimidate him - usually by jumping up his face, or mauling him. Such attempts were always firmly rebuffed.

For the most part - and H&J's wild runs minimised these daily encounters - it was all very good-humoured and friendly, with dog or human; Jason's was a wonderful, sympathetic temperament. And Hector just wanted to mind his own, and our, business, and would respond assertively to another dog only if grievously provoked. Truly, they were models of good behaviour. I trusted both boys completely with humans and dogs, and was proud of each boy's different but equally superb, genuine character.

Each day we would stroll along, enjoying our walk, and always with a friendly greeting for passers by; though sometimes ignored, and sometimes delivering said greeting through gritted teeth. Still, it's worth persevering. We are more likely to talk to 'friends' on Facebook or Twitter than we are to talk to neighbours, or near neighbours. Social media, blogs, texts, e-mail, and i-phone provide a sort of fake intimacy that masks a great deal that is possibly dis-connected about modern life.

Whilst dog walking can expose one to occasional irritations and hassle, it has the major advantage of bringing us into contact with new people, and old friends, in a variety of situations, each and every day. When dog-walking we are obliged to cross paths and, at least, exchange a greeting or two with the people one passes. There are dog walkers who love to - perhaps need to - share their stories. These nearly always relate to family and friends. There, I thought, complacently, walks an adulterer, with many affairs to his name. And there stalks a 'dogger'...whose nefarious activities are *sans* dogs. There, too...but, perhaps, enough...

I'm sure this gentle human contact - of all shades - has benefited my psyche over the years - a small bonus (as with keeping fit) to balance against the time-poverty thus created: *why have I never found time to paint the lounge/clean up the garden/empty the dishwasher?*. But, when all is said and done, which activity has provided most satisfaction, most memories - and most fun?

However, there are downsides. Displacement is a regular theme or, should I say, irritant. What do I mean by displacement?

"I wouldn't want to have to clean those dogs!".
"Well, don't worry, you won't have to!".
"I wouldn't want to have to pay their food bill!".
"Yes, it's a good thing that that's my job".

And so on; is it just me? So much easier to say - as many did - *"what bloody marvellous dogs!"*. How gratifying: such generous comments made up for all those gratuitously irrelevant, throw-away, verbal grenades. Go on - make someone's day. Or else:

"Good God! what a frightful state they're in", he smugly said to me;
"While my own close-cropped mutt is clean as clean can be."
"Why, then, you're doubly fortunate", I ventured to reply:
"Since I must wash my hairy head, while yours is bare and dry."

And then there's the gratuitously offensive. Once, we were approached by a tall, bald chap who enquired: *"Will you have any more dogs"* (quizzical response) *"when you've lost these?"*. (Mmm. *"And will you replace your wife, when you've lost the present Mrs Smith?"* I thought). *"I've really not given it any thought - the boys are still very much with me"*, was my cool reply.

Some months prior to this, another tall, bald, but wizened chap looked at the jauntingly energetic H&J, and remarked: *"Isn't it sad when they reach the last quarter of their lives?"*. *"Why"*, I responded, *"which quarter are you in?"*.

By way of contrast, how often have I seen stressed executives, returning home in their shiny cars and shiny suits, only to set out again seconds later - but this time in their shabby hats and shabby clothes - shining, smiling, dog in hand. It is the essence of the man-dog relationship: a journey of discovery, in harmony, together. One is never on one's own when with a canine companion. A man on his own - particularly in a rural setting - may evoke suspicion; a man with a dog, rarely. It is the perfect - if never a partnership of equals - mammal/mammal relationship.

And how uplifting to exchange a hearty word or two on a grim, filthy morning. We were all exposed to the elements, in dense woodland, and with our dogs, so had at least those factors in common. Whatever the inclement weather - rain, sleet, hail or snow - the universal cry resounds: *"We must be mad!"*. Indeed; but we are also alive, and in love with life. Since dog walking is something in the nature of an escape or release from normal life and its cares and concerns, the chief item of conversation is inevitably the weather. If I knew someone well, then a little topical news, even politics, might be ventured. Still, there was very little that might be termed 'personal' chat since this would penetrate the bubble that surrounds each individual on their little parallel journey, escaping the gravitational pull of worldly concerns.

One of the great benefits of dog ownership is that it practically obliges the owner, or carer, to set forth into the wider world - including parks, commons and woodlands. And, in addition to the exercise, there is the added benefit of being in the outdoors, amidst a plenitude of nature. So it is odd that it is rare for anyone to remark on the beauty of the surroundings - on the delicate light, the wild flowers, the trees in fresh leaf, the intoxicating diversity and constant change, as life ebbs and flows with the weather and the seasons. Perhaps nature is appreciated - but silently, privately; it is our little personal secret, a gift to ourselves, and not to be shared with unbelievers.

One does meet some extraordinary people, and partake of some extraordinary conversations. *"I'd never have another Golden Retriever"* the woman said, rather caustically, her highlights glowing in the afternoon sun. *Pourqui?* *"They moult too much. I could never wear black"*. So there you have it. Put all your cares away.

Please, God, save me from traffic and stupid people,
The stench of endless juggernauts, and diesel;
Give me only birds, and butterflies, and trees,
And a green panoply, and canopy, of trees.

Save me from: "are they rescue dogs, or legal eagles?"
"Good madam, does money flutter down like leaves?"
"Do they do tricks, or do they leap from steeples?"
"No, madam, they run, and run, and then reprise."

And then there is the kerfuffle, as three dogs engage in rough sport, when it is not uncommon to hear:

The angry voices of three gentlemen
Crying sharp, and loud, and clear: Ben! Ben! BEN!

The three Bens, of course, take no notice whatsoever, continuing their mock, or even real, battle, until exhausted, defeated, bored, or called to account by their owners. The other term beloved of dog owners is 'come', in the sense of (of course) 'come here'. Everyone shouting "*come!*" at the same time is a recipe for confusion. Ideally, we should coin our own, unique word, perhaps 'heel' or 'do' or 'get' and train our dogs accordingly. And, if they are really serious, call the dog Benjamin. That would quickly send him scurrying home, tail between his legs. Or perhaps life is too short...

The long years of H&J's development and prime were lived against the backdrop of an economic golden age, bringing with it unparalleled prosperity for most; but it was hard indeed to find any recognition of this good fortune amongst the dog walkers we greeted every day. Collectively, we have an unerring ability to turn silk purses into sows ears. Perhaps this reflects the human condition. For most of us, I've no doubt, Utopia itself would be found wanting.

In saying this, I am assuming that dog walkers are a pretty representative sample of English humanity. So, to the English mind, the problem with (everything) is the mysterious, indiscriminate 'them' - responsible for everything from health and safety and bungling bureaucracy to litter and rising prices. The problem with France is of course the French. And the problem with the weather is...the weather. So, three days of sunshine are viewed as the prelude to drought and famine, while three days of rain are (clearly) the beginning of an almighty flood, and 'the end' of life on Earth.

Whatever the prevailing news and events, this is inevitably viewed with horror and disbelief. To the hundreds of cheerful souls who we've met on our long ramblings, I've no doubt that there was nothing I could have said that would have lightened the burden on their back, or smoothed the creases on their brow. Money, a good roof over one's head, health, fitness - the company of a good dog, on a good walk - are clearly not enough. I try, always, to be cheerful, and to add cheer; life has to be better than the alternative, and our life is so infinitely better, in all its fundamentals, than the lives of so many on this planet, not to mention the countless generations who have trodden the Earth before us.

I often reflect, though, that the English have a 'blue' streak running through their character; a glass-half-empty take on life. Despite decades of prosperity - I hear the grinding of teeth, even as I write - and no war or conflict on the door-step to wreak havoc on our health and happiness, we still find so much to complain about. It is as if the welfare state, the NHS, a free society under the rule of law, increasing longevity, fresh food from across the planet, global travel and - icing on the cake - wall-to-wall TV and the ubiquitous internet - had passed most people by. Don't just take my word for it. In *How Do We Fix This Mess?* Robert Peston writes: *'What we have to recognise in Britain, much of Western Europe and the US is that we are already very wealthy societies, and our capacity to become relatively wealthier - when we face such competition from the vibrant economies of the developing world - is limited'.* Oh dear.

And Andrew Marr, towards the conclusion of his tour-de-force *A History of the World,* reminds us that *'we have to remember the good times brought to hundreds of millions of people who have experienced peace and plenty on a scale that has no historical precedent'.* A little later, writing of the post-war years, and contrasting Western experience with that of Maoist China, Mr Marr reiterates that *'Europe and America luxuriated in a plenty and a personal freedom that humankind had never before known'.*

A conversation - in a dream - between a (deceased) grand-parent and their middle-aged grandson might go something like this:

"So, I hear you own your own house?"

"Well, er, we actually have two, if you count the holiday home in Dorset."

"And a car?"

"Er, we have four, actually. Of course Jackie has her own, as do the heir and spare" (chuckle).

"And, apparently, you enjoy holidays abroad?"

"Yes, let me think, we had...er.. five last year - Nice, Tuscany, Barbados, Rio and a cruise - obviously not counting the Dorset trips. We may have to trim our sails a bit this year (chuckle) - austerity and all that."

"And the world wide web?"

"Don't ask..."

"Well, for most of us, 'abroad' meant the Western Front. A small piece of advice - if you ever do get to the Pearly Gates and meet St Peter, don't greet him with 'Do you know who I am?'

And, oh, if - and I do mean if - you ever enter the said Pearly Gates, be sure to catch up with Buster, and Dolly, after you've settled in."

Though, clearly, we do not live in the 'best of all possible worlds', there can be no doubt that, for most people in the developed world, this is the best moment in human history. It's the same for most dogs, though they, too, may pine for some mythical Nirvana. A dog in Shakespeare's day, or for that matter in that of Dickens, (aka the dreadful Sykes' Bullseye) faced a daily struggle for an existence that was, to quote Thomas Hobbes, *'nasty, brutish and short'.* Today, in the UK at least, a dog is more likely to suffer from obesity than starvation.

Though there is yet more to do, and not all dogs - or indeed people - have come this far, we have already come a very long way.

In truth, there is much to be angry about: the painful death of millions of infants each year, from hunger, disease or conflict; the obscenity of war, and violent deaths suffered by vast numbers of innocent civilians each and every day; and torture, sexual abuse and slavery on a scale that would have astonished Genghis Khan. An unblinking use of terror to murder, literally, innocents abroad. The merciless destruction of wild and wonderful animal species, from lions and tigers, to gorillas and orang utans, to elephants, to whales. But no-one yet has confronted me, and wailed: "*What can we do together to reduce infant mortality/end global hunger/save the planet?*".

Perhaps these issues are just too big for our small but crowded lives. We want to walk our dogs, have a chat, and return home for warmth and a coffee. But, just as we have tried to provide Hector & Jason with lovely lives we have also, I hope, been keenly aware of the big issues that stain the conscience of the world. Perhaps it is me - intolerably smug and insufferable. If one tries to smile or speak to a passer-by, the response - all too often - is one of disdain and distrust. I often thought how many fellow 'walkers' appeared to be both deaf and mute, since they neither passed nor returned any greeting.

Sometimes - ignored or looked at askance after a cheery "*Good Morning!*" - I would shrug my shoulders and mutter: "*Piss off, then!*". My words were often lost on the breeze but, if I was lucky, they might be rewarded with a quizzical backwards glance.

To Loathe, to Love

When the battle's lost and won,
Then, forsooth, the loving's done.

Colin Hill

Why do so many of us love dogs? I have given this question much thought, since love is the inspiration for this book. The relationship is a complex, fascinating, multi-faceted phenomenon. And we continue to maintain a schizophrenic attitude to this most prominent of mammal species. Both a love affair, and a loathe affair. Sweet, faithful Lassie versus the big, bad wolf.

Again, why? Irrefutably, the closeness of the rapport between these two species, man and dog, is unprecedented in any other relationship. You do practically everything together; are together, work permitting, practically 24/7. You invest so much time together, in each other. So much energy, so much intensity is invested in this partnership. You share quality time together, on the most exciting rambles and favourite excursions. You respond to each other; share experience, even memories. At the same time, your dog is dependent on you, for food and shelter, and perhaps for protection in the great outdoors. It is not a partnership of equals, but it is, at its best, a partnership made in Heaven.

Day after day, year after year, the bond between you intensifies, strengthens, grows deeper. If there are closer relationships in your life, they will be with your partner, your children, perhaps with your parents and very close friends; but even they will be, as they must be, different in nature, different in content, different in character. And there are very few of us who can resist love: the knowledge that your dog loves you must, all things being equal, help you to love him. But that love is earned, as well as freely given. It is not the intoxication of a teenage crush, however exhilarating - and painful - that may be: it is deep, and vital, and immensely strong. It is derived from life, is for life, and even beyond life. He is yours and, to a very considerable extent, you are his. Quite simply, this will be one of the deepest, closest, most heartfelt, relationships you will ever experience.

Today - since we are no longer obliged to hunt for our food, or need protection from predators - we are fortunate in being able to concentrate on the essentials of the relationship. The companionship of a dog - where you can give them quality time, and a loving home - will help keep you sane, healthy, and happy - at the least, happier. And the companionship of a dog will take you 'out of yourself' - surely a good thing, since to live only with oneself, 24/7, and forever, is a daunting prospect.

Over the years I have witnessed many, many dog-owners - and their dogs - who seem to be constantly on the move, walking incessantly back and forth; clearly, the man-dog relationship is central to their lives. Perhaps their charges - now Highland Terriers - began life as Irish Wolfhounds. Yet, these pets are, at least, generally content with their lot, and well socialised with other dogs, and their respective owners.

Certainly, the vast majority of man-dog relationships are good, positive, life-enhancing ones - for both owner, and pet.

Sadly, it is to another type of dog owner that I must turn my gaze: dog owners at the extreme end of the spectrum. For, sadly, and inexplicably, many dog owners - and their dogs - are rarely, if ever, seen: the dogs are imprisoned behind gates, in back-yards, even in garages and sheds, rarely seeing others of their kind, and unable to enjoy the freedom of parkland, common or woods. Such owners - and those who mistreat and abuse their pets - inhabit the remotest regions of the canine universe; their dogs lead impoverished and miserable lives. It is often these dogs, however, that, when let loose on high-days and holidays, behave anti-socially - even dangerously.

Whilst, to re-emphasise, the vast majority of dog owners are responsible, caring people, as one would expect, it is the exceptions that always claim public attention: people whose dogs are status symbols, or trained for their aggression, or encouraged to become menacing weapons by their owner's side, for motives which must remain a mystery. So, Hector, Jason and I had a few - thankfully few - nasty experiences. As stated in an earlier Chapter, most of these experiences occurred on Sundays. It is aura time again: this time, bad aura, threatening aura.

One - misleadingly - inviting afternoon, we were striding nonchalantly towards Ridgehill Woods, only a couple of hundred yards from home, when a white, husky-looking dog, only taller and heavier, strode into view, absent of lead. He was followed at a short distance by a middle-aged woman, who remained indifferent, and unmoved, as the said dog launched an unprovoked and violent attack on Jason. Then, as I struggled to extricate the vicious brute, the good woman in turn launched her own unprovoked attack - on me - pummelling my chest with her fists. I retaliated by pushing her away, while telling her sharply to control her dog, and go away. The joys of walking in suburbia - on a Sunday, of course - while (trying to) mind one's one business.

There was a second occasion when we were attacked - an emotionally-charged word which reflects the feeling of personal assault, even if 'only' the dogs are assaulted. That I recall the incident so clearly also shows, I hope, the rare nature of these events. We were about to enter the local woods and I had slipped H&J off their leads. Almost immediately a muscular bull terrier hove into view, accompanied by two women (mother and daughter?) - the younger woman pushing a pram, presumably with a child in it. Without rhyme or reason, the demented animal flew at Hector, grabbing him around the throat, and forcing him back towards the road. Jason was terror-stricken, and unsure what to do: his instinct was to run - again towards the road. I yelled at the women to control their dog, but their feeble calls went unheeded by said dog, which was intent only on savagery.

Taking my life in my hands, I started to assail the dog, hoping that this might check its aggression. At this point, the animal was pulled off a very shaken Hector, and returned to his lead, The chaotic scene was accompanied by much heated shouting and swearing, (in my direction). I remonstrated with these two - er, ladies - that their dog's disgraceful behaviour should have been prevented by its being controlled, and that their animal presented a danger to other dogs. The response? With breath-taking insolence, I was airily informed that my dogs had attacked theirs, and that if I carried on with my accusations I would have cause to regret it. A mobile phone was airily brandished, and one of the 'ladies' began to make a call to her paramour, describing me in suitably unsavoury terms (madman threatens gentler sex).

Seeing that my entreaties had fallen on deaf ears - or worse - I steered the game H&J towards the woods, later examining the stricken Hector for injuries. Luckily, because of the dense fur around his throat, and the speed of my reaction, his injuries were modest, although the flesh had been broken. It's the child I feel sorry for.

The bigger point is that there are many thousands of dog attacks every year - that is, dog on human, with around 7,000 people needing hospital treatment in 2018 for dog inflicted injuries. That is, of course, 7,000 incidents too many. And, in the last 10 years, twenty-one people have been killed by dogs in the United Kingdom; 13 of these were children. These are shocking and depressing statistics that tell a graphic story of neglect, stupidity and worse, since many of these animals have been made violent by their owners. It is the (relatively few) anti-social dog owners who cause dogs, and dog ownership, to fall into disrepute. In today's society, it is surely unacceptable to use dogs as weapons, or as an extension of the aggressive owner, or to wilfully mistreat or neglect a sentient animal. And a shocking 50,000 dogs are abandoned by their owners, annually; it is estimated that around 20,000 of these animals are euthanised each year. This is a sad reflection on our double standards towards dog care and welfare.

Measures to ensure responsible dog ownership - strict licensing, a test or training for dog ownership, perhaps the phasing out of certain breeds - which seem to act as a magnet for anti-social individuals - would all help. However, sadly, the most irresponsible people will nearly always find a way to flout the system, and continue to 'give a dog a bad name'.

There's all sorts of excuses for unacceptable behaviour - frightened dogs, maltreated dogs, neglected dogs, crazy dogs, down-right dangerous dogs - but no justification. Our role, our responsibility, is to encourage the dog to achieve its potential for good in human society. Any less is a travesty. The infliction of injury is unpardonable, and redounds on the owner at least as much as on the dog. Personally, I walk my boys for recreation, not for them - or me - to be attacked and traumatised.

Fortunately, Hector, Jason and I encountered such unpleasantness only rarely. When incidents happen they are, therefore, only too memorable. Certainly, the vast majority of dog carers are at the other end of the spectrum: caring for, and loving their companions; happy, fulfilled pets with happy, fulfilled owners. These owners may be busy, time-poor and pressured: but, taking a cue from their pets - and partly because of their pets - they are in love with life.

But to get back to the dogs themselves: for me, the dogs I have met have always been at least as interesting as their owners, exceeding the latter in variety and often in personality. Their range is extraordinary: from Great Danes to Jack Russells, with a huge diversity of 'Heinz 57 varieties' - cross-breeds, mongrels, or composites - of indeterminate and often exotic parentage. My, or should I say our, situation was a little different, since few dog walkers are immune to their pets being so admired by passers by.

However, of course H&J were generally nowhere to be seen, and I was sometimes identified as a member of the dog-walking fraternity only by the leads slung around my neck. My lonesome treks were the cause of endless banter, and I often envied my colleagues' quiet life. But then I would catch sight of my boys: they heard and saw me, and came hurtling in my direction, huge grins on their excited faces, burning up the ground. My spirits revived, re-born even, we sped home - H&J again charging ahead - until reaching the stile that marked the end of the woodland trail.

One's dogs can be the subject of special, touching, moments, too. One morning, at a local farm shop, a lady approached us and asked whether she could stroke the boys, who were reclining in the back of the car. She explained that she had recently lost her own, 15-year-old, Retriever, and just wanted to touch a fellow creature. *"You think they will go on forever"*, she added, sadly. The brutal facts are that, while good genes and great care can maximise the life of one's beloved pet, 12 years is a 'good' age for a Golden Retriever; 13 or 14 years is heading for the exceptional. According to internet research, a 14 year old Golden Retriever is equivalent to 88 years in human terms. Beyond that is the canine equivalent of a centenarian.

This stark reality can be very hard to accept for the devoted carer, ourselves included, and we will return to this issue later. Suffice to say, now, that the facts of this mortality, which is a given, and the closeness of the bond forged with one's dear friend, can give rise to extraordinary grief. Again, at this point I will confine myself to accentuating the positive: a good, even a great, life, and a life shared, generates a vast wealth of precious memories.

Sometimes our own daily round would be marked by the absence, a sort of pregnant intermission, of familiar faces that, continuing for days and weeks, would become unmistakable in their import. Had little old Bertie passed away? Indeed, was it Bert himself who had shuffled off this mortal coil? More terrible even than the loss of your beloved pet dog would be the beloved pet dog's loss - of you.

Seeing one of my boys, a man grinned and enquired: *"Would you swap him for the missus?"*. *"I wouldn't wish to cause offence"*, I laughed.

And swelled with pride; and rest my case.

PART 2: FRENCH LEAVE

17: To France!

Can this cockpit hold
The vasty fields of France?

Henry V - William Shakespeare

Fair stood the winds for France
When we our sails advance,
Nor now to prove our chance
Longer will tarry.

To the Cambro-Britons - Michael Drayton

We had owned a small cottage in the Normandy countryside since the mid-90s. It was, and is, idyllic: built of granite in the 1840s, roses climbing around the door, and set deep in the bocage countryside. The plot is veritable heaven - a cottage nestling in the 'Suisse Normande': a dream of green.

The fabled Suisse Normande, or little Switzerland, is a defined geographical region of Calvados and Orne. If the sobriquet is a little overblown, it is yet an area of dramatic cliffs and dense, wooded hillsides; swift running streams; picture-postcard villages lost in time; quaint, tumble-down farms, smothered in orchard and pasture; picturesque Norman churches; opulent hedgerows, perfumed with flowers; and bustling markets, brimming with locally crafted cream, cheeses and cider. So, if it's not exactly Alpine, the cliffs and gorges, tumbling streams, and flower-filled meadows clearly echo the lustre of their Swiss cousins.

Elizabeth David, in her inimitable style, sets out the attractions perfectly:

'How deeply our own roots are in Normandy quickly becomes apparent to the English traveller. The churches, the old timbered houses, the quiet villages, the fruit orchards, the willows hanging over the streams...'

I would only add that, in the years since these words were written, in *French Provincial Cooking* (1960) the English landscape has changed far more radically than its Norman counterpart. Some years before we settled in Normandy, I had glimpsed a young waitress step out of a restaurant on to the pavement; in her hand a small parcel. After walking a short distance, the girl turned into the gateway of a small-holding, where she empted the contents of her bag into the midst of a waiting flock of chickens. The flock responded excitedly, and noisily, to this gift of left-overs. I was charmed by this glimpse of a life that Britain has left behind, and instinctively drawn towards it. I wanted a slice of such a life-style - the practical closeness to the earth, and the values that it seemed to imbibe and succour.

We were delighted to acquire the rustic cottage in this little corner of Normandy, and worked hard to make it comfortable and homely. And we established a wildlife-friendly garden, with a small pond, and orchard, with fruit of all kinds. There was a scattering of homes and farms nearby, but all was relaxed and tranquil. In the early days my parents had been among the first guests. My father emerged from the car, and scanned the landscape, before declaring: *"this would make a great caravan park"*. I'm relieved to report that, more than twenty years later, the caravan park has still to emerge.

Apart from electricity and water, there were no facilities; no gas, no telephone, no TV. Perfect, in fact. All that was missing were dogs - it was ideal dog country. From the very start, we had wanted our 'boy' to travel to France, but it had simply not been possible for the travel-loving Victor to accompany us. The 'Atlantic Wall' was impassively still in place. But a new era was dawning. The new, (Labour, as it happened) Government had now passed legislation that allowed pets to journey beyond Britain's shores, to a variety of foreign destinations. We were excited that, at last, the chance had come to venture over the Channel, with the still adolescent H&J. We were eager to introduce H&J to Normandy - and Normandy to them - at the earliest opportunity.

As the clocks and church bells struck midnight on 31 December 1999, firework displays, excited parties and universal great expectations greeted the new Millennium. As always, it was to prove a triumph of hope over reality. But not for us: the Pet Passport Scheme was launched in February 2000. We were determined to take advantage of the new possibilities, to ensure that H&J could accompany us to Normandy from the earliest possible date. We were eager to seize at once the lifetime of adventure and experience that had been made possible. We had two young Retrievers, barely a year old, extravagantly good-looking and brimming with new life. Though mentally still very much teenagers, H&J were now approaching their early physical maturity. It was perfect timing.

As soon as the wheels of bureaucracy permitted we discussed the necessary procedure with our local vet, who had been authorised by DEFRA. The (of course obligatory) rabies inoculation was then administered, and microchips inserted under the skin, in the boys' shoulder area. (Hector's chip always remained where originally inserted; Jason's - no doubt because of his relentless pursuit of the spirit of the forest - moved rather alarmingly, over time, towards the top of his right leg). Frustratingly, the requirements of the Scheme meant a six months wait, following the anti-rabies inoculation, before travel was possible. The vet needed to be certain that the rabies treatment had proved effective. Having proven successful, via a blood test, the necessary forms were completed, checked and re-checked, and by the late Summer of 2000AD we were ready to sail.

In fact, a year earlier, June and I had encountered probably the very first dog to travel to France by ferry, at least in modern times. (I have no doubt that Romans and Normans travelled to and fro without worrying too much about rabies restrictions). The dog in question was a handsome, extremely well behaved, and good natured, German Shepherd - a guide dog for his companion, a D-Day veteran who had been blinded by enemy fire on the landing beaches. The veteran hero was returning to the scene of such powerful history, and memory. This gentleman was sitting with his dog in the ferry's self-service area, very comfortably and, from every point of view, very properly.

We should have had no illusions that Hector & Jason would be travelling in such style. For the dogs that were to follow - no doubt, guide dogs excepted - the travel arrangements were to be very different: we had to make the boys as comfortable as possible for their long crossing within their own vehicle; with bedding, water, windows open, and hopefully a sea breeze blowing through the vessel.

The following February, 2001, brought news of a different kind. Foot and mouth disease had been discovered in various parts of the UK, and the policy response was to slaughter millions of farm animals in order to eliminate the spread of the disease as quickly as possible. The inconvenience to the public was nothing compared to the tragedy being visited upon the lives of farmers and their livestock, but the impact was memorable, nonetheless. With the genius for over-the-top response that has become endemic to the body politic, the Government took a 'shut down' approach, and for around a year the public were prevented from entering the countryside: woodlands, fields and meadows became no-go areas.

Although there were no sheep or cattle within miles of our home, we were essentially denied access to our usual haunts. In fact, we were restricted to our local Park, and the myriad of routes around our urban village. Though - in the circumstances - it was not a great sacrifice, I marvelled at the public's acquiescence in what, on reflection, seems to have been an over-blown reaction to the crisis. Looking back, it's remarkable how the public adhered to these injunctions, which could hardly be rigorously enforced; but public opprobrium, silent but all-seeing, is a powerful force. The public mood resembled the blitz spirit, and it seemed unpatriotic to question it.

So, with Hector & Jason's early trips to France, in 2001 and 2002, we were treated to chemical dips at the ports, with vehicles' tyres subjected to a disinfectant wash as they passed through. But it was a huge relief to actually arrive in France, where there seemed to be no disease present, and where H&J could exercise whenever and wherever we chose. Tasting freedom again - until now taken for granted - was a relief and real delight.

The pet passport process itself was the opposite of straightforward. The multiplicity of forms, demands and rigorous checks seemed designed to ensure that the process was as complex, fraught and stressful as bureaucratic ingenuity could devise. We understood that this was a major innovation, and clearly understood also that rabies must at all costs be kept out of the UK. Even so, the initial DEFRA process was a nightmare that seemed to have little to do with rabies itself. The plethora of forms was based on the premise that (a farmer?) was exporting and importing livestock, and the form-filling and continuous checks - and worry that someone (yourself, or your vet, or the French vet) might have put a comma in the wrong place - generated a great deal of anxiety.

The penalty, if any discrepancy were unearthed, was that the dog or dogs could not re-enter the UK, at least without a great deal of trouble and drama, and possibly six months in quarantine. The slightest error could also condemn us to remain in France - perhaps not such a bad fate, but employers expected our return to duty, on time and without fail. Still, we had no qualms: this was absolutely the right course of action for us. These were risks we were prepared to take and, thankfully, we were rewarded handsomely, with a multitude of new opportunities that would greatly enrich all of our lives.

If the main source of inconvenience - and anxiety - during these early years, in particular, was this continuous checking and re-checking of paperwork, micro-chips and dogs, the odd thing was that the French - and every other nationality in Europe (since dogs travel quite easily throughout the European Union) - were quite relaxed about these healthy, handsome British dogs. And rabies is a distant memory throughout most of France, and a *very* distant one in Normandy. Only the British authorities appeared suspicious to the point of paranoia. On one occasion there was even a DEFRA vet waiting for us at Portsmouth, though the boys, and their paperwork, had already been checked (twice) before leaving France. Despite the terrible events of 9/11, which had just occurred when we started our odyssey, we often reflected that we could have stashed explosives or firearms beneath the boys, so focused were the authorities' on the characterful duo.

Overlaying these anxieties were other, arguably more practical, near-at hand concerns, all concerning H&J's welfare: the weather, and road conditions; the length of the sea-journey to and from France; anxiety about the boys' water intake; possible over-heating and, given the duration of the crossing, a genuine concern about the possibility of toilet emergencies.

I remember how desperately anxious I was in the early days for the boys' comfort and welfare during the crossing. I was worried about the possibility of an 'accident' - concerned on H&J's behalf, not about the clean up itself - and also worried about heat building up in the car. The sea journey was indeed six hours, from port to port. If one adds on the boarding time at Portsmouth, and disembarkation at Ouistreham, the total time without access to a dog's normal toilet facilities was approaching eight hours - and that's without delays, which are common enough. We prepared H&J with meticulous care, with a toilet stop on the journey at Sutton Scotney, and a final brisk walk around the outskirts of Portsmouth itself. And then six hours in the - relative -

comfort of our family Volvo. To avoid the car's becoming too warm during the journey, we always left all four windows completely open, to the bemusement of the ferry company's staff. Then, H&J were on their own for fully six hours - since passengers are forbidden to remain with their cars; but of course they had each other, and a large dish of fresh water.

Hector & Jason were, in fact, amongst the very first dogs to travel this way. In the first year or two we saw few others, and the very fact of their travelling stirred a great deal of interest, and no little admiration, from fellow passengers. There was no shortage of people who just wanted to touch, and stroke, these lovely lads. Many, with pets of their own left behind, wanted to know how easy, or how difficult, the process actually was. Yet others wanted to know about 'arrangements' for the dogs during the six hour crossing. We never tired of telling the prosaic truth.

Our journey to Portsmouth took us through the counties of Worcestershire, Warwickshire, Oxfordshire, Berkshire and Hampshire. And we brushed past some exotic locations: Silverstone race track, Blenheim Palace, famous for the Churchill dynasty, and Highclere, celebrated for *Downton Abbey*. And past Woodstock from where, it is said, hundreds of pensioners fled in August 1969 on hearing rumours of an approaching rock festival... (It may not be too far from the truth: it was in 1980 that June and I were enjoying a quiet moment in a remote Cornish pub when it received a visitation from the dozen, demented hairy bikers who wrecked the joint). Then, past the medieval majesty of Winchester, to be welcomed, finally, by the familiar white sails, blue sky and sea, of that other jewel - the port of Portsmouth. The superb sites we had so blithely passed by, would, hopefully, stay in abeyance for another day: for we had an appointment to keep - with Normandy itself.

But first, Portsmouth. It was Richard the Lionheart who founded Portsmouth, in the 1190s - as a naval base. To sail out of Portsmouth harbour at any time of the year is a memorable experience. To sail at the height of a sparkling Summer day is sheer bliss. The stress of the journey lies behind, and we could at last look forward to the adventure just on the horizon. Portsmouth Harbour, seen from the sea as one edges away from the port, is simply one of the most jaw-dropping sights in the UK - a superb amalgam of the natural and the man-made. Mighty, modern warships are moored on the quayside, almost cheek-by-jowl with the historic *Victory* and the elegant, epoch-making *HMS Warrior*. The glorious shoreline, historic, proud naval buildings, old pubs and churches, and new confections such as the Spinnaker, all jostle for position along the shoreline. Isle-of-Wight ferries chug by, while pleasure boats skim or bob through the white water agitated by the departing ferry. Lowry figures populate the beaches, like stick insects in the sun.

They are images to inspire the mind and lift the heart. This must be among the most impressive panoramas in England, though only too-rarely remarked upon. And this is just the beginning, just the outer-edge, the *hors d'oeuvre*, of the pleasures soon to come.

Portsmouth will always be associated for me with one of England's most celebrated heroes, Admiral Horatio Nelson or, to give him his full title, Admiral Lord Viscount Nelson and Brontë. In 1799, Nelson had been created Duke of Brontë: the word Brontë itself - from the slopes of Mount Etna - is Greek for (appropriately enough) 'thunder'. (Strangely, perhaps, the Brontë name was adopted by the ambitious young Reverend Patrick Brunty, who perhaps calculated that a little of the great man's gold dust might settle on him; the literary family known by that name are now, of course, as renowned as Nelson himself).

Even today, there are features at Portsmouth that would have been familiar to Admiral Nelson, returning home from gruelling voyages chasing the elusive Admiral Villeneuve, to the arms of his darling Emma. As one looks out over Portsmouth harbour there is the Square Tower - a 500-year old gunpowder store - and Horse Sand Fort, the largest of four Forts built in the Solent to protect the City - and country - from a French invasion.

Nelson entered Portsmouth for the last time on August 19, 1805, anchoring *Victory* at Motherbank, after two gruelling years at sea. He would leave the Port, again for the last time, on September 14, in order to confront the combined French and Spanish fleets at Cape Trafalgar. As Nelson departed from the beach at Southsea, a large crowd saw him off, variously cheering, weeping and praying. Nelson had called Portsmouth '*that horrid place*'; no doubt associating the dockyard with the physical and mental strains of war, and leaving behind his beloved Emma.

Before the final battle, Nelson dashed off a poem to Emma, ending with these poignant lines:

'Should conquest smile...
With joyful hearts, upon the beach we'll meet.
No more I'll tempt the dangers of the sea,
But live, in Merton's groves, with love and thee.'

Of course, any romance - in every sense of the word - must be tempered with the ferocity of war, and the daily brutality of life in the British Navy:

'Thirteen of the press gang did my love surround
And one of the accursed crew he lay bleeding on the ground.
My love was overpowered, though he fought most manfully,
Till he was obliged to yield and go on Victory.'

Anon - c1805

These historic, collective memories touched me each little voyage we undertook. The sacrifice of brave men and women - in the Napoleonic Wars and in the massive conflicts of the 20th Century - had made our lives, our privilege, possible. And we were embarking, not to war, but to enjoy the blessings of peace.

Jane Austen, too - her brothers, Frank and Charles, officers in the Royal Navy - knew a thing or two about Portsmouth, and naval affairs. 200 years ago, writing *Mansfield Park*, she talks thrillingly about Portsmouth, through her heroine, Fanny Price. Fanny's excitement is only too evident when she visits the harbour and dockyard with her sailor brother William, who is to join the warship *Thrush*: '*Everything looked so beautiful under the influence of such a sky, the effects of the shadows pursuing each other, on the ships at Spithead and the islands beyond, with the ever-varying hues of the ships now at highwater, dancing in its glee and dashing against the ramparts with so fine a sound...*'. In February 1812 - around the time that Austen wrote these lines - a little boy was born in Portsmouth: he was to become equally renowned - as Charles Dickens.

If the ships and architecture have changed, the effect of the harbour is much the same. Austen's joy echoes down the ages, and is with me as I gaze upon this magnificent scene, changed but somehow changeless. The whole panorama, infused with white light, sea and salt air, is quite breathtaking, quite fantastical. And then there is the expectancy - we are leaving this place, even this place - and travelling to France. With our boys.

We visited our home in France as often as possible. In practice, this meant juggling work pressures, holiday entitlements and family commitments. We managed a Normandy trip on average six times a year. Looking back, I'm amazed that we achieved what we did; it entailed a pretty extraordinary effort, and levels of energy that have probably deserted me, now. However, the excitement, the anticipation and expectancy steels one's resolve, and somehow carries one along. And two excited boys in the vanguard, raring to go, provided added impetus.

These voyages to Normandy were at once a pleasure, and an imperative. We loved being there, period. H&J loved it; extra special. And we saw it - see it - as our future. But it was also an imperative in the sense that homes, and gardens, need looking after, care and maintenance. Normandy weather - warmer than the UK, but with significant rainfall in Spring - is conducive to maximum vegetative growth. It is said that if you put a stick in the ground in Normandy, (and I have) it will grow. Even a month without attention in the Spring or Summer can mean returning to grass and explosive weeds four, five or six feet in height. One can almost *watch* the grass growing. We have photos of (me) apparently drowning in vegetation.

Preparing for and packing for France entailed meticulous care. Clearly, we had to pack food, water and bedding for H&J, and ensure that their Pet Passports were included and up-to-date. Then there was every other sort of convenience for the journey - refreshments, coffee and so on, as well as entertainment for the holiday itself. June packed the car, utilising every conceivable space, filling the vehicle with clothes, gardening equipment, paint, tools, camping gear, records and dvds - even wood for the French fire. The boys' space in the rear of the car - a Volvo Estate - was sacrosanct, so I often ended up with equipment in the foot well beneath my feet; it was a small sacrifice given the anticipated pleasures to come. In addition to packing essentials and desirables, we needed to carefully plan the route - with comfort stops, ensuring that we built-in sufficient time for the boys' needs - whilst ensuring that we actually caught the Ferry.

Once Hector had become accustomed to the routine, he quickly anticipated our plans: half an hour before 'the off' found him in the back of the car, smiling and wagging his tail. Jason, similarly aware, waited stoically for events to unfold. He was often the last piece of 'luggage' to be loaded into the car. The Volvo may have been packed to the gunwales, but the boys always enjoyed sole occupancy of the spacious rear of the estate. And then we were off.

That very first crossing in the Summer of 2000 - indeed perhaps the first two, three or four - were anxious times. Yet, perhaps a little needlessly: the boys were safe, secure, neither too warm nor too cold, and they coped admirably with the experience. And they enjoyed the fuss from passengers and the elegant, smart, (usually female) members of the crew. Brittany Ferries, too, were always very accommodating to our requests to visit the boys during the crossing, in order to check on their welfare. In those early days, the boys would be looking around, maybe a little nervously; they certainly looked-out for, and welcomed, my arrival. I would open the rear door of the car to re-assure them, offer them a handful of water, and moisten their mouths and brows. In later years, familiar with the journey, I might find the boys' asleep, or relaxed, chilling out until reaching our destination. After the first journey or two, not only did H&J get used to, and understand, exactly where they were and what was happening, but they knew where they were going: and they loved where they were going.

As often as we could, we would travel via the *Normandie Express,* the fast-craft that cut the journey time in half. This avoided a good deal of anxiety, and the open nature of this vessel meant that a cool breeze swept through the decks, keeping everything - and H&J - cool and comfortable. The welcome given both to us, and the boys, by staff on this craft was especially warm. On our disembarkation, a smartly uniformed member of staff would be positioned to bid us a smiling "*au revoir!*". One elegantly-attired lady in particular seemed to single out H&J, rewarding them with special attention. Such small kindnesses can make a deep impression. The *Normandie Express* ceases to operate from October to April in view of stormy seas; nevertheless, in view of its speed and comfort, it was a service that we sought out whenever we could.

Our regular route was the six-hour trip via Portsmouth to Caen. Occasionally, we also journeyed via Cherbourg, or Le Havre, but Caen was the most direct. There was always a stop en-route, at Sutton Scotney Services, in Hampshire, which the boys loved. Sutton Scotney quickly became the focal point of our strategy for our Normandy adventures. It was ideal for a stopping-off point for the boys - a welcome walk and toilet-stop, and an exciting rabbit chase - though on leads (the incredibly busy A34 being only an embankment away). I would be pulled along quite mercilessly in search of the mouth-watering largesse of rabbit or even fox. Though H&J always made careful note of our preparations, when we arrived at Sutton Scotney they could be in no doubt that France was their destination.

And then, at Portsmouth, after check in, another short walk - out of the Port, and along a busy road, lined with green spaces. Just the job for two excited, now expectant dogs. Then boarding the ship - usually *Normandie* or *Mont St Michel* for the long crossing. Much excitement when we boarded - lots of questions, lots of stroking the boys. Then six hours on board ship - a curious blend of anticipation and anxiety. We were often asked: *"What happens to the dogs on the journey?". Do they go into kennels?".* One young lady, having been informed that, on the Portsmouth-Caen crossing the dogs were obliged to stay in the car, went on to enquire *"What happens if they need to go to the toilet?".* The response - apart from a grinding of teeth - was rather academic. Whilst pets *are* confined to their cars, Hector & Jason were always impeccable, having prepared themselves, and been prepared, for the sea journey. In addition, we always visited them mid-way through the crossing, if only to check on their comfort, and provide a little moral support. But they were stoically, doggedly 'up for it' and managed perfectly well.

Then, a full six hours later, (with at least one, often two, re-assuring visits to *les chiens*), disembarkment - and another short stop, and walk, along the Promenade next to the Terminal Building. The excited boys knew the routine, and we were quickly on our way. It's just 75 minutes, along the Orne Valley, from the port of Ouistreham to our little cottage, a world away. The return journey was similar, if, inevitably, less exciting - Sutton Scotney was the first available stop, following arrival at Portsmouth. This was a long stretch, without toilet opportunity for the boys: we always ensured that there was a brisk - and productive - walk at Ouistreham, skirting the beautiful beach, prior to embarkation. Again, this fortified H&J for the journey; they were always ready, full-on, full of heart.

On perhaps half a dozen occasions, however, we took the Ferry to Cherbourg, as an alternative to Caen. The sea-going travel time is less, though on arrival we had to traverse the entire Cotentin Peninsula, in order to reach our destination. Cherbourg has many claims to fame. The port was only established as an ocean-going port in the 19th century; in April, 1912, the *Titanic* called in to Cherbourg before setting off on its fateful voyage into the Atlantic.

In Howard Hawks' iconic *Gentlemen Prefer Blondes* Marilyn Monroe - wittily named Lorelei Lee - totters along the quayside to be informed that "*This ship is leaving for Cherbourg, France*". Presumably, in 1953 cinema-goers still needed to be reminded that Cherbourg *was* in France. However, many Americans - and Brits - would have known Cherbourg well: it was captured by the Allies in late June 1944, and an oil-carrying pipeline, called PLUTO, (Pipe Line Under The Sea) laid between the Isle of Wight and the Port. Supplying fuel-hungry aircraft, tanks and vehicles, the pipeline was crucial to the success of the Allied war effort.

We would quickly leave Cherbourg behind, keen to complete our journey. The first stop was always near Campeaux, close to Beny Bocage. Like grit in the proverbial oyster shell, the excited but genial boys provoked a storm of protest from local dogs, shuttered behind their iron gates. Our experience was always the same: as we walked along the grass verges, a doberman-type dog would launch itself against the steel gate to its home, barking furiously at our intrusion. The boys provided an irresistible shot of vigour to a hamlet becalmed in slumber. I almost looked forward to the promised mêlée. However, in this case, familiarity bred content. Hector & Jason took no notice whatsoever of the cantankerous canine, and we never spied the dog's owner, despite the mutt's repeated outbursts.

In fact, everywhere one see the signs '*Attention aux chiens*' (beware of the dogs). Occasionally - presumably tongue in cheek - one may also encounter '*Attention aux lapins*', though I have never yet heard of anyone mauled by a rabbit. But each time we visited this hamlet, we were treated to exactly the same performance. A case of *déjà vu* all over again.

And then, in the gathering gloom, we would head along the valley of the Vire, then through Beny Bocage, St Charles de Percy, and Vassy. Just before reaching Vassy we passed a towering horse chestnut tree, magnificent in its verdure. Each time I saw it I thought: "*we are coming home!*".

When travelling, Jason was Mr Sang Froid, Mr Unflappable, Mr Unperturbable; he was the original SAS dog. Travel was something to be endured rather than enjoyed, though I hope that, over the years, as he sensed the pleasure of the destination, he softened to these journeys. Jason always adapted the attitude of an elite combatant; steeling mind and body for whatever had to be endured. Hector, on the other hand, was energetic, and excitable; a little nervous in the early years, though later this was subsumed by his confidence and eagerness to set paw in France at the earliest possible moment.

Hector invariably sat bolt upright on his seat, and was a familiar figure in the rear-view mirror, his noble head outlined, his quiff distinct. He would look around for features of interest, and keep us, through his society, animated and involved. Hector's head remained in sharp silhouette, a constant feature, even in the gathering gloom. And there he was, still, in the darkness, on the last stages of our journey; ever present, ever stoical and alert. June would sometimes complain that his raised head interfered with her rear view vision, but the fact that he was there, and with us, in being and spirit, always heartened me. No fair-weather friend, this, but someone you could trust with your life. If ever someone was needed to stand steadfast, shoulder-to-shoulder with you in the trenches, that 'someone' would be Hector. Calm in a crisis, tigerish when under attack; the soul of loyalty, always.

And then onwards, and onwards; the very last lap, along dim, windy lanes, and usually dark by now, except at mid-Summer. Quite often, our progress towards La Haute Maison would be slowed, or abruptly halted, as we stopped to avoid a young bull, or a goat, or a peacock, standing astride the narrow road and refusing to budge. Mostly, these animals could (eventually) be encouraged to move on, but not in the case of the peacock, which simply refused to leave its station on the highway. We were obliged to retrace our route, and approach the cottage from the opposite entrance to the road.

Then - arrival at the cottage: silent, except for the clicking of hedge crickets, and sweep of the bats. Arrival always bought a heart-stopping moment. Not only was it always pitch dark, it was always very late - often around midnight. And there were always surprises in store. With or without their owners, houses enjoy a life of their own. Even in our absence, a myriad strange adventures had assuredly unfolded, leaving us scratching our heads in bemusement, or amazement. Four-feet high grass, beyond the gate? A bulbous toad, or slow worm, slithering in the verdant gloom? Mysterious moths, as big as your palm? A dead mouse or two, upon the hearth?

I would unlock the house, and turn on the lights - attracting an array of moths - and re-introduce H&J to their domain. Then, two very, very happy boys. Delighted to have come - home. Hector & Jason, newly freed, would dash into the cottage with feverish excitement and delight, then charge around the garden like whirling Dervishes, expressing excitement and relief: hurling t-towels into the air, and drinking copiously from the pond. They had arrived at their favourite place on Earth. And whatever time we arrived, Hector & Jason were simply ecstatic - it was a joyful culmination of a long and sometimes arduous journey. The immediacy, that transparency with which they expressed their joy at homecoming has always touched me, and does so now, as I write. However many times I saw the boys exult in a tumult of ecstasy, I was never less than moved.

H&J's body language, on arrival, was testament to their deep love of the place. Why, exactly? The sights, the sounds, the smells, the views, the depth of the countryside: all must have played a part in their affections. There were just more dimensions of experience available to them...and then there were the goats...

There were only two small problems with La Haute Maison, as far as Jason was concerned. The first was the floor tiles, which covered much of the downstairs living area (the centre of the room having a deep-pile carpet, beloved of Jas). These tiles were smooth, whereas he was used to wall-to-wall carpet. Tiles were always a trial for Jason, who never overcame his dislike of the *tuiles* so beloved of the French. He would move gingerly from one rug to another - islands in the smooth tile-sea - to where he wanted to get to; then, if cut adrift from one of his rugs, he would edge nervously backwards to the nearest point of safety. Hector had no such qualms. Both lads were on hand, however, whenever food was offered, at breakfast or lunch - even in a rug-free area. Following demolition of his meal, Jason made his way to safety, backwards, whilst Hector simply walked to his preferred destination.

The other problem was the open fire. It's an enormous, black-painted monstrosity of a fire-place. No doubt 50 years ago it was the centrepiece of the home, a warm redoubt, used for cooking as well as keeping warm in a cottage that has never enjoyed central heating. We usually lit the huge, wood fire in the early evening, generally between the months of October and May. So, when the day turns to cool and dark, we light our fire. And Jason hated it. Sparks fly, kindling crackles, and the larger logs emit loud bangs as they spit and fume. June and I love it, but Jason expressed his unease by retiring to bed - climbing a steep staircase to our bedroom, and the comfort of our large double bed. Completely undemonstrative. See you in the morning.

Despite these idiosyncrasies, the boys adored the cottage, and the garden. Whenever we returned from a trip - whether this was a short visit to the local shops, a day out or a week's camping - they went mad with joy, squealing, chasing each other, clutching at familiar objects and running mad-cap round the garden, racing around in a transport of sheer delight. Their hearts were full to bursting, and they needed to celebrate this excess of life. It was heady, unforgettable, wonderful, to witness such bliss, and I can see and hear it still.

From a purely botanical point of view, the garden was a wonder, a natural wonder, to behold: the Spring brought forth, in rampant profusion, daisies, poppies, foxgloves, primroses, cowslips and violets, competing amongst long and fragrant grasses; and apple, cherry, pear and plum blossom, followed by rich fruit, on heavy-laden boughs. This was a gift of overflowing bounty, a sensual feast worthy of Andrew Marvel, and my heart sang with him:

> 'What wondrous life in this I lead!
> Ripe apples drop upon my head;
> The luscious clusters of the vine
> Upon my mouth do crush their wine...'

Seen from a practical, maintenance point of view, however, the garden was something of a nightmare. The average length between visits was about six weeks, and this meant that we were always struggling against the most luxuriant plant growth I've ever seen. While the boys loved galloping through the long grass, the thick vegetation saw off many a strimmer and, (a little before H&J arrived on the scene) my over-worked back, since I suffered a 'slipped disc', and considerable pain on account of too much heavy gardening. Little did I know at the time that H&J were, as it were, just around the corner - and that, among other things, my back would need to acquire a new strength. It may

259

be of interest that the H&J 'power-pulling' method of exercise never aggravated my back condition, but appears to have cured it. Cruel to be kind, indeed.

During the early years, out of a sense of desperation with the rampant fertility of grass and rank weeds, together with my recent back problem and the unavoidable gaps between visits, we secured some external help. In France, professional gardeners, *paysagistes*, are widely available. But, like many a Brit, and sometimes unwisely, I opted for the services of a British guy. He did a decent job, but at a pretty indecent price. The first time he joined battle with the grass he 'phoned me: *"You'll never believe the height of this grass!"* he exclaimed. *"Yes I would"*, I returned. *"By the way, mind the pond"*, I added. *"What pond?"* he replied - *"oh, yes, I can see it now!"*. And so on - after a year or so, we regained sole responsibility for the garden, my confidence improving along with my back condition.

There is a charming story, relating to Bagnoles-de-l'Orne, but which could be true for the rich countryside of Normandy as a whole. The knight, Hugues de Tesse, was reluctant to kill his old charger, *Rapide*, despite his extreme age and infirmity. So, instead, he let the old warrior loose in the forest. To Hugues' surprise, the horse returned - but with new vigour, shining coat and bright eyes. The legend ascribes the horse's new-found youth to the magical properties of the forest streams. The story resonates with my experience: each time H&J returned to Normandy, they appeared rejuvenated: by the clear air, by the sense of adventure and possibility, by the space and sheer difference. We could see them grow in spirit, and respond with their whole being. Hector & Jason, and Normandy, will always remain a special, life-affirming combination.

However long our stay, and whatever adventures we enjoyed, homeward bound was always too soon. Again, H&J spotted the signs, and their body language reflected their spirits. They never wanted to leave.

One scintillating Sunday morning, since we were leaving Normandy via the morning ferry, the boys and I were out at the crack of dawn for our first excursion of the day. It was a simply glorious morning, and deliciously peaceful as we strode out. Despite the early hour, the boys were their normal effervescent selves, happy to follow their usual morning constitutional. Then I thought I heard strains of

Led Zeppelin...where? In my head? On the breeze? What had I been drinking, or smoking, last night? I had, as a matter of fact, 'returned' to *Led Zeppelin* after a lapse of many years, and been playing *Stairway to Heaven* et al on the car's audio system. (Towards the end of 1971, and at the peak of their creative energy, *Led Zeppelin* played Sheffield University. The band had just released *Led Zeppelin 4*, which was to become the biggest selling rock album - ever. And *Zeppelin*'s front-man, Robert Plant, hailed from my native Dudley. Whatever was I thinking? Stupefied by a sort of injection of intellectual embalming fluid, I stupidly passed up the opportunity to see the band perform.

A few months later, and Paul McCartney, and *Wings*, were unexpectedly in town. Apparently, McCartney spent the afternoon relaxing in the student union bar, quite unperturbed; no-one recognised him. I may have been an impoverished student, but I could afford the 50-pence-on-the-door entrance. Maybe I'd had a transfusion, but I didn't miss *that* gig).

So the noises in my head were familiar, but disconcerting, at barely 6 o'clock on a Sunday morning. Everything else was as it should be: the sky wasn't psychedelic, the grass was still green, the boys had not sprung horns.

I thought no more about *Led Zeppelin* et al until, a little later, I called at our neighbours to bid them '*au revoir*'. It was clear that Thierry was out of sorts. "*Heavy rock music all night long! What a disgrace! We didn't move to the countryside to have to put up with this!*". Oh dear. Never mind; at least I was returning to the UK, if sadder, at least not insane. *Led Zeppelin* remained firmly within their protective cover, and we reached home, via *Normandie Express*, without mishap. H&J never appeared to respond to music - whether classical, jazz or rock - they just took it all in their stride, a background to their busy and eventful lives.

On a similar *Normandie Express* journey - in fact, 21 October, 2007 - we found the craft crammed with still-painted, still-partying England rugby fans, freshly disgorged from the World Cup Final at the Stade de France the previous afternoon. England had lost 15-6 to South Africa, but had fought valiantly; a veritable near-run thing. It was the last match for another famous Jason - Jason Robinson, that is. The revellers, high on adrenalin and alcohol, continued their good-natured, good-humoured revelry, re-telling their tales of what was, and what might have been; the mood was cheerful, up-beat, *bonhomie*.

Yet loud rock music - or loud rugby fans - are the least of the range of googlies or inconveniences the holiday home owner may encounter. Owning a maison de vacance, or maison secondaire, can have its drawbacks, as well as pleasures. It may be true that absence makes the heart grow fonder, but this is rarely the case for people with holiday properties who, for obvious reasons, are often absent. While our first neighbours, Annie and Gilbert, were simply marvellous, later neighbours sometimes took advantage of our non-presence: one Autumn, a hundred year-old boundary hedge was bulldozed, to my considerable chagrin. *"Why didn't you ask?"* I remonstrated. *"You weren't here"* - delivered with a Gallic shrug - *"and the machine became available"*.

Rats and mice are another of the minor drawbacks to owning a holiday home. My last, reluctant, job before leaving the cottage, when H&J were safely in the car, was to set down poison; and my first job on returning was to take this up, before H&J were let loose in the cottage. And, before I put on any pair of shoes, I had to check the insides for rodents - dead or alive. A shoe makes an ideal home for a family of mice, or *souris*. As Beatrix Potter well knew, a family of mice quickly becomes a dozen families of mice, in a dry, warm house - and can create absolute havoc. I was once told a true story about a family who, before returning to the UK, accidentally left a carton of milk in the kitchen. An innocent mistake, you may think. The carton was quickly torn open by the said mice. Flies then invaded the exposed milk. On their return to France, the family were greeted by a house full of maggots. So, dead mice were a sad occupational hazard.

Another story was told, rather philosophically, by a guy I met at Portsmouth, who was returning to Normandy to supervise the re-building of his home. On a previous visit, a helpful neighbour had turned on the heating, in order to welcome their returning British friends. Shortly afterwards the Brits arrived to find - shock and horror - their lovely house consumed in flames: mice had chewed through the electrical cables, with devastating effect. There but for the grace of God...

As we departed, I often needed to counsel and soothe the reluctant Jason into the car. But, once at Oustreham, the boys natural spirits re-asserted themselves. I always looked out for the 12th century Church of

Saint Samson - for me, Ouistreham's gem, with its wonderfully graceful lines.

Each time we approached the entrance to the Terminal Building at Ouistreham - H&J pulling me directly towards the entrance - our refection was caught beautifully in the large mirror-glass doors, which then opened magically to let us through. The refection of H&J, advancing forward so gracefully - but as though our reflection was coming forward to greet us - always made me feel so proud. We needed to check in, with H&J waiting patiently whilst our - and their - documentation was intimately, exhaustingly, processed. The ferry company was saddled with the responsibility of ensuring that those pesky pets were not masquerading as some other pesky pets, and had received appropriate, and timely, treatment from an authorised veterinary surgeon.

The whole process was quite unnerving; a single error could spell disaster. Jason's microchip was always evasive - behaving, aka Jason himself, and travelling around inside his leg. And then, checks over, we all embarked upon a celebratory walk along the enticing coastal route flanking the harbour. H&J were carefree and excited; they knew that we would soon be boarding the Ferry, bound for England - but were up for it, and fully prepared.

So many times Ouistreham would be the scene for fascinating encounters with fellow Brits who had intriguing tales to tell. "*We've just bought a house in Brittany*", volunteered one couple. "*Do you think it's a good idea?*". "*Well...*". So many Brits seemed to have acquired farms, Château, even large estates. Many of these people were hardly young, but 'third age': retired teachers, doctors, accountants. Perhaps they needed one more challenge, one more 'project', putting two fingers-up to old father time. I marvelled at their ambition, tenacity, and pluck.

One grey-haired, wizened guy told me that he had just driven ten hours from his place in Portugal, where he had a 100 acre small-holding, growing grapes and olives. Another couple described their 15th century farmhouse in central France, which they had spent ten years restoring; it had ten fire-places - and 1,000 acres of farmland - most of which was let to local farmers.

Such stories took me back to a distant life, and my eye-opening holiday on Mr Jones's Welsh farm, on which the sun hardly set. In a former age, these fellow-travellers might be running a tea plantation in the Himalayan foothills at Darjeeling, or sipping gin on a Kenyan veranda. Now it was France, and Europe. The Old World had become the new frontier.

It was at the Terminal Building - how inaptly named - that a wiry, middle-aged gent stopped us, remarked on how handsome the boys were, and asked if he could stroke them. *"Certainly; please do!"* I responded, charmed as ever. This introduction turned into a casual chat, and it transpired that the chap in question lived on the north coast of Spain, and earned his living as a pet courier. This is now a burgeoning sector, with pets being professionally transported in air conditioned, specially adapted vehicles, largely between the UK and their continental destinations. Imagine my surprise when my genial gent casually revealed that he had lived in Wordsley for ten years, prior to moving to Spain! *"Why, that's where we live!"*, I responded, sounding school-boy amazed. As we so often remark, what a small world it is, these days. Chat over, the lads and I entered upon one of our walks around the splendid coastline of Ouistreham, prior to embarkation.

For some time we had been looking for a handsome carpet to take centre stage on the hearth of the French cottage. In 2007, having found exactly the right pattern, style and quality, we arranged with our local supplier for the 5x3 metre-piece to be edge-bound as a rug. However, even when rolled, the carpet was far too bulky to be transported in the Volvo; so, we acquired roof-bars, and secured the rug soundly to these.

We set off for Portsmouth in due course, loaded with the usual equipment, H&J, and roof-mounted rug. Fate decreed that it was a windy day - it just had to be. Despite the sharp gusts, and travelling at motorway speeds, the rug held firmly within its bindings. I even felt it with my out-stretched arm from time to time, just to reassure myself. Approaching Portsmouth we crossed over a bridge above the estuary - and a savage flurry of wind un-hinged the carpet, which slid slowly down the side of the car. I just managed, manually, to hold the thing in place until we could stop safely, and then rigorously re-tied our bulky package. H&J observed the proceedings with keen but silent interest. Without further mishap - we only had a couple of miles to go - we reached our destination, and the Ferry - and then France.

It had been a heart-stopping moment, but we had won the day. The carpet is perfect in its setting at the heart of the hearth, and much loved by H&J - judging from the constant vacuuming that was necessary.

In later years, fatigued by the mad rush along the motorway to Sutton Scotney, and then the long haul home (often arriving well after midnight) we thought, *'sod the expense'* and stopped-over at The Travelodge in deepest Hampshire. Fortunately, pets are permitted - at an additional cost. Although Sutton Scotney is a pretty un-prepossessing, functional, as-it-says-on-the-tin kind of place, it was always such a relief - literally - to reach the site without mishap.

The boys knew the procedure, with Hector limiting his water intake accordingly and Jason, bless him, in stoic self-denial. Often, we did not arrive at the service station until after dark, when the car headlights, beaming over the wasteland - or meadow, as I liked to think it - would catch the rabbits' reflected eyes; the poor things had imagined they were safe to emerge at night. At those times I had to be particularly careful to hold on to H&J for dear life, as they pulled me excitedly through the undergrowth bordering the A34.

Somewhat to my surprise, the boys loved this arrangement. They simply adored the Travelodge, and were immediately at home in their spacious room. On one occasion I woke to find Hector sound asleep on the sofa opposite our bed. We all slept soundly until the early-hours. Then, at around 4.30am, H&J would awake - and wake me. It was time for a walk. Trousers on, collars on - we would charge out of the building, with the boys, excited as pups, pulling me hectically along the corridors - to the waiting greenery, and into the sparkling, starry night.

What might appear as tedious, or inconvenient, was the exact opposite - the sinuous, joyous expression of life and hope - experiencing the deep night, and quiet countryside, with even the A34 silent under the stars. And Mr Sinatra again pulsing in my head: *Stars fell on Alabama...* Who could have dreamt of perfection in these pedestrian circumstances? Funny thing, life. Then a blissful two hours sleep before further awakening, a cup of tea and, yes, another walk. There was a kind of symmetry to this that kept us all fit, alive and feeling vital.

When returning home in daylight - either because we had caught the morning Ferry, or because we had stayed over at Sutton Scotney - our last stop before home was our local Park. This served two purposes: it gave the boys a welcome opportunity to exercise, off their leads, after a couple of hours sitting in the car; and it provided them with confirmation of a familiar location and environment. The direction of travel may not have been as exciting as the outward journey, but at least

H&J knew where they were. June and I had had that sinking feeling all day (we are not the 'glad to be home' types) but, in their boyish enthusiasm, H&J never betrayed any sign that they were unhappy with life. That said, Jason was hardly as effusive on reaching Maison Wordsley as he was on arriving at La Haute Maison.

A few more observations. We avoided night crossings, whenever possible. Although this is often the most convenient way to travel, from a time-efficiency point of view, asking a dog to 'keep its legs crossed' for nine or ten hours is a tall order, and not one that I'd like to observe, personally. However, the French authorities being so much quicker with the formalities than their British counterparts - but surely no less rigorous - and access to dog-toilet opportunities so much more readily available on the French side, we did manage a couple of night crossings *to* Normandy, when H&J were in their maturity. These passed off without incident or problem, but caused me some anxiety on H&J's account. The boys gave us so much, and it seemed plain wrong to cause them any distress or unnecessary embarrassment.

And we took great care to ensure that nothing that could be construed as a weapon accompanied us. So my Swiss Army knife - courtesy of a little tourist shop in Concarneau - was never ventured to Portsmouth, where it would be at risk of confiscation by officials. *"Do you have any pen knives, sir?"* I am regularly asked by the UK Border Agency staff. Clearly, the Black Country pen-knife maniac.

On the theme of security: I am no expert on firearms, and have no wish to be, but I know a gun when it is pointing at me. Late one Autumn, I was travelling to Normandy alone, since this was just for a few days to focus on boring but necessary tasks, like decorating, that just have to be tackled. Having endured darkness, and wind and rain, I thought that a hot meal in the Terminal Building at Portsmouth would provide a refreshing diversion. I was just about to tuck into a much-anticipated dish of fish and chips when a uniformed officer pointed the barrel of a powerful, automatic weapon directly at my table.

I looked around carefully, but could not spot anyone who looked remotely threatening - except, of course, the officer himself; just ordinary folk going about their everyday business. The gun-barrel continued to point in my general direction. Perhaps my knife and fork had aroused suspicion, or maybe the officer envied my happy lot. I rested said knife and fork on the table, anxious to ensure that they were not perceived as posing any kind of threat. After what seemed like an age, the gun was lowered, and the officer moved away, presumably to repeat his trick elsewhere. Taking a deep gulp of air, I resumed my meal. A woman on the same table muttered under her breath: "*Is that supposed to re-assure us?*". Quite.

Together, in their inimitable style, H&J made more than fifty trips to Normandy. This may not be a record - we weren't trying to set one - but it was a good many trips, over many years, and each one memorable. To be sure, H&J did not travel with us on *every* occasion. Where the trip was confined to a long weekend, for example, (usually in mid-Winter) they would stay at home, with either June or myself for company. We had a rule that, in view of all the travelling involved, the boys should travel to Normandy only when trips took place over at least five, and preferably seven, days. Nevertheless, H&J visited Normandy with us five or six times each year - usually in April, (around Easter); late May or early June, July or August for our main holiday, again in Autumn and sometimes in December.

In every one of our journeys to France, Hector & Jason *shone.* They were simply bursting with life, and affected everyone they met with (in Hector's case) excitement, exuberance, and *joie de vivre*; and in Jason's case with his sheer beauty, and personal magnetism. It struck me that the uplifting swing of *A Foggy Day,* with Mr Sinatra's thrilling delivery, provided a musical parallel to the unforgettable company of two happy, crazy boys - enjoying themselves, and being enjoyed, by everyone they met along the way - fellow visitors to Sutton Scotney, fellow-passengers at Portsmouth, the Brittany Ferries staff on board: all was smiles and laughter. What radiance, what a tonic, was here!

Nowadays, around 100,000 pets a year travel via Brittany Ferries - rather than the hardy handful when we began, in 2000. I hope that they, and their carers, all have the time of their lives; as did we.

18: At Home in France - Halcyon Days

The nectarene, and curious peach,
Into my hands themselves do reach;
Stumbling on melons, as I pass,
Ensnared with flowers, I fall on grass.

Thoughts in a Garden - Andrew Marvell

They order, said I, this matter better in France.

A Sentimental Journey - Laurence Sterne

France has long been our friend and, within France, Normandy has been a special friend. And the French people, too, have proved to be special friends.

Our cottage is on the fringe of Ménil Hubert-sur-Orne. Hubert of Liege (St Hubert) is not only the patron saint of hunting, he also protects against dog bites - some comfort to our happy wanderings. The Bayeux Tapestry itself depicts King Harold hawking with five collared dogs. And H&J lived a dog's life - a dog's true life - at La Haute Maison.

We were first shown the cottage on a bone-shaking, nerve-jangling house-hunting tour of suitable properties by a young agent immobilier. Frank had pretensions to be in Formula 1, and drove his tiny Peugeot accordingly.

Frank roared around narrow country lanes in his turbo-charged tin can, like one demented; June and I hung on for grim death. The tour, one mild, mid-October day, was the culmination of many years of contemplating buying a property in France, and both informal and formal viewings. We had visited Normandy, and wider France, on many occasions before this point, and had developed a pretty sound idea of what we wanted, and where.

The first house that we viewed was the one that we returned to, and bought - the very same day. It was love at first sight, even if the piggy bank quaked at the (actually very modest) price. No formal 'search'; no haggling. We were helped by the fact that the existing (British) owners were keen to extricate themselves for personal reasons. Meanwhile, the property had been on the market, sad and neglected, throughout the Summer months. The cottage had everything we wanted - charm, space and tranquillity. We could *just* afford it, even if I had to write an I.O.U. to the said piggy bank. We returned on a stormy night in late December to exchange contracts, and visited the cottage again on that same wild evening, to celebrate our new house - and changed life.

The cottage was - is - a thing of great simplicity and mystery. A simple stone structure, it seems to rise out of the earth naturally, organically, like so many Norman buildings. The artisans who carved the cottage from granite and oak in the early 1840s would, almost certainly, have remembered the turbulent times of Emperor Napoleon Bonaparte. There remains an old-fashioned charm, together with an acute lack of 'mod-cons' - no TV, no phone, no internet, and a challenging cooker, which (apart from the cooker) suited us perfectly. The main living area comprises a generous space, dominated by a large grate for a wood fire, with a tiled floor, and huge oak roof beams framing the high ceiling. In years to come, the steep, wooden stairs to the bedrooms would be confidently stridden by H&J when we all eventually retired each evening.

In *The Woodlanders* Thomas Hardy describes an old farmhouse as:

'...of no marked antiquity, yet of a well-advanced age...It was a house in whose reverberations queer old personal tales were yet audible if properly listened for; and not, as with those of the castle and cloister, silent beyond the possibility of echo'.

We became acutely aware of echoes of long-ago, and quiet heart-beats; so many generations melded into the walls, so that a living, pulsating presence seemed to invest the fabric of the place. Each time we visited - and we visited every six weeks or so from April to October - I scratched my head in wonder. There was always something different, something strange to encounter. Something might have moved - or been moved. There might be an 'atmosphere', a chill in the air, a feeling of a presence, of something 'other'; or an unrecognisable scent, that had nothing to do with the *souris* who invariably tried to invade every nook and cranny.

The garden, too, was a co-conspirator, and constant surprise. So often, it was the vegetation that had grown, in our relatively short absence, to Olympian heights. Sometimes it was the wildlife, with an owl, or a hare, announcing their magical presence. Swallows nested in the *cave* and, in early Summer, performed their pirouettes in the garden. Often, too, the swallows would career into the house, exploring every space, until exiting through an upstairs window.

On Summer evenings, a toad, attracted by the light, would sometimes crawl over the door-step - on one occasion hiding in the bathroom until my return, some three weeks later. The huge Summer moons astonished me even more - a great globe that beamed its ghostly, greenish light straight into the bedroom. And an overwhelming panoply of stars, more numerous, and more bright, than any I can recall seeing elsewhere. An amateur observatory, half a mile up the road, enjoys unrivalled views over the night skies.

Visitors to our neighbours sometimes referred to our own house and garden as *'le petit maison'*. Indeed, compared to their own architect-designed modernist space, set in 16-acres of rolling landscape, our own situation was modest indeed; yet secluded, and tranquil, and untameably wild. Early on, we planted a small orchard, consisting of apple, pear, cherry and plum trees, supplemented by soft fruit, such as raspberries. It is now mature, and adds lustre to the garden, while providing fresh fruit for us, and food and habitat for the varied bird population. In July, the profusion of ripe cherries can be magnificent - none the worse for the attention of bullfinches during the Spring.

The garden descends towards a long, broad, valley, with a distinct view of the church spire in distant Segrie Fontaine, or Sacred Fountain, with steep cliffs beyond. The garden was the boys' playground: rich with molehills, footballs, myriad forms of wildlife, eerie calls, strange sightings and, best of all, a large space in which to run, tussle and gambol around.

Gardening in France could be daunting, since there was just *so much* garden; and the vegetation grew rampantly, inexorably, almost as one watched. Yet, as long as I was not too expectant, too demanding of orderliness and strict tidiness, the effort was satisfying: whether I spent five minutes or five hours strimming, pruning, or tidying, I could see the results, and feel the benefit. The improvement was not lost on the eye, and the satisfaction was immediate. Then I could relax and watch the birds, butterflies and bees re-assert themselves.

The garden responded heroically, mystically, even, to the roll of the seasons: the so-long Summers, hotter and drier than the UK, (though punctuated by prodigious rains), and the Winters, often bitterly cold, with temperatures plummeting to -20C at times, and frequent, heavy snowfall. The three Christmases we spent at the cottage, with Hector & Jason, were traditionally 'white' and bitingly cold, and we enjoyed them all the better for that. The boys loved walking in the snow, the reflected light transforming a familiar landscape. Enveloped in thick Winter clothing, (the boys naturally comfortable in their own thick coats) we enjoyed these Winter walks as much as their Summer equivalents. This was just as well - heavy snowfall or thick ice could make travelling on our little road, with its deep ditches, a pretty hairy experience.

A handsome round clock dominates the far wall of the living room. I would view the clock from the garden, glancing at it when working among the depths of green. Could it be time for a tea break? Was it time to end the day's *travail,* wash my scratched, blood-streaked hands, and prepare for a pre-prandial evening drink? The clock was a comfort and godsend, though it also reminded me of the remorseless and unforgiving passage of time.

A friend with a house in the rural south of France once complained to me that he had not had a holiday in more than ten years. Why? All his time seemed to be spent in gardening, painting and general maintenance. I have some sympathy with this view. In maintaining a holiday home, one is always 'behind the curve', always playing 'catch up', particularly in the rampant Summer months. Some folk give up the attempt, and employ help, from a gardener (paysagiste). In my case, I calculated jobs in terms of the time-cost: one hour equalled a unit. One unit, or possibly two at a stretch, represented my maximum daily expenditure. The rest of my day would be given over to relaxation, or reading, or sight-seeing - whatever we planned, or fancied. And of course spending time with H&J, whether at the cottage or on our explorations further afield. A question of balance, and enjoying every day - filling it with abundance and interest. As William Blake wrote: *'Damn braces, bless relaxes'.*

There were always fresh challenges in the garden. The beech hedge I had planted near to our boundary with the road had suddenly spurted far above its intended height; eight feet had become eighteen, in the twinkling of an eye. In cutting the twenty trees down to size I had no option but to direct the cut branches into - and across - the road. Since there was always the possibility of a car or tractor bearing down the little highway, as soon as each bough fell I had to run round into the road and remove the offending obstruction. Luckily, we can hear the sound of an approaching car from a mile or so away, which gave me just enough time to avoid a possible collision with an oncoming vehicle.

Even so, unless you've discovered deepest Ruritania, even quite unpopulated countryside can be surprisingly noisy, as motor-mowers, strimmers, hedge-cutters and tractors are wielded into daily action to turn back the spreading green tide. Two or three machines on the go at once becomes an unmelodious cacophony. As always, *my* sounds are music, whilst my neighbours merely make noise. The gritty throb of car engines, too, is more present - in your ear - and more irritating; the less frequently one hears this, the less one becomes accustomed to it - or wants to become accustomed to it.

On this theme we once visited friends who had bought a home, an old farmhouse, deep in the Norman countryside. A small housing development - consisting of perhaps three or four new houses - had begun a mile or so from their property. Despite this generous distance, we could hear only too distinctly, across the crystal clear acoustic, every clink of a brick, every rat-tat-tat of a trowel, every note of the bricklayer's plaintive whistle.

There is another noise of note. Once each week - Wednesday in our case - neighbours put out their refuse for the council cart that careers up the road at about 9.00am the following day. Each family's rubbish is placed in a wheelie bin, which is then trundled to the side of the road. The sound of these bins being wheeled over cobbles always reminds me forcibly of the tumbrils and their unfortunate occupants being led to the *Place de la Guillotine* during the 'Terror' of 1793/94. Perhaps the association always led me to ensure that H&J were well away from the road when this ritual took place.

The garden itself abounds in a profusion of wildlife: swallows swoop in the deep barn, while redstarts, treecreepers, bullfinches, woodpeckers, goldfinches, nightingales, and even hen harriers all populate the generous swathe of greenery. And smooth snakes, frogs, and toads among the amphibian residents lurk among the damp shadows. Then again, flying insects, with long probosci like humming birds, (in fact, the humming bird moth) feed in the hedgerow, and on the buddleia's profusion of spikes, while bats and hedge crickets inhabit the evening air and undergrowth. During Summer evenings, an explosion of moths, such as garden tigers, would glower and gorge themselves on the nectar that offered itself in a seductive profusion from every soft surface of the garden. Fire salamanders - strikingly beautiful amphibians, striped gold and black - smoulder in dark recesses, while glow worms glitter their luminous green light in the darkening grass on Summer evenings. Bats fly balletically under the eves, chasing the myriad, multi-textured moths. Owls hoot and screech all night long, under the star-lit skies.

In 2005, during our long sojourn, I recorded thirty-seven species of birds and, on one glorious July afternoon, twelve species of butterfly. Once, a tawny owl, disturbed by crows, skimmed my head and landed on the chimney top. Peacock butterflies fluttered down the chimney when I lit a fire, and were handed gently to a place of safety.

And there are carpets of wild flowers, everywhere one looks - primroses, cowslips, violets, wild daffodils, orchids - so common indeed that they suffer a kind of benign neglect. In the UK, some of these species would be preserved in a museum, or protected in a nature reserve. The English might say that the hedgerows were 'unkempt'; I loved their freedom, beauty and vivacity.

This modest paradise also attracted more varieties of bees than I had ever seen - not only honey and bumble bees, but buff-tailed and red-tailed species, as well as wasps and hornets, and dragon and damsel flies, with their silent, unpredictable flight, and their blue and red iridescence. The dragonflies and hornets, while pretty formidable, left us well alone, though wasps once chased Hec, Jas and me along a lane, while stinging me twice. H&J had probably disturbed their nest in the bank, but escaped without harm. Fair play.

The only downside to Normandy's rich bio-diversity were the dreaded sheep ticks which one encounters everywhere. We had previously found these only in Scotland. At home in Wordsley, these ticks seem to be entirely absent. In Normandy, by contrast, they seemed to relish the opportunity to pounce on H&J on every walk. The rich grass edges, fields and meadows were teeming with these tiny, spider-like insects, all waiting with intent to ambush our boys.

Arriving home from walks, we would scour H&J's fur, hoping to remove the insects before they took a firm grip. There were always a few which escaped detection. Most of these were later discovered as small lumps attached to the skin, and had to be prized off with tweezers. A very few made it to maturity, when they fell to the ground, gorged and quite grotesque. This plague of ticks lasted all Summer long - certainly from April to October. These insects were probably our only real irritant. In normal circumstances we would have applied a simple ointment to counteract the nuisance but, since the vets would be performing this service in due course, we erred on the side of caution in not over-applying a chemical that may have unforeseen side-effects.

Normandy, it is said, can experience all four seasons in a single day; I can confirm that it can, and often does, at any time of the year. If Summers are generally long, hot and dry, the climate can be unpredictable, and apparently vengeful. When it decides to rain, then the meaning of the word is all too plain. We call a special type of rain in Normandy 'Normandy rain', (obviously enough) since it is not your typical rain, or even the French 'pluie'. It is our term for the mind-changing stuff that can sluice relentlessly from the heavens. Although pluie is an inadequate word, an accurate definition would certainly begin with a 'p'. There is a relentless, apparently endless, vertical momentum that can bombard one's senses for days on end. On returning 'home' to the UK from these onslaughts of wind and rain I was often complimented upon my alleged suntan. I was forced to point out, ruefully, that the complexion was more likely to be rust.

The weather could veer, without warning and in a trice, from brilliant sunshine to ferocious downpour. H&J and I often returned home bedraggled and soaked from one of these episodes, though curiously unconcerned. It was all part of the local tapestry. A quick change of clothes, for me, and a brisk rub down, for them, and all was well again. And then, almost miraculously, the scene changes dramatically, as the sun returns: and a sparkling, magical landscape bursts forth in pristine, revelatory glory.

We know that Jason disliked the open fire, and of course both boys disliked fireworks. Well, they both hated the thunder and lightning that tended to crash over and around the cottage with unerring regularity, and quite alarmingly, on Summer evenings. The thunderstorms were dramatic - sulphurous and ferociously bright, like the anger of the gods - and pulsated through our velux windows. The crackling, roaring and explosive outbursts were awesome in their impact but, for H&J, thankfully short-lived. I would cuddle and comfort the lads, in the knowledge - at least hope - that we were safe, and that all would - soon - be well. With Nature's dramatic display concluded, the boys relaxed, and calm was restored. Only the dripping trees reminded us of the power of the forces to which we had so recently been subjected.

But *vive la différence*. When the sun does shine, it is like the first day, *ever*, so innocent and pure and sweet. So I will forever associate H&J with the perennial beauty of Normandy; with the marguerite daisies that carpet the bocage, with the wild dog roses, orchids and primroses in the hedgerows, with the tall, open, cathedral-like forests, sparkling coasts, and soft sands. Most of all, they will be joined with the bocage itself, in all its inexhaustible diversity and beauty, for the bocage was the chief delight of our walks.

For Hector & Jason, La Haute Maison was home. And France, and our garden in France, was dog-heaven. Normandy is often described as a dream of green. I often counted the diversity of Spring flowers, as we raced past the winding multi-coloured display. My record for a single walk was the same number for the secret of the Universe, at least according to Douglas Adams: 42.

The Spring flowers arrived in waves: first, primroses, celandines, oxlips, and bright clouds of wild daffodils; then bluebells, violets, including dog violets, and early purple orchids - so common in the Warwickshire of Shakespeare that they are mentioned in *Hamlet*, in Ophelia's sad garland. They in turn are succeeded by harebells, foxgloves, and banks of marguerite, ox-eye daisies - the floral expression of Nature at its most exotic and luxuriant. And, finally, the dog roses and honeysuckle that thread and weave through the bocage.

A beautiful, peaceful, morning in May is as captivating, as perfect a day as Earth can create. We can respond anew to the potential that life offers, to the re-affirmation of the possible. H&J responded to each day as though both they, and the Earth, were fresh and new-born.

And sitting on the front step in Spring and early Summer, reading the poems of John Clare, and with Hector & Jason close by my side - perhaps raising my eyes to catch the iridescence of a swallow, or listening to a cuckoo in the valley - was as close to Heaven as I can ever aspire. H&J would gaze into the garden, senses alert to its colours, contours, fragrances and any hint of movement. It was a shared experience; the harmony of man, dog and nature, united in a sweet reverie. *'I love thee nature with a boundless love...'*

And, at night, silence, and stars - millions of stars - their brilliance piercing a black sky. It is endlessly absorbing - a majesty beyond words. And endlessly dramatic: meteors, shooting stars, even the odd satellite, tantalise the eye as they shoot silently across the immensity of the heavens.

For Hector, the trip to France was at first a trial, and then a revelation - a whole exciting, kaleidoscopic country to explore. For Jason, from the first, France was a love-affair; he always equated his other home with gaiety and fun, magnificent fun. It was pure love at first sight. If Jas sometimes looked stern, it was merely concentration, a focus on the excitement of the here-and-now. Every other moment brought a smile of pleasure to his face. France was his actual, but also his spiritual, home.

From the first, Hector & Jason regarded Normandy, and the people and dogs they met, as their own special friends. Thierry and Michele, Loic, and Mozart and Bob (the latter two, dogs), have been excellent friends to us all. What is it that we have all loved? Where to begin? The welcome. The food. The wine. The beauty and variety of the countryside. The culture and civilisation. The courtesy. The shared history. The fabulous Châteaux and cathedrals. The glorious coastline, and variety and 'gallic-ness' of seaside resorts. The freedom and romance of it all...

Whatever one's enthusiasm for French culture, however, one's Britishness intrudes; it's as pervasive as Blackpool rock. Radio 4 was a god-send; a veritable life-support system, declaiming news, weather, and current affairs, but also comedy and entertainment. The beauty of radio is that we could be enlightened, informed, or entertained, without interrupting the normal flow of life. I don't think that our affection for Radio 4 was a case of nostalgia for Blighty, so much as a desire to continue to be part of the global community, be gently amused and entertained, and have at least a vague idea of forthcoming weather. The shipping forecast was always a favourite, with its mysterious but strangely comforting pronouncements of highs and lows in Dogger, Biscay and Cromarty, and fronts 'losing their identity'. The radio provided a constant reminder that the bigger world was still out there, and that we were remotely connected to it.

The mellifluous warblings of Radio 4 provided the sinuous sound-track to the daily lives of Hector & Jason: they were well-used to the cultured tones and, when the familiar pips signalled the 'PM' programme, it was the cue for the long-awaited dog-dinner. The pips were also a sun-kissed cue for a - richly deserved - pre-prandial early evening pick-me-up for June and me.

And Summer evenings were filled with the delicious strains of *Porgy and Bess,* as gloriously sung by Ella and Louis, by Miles's *Kind of Blue,* by Sinatra's *Swingin' Lovers.* The sounds permeated the house, vibrating through the sultry air and mingling with the blackbird's evening song, and the chatter of the hedge crickets. Hector & Jason listened and relaxed, absorbing the sounds and sensations: *'Summertime...'*.

H&J were ever eager for walks beginning from their Normandy home: a glimpse of lead, or me putting on walking shoes, was enough: we were off. In France, it is still commonplace for dogs to roam freely around an extended area. Only the bright, savvy ones survive - perhaps that ability is now embedded in their genes. For me, in charge of two 'super-dogs', this was a step too far: the countryside was vast, the distractions and temptations many and acute, and a sense of security prevailed.

But the boys led on the walks - I let them decide the route, and this varied a good deal. They knew every inch of the local scene for miles around - paths through the bocage, woodland, minor roads off the beaten track near derelict old houses and forgotten ponds, skirting the bulls in their fields or the horses and donkeys in theirs. The boys knew, and loved, it all.

A mere 200 metres from the cottage was our own extensive (almost exclusive) forest, made up of oak, beech and chestnut. It is beautiful, lonely, and with its own special spring, which the locals value for the purity of its water. H&J loved their walks in this forest: there was always something fresh and surprising: - squirrels, deer, a hare, a fox, a badger - all impacted upon, and delighted, their acute senses. The woodland floor seemed to harbour more debris than was helpful for the stick-loving boys, who could never find enough. And, for me, the butterflies - brimstone, speckled wood, tortoiseshell and common blue - dancing in the sun-lit clearings, were enchanting. As was the discovery of the latest waft of wild flowers, or watching buzzards soaring overhead. We always returned home from our walks exhilarated, over-brimming and utterly content with our lot.

While I was occupied in exploring the hedgerows for their profusion of flora, (spotting 30 or 40 species of wild-flowers during a single walk was quite possible, though pretty remarkable given our headlong speed), H&J would be keenly exploring the same hedges for their sights and smells. Often, I would see a hare tearing down one of the country lanes, or a deer passing close by. An encounter with a pole cat was rare, mysterious and exciting; red squirrels also put in a regular appearance. If we often chanced upon hares, bounding along the woodland paths, sometimes these shy, secretive creatures might leap into the garden; they were conspicuous when snow covered the ground, revealing their sleek, athletic bodies. It so reminded me of Keats' *St Agnes' Eve* - '*The hare limped, trembling, through the frozen grass*'. And, if we were extra lucky, we would see a deer or two crossing our path, or a red squirrel, or a polecat disappearing into deep undergrowth.

Fortunately, at these times, the boys would be on their leads, only pulling me that much more purposefully when they saw a hare streaking ahead. Let loose, there was a risk that the boys might never return. Instead, they sniffed, and dug, and panted for more freedom. While H&J enjoyed the smells and anticipation, the wildlife had a welcome respite, and I returned happily home, secure in the knowledge that both H&J, and wild creatures, were safe, sound and secure.

Even so, there seemed to be endless possibilities in the un-peopled and seemingly infinite network of copses, fields, meadows, and hedgerows that spread invitingly before us; a wild pond, a flower meadow, a hare or deer streaking ahead; a fleeting glimpse of a back-side disappearing out of view. The land was teeming with opportunity for two curious and excited boys, and - despite their being tied to me - H&J responded with élan.

There were so many walks, all beginning at our gate. Shall we go to the derelict houses? Or the woodland? Or the farm? Or to see the herd of bulls at *Le Buisson*, that strode menacingly towards us as we passed? Or perhaps the goat walk?

The Goat Walk was Jason's all-time favourite. Knowing where he was headed, Jas would pull even more strongly than usual. With Hector adding to the press, we careered madly down the steep country path, past flower-filled meadows, ruined houses and overgrown orchards, turned right - and there was a herd of goats in their field. The goats spotted us, uttered warning sounds, and continued to stare grimly in our direction. The large billy goats, in particular, horned and menacing, dared us to approach.

Opposite the goat-field were a horse and a donkey in their own enclosure. Perhaps we would pause for H&J to sniff the curious donkey. Then we would power on, eventually coming to another derelict house, a stream, and more goats. We paused - then returned - the boys still pulling, still excited, but making no particular effort to gain closer acquaintance with the goats. Nearness is all. We returned home, step by excited step, H&J pausing for a drink from a bubbling stream; happy boys, happy me.

For Hector, a walk in the bocage was the nearest thing to Heaven. He revelled in the phantasmagoria of smells, sights and sounds that were super-abundant. Every crevice and cavity had to be inspected and explored, and revealed to him a rich and fascinating imprint of nefarious wildlife. What I saw and recorded was minuscule compared to Hector's laser-like senses; just what would we encounter today? Hec was never happier. Perhaps I should have trained him to search for truffles - he would have been brilliant, and we could have made a fortune. Jason would have looked on, perplexed.

On our wanderings we passed the crumbling ruins of ancient houses, once-vibrant communities that were now deserted, and inhabited only by ghosts. Why had they become abandoned? Was it the War? Or perhaps their remoteness, and lack of modern facilities (piped water, even gas)? Or social and economic upheaval, such as in Goldsmith's *Deserted Village*? The mystery lies in my own ignorance; I feel my status as an outsider. But the conjecture is endlessly fascinating to the restless imagination, and energises our every step.

Summer in Normandy is about country lanes, lush forests and exquisite coastlines fringed with gorgeous beaches. Every Summer, we embarked on a mission to explore these beauties for ourselves. The light is cut-glass brilliant, piercing, penetrating to the horizon. And, if the days are not enough, the nights are spectacular: huge, black skies, emblazoned with a million stars - so familiar to H&J through their excursions in the small hours.

H&J have always had a desire to frequent the garden in the middle of the night, and Normandy was no exception. Since I could not see them in the deep gloom of the garden, which an intrepid dog could soon leave far behind, I resolved to take them for short walks in the nearby lane. H&J must have enjoyed this because it often involved two walks per night. These walks were lit by full moons, and the sharp, eerie calls of tawny owls. One walk in particular - a Summer night, balmy, with a colossal full moon - saw us sprinting at our headlong pace for a couple of hundred yards, before the moon revealed the spectral magnificence of twenty young bulls barring the way.

I saw the light-rimmed, sinuous shapes very plainly, as did H&J, but I could only hope that the bulls could not see us, since we were still cloaked in darkness. I dared not say anything to the boys but somehow - perhaps sensing that we might be in a spot of bother - they turned around fluently, silently, and we reversed our tracks. I looked around nervously a few times - charging bulls are utterly dangerous, and there was absolutely nowhere to hide - but they did not pursue us, and we quickly, gratefully, reached the sanctuary of the garden gate.

Back in the cottage, Hector had his own 'spot' - either sitting on an armchair, especially at night, or lying right beside it. There were many times when, vacating that particular chair to visit the bathroom, I returned to find Hector ensconced on same chair: *"my chair, now, bagged it!"*. Jason, meanwhile, was stretched blissfully on our bed, upstairs. Well, as we said, they *were* our family, and they grew comfortably into the role.

H&J loved the viande animaux that is available from French supermarkets - big chunks of meat that appear more appetising than those found in many British pies. Whenever the microwave was set, and gave out its hearty little '*ping!*' the boys would become over-wrought with expectation. Once the meal had cooled, and combined with their usual mixer, they set-too with enormous gusto. The dog version of steak and chips; it never failed. That 'ping' - that always resonated so tunefully for Jason - always reminds me of an early example of marketing spin, a pre-Reformation jingle employed by the Roman Catholic Church:

> '*When the coin in the box (p)ings*
> *The soul from Purgatory springs*'.

When it was time for a trip by car, Hector was always up for it. And Jason always deeply suspicious. He had decided that this was the finest place in the Universe. The garden, and immediate area, had everything - wide open spaces, wild animals, peace and tranquillity, good food - what more did a boy need? If Jason entered the car reluctantly, he always enjoyed the destination - whether this was the mundane supermarket, a picturesque village or a coastal resort. But he always delighted in returning home, and would treat us to a farrago of entertainment as he expressed his boundless appreciation. *"See, isn't it so much better, here?"*.

So, we returned home at the end of each day, from sun-soaked beaches and glittering seas, to the coolest, deepest shades of green. And we returned to Jason's joy - always Jason's joy. Whether returning from the shortest shopping trip, or from a week-long adventure to Brittany, Jason's response was always quite wonderful: *"Rejoice! Rejoice!"*. He would fly round the garden in ecstasy. Hector, too, was excited, and would compete manfully - but Jason's tremendous relief and high-spirits were over-powering. The recollection of this out-pouring of joy, expressed with such heartfelt sincerity, will remain with me for ever.

And, after a long, eventful day, Jason, in particular, would often retire to bed before us. If it proved necessary to light a fire, that was a signal for his early retirement upstairs. On so many evenings I would find Jas, hours later, splayed across our bed, feet in the air, apparently gazing at the stars through the bedroom window.

He seemed at one with the world.

******

It is inevitable that we view France through a prism of Britishness. However, charming as it is, delightful as it is, and no matter how endlessly fascinating, France is a *foreign* country. Despite its geographical proximity, France is indeed, and hopefully will remain - to the average Brit - an exotic and unique country, and culture. That's what makes it so special.

Over the last 25 years, France has changed, and perhaps presented a more open face. When we first attempted to open a bank account, we were met with a Gallic shrug, followed by a polite but firm *"No"*. Now, nearly every bank in every town centre employs an English-speaking young employee, who smiles broadly and says: *"Yes"*. And, for good or ill, France has adapted, flexed and compromised - to accommodate half-a-million Brits, global capitalism, and a veritable surfeit of outlets offering the ubiquitous 'burgers'n'buns'. Quixotically, however, the more France changes, the more it remains quintessentially French.

Not surprisingly, France is the most popular tourist destination on the globe, with more than 85 million overseas visitors per year. It is easy to understand why: superb and varied scenery; wonderful coast-lines and resorts; a civilised, even chic, ambience; a superb historical and cultural legacy. Oh, and great food and wine. Even so, people continue to confide to me (with a knowing smile): *"We really like France, but don't really like the French."*. Strange to come to that conclusion, on the basis of the faintest nodding acquaintance with the French language. In my view, France and the French people are rather inextricably linked. Would we still like France *quite* so much if it was devoid of the invention and genius of the French people? As expressed in French cuisine? Patisserie? Roquefort cheese? Château Lafite, Margaux or Yquem (et al?). Or Mont St Michel? The Eiffel Tower? Notre Dame? No, I thought not.

Most of the finest qualities of our civilisation are defined by words beginning with the letter 'C', as in civilisation itself, together with courtesy, civility, culture, creativity, cuisine, and countryside. And of course champagne. France acquits itself mightily in all these respects. France remains, in its language and culture, a courteous nation; there are more 'bonjours' and smiles per person, per square kilometre, than anywhere else I know. To their eternal credit, Hector & Jason loved France and the French people, who so often made a terrific fuss of them; and they revelled and delighted in all that this magnificent country has to offer.

Never fear: this is not yet another of those excitable, over-effusive tomes about French life and culture that, unintentionally, perhaps, get up one's nose. For all that we were in France, we might have been a million miles away from the familiar tourist haunts. And there is always another side to life and travel: difficult people, (a universal phenomenon), the language problem (don't minimise it); the sheer difficulty of getting things done. One glosses over these things, since they retreat in the memory, in the light of the pleasures and the positives. For H&J, however, the pleasure principle was all-pervasive. When Hector suspected - from the various preparations - that a trip to Normandy was imminent, he would jump in the back of the car, with intense and touching excitement. Even Jason would hover on the path, expectant and not *wholly* averse to the journey ahead.

French people work to live, rather than live to work. Make no mistake: people work hard, but play hard, too. Quality of life is the key thing, and vital to the French psyche. This 'quality of life' centres on culture, in its broadest sense, and relationships with family and friends. This culture is proud, as well as broad: a few miles from our cottage lies the village of Ménil Villement. On the outskirts of the village are the skeletal remains of what was once one of the largest textile mills in the whole of France. A sign proudly reveals the fact that the factory produced school outfits, and military uniforms, for large sections of French society. However, the proudest boast is that the mill also produced the fabric for the wedding dress worn by Brigitte Bardot, when she married Roger Vadim in 1952.

Modern Brits love, they say, French bread, and French cheese - and the French life-style. Yet surely there has to be more to it than that? The countryside, and the sense of space, perhaps? An old-fashioned (to us) ambience? A nostalgia for an idealised past that was more leisurely, less hurried, more fulfilling, always sunny? But, of course, we bring our cultural baggage with us, as surely as we bring our tea-bags and and satellite TV.

Despite these truisms, there are often serious misconceptions amongst Brits about the reality of living in France. The most disconcerting of these is that France is, or should surely be, 'free'. That is, cost-free. This, despite the fact that France is a modern country, with a highly developed, monetized, capitalist economy.

Though the cost of living may, on the whole, be marginally less than in the UK, that cost of living is a certain and inconvenient fact of life. From property to petrol, from a baguette to boules, everything - *everything* - (including - especially - water) has a price tag. It's simply not possible to live on the Euro equivalent of a tenner a week, and still have change for *saucisse et frites*.

If, for example, you feel the urge to visit a *docteur*, that'll be 25 Euros, thanks very much. And bills - electricity, water, and tax - land on the door-mat with monotonous regularity. In order to thrive - even survive - it's essential to have a regular income, from some or other source. And, without marketable skills *and* fluent French, that income is unlikely to be earned in France itself; France has its own (French speaking) unemployed people - including graduates: all anxious for jobs, and eager for salaries.

Certainly, if your idea of Paradise is a tent in the middle of nowhere, getting around by bicycle, you can live pretty cheaply. But it's not a lifestyle that will appeal to many, for long. A baguette, a chunk of cheese and a glass of plonk are all very well, but to enjoy, even sample, France at its best, a reasonable income is a necessity. Only the air is free. Having accepted these 'facts of life', you can now begin to relax, and enjoy.

It is not well-known that that most English of writers, Mr Dickens, was a francophile, inveterate traveller to France, and fluent French speaker (well done, sir). In fact, he harboured a wish that he had been born a Frenchman. At the other end of the scale, the inimitable General de Gaulle, who had lived in London for most of the war, allegedly commented, (in French, of course) upon the liberation of France, "*Don't expect us to be grateful*". This is a very different country to 24/7 Britain, and one had better not forget it. As I reminded my brother on a recent trip, the shops still close between 12 noon and 2.00pm (at least), you're likely to starve if you arrive on a public holiday, and, no, they don't serve malt vinegar with their frites.

In *Landscapes in France,* A.N. Wilson remarks that '*Only in a very few places in France....does one ever quite feel beyond the touch or trace of one's fellow beings*'. I can only say that my own experience is the exact opposite: 'La France Profonde' seems, to this sensibility, extraordinarily 'other', seemingly unexplored, a land of mystery and romance, intensely strange; this imbues ramblings with a frisson of expectancy, sometimes even menace. So many parts of rural France have a forgotten air, in stark contrast to the pristine, manicured (and be-littered) countryside in the UK. Many times, in many places, I have felt a sense of mystery, of remoteness, of the oneness of nature, in Normandy and elsewhere in France - a feeling I have rarely experienced in England. In a country as densely populated as our own, it is hard to escape one's fellow-creatures - especially in beauty spots whose beauty is often submerged beneath a tide of humanity.

As well as greater remoteness, the richness of wild flowers and the sheer variety of countryside ('pays') the French can also enjoy a virtual absence of litter. I have walked amidst some of the most remote and inaccessible landscapes of Britain - to find crisp packets, chocolate wrappers and drinks cans awaiting my arrival. The scourge of litter, a

British disease, always undermines a wilderness experience; but rarely so in the Normandy I know and love.

Ah, let's get back to Normandy, a little universe of it's own:

'Normandy is a rich, lush land farmed by a people apart. Normans never do anything by halves. They work hard, eat heartily and drink deep. That is the essence of Normandy and its people'.

Arthur Eperon's admirably succinct description of the Norman character is as true today as when it was written, over 25 years ago. This is what attracted us to Normandy all those years ago, and why we continue to return, month after month, year after year.

The fields of Normandy produce what may be described as a gourmet's delight. Not only huge quantities of wheat, barley and sweetcorn, but some of the richest milk and butter, and some of the most famous cheeses, on the planet. The famous Camembert, Livarot and Pont-l'Evêque are merely three amongst thirty or so cheeses produced in the area. And Normandy is also a great cider producing area: these are often farm-made, with all the craft and care associated with wine making. Similarly, Calvados, or Calva, the famous apple spirit, when aged and at its most refined, is as rarified and silky as any single malt Scotch whisky. Long before we acquired our Norman property, and following a superb meal in a local hotel one Winter evening, June and I relaxed in the glow of a roaring fire, sipping 30-year old Calva. The experience - and the inner glow - were simply wonderful.

And yet, despite all this dairy largesse, and the great culinary tradition which it has inspired, judging from the evidence of one's own eyes, and the obituaries printed in the local press, Normans generally live healthy, long lives. Many an ancient matron, or gnarled farmer, can be found relaxing on a low wall in the Normandy sunshine, in a tranquil reverie, reflecting on their life's drama.

Even so, however much one enjoys the sheer difference of Normandy, one is never too far from Blighty, particularly during the annual British Summer Invasion. 'Spot the Brit' is only too easy - and I count myself in this. We Brits dress differently, walk differently, and have a different demeanour. Annie, our first French neighbour, once gave an impression of a British (woman) walking in a street: it was hilarious simply because it was so accurate, and so familiar.

And it is a little sad to see, increasingly, a kind of apartheid among supermarket shelves, with 'Brit food' - no doubt by popular demand - stacked separately from French fare, in a dubious aisle all by itself. It seems that our appetite for PG Tips tea, Marmite, marmalade, Hartley's jam, Fray Bentos pies - and curries - has not only transcended national barriers, but survived exposure to one of the finest cuisines, and the highest quality produce, on the planet. This trend really is, if dependable, also predictable, and depressing. We have even seen 'English teas' advertised by the roadside - this in a land whose patisserie, fresh cream and crème fraiche are simply the finest available. And, as we know, H&J's *viande animaux* was far superior, to H&J, than any proprietary dog food, to judge from their salivating expectancy while the viande cooked, then cooled, and their ravenous cleaning of their lately charged, now shiny, steel dishes.

These British food-enclaves go hand-in-hand with another strange phenomenon among Brits on holiday in France - the studious ignoring of each another - that is, even more than is the case in Britain. These Brits will acknowledge, even try to converse with, the locals. But, as for fellow country-men: *"I am enjoying, experiencing, France. You do not exist"*.

On one occasion, we decided to leave H&J in the cool of the cottage, whilst we had lunch at a rural retreat two kilometres away. The restaurant is miles and miles from anywhere on the tourist map. We entered the doorway: practically every table was occupied by family groups. One could hear a pin drop. It was clear to us immediately that the whole place was chock full of Brits - of course, us included. Where on Earth had they all come from? The passable French of a few of them could not possibly deceive us. In the time-honoured tradition of Brits in France, we all ignored each other. *"I'm in France, thank you very much"*.

I have long been fascinated by the pattern of land ownership in France, particularly in Normandy. Most farms seem, still, to be family-run affairs, and it is common to see the farmer accompanied on his tractor by his sons, or his wife. Until quite recently, these incredibly hard-working families were described - offensively - in the British press as 'peasant farmers'. Most often, farms will consist of a patchwork of fields, built-up and augmented over generations, and only loosely connected to a farm-house and out-buildings. Judging from the shining, modern equipment employed on the fields, and with one eye on global grain prices, these farms are prosperous, and flourishing.

How different all this seems from Zola's *The Earth, (La Terre)*, published in 1886, a tale of farm-folk that is shocking in its violence: greed, theft, lust - both sexual, and lust for land - leading to rape, even murder. Vitriol spills across the pages of the novel in an orgy of hate and bile. *The Earth* is set in Napoleonic times, the action taking place in the rural lands around Chartres - itself close to the border of Normandy. The novel creates an atmosphere - imbued with low cunning, and social menace - that is certainly reminiscent of rural Normandy, but of course (nowadays) without the blood-eyed savagery that so dismayed the novel's first readers.

Clearly, *The Earth* describes a fictional extreme, but must have resonated with a contemporary audience. Clearly, also, times have changed. Still, one wonders at the legacy of the past, and what inner tensions and jealousies still tear at families and neighbours, as land is carved up for the rising generation. One senses a great deal of private calculation, and personal agendas rooted in long history; to the foreign interloper, this is a closed book. This is, after all, a foreign country, with deeply-imbued traditions and local and family politics of which we can be only dimly aware. There remains a depth and mystery to this *France profonde* which is closed to foreign eyes; we see only the surface gold and green.

The 'Chasse Guarde' and 'Chasse Interdite' signs, too, attest to the sharp modern debate among the pro and anti hunting lobbies, and give a clue to passions cutting deeply. In the countryside, however, there is an almost visceral attachment to the tradition of hunting, which the Frenchman regards as his birthright, and an even deeper passion for the supremacy of *land* as a birthright. Title to even the meanest patch of waste ground can give rise to extraordinary conflict and melodrama. While it may make us feel uncomfortable, Zola captured the rural French heart in its most primal state.

The Normandy novel par excellence, however, is of course *Madame Bovary*. Though published in 1857, (the action taking place perhaps a generation earlier) and set in countryside not far from Rouen, the novel casts a long shadow. Flaubert describes the area on the borders of Normandy, Picardy and the Ile de France as a *'bastard region'*, lacking charm and fertility. But so much in Flaubert continues to resonate to this day: the rural landscape and hedgerows, the big skies and big moons, the ancient farms, the slate roofs and shutters, the endless rain, the crowing cocks, the dogs barking in the distance. Emma Bovary, too, was given an Italian Greyhound, Yanoda, as a present; though she doted on it, it escaped and was lost for ever.

There is a contemporary place, too, for the confident steeples of mid-19th century churches, the huge crucifixes that pock-mark the landscape, and time-worn bars and restaurants - they are all steeped in history, but live also in the present. And the mind-set of the rural Norman people, historically derived from Norsemen, is as familiar and peculiar as it was to Flaubert. Even the watch-dogs on their chains survive. Only the wolves have gone.

And the landscapes, the bucolic village scenes, and the culture of the countryside, have been captured forever in the rich-toned *pays* paintings by Henri Levavasseur and Andre Hardy, evoking all the colour, rural culture, beauty and passion of this region.

Why mention all this? Well, firstly, it gives an inkling as to what first drew us to Normandy - the lure of countryside, culture, and cuisine. Secondly, it provides a background and context to our lives and wanderings around this diverting, historic *Département.* Finally, there is, for me, an absorbing paradox: an unresolved, evolving miracle of diversity and richness amongst the panoply of human activity; remarkably, of space, still, for nature and wildlife, among the flowing cornfields, pasture and paddocks.

Despite - or perhaps because of - the richness and diversity of its agriculture, Normandy's countryside is simply fabulous. The Suisse Normande contains endless fields of golden crops, nearly all surrounded by thick bocage and ancient trees. There are orchards, paddocks and wild meadows, replete with hoary old fruit trees, and silk-flanked charolais cattle chewing the sweet grass; sumptuous sheep, and handsome horses. There are extensive forests, often coppiced or pollarded, but with great specimen trees that remember the French Revolution. And there are wild, undisturbed places, with streams, ponds, marshes and carpets of wild flowers - bluebells, daffodils, orchids - dancing in dappled sunlight, in a mad profusion, as though this was the very first morning.

And into, and over, and through, these delightful places Hector, Jason and I would roam. Through the fragrant fields and meadows, through the woodlands, over the hills. Around every twist and turn, around every corner, the richness, the natural bounty of France unfolds in all its glory; and through these sun-fringed, luminous, vibrant passageways we would bound. We witnessed the endless skies, and clouds like vast, amorphous galleons, in silent awe. And flotillas of birds - crows, starlings, geese - floating lazily across the heavens. A planet seething with life and energy; and we, spell-bound, in some sort of communion with its spirit.

And Jason, spread out on our bed at night, gazing upwards at the stars...

The Sound of Silent Sundays

The balm of silent Sundays' sunny, sweet serene,
Could smooth the wrinkled brow, inspire a rich tureen.

Colin Hill

Sunday - *Dimanche* - in France, is still a special day. The orgy of consumerism is checked and stilled by close of play on Saturday afternoon. Sundays are given over to hearty hospitality with family and friends, and to fine food and wine. The butcher and baker, and even a Sunday market or two, will minister to your earthly needs on Sunday mornings. But the vast majority of retail emporia remain firmly *fermé*.

Sunday afternoons are tranquil, apart from the buzz of restaurants and the tinkle of glasses and laughter. Two sounds, only, break the rural silence and, in so doing, draw attention to it. There are the church bells, resonating through the valley from Ségrie Fontaine, and always welcome to my ears. The peel of the bells somehow accentuates the silence, most evocatively through the mists of Autumn and Winter. And those cool, misty seasons resound with the sharp crack of gun-fire, puncturing the still air with deadly intent.

This other sound, that from the local hunt, seeking its quota of venison, hare, or even wild boar, is the saddest music to my ears. Hunting in this way is a deeply held tradition in France: Ménil Hubert's very name is taken from St Hubert, the Patron Saint of, yes, hunting. A stone carving of a deer's head is sited prominently on a public building. And there can be no doubt that Hector & Jason - most certainly Hector - would have *loved* to have joined the '*chasse*'.

For me, the glimpse of a roe deer always gave such a thrill; they are so beautiful, and more exquisite still in their sensitive, utter wildness.

The sight of these lovely, sentient mammals being terrorised and killed - even for the table - churns my guts. Call me a sentimental old fool, or a spoil-sport, but I was exceptionally careful to ensure that H&J played no part in these activities, but were mere observers, and from a respectable distance. Give Hector a yard...Fortunately, however, the hunting season passes with the Winter, calm is restored, and the survivors can resume their lives un-molested.

Back in England, June and I celebrate the difference of Sundays almost against the grain of what is now the busiest shopping day of the week. And why not? Each to his own. But in France, we fall in with the natural rhythm of the day, and enjoy, reflect and relax. For Hector & Jason, in England as well as in France, Sunday meant more 'me time'; time for leisurely walks, and a different tempo. If, in England, Saturday afternoons were our big trip day, to a forest or heath, Sunday was the quiet day, with more local, but longer, excursions, less dependent upon the clock.

Long ago, perhaps when Hector's & Jason's grand-daddy was yet a glint in *his* daddy's eye, and before we had even espied La Haute Maison, we were staying in a charming hotel a mere 12 miles or so from the cottage. It was on that very Sunday afternoon that I spied the young waitress carrying a bag of scraps to the nearby yard, where she casually fed the excited chickens clucking around her. This empathy with the earth, and with authentic, real food, affected me deeply; here was a place where I would be happy to live. It still is.

Many Brits move to France to discover a new life, or to re-discover an old one. The book-shelves are groaning with tomes tempting us to sample the rustic charms of rural France, and 'the good life'. There is information-overload concerning the quality of life, the cuisine, the culture, the ambience, the impossibly charming villages, the (to British ears and eyes) eccentric but friendly locals. Certainly, the anticipation of a hearty Sunday lunch would send me meandering to one of my favourite patisseries, in search of a mouth-watering pear-and-chocolate tart.

And it's largely true. I could go on...But there is a 'but'. France is a different country, with different laws, customs, culture - and language - and the Brit, parachuting in, would be advised to get to grips, with as much enthusiasm and excitement as he can muster, at least the basics of the country he is privileged to be able to adopt. Arrogance, and a patronising approach, is not what is desired, or indeed welcomed. If you have made a choice to come to live in France, the very least you can do is to try to adapt to a new lifestyle - to integrate, to grasp the hand that has been so cordially extended. That small human gesture will pay huge dividends in terms of the quality and depth of your French experience.

If we ignore these common courtesies, this natural empathy and reaching out, trying to impose our blunt Britishness on a foreign land, we risk compromising the uniqueness of French culture: turning it into a homogenised sameness, a semi-Anglicised confection. Living the French Sunday - to enjoy the day - would be a good place to start. *Vive la différence*, say I.

Winter, and Christmas, in Normandy

Andaine: So pure and thin the Winter's edge: it shocked surmise; Crack'd like a whip along the ridge; and froze our eyes.

Colin Hill

We spent many Winters, and three Christmases, in Normandy, with Hector & Jason. Winters in Normandy can be, and usually are, severe, and surprisingly cold. 18 or even 20 degrees of frost is not uncommon and, with no central heating and no double glazing in the cottage, Winter evenings tested our ingenuity. Still, we enjoyed the simplicity, the starkness, even, of the season; generations of hardy folk before us had borne these conditions with fortitude, with humour and content, and we did not want to see ourselves as 21st century softies, 'victims' of a hard frost, or a few inches of snow. We were embarking on an adventure and, in any case, H&J loved these bleak but often very picturesque conditions.

Cutting and chopping logs with a great axe and a range of saws kept me not only busy but energised. As soon as darkness approached, building the fire, tending it, and eating and drinking, kept us both occupied and relatively warm. We retired to bed clutching hot-water bottles - not only a nostalgic echo of childhood Winters, but essential to comforting our cold flesh and rattling teeth. H&J seemed to suffer no cold, no icy blast; dog beds and chairs provided comfort enough. The house was closed and barred against the elements, while the embers faded; outside, the owls hooted and hunted, and all was still.

The arrival of Winter in Normandy impresses on every Norman, and every foreign interloper that, outside its major cities, the *Département* is a huge, black space. In an intensely rural area, the days are suddenly very short, and the nights very dark, and very long. The advent of Christmas rouses every town, village and householder to counter the gloom, spiking through the darkness with cascades and strings of multi-coloured brightness and festivity.

This can be a magical, as well as intensely traditional, season in Normandy, with everyone determined to celebrate, reflect, and to look forward to a brand new year, just around the corner. In Britain we often bemoan the lack of a 'White Christmas', with Bing Crosby crooning in the background. Well, Bing can sing his heart out. A mere 600' up in the Suisse Normande, a white Christmas is no longer to be merely a pipe dream.

Yet, despite our best endeavours, June and I always seemed to arrive either just before, or soon after, the Christmas season itself. A mixture of family and personal commitments prevented us - and H&J - from enjoying the true Norman Christmas for a number of years. So we experienced, on occasion, the extraordinary displays - often involving animal 'mobiles' - in French supermarkets; the gorgeous, extravagant, gâteaux and confections in the patisserie; the Christmas trees that sprang up everywhere, dripping with gifts; and the lights, decorations and secret Santas climbing into expectant bedrooms - but we did not savour the Christmas experience itself.

All this changed in 2008, and again in 2009, when we planned to celebrate Christmas in France. There was a certain amount of risk and anxiety involved since, of course, this meant that we needed to travel to Normandy in late December, and return at the end of the year, or very early in the New Year. Quite obviously, this period has the potential for the most adverse weather of the whole year. As we know, severe weather in the UK - particularly snow - can quickly cause chaos, bringing traffic to a grinding halt, and interminable delays. In Normandy, in turn, a fall of snow can rapidly render minor, rural roads completely impassable. Since our house is at an elevation of 640', at the summit of a steep, winding road, the route may be blocked by heavy snow. Fine, if one is snowed in. Traumatic, if one is on route.

In Western Europe, we live in one of the world's most connected, most urbanised areas; yet a thin blanket of snow - a duvet thick - still has the capacity to create mayhem, serious delay, and severe risk. Add the simple fact of responsibility for two dogs, and one can appreciate that an apparently straightforward, routine journey can become discordant - replete with drama, danger, and disquiet. Getting stuck in a blizzard, with the added responsibility of two plucky boys, might be a very serious business.

Three times we made this trip - 2008, 2009, and (a little before Christmas) in 2010. On every one of these journeys we encountered thick snow. On one of them, we were racing ahead of snow-filled skies, and just beat a complete log-jam near Newbury - by the skin of our teeth. On two occasions, we barely made it to the cottage, battling through blizzards and deep snow. Despite every preparation, there was a knife edge between success (and content) and failure (and distress). The journeys were nail-biting, just as the cold, wind and snow were also truly biting. But we did it, and we're glad we did it. The boys loved it, and so did we - eventually.

On each of these visits, we enjoyed a white Christmas - a white-over, one might say - with hares hopping over the garden, and blackbirds, contrasting starkly against the snow, scrabbling for food. My principal impression is of constant daytime sunshine, gleaming on a white landscape; of trips enjoyed, gingerly, on ice-caked roads; and of walks with H&J in temperatures of which freezers can only dream. And of a surfeit of superb food and drink, and mountainous, roaring fires, all the more satisfying given our closeness to nature in the almost raw. It's fair to say that H&J loved every minute - the snow, the sunshine, even the intense cold - well, almost every minute - since Jason hated the fire, whatever the conditions. Even so, since we lit the fire so early (say 4.00pm, just before the light, and the little warmth generated by the sun, began to fade) the flames and sparks soon subsided into a great, warm glow, when even Jason rested comfortably.

On our first Christmas at La Haute Maison, in 2008, Christmas Eve gave us fresh, powder snow, late in the evening. A White Christmas, seemingly imbued with new hope, and thoroughly enjoyed at our snug French home. On Boxing Day we ventured to the lovely Andaine Forest, along roads encrusted with ice, with hedges frozen white. After parking in a woodland clearing, we walked out into the sparkling light. The mighty forest was still, and pristine. The ion-charged air was so chilled that it smarted one's face; the little ruffle of breeze seemed to cut to the bone, like a knife. Even breathing the frozen air, in little snatches, was painful. Hector & Jason pulled on regardless, as remorseless as ever. Despite the conditions, they remained indefatigable, incorrigible.

Within half an hour, though, June and I had had enough; we retreated back to our vehicle for restorative coffee and turkey sandwiches. As always, H&J offered a helping hand. Then, a gingerly retreat home, arriving in a blue, fading light. An early, hearty fire was gladly lit, built-up to withstand the fearful cold of the evening, and to sustain us through the long, bitter night to come. *"Does life really get any better than this?"* was a question I often repeated during these years. The question answers itself.

We decked the house with all the seasonal trimmings, including a highly-decorated, fresh Christmas tree, opened cards and presents with glee, and enjoyed battling with the elements on our rambles. The external hazards, and our relative isolation, somehow made the seasonally special food and drink taste extraordinarily good. These sparkling interludes passed, apart from the alarming anxiety of getting from a-to-b (to shops) and then from b-to-a, (and a-to-c, in terms of our rendezvous with our French vets) almost entirely without incident: we just enjoyed being there, enjoyed H&J, and enjoyed them, enjoying themselves. Happy, happy days.

Christmas was always served up, splendidly, on a Russell Hobbs mini-cooker, courtesy of June's ingenuity. The result - usually locally reared chicken or cockerel - was always worth waiting for, always to savour. And the fayre provided an extra-special Christmas lunch for two special boys.

In 2010, we even enjoyed two Christmases - the first in Normandy, in the first week of December, the second in Britain, at the usual time. Unusually, we had two Christmas trees, two Christmas dinners, two sets of crackers and decorations. On our trip to and from Normandy, the weather was alarming in both directions - surprisingly so, since the outward journey took place on 30 November. We were also able to celebrate the boys' birthday, in Normandy, on 1 December.

Again, we survived the bleakest weather, even more onerous on this occasion, since I travelled alone with H&J, while June followed a couple of days later. At first, all went well - the weather forecast anticipated benign conditions. There was cause for concern, though, as we entered the Newbury bypass to flurries of snow, that soon became more dense and persistent. I put my head down, gritted my teeth, and concentrated like mad. We reached Portsmouth with some relief, and settled down for the Ferry journey ahead. I was even more relieved when, on reaching Ouistreham, there was precious little evidence of snow. So, that great chasm that was the English Channel had come to our aid...

It was dark when we disembarked, and snow-less. A few miles further on, though, the first dread fingers of snow appeared along the hedgerows, and the downfall grew more and more intense. As we progressed towards the minor country roads it became harder and harder to pick out the route, since the tarmac tracks were obliterated by virgin snow, and the dense fall obscured the winding road ahead. Finally, nearing the cottage, and almost blinded by the white deluge, I turned down a track that I had thought led to home - but instead led to Les Bruyeres, a nearby farmhouse. The car slipped and slid dangerously, perilously close to the deep ditches on both sides of the farmhouse track.

Finally, breathlessly, we arrived at the cottage. The lock on the gate was frozen solid. H&J exhibited far more sang froid than I could muster as I ushered them out of the car, and down through the neighbours' dark, deep, deserted garden, lit only by the reflected snow and my torch. We scrambled through the wire fence into our own garden, opened our door, and turned on the lights. Hector & Jason were agitated, but relieved and elated, as they played in the thick snow blanketing the garden. I was intensely grateful just to have made it. I'd never been so glad to see the house, midnight-dark and petrified by cold as it was.

The next day, June had her own difficult journey to make, with deep snow now covering the whole of Normandy, and the little road up to the cottage a sheet of thick ice. For the next few days we negotiated the road with great care, as we made occasional forays for supplies. Thankfully, that long, lone journey, in an eerie combination of blizzard and darkness, was mercifully not repeated.

These anxieties, quietly remembered, are still outshone by the glowing space of Christmas, celebrated with those I love.

19: Normandy '44: Dooms-Day: Dare we Forget

If we can stand up to him (Hitler) all Europe may be free and the life of the world may move forward into broad sunlit uplands.

Winston Churchill - Speech, 18 June 1940

Next to a battle lost, the greatest misery is a battle gained.

The Duke of Wellington

Wandering through the Norman bocage, along the twisting little lanes sprinkled liberally with wild flowers, Normandy embraces us in all its innocence. It appears as a quintessence, a dream of green. The leaves of Summer-clad trees colour the light, infusing it with a refreshing, sparkling verdure, in a hundred different hues.

Yet, sadly, in truth, it is impossible to venture around Normandy's towns and cities - and even its countryside - without encountering, and being compelled to face, and comprehend, the cataclysm of war.

In this context, and strangely, the war came to us. Our first French neighbours, and first French friends, were Annie and Gilbert: a delightful couple, whose warm welcome meant so much to us in those early days. It was Gilbert who would cut our manic grass a day or two before our arrival. And Annie who would greet us at night - on hearing our car - dressed in her night-shirt, and holding a lantern aloft.

One fine Sunday, Annie and Gilbert invited us to lunch. Annie's venerable father and mother were also honoured guests. It was a splendid, warm, hospitable occasion. The food was delicious, the company excellent; all was hearty and happy, until someone mentioned - in the most oblique way - *The War*. Since we were all (British and French) generally on the same side, ignoring for a moment Vichy France, I had not imagined that the subject might invoke controversy, animosity, or anger. But it did. The venerable old chap's eyes filled with tears, and his voice trembled, as he recalled the terrible events of 60 years before. Looking directly at me, (the stereo-typical Englishman), and struggling to contain his voice, he vented his spleen. I knew that he was upset over something, but my French (though pretty familiar with every type of wine and food, and restaurant menus) was not equal to the translation of a full-throttle verbal assault, without expert assistance.

Our friend, his daughter, undertook a brief and, I can be sure, bowdlerised version of his soliloquy. It happened that, in 1940, the gentleman had been serving in the French Navy. The Navy was anchored at Mers-el-Kebir, off the coast of Oran, French Algeria. France itself had - June 1940 - been overrun and utterly defeated by German forces, and had just surrendered to the Nazis. The British Government, scared stiff that the French Navy would be given over to the enemy, and thus participate in the expected assault on Britain, decided to destroy the entire French fleet - by combined naval and air attack. Churchill called this *"a hateful decision, by far the the most unnatural and painful in which I have ever been associated"*. Most of the French fleet was destroyed; 1,297 servicemen were killed in the onslaught. This action may have done more to have saved Britain from invasion than even the Battle of Britain. But, sitting opposite a combatant who had seen fire and death rained upon his friends and colleagues - and to whom the horrific memories were as viscerally fresh some 60 years later as if they had been committed yesterday - caused me to brood on history and time.

This Sunday lunch experience happened a mite before H&J came into the world, but it is nevertheless germane to our story. Sadly, a year or two later, our good friends sold their lovely home, and moved to Nice. I think of this veteran's story often, and thank my lucky stars for the European Union, for all its imperfections. We, and H&J, have enjoyed the freedoms and benefits that, as free-roaming Europeans, we so often take for granted. Our adventures, our pleasures, our freedoms, are only possible because brave young men and women, often far from home - mainly British, Americans, and Canadians, but also French and Polish - sacrificed their youth, health and very lives for their loved ones' preservation, and our future. Visit a Norman town - Caen, or Falaise, or Ouistreham, or Arromanches, or Coleville, or Courseulles - and reflect with grateful humility and pride on the heroism that was - is - the foundation for our lasting freedom.

Criss-crossing the countryside in all directions, observing the unchanging patterns of the fields, rolling hills, farmhouses and churches, it is a mental struggle now to imagine what a bloody but noble part Normandy has played in - all our - recent history. Scratch beneath the surface, or look just a little more closely, and the graveyards and memorials yield their secrets, and reveal the grim if courageous truth. On the beautiful, sometimes bleak, headland at Granville stands an austere memorial dedicated to the fallen of the Resistance; heroes, and martyrs, all. A sadness pervades even the most delightful of scenes, since they have witnessed the most heroic and, at the same time, most appalling violence and bloodshed in an appallingly violent century.

Normandy is a naturally rich area, and blessed with abundant natural resources - so that, thanks to the spirit of its people, the region has recovered remarkably from its nightmare. But from June to September 1944, Normandy was effectively the centre of the world stage. As the Allies invaded on 6 June - 'D-Day' - Stalin wrote to Churchill that *in the whole history of war, there has never been such an undertaking*. That we are now free to indulge ourselves, travel, eat and drink - and muse on history - is due entirely to the huge sacrifice made by hundreds of thousands of Allied servicemen, together with the heroes of the French Resistance, who famously won the war for freedom. And to add - the sacrifice of tens of thousands of civilian casualties.

For once, words are not enough. If war is collective human violence at its most extreme, the campaign for Normandy was war at its most extreme. The cost, in suffering of man - and animals (mainly horses - the truly innocent) - was gargantuan, epoch-making. Antony Beevor's *D-Day*, describes it as *the cruel martyrdom of Normandy*. The deaths of combatants from all sides in the Battle for Normandy numbers a staggering 100,000. As Wellington once observed, *next to a battle lost, the greatest misery is a battle gained*.

The massive assault was code-named Operation Overlord, although the battle for Normandy is referred to by the French as *The Dénouement* (The End). We know well the towns made famous by the D-Day landings: Ouistreham, Courselles-sur-mer, Luc-sur-mer, and Arromanches, and the beaches where the liberation of Europe began: Sword, Juno, Gold, Omaha, Utah.

The 100 days of the Battle for Normandy was preceded by ferocious aerial bombing. In the months leading up to D-Day itself, many towns were reduced to rubble. Or, following the landings, pulverised in the desperate fighting to wrest control from the occupiers. 19,980 civilians perished over these three months, in addition to the 20,000 killed during the five months of preparatory bombing. Many more suffered horribly from deprivation and the loss of their homes and all they possessed. The physical scars may have been smoothed over, the fissures covered by new brick and concrete, but the power of collective memory has an altogether deeper resonance.

The innocent, beautiful bocage that I love was central to the battle for Normandy: the conflict took place around it, through it, behind it. It was called *'the battle of the bocage'*, or hedgerows. The barrier formed by the bocage played a leading role in the Normandy campaign, and shaped the tactics of the opposing forces. The high, dense, connected hedgerows could be - and were - used to hide Panzer tanks, combatants and snipers, and seriously frustrated the Allied advance. Because of the formidable bocage, the Allies progress was more protracted, difficult and painstaking than expected. Finally, a special implement was devised and fitted to tanks in order to force a way through these tall, deep hedges. An American sergeant is credited with inventing this device - leading to greater mobility, and fewer surprise attacks.

Poetry needs time in which to flower, or fester, and the ferocious Normandy Campaign yielded precious little time for reflection. So it is not altogether surprising that much of the poetry that recollects this campaign was created in the years following the Normandy campaign.

Louis Simpson was an American infantryman and D-Day veteran, whose poems were written following the amnesia he suffered after the end of the War. *Carentan O Carentan* re-lives the the trauma of conflict: juxtaposing an idealised past, of trees almost watching over young lovers as they wander along shady lanes, with an ever-present, eviscerating nightmare - where the whistling in the leaves is caused, not by the wind but, we can be sure, by artillery and tank fire, bullets and bayonets, that brutally cut down both young men, and the majestic trees themselves.

Mercifully, the forests shredded by artillery fire have grown strong again; and hedges, the glorious bocage, have survived and recovered, so that they remain an integral part of the Normandy landscape. Although there is no escape from the trauma of 1944 - and Louis Simpson's poetry, and the collective memory, deny that escape - the trees, and the flowers, have somehow redeemed the suffering, and transformed the blood shed on all sides, returning nature to its innocence and beauty. I brooded, again, on the (to my eyes) vandalism of our French neighbours, who had treated me to their own take on bocage destruction when they hired a JCB to remove our ancient boundary hedge. The hedge was laboriously replanted the following Winter, tree by tree - my own little bit of due honour to the bocage.

June and I have traversed practically the four corners of Normandy, but always with a respectful eye to history, and the suffering inflicted on combatants and civilians alike. Place names will ring out long into the future, and evoke the heroism, and steely desperation, of those times: Pegasus Bridge. Caen. Villers Bocage. Mont Pincon. The Falaise Gap. Hector & Jason have accompanied us to these sites of conflict and renown; we have visited in order to honour courage, heroism, and selfless resolve, and to pay our respects for the sacrifice made - so that we fortunate successors could live as we chose, without fear of bomb, bullet or oppression.

Rivalling only the oppressive crucifixes scattered throughout the bocage are the innumerable monuments to those fallen in war: painfully realised warriors in bronze, weapons raised, charging towards a vanished enemy. These stark, sobering memorials to, mainly, the 1914-18 conflict, reflect the agony of a blood-letting that traumatised the nation.

Many memorials, poignant and often quite discreet, can also be found scattered liberally throughout the countryside: these are dedicated to the civilian as well as military casualties incurred during World War II. But it is the military cemeteries that provide the most vivid and heart-rending testimony to sacrifice. And these cemeteries are a-plenty - 27 in all - to commemorate the fallen: German, British, American, Canadian, Polish and French.

The ravages of war seem to have spared no-one and nowhere; even the smallest, prettiest of towns and villages has its page in history. Every visit to boulangerie, epicerie, mairie or bar is redolent with the shades of the past. Every hedge, every field, could yield a terrible story. Thumbing through a recent book on the Normandy campaign, I came across a photograph of Athis-de-l'Orne from August '44: one can clearly see the fountain, and boulangerie, as they remain - only the clothes give away the historic nature of the picture.

The town of Arromanches, impressively set between mighty headlands, remains a powerfully memorable place. The town, now awash with visitors and students of history from around the world, was pivotal to the Allies' ultimate success. Apparently the idea to create an artificial harbour was Churchill's own. The massive concrete sections that were to make-up the harbour were towed over by a flotilla of ships shortly after D-Day itself. Once formed into a huge arc, the DIY harbour provided a giant, weather-protected conduit for massive supplies of men, armour, and fuel. The broken line of the Mulberry Harbour still dominates the horizon. A plaque unveiled by Lady Soames, Churchill's daughter, on 6 June 2000, says simply: '*Without Mulberry B, the liberation of Europe would not have been possible*'.

Hector & Jason gambolled along the vast beach at Arromanches, running around and between the huge, displaced sections of the harbour. Though oblivious of the role that these leviathans had played in modern history, the boys were nevertheless deeply aware of the brooding, enormous physical presence.

The famous Memorial above Omaha Beach, near Coleville-sur-mer, which commemorates fallen American heroes, touches us with an acute power. The war cemetery contains 9,387 perfectly aligned headstones, while the Garden of the Missing contains a further 1,557 names. The *Blue Guide to Normandy* describes this place as '*an impressive sight*' - for once, an understatement. The Cemetery is immaculate and hugely dignified; the atmosphere is tranquil and reverential.

An early visit with Hector & Jason was to Pointe de Hoc, near to Omaha Beach. It was here, at 6.00am on 6 June, that Lt.-Colonel James Rudder and 225 US Rangers climbed the imposing sea cliffs before engaging the enemy in order to knock out the awesome gun battery that protected this section of the Atlantic Wall. The fighting was ferocious and, by the time the Rangers were relieved on 8 June, only 90 men were left alive. We walked around the site - which is remarkably well preserved - in something approaching awe at the scale of the achievement. To comprehend the astonishing feats of arms accomplished here is truly jaw-dropping. What courage, and what single-minded determination. And at what cost.

These days, swallows and sea-birds dash across a blue sky, unperturbed by the gaily-coloured visitors, or the jagged concrete of the shattered bunkers, which brood in sullen silence on their deep memories.

Living, as June and I do, near the Staffordshire border - and with most of our dog-walking performed in Staffordshire - we have taken a keen interest in the brave exploits of the Staffordshire Regiment in Normandy. The Staffordshire Regiment's 59th Battalion played a notable part in the battle for Caen - and then for Thury Harcourt, and the Suisse Normande - and witnessed the dreadful aftermath of the Falaise Gap, around Trun and Pierre sur Dives. The Staffordshire's own mascot happens to be a dog - a bull terrier called Watchman - who is now enjoying his fifth re-incarnation.

The bloody fight for Thury Harcourt, a restored and now-handsome town at the entrance to la Suisse Normande took place between 9th and 14th August. A plaque commemorates the (59th) who, after bitter fighting, liberated the town:

'TO THE GREATER GLORY OF GOD AND IN MEMORY OF THOSE WHO DIED WHILST SERVING WITH THE 59th STAFFORDSHIRE DIVISION'

A further, desperate and bloody action took place at the hamlet of Berjou, only five kilometres or so from what is now our cottage. Between the 15th and 17th of August, British soldiers from the 43rd (Wessex) Infantry Division and the 8th Brigade of Sherwood Rangers distinguished themselves in a ferocious action with German forces determined to maintain their grip on the area. This was the penultimate battle before the closure of the 'Falaise Pocket'. The Liberation Museum pays tribute to the courage and sacrifice of participants.

The operation to surround and destroy the German 7th Army, consisting of some 200,000 retreating soldiers, was code-named, chillingly, 'Operation Totalise'. The German army, enduring withering fire from all sides and facing catastrophe, pressed grimly forwards towards a narrow escape route dubbed 'The Corridor of Death'. The desperate fighting continued under cover of darkness.

The 59th Division were not directly involved in the fighting at the Falaise Pocket between 19th and 22nd August; instead, they were part of the huge and grisly 'clean-up' operation that followed. Peter Knight, who recounts the story (1954) of the 59th Division, paints a picture of the countryside that remains accurate, and memorable:

'Normandy, in the area immediately south-east of Falaise, is very little different from the average countryside to be found in agricultural parts of Great Britain...

The population of the Falaise Pocket consists in the main of ordinary French peasants, living with their families in farmhouses which are generally grouped into small villages, to which the only access is along winding, narrow, unkept lanes. '

We have stood on Mount Ormel, at the Memorial that looks out over the vast Falaise Pocket. There is an impressive monument to its Polish defenders - a monument to indescribable violence and unbelievable suffering.

The courage, and the carnage, were beyond belief, or description. A vast, empty panorama stretched out before us. There are immense views over the Dives Valley. It is a lonely, windswept place, peopled with ghosts, with only a couple of redundant tanks to share the vibes, and the view. One is overcome with the immensity of suffering that took place. The sense of heroism, and of incalculable, terrible death, is overwhelming. I remember patting our boys, in a small act of sadness and gratitude, and looking over the valley that had witnessed almost unprecedented destruction. Here, in August 1944, almost unimaginable horror had taken place. Here, a vast Army, the German 7th Army, had perished. Here, a World War had been won, and lost.

The Memorial reads starkly, (in Polish, French and English):

'AT THIS HISTORIC SITE, ON AUGUST 19, 20, 21 AND 22 OF 1944, THE HEROES OF THE 1ˢᵗ POLISH ARMOURED DIVISION IN BLOODY AND VICTORIOUS COMBAT, SEALED OFF THE FALAISE CHAMBOIS GAP, WHERE THE ENCIRCLED GERMAN 7ᵗʰ ARMY SUFFERED TOTAL DEFEAT.
THIS FINAL BLOW DESTROYED THE GERMAN STRENGTH AND WAS THE DECISIVE ELEMENT IN THE VICTORY OF THE WAR OF 1939-1945'

The soldiers of the 59th Division encountered scenes of destruction that defy imagination. In the words of Peter Knight:

'Typical of one of these villages is Tournai, lying just south of the main Falaise-Chambois road. It was here that the signs of real devastation first became apparent, and journeying further east the terrible sights became far worse and unbelievably fantastic'.

In the Summer of 1944, great numbers of enemy combatants lay where they had fallen, along with many thousands of their horses:

'They lay where they had been shot down, and here, surely, was warfare in its most useless form. These beasts, particularly the horses, had been man's assistant in war and peace; they had no connection with the reasons for war; they were not human and so could in no way help what was happening'.

Though it was Spring, a fierce, gusty wind bleared my eyes.

And then - because we had been privileged to be saved through the spilling of so much blood, so much of it totally innocent - we continued our journey. Only a few miles away lies the charming, flower-filled village of Camembert, now seemingly a world away from war's blood and iron. And then we travelled through a delightful and unembarrassed landscape, and so to home: to our own *'winding, narrow, unkempt'* lane; to our little home comforts, and the same birdsong that had greeted our forebears in 1944.

Some time before, we had visited Mont Pincon. The Mont is a steep, deserted hill. It was the site of some of the bloodiest fighting, taking place between 6/7 August. Little wooden crosses, with poppies, were studded into the landscape: left by colleagues or relatives in honour of fallen comrades. The little crosses are stark testament to the extreme heroism displayed here in the Summer of '44. Ghosts and shadows swirl in the mists that surround the site. The wind blows fiercely across the furze-covered hill.

As well as the national euphoria that greets the 14th July each year, around 6 June, the exact date depending on local Liberation, commemorations take place in towns and villages across Normandy. The Liberation is celebrated with the utmost dignity, honour and ceremony. Flags and flowers accompany local dignitaries, veterans, gendarmes and brass bands as they remember the sacrifice of civilians and soldiers that led France, and Europe, to freedom.

Hector & Jason had a strange, if distant, connection with these epoch-making events. As we know, they began their lives near Uttoxeter. Not far from here, in the village of Fauld, an extraordinary event took place on 27 November 1944, when a gigantic ammunition dump accidentally ignited, setting off the largest man-made explosion ever recorded up to that time. The severity of the blast has only been exceeded by the nuclear cataclysms that have occurred since. Seventy people lost their lives, and the village and its environs were completely destroyed. The very fact of this tragedy is now buried almost as deep as the reservoir that disappeared as a result of this climactic event.

I began this Chapter with a personal anecdote, and will end it with another.

I recollect my old allotment-eer in arms, one fine September day many years ago. Leaning on his spade in the sunshine, the old chap told me - sketchily - about his service on the Russian Front, and then in Italy. Suddenly, everything clicked into place. The gent everyone referred to affectionately as 'einz' (as in the baked beans, but with silent 'h') was in fact Heinz, pronounced (Highntz) as one would if, in, well, Germany.

Heinz - one of the lucky ones - had been captured in the Autumn of 1944, while eating grapes in a vineyard: he compared the sunshine we were basking in with the weather on that fateful, perhaps fortunate, day. Shortly afterwards, he had been transferred to a prisoner of war camp in Brierley Hill (of all places) and, on his release several years later, stayed on, married a local girl, and raised a family.

I pondered his incredible story, stood, as we were, on a patch of ground in the middle of the Black Country, a million light years from the cataclysmic events of his early adult life. "*You should write down your memoirs - publish them*", I suggested. He laughed, and shook his head: "*I couldn't do that*" he replied, elliptically. "*But I'll tell you one thing - they thought more of the horses than they did of us - they could replace us*".

Heinz, who had survived the almost unimaginable, was later run down, whilst waiting for a bus, by a 17-year old, uninsured, youth. Heinz survived, just, but all but the outlines of his incredible story are now lost to time.

It was Heinz's reference to 'war horses' that tugged on my memory, when I reflected on the killing fields of the Falaise Gap. It is surely fitting that, in addition to The Cenotaph, and the thousands of war memorials erected throughout the UK to honour the fallen, there is now a National Memorial - in Hyde Park - to commemorate the millions of animals that served Britain in man-made conflicts. These sentient creatures included enormous numbers of horses, mules, donkeys - and dogs. Animals served, and suffered, and died, in great numbers. In the terrible conflagration that we call the First World War, eight million horses perished. On the final day of the Allies withdrawal from Gallipoli, on 8 January 1916, 35,268 men, and 3,689 horses, were successfully evacuated, without loss. At the very same time, 508 mules were shot, apparently to prevent them from falling into enemy hands.

More recently, but upliftingly, in the 20ᵗʰ Century's second great conflict, dogs were parachuted into enemy territory along with Airborne Divisions: they descended on their own parachutes, and ordered to 'quarter' the ground, seeking out injured paratroops.

The humble pigeon, too, made an enormous contribution during two World Wars - greatly assisting communications, when radio was still in its infancy, and collecting vital intelligence, with the help of (mainly French) collaborators. Between 1941 and 1944, 16,554 birds were dropped (by plane) over Europe, by British intelligence operatives. One, British, pigeon - Cher Ami - was donated to American forces on the Western Front: she flew through atrocious enemy fire, and was shot down. Though wounded in the breast, blinded in one eye, and carrying a badly damaged leg, Cher Ami got up and flew on; her action saved the lives of an entire battalion, who were surrounded by German forces. The pigeon, too, survived, and was fitted with an artificial leg made specially by grateful soldiers.

The National Memorial is not only fitting, but beautiful, and intensely moving. The inscription reads:

'This monument is dedicated to all the animals that served and died alongside British and Allied forces in wars and campaigns throughout time.'

The second, smaller inscription, simply reads:

'They had no choice.'

A respectful and affectionate footnote:

British War Dogs

British War Dogs, by Lieut-General Edwin Richardson, describes the valiant role played by dogs in serving British forces during World War I. Richardson was ideally placed to record the role of British War Dogs, since he himself was largely responsible for persuading Army chiefs that dogs could perform valuable service in supporting the Army. The Lieut-General then played a vital part in sourcing and training the recruits themselves. The 'War Dog School' was the result.

Whilst the title itself may rattle modern sensibilities, *British War Dogs* is a remarkable book; it tells an astounding, indeed inspirational, story. And it is a story that deserves to be much better known. Richardson's expert account is told with appreciation, even affection - but without sentimentality. The bare facts are impressive in themselves. By the end of the Great War in November 1918, many thousands of dogs had served their country with great distinction. Their brave, selfless service contributed to a successful outcome; and saved the lives of countless British and Commonwealth soldiers.

In the early days of the War, dogs were recruited from the 'Home for Lost Dogs' at Battersea; then, from Birmingham, Liverpool, Bristol and Manchester Dogs Homes. Ironically, recruitment as war dogs saved many of these super dogs from almost certain death. As these dogs proved their worth and the need for more recruits grew ever more acute, ordinary British citizens were encouraged to send their family pet for service on the Front. Writes one good lady: *'I have given my husband and sons, and now that he too is required, I give my dog'.*

The British were not the first, or only, nation to employ war dogs for service in this way. In fact, the Germans were the first to do so, having prepared and trained large numbers of dogs before the onset of hostilities. And the French army employed 150 'chiens sanitaires' whose sterling role was to search and find soldiers who had been wounded and stranded on the battlefield.

British war dogs carried out three distinct roles, depending on their individual talents: guard dog, sentry dog or messenger dog. All dogs required careful training for such responsible roles. Lt-General Richardson writes: *'It should clearly be understood...that the trained dog considers himself highly honoured as a servant of His Majesty, and renders no reluctant service'.* Meanwhile, he says, the dog's Keeper will understand that *'while regarding it as a dog, (he) also realises in it the presence of qualities, such as reason, honesty, wit, affection, pluck, - in fact, the like qualities of the human mind - the desire to exhibit these manifestations of intelligence becomes very strong'.*

The role of the Guard Dog was exactly that: to guard and protect property and military assets from any approach or threat from unfriendly forces - a serious and responsible job in wartime, and one which the chosen dogs provided with conscientiousness, concentration and a strong sense of duty - at the same time freeing many soldiers from this laborious task.

The Sentry Dog performed a quite different role: helping to prevent or warn against attack; this included accompanying soldiers whilst out on patrol. Often, the Sentry Dog would warn his companions of danger from enemy raiding parties; many lives were saved in this way.

However, it is the dogs trained as messengers that attract the greatest admiration. Since field telephones were often useless, and human messengers not only relatively slow, but extremely vulnerable to enemy fire, the role of dogs was crucial. Messenger dogs carried their vital messages day - and, remarkably, by night - negotiating miles of mud, water, shell-holes, and swathes of barbed-wire, while always at risk from enemy fire and exposure to gas. Richardson writes of these remarkable, valiant messengers: *'There have been many occasions when a situation, at one moment so full of anxiety and uncertainty, has been completely transformed by the arrival, out of the chaos and darkness, of one of these brave dogs bearing its message of information and appeal'.*

This dangerous, difficult work has been dutifully recorded. The record of the dogs valour is sometimes unbearably poignant. One Keeper - Keeper Brooks - reports that Tom *'has been gassed and got a bit of shrapnel but is quite well again'.* Keeper Osbourne reports that *'Jim was instrumental in giving the first warning of gas, due no doubt to his highly sensitive nose, whereupon he was immediately released with the warning to Hdqtrs., arriving there a little more than three-quarters of an hour earlier than the warning given by wire. His worth is beyond value and his services beyond praise'.* We are proudly told of Nell that *'this dog alone saved hundreds of lives'.* Keeper Dowdeswell reports that his dog Smiler *'brought his message in safely although severely wounded'.*

Keeper Corporal Coull, recording his charges courageous service, states that *'a black retriever dog called Dick had a wonderful record, worthy of the VC... Through all his sufferings the dog carried out his duties cheerfully and most faithfully until he was overtaken by death'.* In writing about his own experience, Keeper Sergeant Brown testifies that *'The old idea was that a dog's life was nothing, but after my experience I have had with them in the field it has taught me to love and respect them as never before'.*

Writing about the messenger dogs unerring 'homing' instinct - despite conditions that included total darkness and featureless terrain

- Richardson concludes admiringly: *'It must be confessed, that in trying to account for the cause of this wonderful instinct in his four-footed friend, man is hopelessly nonplussed, and can only admit with admiring humility, that in this respect at all events, dog beats man completely'.*

Remarkably - he must have had many weighty issues on his mind - in his final Despatch of the War, Field Marshal Haig paid tribute to the contribution made to the war effort by the Army's messenger dogs.

In a story that I read with no little pride, Keeper McGregor writes of his dogs that: *'I wish to let you know that my dogs are doing very well over here. I have them running from one company to another. The retriever did 8 kilos in a little over half an hour and the other in 20 minutes'.*

Finally, Keeper Ferriby's dog, Sharp - how aptly named - won a competitive race, and a silver cup, for his speed, covering a mile in 1 minute 50 seconds.

The great Roger Bannister - the first man to break the four-minute barrier - would have been left trailing in his wake...

20: 2005: France without End: a Vintage French Year

Lads! Were we ever so impassioned, so alive
As on our wild and wondrous walks in Two-O-Five?

Colin Hill

Two Paradises 'twere in one,
To live in Paradise alone.

Thoughts in a Garden - Andrew Marvell

In March, 2005, I enjoyed what is often euphemistically styled a 'career break'. In other words, the money had run out and I had been declared redundant. For a man in his early 50s, this might be regarded as little short of a disaster, since new jobs and oldish men are rarely a marriage made in Heaven.

This is not how it appeared to me at the time, or since. My role - essentially involving economic regeneration - had become purgatory. Spring was approaching, and it was decided that I should spend some quality time in Normandy, with my little pot of redundancy money, and my boys. Hector, Jason and I were resident in France for a total of seven weeks - short enough, you may think, but by far the longest break I had ever enjoyed. Following feverish preparations, we sallied forth on April 16, excited and expectant.

Although H&J knew the cottage and its surroundings very intimately by now, for them, too, it gave opportunity for a lengthy period of recreation and tranquillity. Together, we could enjoy simple pleasures - the newly-awakened garden, the burgeoning woods and meadows, and, in our ageing Volvo estate, meander around the countryside in all its emerging Spring glory.

I had thought that I might pick up some casual gardening or DIY work whilst in Normandy, particularly amongst the British ex-pat community. I placed some hopeful adverts in one of the magazines so beloved of Francophiles, and began to look forward to tootling around the countryside with H&J, and the frisson of discovering exciting new corners of Normandy, prior to the mundane business of cutting grass, or painting walls. In fact, while I received a number of replies, the offers were extraordinary. Did I really want to hire a JCB in order to move earth around someone's garden? Did I really want to be engaged in clearing mouse traps that had been baited weeks before? I decided, instead, to concentrate on our own property maintenance, and leave my honourable countrymen to theirs.

These issues settled, this was my - and our - time, when I could arrange for some long overdue projects to be completed. In particular, the garden gate, which was way past its sell-by date, needed completely rebuilding. (The broken double-gate had even attracted caustic remarks from the local Mayor). In addition, the cottage urgently needed a new roof to replace a terminally old and leaky one. The superb new gate was fitted during this time by a M. Serge, a self-employed artisan. The roof - or at least part of the roof - was replaced later that Summer, by the same hard-working builder.

But, with no access to new income, I set my budget (gate and roof aside) at a modest 100 Euros per week, spending this mainly on food, dog food, petrol and alcohol, (not necessarily in that order). The budget was a challenge, but one I relished. My new status as a 'non-employed' person made me keen to tighten my belt but, quite honestly, neither I - nor certainly H&J - endured any hardship.

This idyll, spent largely on my own, though in the inimitable company of H&J, also gave time for sober reflection. What did I want to do in the future? How earn a living? How live my life? It was a rare moment of repose and inner and outer peace; I savoured every sparkling day. Each morning, I listened for the church bells drifting up the valley; heard their rich, resonant, mystical voice. What did they suggest, what did they say? And each day I would observe the sleepy old oak at the bottom of the garden. When would it awake? Then, on 1 May, the giant tree un-sheathed and burst into vibrant life. It seemed like a welcome sign of good things yet to come.

Although I was pretty content with the novelty of my own company, and my own reflections, Hector & Jason added a dimension of loyalty, affection and companionship that turned what might have been a lonesome sojourn into a deeply memorable and satisfying time. Hector & Jason were in their glorious Summer years of what was to prove a gloriously long Summer. We exulted in this brimming of life; our cup over-flowed.

The cottage remains relatively isolated, with very few people to be seen - especially at night, after darkness closes in. These nights are deeply silent, and a sudden sound can startle. I am not a naturally nervous type. Even so, the physical presence of H&J was always immensely comforting, and re-assuring, during these otherwise lonely vigils.

I have clear, strong memories from this time, but, surprisingly - since this was Hector & Jason - little that one might call eventful. This was at least due in part to my exercising H&J on their leads. Whilst cars were a rarity on the road near the cottage, and fields and woods were evident everywhere one looked, I was genuinely worried about one or other of the boys going missing. Outside of our immediate area, we were hardly known, and (though they were micro-chipped) anyone finding the boys - possibly several miles distant - may have had no idea where they came from.

And, dare I say, H&J were so exceptional that the finder may have chosen not to return them. They were potentially very useful, either 'in the field', or as guards. In addition, they were of course strikingly handsome, the canine equivalent of model-on-the-arm trophies. How many people, finding a gold sovereign in the road, would be honest enough to hand it in to the police? And it is not uncommon to see a 4x4 criss-crossing the country roads, its anxious occupant making urgent enquiries of passers by about a missing canine friend.

Although it is a legal requirement in France that every dog is tattooed on the inside of its ear with a unique number, I suspect that only the super-intelligent and the lucky-lost are fortunate enough to find a Mairie or police station. Unlike foxes or wolves, domestic dogs are not attuned to the natural environment. They are used to being fed, housed and pampered. Exposed to an alien, hostile, and unforgiving natural world, most strays face an uncertain future. Only Hector, of all the dogs I have known, would have had the guile and instincts to have survived, possibly even thrived, on his own. But this was not an experiment I was keen to undertake.

Looking back, my anxiety may have been a little over-done. At home in the UK, H&J were nearly always exercised off-lead. However, I already had experience of an attempt to steal my Jas. And, 'given their heads', H&J could, literally, be miles away within minutes. Perhaps further inhibiting factors were my being alone - no-one to share any headaches with - and my relative lack of fluency in the French language. These guys were very special to me, and their safety was paramount.

So our daily routine was simple, and similar. Each day was enhanced by our three long walks; in-between we would shop, garden and enjoy each other's company. The weather was fine and bright, and the long sojourn and increasingly long days gave me opportunity for some concerted DIY. The garden had never looked better, and positively glowed with fresh Spring health. We cruised around the lush, rolling countryside in the comfort of the Volvo 940, which gave the boys a spacious, flat capsule for travelling, with a superb all-round view.

This was a time of serene contentment, and we discovered new, lengthy rambles in and around the bocage. One of the most memorable walks took place near to Conde-sur-Noireau, in the hamlet of Proussy. It was as though I had stumbled on a world forgotten by time, or some far-off, undiscovered country: the *pays* seemed so detached, so incredibly remote. That morning, having loaded the car with all manner of detritus from the *cave*, the boys and I had embarked on a long-overdue visit to the déchetterie. We arrived at lunchtime, to find it closed. No surprise there.

So, with a couple of hours to fill, I headed out of town, and parked in a quiet spot a couple of miles away. I found an inviting-looking walk along a minor road, and off we went. Suddenly, we became immersed in some of the most remote countryside I have ever seen. Fields and woodland passed us by, as we continued our long march through goodness-knows-where. Such loneliness, such emptiness is hard to describe - except, of course, the countryside was *not* lonely or empty, save of people; it was full of nature, in its glorious Spring raiment, and the multi-melodies of birdsong.

Occasionally, we came across a lonely-looking house, or farm - where we were invariably greeted by an angry looking dog, tugging on its chain. The dogs, secured on chains, were linked to an inevitable kennel.

If the purpose was to warn residents of the approach of strangers, the straining hounds certainly served their purpose. For once, I was glad to see the dogs actually on chains, since their frantic barking warned that they were none-too-pleased to see Hector & Jason - or me.

Fascinating as it was to see a glimpse of old rural France at its most profound and enigmatic - veritably 'France profonde' - it was gradually becoming apparent to me that I had lost my way. I had intended a sort of circular walk that would return us to our vehicle in about an hour. Three hours later, and with some relief, we re-located our waiting Volvo. The boys - who had of course remained on their leads throughout, and had served to pull me along as though I had been a manikin - were as fresh as the daisies lining the hedgerows. I was a little fatigued, rather relieved, and just a little annoyed with myself. Yet, overall, it had been an insightful experience into a way of life that I had imagined had disappeared decades earlier.

We now completed our original intent, and returned to the déchetterie. These French refuse centres are, given their purpose, extremely clean and well-managed. And the staff are remarkably friendly and helpful. The chap who approached me, seeing that I was British, greeted me in halting English - far better than my own French - and ushered me to his car. He informed me that he had a number of English friends, and reached into the vehicle to show me something: it was a bobby's (policeman's) helmet, a present, he told me proudly, from one of his English friends. The helmet was professionally inscribed *Yorkshire Constabulary*. Impressed, I shook the man's hand, deposited my rubbish, and returned home. All in a day's work.

One sunny evening I decided that an exploration of the Rouvre river, a mere two miles from the cottage, would provide an absorbing ramble. At this point the Rouvre becomes wild and tumbling, and in Spring becomes a foaming torrent. Parking the car on the outskirts of the village, Hector, Jason and I began our trek. We quickly passed a few holiday cottages, seemingly abandoned, perched above the river. Then, nothing but the river, and the surrounding meadows, and endless lush woodland. After an hour's walk, seemingly following our nose - though the boys, as usual, were excitedly pulling me along - we arrived at the most amazing little village.

Steeped in history, and apparently lost in time, with a couple of ancient churches and a statue of the tormented Christ, St Philbert-sur-Orne greeted us with a phalanx of barking dogs. Residents craned their necks from upstairs windows to see what the fuss was about, and who might be the cause. The fuss was about a guy being pulled along by two Retrievers - not a very unusual sight - but in this village, maybe. It seemed that I was the first stranger they had seen for months. No doubt everyone knew each other, but they didn't know me. This was a brief, enigmatic glimpse into another way of life. 'Glimpse', because I thought it best for all concerned that we departed as quickly as we had come, and start the peaceful journey towards home.

In these sunny uplands of 2005, June was still working furiously, but squeezed in a two-week visit to the three of us in the middle of our extended break. I was eagerly looking forward to this visit, and the boys were certain to give June a royal welcome.

On the very morning of the long-anticipated arrival, a (British) neighbour suffered a heart attack. Within an impressively brief space of time our little road was rammed with ambulances, police cars and sundry vehicles pulsing and shrieking. Emergencies are emergencies, but there was no way any - other - vehicle could negotiate the crammed road. June 'phoned to announce her imminent arrival, and I explained the situation. Barely a minute before her arrival, the road miraculously cleared; not a gendarme or ambulance in sight. June breezed in, in her newly-acquired Ford Focus, querying what all my fuss was about. As expected, the boys went berserk with pleasure in greeting her. We have photos of the very moment of June's arrival, her car surrounded by an excited Hector & Jason.

There was an unusual and happy(ish) ending to this particular tale. The 60 year-old patient made a complete recovery but, perhaps reminded of his own mortality, 'eloped' soon after with a 26 year-old French woman. This must give the lie to those who loftily declaim that, without command of fluent French, we have no hope of communion with our French counterparts; and that one cannot '*mange votre gâteau*' and still have it. The erstwhile neighbour is nowadays referred to by his said nearest and dearest, aka *The Scottish Play*, as "*he who shall not be named*".

A few days later, we all embarked on a 'grand day out', that took us to the famous oyster-producing resort of Cancale, nearly a 100 miles away along the coast. It was a splendid day out. The very next morning, the car refused to start. The local garage prescribed, and supplied, a new battery, that was to serve the car for many years to come. However, it had been a close call, since the old battery could have expired on the trip itself. Another reason why - especially with H&J on-board - we always carried European vehicle breakdown cover.

June returned home ten days before Hector, Jason and myself. It was an emotional moment, I think, for all of us. Yet I - we - eventually left Normandy with great regret. Summer had blossomed; the countryside was alive with birdsong and butterflies, and we were all blissfully happy. On that final day, the boys sensed a momentous occasion, and scrambled into the car with marked reluctance. There is no doubt that, given the choice, H&J would have stayed at the cottage, happily, and for ever. But I could stay no longer; livings had to be earned, and there was no way that I could yet retire, or earn a viable living in France itself.

We returned to the UK on 23 May - the evening that Liverpool beat Inter Milan 4-3 in the European Championship Final. On the return journey I was be-friended by two little old ladies, who were enchanted by the boys. I happened to re-unite the ladies with a mobile phone that they had left in one of the ship's lounges. The ladies likened me, implausibly but hilariously, to the celebrity cook and campaigner, Hugh Fearnley-Whittingstall. My hair, which had grown wild and over-long, was the probable cause of the confusion. An omelette, or a barbecue, stretches my culinary pretensions.

We arrived home at the awful hour of 2.00am. The Ferry had been delayed by an hour and, in my tiredness, I had taken a wrong turn off the motorway. We edged back through Birmingham and Sandwell; strange, even hostile, territory compared to that we had so recently left behind. Still, late as we were, we tumbled into the house to a hero's welcome from June and the cats. Adrenalin overcoming tiredness, we re-lived the match I had earlier abandoned at 3-0 to Inter, before finally sinking gratefully into a strange bed.

It was the start of a new Chapter for me: I had re-branded as a 'consultant' - a euphemism for hired-help, but which would help me to carve out a living for the next few years. From now on, Normandy would see us at every opportunity. But many years would pass before I could re-live the experience of this long sojourn - and then, fate decreed, on very different terms.

The brightness and optimism of Spring, 2005, continued through the year. Later that Summer, we would undertake our 'assault' on Tafolog.

And, in July, we would embark on our first visit to the exquisite resort of Keranterec, in Brittany, recounted in a later Chapter. Life was yet young, rich, and joyous.

In mid-September, we returned to Normandy in convoy with our friends Margaret and Trevor, and of course H&J, to enjoy a blissfully serene period of late Summer. The roofing work was complete, and we settled our dues with our builder. The short trip was a frenetic blur, as we toured local beauty spots - including Deauville - in sparkling sunshine. We departed very early one morning for the first ferry of the day, shocked to find the not-yet departed night complemented by the thickest of fogs. We inched our way through the almost impenetrable murk, eventually finding a glimmer of light, and a loosening of the grey blanket that had threatened to smother us.

April 2006 saw the Red Volvo's last outing to France, before a well-earned retirement to lighter duties. Some friends of June's had bought a large, rambling house an hour or so distant, and we motored to see them, veering across the quiet, undulating countryside. Despite all our preparations, Hector, true to form, left his calling card upon arrival. All cheerfully dealt with, we left after lunch, with H&J - and a plastic bag - to make our return journey home in the faithful old carriage.

The New Roof

Summer time, my lad, is time to mend the roof;
Afore the Winter's wails, ripping with jagged tooth.

Colin Hill

At 6.00am on 26 December, 1999, northern France experienced the 'storm of the century' - any century. It lasted barely an hour, but was devastating. That hour was interminable. In that moment of horror, terrible destruction was wreaked: homes, like dolls houses, blown over; roofs ripped off; whole forests smashed down, as though hundred year-old trees had been mere matchsticks.

In view of the early hour, mercifully relatively few people were up and about. Even so, there were many casualties. Some were killed in their beds; others by deadly, flying roof slates. Our nearest supermarket, 10 kilometres or so away, had been, literally, flattened by the ferocious onslaught. Fortunately, perhaps, for us, we were absent from Normandy on this occasion. We heard about the storm from the usual sources -

radio and TV news and, yes, from friends in France itself. So we were anxious to return to La Haute Maison as soon as possible, in order to get to grips with any damage.

We travelled to the cottage early in the New Year. Hector & Jason were still not - quite - able to travel with us, so we journeyed on our own. As it turned out, we were among the luckier home owners. The position of the house, partly protected by the buffer of nearby deep woodland, had helped to shelter it from the violent onslaught. True, a large swathe of slates had disappeared from one corner of the roof, and a mature buddleia had been flattened to the horizontal; but that was pretty well the extent of the damage. With devoted care, the buddleia would survive, and again thrive and delight the butterflies. Fixing the roof would present a problem in the short term, since roofers were like gold dust, and under enormous pressure. But repaired it would be.

Even so, considering that several weeks of clean-up had already taken place by both the authorities and residents, we were pretty shocked by the visual evidence of destruction. It was the worst natural calamity I have personally seen. Since many people had lost their homes, or their houses had become un-inhabitable, we saw our own needs in perspective.

Yet we were so impressed by the energy and resilience of our French community. Large old trees had blocked our road at several points; they had been quickly cut up and removed. Debris was also being removed, and houses painstakingly repaired. Plans were quickly under-way for re-planting the forests trashed by the storm. There was an air of calm, and focused, practical, business-like activity. Everyone had rallied round, in what we would call in Britain a resurgence of 'the Blitz spirit'.

This natural calamity underlined our own vulnerability, and the risks we faced, particularly in Winter. In acquiring a stolid, stone-built cottage, we had also inherited an ancient slate roof that was already well past its sell-by date. As the years passed, we arranged for the slate to be patched and re-patched, but ultimately the roof was no match for the fierce Normandy rain, which, at any time of the year, can be almost tropical in its torrential force. This was all deeply ironic, since Normandy weather is generally more clement, more clear and sunny, than that of the UK. I'm sure that the old Kings - the likes of Henry II and Richard I - lived in Normandy, and on the Loire, for very sound geo-political reasons. But part of me suspects that the benign climate may have had something to do with it. *"Where would you like to spend the Summer this year, my dear?"* one imagines Henry asking Eleanor. *"In (damp, foggy, wet) London, or in Loches? In Birmingham, or in Blois? In Canterbury, or in Chinon?"*.

However, while Summers are long and warm, and Winters - though often intensely cold - short, and brilliant, the weather itself can be another matter. That 'four seasons in a single day' motto is only too true. And the rain is often a deluge, an utter torrent, that can come from nowhere, at any time of the year, and continue for 24 or 36 hours, without a break.

These extremes of weather had begun to find weaknesses in the ancient roof of our cottage. The natural slate roof had begun to look fragile and tired - fatigued. During heavy spells of rain, there were a few drips that I was forced to intercept with buckets and dishes. Repairs were many, but were only a temporary solution to a systemic failure. The old roof was simply giving up the ghost. Worn out. Past it. The roof had struggled manfully against the elements, but had been left to cope for too long. We feared the next deluge or, particularly, the next deluge when we happened to be absent. A domestic catastrophe seemed imminent. The 'Great Storm' represented a last wake-up call - we needed to act.

Even so, it still took us until 2005 - that year again - before we had the time, focus and contacts to deal with the roof. We were fortunate that 'the Great Storm' had been exactly that, and that there had been no further serious shocks. Now, my relationship with the French language has always been light-touch; that is, skin deep. But when, artisan by my side, I pointed to the roof, and said: *"Nouveau toit, s'il vous plaît"*, I believed that I had successfully conveyed my meaning. Unfortunately, I had only conveyed half my meaning, since the outcome was *half* a new roof. I supervised M. Serge for a few days that September and, entirely satisfied with the progress made, journeyed home. Returning with June, and friends, barely a couple of weeks later, I witnessed said roof. That new half was indeed well-done, and most handsome - but it was still only half a roof.

It was a full six years later, in May 2011, that we had time and opportunity to complete the job. Spring had advanced and, as the man said, the time to repair your roof is when the sun is shining. Through a mutual French friend, we engaged the excellent Patrice, a roofer by trade, who was now semi-retired. In fact, the completion of our roof would be his last major job. We easily agreed terms, on the most amazingly reasonable basis. In view of the very fair terms, and the scale of the task - not least, heaving thousands of new tiles on to the roof, ready for placement - it was agreed that I would act as labourer. In French terms, I would be *jeune* to the master artisan. Certainly, *jeune*, or naïve, in my mind: if I had known exactly what was in store I may have had second thoughts. However, in reality there was probably little choice.

The task began by stripping off the old roof - slates, and the old lattice woodwork beneath. This was a scary task - Patrice was a man in a hurry, and slates, and bits of slate, were slewing everywhere as they came off the roof in sheaths. I had already decided that the best place for the inquisitive H&J was indoors; flying, skimming, wind-blown tiles are incredibly dangerous, and have been known to wreak havoc, and cost lives. I had enough to do ensuring my own safety, without having to worry about the boys. And Patrice needed to know that the risks around him were minimised. So, H&J were kept well out of the way. Patrice ripped off the old tiles with alarming speed, throwing them down for me to remove. My task at this stage - apart from dodging the flying objects - was simply to collect up all the old tiles, and to cart them in my wheelbarrow to a specially designed receptacle - hole - at the bottom of the garden.

I was worried about heavy rain since, for a short interval, the roof had minimal protection. Still, the weather held and, a day or so later, we were ready to apply the 'paper' or plastic membrane as the first layer of defence against the elements. There followed the intricate and time-consuming work of creating a new network of wooden lattice, in a criss-cross framework on the exposed roof. I had hoped to be an observer at this point, but I was sadly mistaken. Each part of the new framework had to be carefully and exactly spaced. My job was to hold one end of a little device, a special tape, that left a green mark on the vertical lathes, in order to determine the spacing for the next row of horizontal lathes. I hope you are still with me. My head for heights is not what it was and, balancing on the wooden framework already laid - since Patrice had started at the bottom - we gradually made our way, inch by inch, towards the top of the roof.

Now, the two-storey cottage is not particularly high but, looking down from its apex, from my precarious foothold on a one-and-a-half-inch wide wooden lath, I began to feel pretty exposed. There was no mattress beneath, no safety net. I had to trust to my mountaineering experience (though I have far more confidence in rock than in thin strips of wood) and my natural sang-froid. I hope I did not betray too much of my anxiety to the cool, chirpy Patrice, who was himself taking a risk in 'taking on' such an inexperienced partner.

And then - balanced precariously on the very apex of the roof, with disturbed hornets buzzing angrily around, and with buggar all to hang on to - I heard the most extraordinarily loud engine-like noise, coming as if from everywhere at once. It was no car or tractor, making its way up the road. This was far, far louder, quite terrific, and seemed to fill the whole sky. Surely I was safe, up here? And then it emerged - a Hercules transport plane, or similar. Oh my God! I could see every detail of the underside; I could see the markings.

I could see the pilot. I could see his eyes. The wind-displacement from the plane ruffled my hair. The thing passed over, with a huge, four-prop energy and blast of noise, just a few tens-of-feet above my head. "*What the...!*". And then it was gone. "*Holy Moses!*" - I just clung on, and shook my head. I had never seen such a sight before, so near the house. Though I have observed one or two planes since then, they were not so close, or so low. I'm sure Richard the Lionheart never had to face such giant dragons in the sky.

The plane fright proved to be the high point - or the low point - of our roof project. When we left Normandy a few days later, Patrice had begun fixing the new roof slates. They looked great. I was, even more than usual, sad to leave - I would dearly have loved to have seen the project through - but, when we returned in early Summer, the job had been completed to perfection. Glinting in the sunshine was a smart new roof that will see out our days, with no more worries about rain, or damaging leaks, or Winter's rages. It is as handsome, and sound, as a roof can be. Patrice had also spent two days re-pointing our ancient and wobbly chimney, which now stands proud against the fearsome Normandy gales.

H&J's role in all this was minimal: they were inquisitive spirits and, between bouts of activity, I encouraged them - they needed no urging

- to enquire into the latest progress, and to make their report. They seemed happy with the improvement to their home.

Meanwhile, a large toad had taken up residence in the pile of old slates that neatly filled a natural crevice at the bottom of the garden. Everyone and everything, it seemed - save for the hornets - welcomed the splendid new roof.

Spirit of Portsmouth: we are sailing

The cottage: a study in scarlet

At play - La Haute Maison

At play - with friend Mozart

Spring in the bocage

The goat walk - with resident goat!

The Chateau at Lessay

The magic of Mont St Michel

Medieval market marvel

Gaiety at (Château) Ganne

Electric Jason hits the beach!

And again!

Hector braving the waves

Hector at St Aubin - Juno Beach

Life's a beach

Jason in his redoubt

Happiness at Merville

White Christmas at La Haute Maison

Jason - in his element

Hector in the snow

21: ADVENTURES IN RURAL NORMANDY

Green, green the grass grows, in fragrant Normandy;
Sweet, fleet, the breeze blows, 'cross perfumed Normandy!

Colin Hill

The sun does arise,
And make happy the skies;
The merry bells ring
To welcome the Spring.

The Echoing Green - William Blake

Napoleon himself regarded Normandy's countryside as the finest in France. Two hundred years later, the Emperor would be astonished to find his dominions almost untouched, almost unblemished by progress - but, with his military eye, delighted to see the vastly improved roads.

While our Summers in Normandy were spent in the garden, or under the gazebo, they were also on the beach, or promenade. And there were notable other visits, of course - through the lush landscape of the *pays* - to lakes, and superb forests, of which more anon, and to spectacular sites such as Mont St Michel, and Normandy's awesome cathedrals and Châteaux.

I loved wandering around the bocage countryside near to our house, in the educated company of Hector & Jason. 'Educated', because while I noted the amazing diversity of wild plants and flowers in the hedgerows, they showed me the hidden things, a secret dimension of wildness, intricacy and intimacy.

H&J soon became familiar with all the pathways that radiate from the house: the woods, the country lanes, the strange old derelict and ruined houses, half-hidden in overgrown orchards. And of course the half-wild, but seductively near-at-paw, herd of goats.

Even in the most mundane of circumstances - regularly, in supermarket car parks, or walking in villages - H&J would attract the attention of strangers, and generate popular affection. We would be hailed, or people stroll up to us, quite purposefully, and make eager, detailed enquiries. What were their names? What was their breed? Where did they come from? Were they related? We were only too pleased by this interest in the boys; it provided an opportunity to share H&J with the world, and we responded with alacrity to such well meaning entreaties.

Although we always looked forward, almost every Summer, to travel with boys and tent in order to explore further afield, most of our trips to Normandy involved shorter stays, responding to weather and opportunity. There are so many local beauty spots, accessed by a short drive - such as Chante du Cailloux, or the exquisite Maison de la Paysage - both set on the banks of the rushing, winding River Rouvre. Here, kingfishers may be seen whizzing above the pure, bubbling waters, while otters glide smoothly along the stream. A profusion of wild daffodils and orchids clothe the riverbanks, while butterflies dance in the warm Spring breeze, and kiss the grateful flowers.

Nearby, the enchanting village of Clécy was a favourite destination: a local focus for tourism, centred on outdoor activity around and upon the River Orne; it is delightful and spirited in Spring and Summer. Little gift-shops and bars - straight out of Manet's *Bar at the Folies Bergeres* - grace the picturesque river, whilst pleasure-seekers in canoes and motor-launches meander along the languid flow. H&J enjoyed innumerable strolls along the river-bank, absorbing the local colour and abundant street-life - and wildlife.

Approaching Clécy, the view is dominated by the massive cliffs of the Pain de Sucre. We often visited the summit of the Pain, both for the stunning views over the countryside below, and to watch the hang-gliders, launching into an empty blue sky. The *Route des Crêtes* offers amazing views over the Orne Valley, a vertigo-inducing 500' below.

Needless to say, H&J enjoyed heady walks along the airy summit of the 'Pain', but without ever being set free, or putting themselves at risk. Even so, dramatic and exciting places always seemed to energise them, and the boys would be on maximum alert, beguiled by the big skies, inviting breeze and bold action of the hang-gliders.

While visits to, for example, Mont St Michel were spectacular, day-long outings, many more trips could be accommodated in half a day, or incorporated into, perhaps, a simple shopping trip. June wrote a brief diary for our Easter, 2004, visit, which is set out below. It contains only the bare bones of what was a delightful week:

Sat 10 April Shopping in Condé - cool, sun & cloud
Sun 11 April -   Arthour's Fosse - sunny, cool

Arthour's Fosse is an impressive, natural feature comprising cliffs, river (the Sonce) and placid lake. Here, King Arthur is said to have held his court; Camelot, perhaps. I wouldn't be surprised - it's such a remote and remarkable area; the boys loved trotting around and, in Hector's case, sampling the cool, deep lake. The 'lac' is so tranquil - one could imagine seeing Excalibur rise from its waters.

Mon 12 April - Domfront, Andaine Forest - long walk, then to Champsecret - vide grenier. Sunny and warm.

Domfront is a superb medieval town, set high above the surrounding countryside, and with remarkably preserved castle walls. The Andaine Forest is an enormous area of mature woodland - perhaps 600 square kilometres in extent: the graceful, slender stands of oak and beech, and the lonely aspect, spirit one back to a former time. The boys loved their forest walks, though - with the possibility of coming across deer or even wild boar - they remained securely on their leads.

A vide grenier is the French version of the English 'car boot', but usually more fantastical and eccentric. We chanced upon this one at the lovely village of Champsecret quite by accident; I purchased two porcelain figures of Napoleonic marshals - very fine, although they turned out to be 'Made in Korea'.

Tues 13 April - Thury Harcourt - garden centre for trees and shrubs. Condé sur Noireau -   Pont Vert - (i.e. garden centre/DIY) - sunny.
Wed 14 April - Villers Bocage - (market) - very misty, then sunny.
Thurs 15 April - Fougeres Forest and Vitré– fine, sunny day.

Fourgeres Forest, on the border of Brittany, is probably my favourite French forest - as beautiful as the enchanted forests re-created in Walt Disney films. Vitré is another fine town with strong medieval traces, including a well-preserved castle. Unfortunately, dogs are not allowed in the Château. However, we did acquire two fine wooden chairs for the cottage that harked back to medieval styles. A varied and fascinating day for all of us.

Friday 16 April - Condé (déchetterie) and Flers (shopping). Warm, sunny day.

Sat 17 April - Condé (shopping). Thury Harcourt (vets). Sun and cloud.

Thury Harcourt provided our first French veterinary experience, before we switched to a practice in Falaise.

The reader can be assured that this was a pretty stretching schedule; but there was something of interest and entertainment for H&J in every single trip. Hector was eager for every excursion: bright eyed, alert, excited, expectant. Meanwhile, Jason re-focused himself for each fresh challenge.

We travelled far and wide within Normandy, whenever opportunity and the stars aligned. Here is a flavour of some of the delightful and varied excursions we embarked upon together - to country retreats, Châteaux, pageants, historic towns and medieval extravaganzas...

A visit to Rabodanges was always a favourite: this is the site of a lovely, man-made lake, where the dammed River Orne burgeons into a massive reservoir. A large steamer tours the lake in peak season, gay with an excited entourage. The lake formed the scene of many fine walks with H&J on sun-lit afternoons. Rabodanges always made a very pleasant excursion, as we wander through idyllic countryside towards the lake: all is very relaxed, with a typical Gallic ambience. H&J were probably the only discordant note as, with boundless excitement, they raced over the main bridge and around the perimeter of the lake, as though on a mission to explore the whole area for the very first time.

A short distance from the Norman town of Carrouges is an impressive Château, a magnificent brick-built edifice dating from the end of the 16th century.

The imposing, red-brick Château of Carrouges, surrounded by a carp-rich moat, glows warmly in the Norman sunshine. The Château dates from the reign of Henry IV. Louis XI stayed here on August 11, 1473, a guest of the de Tillieres family. The Château's most famous feature is a monumental staircase. Nowadays, cared for by the French state, the Château basks peacefully in its own grandeur, untroubled by the tourist hordes of the Loire's Châteaux-hunters. Another splendid day-trip for the intrepid H&J.

Nearby Pontécoulant Château is an impressive 17th century pile with the usual manicured gardens in formal French style. Having visited many years before, and only thirty minutes from home, we decided that an afternoon visit with H&J would prove an enjoyable diversion.

We understood, of course, that the Château's interior would be out of bounds for the two lads, so we strolled nonchalantly through the gardens. A young lady chased after us along the sweeping path. This promised to be intriguing but was, in fact, disappointing: *"Je suis désolé - no chiens!"*. Perhaps understandable, though the French are generally dog-tolerant - *and* dog mess can be easily cleared up. No place for the boys? No place for us. We shrugged our shoulders, took a parting photo, and meandered back to the homely cottage.

The 15th century Château d'O is a romantic, jaw-dropping architectural jewel. It rises like a crazy confection, reflected in the mirror-like waters of its wide moat. Sadly, it was closed when we visited with H&J; on a previous visit we had marvelled at its flamboyance and outrageous lines. The Château's overblown Gothic romanticism has echoes of the Taj Mahal.

The Château's broad, translucent moat contains the most enormous pike I have ever seen. It was a real shame that it was closed on this occasion - I had special plans to prevent Hector diving in the lake and tussling with those giant fish.

Bagnoles de l'Orne, a mere half hour's drive away from home, is a popular spa town, with very pretty gardens that always look manicured and pampered; the resort is immaculate in its prim prettiness. The many, mostly elderly, visitors are here to take the waters to rejuvenate their health. The visitors wander round the town in leisurely fashion, admiring the cut-crystal finish of the pristine flower beds.

The spa waters are reputed to be beneficial for circulatory disorders - perhaps induced by the presence of the prominent casino. In all honesty, it's not prime dog territory. For the fit and energetic, the town provides a whiff of ennui: it was always a touch boring for H&J, who were anyway in far too rude health to need to 'take the waters'. Luckily the town is surrounded by deep forests, which definitely required a visit, and provided an energetic walk before the inevitable journey home.

The little market town of Mortain provides another absorbing excursion. Famous for its tumbling waterfalls in a steep, heavily wooded setting, the Grand Cascade (which tumbles 25 metres) and

Petite Cascade offer some pretty spectacular sights. The small wooden bridges over the river provided no obstacle to H&J, who charged over the area to view the attractions.

I remember admiring a gorgeous little cottage set in luscious woodland on the edge of town, only to hear English voices emanating from the garden.

La Ferté Macé is another characterful old town, dominated by the towering spire of its eglise. There is a superb weekly (Thursday) market. We always took care to ensure a wide birth for H&J around the penned but noisy poultry and ducks that are a distinct feature of this, and many other, French markets.

Near the town lies a splendid community lake, with its own beach, and small yachts. The lake provided a bracing promenade for H&J, during one of our many shopping trips to the nearby hyper-market. We always found it neat, and enjoyable, to fit in two or preferably three points of interest on every excursion - at least one of these specifically intended for H&J. Hector, eyes and nostrils alert, was always on the lookout for water-borne ducks whilst we circuited the impressive, man-made lake.

The small city of Sees, situated on the River Orne, is famous for its 13th century Cathedral, which dominates the landscape. The Cathedral of St Latrium's is certainly one of the finest in Europe, and has outstanding 13th century stained glass windows. The cathedral's two sixty-metre spires provide a hugely impressive landmark, and dominate both the city and the skyline for many miles around.

In different circumstances, we would have been eager to explore the cathedral's magnificent interior but, perhaps swayed by H&J's insistence on viewing the surrounding town, we simply marvelled at the glorious exterior on our visit there. As we know only too well from Hector's visits to Hereford and Bayeux, dogs and cathedrals do not a perfect marriage make.

In the Footsteps of Henry II

A day-trip to Argentan - now a pretty, but busy, purposeful, town, centred on the youthful River Orne - was long in the mind. There was no particular reason to visit, except that I had once (2003) travelled to Argentan by rail, on my way to the cottage, in an attempt to discover how easy, or otherwise, it was to travel to La Haute Maison, and back, entirely by public transport. The answer? The (crazy) venture - finishing with a 40 mile - £100 - taxi ride - was never attempted again. So, on this occasion we took the sensible option - car - from the cottage, in order that I could reminisce on the earlier experience, admire again the River Orne, which flows prettily through the centre of the town, and point out some of the finer architectural and natural features, such as the church of St Germain, sensitively restored following extensive war-time damage.

One of Argentan's chilling claims to fame is that it was here, in his castle or donjon in 1170 (a 12th century Marguerite Tower and donjon still exists) that Henry II demanded of his retinue: "*Will no one rid me of this meddlesome priest?*". A short time later, four knights set out on their deadly mission to murder - no doubt, in their view, 'execute' - Thomas Becket, Archbishop of Canterbury, and erstwhile friend of the King. The Archbishop had become a thorn in the King's side, in his strong defence of, as he saw them, the rights of the Church. This infamous event took place on 29 December 1170, at the altar of Canterbury Cathedral; and here we were, nearly 1,000 years later, in the bustling town, pondering these momentous events.

How many residents, passing busily from boulangerie to boucherie, spared a thought for these historic bombshells? If they were thinking about anything other than their next meal, or how to pay the gas bill, they might have thought, with something approaching wonder, how Argentan had recovered so heroically from the (Allied) aerial bombardment that had destroyed 80% of their town in the months leading up to D-Day. The town is now restored but, sadly, no longer Henry II's medieval jewel.

This would not be our only encounter with Henry - Domfront was another of his favourite castles, or Châteaux, as was Falaise. And the fierce old chap breathed his last at Chinon, on the Loire, near to the dog-tower, in 1090. Henry bequeathed his kingdoms in France and England to his Plantaganet heir, Richard 'the Lionheart'. June and I had visited this impressive Château in earlier years but, on our only visit to the Loire with H&J, we focused on a different stretch of the famous river valley, and have never returned to the lovely town of Chinon. The distances are considerable, especially when travelling with pets and, for good measure, the weather is often blisteringly hot. Besides, if we had returned to Chinon, we could never have seen Chambord. Choices, always choices.

The town of Domfront, a medieval gem, was the focus of regular visits. Set spectacularly on a steep rocky spur above the River Varenne, thirteen of the original castle towers from the medieval Château-fort still stand. The remains of its castle, at the high point of the town, quite dominate the settlement.

There is a grim story associated with Domfront's Castle, since it was the scene of an infamous 16th century siege. The defenders, led by Robert de Montgomery, fought heroically against overwhelming forces. Their numbers reduced to single figures, the survivors wounded and starving, they surrendered on receipt of a promise of safety from the formidable Catherine de Medici. Predictably, she reneged on the undertaking, and promptly executed the gallant Robert. Years earlier, this knight had accidentally wounded Catherine's husband, King Henry II, in a joust. The injury was to prove fatal. On his deathbed, Henry had magnanimously forgiven Montgomery. Catherine, however, had her revenge. The dénouement (end) probably came as no surprise.

400 years earlier, forbear and namesake Henry II and his wife Eleanor of Aquitane were regular visitors; Thomas a Becket also visited at Christmas, 1166. I was pleased with these associations, since we had always intended that H&J should visit the Dog Tower at Château Chinon, where Henry II's hunting dogs had their home, near to the King's eventual tomb. Although we did visit the Loire Valley with H&J, sadly this ambition remained unfulfilled, mainly due to the intense heat in July and August. Our wanderings would be confined to the eastern Loire.

The shadow of history, and historic events, continued to confront us at Vitré-Ille-et-Vilaine; history appears so up-close and personal, though the famous characters and events we recall are of course hundreds of years distant.

Vitré is a little jewel of a town, located a few miles over Brittany's border. We must have been inspired by *The Blue Guide,* or similar, since it was quite an arduous trip. The Castle has its origins in 1070, the work of Robert I. It's in impressively good order, and one can visit the Château, tripping over the drawbridge to pay one's dues. I quickly noticed that *chiens* were not welcome in the Château so, while June visited the impressive edifice, I had an energetic foray around the wonderfully preserved medieval heart of the town, in the company of the ever enthusiastic H&J. How I managed to take a few half decent photos of our visit I will never know.

In *The Hunchback of Notre Dame,* Victor Hugo describes this place as one of the best preserved medieval towns in Europe. Even its ancient ramparts are still largely intact Well, let me tell you, we've probably seen more European towns than Mr Hugo - but he's quite right.

To keep Vitré up to date, and keep it looking at its best - I can't imagine this in the 14th century - we encountered a machine that dispenses dog-poo bags - the very first that we'd come across.

Re-united with June, and staring into the pot-pourri of shops that nestled in ancient alleyways, we chanced upon a store selling old-style (we'd say 'reproduction') furniture. We were attracted by a solid wooden chair with leather upholstery, and promptly bought it, quite to the delight of the sales women, who had been looking quite subdued. On getting the chair back to the car - a mere 300 hundred yards away - we decided to return for a second chair, its near-twin. Encouraged, the sales lady asked whether we also wanted the large sofa that followed the same style. Sadly, we couldn't accommodate this in the car.

Having taken our fill of local plunder, and having exhausted the well-intentioned, obligatory tourist trail, we turned for home. H&J were exercised and happy, and a gin and tonic awaited us - 50 miles hence.

The two handsome chairs, a small but pleasing part of our history, have since enjoyed pride of place at La Haute Maison, alongside a handsome oak cabinet purchased locally, and a traditional English dining set brought over on a white-van trip. Possessions are, ultimately, of little value, but that little value consists not only in their functionality, but in their story, and the warm memories that we fondly recollect each day.

In the Footsteps of King Arthur

Fosse Arthour, near Lonlay l'Abbaye - still in the Orne region - is another favourite destination. With its rushing torrents, the Sonce river, steep cliffs and tranquil Lac du Lancelot, the Fosse seems like a world away. It is quite easy to imagine Lancelot, Guinevere, and of course Camelot, on these romantic shores. The Fosse is so peaceful, beautiful and remote. Hector & Jason loved the surge round the lake, and along the many footpaths.

The 12th century French poet, Chretien de Troyes, seriously embellished the Arthurian legend in his poems. Before him, there was no Lancelot, no Guinevere. No-one really knows whether there was an actual King Arthur, or a real Camelot. Many claims have been made as to Camelot's possible location - Cornwall and Wales chief among them. But in the far off period supposed to constitute the Arthurian Age - somewhere hazily between the 5th and 8th centuries - Britain, and much of modern day France, were dominated by the Celts, and Celtic culture.

So it is not entirely fanciful to believe that Arthur and his kingdom spanned parts of England, Wales and northern/western France, such as Normandy and Brittany, seats of the Celtic culture. We read in Mallory - and de Troyes - that Lancelot himself was (in the heady mix of alleged fact, fiction and myth) the son of the King of Brittany. At any rate, Fosse Arthour is a wonderfully evocative location, and one can readily envisage a faery kingdom, replete with crags and torrents and wild, mysterious places, complemented by witches and magicians. And - real - magnificent castles, within a day or two's ride, at Falaise, Lessay and Fougeres.

H&J took to the Fosse at once. Not content with the acquaintance of an array of historic royalty from their travels, the boys had to rub their excited shoulders with the most romantic legend of all. In his beauty and his courage, Jason may well have inherited the soul of the great knight Lancelot himself.

One walk at Fosse Arthour that sticks in the mind saw us climbing the crest of a steep hill, where we encountered an enormous white crucifix gazing pacifically down on the valley below. As always, after the first shock of the new and unexpected, we powered past, intent on the next spectacle - the view or encounter around the next corner.

Storming at Lessay

One fine afternoon in mid-July (2004) we travelled to a favourite destination, the exquisite little Norman town of Lessay-les-Château. The town has a 14th century castle. This Château, built in 1458, in the reign of Charles VII, is impressively well-preserved, with a formidable, almost threatening, medieval presence. The Château fort - with battlements, turrets and moat - is in a state of remarkable preservation, and impressively un-touched by modern attempts at refurbishment.

This particular day being the anniversary of the 'Storming of the Bastille' in 1789 - the iconic event that sparked the French

Revolution - vividly dressed actors were re-creating the said Storming, at the eminently authentic Castle, and providing a sure recipe for an entertaining afternoon.

We travelled cross-country, along mainly minor roads, and through tiny villages, for the 30-mile journey to Lessay. The sun beamed down as I played Ella Fitzgerald singing the *Irving Berlin Songbook*; it somehow accorded with, anticipated (in my view) the pleasures soon to come. The music emerged joyously, mellifluously, from the car's speakers as we weaved along the winding country road.

In the late 1980s - I have to pinch myself - we had experienced the great Ella Fitzgerald in concert, at Wolverhampton Civic Hall. How could it have been possible? And how possible that there were a scattering of empty seats? And now, here we were, on the road to nowhere, with Ella - and Hector & Jason.

Ella was still gaily singing her way through the *Songbook* as we approached a herd of cattle, nonchalantly crossing the road. I turned off the CD player - all top hats and white tails - as suddenly inappropriate to the scene. The soft-flanked, brown and white spotted cattle were escorted by two young girls. (To my suspicious mind, they wore oddly British-style clothing). The large herd, in no particular hurry, and eyeing us with some disdain, took a full ten minutes to cross the road. In that time, no queue of cars - not a single car - pulled up behind us. In fact, we encountered no other vehicles, and no other people, until we reached the outskirts of Lessay itself.

Then, to my consternation, Lessay was simply heaving with vehicles and people. The town, usually a sleepy backwater, had become a magnet for tourists: cars and coaches fought for space in every public nook and cranny. It was as though word had reached the whole of Europe that *the* Storming of the Bastille was about to be re-enacted, and must be seen to be believed.

We parked on the road a good distance from the centre of town, pointed the excited H&J in the 'right' direction, and marched towards the action. The town centre's cobble-stones were almost invisible beneath the throng and weight of humanity, which jangled and jumbled around the hundreds of stalls purveying steaming fast-food and every type of bric-a-brac, freshly discovered from attics and *caves* far and wide. To my astonishment, the dominant faction was American. We recognised the accents, the thunderous, possibly ponderous, style of walking, the colourful clothes, the obligatory hamburgers - in just the same way that one spots a Brit in France: the look, the walk, the attitude - speak loudly of a different culture. And English accents, too, were thick on the air, in the sun-filled market place.

Quite how so many hundreds, thousands even, of American citizens had descended on such a (normally) remote place was a mystery. Where had they come from? How had they arrived - by parachute (hardly)? And why, exactly - were there no other Bastille re-enactments, nearer to, or in, Paris, perhaps? Of course, the visitors were all most welcome - it was probably the town's biggest jamboree and pay-day of the year. And once I had become accustomed to the idea of a bustling, heaving, noisy town, full of American citizens, rather than the peaceful French village we had expected, I warmed to the atmosphere, and we joined in all the hustle and bustle. H&J were in their element - people, scents, bits of food strewn along pavements: pure bliss. Let them eat cake, indeed.

We never did see the actors re-enacting the 'Storming', though the ranks of expectant, empty seats in the castle courtyard did argue that the said storming had happened, or was about to happen. Instead, and with some relief, we left Lessay and its burgeoning crowds in late afternoon, eager to return at last to quietude. Within seconds we were swallowed up again by the empty French countryside.

Nearby St Leonard des Bois was the destination for an annual visit - usually on a glorious day in Spring. It's at the heart of the lovely Mayenne Region, which we reached along straight, fast roads that were almost deserted. Passing through verdant, fertile meadows flanked by thick forests, with big, open skies, often several minutes would go by without us seeing a single car.

The small village nestles beside a bend in the impressive River Sarthe. There is (or was) a small hotel, *Touring Hotel*, situated on a bend in the road, and a camp site over the way. We would enjoy our picnic with Hector & Jason, while relaxing near to the river bank. All around are lovely walks, with carpets of bluebells and oxslips gracing every winding lane. We strolled through a paradise of scent and colour, with two entrancing boys.

A short drive from St Leonard de Bois, St Céneri-le-Gérei is reputed to be amongst the most beautiful villages in Normandy, and perhaps the most lovely in all of France; it was a favourite destination. The setting, on a tranquil river, is simply enchanting. The historic, but quiet, village is almost chocolate-box idyllic. There is a lovely, 15th century, Romanesque church - Chapelle des Céneri - and a pretty bridge over the equally attractive river Sarthe, meandering blissfully through the centre of the village.

H&J love charging around the ancient streets, and zooming down to the exquisite little chapel, set in its own enchanted garden beside the river. Yet, if not exactly quiet, this little treasure is neither over-run or taken over by day-trippers, since the chief attraction lies in the sheer beauty and tranquillity of the village: there are no frivolous attempts to whip up further tourist frenzy to its environs.

One balmy afternoon, returning home from St Céneri, we deviated to the nearby Belvedere Des Avalon, a stone latticed tower that offers unrivalled views over the surrounding countryside. I wound my way around the spiral, ascending slowly but surely, my laboured progress watched with amazement by H&J, straining their necks a dizzying distance below. My head-for-heights failing me with man-made structures, I decided to descend before reaching the exposed summit, to the no-doubt relief of all my companions.

The return journeys from this area were often uneventful - tranquil and peaceful forays through deep countryside - except for one trip when we were pursued by a 'twister'. This is 'big country' France, so the presence of a tornado did not seem so far-fetched. Fortunately, the storm gathered itself and passed elsewhere.

In the Conqueror's Footsteps

Over the years, we have visited the market town of Falaise perhaps a hundred times. There should be no surprise in this, since Falaise is a large, vibrant town with a surprising number of high quality, distinctive shops, and is a magnet for residents from the surrounding plains.

Today, Falaise is best known as the birthplace (in 1027) of William the Conqueror, whose impressive, horse-mounted bronze statue rears above the cobbled main square. However, it is the enormous Castle which dominates the town. The present, gigantic, edifice, actually begun by William's son, Henry I, is widely regarded as one of the finest examples of military architecture in the whole of France.

There is a charming story concerning the Conqueror's origins. Returning from a hunt, Robert, 17 year-old son of Richard, Duke of Normandy, espied a girl washing clothes in a stream, her skirts held provocatively high. Robert let it be known that he desired the girl - Arlette, daughter of a rich tanner. Eschewing protocol, the proud Arlette put on her finery, and rode on horseback, through the Castle gates. It was to prove a productive encounter. Arlette, famously, had a dream that a tree grew from her belly - until it encompassed not only Normandy, but the whole of England. William - henceforth jarringly known as 'William the Bastard' was the fruit of their union; a man destined to unite his French dominions with those of England. Arlette stayed to bring up her son. The pretty Fountain of Arlette lies a little distance from the walls of the Castle Keep, on the River Ante.

The rest, as they say, is history. William was perhaps inspired by his unbecoming suffix to earn the sobriquet of *Le Conquérant* following his successful invasion of England, and crowned as William I. Falaise was later the favourite seat of Henry II and Eleanor of Aquitane. In 1159, they held a Court of Love within the castle walls, with troubadours and great merriment.

The ancient town will, however, reverberate for all time in the annals of history as the scene of one of the bloodiest confrontations of World War II.

This battle, fought in mid-August 1944, brought the battle for Normandy to a decisive but grotesquely violent conclusion. Those with even a passing knowledge of history may well enter the town with some surprise, since 85% of the infrastructure was destroyed in that fateful campaign, largely by Canadian forces engaging with the German 7th Army. Medieval Falaise, built mostly from timber, was almost completely lost, and has been replaced over the decades by modern structures. Although the town now seems so serene, and there are few outward traces of the pulverising calamity and destruction wreaked on the place, there are bullet holes a-plenty in the soft, Caen stone of the few original buildings that remain.

The Château itself came under heavy bombardment, since the Talbot tower, with its commanding views over the area, was used by the Germans as an observation post. It is testament to the strength of the fortifications that the tower, and Castle, survived in such good order. Perhaps fittingly, the magnificent equestrian statue of William the Conqueror was one of very few structures to survive the convulsion intact.

On a lighter note, Falaise hosts - yet another - superb market each Saturday; the food market is simply one of the best of its kind that we have encountered - superb cheeses, farmhouse bread, great vats of crème fraiche, heaps of vegetables harvested that very morning - along with poultry, ducks, turkeys and rabbits all awaiting (one hopes) new homes.

Falaise market has a fromagerie, belonging to the Mercier family farm at Carrouges: it's probably the finest we have found, anywhere. The range and quality of the cheese is unparalleled. We - and H&J - always looked forward to our visit - it's certainly worth the 30-mile round-trip.

The town also boasts an enticing photography shop, in the market square, via which I took my first plunge into digital photography. It was in 2008 that June bought me a first digital camera - my proud birthday present. Thank goodness - since I now possess hundreds of digital images of the immortal H&J. The camera was immediately, and continuously, employed, and H&J helped me capture some of my favourite, unforgettable, images of all time.

Falaise often treated us to a surreal sight; zebras and camels grazing on the grass beneath the brooding castle - the circus had arrived, and the stars of the show needed to be rested and fed. As always, we steered the boys carefully away from the circus animals, curious and fascinated though they were.

Hector & Jason were frequent visitors to Falaise - they knew the great Castle, the surviving medieval churches, and the contours of the vibrant market place - all exciting prospects for two exuberant boys. To avoid over-excitement, however - as with the circus animals - I carefully steered them away from the afore-mentioned chickens and rabbits that, in their respective cages, were a familiar feature of the market place.

While we appreciated the historic and the modern day charms of Falaise, our visits were often for an altogether more prosaic purpose. DEFRA, in its wisdom, decreed that every animal subject to the Pet Passport Scheme has to be checked by an authorised vet before being permitted to return to the UK. This check had to be carried out between 24 and 48 hours of the intended embarkation, and had to be duly noted in the Pet Passport. The check consists of confirming the identity of the pet via its micro-chip, confirming that it is in good health and able to travel, and treating the pet against possible worms and ticks. O, yes, and confirming that the animal has been inoculated against rabies.

We found a friendly veterinary practice in the middle of Falaise, and remained clients when they moved to a purpose designed, state-of-the-art practice on the outskirts of town. The boys never enjoyed visits to the vets, to put it mildly, but were relatively relaxed there, and exceptionally well-treated.

As often as possible, for purely recreational reasons, we visited this historic town on bright, sunny, Saturday mornings. Then, we could meander around the fabulous market with our two boys, and walk admiringly beneath the enormous stone walls of the Castle's Keep. Returning to the car replete with some of the finest quality produce in the world - including crème fraiche and cheese - we would take the scenic route back home, along empty, forested roads.

If this was all a world away from 1944/45, it was sure proof that life could get better, as well as worse. And, in these years, life was very, very good.

The small town of Tinchebray provided further proof that we bump into history with every undulation in the road. In Tinchebray, we encountered an apparently unremarkable, but actually quite remarkable, town; in fact, a hardly less fascinating place than Falaise itself. We had so often by-passed this small place, usually on the way to somewhere else. So, one April morning (2012) we decided to pay a visit. As it happens, in appearance it's a small, pleasant but unprepossessing town, about the last location imaginable as the site for an earth-shattering event.

But we knew that, in 1106, Tinchebray was the scene of a momentous battle, now almost forgotten. However, the Battle of Tinchebray changed the world. Following the strange death of the eldest brother, William Rufus, in an apparent hunting accident, the youngest son of the Conqueror, Henry, became, rather dubiously, King of England, while his elder brother, Robert 'Curthose', was obliged to make-do as Duke of Normandy. They both wanted the same thing - power, and each other's thrones and dominions. Following a failed attempt at an English invasion by Robert, in 1103, Henry invaded Normandy. On 28 September 1106 the decisive battle took place - its epicentre at the heart of the present town. Henry's forces were victorious, and destroyed or captured most of Robert's army. For his pains, the captured Robert was imprisoned in Cardiff Castle until the end of his days, nearly three decades later.

Curiously, a year later found us in magnificent Gloucester Cathedral where, quite by chance, we came face-to-face with the superb, life-like effigy of Robert, Duke of Normandy, carved from almost indestructible bog-oak. The effigy is directly above his tomb, which had lain undisturbed for 900 years.

The Battle of Tinchebray, one of the most decisive battles of medieval times, is commemorated by a very small - and easily missed - metal plaque, fixed to a wall. I guess it's tiny, not because of the battle's insignificance, but the opposite: French historians clearly regard Tinchebray as the day that the Norman Conquest - barely a generation earlier - went into reverse.

Tinchebray is now a tranquil place, almost ghostly quiet in a very rural, French way. It's hard to appreciate that the bloody and momentous event that occurred here not only united England and Normandy once more, but put England firmly in the driving seat in the relationship - where it would remain until King John 'Lackland' lost his French dominions. The consequences were to be even greater, in terms of the emergence of England, then Great Britain, as an independent nation, and an emerging world power. The tail had not only wagged the dog, but morphed into something very large, and very fierce. The site where hundreds - if not thousands - of brave men shed their blood is now a children's playground. Sometimes, irony just can't get any deeper.

A millennium later, the Americans were the next to invade, taking the town from the occupiers on 15 August 1944. This was pretty well the last Norman town to be re-captured before the great drive westwards, towards Brittany, and eastwards, towards Germany itself.

Beauty in Bayeux

We have visited Bayeux many times, to savour its medieval magnificence. A visit to see *La Tapisserie* should be on everyone's 'bucket list'. And the 11th century Cathedral de Notre Dame - begun in 1040 - is a medieval masterpiece. The Cathedral dominates the small City, and maintains its dignity and sense of purpose, despite the inevitable hordes of visitors.

The City's more recent claim to fame is that it was the first important Norman community to be liberated, in early June, 1944. Since it was liberated quickly, miraculously, it suffered little loss of life or collateral damage. This meant that the exquisite little City's medieval structure remained proudly intact.

However, on a singular occasion we visited the City in August, in order to savour its glorious Medieval Pageant. It was exactly my kind of occasion - colourful, vibrant, full of life and energy - and very hot.

Our introduction to medieval pageants had began at Château Ganne, a mid-Summer treat, and short ride from home. The picturesque ruins of Château Ganne host a weekend nostalgic tilt-of-the-habbard recreation of life a millennium ago. Jousting, troubadours, poirrots, peasants - the pageant is a riot of rustic, vivid colours, and French bonhomie. Bows and arrows, mead and honey are amongst the tempting goods on display - and sale. One's senses are assaulted by the music of lutes, while the savour from ox-roasts is carried on the warm breeze. These visits were, perhaps, a little reminiscent of our trip to Berkeley Castle several years earlier.

Since the Ganne extravaganza was so exciting, in sensory terms, and with horses, goats and chickens all a necessary part of the atmosphere, Hector & Jason required acute attention. Even so, there we all were, standing upon a hillock, watching a troop of entertainers in the dip below: a troop consisting of two men, two women, and a monkey. It was all urgent, physical and verbal action: wife-husband scolding - a universal language. We returned home after two hours of fun, and several miles of exercise along the winding paths of the site, relaxed and happy.

The Bayeux afternoon was sultry, and humid, and the boys enjoyed the thick shade thrown by the long bench that we found, adjacent to the great Cathedral itself: there had been sufficient exercise on the long romp from the car park, a mile or so away, and the pressing crowds deterred too many forays into the melt of activity, colourful as it was.

In the cobbled square and streets outside the Cathedral, a beautiful, raven haired young dancer, in flowing purple silks, danced and gyrated at the head of a line of drummers, minstrels and troubadours. The vibrant, animated procession proceeded through the streets, squeezing between the crowds of tourists and the hundreds of stalls that sold everything from steaming, succulent dishes, to crossbows, medieval themed textiles, leather, swords and shields, and exotic ceramics. At intervals, the procession would halt, and intensify its dancing and music-making, before moving ahead once more, ultimately returning to the Cathedral entrance. H&J spent an hour or so in the midst of this tumult, absorbing the atmosphere from the relative haven of their bench adjacent the Cathedral.

June and I enjoyed separate forays into the throng, and I snapped the colourful procession as it stopped along its route. I also hurriedly cleared up Hector's 'folly', which occurred right outside the magnificent entrance to the Cathedral.

The joyous afternoon was rounded by an hour's drive home - past the remote and sobering Mont Pincon, scene of brutal and courageous fighting in August 1944.

We gave thanks for our blessings, returning to our refuge as grateful descendants of the brave warriors who had made our very lives, and travels, possible.

These day-long excursions, in Normandy, Brittany, and the nearby Pays de Loire were, in all their richness and diversity, almost inexhaustible. We could have explored these historic places, and lovely scenes, in the exalted company of Hector & Jason, for ever and ever.

22: Fabulous Forest Frolics - and Market Mania

All four of us loved French forests - and French markets. The 'French' is important, since French people do things differently. Whilst forests, and markets, of course offer contrasting experiences, in some ways the affect on one's senses is similar. Both forests and markets provide a conduit for adventure, excitement, fun and pleasure within a civilised - and civilising - ambience.

I hope that's not too 'high-fallutin'. Hector & Jason were not intellectuals, and were certainly not high-brow. But they loved their fun and frolics, and forests and markets offered both, in spades. Simple, deep pleasures, innocently enjoyed.

Fabulous French Forest Frolics

Forests, bright as beaten gold, your lovely limbs unfurled:
Unfold those loving arms, embrace, surround the world!

Colin Hill

Anyone with even the most sketchy acquaintance with French history will know that, when French kings were not 'warring', they were hunting - in their magnificent forests.

Travelling through, or roaming around, the forests of Normandy and the Loire is to be struck forcibly by the beauty and immensity of these ancient natural spaces. Hunting apart, who would not want to be exposed to the grandeur and possibilities offered by these natural marvels? According to a survey conducted by *BBC Gardeners' World,* 98% of adults in the UK find it impossible to name just five common tree species. So, the forests are a natural place to learn, as well as to marvel.

As well as repositories of nature, tranquillity and beauty, forests are resonant with risk, with mystery, perhaps with sexual desire. In

Grimm's fairy-tales, it is the forest that is always the source of adventure, excitement, potent danger and keen apprehension. Until recent times - and perhaps including them - there was the possibility of a surprise lurking in the undergrowth, around every leafy corner.

In modern times, we have sought to emasculate, tame and domesticate forests. However, left to their own devices, allowed to become meaningful and wild, forests have a strong sense of the 'other'; of forces, life-forms and intelligence beyond our knowledge and control. Hector & Jason sensed these qualities in forests and woodland; their excitement was evident in their faces and the sheer power and urgency of their bodies as they turned off the beaten track and entered a rich, fascinating, and unknown natural space.

French forests were amongst our favourite places to visit - how delicious, how delightful they are! Perhaps a little manicured and managed, but still how deep, remote and magnificent. The very names are redolent with mystery, and pleasure: Fougeres, Andaine, Ecouves, Grimbosq. These forests are enormous: Andaine, for example - a mere half an hour away from our 'base' - extends for some 600 square kilometres. One could easily spend weeks exploring these mighty places, or get lost among their seemingly endless pathways and vistas.

These forests are straight out of Disney, or the Brothers Grimm: huge, impressive, majestic, lonely. And yet so civilised. The tall, slender oaks and beeches reach to the sky, their natural architecture providing nature's cathedrals; so lovely, elegant and intricate. The forests are so immense that one's experience is shaped by the specific attributes of the space before one's eyes. And yet they're so individually distinct: Ecouves has a World War II Sherman tank at a central crossroad, or carrefour, (the 'Croix de Medavi') while Grimbosq has a pretty lake at its centre. In addition, this forest boasts an Arboretum, with 125 species of tree from four continents, an 'Animalerie', and a pet Cemetery - where dogs, cats and *poisson rouge* (goldfish) are all laid to rest.

The small town of Fougeres itself contains one of the largest, and one of the most complete, medieval castles in Europe; it will always be associated with our old friend Henry II. It is easy to imagine ramparts filled with medieval villagers, knights, damsels, and jousts. But our attention, on the several occasions we visited Fougeres with the boys, was on the area's fabulous forest which, like the Castle itself, is a fairy-tale confection - of perfection.

Fougeres is situated just inside Brittany - so, for us, a two hour journey away. But so worth the visit. Fougeres must be my absolute favourite forest - though rivalled by Andaine; it's a simply magnificent creation of oak and beech. Around every corner, along every path, unfolds a superbly varied landscape, with impressive new perspectives and intriguing, disappearing pathways. The lovely, pale limbs of the tall trees reach into the blue yonder, like ballet dancers caught in slow motion; the tall, graceful boughs reach skywards into shafts of sunlight that model their elegance to perfection.

It would be only too easy to become lost in the vastness. Though feeling free, H&J could not possibly be released from their leads in these most civilised of wildernesses. They were none the poorer for that, being super-alive to every moment, every possibility. So it was fitting that H&J hurried us along in a straight line, guided by the occasional command - when we were obliged to choose among the many enticing paths on offer. We kept determinedly to the well-marked routes: not only were the forests vast, but there are deer and even wild boar living in their depths and, with H&J firmly in mind, we wished to avoid the wrong sort of contact. Inexorably, the boys would pull me along the forest trails for all they were worth, their excitement palpable, their enthusiasm unquenchable.

Though the paths are clear and numbered, in Fougeres as elsewhere, we did manage to lose our way on one occasion. The sheer scale of the forest, with its millions of trees, was simply over-whelming. As relative new-comers, we became confused by the dappled depths and endless vistas: a troop of knights on horseback might have crossed our path, or characters from *Lord of the Rings*. We paused, then burst on, H&J leading until, at last, we found our way - a beam of sunshine lighting our route. O the space, the crackling air, the beauty, the freedom, the joy!

We rarely stumbled across another human being; an isolated dog-walker, perhaps, or a family collecting wild *champignons*. We collected our own little treasures: huge pine cones, great chunks of tree bark, and a few strands of aquatic plants, to diversify our little pond. I can only guess what stimulation H&J derived from these walks: a plethora of exotic smells, the excitement of a vast amphitheatre of wilderness, the possibility of the unexpected. Certainly, in Grimbosq Forest, we encountered wild boar, and the forests are rich in wildlife: deer, badgers, foxes, red squirrels, pole cats, pine martens and more. To H&J, a rich tapestry of life must have been apparent, though - apart from a myriad of bird life - the forest's mysteries were mostly hidden from June and myself. We were the 'muggles' of the forest; it was Hector & Jason who were at once in tune with its spirit.

Situated near Argentan, Ecouves is another vast forest comprising 15,000 glorious hectares. Part of the *Parc Naturel Regional Normandie-Maine*, in all spanning 230,000 hectares, Ecouves Forest itself is the largest oak forest in Normandy - and that's saying something.

At the centre of the forest is the the Croix de Medavy itself, with its bizarre icon, the Sherman tank. It is a graphic reminder of the clash of fire and steel that took place nearby. The tank saw action in August 1944, at the Falaise Pocket, under the French General Leclerc, and was part of the force which went on to liberate Alencon on 12 August.

The forests have regained their natural peace. Our almost numberless walks with H&J in these seemingly endless, ion-charged spaces were amongst our most joyful, and most perfect.

Mad Market Mania

Marché: colour; scent; exuberance. A Manet?
Acheter? A feast for heart, ear - and eye. Parfait.

Colin Hill

It is often said that the French work to live, rather than live to work. That quality can still be seen, in the annual August migration, in the high appreciation of food and drink - and in the love for markets, and the sensory experience these provide.

The sheer delight that is French markets whets the taste and sensory buds. Wherever we travelled in France, we relished the opportunity to visit these visual and sensory treats - sometimes, deliciously, we just chanced upon a market in full swing. Except for the tourist haunts in mid-Summer, markets are served by, and serve, their local communities: from a myriad latticed tributaries, all and sundry converge, as it were, on a big fork in the river. These folk provide the core and enthusiastic custom for the multitude of traders who - descending on particular towns in a strict pattern laid down by a thousand years of history - cascade a kaleidoscopic range of produce on to the waiting and (in my case) salivating recipients.

What is it that makes these markets, Marché, so appealing? There is so much that is seductive - the quality, colour, profusion, and sheer diversity of the produce and products. Together with a real vitality, and lively, animated atmosphere. But there is an extra, almost indefinable, ingredient that makes the major Summer markets so special and attractive - a kind of sense of occasion, excitement, even. '*The market has come to town - let us feast our senses, open our mouths, hearts - and purses!*'. The markets offer a cornucopia, an Aladdin's Cave of delights for the senses. All is for sale: handbags and purses, jewellery and watches, perfumes, records and films, lingerie and clothes, fabrics, leather goods, bric-a-brac, antiques, toys, flowers and potted shrubs, cutlery and tableware, carpets, beds, furniture, hand and power tools - even air-pistols.

There are food vendors to tempt every type of taste-bud: steaming cauldrons of couscous, saucisse et frites, crêpes, and paella. Specialist meat stalls offer andouilles, boudin noir, and tripe; fish stalls with this morning's glistening catch resting on a deep bed of ice; specialist stalls selling country honeys and preserves, yoghurt and crème fraiche; and tables groaning with huge loaves of freshly baked bread, or barques of strawberries and raspberries. And fruit and vegetables and flowers in a profusion, and an intensity of colour, that might have inspired a Renoir. And, to cap it off, an accordion or barrel organ infusing the fragrant air with the inimitable sounds of France.

No-one writes more vividly - more passionately - about French markets than Elizabeth David, (in *French Provincial Cooking*) revealing their 'infinite variety' to the sensory imagination:

'The fish is particularly beautiful in its pale, translucent northern way. Delicate rose pink langoustines lie next to miniature scallops in their red-brown shells; great fierce skate and sleek soles are flanked by striped iridescent mackerel, pearly little smelts, and baskets of very small, very fresh mussels. Here and there an angry-looking red gurnet waits for a customer near a mass of sprawling crabs and a heap of little grey shrimps. Everywhere there is ice and seaweed and a fresh sea smell.

Outside, the vegetable stalls are piled high with Breton artichokes, perfectly round with tightly closed leaves; long, clean, shining leeks; and fluffy green-white cauliflowers. At the next stall an old country woman is displaying carefully bunched salad herbs, chives, chervil, sorrel, radishes, and lettuces.'

The description is taken from a market near to Caen. Mrs David continues to rhapsodise about the:

'astonishingly productive province' of Normandy, *'where bowls of thick white cream and the cheeses of Camembert, Livarot, Neufchatel, Pont l'Evêque, Rouy, Isigny and a dozen other districts ooze with all the richness of the Norman pastures.'*

The great French public, of every age, size and shape, and in their teeming thousands, relaxed but excited, and focused like you've never seen them before, respond with every fibre to this sense of occasion. A surreal social spectacle unfolds, replete with smiles, bonhomie, banter, handshakes and much (French-style) kissing. The jolly live music helps to create an ambience that one could cut with a knife. There is more colour than on an artist's palette, and more types of meat, fish, cheeses, vegetables and fruit than one has ever seen assembled in a single place. The larger markets are veritable *supermarché*, except that the term is now associated with shopping from pre-fabricated sheds. But these markets also provide a bewildering and exotic array and display of just about everything one needs, or will conceivably ever need in the future. They are a feast for the senses, a lift to our animal spirits, and a (quite deliberate) sweet temptation to the pocket.

Hector & Jason responded as only they could to the excitement, profusion and confusion of the markets, exploiting every sense, and dashing around like beings possessed among the milling people. It was a case of one of us - usually me - taking the boys for a quick spin round the aisles to sate their curiosity, then retreating to a strategic point, in order to watch from a point of safety, and relax, whilst June sought some fresh food or other treats - leather, ceramics, table-ware. We have bought bright ceramics, fine tablecloths - all sorts of paraphernalia that would be impossible to find elsewhere - amongst the heaving, absorbed and loud coterie of people who descend on these exotic gatherings that have met without interruption since medieval times.

If one aspect of our market ritual was yours truly charging around the crowded aisles with the never-daunted boys, the other aspect was actually looking and buying. While June was thus engaged in Falaise one fine Saturday morning, I was performing 'dog duty', taking time to stand and stare, when two smiling Frenchmen approached, and began to fuss the boys. Then, turning to me, one gent enquired: *"Can we interest you in Jesus this morning?"*. *"Sorry,"* I smiled back, *"it might be a very long conversation…"*.

British sensibilities are probably offended by the serried ranks of chickens, ducks, turkeys and rabbits, confined in cages, that are offered for sale at most country markets. Many of the chickens and ducks are just weeks old, and probably purchased for fattening, and ultimately for dinner. However, they will experience a decent quality of life, striding around a yard or garden, before that time arrives. And, hopefully - especially if purchased by the occasional Brit - they may even be regarded as pets, or valued for their eggs, adding substance to 'the good life' that so often brings our migrating countrymen to France.

With Hector & Jason lording it over our garden, there was never any question of adding chickens or ducks to our patch, however wistful the prospect seemed. Indeed, my major pre-occupation when visiting these markets with H&J was in steering them away from the areas where livestock were being sold; it would not do to add to these creatures' stress by confronting them with two panting and straining demi-wolves.

The most spectacular markets we have visited in Normandy have been at Falaise, La Ferté Macé, Villers Bocage and Condé sur Noireau. Character and tradition remain strong features: La Ferté Macé, for example, is famous for its tripe, which is sold, grilled on skewers, at Thursday's market.

Yet some of my favourite markets, and those I remember most fondly, have been in Brittany: at Carnac, Le Forêt Fousnant, and Penmarc'h, the last two accidental visitations, chanced upon in the midst of our travels.

We encountered the Sunday market at La Forêt Fousnant almost by accident. From our base-camp at Keranterec, one glorious, expectant Sunday morning, we decided to visit the pretty little port of Le Port Forêt, just a few miles from camp. After admiring the attractive harbour, with its smart yachts, we followed our nose, as it were, into the surrounding countryside.

A path soon emerged, with people moving purposefully in the same direction. Before long the path opened out, and we found ourselves in the super little village of La Forêt Fousnant, set in a quiet harbour, where river meets the sea. An egret waded in the shallows.

And there it was: a sprawling, bustling Sunday market, one of the most inviting we had encountered. The displays were more artistic - rustic and bountiful in character - than almost any we had seen, perhaps with at least one eye on the tourist market. A veritable profusion of ceramics, paintings, clothes, furniture, and jewellery were displayed, tempting both eye and wallet.

In view of the mid-day Summer heat, June and I took turns in shopping, the other minding H&J, who could observe all from their shady seat, along with their 'guardian'. Hector, Jason and I sat back and enjoyed the cool shade of the local river, with egrets fishing silently. It was a simply delightful morning, perhaps more so because our discovery was so unexpected. Bold colours gleamed in the sunshine, and the setting perhaps merited the palette of a Renoir. I had only my trusty *Canon*, which I deployed with some enthusiasm.

We still have the large, ceramic dish acquired that day - and the dish, of little intrinsic worth, has a value for us that is enhanced by the memory and pleasure of happy times.

We returned to our camp-site at lunchtime via the same meandering route, truly content with our morning's work, and its sheer innocent pleasure. H&J always exalted in the unexpected and in pleasant surprises. In fact, life was a game of unexpected surprises, and this market had offered up yet another delightful experience.

While exploring the remote western edge of Brittany, we stumbled on the market at Penmarc'h, in the middle of a hot and dusty day. Sited, apparently, in the middle of nowhere, it was as large and attractive as a souk in remotest Araby: all noise and colour. We just had to stop and *regardez*.

However, it seems that others came before us. There is an impressive, 64 metre-high lighthouse built in 1897, and named in honour of Marshal Davout, one of Napoleon's finest generals. And this is also reputed to be the very place where Tristan and Isolde died.

On that sultry, dusty day, when we were all - H&J excepted - wilting in the heat, and oblivious of the weight of history, the market provided a welcome diversion. I remember the boys hurtling around the narrow, crowded aisles, me in tow. As a consequence, I don't believe that we bought so much as a croissant, though as usual I did grab the odd photograph.

Carnac is, of course, a magnet for over-Summering Brits. The resort's market is held every week in Summer; it stretches as far as the eye can see, and delights the eye with its brightness, profusion and vibrancy. The market is actually held in two sections - the food market, and everything else - the two parts being separated by a narrow road.

The food market is truly spectacular, even for connoisseurs of such events, with thousands of stalls, a dizzying array of choice foods being cooked and roasted, mountains of fresh fruit and vegetables, cheeses, wines and ciders - everything to tempt both palate, and purse. Parting with one's cash has never been so painless. I do believe that we bought a roast chicken for lunch, (to be eaten on this occasion at Camping Kervilor) but also two fine tablecloths, still used frequently in Normandy. Again, the memory is refreshed every time we spread one of these cloths in preparation for dinner.

It still amazes me that H&J waded into those throngs of people, all that hubbub and apparent confusion, with the confidence and zest of athletes at the top of their game. The waft of meats cooking on the breeze no doubt helped, but they treated each stall with equally brief attention as they urged me along in their matchless, inimitable way.

However, matching the market's fame is that of the town's only, but illustrious, supermarché. Everyone who knows Carnac will be familiar with the 'Super U' supermarket, the town's own goldmine, or Comstock Lode. From *Lundi* morning, through to *Samedi* evening, (of course closed on Sundays) the shop's aisles would be crammed with sweaty tourists, and its tills crammed with sweaty euros. I often joked that a single day's takings would feather-bed me for life. While June bravely joined the milling throngs, Hector, Jason and I, bathed in warm sunshine, would sit in the car park and marvel as the multi-hued customers, armed with their 'chariots', engaged in battle in the surfeited, almost smirking, emporium.

Vive la différence: whatever the style of market, whatever the occasion, the boys were ever eager to relish each and every atom of experience.

23: Sun, Sea, Seduction...

A promenade; a picnic made; dizzy runs along the strand;
A sea bird's cry, a beach belle's sigh; tides of joy by breezes fanned.

Colin Hill

What is love? 'tis not hereafter;
Present mirth hath present laughter;
What's to come is still unsure...

Carpe Diem - William Shakespeare

Forests and markets not-withstanding, it is our annual adventures to the resorts and beaches of Normandy and Brittany that linger in the mind and senses. The French seaside has a curious, nostalgic allure, a delightful poignancy, that is hard to pin down, but totally seductive.

The visits to Normandy's beach resorts were all the result of day-trips from the cottage: waiting for a fine day and then setting off early, towards one or more coastal resorts. They are all so charming and irresistible. We were spoiled for choice...

The wealth of options included the resorts along the Côte Fleurie, those adorning the Côte de Nacre, and a further bevy of seaside haunts nestling along the Cotentin or Cherbourg Peninsula. Hector & Jason adored the atmospheric sea-fronts and the huge, empty beaches that we found, tucked away from the more excitable tourist magnets such as Deauville, Trouville and Cabourg. The resort towns of Granville, Franceville-Merville, Houlgate and Courseulles-sur-mer all saw us frequently - but Cabourg, Trouville, even glamorous Deauville, almost too chic for its own good, saw us too. Oscar Wilde, yet again.

The coasts of Normandy offer some of the most delightful resorts in - at least - Europe. From the sophistication and 'chic' qualities of Deauville and Cabourg, to the Third Empire charm of family resorts such as Houlgate and Trouville, to the historic and impressive

Arromanches, or yet the wild, unspoiled coasts around the Cherbourg Peninsula, Normandy's resorts have an atmospheric attraction that is deeply and uniquely French. The boys loved the promenade in Houlgate, Luc-sur-mer and Courseulles-sur-mer, and the beaches at Granville and Merville-Franceville, near Pegasus Bridge. They also loved the south Brittany beaches at Carnac and Bénodet, as we shall discover. My memories of our visits gain added lustre from the sheer pleasure these great spaces provided, visually, culturally and socially, combined with the pleasure that H&J, in their turn, both received and conveyed.

The resort of Granville is a grand, stylish if slightly austere town on Normandy's Cotentin Peninsula. After a coffee in an open-air café, near to the ubiquitous Casino, we would stroll around the magnificent headland with H&J. At the command to '*stay!*' our caravan would shudder to a halt, and we would admire the sparkling seas and unimpaired views in every direction. Once more John Keats springs to mind:

> *'Then felt I like some watcher of the skies*
> *When a new planet swims into his ken;*
> *Or like stout Cortez, when with eagle eye*
> *He stared at the Pacific - and all his men*
> *Look'd at each other with a wild surmise -*
> *Silent, upon a peak in Darien.'*

We would return for a delicious lunch at a bar adjacent to the Casino - more James Bond than Cortez.

Some years earlier, when June and I were looking anxiously for accommodation in the town, (the whole of France downs tools in August), we enquired at several hotels without any success. Having almost given up hope, I spotted an imposing, gleaming place - almost palace - situated invitingly above the beach, and facing the sea. Excellent! This would do nicely. I strolled in to the reception and enquired of the concierge, in my best French, "*Do you have any rooms available, please?*". "*Monsieur, this is a hospital*", he replied nonchalantly.

The resort also hosts a 'Shrine' and excellent Museum dedicated to the fashion icon, Christian Dior. Needless to say, the Museum does not offer accommodation.

The choice little resort of Luc-sur-mer, part of Sword Beach, is charmingly characterful, and only a short drive from Ouistreham, on the Côte de Nacre.

Luc sur Mer is a breezy, traditional seaside town, rich in charm, history and nostalgia; it is headily perfumed with that special Gallic seaside *bonhomie* which, if one could bottle it, would make one a fortune. The town has a faded grandeur - a place where I could imagine writing poetry, or a novel (in the style of Proust) in an antique-furnitured hotel bedroom, looking out onto the promenade, beach and speckled sea beyond: the resort positively reeks of French tradition and atmosphere. Rows of pointy-roofed, regimented, bathing huts line the promenade; they stand sparkling - almost smiling - in the Summer air.

Luc is a quiet little resort - there is world-class competition for sun-worshippers along this coast - but the shops, cafés, restaurants and hotels that string along the main street that faces the beach, make a lively and indelible impression. We could stroll along the promenade with the boys, then sample a coffee, and watch the world go by, without a care. Even the boys, excited on arrival, seemed to absorb the relaxed atmosphere of the place.

If the weather was sufficiently inviting, we would wander on along the road that winds along this superb coast towards St Aubin-sur-mer, and then Courseilles-sur-mer, and onwards to historic Arromanches and pretty Port en Bessin.

How many visitors to the smart resort of Courseilles-sur-mer are aware of its place in history? Perhaps the boldly positioned, beautifully maintained, traditional (bright red) English phone box on the promenade provides a clue. Churchill visited here on 12 June 1944; General de Gaulle followed on 14 June, and George VI on 16 June, following the historic Normandy landings that had begun only days earlier.

It was Canadian forces that had stormed ashore and captured Juno Beach. When we visited the vast stretch of sand that lies at Bernieres-sur-mer - mid-way between St Aubin-sur-mer and Courselles - for picnic lunches, there was hardly a soul to be seen along the windswept beach. This was the scene for Jason's irresistible, epic gallops across the spume-flecked sands, watched in amazement by his anxious friends. Given his sensitive antennae, I'm quite convinced that Jason's dramatic runs along Juno beach were somehow inspired by the spirit of the place.

Arromanches is a small town on the Côte Fleurie that will forever be famous as the site for the Allies' main supply base. The town was affectionately nick-named 'Port Winston'. The Allies transported an entire harbour - huge concrete platforms, towed by cargo ships - and with them built a storm-proof haven for landing military hardware and that precious substance that kept the invasion mobile - oil. The 'Mulberry Harbour' proved crucial to the juggernaut Allied war-effort, as it continued its relentless advance across Normandy. Today, the concrete *caissons*, remnants of the famous harbour, retain their formidable, algae-crusted presence along Arromanches's beach.

The resort has an impressive setting in its own right, nestling between superlative headlands. The cliffs above the town provide a magnificent panorama. This dramatic backdrop is entirely in keeping with the enormity of events that occurred in this historic place, a mere 75 years ago.

The whole town, whilst clean, prim and proud, is now given over pretty much entirely to celebrating its unique place in history, with an absorbing museum and a heady array of gift shops, with a predominantly historic-military theme.

Of course, the boys were blissfully unaware of the town's dramatic, even pivotal, place in world history. On all the visits made by H&J, the main attraction was always the beach. Because this is not a prime bathing beach, the boys were free to run around the large expanse of sand with gay abandon. Hector & Jason played happily on the sands, darting between the seaweed-plastered sections of the artificial Mulberry harbour, quite oblivious that they were rubbing shoulders with history at its most monumental.

Port en Bessin is a charming, but busy, active, fishing port, where the young Jason first witnessed the sea at first hand. Needless to say, he was startled and shocked by it. Was it alive? Certainly, no place for a highly-strung and sensitive boy...

Nowadays, it is hard indeed to think of the Port, with its lively little bars and restaurants, and sleepy fishing harbour, as the scene of some of the most intense fighting around D-Day, with British Commandos engaged in a desperate struggle for the town between 6 and 8 June.

Two days of heavy fighting followed the D-Day invasion, with the British forces at Bessin heavily outnumbered. Then, the Commando leader, the gallant Captain Cousins, discovered an apparently undefended zigzag path, leading towards enemy positions. Under cover of darkness, Cousins led a party of 25 men as far as he could, up the hill, unobserved. In true commando style, the men then charged - yelling, screaming and firing from the hip - and over-ran the enemy bunkers. The much-loved commander was fatally wounded in the assault. Many in the Commando believe that Captain Cousins should have been awarded a VC for his selfless action.

Today, sitting outside one of the fish restaurants that line the cobbled road by the inner port, you would really never guess that so tranquil a resort could have seen such bitter fighting. Oh, the pleasures of peace and freedom...

H&J would lead a charge along the aptly named *Promenade des Chiens* that follows the graceful contours of the harbour.

I'm really chuffed with the pictures I took of the young H&J there, on our very first visit: there they are, looking proudly at me from their seat in the rear of the Volvo, vital and brimming with life and expectancy.

Deauville itself is the most chic, sophisticated, luxurious, elegant resort in northern France, and one of the most celebrated in the whole country. The town exerts a magnetism for Parisians, celebrities, would-be celebrities and celebrity-watchers from all over the world.

The resort was founded by the Duc de Morny in 1866, and was intended to be special from the outset. The resort is oh-so-chic, but is admittedly a smart, exciting place to visit. People-watching from the impossibly expensive bars on the *Promenades des Planches* is *de rigeur*. July is high season, when the famous racecourse has its premier meeting, and the casino is in full swing. Again, the boys were there: the boys were there!

Deauville's elder, more sedate sister, Trouville, is a splendid, elegant, *fin de siecle* resort, which has retained its 19th century charm. It is famous for the patronage of the Empress Eugenie, wife of Napoleon III. Indeed, a painting (by Boudin) of the Empress strolling on the beach with her retinue, all elegantly dressed and with open umbrellas to offer protection from the sun, graces our humble cottage. 21st century Trouville still boasts many elegant buildings dating from this Third Empire period, imbuing the town with period charm.

We once bought fresh prawns from the local fish-market - purchasing far more than we intended, because of a mix-up over weight or money. Never mind - they were delicious.

I'm afraid that Hector experienced a toilet emergency on the sea-front. Strange how one recalls these little incidents - and how that ushers in all kinds of reminiscences, local colours, and, yes, fragrances.

Merville-Franceville sur-mer is an attractive, inviting resort, accessed via Benouville. On the journey we always passed over historic Pegasus Bridge, with its famous café and proudly be-medalled war veterans. Then, almost immediately, we passed through the impossibly pretty village of Sallenelle, filled with flowers and tempting shops full of choice patisserie.

And then, turning off the busy, tree-lined road, we are at once in a resort which is essentially modern, with a few bars, restaurants and gift shops, and a superb beach, promenade and delightful coastal walks.

Merville-Franceville is charmingly informal and relaxed. There is the familiar 'No Chiens' signs along the beach, but dogs are permitted beyond the main bathing area. The promenade itself was enjoyable for the boys, and the coastal walks are simply superb. From here, we could watch ferries steaming into nearby Ouistreham. And how we would admire the golden, cliff-top flowers, with a myriad butterflies fluttering in a refreshing Summer breeze. Not for nothing is this coast deemed the 'Coast of Flowers'.

We spent so many happy, care-free days at Merville with Hector & Jason. The resort was one of their very favourite places, and the scene of some of our most blissful days together; quintessential, happy-go-lucky, bucket&spade-ville.

Some of my favourite pictures of H&J were taken here. On these images, the lads always look supremely happy.

A mere few minutes from the languid resort and its pleasure-seeking trippers lies the famous Merville Battery, and its impressive Museum. The Merville Gun Battery provided a fearsome emplacement in the Atlantic Wall, and one that needed to be neutralised quickly, if Sword Beach was to be won without huge loss of life and equipment. Elaborate plans had been made to capture the Battery - plans that, given the sheer logistical difficulties of the operation, went badly awry.

In the event, in the early hours of 6 June '44, Lieutenant-Colonel Terence Otway led 160 men of the 9th Battalion of the Parachute Regiment - a force that had originally consisted of some 600 Paras - into a fire-fight against the fearsomely protected coastal Battery.

Within minutes, Otway's small force had suffered 75 casualties, but had succeeded in taking their objective: the Battery had been disabled.

The nearby towns of Houlgate and Cabourg are 'bourgeois' resorts par excellence. Houlgate's fulsome and spectacular late 19th century architecture is most impressive. We often used to walk through the town, admiring the splendid buildings, as well as promenading along the beach. This was another favourite destination, since the boys were permitted free access to the broad beach; the atmosphere was always convivial.

We first visited Cabourg with H&J in July, 2004, on a hot, sunny morning. The resort was buzzing, and could not have looked more impressive - manicured, immaculate, with a sort of regal elegance and restrained energy. Almost immediately, the promenade and beach made a deep impression.

Cabourg is imbued with that Gallic chic and elegance, but in a more rarified form; in competition with nearby Deauville, perhaps. The pride - and prejudice - of the resort always lifts my spirits.

The resort was laid out by Robinet in 1860, very much like its rival Deauville. Yet, there is an air of faded gentility, that perhaps lends the resort an added charm. We would stroll purposefully along the grand (and very long) *Promenade Marcel Proust.*

Marcel Proust paid long Summer visits to the The Grand Hotel, (which remains rather grand) and wrote *Remembrance of Things Past* while staying there. In August 1914, with the Kaiser's army threatening France, the Government and a million Parisians residents de-camped from Paris. Proust, too, departed Paris. However, whilst the Government established itself at Bordeaux - as far away from the advancing Germans as possible - Proust headed to his beloved Cabourg. There, he found the town's little hospital over-flowing with wounded soldiers. Each day, he took them gifts of chocolate, games, and playing cards.

Though Cabourg is very posh, and manicured, it perhaps takes itself a little too seriously. On that first visit to Cabourg, we had been strolling for only a matter of seconds along the glorious promenade when we were approached by a uniformed chap, asking us to ensure that we cleaned up any incidence of dog poo. It seemed almost unnecessary: not only were the boys impeccably behaved, it would have been sacrilege not to have cleaned up, when faced with the couture of the flower beds, and those grand, if rather pompous, Third Empire façades.

But it was another small incident from our first trip there that I recall most warmly. We had been preparing H&J for their walk (water and fuss on a hot day), when an elderly French lady approached us, and complimented us excessively on our care and attentiveness to the boys. O, the kindness of strangers. Thank you so much, madam.

Taken much later, my photos of Hector & Jason, snapped outside The Grand Hotel, are some of my most cherished. I can still smell the sea-salt, still picture the elegance, still see the race horses pulling 'chariots' elegantly across the broad sands; still sense the thrill of my boys. As it happens, most photos of Hector & Jason reflect our adventures in France: this is not a coincidence, but a testament to our happiest, most special times together.

We visited Villers-sur-mer on so many occasions during the Summer, starting out early in the hope of finding a parking space. The town lies a fair distance beyond Cabourg and Houlgate, but along winding country roads. Thank goodness it's a lovely drive, because we only managed to find space on the car park on a single occasion! In July and August the locals, and in-situ tourists, will always arrive first. The resort is smart and exclusive - and predictably gorged with visitors. On that single, successful, occasion we set off with H&J for a well-deserved walk along the resort's elegant promenade.

Portbail, on the western Cherbourg Peninsula, and once an important Gallo-Roman town, is now a small port, but with a pleasing sense of remoteness. Just a few scattered buildings and yachts, their fittings clinking in the breeze, provide a relaxed ambience. We enjoyed a quite wonderful day here, with H&J, magnificent in their power and sense of freedom, thundering along the fine, broad beach of powdered sand.

The little church of Notre Dame, now secularised, dates from the 11th century, and is a fine example of the Romanesque style. When we visited, a modern art exhibition took centre stage. A little knot of English tourists ate their ice-creams on the green sward outside; H&J looked longingly at the tempting ices.

And there are super pictures of H&J pounding excitedly around that vast, empty beach...

The Marvellous Mont

Mont St Michel, rising on the very border between Normandy and Brittany, seems a world away from the northern Normandy resorts.

What more can one say about this iconic site? The superlatives have been exhausted.

The Mont was first conceived in the 8th century, (708AD) as an oratory, by the Bishop of Avranches. It became, first, a fortress, then an Abbey, and an immensely important focus of pilgrimage. The site remains a quite fantastic destination to visit, and explore. Mont St Michel is a veritable magnet for visitors - not only the biggest single attraction in Normandy, but the third greatest tourist draw in the whole of France, attracting 3 million visitors each year.

Certainly, a visit to Mont St Michel has always been a much anticipated pleasure. The journey to the Mont, via the coast road south of Granville, is almost as spectacular as the immense and magnificent edifice that one confronts on arrival. Viewed from the bay, the Mont appears as a ghostly, impossibly romantic presence, rising majestically from a shimmering, silver sea. In purely picturesque terms, this is as good as it gets.

On the journey, we always exercised Hector & Jason on the lovely, lonely, sands at Kairon, with its superb views over to Granville. How they loved ripping along the windswept beach! The boys vented their pleasure, eagerly galloping and tussling on the sands. H&J would grab the cuttlefish that littered the beach with their white, chalky shells, and race around, triumphant, fish-in-mouth.

And then on to Genêt, with yet more superlative, mesmeric views of the looming Mont, within its majestic bay. We shared the views, and the experience, with the sheep, which grazed on the salt flats, and with the swallows, which darted in a clear blue sky.

And finally along the long, winding road, with Mont St Michel losing its misty aura, and becoming a massive stone edifice rearing supremely from the waters, and commanding one's every attention.

Mont St Michel fully deserves its huge popularity. Any description can only provide a vague idea of the magnetism and magnificence of this great Abbey and walled town, isolated on its rock, and jutting dramatically out of the sparkling sea. The inevitable commercialism is quite tasteful by British standards, and hardly detracts from the unique impact of the Mont. If one does not quite capture the excitement - and danger - of the early pilgrimages, a traveller, nevertheless, must be suffering a special kind of ennui not to be awed by his visit.

The Mont, a World Heritage Site, is one of the very few places in Normandy where there is actually a charge for parking - Arromanches is another. In the midst of this splendour, one pays up gladly.

We did not enter the steep, mighty fortress with the boys in tow - simply, too many distractions. Although they would have loved the steep, narrow steps and frenetic atmosphere, we were content to patrol the perimeters of the awesome walled fortress. We had arrived at the end of a marvellous journey, and were happy to be photographed, with the boys, against the immense edifice of Mont St Michel. An immortality, of sorts.

Once, and once only, we ventured on the superb Grand Day Out that took us right around the marvellous Bay of St Michel, via the magnificent coast road. Once only; but unforgettable.

We chose our day well: Spring, and bright as a button, with a gentle breeze. Our route passed through the attractive village of Teilleul, then Buats, followed by the mysterious St Symphorien des Monts, with its ancient park and walled Château.

There is a wildlife park in the grounds of the ancient Château, including bison, white (wild) boar, and rare red pigs, all the way from Tamworth. The Park's charming motto is: *'Nature counter-attacks!'.* Then we arrived in the quite substantial precincts of St Hilaire du Hacouët. If you are lucky - and we were - it will be a Wednesday, and a bustling market offers the town local colour and gaiety. St Hilaire, together with its twin-towered church, was almost completely wrecked during the German counter-attack on 6-7 August 1944. Some commentators describe the restored church as 'ugly'; I would describe it as heroic.

St Hilaire was quickly followed by a welcome stop at the Aire de Repos, where toilets and a green carpet of lawn proved very acceptable, variously, to all four of our party. Refreshed, we headed on through the splendid, fountain-and-flower-filled town of Ducey, set on a clean, sparkling river, with a superb weir; and yet another impressive church.

At St Broladre we stopped at a boulangerie for a baguette, to complete a picnic lunch. And then, the road clung to the coast, and its rich hinterland, with windmills, and former windmills, situated prettily along the road-side. Garlic, onions, and leeks seem to dominate the fields, though there are also extensive patches of cabbage, maize and wheat growing on the rich, alluvial soil.

A little way beyond Le Vivier sur mer, at Hirel, is the Air des Nouettes - situated right on the bay - we all decanted on to the huge plage, to enjoy a leisurely picnic lunch on one of the wooden benches thoughtfully provided for the purpose. Hector & Jason, meanwhile, ran along the beach together in glorious abandon. And, in the distance, glittering in the bay, the unique Mont St Michel itself.

The next stop was a mere blip away, a tiny development - Saint Benoit des Ondes - which we explored exhaustively. I took an 'arty' picture of the algae-encrusted, characterful, and ancient, wooden stockade that, twice daily, attempts to disrupt and reduce the power of the tide.

And then, at last, we found famous Cancale, nestling in its own neck of the Bay, and heaving with holiday-makers enjoying its oysters and 'moules'. Cancale is the oyster capital of Brittany; Louis XIV had his oysters bought from Cancale to Versailles. Three hundred years later, we too can savour the food of kings. There are terrific views of the town from the cliffs above, on a little car-park dedicated to a former mayor, Olivier Biard.

On a clear day, there are stupendous views of Mont St Michel from Cancale. I recall stopping, and staring, with H&J. But one is never far from Blighty. June spotted another couple strolling along the seafront, a *Morrison's* carrier bag to the fore; clearly, the British at play. Strange how these oddities stick in the memory.

Though we did not find - did not then know - the spectacular cliffs and sea-views of Pointe de Grouin, only a mile or two away, this was a marvellous, heart-brimming day out, and we headed joyfully for home via the direct route, along the fast and true A84.

As always, Jason was delighted to see his home again; there was nothing, and nowhere, better. Even so, I suspect that he had enjoyed a day in this wild and wonderful environment that had matched even *his* spirits.

Chapter 24: French Odyssey: Adventures on Far-flung Shores

The Clarion of Adventure draws me to her breast:
'Seek! Desire! Explore! dear child. And then - eternal rest.

Colin Hill

Let us yet sing, and dance, and laugh, and play -
And kiss the sun, and love this merry day.

Colin Hill

I have spent most of my adult life in effect re-butting my father's imprecation that "*You can have too much scenery*". If, as a Black Country lad, you *do* love scenery, and the natural world, then you have little choice but to travel beyond the confines of our sub-region to discover the charms that lie on distant horizons.

Hector & Jason would have accompanied me - or more accurately, led me - to the ends of the Earth. But the pedestrian reality is that we explored no further than Normandy, Brittany, and the Loire Valley. That in itself was no mean feat, and is not undertaken lightly - the distances between major towns and places of interest in France being really quite daunting. How many news bulletins have you heard where a - usually troubled - part of the world is described as being "as large as France"? In practice, despite the relatively light traffic, it can take many hours to travel from one region to another. And we are - all - usually travelling when the whole world seems to be on the move and, as often as not, when the weather is at its hottest. Though Hector & Jason were fabulously fit, we were careful not to make their travelling overly arduous. At all times, one is conscious of heat and fatigue and its effect on boys with thick fur coats; we had to think of them, and with them, every minute of the journey.

So our adventures were never more than a day's drive from our French cottage, and never needed to be: wherever we ventured, we were sure to discover lush forests, cooling lakes and pine-fringed seas. It is fair to say that I have never felt constrained or limited by our travels - finding a wealth and remarkable diversity of scenery - and culture - everywhere we wandered. For us, and the boys, every day's adventure promised unexpected delights; we found new treasure each and every day. Hector would sit up on his seat throughout each journey, searching the horizon with keen interest. He was a confident, curious traveller: Jason would relax, chilled out, waiting for events to unfold. For them both, the journey was merely the prelude: arriving was easily the best part of the experience, the beginning of excitement, ecstasy, even.

For sound reasons of practicality, hot weather, and the wear and tear of travel, we tried to arrange a schedule that combined new and exciting environments with a not-too-stretching timetable. Four or five hours in the car, in achieving our destination, even with breaks on the way, was quite challenging enough. That little square on the map - bordered by Normandy's coasts, and extending to Brittany in the West, and the Loire Valley in the South - framed our decade and more of wanderings. But, believe me, there is more to interest, excite and inspire within these parameters - coasts, cities, countryside, history, culture - than can be explored in a lifetime.

It seems strange to think that, over the first decade or so of the new Century, June and I spent only around 10% of our time in France. And only around 2% of our time was spent on our high-Summer 'missions' to camp sites in Brittany in particular - and to our favourite sites at Camping Kervilor and Camping Keranterec. Yet those relatively modest percentages possess a technicolour, sharply three-dimensional status in my mind, crowding out a large chunk of the remaining 90% - which largely consisted of the repetitive daily pattern of working life.

I will attempt to give a flavour of these forays into French holiday life, so full of anticipation and vitality, and so enriched by the companionship of Hector & Jason. Every year, just as the Summer was reaching its most enchanting, the days warm, enticing and endless, we would set off on our annual migration from La Haute Maison to deepest Brittany. These trips to Brittany were longer - camping holidays - and we were equipped with all the essential paraphernalia required for an extended break, to either of our favourite destinations - Camping Kervilor, near to Carnac, or Camping Keranterec, close to Concarneau.

Together, we travelled the highways and byways to explore Brittany's glorious coasts, and would later venture to the Loire, and the region's fabulous Châteaux. If the boys loved these trips, Hector loved every moment, and every aspect, while Jason, as we know, loved *arriving*. It would take a day or so to prepare and plan for the journey, and we would set out early on the appointed day with the car stacked to the gunwales with camping equipment: tent, sleeping bags, tables and chairs, but not forgetting dog-dishes, dog-food, copious supplies of water, and (one excited, and one expectant) Hector & Jason. We would depart from La Haute Maison quite elated, full of anticipation; and with 'excited and expectant' boys on board.

Wherever we travelled, we trod In the footsteps of famous figures - kings, statesmen, artists - who had left their indelible mark on history: William the Conqueror, Henry II, Joan of Arc, Leonardo da Vinci, Francis I, Proust, Churchill, De Gaulle - all spectres whose ambitions and achievements guided our path, and filled our vision. Sometimes, it's true, we needed to exercise a little imagination, to scratch away the accretions of history, and look, and listen; to allow the past to reveal itself, breathe, and speak.

Our journey along main roads, planned to include coffee and toilet stops, with opportunities for the boys to stretch their legs, would take around five hours. As we never fail to appreciate, France is a large country, and travel time expands accordingly. Service stations, or 'air de gaps' are therefore most welcome though, in Summer, along the main routes, these become crowded with coaches, trucks and motor-homes jostling for space. Everyone is eager to rest and recuperate on this brief interlude to their journey west or south.

Clearly, we are atoms in the flotsam and jetsam of a vast human tide. Europe's vast populations are on the move - from Britain, the Netherlands, Germany, Spain and elsewhere - to France's western coastline: from Dinard to Biarritz. It is an exhilarating and rather daunting migration, involving millions of people, each intent on finding the elusive Holy Grail of sunshine and happiness. But it is an unedifying, unlikely route to the Elysian Fields, and sometimes more resembles the Augean Stables. If one chances to visit the smaller air de gaps, often mere lay-bys without toilet facilities, the stench of human urgency is all too apparent. Needless to say, despite my trepidation, Hector & Jason loved these 'pit stops'. For them it was fun-time; they found a doggy fascination in these walks, garnished with the choicest, most moist and sweet scents.

Our main 'stop' on the journey to Brittany's west coast was the Broceliande Air de Gap. Broceliande itself is an ancient, medieval forest, long associated with the Arthurian legend. The legendary knights of the Round Table were in pursuit of the Holy Grail, deep within the forest. It is said that King Arthur's sister, Morgan la Fay, ruled here, and ensnared Arthur's knights with her cruel wiles; the victims were often rescued by gallant Sir Lancelot. In this forest - modern day Paimpont Forest - Merlin fell in love with the Fairy Viviane, who robbed him of his powers and entombed him in the forest, where he allegedly still lies.

Although it still covers an impressive 9,000 hectares, Paimpont Forest's secrets remain hidden to the cars thundering along the A84, before they take refuge in the concrete and tarmac of the Air de Gap. Here, one finds only an incredible bustle of vehicles and people, and little trace of knights, magicians or fairies. These earnest seekers arrive in pursuit of their own Holy Grail: the modern cult of seeking pleasure and fulfilment.

Valuable as the Air is as a modern utility, and a boon to the weary traveller, it is another sad example of how the marauding tourist effectively concretes over his goal, and destroys the appeal that first made it a destination of desire. Paving Paradise, as Ms Mitchell might say. Yet H&J were content enough here, rooting around the car park for smells, and happy for a break and to share a simple meal. If, unlike in our Normandy home, there was no hint of magic, we recognised that we were part of the herd; and were now only a couple of hours away from our destination. A tranquil camp-site awaited us: a site close to a dramatic - and hopefully magical - coastline.

Despite the rigours of the journey, the destination - camping in coastal France - is almost synonymous with adventure. For the suburbanite, keen with anticipation, the journey to new places is irresistible: promising warmth, vibrant colours, a diverse, undiscovered countryside, and a simple, close-to-nature camping experience. At the same time, the traveller (tourist) knows that he is travelling in one of the most sophisticated and culturally-rich countries in the world. This juxtaposition - under canvas, but with the possibility of high culinary experience only minutes away - gives French camping a real extra fizz. And a well-run camp site, with modern facilities, is a real treat, attracting holiday makers from across Europe - as well as French tourists themselves. Every visitor is intent on enjoying him or herself to the highest height, and the camp-sites are eager both to attract, and to retain, their clients. The camps offer tempting swimming pools and water features, bars, restaurants and sports facilities, and a variety of entertainment to keep both adults and their children amused, engaged, and beatifically content as can be.

Our own camping arrangements were simple, and modest, certainly compared with those campers, involved in 'Glamping' - ensconced in mobile homes, enormous caravans or voluminous tents complete with every modern facility. We were comparatively down-at-heel neighbours: a four-birth tent, sleeping bags, chairs, table and enough cooking equipment to ensure our relative comfort. This was really all we desired - and all we could cram into the car. We were, after all, travelling with two large boys, who required all the space in the rear of the vehicle. But a camping we-would-go, every July or August; and we loved it. Just as importantly, Hector & Jason loved it. The adventure, the sheer variety of sights, sounds and smells were all just so exciting to these life-loving boys.

While June and I loved the camping experience, Hector & Jason shared, for a very long time, a dislike of the camping element itself. From H&J's perspective, they had recently left a comfortable, spacious home behind, only to be squeezed into a small, quivering, canvas box. Whilst quickly recognising their new territory, and becoming experts at people watching, for many years H&J refused to settle at night in these uncongenial quarters. Instead, they preferred the familiar surroundings of their secure metal box, where they would snuggle down happily at the darkening, peaceful end of each perfect day.

This comfortable repose would not, however, prevent H&J's waking me at least once each night. Hector & Jason would begin barking - in unison - at around 2.00am or 3.00am in the morning. The night would be pitch black, with thousands of fellow-campers sound asleep, and only separated from us by thin strips of canvas. So I needed to respond quickly: I was on pre-planned auto-pilot, grabbing trousers, shoes, car keys and dog leads and, in an instant, opening the car. A quick fuss, to quell the noise and reassure, and we were away - for a twenty-minute walk. Since we were deep in the countryside, or near the sea, the skies were usually full of stars, or a full moon, to light our way. Despite the break in sleep, in so many ways this was a more vivid, certainly enriching, experience than the equivalent time spent moronically asleep.

There was also a convenience element - literally: I would take the boys on a small detour to the nearest toilet block, to spend a penny, or a cent. Only, I had to take H&J inside with me. I would rather have gone to Hell than leave them outside - to 'explore' on their own. Embarrassment is, in my experience, usually a cheap price to pay for peace of mind. Amazingly, even at 3.00am in the morning, there are always people at large (the intake of alcohol being pretty prodigious on these sites, encouraged by the blissful absence of hangovers). But the sight of this chap standing at the urinal with two dogs certainly raised a few eyebrows. Next morning, it was probably a case of: *"You know, I had a funny dream last night. Thought I saw two dogs visiting the bog. Must have been the vin rouge.."*. Then, it was a return to the car for the boys, and hopefully a couple of hours rest for me, before the inevitable dawn awakening, and a longer, invariably inspirational early-morn outing along the sparkling coast.

At this hour of the day, perhaps 6.00am or 6.30am, it is too late to return to bed, but too early for conventional day-time activity. Campers sleep well - all that fresh air and good wine - and at this hour no-one is about. It is a magical time of day, with the sky and clouds reflecting the return of the sun, and a myriad birds energetically pouring forth their thanksgiving. Time for a cup of tea, (since the boys had already bounced into the tent to wake June), to contemplate life, and to plan for the day ahead. The boys had an acute sense of their territory, and were now content - unless tempted by a passing dog (or rabbit) - to sit or lie near to their tent home.

For me, these quiet early morning walks, in the tranquillity of nature, and even quieter moments in the serenity of the still-sleeping camp site, were pure heaven. Even H&J seemed to be affected by the atmosphere, and were unusually still and quiet. These times, so unremarkable, so lacking in detail or incident, were times of peace and reflection. Together, Hector, Jason and I shared more starry skies and delightful dawns than is decent in one lifetime. It was the fruit of long days and unusual hours, spent often in the most beautiful places.

"There are more things in Heaven and Earth than are dreamt of in your philosophy", opines Hamlet to Horatio; and that's exactly how I felt.

The memories of such unalloyed, perfect happiness are inseparable from Hector & Jason.

Adventures at Camping Kervilor, and Carnac

Carnac! Your granite mysteries, too deep for laying bare,
Juxtaposed with japes and jollity, at Trinité-sur-mer.

Colin Hill

Camping Kervilor was the scene of the boys' very first camping trip in France, and our favourite location in the Carnac region of southern Brittany.

Kervilor itself is a large, friendly site with spacious pitches, and excellent amenities, including a superb outdoor pool and water slide where, sadly for them but not for other guests, H&J were not permitted. What larks they would have had!

Campers are, almost invariably, a friendly species of people; thrust together in their make-shift world, they have much in common, and a common desire to enjoy this brief sojourn in the sun. I vividly recall an early holiday at Kervilor where H&J were be-friended by two young brothers of, I suppose, about eight and six years of age. These bright, out-going lads were the proud offspring of a French father and a Polish mother. Already, at such tender ages, they were fluent in French, Polish and English, and spoke to each other in each of these languages, sometimes mixing several 'tongues' in the same sentence. The brothers were mesmerised by young Hector & Jason, perhaps identifying kindred spirits, and came to see them every day, making a great fuss of the boys. H&J responded enthusiastically, and it was touching to witness the mutual affection and tenderness shared between different but sympathetic beings.

One glorious afternoon we found ourselves on the same beach with this family, and the young brothers ran over excitedly to see their doggy friends. I've often wondered what became of these delightful little boys (now grown men, of course), where they're living now, and how their lives have developed. I'm sure that they have made successes of their lives, and will now have families - and surely dogs - of their own.

It was Carnac Plage and its environs, and the sailing mecca of La Trinité, that saw our most vivid adventures. From Kervilor it is merely an invigorating mile-and-a-half stroll down a steep road to the impressive Trinité-sur-mer - a fashionable and brilliant marina, with hundreds of equally impressive leisure craft that, collectively, must be valued at tens of millions of £ - or Euros. June laughingly calls the marina a 'boat park' but, in its way, it is certainly the most glamorous of its kind in this part of France; a magnet for the excessively well-heeled and their super-yachts. H&J would enjoy a walk around the quay-side, then along the bay, where a clutch of magnificent mansions - teetering on Château status - enjoyed what estate agents like to call 'uninterrupted' views over the Atlantic. After a breath-taking walk, it was a steep hike back up the narrow, winding road to Kervilor. These days were roasting hot, but the young boys insisted in pulling me up the burning, dusty road. These trips proved a good workout even for these young meteors.

Near to Kervilor, and after an intriguing walk through open country, adjacent to an ancient, walled Château, one comes suddenly upon an exquisite little harbour, so perfect that it could have been designed by a divinity. A few tiny boats clink on their moorings; and beyond them there is a blue sea stretching forever, between pine-clad shores. This was a favourite little walk - a mere mile or so from our camp. The bay formed a perfect diversion, when a drive in a hot car, on crowded roads, to crowded car parks and crowded beaches, seemed less than tempting. Hector & Jason loved this Elysian ramble, and were even content to allow the exquisite scene to calm their enthusiasm.

Kervilor itself was a pretty inclusive kind of camp-site. It was easy to see why many guests hardly left the site during their stay; they played, ate, sunbathed, drank and slept in a playground that accommodated their every need. Although the boys were always happy to sit close to the tent - dogs have an amazing ability to determine their property and sphere of influence - they were also keen to walk out with us and explore the wider environment. And, of course, they shared a pretty dim view of our modest camping arrangements. So, the nearby and seductive coastline, and the enticing Celtic countryside, became *our* playground.

Despite the attractions of the camp-site itself, human beings seem to have an innate need to explore. From our base at Camping Kervilor, the pretty, granite tourist village of Carnac, merely three or four miles away, drew us like a magnet. Carnac's international reputation is founded upon the significance of its globally celebrated megalith sites - alignments of ancient stones on a scale that is unique in Europe. 1,169 stones are to be found in an alignment at le Menec, 1,029 at Kermario, and 594 at Kerlescan. The bare facts can give little impression of the scale, marvel and mystery of these sites, which are thought to have a religious significance. Sun-worship and fertility are the favoured explanations.

Carnac is world famous for these three fields. Imposing, and awe-inspiring; this is a very special and mysterious place. We bought a large map of the history of human civilisation from the tasteful little gift shop that serves the monument. The ebb and flow, the beginning and fall of empires and civilisations is recorded by the map. *My name is Ozymandias...look on my works ye mighty, and despair!*. Indeed. Framed, the map adorns a wall of our lounge in Wordsley, and always inspires reflection and wonder.

And today, of course, Carnac's magnetism is largely due to its superb coastline, awesome when bathed in sunshine, and we headed to the coast as often as possible during each stay. Like most popular French beaches, however, that of Carnac is banned to dogs. Luckily, the coastal strip just around the bay, studded with mature pines that cooled the scented air beneath, had no such restrictions.

This was the scene for Jason's swimming lesson, described in an earlier Chapter - his first and only experience of swimming. On that very first visit, however, on one quite beautiful, pine-scented morning, we arrived to find a large festival in full swing, with gymkhana, massed bands and thousands of spectators milling around. A normally very tranquil place was overwhelmed with all kinds of arenas, officials, vendors, vehicles and excited spectators. We skirted around all this activity and, boys on leads, walked near to the water's edge, along the vast, empty, un-peopled beach of soft white sand.

On the return journey along the beach, I spotted a slope of sand that had been fenced off, to allow marram grass to re-establish. I had sensed for a while that Jason might need to relieve himself, and knew that he preferred to do this 'off lead'. I spotted a gap in the rectangular wire-and-stale fence, and let Jason in, convinced that he would be secure. O dreadful mistake! A bolt of electricity charged through him, and he was off - through the fence, and heading like a missile directly towards the gymkhana. Horrified, we leapt after the runaway - there were countless dangers lying in wait, including being trampled under a horse's hooves - and the busy coastal road was only a couple of hundred metres away.

Running this way and that amidst the tumult of people - loud-speaker addresses, music, horses and the press of human activity - and frantically calling, I chased after my scatter-brain boy. Jason re-appeared a full ten minutes later, slightly out of breath, but insouciant; what was all the fuss about? He was unharmed, and the gymkhana seems to have continued regardless, untroubled by a mad dog on the loose. There was no explanation, no rhyme or reason, for his mad-cap adventure. It was just pure, inexplicable Jason. Shaking our heads and much relieved, we returned to our camp-site, older but no wiser.

Less eventful, but delightful, were our trips to Auray, a deliciously pretty village. Auray is famous as a 'holy' town. In 1364 Charles of Blois died here in a battle that marked the end of the War of Succession of Brittany; he was later declared a Saint. Also, in 1625 a statue of St Anne was discovered in a field by a 'peasant', Nicolazic. A monumental basilica now dominates the town, and pilgrims flock here each year.

We would stroll briskly up the steep road, looking curiously into the tasteful art and gift shops that dominate the winding, narrow street. Below the street, after negotiating a vertigo-inducing stone staircase, lies the delightful little fishing port, once visited by Benjamin Franklin. This Port town of Saint Goustan now proudly boasts the *Quai Benjamin Franklin*. Franklin sailed from Philadelphia and disembarked here in December 1776 - his purpose being to seek a French alliance against the British in the American War of Independence. He duly received the enthusiastic support of Louis XVI - though the consequences were momentous. The war resulted in Britain's defeat, in 1783, in the American War of Independence, and a newly-formed United States, with all its historic repercussions. The war also ruined France, financially, and proved a catalyst for the French Revolution a decade later, and the overthrow and execution of Louis. And the rise of Napoleon, and the climactic Napoleonic Wars. That's quite a burden of responsibility for a little Quay to bear.

The precipitous route down the stone staircase to and along the Quay was the favourite aspect for our enthusiastic boys, who raced along Ben Franklin's Quay with great aplomb, and without a care in the world.

We also loved to explore the Gulf of Morbihan and, quite close to Carnac, the long, narrow isthmus that is Quiberon, which juts dramatically into the Atlantic. The 14 kilometre-long long isthmus is accessible and popular, though at its narrowest is only just wide enough for the road itself. Quiberon remains, somehow, wildly romantic and exciting. The boys loved its terrific coastline, and the soft sands that were an open invitation for mad, uninhibited frolics.

At the extreme end of the isthmus - half an hour's drive along the narrow road - one finds the dramatic coastline of the *Côte Sauvage*, with the powerful sea pounding incredible rock formations, and superb daubs of coastal flora dancing in the breeze. It was here, among the wild flowers and the breakers' spume, that I would recall lines from John Masefield's *Sea Fever:*

> *'I must go down to the seas again, for the call of the running tide*
> *Is a wild call and a clear call that may not be denied;*
> *And all I ask is a windy day with the white clouds flying,*
> *And the flung spray and the blown spume, and the sea-gulls crying.'*

This being France, no matter how sublime the setting, there is an unobtrusive but very smart little brasserie. We looked longingly at the guests savouring their lunch - as did H&J - but were quite unable to participate in their pleasure, since H&J's frenetic energy was a little on the rare side to be accommodated in most French restaurants.

We did, however, all enjoy lunch at a pavement café in the narrow, windy streets of Ile Tudy, with its white-washed, blue-shuttered old cottages. Hector & Jason sat by our side, fascinated by the hubbub of people passing by, by the reputed 'Venetian' atmosphere, by the salty sea air and, no doubt, by the smells of wonderful fresh food.

H&J were wildly excited by their adventures along this coast, and pulled me hither and thither. And excited, also, by their crazy, free runs along superb, empty, wind-swept beaches. There were no dramatic incidents - just huge enthusiasm and enjoyment. Four sentient beings experiencing a fabulous environment together, with no other object than to seize the day.

Adventures at Camping Keranterec and Concarneau

> Keranterec! - *Where luscious greens meet, kiss, the glitt'ring bay,*
> *While lovers take their ease, and rabbits play.*
>
> Colin Hill

As we know, France is a large country (all those news items, baying breathlessly: *'It's the size of France!'* - as though we know what that is), so travelling from (a) to (b) generally takes longer than one would expect, even with, by British standards, quiet - and good - roads.

The town, and camp-site, of Keranterec - a mere few inches from La Haute Maison, even on a large-scale map - is actually 246 miles, and a good six hours of journey time, when including three 'comfort break' stops. It's a stretch of a car journey, but not without passing interest, as one travels through bustling, flower-filled towns like St Hilaire and Ducey, then skirting Mont St Michel Bay before scudding along the arterial A84, and the inevitable Air de Gap at Broceliande.

Broceliande was our third 'pit-stop' along the route, the boys comfort always being our priority. From there we continued on towards Rennes and Lorient, and another quick stop in a lay-by, before reaching the constricted little roads around the Brittany coastline, and our final destination.

Of course, the return journey was also 246 miles - though inevitably it seemed longer. Our last 'rest' stop on the route home would be at a lay-by at Domfront; on reaching there, the excited boys always knew that we were approaching home.

H&J always thought the Air de Gaps - for them a wooden table and a bench - a 'rum do' after the comparative luxury of the cottage. *"We are reduced to this?".* Worse was to follow: a flimsy film of flapping canvas (our *tente*) that brought no re-assurance whatsoever - only the certainty of noise, or rain, or Dubai-style heat, depending on the vagaries of the weather. Only in later years did H&J acquiesce, or humour us, by actually entering, and occasionally deigning to sleep within, the (by now much roomier) tent.

Camping Keranterec lies on the southern coast of Brittany, near Fousenant. Keranterec, family-run, was our other special site, with its own ancient orchard of gnarled fruit trees, stunning sea views, and a pretty little beach all to itself. Cider is made from the orchard's apples; this is locally prestigious, and sold throughout the area, as well as from the camp-site shop. To this day, this is the finest cider I have ever tasted. The camp-site lies adjacent to the stunning beach at Keranterac village, a short walk away.

Keranterec is situated at the heart of a superb, concentrated niche of villages and resorts: Fouesnant; Le Forêt Fouesnant; Port le Forêt, and Begmeil. The site was also superbly placed for tempting trips along the coast - to Concarneau, Bénodet and Pont Aven, as well as to the extreme west of Brittany, which still has the feel of a wild, remote, lonely and 'sauvage' coast: Penmarc'h, the Crozon Peninsula, Pointe de Penhir, Camaret sur mer, and Pointe des Espagnol are all delightful, inspiring places, and all within (fairly) easy reach.

The first, memorable, visit to Keranterec took place in the Summer of 2005. We were shown our pitch by a smiling young guide, who rode ahead of us on her bicycle. Then, while every other camper relaxed and 'chilled', we set-to, erecting our shiny new tent in the sweltering afternoon heat. This was to be the last sunshine we were to see for quite some time.

Our camping arrangements at Keranterec were eccentric, to say the least. As we know, Hector & Jason rather resented a home consisting of flapping canvas, and preferred their sleeping arrangements to be Volvo-based. So, though we had a comfortable tent, with camp beds and sleeping bags, I would often find it more convenient, and comfortable, to sleep in the passenger seat of the car, in readiness for the inevitable wake-up call that I knew would come at around 3.00am. There followed a quick tour of the silent site, under the stars - perhaps taking in the toilet block for good measure - before returning - this time to the camp bed, for three hours of oblivion.

At 6.00am, H&J would call me again - just in time for the dawn chorus. Another tour of the site, this time lit by a strengthening young sun. In the dawn walk beloved of H&J, we would cavort along the coast road on the perimeter of the camp, mesmerised by the breath-taking prospect opening before us: the jewel of a bay, blue waves breaking on a fringe of soft sand, with white-washed houses framing the view. We never tired of this walk, half an hour of bliss before the day's first cup of tea. On our return, the boys would pad excitedly into the tent, greeting the recumbent June to the new morning. Hector & Jason were always intensely excited: they knew that a new day had dawned, and were glad in it.

Even in high Summer, we would return from our walk to a glistening dew on chairs, tables, glasses, radio - anything that had been deliberately or inadvertently left outside the tent. This would not deter us from a steaming cup of tea, while quietly watching the magical unfurling of the day, with its strengthening light, unburdening its promise. The warmth of a burgeoning sun would quickly chase away the beads of moisture from every exposed surface. It was simply glorious to sit silently in the still, unutterable calm, and watch the day unfold: the intensifying sun filling in the shadows and absorbing the dew, the birds awaking from their all too-brief rest, the campers rising, zombie-like, and meandering sleepily to the wash-house.

That very first visit to Keranterec, in 2005, proved eventful. Every day, as part of our daily routine, we would visit the site's small beach, where H&J could run and play. One fine morning we were approaching the beach, the ranks of tents and caravans at long last petering out, and the route becoming clear to the boys. At this point - the beach itself mere yards away - I released Hec and Jas from their leads. We reached the beach and, suddenly, I was distracted by my familiar role of toilet attendant, this time to Hector. Jason, however, apparently saw or heard something, because he shot off to the right, and was soon atop a small cliff, rising perpendicular above the beach - and quickly found himself in the midst of a dense thicket, made up of brambles and thorn bushes.

It was clear that Jason had glimpsed a rabbit, but equally clear that he was having difficulty in extricating himself from the thicket. Realising that the only way was down, Jason let out a yelp, and half-leapt, half-fell, over the edge, and into space. The cliff was sheer, and at least eight metres, or 25' tall: not high for a cliff, but high enough for a leaping dog, minus parachute. I was a mere forty yards away, but events unravelled so quickly that I was powerless to reach Jas before he fell. So it was fortunate, to put it mildly, that a camp-site worker - who had been changing a litter bin, and who was almost directly below Jason - moved quickly to break the boy's fall. Jason was shaken but not stirred. He suffered a small cut as a result of his misadventure; but no broken bones or worse. I was, of course, hugely relieved and grateful. There were to be no repeats of this mishap; in future, access to the beach was strictly by lead. And, (if we except the 'stabbing' *debacle*) fate decreed that this was to be the first and only time in Jason's life that he found himself in such danger.

However, we had not yet quite done with rabbits. They were quite a feature of the camp-site. Keranterec seemed to be home to more bunny rabbits than *Watership Down.* Had I been a rabbit, I might have chosen this delightful spot myself, with its orchards, thickets and lovely sea views. One particular rabbit hopped by our tent each day, for reasons best known to itself. June and I were always pleased to see the little chap; he really looked like something from a Disney film, even cuter than the cuddly toy version. One lunch-time, we were all rather *too* relaxed when said rabbit ambled past the tent. Like a young lion, Hector pounced. Despite my best efforts to revive it, the dear, poor thing died instantly. We were upset with Hector; perhaps upset with ourselves, for not responding more quickly, or keeping closer watch over the boys. But it is hard to blame a dog for acting in accord with his nature; and Hector's nature in this respect was pure wolf. *Hound Dog*, as ground out by Elvis, is a rather surreal exposition of a man's rejecting his lover, on the bizarre grounds that she has not caught a rabbit. I had rather wished that Hector had been similarly unsuccessful. *Lapin* is, of course, a delicacy in France. In a different context, Hector would have been a hero. But, for me, it was all just very sad.

A day or two later, another rabbit - there was no shortage of kamikaze bunnies - ran past the tent like the hare at a greyhound track. H&J both set off in furious pursuit, (quickly followed by yours truly). For the next ten minutes they criss-crossed the site, chasing the creature, barking excitedly. and creating mayhem: tents, barbecues, washing - even people - were of no concern as, in mad pursuit, H&J homed in on their jinking, diving, objective.

In hot pursuit and with huge relief, I managed to retrieve the boys before they destroyed the camp site or the rabbit. This end-of-fun was much to Hector's disgust. Youthful exuberance in action; a rabbit, or a hare, never could be resisted. Oscar Wilde; deja vu all over again.

Looking back, it's astonishing quite how much we accomplished during these visits, particularly given the boys' rabbit fixation. On our first trip to Keranterec, however, we had erected the - brand new - tent on an almost unbearably hot afternoon and, following a couple of hours hard labour, were looking forward to several days of sunshine and relaxation. No; many days of torrential rain and glutinous mud were in prospect. The Atlantic weather closed in with a vengeance, and the *pluie* poured down practically non-stop for five whole days.

There was a single bright, sunny day by way of grateful intermission. I recall that bright day well: we undertook our first visit to the spectacular walled town of Concarneau, France's third largest fishing port. We parked on the outskirts of the town, a mile or more from the old quarter, along the promenade wall, and looking out towards the vast *plage*. Across the road, in the estuary, a white egret searched for mussels.

How clearly I remember H&J racing excitedly along the sunlit promenade leading into the town, like two thoroughbred racehorses on a mission, yours truly in tow. The twin pleasure and physicality of the boys, and the prospect of the magnificent old port, heightened the senses with the sheer exuberance of being alive. We toured every inch of the spectacular, walled town, admiring Concarneau's handsome structure, and its magnificent granite ramparts. H&J, with me in tow, charged up and down a multitude of stone staircases as we explored every nook and cranny. I managed to negotiate a brief stop in order to buy a keep-sake pen-knife. The whole place was zany, it was colourful, it was full of noise, excitement and hubbub; Hector & Jason adored every charged moment.

But magnificent Concarneau turned out to be the summit of our visit: a visit mired in rain, beneath a leaden sky. At the end of the fifth day we decided to cut our losses, since there seemed to be no end in sight to the foulest of foul weather. Keeping ourselves, the boys and our clothes dry had become simply too wearing. Brittany is fabulous when the weather is fine; but when it is bad it is very, very bad - and the vile weather can stretch beyond the tourist's powers of endurance.

Since Concarneau was the highlight of that first, truncated adventure, on returning to Keranterec a couple of years later the resort was firmly on our radar. To re-visit is to be captivated again by the charms of this delightful, medieval walled town. It is only a pleasant, short-ish drive from the camp-site to the outskirts of Concarneau, where we parked and re-traced our steps along the long promenade, towards the fabulous, fortified town.

The resort is a tourist magnet, but in the most civilised and picturesque way, so that the experience of wandering around remains distinctly pleasurable. There is enough diversity, atmosphere, and French eccentricity on offer in this resort to please all but the most jaded palate. In any case, 'jaded' is not a term that ever applied to H&J, who were happy to zoom around the narrow streets, expecting more excitement around every corner, every steep staircase, and every viewpoint. And excitement there came - from the encounters with people, with other dogs, and a profusion of sights and, no doubt, smells.

A short distance from Concarneau lies the exquisite little resort of Bénodet. The familiar 'No Chiens' signs are in evidence along the magnificent beach but - a short drive and delightful walk along a majestic coastal path and - there we are, another magnificent beach, this time dog-friendly. H&J spent some superb afternoons on this glorious coast, with happy holiday makers and some equally happy dogs. I have the memories, and I have the photographs to enhance and inform these. But life is lived in real time, and I can only testify to the sheer vitality and happiness of H&J on these excursions. We eventually returned to our camp site, to chill out to the sounds of the radio news, accompanied by a meal and a bottle of wine kept chilled for the purpose in a cool-box. Another perfect day.

And we travelled further afield - for example, to the superb Pointe de Crozon, close to the extreme western edge of Brittany, and France. We gazed out over the calm, vast Atlantic, with no land between the Pointe and America. Then on, through a wild, strange, landscape, to the multi-coloured, compact town of Camerlet, twinned with St Ives in Cornwall. Camerlet - an important fishing port for spiny lobsters - might have been dropped from the air by helicopter, so improbable and fantastical it seemed.

We also took the opportunity to visit Pont Aven. This beautiful village, near to Concarneau, became famous among the artist community from the 1860s. Paul Gauguin began to visit from 1886, and a 'Pont Aven School' quickly emerged - founded on innovative use of colour, and symbolism.

This is a gorgeous spot, and it's fascinating to compare the photographs taken of today's Pont Aven with the essence painted by such as Gauguin and Bernard. We arrived on a blistering day, but the boys took it all in their dashing, powerful stride - another gorgeous new place to explore.

On the fifth day of that first, 2005, trip, we reluctantly decided to pack up camp, and return to Normandy. We struck camp in the most miserable weather, and headed home in a complete washout. Our return to Normandy took place in a rain-machine downpour, vindicating our decision, but making driving itself an anxious affair.

We stopped at rain-soaked but welcoming Broceliande for lunch. Maddeningly, on leaving, we suffered an accident at the good-old Aire-de-Gap, when an elderly woman reversed her car into our (stationary)

Volvo - and hurriedly drove off, without the small courtesy of exchanging details. The boys, whose quarters had been bumped, looked on with incredulity.

The mood lightened as we returned to Normandy. A bright, warming sun miraculously re-appeared. We celebrated with a 'relief' barbecue.

Jason, of course, was truly, madly, ecstatic.

My abiding memory is of H&J stamping their personalities on everywhere we trod: forever, and for ever, Hector & Jason will roam the bocage, and imprint their brave, fearless, giant strides at Kervilor and Keranterec.

Larks on the Loire

Châteaux, gâteaux, and stately, burnished Blois -
We marvel as we survey the mighty Loire.

Colin Hill

Everyone should visit the Loire Valley at least once in their lives. The breathtaking loveliness of Chenonceaux, the grandeur of Chambord, the almost other-worldly perfection of Villandray - and a hundred other Châteaux - are practically beyond compare. And then there is the countryside - lush, fertile, filled with flowers, fruit, birds and butterflies, and on a grander scale than anything we can experience in the UK. And finally - providing unity, fertility and immortality to the whole region - is the magnificent River Loire itself, and its almost equally impressive tributaries.

June and I had visited the region years before - pre-H&J - touring fascinating towns such as Chinon, Saumur and Tours. We now decided to tour the eastern Loire, particularly the area around historic Blois. Knowing how searingly hot the region becomes in Summer - with an absence of coastal breezes, and virtually in the middle of France - we decided against camping on this occasion. Forty degrees under canvas can feel like being cooked in a microwave. We recalled a previous trip, where we had almost baked in the town of Richelieu - a town created by the Cardinal, and modestly named, by him, after himself. So, after making extensive preparations for our longest single trip ever with Hector & Jason, we set out from the cottage one sunlit morning in July, and headed brightly towards Le Mans.

Five hours and several pit-stops later, we found ourselves near to our destination of Blois. The next step was to find a small, family hotel. We visited village after village but, to our surprise and consternation, hotels were very thin on the ground. There were a few very grand, palatial hotels, that would probably not be welcoming *pour chiens*, and a few more modest hotels that, unaccountably, were closed. For an area famous as a tourist magnet, this was puzzling indeed. The afternoon had become exceedingly hot, and we were all - excepting H&J, of course - getting rather fazed and fractious.

Then, suddenly, a hotel sign: we follow a small road - and there it was, a smart-seeming establishment, looking rather pleased with itself, in a perfect, quiet location. The hotel was dog-friendly, and the smiling proprietor found us a comfortable room on the ground floor that opened directly on to the spacious garden. Perfect for the boys. As the afternoon heat dispelled and a welcome coolness descended, H&J were fed, and June and I looked forward to our own *déjeuner* with some anticipation.

I've always enjoyed the experience, the theatre, the sense of occasion, of dining in French restaurants. After such a gruelling day, we were certainly looking forward to an evening's taste sensation. We sat down at a beautifully laid table, already immaculately placed with elegant cutlery, sparkling wine glasses and fine china tableware. The setting promised an exceptional experience. We ordered, perhaps not the most expensive dishes, but still lump-in-throat pricey. Almost immediately, the large plates were whisked away, and replaced with others little larger than saucers. Even so, when it arrived, the food barely did justice to the tiny dishes. I think we ate three courses that evening, and I confess I've never left a French restaurant feeling quite so miserable. A touch of genius was needed to achieve such an effect, after such an exceptional day. The food itself was interesting and tasty - it's just that the portions were designed for Lilliputians. This was very odd since, in our extensive experience of eating in France, portion control, and value for money, is rarely an issue - and the Loire is renowned as the garden of France. It was the worst of both worlds: the portions eye-wateringly minimalist, the prices, eye-wateringly staggering.

Still, on the bright side, the hotel itself was charming, and its location ideal for our needs. H&J enjoyed a further walk after dinner - plus a couple more during the small hours - in the hotel's attractive garden.

With that, we were refreshed and ready for the new day's adventures. The day began, obviously, with a vigorous, exploratory walk for H&J, a walk where we found a pretty little river, and an ancient bridge, before returning for breakfast. Since *petit déjeuner* is generally a modest repast in France, and given the experience of the evening before, my expectations were hardly high. Remarkably, breakfast was superb; a Balthazaar's feast of every imaginable type of breakfast goodies. Quite one of the most memorable breakfasts I've experienced, and I indulged royally. So, honours even, inexplicably.

Another glorious day had dawned. In great spirits, we set off for Blois, and its Château. After parking near the banks of the Loire River, Hector, Jason and I strode up the steep stone staircases that led to a Château steeped in history. This had been the residence of ten Queens and seven Kings, including Louis XII and Francis I. Louis married Anne of Brittany at Blois in March, 1499. Caesar Borgia also married here in the same year, whilst Machiavelli visited the Château in 1501 and 1510.

Following his coronation in 1547, Henry II entered Blois with naked women astride oxen. Naked women notwithstanding, it struck me forcibly that Leonardo da Vinci had also been here, and had known this view. All these ghosts, and many others, from Blois' glittering Renaissance heyday swarmed before us. I took the best photographs that I could, given that I was managing two powerful, inquisitive boys. All that sweep of history re-visited on a sparkling July morning, that was witnessing our own modest passing by.

Curiosity satisfied, we returned down the steep staircase, and hugged the banks of the River Loire, in the direction of the car. Mid-morning by now, the sun was broiling hot. H&J tripped happily alongside one of Europe's most impressive waterways, and drank deeply from the eternal river, before returning whence we had come.

Next stop: Francis I's 16th century Renaissance masterpiece, Chambord, an hour or so away. We travelled through the most picturesque and serene countryside, seeing hardly another vehicle or person. Then, suddenly, we were on a self-important road, with vistas of imposing grandeur - clearly designed, literally, to impress. Pictures in guide books can hardly prepare one for the visual impact of this magnificent Château, the brainchild of the ambitious French King. It is awesome. Surely, Leonardo (who Francis I had brought to France, Mona Lisa in his knapsack) had had a hand in this?

And suddenly, the whole world was there. Where on Earth had all these people - Americans, Chinese et al - come from? But the site is so vast that it easily absorbs many thousands of tourists each day. I greedily took many, many pictures. It was simply world class, and I was delighted that we, and Hector & Jason, had 'made it' to this incredible space.

Eventually, reluctantly, we departed, and were at once absorbed into the huge royal forests, with signs bidding us to beware *sangliers* - wild boar. We were fired up by this time, and decided to ride our luck.

We toured through the Sologne, an area rich in unspoilt lakes and crammed with wildlife: 220 bird species have been recorded here, including booted and short-toed eagles, and ospreys. There are 50 species of mammal, 30 species of fish, ten or so of reptiles and 56 species of dragonfly. Three-quarters of the area is forested, while the lakes themselves - all 3,000 of them - cover 12,000 hectares. The bare statistics alone cannot prepare the visitor for the wildness and magnificence of the Sologne region; even driving near it, through it, is an exhilarating experience.

We headed for and eventually reached our third Château of the day - it can become addictive: the very beautiful Château of Cheverny. It was mid-afternoon by now and, again, baking hot. We explored the gardens and gift shop (buying some estate wine) with two excited boys, but declined the tour of the Château since, of course, dogs would not be admitted to the impressive edifice. The Château, which remarkably has stayed in the hands of the same family since its foundation, was cunningly kept out of view of the non-fee paying public, which included us. However, I managed to get a sneaky photo, nonetheless: Hector, Jason and I took a long walk around the perimeter of the Château's high walls, and I pointed a camera literally through the key-hole in the (steel-meshed) main gates. We returned happily to the car, and journeyed back to our modest, but comfortable, hotel.

And so it was home, Jeeves, to chill out following a wonderful day, and to enjoy another perplexingly miserable meal. Then a final walk with H&J, who were still remarkably fresh, followed by retirement to bed - a 'retirement' punctuated by further walks into the balmy night. Who cares? It was great.

We departed for Normandy the next morning, following another stupendous breakfast. We could have extended our stay, but the law of diminishing returns, the sheer expense, and the wear and tear of continuous travel, argued for a return to the peace and sensible prices of our home turf. Following a long but uneventful drive (often the best sort), we descended on La Haute Maison, beaming in the sunshine, late in the afternoon.

Touchingly, Jason treated us to his dance of gratitude and delight.

Dinner at Dinard

Glam'rous Dinard! A jewel, lit by a silver sea;
We cherished the precious hours spent with thee!

Colin Hill

Once more, we decided to abandon the tent that had provided such sterling service, and enjoy the comfort of a hotel for our trip to Dinard - an exquisite resort in northern Brittany, across the estuary from the fine port of St Malo.

Alhough not far from the border with Normandy, Dinard has a different 'feel' to Normandy's resorts; perhaps a more southern ambience. Immediately, the town strikes the visitor as well-heeled, up-market, and a little exclusive, with its elegant clientèle, posh restaurants and bars, and luxurious, almost tropical, vegetation. It came as no surprise to find that the great Picasso was inspired to paint here - his beach scenes imbued with an almost Mediterranean feel.

And Brittany itself is certainly different to its neighbour, and indeed to any other region of France: Dinard excepted, the natural flora is colourful but tough and resistant, to withstand the whipping winds of Winter; even the trees appear stunted and gnarled. The softness and luxuriance that characterise Normandy have disappeared, and been replaced by something *'rich and strange'*. The landscape is weathered, rocky, and spartan, and ultimately climaxes in wild, end-of-world coasts. The overall impression is of the dramatic; of spare, powerful beauty. In Summer - and when the weather is on its best behaviour - the effect of light on sea and scenery can be ethereal, breath-taking. That is why, in August, especially, the whole world seems to beat a path to these shores, to share the magic, to bathe in the gold-dust.

Our decision to stay in a hotel was based on pragmatic concerns. This would be a shortish-trip - perhaps five days. Setting up camp, and dismantling the same, can be time-consuming and tedious, and then there is the packing, un-packing, and the hassle of loading every conceivable item of equipment into, and onto, the car. And we recalled that 2005 trip to Keranterec, when we were be-devilled by incessant rain. As luck would have it, the no-camping option turned out to be an excellent decision. Although the weather in Brittany is nothing if not unpredictable, sunshine - in July - is clearly what we were hoping for, and expecting.

We arrived at Dinard at lunchtime, following a tedious drive, and parked just off the main street. It was a blisteringly hot day, and we were all glad of a break. Jason himself launched into the water bowl. Even so, both boys took a lively interest in proceedings, since the town was not only steaming but thronged with tourists. Predictably, the resort was packed to the gunwales with folk eating, drinking and enjoying the ambience of the plethora of bars and restaurants. We conducted a quick recce before satisfying ourselves that this ultra-smart town was not a promising venue for H&J themselves: the hotels positively reeked of class and decorum, and we suspected it would be futile to enquire about their hospitality to *chiens*.

So, after a brief respite, we set off for the hinterland to search for hotels that might welcome the boys. An hour later, in an unprepossessing village a couple of miles out of Dinard, we came across such a place: the proprietor was only too happy to oblige, and soon we were established in a very French-provincial bedroom, where the boys found it easier to leap across the large double bed than to clamber around it. The views over the village from the balcony positively reeked of old France. House-martins screeched and flew backwards and forwards on to the guttering that fringed the ancient roof: natural surround-sound and an aerial display were ours at no extra cost. Five star character, and atmosphere, at bargain-basement prices.

The afternoon was still young and inviting, so we drove down to the nearest beach, just along the coast from Dinard itself. Here was cosmopolitan Europe at play: Germans, Italians, Dutch and British, all enjoying the sun, sea, sand and the many little bars that lined the promenade. We strolled along the elegant promenade, chocked with people intent on relaxing in the golden glow of mid-afternoon. The boys were excited to have their first extended walk of the day, and in such a stimulating environment. Though H&J were not permitted on the beach itself, they bade a brisk '*hello*' to a number of other boys and girls of their kind who were similarly promenading, and taking in the social whirl and sparkling air.

The walk adjourned for refreshments. I remember us all sitting at a bar, and striking up a conversation with a young Dutch family who, as is so often the case, spoke fluent English - and with such perfect manners. We ate ice-cream and relaxed; bliss. The mid-afternoon sunshine was simply glorious and, secure in our situation, we mused brightly on the delights to come. Things just could not get any better. As things turned out, this was an unusually perceptive conclusion.

We returned to the hotel late in the afternoon, as happy, as content as could be. Apparently we were the only guests, and we sat down to excellent *steak et frites*, eased down with a decent bottle of claret. H&J were ensconced in our room for an hour, followed by the obligatory evening walk around the rather dusty town centre, with its surprisingly busy main road. However, we looked forward to tomorrow, and tomorrow...

At dawn, around 5.00am, I was aroused by H&J - they seemed to work in tandem on this - and we rushed out, me in t-shirt and shorts. Given the absurdly early hour, I closed the hotel door firmly behind me. Rain - *pluie* - was absolutely ripping down, and bouncing off the pavement like bullets. We re-emerged five minutes later, (I must have had a key) soaked to the skin - an unexpected and unwelcome twist to our fortunes. It was only too clear that the rain was here to stay. After breakfast, we sadly checked out and visited Dinard proper: the classy resort looked be-draggled, and almost deserted in the relentless downpour.

What a difference a day makes! For a few, hardy souls, umbrellas, raincoats and down-cast looks had replaced bikinis, sand-castles and smiles. An hour or so later we made the reluctant decision to return to Normandy. Meandering around town with two soggy 'boys' was not what we had bargained for; neither was sheltering in a cramped hotel bedroom from the acutely inclement weather. We had no idea how long these conditions would last, but past experience did not provide any re-assurance.

It had been a brief but somehow memorable visit. Sunshine transforms places and situations. Even the most glamorous of resorts loses its lustre and looks down-in-the-mouth in a prolonged downpour. I took a few photos around the be-soaked, be-smirched Dinard as pure memorabilia. Several hours later we emerged in Normandy, where we were greeted by wall-to-wall sunshine.

As always, and to my infinite delight, Jason greeted his return with wild ecstasy.

PART 3: ALL YOU NEED IS LOVE

25: Pictures in Time

Such poignant pictures, shimmering still,
Upon the shining sea, along the sunlit hill.

Colin Hill

I remember: still glowing and still loved -
Seared on my soul, and forever proved.

Colin Hill

There are many millions of camera-users, scouring the world for an interesting photograph. If we overlook the familiar, it can be a daunting prospect. How many pictures have we seen, of the endlessly-reproduced Parthenon, Pyramids, Taj Mahal, or Canaletto's Grand Canal, and thought: *"So what?"*. The exotic has become the banal; their contours commonplace to the jaded eye. So, if a picture is still to be worth a thousand words, it had better have an impact.

I came to photography at nine years of age, surprised and delighted when my parents presented me with a Kodak box brownie for Christmas. They probably regretted their decision a few months later, when I 'shot' a whole roll of film on the fascinating prospect of my youngest brother, recumbent in his push-chair.

My impecunious youth prevented any serious interest in cameras and pictures. My next camera was a Kodak Instamatic, acquired soon after June and I were married. My interest quickening due to Summer holidays spent on the dramatic Cornish coast, with its stupendous scenery and magical light, I quickly graduated to a second hand Russian Zenit. The clunky Zenit, an ideal 'training' camera, was quickly succeeded by more sophisticated Canon SLRs. I was hooked, and have always been grateful for the ability of photography, aided by a lively interest in people, nature and travel, to record what has been important to me. These days, I take a camera wherever we go, and try to capture images that record the essence of place and subject, in a context of irreplaceable time. Not *too* pretentious, I hope.

We tend to record what most engages us as human beings. Some photographers focus on people; others on landscape, others on architecture of various kinds, and so on. I'm pretty eclectic - any and all of these may interest me: a fine view over a river valley, or a mountain range; a cathedral rising sheer above the landscape; the human activity imbuing life and variety to a village, street, or festival, or fairground. Looking through our albums, all of these subjects have triggered a human, possibly even aesthetic, response.

Just as most photo albums are exclusively made up of pictures of husband, wife, and family, with a variety of backgrounds and lamp-posts growing out of their heads, in recent years I have found that our photographic memories are dominated by...Mont St Michel - and Hector & Jason; Mount Ormel - and Hector & Jason; Grand Hotel, Cabourg - and Hector & Jason. I can make no apology for so disturbing or corrupting the classic subject matter. For me, capturing these images was absolutely fitting. I was proud that Hector & Jason were there, and felt that they were as important, and as unique, as any of the historical personages who dominated or graced these iconic places before them.

Now, this might seem naïve, silly, pompous, even. But I loved it. Our boys were there - seen that, been there, shared a setting or an experience with the great and the good. And, as far as I was concerned, they were the Princes of their race, innocently exploring, and adding their lustre to, some lovely, historic or infamous place; enjoying themselves, and enhancing our enjoyment.

And we have many fine pictures of Victor. Some of my favourites are of Vic near Lake Vyrnwy, beside a wonderful cascade - the waterfall at Rhiwargor. Another favourite is of the young, athletic Vic a-top the Malvern Hills, one fine but extremely windy afternoon:

Buffeted, battered on Malvern Hill:
Bravely battling the storm gusts, still.

Another gem - that must abide only in my mind's eye - is of a soaked-through Victor, on a bright afternoon at Dovedale, shaking his fur against a declining sun, the water-drops flying like diamonds from his coat.

Shortly after we lost Victor I had some of my favourite photos of him enlarged, and framed. When the shop assistant showed me the results, she exclaimed: *"What a handsome dog!"*. So he would always be. I beamed with pleasure. And, from his stand-point on the sofa, the mercurial young Victor is still looking at me, across the span of years.

If we have many, many photos of Vic, H&J were probably the most photographed dogs on the planet: Princess Diana was hardly more photographed. Now, there are many cultures, communities (or 'tribes') in the world - and many individuals - who regard being photographed with disdain, fear or anger; often, this is because they feel that the photograph is stealing their soul, or at the very least invading their privacy. Fortunately, although H&J were aware that I was doing something different, they were generally happy subjects. Perhaps fascinated and intrigued by a process that (in my case) involved hiding my face behind a lump of glass and metal, they did sometimes become shy and self-aware. If they had been human, all this attention might have gone to their heads. Had he known the truth, Hector would have been a little puffed up; he always knew his value, and would have revelled in the attention - as he did, to the expected degree. Jason, ever modest, would have shrugged his shoulders and continued with his life - his exploration, his running. While they knew they were in the limelight - and Hector always loved the attention - Jason forever remained his modest, demure self.

So here they are again, at Falaise, birthplace of William the Conqueror; at Pont Aven, beloved of Gauguin; at Courseulles, following in the footsteps of Churchill and de Gaulle; at Arromanches, playing on the beach that has witnessed truly world-changing events. At Berkeley Castle, rubbing shoulders with medieval kings and queens, and at Chatsworth, mingling with the ghosts of English aristocracy - fancifully, the bewitching Georgiana, Duchess of Devonshire.

But there are other types of picture, more personal, even 'cheesy'. Pictures that give context, time and place to a particular phase in our lives, and that release a precious nugget of memory. Pictures that tell a story, or merely say: *'this was then, wasn't it great?'*. Hector looking askance at me, whilst lying on our bed; or the boys playing and tussling, with spirit and enjoyment, in their garden in France. Even the still photos crackle with fire and energy.

And there are pictures - fewer in number, but utterly precious - that fuse a connection between photographer and subject, that have a directness and depth that makes these images immortal; as a perfect moment in time, as an emotional connect, even as 'art'.

These are the most intimate pictures of H&J: relaxing, contented, reflective, even: Jason in his redoubt, in his French garden; or rushing to greet me; or H&J looking out, happy, from their den in the car. These pictures can reveal, again, as if I didn't know, their playfulness, with us and with each other, their sense of adventure, their fathomless affection. In these images, Hector & Jason appear luminous, radiant; they burn a hole in the screen.

My only regret, in terms of photographs, is that, inevitably, I missed some important moments, because these - unforgettable - moments happen so quickly, so unexpectedly. And that there are never enough pictures. I remain greedy for immaculate images of my fabulous boys. Every existing image is different, capturing the boys in a different place, in different perspectives and 'poses', and in a variety of moods. I could have photographed H&J until Domesday, and still felt that I had missed something, failed to capture a likeness, an essence, or the most memorable moment of a memorable experience.

Successful pet photography depends, to varying degrees, on equipment, technique, patience and skill. Remember that each pet has its own personality, and will respond in its own individual way to the experience of being photographed. He or she may not know exactly what you are doing, but they know that you are doing something different, that involves them, and that somehow intrudes on them.

Certainly, from an aesthetic point of view, 'shooting' a pet is best done either at the subject's eye level, or below the eye level. Since I was more than twice as tall as H&J, this meant that, for best results, either I had to get down very low, probably on my knees, or that the boys were photographed on top of a mound, or rise, or hillock. These ideal conditions rarely occurred for me, since they are achieved most regularly with a very pliable, eager-to-please subject, or with a little bit of engineering - i.e. setting up the photo. The very best results are obtained by exercising patience, showing respect, and loving your pet. The images that result will keep you spell-bound forever.

There were several challenges, however, that made H&J photography a fascinating, complex subject of its own. Only remember that these were the most *alive* dogs on the planet, with huge energy and style. So they were often difficult to capture - it was akin to bottling quicksilver, or moonshine. To catch them in the flux of action, or to create a little stillness and space, took time and patience - or a good slice of luck.

A further practical constraint was that, on our walks, I was nearly always behind the boys - and the rear (and retreating) view of any living subject (person or dog) is rarely as edifying as the smiling, shining front. Even when I chanced to be ahead of H&J's on-long gallop, the results were always going to be a bit hit-and-miss - more in the way of action or candid photography than anything formally posed.

And, when I did have the boys' attention, say in the French garden, their desire was always to come towards me - so I had to be quick - before Hector, Jason or both lads were practically on top of me. Looking again at the sheer numbers of pictures, in different locations and showing the boys in different aspects, I am pretty pleased with what we achieved, together, and with the quality of the results. I relished the challenge, and caught their characterful and delightful images as often as possible, to the apparent satisfaction of all present. I think the boys themselves would be quietly - no, loudly - happy with the images that continue to smile back at us, with pleasure and anticipation.

We were fortunate, in that so much of our photography was conducted in France. A case of: Light. Action. Atmosphere, Ambience. The country is so richly photogenic, crammed with character, the unexpected, the fantastical, the unforgettable, as to make photography there a delectable dream.

And, even though I may never have created sufficient images, never *quite* took the definitive photograph of Hector or Jason, I can be content with the many hundreds of glowing images that help to tell their story - especially those where the boys are doing what they did best - being themselves. These pulsating images assume another small aspect of their immortality.

Looking at, and marvelling at, a vital image - all that energy reflected back at the viewer - it is hard to believe that those luminous beings can ever be less than fully, breathtakingly, alive.

I hope you take a close look at the pictures in this book: they represent glowing memories of two immortal heroes; and they represent the best of me.

The Portrait

Painting, portrait, luminous to view
For eternity it will 'capture' you!

Colin Hill

June was planning to retire in the Summer of 2011. In February, I took a call from one of her closest colleagues: the subject - broached with a conspiratorial air - the type of gift that June might like to receive. I confess that I was completely stumped. The colleague, Ava, called me again, soon afterwards. *"What about a portrait of the boys?"* she asked. Of course, everyone knew, or knew about, Hector & Jason.

Ava explained that she had come across an artist, living in Scotland, who was renowned for her portraits of dogs, and who had recently completed a commission for a friend. The friend had been delighted with the result. The name of the artist was Grace-Craig Ward.

It was certainly a very generous suggestion - I had no doubt that this would be a pretty expensive commission. The main risk, for me, was: would the finished work accurately represent Hector & Jason in June's eyes? We all have our very personal perception of our pets, which goes beyond the mere physical likeness. But even the perceived 'physical' alters all the time - according to mood, circumstances, age, even lighting conditions. And would the boys' personalities somehow shine through? It seemed a tall order and, if June was disappointed, there would be no place to hide...

I looked at the artist's web-site, and was immediately impressed. Provided that Grace could execute a similarly excellent portrait of H&J, I was pretty confident that June would be delighted with the outcome. So, though not entirely sure - this is a very subjective field - I'm glad that I quickly warmed to the idea. I 'phoned my co-conspirator: let's go ahead, please. What was needed from me? Answer: as many photos as possible, to show the boys in different positions and circumstances. I carried out this operation in some secrecy, delivering the photos to the home of my confidante. Fine. That was not, however, the end of the matter. Over the following weeks I answered a variety of questions, in quick succession. Which was Hector, and which was Jason? Could I confirm their respective eye colour? What more could I say about their respective characters?

In due course, the commission was completed, and on time - a relief, since the artist was a very busy lady. I was informed, in excited tones, that the portrait was a complete success. Of course, I was relieved to hear this, but still a little anxious, since not only had I not seen it, but felt that June, on seeing the portrait for the first time, would know immediately whether the outcome had been a success. Had the essence of the boys been 'captured'? The unveiling would be on the occasion of June's leaving bash - if the result, and impact, was less than perfect, it would be too late to change anything.

I was fortunate to attend June's retirement event - a wonderful celebration, and very happy occasion. Following some very warm words from colleagues and friends, it was at last time for the presentation - and unveiling. June was thrilled - delighted - the main consideration. And so was I. More than a relief. A memorable occasion, capped by the unveiling of a super portrait that will be with us for ever.

The painting does reveal an amazing likeness of Hector and Jason, and also reveals aspects of their personality. In the picture, Jason is wearing his 'stern' face - really one of concentration and focus - while Hector looks deep in thought. The boys had many different expressions, but these are real, and typical, enough. If there is the merest hint of anthropomorphism in the picture, it could hardly be inferred more suitably than in two such characters as Hector & Jason.

There was only one place for this imposing, impressive portrait. The picture now takes centre stage - where else? - at La Haute Maison. It is the perfect setting for this lasting tribute to wonderful friends. When I first displayed the painting, I had leisure to ponder the image: the picture itself, with the (pictured) boys looking down from a special setting above the stairs; and the real-deal H&J looking up, apparently admiring the art-work.

The portrait is a triumph and, as time goes on, in its ineffable way, the picture - and its subjects - grows ever more intense, ever more luminous.

26: God Smiles, and Summons

Dogs are our link to paradise. They don't know evil or jealousy or discontent. To sit with a dog on a hillside on a glorious afternoon is to be back in Eden, where doing nothing was not boring—it was peace.

Milan Kundera

If I have any beliefs about immortality, it is that certain dogs I have known will go to heaven, and very, very few persons.

James Thurber

Hector & Jason were as complementary, as necessary, as vital, each to the other, as salt and pepper, or sugar and spice. They were as mutually indispensable as Roland and Oliver, D'Artagnan and Aramis, or Lancelot and Gawain. It was almost impossible to conceive of an independent existence for one, without the presence and interaction of the other. But yet it came to pass.

Hector aged gracefully, remaining young in mind and body for many dog-years. From the age of ten years he did need medication to help his mobility, and he grew a little grey around the muzzle. He continued, though, to enjoy the trim figure and lively outlook of a much younger dog. Jason, however, seemed to have the gift of eternal youth; there was no trace of grey, his spirit remained young and animated, and he continued to enjoy long walks and crazy runs, both at home and on Normandy's endless beaches.

My retirement had been some time in the making, and suddenly it was upon me; fixed for 20 June 2012. Retirement is a strange phenomenon, but mine had been long in the planning. Could the world cope without me? You bet. Could I cope without the world of work? Time will tell.

We had all travelled to France at Easter, 2012: we were then unaware that this would be our very last trip together; a dream of gentle joys. The long-matured plan was that I would share Summer in France with Hector & Jason. For my darling Jason, it was not quite to be. A lightning-bolt shot from a clear blue sky. At the very last, he had run into my arms.

At my powers' princely height,
My muse, my rock, my light,
My very soul's delight -
My Jason.

What a mighty heart beat there! A bright, smiling day dissolved into a vale of tears. From a clear blue sky came a howling storm: a great, globular torrent.

It was 12.42. Time stood still.

'Did he who made the lamb, make thee?'

During what transpired to be the last weeks of Jason's life, Hector, eschewing his usual manliness, had treated his brother with extraordinary tenderness. Our little lives are rounded with a sleep.

For me, Jason was Donatello's *David;* he was Scott's *Ivanhoe;* he was Shelley's *West Wind,* he was Van Gogh's *Starry Night;* he was Jimi Hendrix playing Woodstock. Yet no single word can capture, can conjure up, his essence. Adorable. Charismatic. Exquisite. Entrancing. Sensational. 'Sensational' comes closest. Only the three of us knew just what we had lost. Where could I find his like again? Where could I find such love again? Never. Never. Never. Never. Never.

'And there is nothing left remarkable
Beneath the visiting moon.'

I had arranged to spend a long weekend in France to, literally, prepare the ground for us: bringing the house and garden up to scratch. I departed for France, leaving Hector at the gate: eager as ever, and smiling through his grief. He was anxious to be with me, having picked out the signs of imminent departure. Sadly, a long weekend could not warrant the travel weariness and risk that would occur to my elderly boy. So, regretfully, I travelled on my own, alone with my thoughts. I departed with a heart filled with sadness; all my joys seemed left behind.

It happened to be Le Mans weekend, and when I arrived at Portsmouth on a cloudless evening it was to find the port heaving with gleaming super-cars, panting in proud ranks, awaiting embarkation. All of the grand marques were there, along with their testosterone-fuelled owners: Aston Martin, BMW, Jaguar, Ferrari, Lamborghini, Lotus, Maserati, Porsche. The most expensive, fashionable, lusted-after cars, in a profusion I had never seen before. In terms of 'breeding', they were the super-car equivalent of Jason, if *sans* spirit. Yet I would have traded the whole expensive extravaganza for a day in his magical company.

On my own - the very words seem desolate - I repeated the St Philbert walk of 2005. Unaccompanied, and in foul weather, though it was early Summer. Rain sluiced across the landscape, so that the very air was drenched and colourless. Yet everything was as I had remembered it - the almost eerily lonely, winding walk, the holiday cottages (still in their dilapidated state), the tumbling river, the opulent, if bedraggled, woodland: and the curious, ancient, village. The only difference was the roads - dug up to renew electricity cables. And the absence of my boys.

But the desolate figure of Christ remained, rain like tears dripping from his face. I started the journey home, dispirited; alone. Though I knew, across the miles of land and sea, that my boy awaited me.

A Golden Summer - Glorious Coda

These sweet perfect days, I'll give to you;
These perfect days I'll live for you.

Colin Hill

Under the wide and starry sky
Dig the grave and let me lie.
Glad did I live and gladly die,
And I laid me down with a will.
This be the verse you grave for me:
Here he lies where he longed to be;
Here is the sailor, home from sea,
And the hunter home from the hill.

Requiem - R L Stevenson

There was hardly time to think. After frenzied preparations, for which I was grateful, Hector and I sailed to France on 3 July, for an extended stay. The journey, as usual, was long, but thankfully uneventful, with Hector, knowing the routine and wise in his years, playing his part with aplomb. We arrived at the cottage in darkness at about 10.30pm. I fed and fussed Hector, had a drink, and went to bed.

Hector bore the loss of his twin brother and soul-mate with immense fortitude. In the days and weeks that followed we became, if anything, closer than ever before. I was hardly ever out of his sight. The new reality was painfully strange. At every moment, Hector reminded me of what I had lost, and what I still had. We were united by an unseen shadow, and intense, internalised grief. I had made Jason a solemn promise - that I would look after his brother (as he had done) better than anyone had ever looked after a brother. And that is what I believe I - and we - did.

I laid Jason in the most exquisite natural space, near to his den in his Normandy garden: where the sun shines on him by day, be-jewelling the very grass, and where the moon shines on him by night. It gives some solace that the loveliest of beings is united with the loveliest of places. As soon as I had laid Jason to rest, Hector lay on the very spot. There could not have been a more fitting consummation of their lifelong partnership. Far in the distance, a dog barked.

******

Several days into our sojourn, I was rudely reminded that trivial, worldly events could still mess up one's plans. Setting off early for a quick visit to the shops, I felt the car vibrating strongly, and awkward to steer. Getting out to inspect, I found a completely flat - punctured - tyre. Fortunately, we were only a mile or so from the cottage. Even so, I was concerned about Hec's ability to get home, under his own steam. I need not have worried: leaving the car on a grass verge, we practically bounced home. Heaving with pride, I called our emergency service, and they - and later the local garage - sorted out the car and its ruined tyre. A new tyre replaced what had been a new tyre. In our circumstances, and since Hector was showing such splendid form, it was inconsequential.

What followed were 80 days of glorious weather, perfect in their purity, their warmth, their cloudless skies, their colour and perfume. Hector and I would spend whole days beneath the gazebo, watching clouds of intoxicated butterflies feeding on buddliea, lavender and bramble flowers. I would read Dickens, absorbed hour after hour, with Hector by my side, beatifically content. Hector was clingy, close; we revelled in each other's company. We shared a common loss, a common purpose.

It gave deep pleasure to watch Hector gain in strength and vigour under the influence of sunshine, fresh air and rich countryside. He was the Lion in Summer, sleek, supple and super-absorbed in the minutiae of the turning days. His coat gleamed, again, with gold; he regained a zest for those three walks a day, along the familiar winding paths of the bocage. For the first time since 2005 I was able to devote every waking moment to his care. This was the last, precious flowering of his spirit. It was - almost - a dream come true, and I savoured every moment.

Day followed day, each as perfect as the one before; we lazed under the gazebo, listening to the peace, and admiring the effect of changing, shifting, light, and the subtle palette of the Summer garden. In the clear, sultry air, shimmering clouds of butterflies - peacocks, red admirals, commas and tortoiseshells - alighted on one's hand and book, in a profusion that was almost dream-like, a kaleidoscope of purple, gold and blue.

We were not entirely, or always, reliant on our own company. June, who had a variety of business commitments, made three separate visits to see us, and my youngest brother and his partner joined us, with June, for two weeks in August. This arrangement, quite accidentally, provided the variety and stimulation beloved of Hector. He was in the place that he loved, surrounded by the environment he loved, and bathing in the weather that he loved; and was close to the people he loved. And, on most days, he ate his favourite viande animaux.

Hector revelled in life, and all its rich pleasures and gutsy possibilities. We journeyed everywhere together: even to the local shops, which always took in a walk around a small lake, a beech forest or a village. Hec's favourite walk, during this memorable Summer, was along the banks of the serene River Orne at Pont d'Ouilly, with all its colour and sweetness. Most days would find us visiting this picturesque tourist haunt. Hector would try, and often succeed, in inveigling himself into the little café, *Carpe Diem,* which nestles on the riverbank. He would wander nonchalantly into this little river-side bar, before being just as nonchalantly shown the door by the smiling lady owner.

'Carpe Diem' - seize the day - might have been the motto, the mantra, for the band of brothers. 'Seize the Day' was certainly their practice. Hector, certainly, was as game as any dog ever was. Genetics can create magic. Jason's magic was his special gift, his genius. Hector's was the magic of deep, complex character. When Elgar completed *The Dream of Gerontius* he wrote: "*This is the best of me*". In terms of greatness of character, this was Hector's glorious best.

'Carpe Diem' is often used as the title for a lovely song from *Twelfth Night*, that reflects wistfully on the fleetingness of youth and beauty. It was sweetly apposite, now:

> '*What's to come is still unsure;*
> *In delay there lies no plenty, -*
> *So come kiss me sweet and twenty,*
> *Youth's a stuff will not endure.*'

There were frequent visits, too, to the ever-popular river resort of Le Vey, with its charming bars overlooking the river, and its bobbing *bateau*, alive with excited day-trippers. Each scene, in the mind's eye, became a Renoir canvas. And we ventured further afield, again to Rabodanges, and to our favourite Fosse Arthour, with Hec circumnavigating the Lac du Lancelot with typical *élan*.

'*Le Weekend*' at Le Vey, in the sunshine, I took to calling '*Show off Saturdays/Sundays*'. There is a long promenade that snakes beside the bars and along the river. There, the young bloods would show off their girls, the young parents would show off their *nouveau bébé,* and the single guys would show off their garishly decorated, extravagantly distended Harley Davidson bikes - the symbolism all *too* blatant. Hector walked manfully, diligently, beside the river, which was awash with pleasure-boats. Despite the heat, he was now too wise in his years to attempt to venture for a dip.

When June arrived, at the height of Summer, all three of us visited the medieval festival at Château Ganne, more authentic than any such I had seen. And, remarkably, free of charge. Hector took it all in - the strange sounds of medieval instruments, roast meats over wood fires, dancing, duelling and jousting, and general hubbub. He had seen it all before; he was confident and, as much as he could be in this strange new world, content.

And, in August, we re-visited an old haunt - the towering, dramatic cliff-edge that is Roche d'Oeutre - set high above the valley of the River

Rouvre, and clothed in thick forest. Chancing across this sight for the first time, one might think oneself in the middle of a tropical forest, or a lost valley. But, this being France, there is a restaurant nearby, to refresh the weary traveller, and a gift-shop, to commemorate the visit. Hector sauntered around the site with a proprietorial air; this was *his* country.

And we travelled further afield yet, crossing Pegasus Bridge, and wafting through Sallanelles, to our favourite sea-side resort of Merville-Franceville, a peculiar mix of chic and bucket-and-spade family fun. On the 30 August 2012, Hector enjoyed three separate excursions or promenades around an overcast, atmospheric Merville: along our favourite coastal path, and in the attractive little resort itself. And we explored hitherto undiscovered places in the resort's hinterland. Why had the *Chez Marion Hotel* lain undiscovered for so long? A few photos to mark the occasion; our only visit as a 'team', but remembering our lost brother with every step. Then a last photo to mark the day, with Hec looking directly towards me from his seat in the car; the shade of his brother by his side.

On a special Sunday every year, in mid-August, it is customary for French churches and chapels to hold a service to 'bless the animals'. I have observed this at, for instance, the beautiful little *chapelle* at St Roch. With their beaming carers, a line of dogs stand patiently, waiting in turn for the priest's blessing. It is the Grand Pardon: at the garlanded altar, with due ceremony, a priest gives each pet a benediction. These little ceremonies have a resonance that I find deeply touching. As a child, I loved to read stories about St Francis, and his tending and care for animals. I was reticent in taking Hector to be blessed, from a probably misplaced sense of embarrassment, on many levels; but, proudly, I stood with him, in spirit.

At the beginning of September - end of August, even - like a trap door slamming shut, everything changes. The French call this *'La Rentreé'*. Workers return to work. *Les Scolairs* return to school. The harvest has been gathered in. The weather becomes melancholy, as though in sympathy with the changing seasons. Nowhere is this change more dramatic than on the sea-fringed shores. The bikinis and beach-brollies are replaced by beach-combers, joggers, and the odd man walking the odd pooch along a deserted shoreline. The atmosphere is spread thickly, with the palette of a Monet, or a Renoir. The shore is re-claimed by the gulls, waders, and the endless tides. If there is a tinge of sadness in the air, a new life, a new chapter, has begun. The raucous cries of the gulls proclaims their triumph at the re-capture of the coastal fringe, the battlements betwixt sea and sky.

Such was this Sunday, 30 August, 2012. On our return journey from Merville, I stopped for a moment to take a look at the impressive Museum at Pegasus Bridge. For Hec, this was a step too far. The day had proved an emotional roller-coaster, and Hector barked with annoyance at being left alone. I had not left him for a moment in two months, and this was not the time to start. I quickly rejoined him and, without further ado, we journeyed home.

Still, on Sundays, when on our own, Hector and I our would retire to our favourite bar, on the river at Pont d'Ouilly. While we watched the kayaks gliding by, and the ducks evading the kayaks, Hec and I would share a plate of *saucisse et frites,* while the sun shimmered on the placid river. *Parfait.* Hector's condition responded to all these stimuli; his coat regained its golden lustre, while his walking continued to gain in strength and resolve.

And we visited a much-publicised Ball-trap, at Cahan - through the farm yard, in the middle of nowhere. Hector looked interested as we approached the ball-trap, a colourful and traditional community sport. But all those people excitedly firing their rifles was hugely noisy, and I decided to steer the car, and Hector, to more peaceful pastures - a homely bar, a grandstand seat by the river, and yet more saucisse et frites.

Each evening, after our day-long family frolics, rounded off with games and a few drinks, I would assemble the camp-bed and sleep downstairs close to Hector. I had found that he was unhappy sleeping on his own, and my physical nearness made for a contented night's sleep. Each morning we woke ridiculously early; switching on my life-line, Radio 4, I became quite well informed on modern farming practice, news from around the globe, and even the latest theological debates.

Piled high beneath the gazebo were weeks and weeks worth of newspapers, frazzled and yellowing under the sun. They were my concession to my native culture. Their contents were awaiting another re-read, and pondering, and reflection. Strange how one attains mental clarity when reading old news, and when reviewing developments after the passage of time.

It was around this time that our neighbours acquired a goat, ostensibly to help control the grass. Given the size of their estate, it would have required a veritable army of goats to have accomplished this mission. As it was, given the porosity of our borders, my main task was to ensure an absence of hostilities between Hector and the goat, since the latter, despite Hector's advanced years, had quickly come to his attention.

One night, I heard deep, pitiful moans coming from the valley below. I was tired; Hector and I had just 'turned in', and I listened from my bed. I ran through my lexicon of animal noises, but none fitted. A fox? A badger? A cow in distress? Surely, pointless to investigate, in the darkness; I fell asleep.

Next morning, I bumped into Thierry, in the road. "*Bonjour. Did you hear anything last night? Our goat has been killed, and half eaten. All the marks suggest that it must have been wild dogs*". Shaken, I confessed that I had heard sounds, but had obviously not realised what was afoot. I expressed my sadness, and sympathy; it must have been a ghastly find. I felt dreadful. Then, as an afterthought, I added: "*Hector was in the house, all the time*".

I could tell from Thierry's response that Hector was not a suspect; it was probably a first, but - on this occasion - he was as innocent as virgin snow.

And so each day passed, as pure, as perfect as could be. When Hector and I finally left the cottage, on 19 September, the weather remained warm and bright. Again, we had a smooth crossing, and again, we stayed overnight at The Travelodge at Sutton Scotney. And, again, we enjoyed a quick walk by starlight. While I ate a hearty breakfast, Hector's eyes were focused on me throughout, from his viewpoint in the car; he was rewarded with choice tit-bits from the table. We arrived home on the morning of 20 September, to the usual slate grey skies, and unsettled weather. Autumn had arrived early, but the sun was still in our hearts.

During the endlessly drab, dour, darkest days of the year, Hec and I remained as restlessly active as we could possibly be. The weather briefly rallying, we re-visited the National Arboretum near Tetbury, at the glorious, riotous height of the Autumn. Proudly, I photographed the equally proud Hector under the spreading boughs of a magnificent beech tree. There he is - practically standing to attention - beneath the spangled canopy of the majestic beech.

And, needless to say, Hec and I continued our regular, time-honoured walks, to our local woods and Park, paying little apology to the passing years. We continued, too, visits to my parents, to mutual delight, and our jaunts - crowded with memories - along the banks of the River Stour. Naturally, Hector continued to relish his dinner, his biscuit treats - and my breakfast.

On his 14th birthday, 1 December 2012, we took Hector for an outing on his old stomping ground, Highgate Common. He strode energetically, purposefully, in the Winter sunshine, looking exactly what he was - a proud, un-bent, elderly gent. I snapped a few images, stirred by the knowledge that time was fleeting. Later that day we strode again in our local woods. Again, the same proud, keen, wise boy. I collected two large sycamore leaves - one for Hector, one for Jason, and stored them carefully. Ripeness is all, sayeth the bard.

On the evening of Thursday, 27 December, 2012, Hector and I embarked on our final walk of the day. It was dark but mercifully dry, and Hector led me down the main road: Christmas lights radiated and twinkled as we passed. On reaching our usual turning point, Hector decided to press on. We reached our second turning point, and still he wanted to go on. The Park was now close by, and Hector decided to enter. We walked around the Park, as we had done a thousand times before, and then returned whence we had come. Hector was remarkably robust; this was his longest walk in many a month. I responded with incredulity, awe, almost with reverence - *how?*

On this day, Hector happened to be 14 years and 26 days of age. This was the exact age - to the day - that we had lost Victor. 27th December was also Victor's birthday. It was a homage to past glories, to a great tradition; to deep memory, and deep content. But it was also pure Hector. At the time, and since, I was struck by this brave, defiant gesture, in the face of Old Father Time. Though Hec was by now a very elderly gent, an unquenchable spirit shone in his eyes, and energised his being. There was to be no *'going gentle'*, no *'dying of the light'*.

And Hec found his last badger - this time, already dead - hidden deep within a field, but still attracting my boy's curiosity. Days later, sniffing around in the leaf litter, deep within the woods, Hector discovered one half of an enormous koi carp. Since there are no lakes within the wood, or even pools, I can only imagine that a wily fox had raided a neighbouring pond, and fished out the unfortunate carp for his supper. One of our cats - the dear Oscar - did just that with a neighbour's goldfish, which were seen squirming in the jaws of the triumphant hunter. What well-fed cat can accomplish, hungry reynard can surely emulate.

In the midst of Winter, Hector found a football in the local Park. Unfortunately for him - and me - the thing was stuck firmly behind the high perimeter fence that surrounds the local primary school. It happened to be a Sunday morning. The shiny leather object of desire was pretty unrecoverable, but Hector would not budge. So, I set to work with a stick, to encourage the ball towards a small cavity between the bottom of the fence and the earth. While I toiled, other dog-walkers homed in on us, enquiring what I was about. *"Is it his ball?"*. *"Well, it is now!"*. Having manoeuvred the recalcitrant spherical object to the right place, we had to dig a further small dent in the soil, to ease the ball out. By this time, a small crowd had gathered. I have always had this 'gift' - a rather inconvenient one - of attracting numbers of curious people when I am engaged in quite innocuous pursuits, and this was no exception. The ball was triumphantly recovered, and a delighted Hector dribbled the thing around the Park like a young blood. It added to a large collection that continues to 'adorn' our garden. Perhaps I should enter them for the Turner Prize: 'Hector's Collected Balls'. Or perhaps not.

At Christmas 2012, my parents - my father, 91 years young - joined us to celebrate the occasion. But, whatever - parents, good cheer, roast turkey, a cracking '70 vintage port, decorations, crackers and all - it was Hector who stole the show. He loved people, and insisted on being the centre of attention, and of attentiveness. He was the centre and soul of a special day.

Then, in the depths of Winter, Hector discovered yet another superb football, but quite out of reach behind the Fort Knox-like steel fencing of the local school. Day after day he returned to the scene of this football, observing it with lustful eye, and looking towards me for inspiration. Not being a pole vaulter, I muttered to him that retrieval of the ball was impossible. A day or two later, the school gate being open to permit the exit of pupils at the end of the school day, Hector seized his chance, darting through the gate and scurrying towards his prey. He gained his prize with relish, and played with it happily until the end of his walk. As always, he then forgot about it. There would be a new temptation, anon.

A full eight months following Jason's grievous loss - in bleakest January - Hector and I had set out on our final walk of the day when we were greeted by a neighbour in the street below us. He asked how Hector was, and reflected sadly on Jason. He remarked, with feeling, that it must be like losing a child. I had not had that exact thought; many people would perhaps deplore the comparison. The loss of a fourteen-year old dog, for whom nature has run its course, may be different in kind to the loss of a fourteen year old child. Yet, for those who have loved and lost their canine son or daughter, the emotional impact can be incredibly, almost impossibly, severe. And until that moment, I had studiously avoided the use of the emotionally-charged word, 'Jason'. But on this occasion my voice tripped over it; Hector wagged his tail for all he was worth. Sometimes, words cannot express one's depth of feeling.

For a number of months before this, Hector had battled against several serious conditions, any one of which would have sapped the spirit of most people, and most dogs. And, for every one of these days, I am convinced that he grieved for his brother.

Hector responded to these illnesses with great psychological resilience, and raw courage. Until the last, he was himself - cheeky, affectionate, brave. In these weeks and months Hec demonstrated a depth of character that was truly remarkable. At night, snug under his quilt, he would smile and turn his head when I stroked him. His example is an inspiration to me, as I face the journey ahead.

And he remained a fighter to the very last. Despite my misgivings, Hec continued to insist on attending his old walks. I marvelled at his courage, which propelled him beyond what should by rights have been his powers of physical endurance. Increasingly, and touchingly, Hec became reluctant to let me out of his sight. I slept beside my precious boy every night of that long Autumn and Winter.

We embarked - just Hector and I - on a ten day trip to Normandy, on 6 February. Hector seemed up for it, and enjoyed the welcome sunshine; my very last pictures of him show him contentedly lying on the doorstep, near to his brother. But he was not to return to England. He was, in fact, already home - the home that he loved.

We eventually 'lost' Hector on 11 February, 2013, aged 14 years and three months - 90 years old, in human terms; 257 days after his beloved brother, whom he had remembered, and revered, on each and every one of those days. Hector died as he had lived: bravely; unflinchingly. It had been a glorious, honeyed, golden goodbye, for which I was intensely grateful and proud. But my preparedness was no preparation at all.

Through force majeure I loosed my hold;
Your eye still glittered, your coat still gold.
My heart shock-froze; my blood ran cold.
What mighty seer this tale foretold...?

On our return to the cottage following his loss, I paid a short visit to the exquisite Chapel Saint Vigor, in order to say '*thank you*' to whoever, or whatever, had given Hector his life. Then we returned home, to La Haute Maison.

Within a few minutes, I was visited by our neighbour, Michele, who introduced me to her new, two months old border collie - Hikou. Wonderful. New life. Hikou eyed me with true doggy mistrust - I must have looked a complete fright - it made me laugh. And then the French air-force made a grand, low-level, fly-past. And then the ancient church bells tolled. And then I laid Hector to rest.

I laid Hector in a lovely, sunny, spot, where he had loved to 'mooch'. He was laid to rest with the utmost dignity, immense honour, and all reverence. His grave lies beneath a mature cherry tree, '*the loveliest of trees*'. He looked asleep, at peace, in the afternoon sunshine, and that is a picture my heart will always treasure. All seven of his latest prizes - tennis balls, all - accompanied him. Over his grave, I read Byron's *So, we'll go no more a roving*:

'*So, we'll go no more a roving*
So late into the night
Though the heart be still as loving,
And the moon be still as bright.'

The sun shone on the spot, and birds sang. And Shakespeare came to mind: '*Our little life is rounded by a sleep*'.

He was at one with nature. In eternal sunshine, enveloped by flowers, and butterflies, and bird-song; there is only gladness, and sweetness.

Je suis désolé. Borrowing Hector's courage, and through the sorrow, I need to shout out, to celebrate one *helluva* life:

The smile through which your spirit shone
That heart and soul conjoined as one:
That strength, survived the glassy stone:
My love, my lore, my Hector.

I had promised Jason that I would love him forever. It hardly needed to be said. And my sacred promise to him, that I would care for his brother, better than any brother had ever been cared for, I believe was honoured in full measure. I pray, truly, that I succeeded. As for my first promise, honouring it is a daily passion. Most earnest of all is my desire to thank Hector & Jason for their great hearts, and great souls, inspired from within, and so freely given.

That February day was unseasonably warm, and sunny. I saw the first peacock butterfly emerge, hesitant, from hibernation. The hellebores were in flower. Everywhere there were signs of life: in the very grass, in the tree peony; even in the first gold of the primroses; and Jason's rose was in new leaf-bud. Nature - season, plants, birds - was burgeoning back to renewed life, in all its glory, all around my lovely boy. The poignant final lines from *Wuthering Heights* welled into my mind:

'I lingered round them, under that benign sky; watched the moths fluttering among the heath and hare-bells; listened to the soft wind breathing through the grass; and wandered how any-one could ever imagine unquiet slumbers, for the sleepers in that quiet earth.'

The following day, I re-traced some of our favourite walks. The goat walk, of course. So evocative, and alive with memory. And a walk, in bleak sunshine, along the River Orne at Pont d'Ouilly; of course. The river was swollen with Winter rains, and glinted with pale, late afternoon sun. Sunlit, serene; empty. Walk after walk, accompanied by Hector's lead, and Hector's spirit.

Hector had travelled to his French home for 14 consecutive years, and Jason for nearly as long. Now Hector was united with the home that he loved, in the earth that he loved; and close to the brother whom he adored. Each day, they will still witness a world full of light, and full of life. They are not, to be sure, in eternal peace, but in eternal watchfulness, eternal motion, eternal grace.

How to remember them? Well, there is a glorious rose bush, planted near to the front door of our French home, and close to Jason's grave: each season the rose offers a profusion of deliciously perfumed, elegant, deep crimson blooms. There is an oak tree, to commemorate each boy, specially selected, and planted in a lovely spot, at Tafolog. There are hundreds - many hundreds - of photographs of these adventurous, fun-loving boys, some of them reproduced here. There is Grace's fittingly superb portrait of our sensational boys, always to be admired and enjoyed. There is this memoir, which has been a joy to write. There is the *Spirit of Jason Trust,* established in his memory, and which will continue far into the future. And there is the *Heart of Hector Trust*, established in *his* memory. And there are my memories, crowding in, sublime, and with me forever. I hope that that is enough to comfort my grieving soul, and to leave a legacy of goodness to the world.

I can recall Jason's tender, luminous nature whenever I listen to the lovely Cavatina from Beethoven's miraculous Late Quartet, Op 130. The Cavatina itself is followed immediately by the stupendous Grosse Fuge. Hector was a serious case of a multi-faceted, deep and complex character. I am instantly reminded of Hector, every time I hear the Fugue's profound, unstoppable life-force.

An unforgettably enduring memory of Hector is his handsome head, complete with quiff, always in the rear mirror as we motored along - alert, vital, responsive, whether visiting a favourite, familiar place, or on safari through deepest France. I look in the rear mirror, and the image is with me yet.

Standing in the garden near to the brothers on a cold, dark night, I look up at the night sky. The stars are overwhelming in their majesty. All that power. All that unimaginable power. I feel humble, utterly humble, and grateful again for my sweet boys.

It was the end of a heroic age. But the courage and spirit of my superb boys will give me the strength, for all time, to celebrate two magnificent lives.

Shortly after we lost Hector, a fellow dog-walker asked me the inevitable question, and received the inevitable reply. *"I'm pretty philosophical about these things"* she confided. Well, time will tell how deep that philosophy runs. I'm reminded again of Hamlet's injunction to his friend: *"There are more things in Heaven and Earth, Horatio, than are dreamt of in your philosophy"*.

"Hector was fabulous; I loved him", a lady said to me, without prompting. Though she did not know me especially well, she could not have said anything that would have provided greater comfort, or inspired greater pride. I would have given much for such a golden

tribute, delivered so simply, without affectation or artifice. I hope that Hec was listening; he too would have swelled with pride.

Fifty days after I lost Hector, I was walking alone in Ridgehill woods when a fit-looking woman, well known for her almost incessant dog-walking, confronted me:

"Have you lost your dog?", she demanded.

"Yes, I'm afraid I have."

"Well, I'm sorry, but I've just lost my husband. With respect, you can always get another dog".

"With respect, you can always get another husband."

We both laughed.

Then I experienced a strange dream, which might have come from the Brothers Grimm. Hector and I were on the banks of a swollen, muddy river. It could well have been the Severn at Twyning. A few other people were there, too, walkers and fishermen, among a scattering of old houses and inns. A fisherman caught a huge pike and hung it, still quivering, from a fence. Suddenly, a mongoose darted from the undergrowth, and attacked the struggling fish. Just as suddenly, Hector latched on to the mongoose. With some persistence, and much reluctance on Hector's part, I slowly eased him away from the surprised predator. We left the scene. I awoke. It was all strikingly real: how very Hector!

For some time after I had lost him, the singular youth of the area would greet me with: *"Hector! Hector!"* each time our paths crossed. A case of the immortal gracing the lips of the immutable. Out of the mouths of babes and sucklings...

Soon after our loss, I saw a neighbour, a strikingly svelte and sassy lady, departing for work one morning. *"Have a good day!"* I ventured. *"I'm sure your day will be better than mine"*, she replied, ruefully. *"Well"*, I continued, (it must have been my 'stupid' day) *"I'm sure you'll get your reward in the next life".* She laughed and, shutting the car door, looked at me narrowly, before responding: *"I'm going to come back as your dog..."*

Maybe, after all, we did something right...

Much Wenlock Memories

I wept, and wondered, on Hector, Prince of Troy;
Sought brimming churches, brave flowers for my boy.

Colin Hill

The small village of Much Wenlock, in Shropshire, is quite delightful in itself. A Norman church dominates the village, together with an ancient abbey.

However, Much Wenlock has a quite extraordinary claim to fame - breathing new life into the Olympic Games, which had not been held since ancient times. The renowned William Penny Brookes revived a form of the Games, which re-commenced in the village from the mid-19th century.

Brookes's life-long campaign to get athletics on to the school curriculum brought him into contact with Baron Pierre de Coubertin. In 1890, the young French aristocrat visited Much Wenlock and stayed with Dr Brookes at his home in Wilmore Street. A Games was staged especially for the Baron and, inspired by the event and his discussions with Brookes, Coubertin went on to set up the International Olympic Committee in 1894. The Much Wenlock Games therefore had a direct influence on the decision to revive the modern Olympics, which first took place in Athens in 1896.

As we know, Lord Coe was the Chair of 'LOCOG', the London 2012 Organising Committee, which delivered the most superbly successful 2012 Games in London. In the Norman Church - which reminded me so much of the churches in Normandy - a plaque has been placed by the 2012 organisers to commemorate Dr Brookes' and Much Wenlock's role in reviving the Olympic movement. It is a very fitting tribute.

We visited the church, in silent appreciation, remembering the absent Hector & Jason. Suddenly, a variety of memories, and strands of memories, seemed to come together, as I read the memorial plaque and, once more, thanked *whatever* for our two golden boys.

My mind still swimming in memory, I bought crocuses and cyclamens from a local shop. They were, of course, destined for France. The flowers were planted in the deepest, purest, whitest, snowfall that I had ever seen in the Normandy garden.

******

Shortly after this visit, June and I travelled to Gloucester, and then to Winchester, to visit their magnificent Cathedrals, perhaps to ponder and, in my case, as the passionate pilgrim. It was at Gloucester that, to our surprise, we came across the effigy, and tomb, of Robert, Duke of Normandy. And at Winchester that we saw the gravestone of Hampshire's most famous daughter, Jane Austen. I assiduously avoided walking on the engraved gravestone - which is set in the floor of the Cathedral - but noted with chagrin that others were not so particular.

27: Art and Grief

No symphony orchestra ever played music like a two-year-old girl laughing with a puppy.

Bern Williams

If music be the food of love, play on;
Give me excess of it; that surfeiting,
The appetite may sicken, and so die.

Twelfth Night - William Shakespeare

We associate art, the greatest art, with the most profound and sublime human thought, creation, and expression. So it is inevitable that we seize on art when we experience grief, in a desperate effort for solace, for *any* possible comfort.

Since art essentially centres on human relationships and experience, it can be no surprise that the eternal themes of love, loss, grief and pain are at the forefront of artistic endeavour. Visual art - paintings, say, by Rembrandt, Goya or Van Gogh - explore these subjects with profound compassion and sensitivity, as well as with awesome skill. So, too, does great poetry explore every emotional state in ways that are as complex as they are wonderful, and that resonate with profound feeling and meaning.

The most famous architectural monument, almost the epitome to love and loss, must be the Taj Mahal. Mumtaz Mahal, beloved partner of Shah Jahan, died in 1631, while giving birth to their 14th child. The construction of the Taj Mahal started in the same year; it was completed 22 years later, in 1653. This was a stupendous project, carried out at almost unimaginable expense. Construction occupied 22,000 masons, stonecutters, carvers, painters, calligraphers, and dome-builders, and 'employed' 1,000 elephants, which transported marble and materials from across India. The Taj Mahal is an exquisite white marble mausoleum, demonstrating the depth of feeling that one sentient being may have for another.

Yet it is to music, the soundtrack to our lives, that we rely on in our extremity. We listen to music when we are in love, when we are out of love, when we are happy, when we are sad. There are a myriad songs, and sounds, to reflect and enrich every emotion, every mood. Music energises us, seems to empathise with us. At critical times in our lives - birth, marriage, death, war - music fortifies and inspires. Music engages us intellectually, emotionally, even spiritually, enhancing our lives, enriching our experience. According to academic research, we actually enjoy crying in response to art. And we are more likely to shed tears in response to music, than in response to any other art form - such as a poem, a painting, or magnificent architecture.

Certainly, it is music, particularly classical music, that most of us turn to in moments of extreme emotion and adversity; music that is not only beautiful, but which has genuine depth, and genuine power to 'move'. This music is also (generally) 'abstract': where there are no words or images that may act as a barrier or filter between artist and the listener; where communication is immediate and personal, and understanding, though often very subjective, no less real for that. I am thinking, for example, of Bach's Partitas for violin, Mozart's String Quintets, and Beethoven's Late String Quartets. There are many, many other possible examples.

There is also, of course, great opera, song-cycles, passions and requiem masses that take this extreme-human subject matter and give it the most profound expression. Examples might include Bach's *St Matthew's Passion*, Verdi's *Requiem*, and Schubert's *Winterreisse*.

In moments of extreme emotion, we are seeking to escape our grief, to be taken to other spheres ('taken out of ourselves'), searching for solace and consolation, or seeking a deeper awareness as to *why*: why things are as they are, why we feel as we do. How should we respond? What should we do? How can we achieve even some consolation? How can we rise up from the depths of despair, and seek understanding?

Yet, as with most modern popular music, most classical music was written to please, to give delight, to uplift and create enjoyment. As Howard Goodall explains in *The Story of Music*, Mozart's music was written in order to enchant humanity: *'His music...wants you - whoever and wherever you are - to feel good'.*

And, God knows, our forbears needed it: any *soiree* into European history will reveal a panoply of misery, suffering, poverty, disease and early death. So most of the secular music written by, for example, Mozart, Haydn, or Beethoven, is written to delight our hearts, to gladden and lift our spirits. And a good thing, too.

Great sadness, sorrow, and grief, can also be reflected in music: in opera, or lieder, the tragedy involving the - often innocent - main protagonist is often the central theme. The music, the feelings expressed, are deep, powerful, intense. And we cry. We cry because, in that instant, we believe the artist, we are immersed in the art. It may be harrowing, yet so exquisitely beautiful. It may be Dido, or Idomeneo, or Tosca.

Even great, tragic, opera - say *Tosca*, or *Rigoletto*, or *Don Carlos* - operas soaked in blood, with gruesome murder, torture, rape and appalling executions - are nevertheless meant to transport and uplift - entertain; so that we leave the theatre smiling, and ready to return for more. Poor Flora Tosca leaps to her death - and the audience gasps, and applauds. Puccini and Verdi would never have apologised for this - while wringing us out, they wanted to leave us thrilled and delighted.

Strangely, we feel better for the experience. It is the greatness of art, it is the greatness of the composer, that has lifted our hearts; in that moment, we have become better human beings. On the first London performance of *Messiah*, Handel was complimented on his providing such *"noble entertainment"*. The master responded: *"I should be sorry if I only entertained them, I wished to make them better"*. What we have felt (from the music) is not perhaps schadenfreude - experiencing a malicious pleasure at another's misfortune - but it *is* getting a high - perhaps even a moral high - from the most desperate experience, expressed in the power and empathy and directness of music. And then, returning home from the performance, we pour ourselves a drink and turn on the TV. There has been a violent attack somewhere in the world; dozens of innocents have been 'slaughtered'. Do we cry? Or just curse, and switch over the channel?

Though a great deal of music, inevitably, was written on the subject of death - since it is such an ever-present part of the human condition - masses, requiems and the great oeuvre of church music were written to inspire, or to give comfort to the living. What could be more horrible than the story expressed in *St Matthew's Passion*? Yet, while we are horrified and overwhelmed by the tragedy and cruelty of the Passion, we are uplifted by the power and tenderness of the music. It's called genius; you engage with it, are engaged by it.

And yet. And yet. When a raw, visceral grief, a personal grief, overwhelms you, and you demand that the music responds then, inevitably, there is a disconnect. The miracle has faded, shrivelled before you. In my humble opinion, there are scant musical creations, or any other works of art, that are cathartic to utter grief, to great personal loss; even fewer that enable one to genuinely understand and come to terms with what is being experienced. While it is only natural to seek relief, to search for comfort, a gnawing problem is that the state of grief may not be consistent with the response to even great music, since this requires the exercise of intelligence, thought and an ability to engage with the art.

In other words, the music also requires a response *to it*. Great music cannot be a kind of nicorette patch, to lessen or assuage our grief. My experience is that even the most wonderful music can become '*a thousand twangling instruments*' - inchoate, irrelevant, irritating, if we try to engage with it at a time of almost insensible grief. At best, music may be a flag set in a howling storm.

There is music, certainly, written by artists who themselves are experiencing profound grief - in a variety of personal circumstances, including the loss of loved ones, and their own soon-expected demise. In the 18th and 19th centuries life expectancy was much shorter, and artists themselves were not spared the loss of their loved ones - including children - in infancy. We should not think, because this experience was all too common, that such tragic personal loss did not have a traumatic effect on the artist, who by definition is also a sensitive human being. Equally, although great art has somehow arisen from such ghastly circumstances, I do not wish to imply that there is some kind of quid pro quo, that the art somehow cauterises the human tragedy. Rather, I see it as humanity's heroic response to profound loss. This is not always sad or sorrowful music. It is beyond sadness and sorrow, and, whatever its form, explores and often reveals the deepest emotional response.

Most 'sad' music (however we interpret that word) is written by artists of huge talent who transmute their human experience into art through creative energy. The interpretation of that art form involves an energy and intelligent sensibility of our own; this may desert us at certain times in our lives. The structure of music, the creative energy expended, the would-be-ness of the finished art, may be antipathetic to the consuming chaos of grief. No matter how tragic the piece, almost invariably the artist wishes us to be uplifted by it, through it - and this may not be possible in all circumstances. After all, art - and music - is organised, structured: thought-through. Grief is destructive and de-constructing, a meltdown towards chaos; at that stage, we are almost beyond help. Grief is at the opposite end of the spectrum from the creative process, or the cognitive, interpretive and appreciative faculties.

This is not to deny the pain and tragedy in all of our lives: Verdi, for example, lost his wife, Margherita, in 1840. She was 26 years of age. Only a short time before, the couple had lost their infant son and daughter. I have no doubt that this life experience, if such it be, somehow shapes, somehow *is,* the operas. I make no simplistic connection between the art and the life. The music is sublime. If it somehow helps you in your grief, perhaps inspires you to do good, this must be a real comfort.

But just as the crime novel will go down like a lead balloon in a country racked by war and chaos, so music will struggle against mesmeric grief. If there are exceptions, they are few indeed. In my view, only a very few, supremely great, artists have managed to explore, and communicate, the most profound human truths. And our own grief may, at least temporarily, disrupt our intellectual, even our emotional, response.

There are, indeed, a few masterpieces, by Bach, Beethoven, Mozart and Schubert - there will indeed be others - that have offered me, perhaps not consolation, but understanding, and I revere them and their creators for this miracle of enlightenment. I hesitate to name the works, since each individual is different, and I feel it would be unwise - even patronising - of me to suggest something that may be seized upon as some sort of healing balm, rather than a path to explore. We all need our own time, our own space, to find a way through the most painful of human experiences.

While it is probably asking too much for art conceived by man to speak to us, to support us, during our darkest days, I will contend, with humility, that a few immortal creations, through their depth, their complexity, their beauty - often all three - have touched me deeply. Bach's astonishing Partitas for solo violin; Mozart's string quintet in C

Minor; Beethoven's Late Quartets; Schubert's string quintet, and song cycle *Winterreisse*.

The reason I am drawn to these works varies: Bach offers a complexity and unity which is almost beyond expression and human power; Beethoven seems to offer pain - and perhaps comfort - the extreme rendered bearable through soul-searching and profound thought, somehow synthesised in intense musical expression. Mozart provides a depth of beauty - in the midst of personal tragedy - that seems to transcend grief, with a life-affirming profundity. Schubert offers bleakness, pure and simple: ashes in the mouth, and the same tomorrow, endlessly; come to terms with this spiritual misery, through the music.

Bach's Chaconne to his Second Partita for violin is one of the undisputed masterpieces for that instrument, and is thought to have been written in memory of his wife, Maria Barbara, who died whilst Bach was on a business trip; the work was composed shortly afterwards. This is one of the few pieces that has provided consolation - nay, enlightenment - for me at a time of deep personal grief at the loss of a loved one.

The final movement of Beethoven's last completed work, the awe-inspiring Op 135 String quartet, has a motif: '*Must it be?*' which is answered: '*It must be*'. Now, that may be Beethoven's light-hearted response to his cleaner's asking for her dues, or his riposte to a music enthusiast's trying to wriggle out of payment for a copy of a manuscript. Yet this Quartet, and a small number of other such works, have given me a solace beyond words.

When, after we had lost Jason, Hector and I travelled to the shops, or for a walk, or to my parents, the only music I would - could - listen to was Beethoven's Late String Quartets. These astonishing creations have an extremism, a unity and an unplumbable depth that my own extreme emotions could somehow key into. One hundred days after losing Jason - on a sunny Sunday morning in Normandy - I listened to Mozart's *Requiem*, music that the composer struggled to complete as, literally, he lay dying. This music is unutterably sublime. Listening to such an effusion seemed fitting in commemorating a wonderful life - Mozart's, obviously - but it speaks across the ages, for all those we have loved and lost.

In such extreme circumstances, I could also listen to Schubert's *Winterreisse*. Schubert's friends were shocked when he first played this song cycle to them. The music is remorselessly, hopelessly bleak. Words and music express a grief that cannot be enjoyed because of its musical expression, or wallowed in, because of its exquisite intensity. The landscape, and prospects, and soul, are laid utterly, and unutterably, bare. An utterance of stripped, shredded, pathological despair. Life: *sans* meaning, *sans* hope. What had dragged-forth the unrelenting hopelessness of *The Hurdy-Gurdy Man*? A pack of growling dogs - none else - surround and threaten a poor old man on a bleak Winter's day. Such alienation. Such desperation.

In a different medium, but at around the same time - 1823 - came an astonishing creation from Francisco de Goya. We can only conjecture from what deep recesses of being sprang one of the most poignant masterpieces in the history of art. The painting is called, quite simply, *The Dog*.

At a different end of the spectrum, the only other music I could bear to play at this time was Sinatra's *I Remember Tommy*, his 1961 tribute to his former band-leader, Tommy Dorsey. I could bear it, since it was the opposite of maudlin or soulful; it is exuberant, life-enhancing. And it embraced *our* past like a comforting, cosy duvet. Sinatra, of course, is no longer 'alive', a phrase that sounds strange, even as I write it. He often joked: *"I hope you live to be a hundred, and that mine will be the last voice that you hear"*. The centenarian is rather unlikely, but 'The Voice' may well be the last that I hear. Immortality, of a sort.

For me, ultimately, whether it is gay or sad, light or deep, music is for the good times, the happy times: to gild our lives and experience, stimulate our every mood, somehow extend and lift our spirits ever upward. Music is entwined with our fondest memories, enhancing and perhaps even flattering them. Given a fair chance, music can help tilt your heartstrings - or your braincells - to a happy, or beatific, or exalted, state. In fact, music helps to celebrate the gift of life. And those gifted individuals who can bring us joy, who can inspire, more than even the drawers of water, and the hewers of wood - more even than the scientists and engineers who have shaped our comfortable modern lives - *they* are the best of us.

And H&J were the good times: so their soundtrack - in England or in France - was the breezy and the elegant, the deep and soulful: Frank and Ella, Miles and Louis, Nina and Joni. Great voices, great music, great fusions of memories - at home, and whilst cruising in the car. '*That's life....*'

If June and I needed to leave H&J alone at home, usually for something necessary or rather mundane such as work or shopping, we left Radio 4 playing in the background: the rich, cultured sounds emanating from the *Today* Programme, *Woman's Hour* and *Gardeners' Question Time* created a human sound-wave that seemed to calm their waking hours, at least until their peace was fractured by the arrival of the postman or paper-boy.

Our return home, whether individually or together, was invariably greeted with wild excitement: Hector and Jason would seize towels, oven gloves, pieces of wood or a favourite toy, and gambol round and round - Hector making his various squeaking noises, while Jason displayed his matchless *joie de vivre*.

The mood was just as delicious when, on returning to our French cottage from a minor shopping trip, the boys would bark a greeting on hearing our approach, and continue this excitement on our entering the house; round and round the garden they would go, gurning and grinning, t-towels swinging from their jaws, with Hector trying to rob Jason of his spoils. The royal welcome was always a delight to witness, even if it resulted in a great deal of repeat-washing of clothes that had been paraded triumphantly around the garden.

It is that music, *their* music - the music of pure joy - that I will remember longest of all.

28: Love and Memory: Loss and Legacy

The stress of red mist and the fog of the stress;
Through grindstone and sweat and the absence of bliss;
Remember this, young man, remember this:
What you miss, young man, you will miss.

Colin Hill

My grief lies onward, and my joy behind.

Sonnet 50 - William Shakespeare

For thy sweet love remember'd such wealth brings
That then I scorn to change my state with kings.

Sonnet 29 - William Shakespeare

Tis better to have loved and lost
Than never to have loved at all.

In Memoriam - Alfred Tennyson

If you have a dog, you will most likely outlive it; to get a dog is
to open yourself to profound joy and, prospectively, to equally
profound sadness.

Marjorie Garber

A good dog never dies. He always stays. He walks besides you on
crisp autumn days when frost is on the fields and winter's drawing
near. His head is within our hand in his old way.

Mary Carolyn Davie

Yet thy love shed upon me
Life more than mine own
And now thou art from me
My being is gone.

Love and Memory - John Clare

Hector & Jason had a zest for life that was boundless, infectious, as joyously relentless as a torrent in Spring. Their white-heat intensity was life-enhancing, life-changing. And they honoured every day, as though it were the first, or the very last.

Once, strolling along the street on my own, a passer-by remarked: *"I've never seen you without your dogs!"*. *"No"*, I smiled, *"I don't feel quite complete"*. But I knew that they were *there*. Now, a new, terrible knowledge possessed me: without my boys by my side, I was not quite complete. How can they be gone? How can such restless energy be stilled? Can the suffocating darkness recede, and allow light to illuminate the contours of great lives? For so long I had breathed the magical air, been immersed in fantasy, and explored wonderland; emerging from the rabbit hole means painful, gut-wrenching re-adjustment.

It is often said that the best things in life are free - a platitude that's also true. But because these 'best things' are often so familiar - like beauty, or nature, or love - in the minutiae and pressure of life we often begin to take them for granted, to see through them. Yet to share my life, to unite it, with Hector & Jason, was an extraordinary privilege, and one that I *never* took for granted. Though I could not see the end, yet I trembled at the prospect.

Hector and Jason lived life in the fast lane; *'seize the day'* was their thing. They were both endowed with a gift *for* life. Both were so full of vivacity and vigour, and enhanced the lives of their nearest and dearest on an intense, 24/7 basis. The happiness merry-go-round truly never seemed to want to stop, but to project ever forward. Moreover, in a world that is so overwhelmingly consumed - no pun intended - with material things, the tangible intangibles provided by H&J were priceless: their spontaneous affection, and intensely-felt welcome; their joy, almost gratitude, for life and for one's friendship and love. The thrill they gave, across the species barrier, remains seamless and timeless. And I experienced this colossal privilege for, collectively, 28 years - as long as any single dog has ever lived. So, it was - is - hard to believe that H&J are no longer with us: to touch, to stroke, to show a lead to - to inject instant excitement into the moment. We continue to celebrate them, but their departure has brought an emptiness that is desolating.

I am often reminded - usually with a rueful smile - that *'life goes on'*. Indeed it does, and always will do, on other planets as well as our own. But that little truism often reminds me - that I can withstand any amount of someone else's pain. And the reality of loss should not be an invitation to forget the past, which in some respects is more real than the future - because it has actually happened, and has shaped who we are. As the great Bard wrote, '*What's to come is still unsure*'. If one has ever been truly loved, then that love is boundless, and infinite. It is a gift that goes with you into that future, and which will temper your response to whatever vicissitudes lie ahead.

It is true that, in sixty, seventy or eighty years time, at the extreme, each and every one of us will cease to be a memory of anyone then alive. At best, we will be a memory of a memory, and already crowded out by new life, and its own demand for recognition. And then, nothing. And it has been (well) said that to be born is a miracle, and to live to old age is a privilege. And that's it; bye, bye, baby.

As life is so precious, squeeze the last drop from every day. Savour every moment: - that endeavour gives our memories of Hector & Jason the quality of intensity. The greater the quality and quantity of life you give your dog - the greater the experience and variety - the more life you give yourself. Whoever said, at the end of their days: *"I wish I'd spent more time in the office"*, or *"I wish I'd spent longer in bed"*?

Without H&J in our lives, sharing our lives, life could not have been quite complete: though, Heaven knows, my life has been blest. Without them, life would have been more comfortable, more composed, more mundane, more relaxed; certainly, not as energised or challenging. And the challenge could at times be almost over-whelming. But, as I have said, there will be time, a world of time, in which to relax.

From the earliest times, human beings appear to have decided that the prospect of eternal oblivion is unpalatable, unacceptable, and perhaps unnecessary. The world's religions therefore hold out the prospect of eternal life, in some shape or form. Well, if Heaven is available to the flesh, or the spirit, of homo sapiens, then rationally it ought to be available to sentient animals - again, in some shape or form. There will be no blinding revelations here, or dogmatic assertions (forgive the pun) - just a few, gentle thoughts to ponder, as you will.

One can assert baldly that most human beings may regard themselves as lucky - I jest not - if a park bench is 'erected' and named in honour of their memory. And the word 'jest' brings me to a scene in *Hamlet* - Act V, Scene 1 - where, in a graveyard, Hamlet chances upon the skull of the (late) Yorick, jester to the King. After musing on the nature of life and death, Hamlet challenges the skull: *"Now get you to my lady's chamber, and tell her, let her paint an inch thick, to this favour she must come; make her laugh at that"*. Lines that should perhaps be inscribed on our foreheads, so that, whenever we peer in the mirror, we are reminded to love and, like Hector & Jason, seize the day.

Love *for* a dog is special: there will be few people who you will ever love so much. And the love *of* a dog is special: there will be few people who will love *you* so much. Make no mistake - this will be one of the deepest, closest relationships of your life. Next to your relationship with your partner, and your feelings for your children, maybe different in nature, this may well be the most important, most heartfelt, relationship you will ever know.

The loss of Jason was still very fresh and painful when, eight and a half months later, we lost Hector. If it was possible, in view of his extraordinary nobility and courage, my love for Hector deepened even further in the months following Jason's loss. The timing of loss comes like a googly, bowled from behind - you don't see it coming. Looking back, there was a long, honeyed goodbye; *a bientot*.

But there and then Hector's loss hit me like an implosion, leaving in its wake a vast, dreary chasm that stretched into the future. From being one of the happiest, most fortunate guys on the planet, with my two fabulous boys, I was suddenly struggling for air. Pleasure, and pain, seem to be on opposite sides of the spectrum, but in fact are so close, so threateningly close.

Except for the simple but inescapable fact that we are all biologically programmed to die, Hector & Jason would have stayed loyally at my side for all time. With them, there was no compromise, no moderation, no negotiation, no prevarication, no *'yes, but...'*. It was pure adoration, and it was mutual.

Nothing could prepare me for the hurricane that engulfed my being. I had two in-your-face, adorable dogs. Then one. Then none. Two, fabulous boys, eternally in my heart. But still nothing. *Rien*.

Everyone knew Hector and Jason, and missed them, asked about them. Their energy and electricity lit up the world; at least, they lit up my world. A vile, eviscerating grief overwhelms the senses. One's spirit is laid to waste; one's strength lies in ruins. The very foundations are under attack - from within. Resilience is a second-hand mattress. If one has loved, this is the price that must be exacted, even while positive forces, so battered and be-battled, oh so slowly, re-group.

On a single walk, long after I had lost them, I was asked about H&J on three separate occasions; the enquiries made gently, and always with warmth and appreciation. Nuggets of memory lingering on the mind... what an impact they had made, what an indelible impression!

We are in good company: Presidents, Popes, Princes, potentates, pop-stars (especially pop-stars), yea, the greatest celebrities, will all fade away, and be gone: however powerful, however wealthy, however well-connected with God; whether saint or sinner, it is all the same. Harry Houdini, the great escapologist, said that, if it was possible, he would send a sign from beyond the grave. He didn't. So the only difference is in the quality of life; the good that we do with it; the way we employ spirit and energy to make a difference - that is worth honouring, treasuring, remembering.

I have, sadly but inevitably, attended a great many funerals over the years. As we grow older, we become painfully aware that the next funeral may be our own; and this gives an added urgency, if not poignancy, to our daily experience. Deaths, and funerals, have much in common with a pebble falling into a pond: there is a splash, followed by ripples on the surface. Then the pebble is submerged, and the surface of the pond becomes smooth again. More prosaically, a ten minute oration, a brave attempt at humour, and that's it - you're buried, literally. For me, the pleasure felt by feeding a robin will always far exceed the spiritual nourishment provided by any type of formal funeral service.

The life-span of human beings is long by the standard of most mammals and, though life-expectancy is increasing, our time on Earth still seems - to us - indecently short. Still, 80 or 90 years seems pretty good, compared to the 10 to 15 years accorded to most dogs. By contrast, some trees have a recorded age of 2,000 years or more. But dogs - and many human beings - live so intensely that, in their brief existence, they are consumed by activity and, hopefully, by their achievements. This is the most we can hope for ourselves and for our dogs - that their every second is a second well and passionately spent. A mammal has the potential for 1.5 billion heart-beats. For a dog, that's 5,000 days. Treasure, savour, every moment. It has been well said that the currency of love is time - quality time.

This is worth pondering: what do we leave behind? Children? Good works? A body of work? And which of us is remembered, and why - daily, even yearly? And with what thoughts, what memories, what tenderness? And how many of these lost souls leave a lasting legacy of any kind, of any significance?

From the tortured, incandescent cry of *Dido's Lament* - *"Remember me! - when I am laid in earth"*, to the poignant, sun-and-shade of Christina Rossetti's *Remember me when I am gone,* our most urgent, plangent desire - next to immortality itself - is to be remembered:

'Only remember me'

It is a desperate, heartfelt desire, based on the worth we place on our own existence; the impact of our having lived. But why should, and how can, this crowded, hyper-fast-moving world remember anyone but for the briefest time, when that life force is spent; when we are no longer here to say 'yea' or 'nay'?

And given the inevitability, why do we grieve? Do we grieve for the life that is lost? Do we grieve for the love that is lost? Or do we grieve for the loss that *we* have sustained? Surely, for all of these reasons, and more. And is our grief tinged with regret, or guilt, or relief, as well as sorrow?

How you choose to respond to the loss of a best friend - your pet boy or girl - and how you rise to this appalling 'event', may offer some insights into your own legacy, your own memorial. In the final analysis, it will be for others - your own loved ones - as here it is for you - to take responsibility, and to treasure the remembrance of a precious flame.

The moment and experience of loss is shot through with a charge of adrenaline compounded in shock. The seismic nature of this 'experience' sustains - or numbs - us for a short while. Then, as the weeks and months pass, these natural emergency defences can no longer be sustained. There is no comfort. There is no consolation. These crumbling defences are replaced with an inevitable but horrible grief, an endless emptiness; an aching sense of irreplaceable loss. There may be a sense of desperation, a deep need to re-unite; but we are on either side of an unbridgeable divide.

This grief will never be totally expunged - why should it be? - though the nature of it will change. It is said that human beings grieve for close relatives for between 12 and 18 months. This is a materialistic view, based on the notion of human beings as rational machines that eventually adjust and 'move on'. Similar time-scales have been suggested for our grieving for a beloved pet. It's a fair point, and intended kindly, and helpfully. But the sentient being has no defence, no resilience, against the loss of a friend so greatly loving, and so greatly loved.

I only know that grieving for one's pet may take much longer than the time-spans suggested, and perhaps may never truly be over. This may sound selfish, self-indulgent, even silly, to some. I call it real, though it does not, need not, prevent the continuance of life, particularly life that is determinedly good, and, in some ways, lived better than before. That is surely the best tribute you can pay to your (physically) absent friend.

Sharing Jason's and Hector's lives made me a better person, a more compassionate person, and a more complete human being. Without them, I am diminished; not their responsibility, but proof of the extraordinary dimension, the love and thrill that they brought to our lives.

So you will never truly 'get over it'. You have to endure it, and you have to remember with pride; and the love will go forward with you, and the life-force will go on, stronger than death. The presence, the physicality may be missing, except in the mind's eye, but the spirit remains: in you, with you, beside you. Expressions of condolence from people you respect *do* help, in acknowledging not only your loss, but the worth of what has been lost. Sometimes, surprisingly, even people you were only vaguely aware of walk up to you, and tenderly express their sympathy. I always responded to such kindness with sincere gratitude.

One near-neighbour enquired about the loss of Jason, then shook his head in sympathy: "*I can imagine*", he said. "*No you can't*", I thought, but thank you so much for your solicitude. Another man, a good-hearted fellow dog-walker, told me proudly: "*They're the most handsome retrievers I've ever seen*". Many thanks indeed. An elderly lady confidentially informed me: "*I cried more when I lost my dog than when I lost the old man*". Another elderly lady enquired whether "*you will be getting another*". I replied gently that, just like a husband or wife, a beloved pet cannot be replaced. She responded by pointing out that, in many cases the missing partner was 'replaced' "*within weeks*". In truth, it brought a smile to my face.

There is much poetry, and much art, on this perennially powerful matter: the tension, the agony, surrounding Love and Death. Can love ever succeed, ever triumph, over death? Can it be so? Or, in our abject misery and desire that it should be so, do we merely convince ourselves that it can be so? Imagine, if you dare: you have lost the most beautiful, devoted, gentle, woman in the world - or perhaps the most handsome, devoted and gentle man. Grief is the visceral reflection of love. What to do, in your agony? To succumb to loss, curling up in bed and hoping to die? Or grieve, and commit to good works for the rest of your days? To suffer, silently, guilt and regret? To press on in a whirlwind of activity? Or search the universe for one (almost) equally beautiful, devoted and good?

And so with a beloved pet. The grief, and the emotions, are comparable. We can love the friends that remain, even more than before. We can honour one's absent companion by adopting another - but not a replacement - boy or girl. We can create a memorial, a shrine, a lasting legacy. We can use our energy and strength of purpose to achieve some permanent good - for human beings in distress, for homeless dogs and cats, or to help ensure the diversity and permanence of nature. We can do all of these things - and more, in continuous praise for the ones we love.

When, ultimately, dog owners lose their cherished friends, many retreat into the privacy of their homes, to grieve in peace. One may not see them again, ever, or perhaps six months later - in the company of a bouncy new friend. Others determinedly continue their routine, desiring to remember through the familiarity of shared walks, and refusing to allow their loss to subdue the spirit, or to undo the past. When meeting such colleagues, they are often eager - and brave - to share their experience, to remember their loved one and the experience of the last days, the final illness, and to discuss their future plans. It is as though only fellow dog carers will understand, empathise and share in the loss of a unique boy or girl, while the rest of the world seems to move carelessly, remorselessly on - as indeed it does.

As with people (sometimes) so with dogs. Is the very thought of a new dog an act of treachery, or conferring an honour on the memory of your lost treasure? We're all different, with different needs, views, values. Each person must take their own counsel, make their own best decision. You will not be honouring your lost friend the less if you decide to bring another companion into your life, to give another boy or girl the chance - the certainty - of happiness. But, if you decide to be content with your love, which still burns bright, and to honour that memory exclusively, that, too, should be respected - and applauded.

I have sometimes been puzzled when seeing, over the space of 20 years or more, increasingly grizzled old chaps, out walking their charges; often these will be a West Highland Terrier, or a Jack Russell. They're usually called Ben or Mitch. I've marvelled at the longevity of these dogs. Then, in casual conversation, it emerges that, in fact, Ben is actually Ben III - the third such dog in the line. The pet in question may be a living reminder of Ben I or Ben II, sharing the breed characteristics, or may even be a descendant or relative - daughter, grandson or grand-nephew - of the earlier pets. Either way, the practice provides a touching example of the power of familiarity, affection and shared experience. They simply can't live without Ben, his memory enshrined in the physical *actualité* of... Ben.

There is also what I call the clone factor, where dog carers will acquire a new, young, look-alike dog as a companion to an ageing companion. Through this process, the dog owner knows that he will never face the future alone, but will always have the immediate comfort of a dog, that looks, and possibly shares, similar characteristics to the one he has lost. It may not be perfect but, if it works for some, that's good enough for me.

There is a special camaraderie amongst those folks who share a particular breed. To re-connect with life, with the familiar, with the empathetic - dogs of similar temperament, and distant cousins - is a real tonic. I am always touched by these simple human gestures. As human beings, we need to connect much more than we do, and dogs can provide a welcome means of levering shared experience.

When I lost Hector & Jason, every day I would echo Caliban's poignant cry to lost perfection:

'Be not afeard. The isle is full of noises,
Sounds, and sweet airs that give delight and hurt not.
Sometimes a thousand twangling instruments
Will hum about mine ears, and sometime voices
That, if I then had waked after long sleep,
Will make me sleep again. And then, in dreaming,
The clouds methought would open and show riches
Ready to drop upon me, that when I waked
I cried to dream again'.

In practical terms, what can we do to ease this torment? And should we even try?

These are very personal decisions. I would only say - *do something* - something of which you will be forever proud, and which will, if anything, enhance your love, and the memory of your loved one.

Treasure photographs and video film. Cherish their lead and collar. We still have the boys' first, teething toys - their practically indestructible Nylabones. And you could write a memoir, or crystallise memory into a poem. You can light a candle, every day, every week, or on special occasions. You can commission a painting. You can frame a favourite picture, or create a dedicated photo album. You can celebrate the birthday of your pet, or the anniversary of your first meeting.

There are so many decent, honourable, good things you can do to commemorate your friend, and to project their memory into the future. You can support a charity - perhaps a charity that reflects the character of your friend. You can leave a legacy to a charity in your will. You can create a charitable trust, which can continue doing good deeds long, long into the future. You can do a good deed - preferably a series of good deeds.

You might plant a tree in your garden, or in a woodland managed by your local Wildlife Trust, or the Woodland Trust. Dogs and trees are a happy combination, and an oak tree - and its own progeny - can live forever. An ancient oak near to our home in Normandy is over 500 years old. If you bury your friend's ashes when planting the tree, a certain type of immortality is assured. Or, in a marvellous scheme run by Dogs Trust, you could even adopt a canine friend. There are pet cemeteries where your loved one can be remembered. Or a memorial in your own garden. A candle-light vigil to remember his birth, each year. And a 'memories' evening, with suitable prayers and poetry.

Presenting framed photos of your pet to your 'nearest and dearest', recalling happy times, is another way of ensuring that treasured memories remain alive: these small gifts will celebrate your friends' and relatives' connection to the lives of (you and) your loved one. This is not just about the past: it is fresh, living, real.

A theme of mine was to buy (investment) shares in the memory of Hector & Jason. For Jason, the shares were called 'Perpetual' - as fitting as could be. For Hector, the shares began with the word 'Rothschild', again perfectly fitting. If you go down this route, it is important to acquire shares that will (hopefully) gain in value over time, and that will still be around for the very long term. Every time I look at these shares I think of my boys. Because the shares are bought in their honour, the income gained can be put to the best possible use, to a favourite charity, or trust.

I once read about a guy who bought shares in the name of his dog, which appreciated over time. Eventually, the pet died, but the value of the investment, with income rolled up, continued to grow and grow. Of course, these shares could not be sold or unlocked, so they will continue to grow forever, like a star spinning through the Universe. A nice story: but H&J's shares can be employed as a force for good, and permanently.

So we have committed to many of these things, and more. I treasure the two maple leaves that I collected on Hector's 14th birthday - one for Hector, the other for Jason. The more you do, the more pleasure you will derive. Life should lead to goodness, to gifts and rejoicing.

And at the micro level, that of real, physical imprint, the impact of Hector's early anxiety is still with us; the deep etching of his claws into the kitchen floor tiles in France is a permanent reminder of the youthful, exuberant boy. As is the stone that Hector managed to swallow, all those years ago - a reminder of his youthful madness. And I continue to hear Jason's deep, resonant bark, even as I write.

John Keats wrote:

> 'WHAT can I do to drive away
> Remembrance from my eyes? for they have seen,
> Aye, [but] an hour ago, my brilliant Queen!
> Touch has a memory. O say, love, say,
> What can I do to kill it and be free
> In my old liberty?'

Touch does indeed have a memory. My fingers still feel the tenderness, the frisson of Jason's extraordinary, fine coat, along his rippling frame.

Some traditional societies attach far greater importance to the past than to the future. What, indeed, is 'the future'? A hope? A prospect? Potential? An illusion? But the past is real. It is vast, intricate with people and place, an almost infinite storyboard of lives, adventures, exploits - of our families, of those we love, of our younger selves. Hector & Jason are ever beside me in that past - that present.

I continue to believe that the force of life, and renewal, is stronger than death. At the same time, as a non-believer, I cannot accept that death is 'nothing at all'; it is viscerally real and painful. But, assuming that Heaven exists, is there room there for my innocent dogs? *'In my father's house there are many dwelling places'*. I suspect there is not room enough, in the conventional mind-set. The Book of Revelation thunders: *'Outside are the dogs and wizards, and the sexually immoral and murderers and idolaters'*. And yet I feel that Jason - & Hector - will always be alive, not just in memory but in spirit. They that have been here, are here, and will always be here.

And a strange thing did happen, shortly after we lost Hector. Early on the morning of Saturday, 2 March (2013) I was lying in bed, half-awake, when I heard Hector's bark - just once. My whole body tensed. What was that? Had I been dreaming? Was it a neighbour's dog? Was I mistaken? Five minutes later there was a second bark - distinctively Hector, and emanating from downstairs.

Then, on Monday 4 March, again lying in bed, but fully awake, I again heard the bark. This time, I was thrilled. June heard it, too. Don't look to me for explanation - I have none - but I heard what I heard, and was glad:

'Fled is that music - do I wake or sleep?'

Genetics is a mysterious, wonderful, mind-numbing phenomenon. So there may never be another Hector: his mix of spirit, guile, loyalty and independence was a pretty unique blend. There will never be another Jason: unless serried ranks of chimpanzees, randomly tapping zillions of characters into their Apple Macs, suddenly re-create *Hamlet*. Go to it, guys.

And, just as there are trillions of stars in billions of galaxies, so there are numberless planets orbiting these suns. How likely is it that there are countless planets like our own, with advanced life forms leading civilised lives? The richness of possibility is endless. Indeed, so vast are the possibilities, how likely is it that there is a being on one of these planets, typing the exact same words as I? And, if this may be the case, there may well be a Hector, and a Jason, playing happily in a sunlit garden.

The bottom line is that we had all - June & I, Hector & Jason - particularly Hector & Jason - all delivered. The promise of their lives was secured. Their destiny had been fulfilled. And like a few, very few, gifted people I have known, Hector & Jason made everyone around them feel special. That must be their legacy.

And Hector and Jason are with me, wherever I go, in everything I do, in everything I am; in every thought, movement, and action. They are within me, beside me, have become part of me...

I think of you each day
And know you think of me:
Of the great days that stay
Enshrined in memory;
Seductive days, sun-swathed,
And days that are yet to be.

A little while after Hector's bark, I had a dream. And in that dream, God said unto me: "*My ME, that Hector is a deep one! As for Jason, well, it's a good thing this place has no boundaries...!*"

******

Our cat Louis had an instant and life-long devotion to both the boys, a devotion which was reciprocated. A year or two after the loss of their companions, Louis, Oliver and Lenny would fulfil their destiny and undertake the hazardous journey to France: in a silver car, on a silver ship, on a silver sea...to see and experience for themselves. At once, they found, and *knew*; they knew the vibe, and were happier than I ever remembered them to be. Louis Quatorze, Richard (Lenny) Coeur de Lion, and Crusader Oliver had at last found their temporal - and spiritual - home.

And somehow, I knew that they knew, that Hector & Jason were in the cottage, part of the living, breathing fabric of the place...

You do not know me
But I am known
In those dreams, so rich, so rare,
And wild adventures everywhere.

You do not hear me,
But I am here,
On the path towards your lair:
I am the light that leads you there.

You do not see me,
But I am seen:
I am the wind that ruffs your hair,
The muffled tread upon the stair.

You will not love me;
Yet our strange love
Burns brighter than a solar flare:
None can equate, and none compare.

29: IMMORTAL IMPRESSION

You think dogs will not be in heaven? I tell you, they will be there long before us.

Robert Louis Stevenson

I think God will have prepared everything for our perfect happiness. If it takes my dog being there [in Heaven], I believe he'll be there.

Rev. Billy Graham

The dog is the most faithful of animals and would be much esteemed were it not so common. Our Lord God has made his greatest gift the commonest.

Martin Luther

If there is no God for thee
Then there is no God for me.

Anna Hempstead Branch

Dogs don't know about beginnings, and they don't speculate on matters that occurred before their time. Dogs also don't know—or at least don't accept—the concept of death. With no concept of beginnings or endings dogs probably don't know that for people having a dog as a life companion provides a streak of light between two eternities of darkness.

Stanley Coren

If we were to assemble a representative council of fellow citizens, and task them with advising on the most important goals of human existence, they might reply, with due gravitas: the pursuit of prosperity; or the pursuit of fame and power; or the search for love and friendship.

Ask the same august body what were the most important goals for our humble canine companions, and they would most likely suggest: food; shelter; sex and procreation; companionship; play. Yet those goals are primary human concerns, too.

After the satisfaction of basic and intrinsic needs, I would submit that the fulfilment of individual potential, in all its forms, is the greatest single imperative. The true expression of one's talent and abilities, to their highest degree, must surely be life's greatest object. Those individuals whom we celebrate, those we remember, strove to achieve the maximum possible, rather than slide by on the minimum. Do we know how much money Elvis Presley left behind? Do we care? Does Roger Federer play tennis in order to be famous, or is fame the consequence of his majestic talent? Can a tiger in a zoo fulfil its potential? Or an eagle in an aviary?

Again, no-one would deny the central importance of love, but we do not pursue it for its own sake; we are loved for who we are, for what we are, and we in turn give love on those terms. The great 'Romantic Poets' - Wordsworth, Coleridge, Byron, Shelley, Keats - continue to be read not just because they are required reading, or even because of their subject matter; or because they desired fame and fortune (though they did), but because of their indefatigable striving to combine the most noble thought and emotion in the most exquisite forms.

"I have left no immortal work behind me - nothing to make my friends proud of my memory - but I have lov'd the principle of beauty in all things, and if I had had time I would have made myself remember'd.". So wrote John Keats in February 1820. It is a cry from the heart. He had a year yet to live - though a year of physical pain and psychological despair. His words remain painful to read. His personal anguish was real enough; yet his astonishing body of work - despite his death at the age of 25 years - remains immortal in the pantheon of English poetry.

Even more surely, Mozart is immortal; Jane Austen is immortal. Although strikingly different people, with different lives and a different genius - and whilst their mortal lives over-lapped - to enter their worlds is, in either case, to engage with a sublime, timeless spirit. Although almost unknown in her own life-time, beyond her immediate, intimate circle, you don't have to be a 'Janeite' to feel that you are communing - still - with an acute sensibility, a distinctive 'voice', penetrating the ether.

Or a Mozart-fetishist to feel that the great operas, piano concertos and string quintets continue to express the most profound human truths, in a glorious, eternal language.

And there are some who are immortal purely by association: the singer, Nancy Storace, (born in London to an English mother and Neapolitan father) who 'starred' in the first production of *The Marriage of Figaro*. When we watch and hear again the unfolding miracle of the opera, be assured that it is the soul, spirit and even sound of Nancy that are present in the heroine, Susanna - a part written for the 21 year-old soprano. When Mme Storace departed Vienna for London early in 1787, Mozart's parting gift was the *Scena con Rondo - 'That I should forget you?';* its ravishing strains remain as luminous now as when composed in December, 1786.

Similarly immortal, Mozart's fellow Mason and financial saviour, Michael Puchberg. Even the Mozarts' dog, Gauckerl, (who accompanied Wolfgang and his wife Constanze on their triumphant tour by carriage to Prague in January 1789), has a small but unassailable place in history. The self-important Archbishop Colloredo, of Salzburg, meanwhile, remains fixed in the collective memory, like an insect encased in amber, simply because, in dismissing his 'servant', Mozart, he kicked the young composer down the stairs. Immortal, too - but in the most positive possible sense - are Cassandra Austen, Keats' steadfast friend Joseph Severn, and Emma Hamilton, (George Romney's muse, and Nelson's beloved) to name but a scattering of stars who beamed upon, as well as reflect, eternally shining suns.

These relatively few exceptions to our notion of mortality only prove the rule: just as Mozart will live for ever, through his music, so will Bach. And Beethoven. So will Michelangelo; and Rembrandt. Of course, John Keats. So, perhaps, will Pelé, or Ali, though I concede that sporting genius lives in the moment, in the memory, and in the (evidential) record. All of these exemplars achieved their true, their ultimate potential, through the furious exercise, practise, and revelation, of their innate genius.

So I return to Hector and Jason. They needed all the conventional stuff - food, water, shelter, friendship, love. But, as with human beings, the reality is more complex and more profound: June and I recognised from an early stage that we must allow them, encourage them, even, to realize *their* potential. Therein lies fulfilment, and happiness. I am proud that, despite the risks and the anxiety, their potential flourished and flowered, so that we can continue to celebrate Hector's heart, and Jason's spirit.

Is that it? If immortality lies merely in the direct remembrance by others - perhaps on a birthday, or an anniversary - then it wouldn't amount to much more than a candle in the wind - soon extinguished. The connection grows more and more tenuous - less and less real: a shadow, the shadow of a shadow. A name, dates; a half remembered story, garbled in the telling. A curiosity; a little amusement or winsomeness, a smidgeon of sentiment; a question, vaguely answered.

Our greatest writer, living more than 400 years ago has, arguably, left too little of life's traces and travails behind, despite a life lived fully, and exhaustive research into his history. However, most obviously, he has left behind a body of work that is unparalleled in it's eviscerating power. Indeed, Shakespeare's 'star' is so bright that it has cast a long shadow over the reputations of even the most brilliant of his contemporaries - including Ben Jonson, Christopher Marlowe, Thomas Kyd, Edmund Spenser, Francis Beaumont and John Fletcher. Such are the vagaries of time, circumstance, and literary fashion.

By contrast, many of us, living in the information-supercharged 21st century, generate so much 'noise' and data on social media sites as to apparently create a major imprint, that appears to stride confidently towards the abyss. However, we may find, even if technology remains constant, (and assuredly it will not) that the sandstorm blowing across this footprint will obliterate it soon enough, leaving not a jot behind. Shakespeare himself knew this, as in *Macbeth*: *"It* (life) *is a tale, told by an idiot: full of sound and fury, signifying nothing"*. D. H. Lawrence, too, in *The Ship of Death*: *'The voyage of oblivion awaits you'*.

Yet the notion of immortality fights back, and takes many forms. We like to think that immortality is bestowed by genetic transfer, or reproduction, through our children, and our children's children. This genetic immortality is expressed, in a sense, through one's off-spring, who will look out on the future with something approaching your own eyes. Similarly with dogs, since no dog can continue the same life forever. Even Maggie, a lovable Australian kelpie, and the world's oldest dog, passed away in April 2016, aged 30 years.

H&J, however, had no offspring. It is not only that they showed no interest whatsoever in the opposite sex; breeding pedigree dogs is all about dog shows, rosettes and awards, apparently as a means of ensuring and maintaining the standard, character, trueness and good health of particular breeds.

But I have no doubt that some of H&J's brothers and sisters will have had progeny; certainly their father, and probably their mother, Jess, too. So their genes, and some of their characteristics, will live on. That forward-moving life-force gives me a degree of comfort. However, even natural reproduction has its limitations: gilded attributes are diluted, softened, flattened, through the generations, until they merge into the plodding and pedestrian.

Yet there is also the immortality of personal or family remembrance that filters through the generations. Or immortality enshrined in a memorial to an individual, and their life and times, that inspires memory, affection, or gratitude.

And eternity may be perceived, as well as the genetic 'real'. If you were to strap me in to an uncomfortable chair and force me to watch motor racing, or participate in an interminable game of Monopoly, or perhaps view 'soaps' until the crack of doom, *that* would indeed seem like eternity - though not of the highest quality. It reminds me of Mark Twain's response when asked where he wanted to die - "*Wolverhampton*".

And there is the immortality forged in the white heat of creative flux, so that:

> '...*thy eternal Summer shall not fade*
> *Nor lose possession of that faire thou ow'st,*
> *Nor shall death brag thou wand'rest in his shade,*
> *When in eternal lines to time thou grow'st:*
> *So long as men can breath or eyes can see,*
> *So long lives this, and this gives life to thee.*'

There is also the immortality derived from being a vital atom on a planet, spinning in time and space. There is the immortality of the soul, imperishable and indestructible. And the immortality of making an indelible impression on the Universe.

How real is this view of immortality? Is it mere fancy, or conjecture, or hope, or desperation, or wishful thinking, or whistling in the dark? Is there any real sense in which Hector & Jason were - are - immortal? I hope and believe so. H&J created an unforgettable impact. We never truly get over the loss of a loved one; it becomes part of us, absorbed into our DNA. They will live on in our memory, in the collective memory, and will continue to live in our hearts, until those hearts stop beating.

Jason's life on this planet of ours spanned fifteen calendar years; Hector's, sixteen calendar years. Are those years now gone, and of no account? Take the last decade of your life. Are these years now completely finished, complete, exhausted, dead? Or are they still connected with the still-living you, by influence, by memory, by blood; shaping and still connecting you to the present, and the future? Surely, the past still reverberates in the here and now, and for all time? Just as surely, every life is immortal, since it has been lived, and in that dimension, continues.

Heaven has been described as '*Pie in the sky when you die*'. But we now know that the Earth, and everything in it, is composed of elements derived from dying stars; we are stardust, and our living matter is continuously recycled. This as is true for H&J as for all of us: their indestructible atoms will be endlessly transformed into new structures and life forms, for the rest of time. That may sound trite, or mind-boggling, but it is also true. Hector was earth, and Jason pure spirit. They are both immortal diamonds.

Plato argued strongly in *The Republic* that the soul is immortal. He states that the soul '*must exist for ever; that is to say, it is immortal*'. For Plato, the soul has always existed, and will continue to exist, though it will assume various physical forms (hence Shakespeare's quip, through Malvolio, in *Twelfth Night*, '*that the soul of our grandam, might haply inhabit a bird*'), though here Shakespeare quotes Pythagoras as the philosopher in question. For me, it's a powerful argument, that does not require conventional religion to support it, to give it meaning or validity:

'*This at any rate is my advice, that we should believe the soul to be immortal, capable of enduring all evil and all good, and always keep our feet on the upward way and pursue justice and reason. So we shall be at peace with God and with ourselves, both in our life here and when, like the victors in the games collecting their prizes, we receive our reward, and both in this life and the thousand year journey which I have described all will be well with us.*'

In the more worldly 17ᵗʰ century, in an urgent plea *To His Coy Mistress*, Andrew Marvell was inspired to write:

'*But at my back I always hear
Times winged Chariot hurrying near:*

> *And yonder all before us lye*
> *Desarts of vast eternity.'*

After this fearsome utterance on eternal oblivion, a note of (no doubt self-serving) optimism intrudes, as a final clincher to woo (or at least persuade) his equivocating lady:

> *'Thus, though we cannot make our Sun*
> *Stand still, yet we will make him run.'*

If the worldly-wise Marvell strikes a note of heroic desperation, the Brontë sisters viewed life very differently. Charlotte, Emily and Anne - who never ceased to be young - never ceased to be absorbed with the idea of immortality. Death must have seemed to be all around, pressing, and omni-present, claiming their mother and, particularly, their two older sisters at horribly young ages. One form of immortality was to be found in writing: in December 1836, though unworldly, and unknown to the world, the aspiring Charlotte wrote to the Poet Laureate Robert Southey that she wanted no less than *"to be for ever known"*.

In a remarkable series of poems, Anne Brontë explored the concept of immortal life. In *Farewell to thee* the (departed) loved one's continued presence is manifest - made real, and whole - by the fusion of memory and continued love:

> *'Farewell to thee! But not farewell*
> *To all my fondest thoughts of thee:*
> *Within my heart they still shall dwell;*
> *And they shall cheer and comfort me.'*

In *A Reminiscence*, Anne seems to take a step further:

> *'Yet, though I cannot see thee more,*
> *'Tis still a comfort to have seen;*
> *And though thy transient life is o'er,*
> *'Tis sweet to think that thou hast been.'*

Here, it seems that the life, though over, has left a residual energy. Immortality rests not merely on the comfort of memory, but on a realisation that the life is somehow irreducible, because *'thou hast been'*.

In the austerely titled *Severed and Gone*, Anne Brontë transforms the base metal of memory, and even the silver of the always-lived life, into the pure gold of immortality:

'Life seems more sweet that thou didst live
And men more true that Thou wert one;
Nothing is lost that Thou didst give,
Nothing destroyed that Thou hadst done.'

What is done, cannot be undone. This is not dependent on memory. What is achieved, is secure; the heroic giving, and achieving - doing - cannot be wiped clean from the face of time and history, but must remain irreducible - because it happened. These poems were composed following the death, in September 1842, of William Weightman, an engaging, perhaps inspiring, young curate, and dear friend of the young writer. Weightman had contracted cholera, through having dutifully, and bravely, visited his sick parishioners.

As it happens, Anne Brontë owned a dog called Flossy, to whom she was devoted. Her sister Emily had a fierce love for her huge bulldog-mastiff, Keeper. Each day, Emily and Anne would place their half-finished porridge on the kitchen floor, to be devoured by the expectant Flossy and Keeper. In 1843, homesick and miserable in Brussels, Charlotte wrote to Emily that, compared to her situation as student and teacher at the 'Pensionnat' she would prefer even to be cooking hash at home at Howarth, where she would *save the best pieces of the leg of mutton for Tiger* (cat) *and Keeper; the first of which personages would be jumping about the dish and carving knife, and the latter standing like a devouring flame on the kitchen floor...How divine are these recollections to me at this moment!'*.

The dogs would accompany the sisters on their long walks over the wild, wind-swept moors, so familiar to readers of *Wuthering Heights*. When Emily became seriously ill, Keeper kept watch by her bedside. When she died in December 1848, aged only 30 years, Keeper was inconsolable, and howled outside her bedroom door. He would later follow the coffin of his mistress, on its journey to the churchyard. In turn, when the now enfeebled Keeper himself died in old age, three years later, Charlotte Brontë records that *'he went gently to sleep, we laid his old faithful head in the garden. Flossy...is dull, and misses him'*.

Anne, the youngest of the Brontë sisters, was herself to succumb to consumption in May, 1849, at the tender age of 29 years. She bore her illness with immense fortitude: Anne Brontë's poignant poetry continues to ring with an eternal truth.

In the words of John Clare's *An Invite to Eternity* '*past and present all as one...we're wed to one eternity*', As if that were not enough, the Brontë sisters' desires were amply fulfilled: they became immortal through their prose and poetry. Each time someone reads *Wuthering Heights* or *Jane Eyre*, that immortality is refreshed, through contact with the unique force of their creators, and through familiarity with the personalities of Charlotte, Anne, and Emily, most notably, in *Shirley;* thinly disguised, they yet inhabit these pages.

I've recently taken up violin studies. I've never before played a musical instrument, and 'played' is probably too strong a word for the sound that I wring from the instrument. But it will get better; and every note, every expression, is my song of gratitude for my own immortal heroes, Hector & Jason. And these are my hard-fought for words:

Immortal Vibes

Sept billion preening people, prattle on,
Careless of each flickering hour, each blood-soaked sun.
Time partners every life, but when each race is run
Time stands astride the finish line, alone. Alone.
The bell it tolls for thee, blithe spirit, tolls for thee
Through 'paint' and artifice, and cunning surgery;
Through champagne calendars, air-kisses, flummery:
The bell it tolls for thee, lithe spirit, tolls for thee.
I am the keeper of the flame
The rock on which remembrance laps
The cup that sacred spirit charges new
The watch whose every vigil keeps.
'Immortal'. A word. A hope. A fervent prayer.
A wish. A vanity. A desperate dare.
An ache. A thread that's frayed. An empty place.
A memr'y. An inner cry. A silent space.
A meditation, that time, and love, may prove;
A paean to the power of love, to move.
But at the end of day, a double death:
An end to sentient and hopeful breath.
An end to everything, 'cept agony and care,
Though thought may burn and rage with wear -

And memory will shed a soft-soothed tear:
Yet - through eternity - stardust, everywhere.

In our local woods, lovers' names are often carved on the trunks of trees: *"I love Lucy"*, or Emma, or Tamara. These incisions, these messages, will undoubtedly stand the test of time; many will outlive the passions which inspired them. Still, they are hardly immortal, and give great offence to the noble trees themselves, by defacing their beauty. In *As You Like It* - a play with a strong environmental theme - Shakespeare writes:

'*There is a man haunts the forest, that abuses our young plants with carving 'Rosamund' on their barks...*'

H&J caused no offence - or abuse: their shades have passed this way, and will pass this way for all time.

We now know that time is not a constant; that the certainty, comfort, even, of the ticking clock, is somewhat illusory. Even in our everyday experience, one hour or period of time seems to be elongated, or shortened, depending on the type and quality of our activity. But there were times, with H&J, when the searing intensity of activity seems to have given certain experiences a shimmering life of their own, and somehow removed them from 'normal' time. In the long annals of planet Earth, the memory of your dog is assured. If you yourself forget, then you have lost a part of yourself.

There are 3,000 billion galaxies in the observable Universe, each containing between a mere few million to over a trillion stars. To step out of doors on any warm Normandy evening is to be enveloped by the deep black sky, and its zillions of stars. And I say again: all that power. All that unimaginable power.

And there is one star in especial that I seek out; it shines more brightly than any other, and seems to beam down directly upon us, glinting its majestic presence. This is Sirius: deliciously, the Dog Star. Through this act of history, the Dog Star is the brightest star in the firmament. It is, perhaps, Keats' *Bright Star*. How utterly fitting.

Their own star will bathe Hector & Jason in celestial light for all eternity. Again, the scene recalls those lines from Blake's *The Tyger*, which will always have a special place in my heart.

During our long Summers in France, I experienced the intense pleasure of reading some of Dickens's greatest novels: *David Copperfield, Bleak House, Little Dorrit*. All human life is contained in these pages, peopled with unforgettable characters, an infinity of humanity, and life in all its aspects. Hector & Jason, with their distinctive personalities, could even be characters in these fantastic artistic confections masquerading as reality. H&J would lie beside me, under the gazebo, as I read quietly - my mind gasping at the writer's daring, innovation, astonishing creativity and humanity. I will continue this tradition; in the knowledge that every time I open a page, H&J are with me, not only by association, but in memory and reflection on every line of text.

In our little lives, if we are lucky, we will experience a maximum of 1.5 billion heartbeats. We leave a shallow impression with our lives, and that impression may soon be erased. For me, that carries a responsibility to do useful things - to do a little good, where possible, to make a beneficial impact. Quite simply, H&J have inspired us to do more, to give more, to help more, to love more. June has long been a keen supporter of Dogs Trust. And now we have The Spirit of Jason Trust, and Heart of Hector Trust, to which any proceeds from this book will be directed. Good has come from their lives, and will continue indefinitely.

In a modest way, I hope that this book, too, and its photographs, provide a gentle reminder to a restless and careless world of the wonders that were, and are, Hector & Jason. Jason will always *be,* leading his brother on wild wanderings across the Universe. And their unique timbre will echo through space and time for ever.

For ages after I lost him, the singular youth of the area would greet me with: *"Hector! Hector!"* each time our paths crossed. A case of the immortal gracing the lips of the immutable. Out of the mouths of babes and sucklings...

Hector & Jason are forever young. They are, for ever, one with the Universe.

No-one expresses this more vividly than Emily Brontë, in evoking eternity:

'When I am not and none beside -
Nor earth nor sea nor cloudless sky -
But only spirit wandering wide
Through infinite immensity.'

And so, now, welcome - Bright Star Henry.

30: Cats and Dogs: Poetry and Prose?

I have found that when you are deeply troubled, there are things you get from the silent devoted companionship of a dog that you can get from no other source.

Doris Day

My dear old dog, most constant of all friends.

Maria Callas

I have always felt that cats are poetry, and dogs, prose. That cats are poetic - in their sheer feline beauty, their grace, their exquisite personas, can hardly be doubted. The 'big cats' - tigers, leopards, jaguars - are amongst the most iconic of all mammal species. And that dogs are prose - in their loyalty, their honesty, their steadfastness - seems just as true. And, in me at least, cats inspire poetry, while dogs inspire (this) prose.

To illustrate my own predilections, the (groovy), mercurial, dog-loving personality of our Burmese cat, Louis, (pronounced as in The Sun King, Louis XIV), and the legendary jazz artist, Miles Davis, inspired the following confection:

Louis' Land

Welcome to Louis' Land, the place where it's at,
The Club where cat chums blast cool and fast
And Oscar and Ollie play sweetly and sing
Accompanying Louis, the lover of swing.

For Louis on stage is the crème de la crème –
The star in his spotlight, most groovy of men:

A mike in his paw, a swish of his tail
As they eagerly wait his waul and his wail.

His beat is superb and his timing sublime
Mewing through standards of song and of rhyme –
Rogers and Hart, Cole Porter, Berlin –
From 'Stompin' to 'Stardust', reprise 'the Beguine'.

He digs Ella and Duke, and Basie and Miles
And knows their rhythms so well he just smiles
As lights beam and glow, while he taps out the beat
Of 'Chaser' and 'Train', while he piles on the heat.

The audience applauds and cheer where they stand –
Let's hear it for Lou' and his friends in the band!
They bounce through more classics, with brio of youth –
Climaxing with 'So What?' and raising the roof.

Lou' prances and swirls with the beat of the jazz
While his paws deftly move, finessing the brass.
Then round 'bout midnight he croons deep and low:
"Dear ladies and gents, it's the end of the show."

The concert erupts, then embraces the night –
Deep furs shelter eyes still excited and bright:
Impressions long burnished will beam down the years
As they fashion fond tales of Lou' and his peers.

My own proclivities apart, in researching the genre of 'pet poetry', I have certainly found a far wider canon representing cats than dogs. I had thought that this view - cats-poetry, and dogs-prose - might be a purely personal taste. However, the current edition of *Poetry Please* - an anthology of the nation's most requested poetry - contains not a single poem on the theme of dogs, or a dog. Perhaps the 'dog poems' that do exist are just too personal, and not sufficiently universal, in nature. The anthology does, however, contain copious numbers of poems on the theme of cats - and various birds, donkeys, and horses. The same is true of *Palgrave's Golden Treasury*.

Cats seem to have generated a niche - or rich seam - all of their own. Probably the most famous book of poetry on the theme of cats - though there is the lurking suspicion that these cats are all too human - is T.S. Eliot's delightful *Old Possum's Book of Practical Cats*. The book was first published in 1935, and has never been out of print. There is, too, Paul Gallico's superb collection of poems, *Honourable Cat*.

Sadly, I am not aware of any similar, popular, or highly regarded, tome on the theme of dogs. The omission of dog poems in anthologies is not accidental, but the result - for whatever reason - of a paucity of high quality material. The oeuvre of really good dog poetry is indeed a slim volume. T.S. Eliot himself highlighted one possible cause, when he said late in life that *"dogs don't lend themselves to verse quite so well, collectively, as cats"*.

The sheer quality - as well as quantity - of poetry on the theme of cats seems to me far superior to the collective dog *ouevre* - from Christopher Smart's celebration of his cat Jeoffry in *Jubilate Agno* to Thomas Hardy's *Last Words to a Dumb Friend*, written in 1904:

> *'Never another pet for me!*
> *Let your place all vacant be.'*

In parallel with the lives of Hector & Jason, and my enjoyment of them, I wrote a long series of Cat Poems, *Cat Crazy*, celebrating the very cats that H&J knew, and who knew them. Perhaps my favourite is *Eternal Cat*:

Eternal Cat

> *Eternal cat! What god first bore you,*
> *Enjoying her delight in shaping you?*
> *From Pharaoh's halls to Privet Avenue*
> *That sacred soul burns bright and true.*
>
> *Exquisite cat! what stars first awed you*
> *Exploding their rich vaults to welcome you?*
> *From Eastern moons and milk and honey-dew*
> *To English shires, in vibrant, verdant hues.*
>
> *Enduring cat! what man first spied you*
> *Exploring spectral forests, dim to view?*
> *From golden frieze in Fez or Xanadu*
> *To adoration in suburban mews.*

Yet there is nothing in this view that should lead to favouritism, or the idea that cats - or dogs - are somehow 'superior' to each other. There is great poetry - Shakespeare's Sonnets, or Keats's Odes - and there is great prose: Dickens's *Great Expectations,* or Jane Austen's *Emma.* Hector was certainly heroic prose, and I would associate him with Dickens' muscular, witty and staggeringly intelligent creations. Jason is a more difficult case entirely. Ultimately, I associate him with poetry - but a poetry that is strong, pure, passionate, reckless, romantic - Byronesque.

The following poem, written when H&J were young boys, was in fact inspired by our beautiful Burmese boy, Jack. However, on re-reading, it is also pure essence of Jason - expressing his elegance, coolness, and wonderful, deep affection:

Mister Flashman

You came, you saw, you conquered all:
More looks than Valentino
More class than Fred Astaire;
More style than Yves St. Laurent
In his evening wear.

You're Mr Wonderful, you are
Exquisite as a star
More beautiful by far
Than any plane or car.

You gave, you loved, bewitched us all:
More cool than Frank Sinatra
In his swingin' time;
More show than showman Ali
In his showboat prime.

You're Mr Fabulous, you are,
Swingin' on that star;
More beauty in your paw
Than any prince or czar.

You gazed, you spoke, delighted all:
More eloquent than Miles

At midnight on the moon;
More tone than Pavarotti
In Traviata's tunes.

You're Mr Gorgeous boy, you are:
That insouciant charm
Spreads joy like sweetest balm
From opera or psalm.

You came, you loved, amazed us all:
More love than ardent Romeo
Beneath Verona balcony;
True as a Shakespeare sonnet, or
A Mozart symphony.

Mr Adorable, we adore thee -
In all you are, sublime:
Come, wind yourself around me;
Forever, love, be mine.

There are, no doubt, many poems on the theme of dogs, or of a particular dog. But there are not too many well known poems, and very few objectively good poems about dogs, let alone great ones. When I reviewed dog poetry, it was to find that even great writers such as Kipling and Chesterton, and even great poets like Burns and Kipling, were able to write the most maudlin, mawkish, even awkward verse. Even Alexander Pope - whose Argus is quoted in the final Chapter - gives proof that, as far as dog poetry is concerned, even the greatest poets have their dog-days.

This is not a criticism: it reveals how near to the heart, how personal many of these poems are: they are so often not about dogs, but about *the dog* - and the loss of a close friend. The authors are de-stabilised by events: the poems are direct, raw, intense, emotional, touching, heart-rendingly honest. Whilst the profundity and objectivity of great poetry may not be present, one can feel the pain, empathise with the heartbreak.

One of the few, truly high-quality poems *about* a dog was composed by William Wordsworth - *Fidelity*. The artist, Charles Gough, set out on a strenuous Lakeland walk in April 1805, with his dog, Foxie. Gough was never heard of again. Months later, a shepherd heard a dog barking, and discovered Foxie guarding her master's remains. The poem commemorates the dog's steadfast loyalty. (Sir Walter Scott, in his poem, *Helvellyn* celebrates the same event). Although Wordsworth changes the dog's gender, (Foxie gave birth to a pup whilst on the mountain!), this has little effect on the nobility of the sentiment expressed. The last stanza of *Fidelity* sums up the tone of the poem:

> 'Yes, proof was plain that since the day
> On which the Traveller thus had died
> The Dog had watch'd about the spot,
> Or by his Master's side:
> How nourish'd here through such long time
> He knows, who gave that love sublime,
> And gave that strength of feeling, great
> Above all human estimate.'

Sir Walter Scott's poem is similar in tone and sentiment:

> 'Nor yet quite deserted, though lonely extended,
> For, faithful in death, his mute favourite attended,
> The much-loved remains of her master defended,
> And chased the hill-fox and the raven away.'

Both dog poems, though romantic and noble in tone, are at several removes from the author: Foxie did not belong to Wordsworth, or Scott, neither of whom, as far as I am aware, had ever met the dog. In fact, Foxie - who is not named, in either effusion - is not a personality, or an individual, but a stereotype for the best qualities of man's best friend. So no thought is given to the practicalities of how Foxie survived whilst on the mountain for so long, and no mention is given to the awkward fact of her giving birth. Such inconvenient truths are inimical to the romantic's view, purpose and intent.

We have come across the poet Shelley earlier in our story. Shelley's good friend, the brilliant, but notorious, Lord Byron, owned a Newfoundland dog called Boatswain. Unfortunately, Boatswain (pronounced Bosun) contracted the dreaded rabies after having been bitten, and died in 1808. Throughout Boatswain's last illness, Byron nursed his friend, oblivious of the risk to his own life. The famously 'dangerous' poet wrote affectionately that his dog died *retaining all the gentleness of his nature to the end, never attempting to do the least injury to anyone near him*. A large monument to Boatswain's memory was erected at the poet's ancestral home, Newstead Abbey. Inscribed on the monument is the following poem. It's surely one of the finest and most touching of its kind:

Epitaph to a Dog

Near this Spot
are deposited the Remains of one
who possessed Beauty without Vanity,
Strength without Insolence,
Courage without Ferosity,
and all the virtues of Man without his Vices.

This praise, which would be unmeaning Flattery
if inscribed over human Ashes,
is but a just tribute to the Memory of
BOATSWAIN, a DOG,
who was born in Newfoundland May 1803
and died at Newstead Nov. 18, 1808.
When some proud Son of Man returns to Earth,
Unknown to Glory, but upheld by Birth,
The sculptor's art exhausts the pomp of woe,
And storied urns record who rests below.
When all is done, upon the Tomb is seen,
Not what he was, but what he should have been.
But the poor Dog, in life the firmest friend,
The first to welcome, foremost to defend,
Whose honest heart is still his Master's own,
Who labours, fights, lives, breathes for him alone,
Unhonoured falls, unnoticed all his worth,
Denied in heaven the Soul he held on earth –
While man, vain insect! hopes to be forgiven,
And claims himself a sole exclusive heaven.

Oh man! thou feeble tenant of an hour,
Debased by slavery, or corrupt by power –
Who knows thee well must quit thee with disgust,
Degraded mass of animated dust!
Thy love is lust, thy friendship all a cheat,

Thy tongue hypocrisy, thy heart deceit!
By nature vile, ennobled but by name,
Each kindred brute might bid thee blush for shame.
Ye, who behold perchance this simple urn,
Pass on – it honors none you wish to mourn.
To mark a friend's remains these stones arise;
I never knew but one - and here he lies.

The reclusive American poet, Emily Dickinson, loved her Newfoundland, and wrote: *'The dog is the noblest work of Art, sir'*. Nana– also a Newfoundland dog, features in J M Barrie's *Peter Pan*.

The lesson is - if you're a dog and want to be immortalised - make sure you adopt a poet. Yet, my view remains that the most memorable portraits of dogs are in prose fiction - such as Dickens' *David Copperfield* and *Bleak House*. There is ample evidence in his novels that Dickens was a great fan of dogs: witness the characterful Diogenes in *Dombey and Son,* or Dora's devoted Jip, in *David Copperfield*. (Dickens himself owned a menagerie of dogs, which he appears to have doted on). Not so 'Aunt' Jane: Lady Bertram's spoiled pug in *Mansfield Park* is an artistic device, replete with meaning but, like its owner, lacking humanity. Contrast *The Jungle Book*, where Kipling invests the wolf-characters with real characterful feeling: we see the world from their perspective.

Everyman Classics has published a collection of dog stories called, well, *Dog Stories,* a compendium of delightful dog tales told by writers from Chekhov to Chesterton, and Kipling to Mark Twain and P.G. Wodehouse. Kipling's story, *Garm - a Hostage* is possibly the most famous of these stories, but they all make superb reading - poignant, sad, wistful, inspiring. And every one - prose, magnificent prose.

But to return to the poems: the best (personal) poems about their dogs are probably Lord Byron's, and Elizabeth Barrett Browning's - *To Flush, my Dog,* surely one of the truest, and most touching, of the genre, if bordering on the cloying and sentimental. Flush seems to have provided ardent service, in faithful attendance upon his sickly mistress - before she met and was swept away by the poet, Robert Browning. The six stanzas reproduced are from the middle of the 19-stanza piece and, in my view, are the most memorable of the poem:

'Yet, my pretty sportive friend,
Little is 't to such an end
That I praise thy rareness!

Other dogs may be thy peers
Haply in these drooping ears,
      And this glossy fairness.

But of thee it shall be said,
This dog watched beside a bed
      Day and night unweary,--
Watched within a curtained room,
Where no sunbeam brake the gloom
      Round the sick and dreary.

Roses, gathered for a vase,
In that chamber died apace,
      Beam and breeze resigning--
This dog only, waited on,
Knowing that when light is gone,
      Love remains for shining.

Other dogs in thymy dew
Tracked the hares and followed through
      Sunny moor or meadow--
This dog only, crept and crept
Next a languid cheek that slept,
      Sharing in the shadow.

Other dogs of loyal cheer
Bounded at the whistle clear,
      Up the woodside hieing--
This dog only, watched in reach
Of a faintly uttered speech,
      Or a louder sighing.

And if one or two quick tears
Dropped upon his glossy ears,
      Or a sigh came double,-
Up he sprang in eager haste,
Fawning, fondling, breathing fast,
      In a tender trouble.'

Flush is a deeply felt poem, but doesn't usually figure in anthologies of the poetry of Elizabeth Barrett Browning. The reason is simple: touching as it is, as poetry, it simply isn't good enough. Barrett Browning's most notable poem - Sonnet 43 - is powerful indeed, and justly famous. It begins:

> 'How do I love thee? Let me count the ways.
> I love thee to the depth and breadth and height
> My soul can reach, when feeling out of sight....'

The Sonnet was not, however, written for the faithful Flush, but for Miss Barrett's no-doubt equally faithful lover, later husband, Robert Browning. Perhaps it's not too surprising that, at the deepest level, men and women inspire each other to greater poetic heights than they can summon for even a much-loved canine friend. Different her love may have been, but there can be no doubt that Miss Barrett's love for Flush ran madly, deeply: when the cocker spaniel was stolen - 'dognapped' - from the family home at Wimpole Street, and held for ransom, the poet - a delicate figure, and an invalid - braved the dangers of deepest, darkest London to rescue her beloved boy.

To return to prose. Taking up the theme of Flush, Virginia Woolf, herself a noted dog-lover, wrote a novel - *Flush - a Biography*, purporting to tell the life of the pet dog, through its own eyes. Published in 1933, *Flush* was an instant best-seller. It has since been almost entirely forgotten. I suspect that there's an element of intellectual snobbery about this, since the novel is touchingly, beautifully written; a kind of *Black Beauty* for dogs.

On 29 October, 1940, Virginia Woolf noted in her diary that their dog, Sally was an *'old fine trusty crone'*. Sally was to outlive her mistress. Only five months following that diary entry, on 29 March 1941, Virginia Woolf took her own life. Immortalised by great novels such as *The Years* the author was laid low in sustaining the terrific creative energies demanded by her muse.

Finally, we return to Thomas Hardy. In December 1913, Hardy, along with his soon-to-be new wife, Florence Dugdale, acquired Wessex, a rough haired terrier. (So much for *'Never another pet for me...'*). Both Hardy and Florence doted on and indulged Wessex, even feeding him from the table. Meanwhile, the errant dog terrorised the neighbourhood. Says Hardy's biographer, Claire Tomalin, disapprovingly: *'They indulged him in every way, like a delicate, delinquent child, and he behaved accordingly'*. Wessex eventually died on 27 December, 1926. He was deeply mourned by the Hardy's at his passing.

Hardy wrote the following poem in commemoration of Wessex. Since Hardy was born on 2 June 1840, the poem was written well into the poet's 87th year. The poem is deceptively simple in construction: poignant, yet free of sentimentality. The verse expresses, exposes, a chasm in Hardy's life, as well as alluding to Wessex's own indomitable nature. Written in the (dog's) first person, it also offers the intriguing possibility - despite the poem's insistent denial - that Wessex is still 'out there' somewhere:

Dead 'Wessex' the Dog to the Household

Do you think of me at all,
Wistful ones?
Do you think of me at all
As if nigh?

Do you think of me at all
At the creep of evenfall
Or when the sky-birds call
As they fly?

Do you look for me at times,
Wistful ones?
Do you look for me at times
Strained and still?

Do you look for me at times,
When the hour for walking chimes,
On that grassy path that climbs
Up the hill?

You may hear a jump or trot,
Wistful ones,
You may hear a jump or trot -
Mine, as 'twere -

You may hear a jump or trot
On the stair or path or plot;

But I shall cause it not,
Be not there.

Should you call as when I knew you,
Wistful ones,
Should you call as when I knew you,
Shared your home;

Should you call as when I knew you,
I shall not turn to view you,
I shall not listen to you,
Shall not come.'

My youngest brother, though never a natural bedfellow to poetry, was nonetheless inspired by contemplation of his lady-love to a poetic effusion. Having declaimed the said verse from a fragrant sheet of vellum, he promptly fell asleep, no doubt overcome by the emotional sensibility of the moment. Hector, also never a bedfellow to the poetic muse, took the copy from the prostrate grasp, and promptly ate it. The action was quintessential Hector - pure, muscular prose. Jason could never have contemplated such an act. Of all and any dog I have ever known, Jason was poetry, pure and simple.

Since this book is written for, about, and dedicated to, Hector & Jason, I must end with two poems dedicated to them: *Prayer for J,* written 200 days following the loss of the incomparable Jason; *Hector: Bravest of the Brave,* written shortly after we lost that mighty boy.

I hope the poems speak eloquently for themselves.

These are my small memorials to these passionate brothers, my fabulous, unforgettable boys.

Beginning with Jason:

Prayer for J:

Lord, at this journey's end
I lay my son before thee.

I thank thee for the life
He lived so fervently;

I thank thee for the love
He gave so ardently;

I thank thee for the gifts
Returned so graciously;

I thank thee for the joy
Rejoiced in joyfully;

Lord, I do beseech thee,
To take him in thy breast:

And kiss him lovingly;
He has served thee mightily.

Pure, purple prose that he was, Hector inspired this passionate verse:

Hector: Bravest of the Brave

Hector! brave Prince, and mighty pride of Troy
And fitting sobriquet for this magnifique boy:
A life that witnessed feats to blush fair Helen's maid:
Bravest of the brave, my boy, bravest of the brave!

So bold a nature: steadfast as sun; never cool or coy
Leap in the car again, and smile that smile of joy.
Immortal! bold, and true of heart, and never cur or slave -
Bravest of the brave, my boy, still bravest of the brave.

Always - always! - that chiselled countenance, that manly flow,
That beam of bright and gold that lit across your brow,
Each day a golden dawn, inspired a dashing blade
Gamest of the game, my lad, bravest of the brave.

A heart of hearts, as Braveheart or Rob Roy -
Yet never beat but once, but mischief bade 'enjoy!'
Burst like a meteor in our lives, you came, you saw, you gave:
You are the very bravest, bravest of the brave.

Through thicket, gorse and stream, plunging quickly, now:
That headlong search: that ball, that rock - that crow;
Be damned, I tell you, for at my death I'll rave
"He is the very bravest, bravest of the brave."

One paw in Love's sweet Court, the next in Mars' enclave:
Still loving your dear child again, while in his love you bathe;
My dying wish, whe'er near or far, that on my heart engrave:
"Bravest of them all, my son, bravest of the brave!"

PART 4: PAUSE FOR THOUGHT

1. To have, or not to have?

To have, or not to have, a question as profound
As falling forest giant - did it make a sound?

Colin Hill

Acquiring a dog is a serious business. Therefore, the question: "*should I get a dog?*" must receive very serious thought. Indeed, you need to consider why, and how, that very question arises. What, exactly, are you looking for? What is missing from your life? What can you offer? This should be a positive, memorable, exciting moment in your life's trajectory. But a dog is not a toy, or a fashion accessory, but a living, breathing, being - and responsibility. This will be a demanding, ten to fifteen year commitment, that will change the shape and content of your life.

For many people, dogs are unpleasant, fearsome, even hateful; the hounds from hell. The pejorative term 'Black Dog' can denote either acute depression, or a testosterone-fuelled young man on the make. And a few individuals - Angela Merkel is a famous example - suffer from cynophobia, or fear of dogs. Not even Lassie would persuade such people to view dogs with a kindlier eye. Every encounter, every 'dog report' on the news, only confirms what some believe they already know: dogs mean danger.

For yours truly, this represents a strange, startling conclusion - since the great majority of news reports concern the nefarious activities of homo sapiens across the globe. No doubt murder, rape and pillage is - shoulders shrugged - seen as part of the warp and weft of human behaviour.

However, if - despite these cautions - you still feel inclined towards a dog and, following deep and mature reflection - and maybe a lie-down in a darkened room - the question *why* still causes fundamental doubts, (to more than exploring the quality of home, care and love you are able to offer), then you should probably look to extending your family, or enlivening your existence in other ways - a new car, perhaps, another foreign holiday - or a new partner.

Certainly, before committing yourself - or the dog, which after all has no say in the matter - you need to examine your circumstances and priorities, and the suitability of your home, garden and local environment. This lifetime obligation requires that you look up to fifteen years ahead: is this commitment and responsibility really for you? Can you look so many years ahead, and pledge that you can, and will, provide a loving and stimulating environment for your friend? Next to getting married or having children, this could be the most important decision of your life - because it involves, very intimately, the future happiness of another sentient and dependent being. And it will also, of course, affect your own happiness - either enriching your life, or creating the bane of your life.

There are so many dis-benefits to dog ownership - so many reasons for *not* sharing one's life with a dog - that they bark from the rooftops, and demand mature, honest reflection. The disgracefully large number of abandoned and unwanted dogs speaks volumes about the often casual and unthinking way that the public approaches what should be a major decision. Each year, tens of thousands of dogs are abandoned and placed in rescue kennels. Six thousand dogs are needlessly destroyed in the UK each year. The RSPCA is now calling for a system of licensing for pet ownership, on the basis that pet ownership is a responsibility and a privilege - not a right.

Dog ownership involves responsibility, trust and privilege. You may well want to discuss your plans with your local vet, with friends, or other dog owners, before making a final decision. Certainly, should you enquire with dog rescue charities, not to mention reputable breeders, they will certainly ask you some direct questions designed to assess your suitability. Websites such as those of The Kennel Club, or Dogs Trust, provide invaluable information on the responsibilities and commitment that dog ownership entails.

So I must remind readers of the headline reasons for not acquiring a dog, or dogs. The main point remains that you should acquire a dog only if you know, deep inside, that you will remain dedicated to your pet, and that your personal circumstances can provide the time, stability, and meet the cost, of caring for a dog. It's a pretty tall order - but then it's a pretty big commitment.

OK, cost. If you make a decision to have a baby - or two, or ten - then you do so in the knowledge that, even before day one, the child's health care costs will be funded by the State. No need even to apply; it's a done deal. If, however, you decide to have a pet - cat or dog being the most obvious choices - then you're on your own, baby. Indeed, that is just as it should be. But you need to recognise the fact beforehand, and to factor it into your long-term - that is, ten years or more - financial planning.

If you think that, compared to the costs of gym membership, acquiring a dog for exercise is a free no-brainer, think again. Believe me, a year's subscription to the local gym will prove far less costly than a year's membership of planet dog! Unlike your 'training', a dog will cost you - in food, vets bills and possible boarding costs - at least what gym membership will and, unlike gym membership, the cost of caring for your dog may rise unexpectedly. And you can hardly cancel your dog, unlike your membership of a club. Likewise, while you may decide you have better things to do than go to the gym - there's a football match on telly - your dog will come to expect - indeed, need - his daily walks, regardless.

Let's itemise the costs. Say £500 a year for food, and the need to set aside at least £500 a year - £1,000 would be more realistic - for veterinary bills. If you're planning to go on holiday abroad at least once a year, then you need to factor in a couple of hundred pounds for boarding kennel costs; if the dog is to accompany you on holiday, then the cost of preparing them for these adventures, and vets costs on the (for example) French or Spanish side, amount to another few hundred quid. So, though you don't need to be rich, you do need fairly deep pockets, or at least a clear priority on the canine front.

In addition, the veterinary costs involved in dog ownership may be not only large but (worryingly) unquantifiable. Pet insurance can provide some re-assurance here, though it is not a panacea, and of course the insurance is itself an on-going cost. Over a not inconsiderable lifetime, that bundle of fun and fur may (at 2019 prices) munch through, be treated for, and be pampered by, around £15,000 of your hard-earned cash.

After cost, there's the wear and tear. Puppies and adolescent dogs nearly always generate a good deal of collateral damage - of wear and tear on your house and garden, particularly when the dogs are growing and learning. This damage is pretty unavoidable. If you are particularly house-proud, and will be upset by damage to your furniture, curtains, carpets, shoes and so on, especially at the formative stage, then why put yourself through it? In our case, with H&J, this damage included curtains being torn down, carpets being ripped up, damage to paint-work, and mud everywhere. They were worth it, of course, but at the time it's tough, and wearing on mind and body - and wallet.

And, inevitably, when the dogs are learning self-control, before you reach that happy point when they realise that the garden, and outside, is the place for relieving themselves, you can expect copious deposits of poo and pee - not the ideal accompaniment to fitted carpets. Of course, if you can be at home with the new pets full-time, and particularly during the main growing phase - up to nine months - this can help to minimise the disruption, damage and upset, as well as minimising the toilet-learning phase itself. But, if you have read this paragraph with mounting horror, perhaps dog ownership is not for you.

An associated issue is that of doggy perfume. That is, the peculiar smell dogs confer; dogs love to smell 'doggy', and may make things worse by rolling in unpleasant substances, like horse manure, or fox poo. Then again - since dogs can't generally use human toilet facilities, there will - trust me - be the occasional accident. If you leave the house for any length of time, or are absent at work, you expose your home to this risk - and yourself to the inconvenience of cleaning up. It's not a Greek tragedy, but it is unpleasant, and can be upsetting, both for you and your dog.

If cost itself is a big issue, it's not the biggest. A far bigger issue than any of the above is time - and convenience - your time: hours and hours a week - every day, every week. And your convenience - or inconvenience. Time for walks, time for clearing up, time for grooming, time for the constant vacuuming of carpets. And of course quality time for him, her or them. According to the animal charity, the PDSA, caring for a dog involves a commitment of five hours per day; that is, every day. I do not think this an exaggeration. For me, caring for my boys was always the big deal, the real deal; they were at the centre of my universe. Almost every other activity had to fit around their needs. Balancing the demands of work, home, family commitments, and leisure time, will prove even more demanding - if also strangely pleasurable - with the added dimension of a family dog.

Frankly, work - that most intrusive of four-letter words - can be the major headache, in dog-care terms, just as it is with child-care. If you and your partner work full time, how is your pet supposed to cope throughout the day, both physically and emotionally? Your pet is not an accessory, but an integral part of your life. And you are an integral part of their life. They will want, and need, your company, as much as possible. If you haven't got the time to care for them properly and fully, or if you will begin to resent their on-going needs, then don't do it. Cuddly toys, or those nice, porcelain Staffordshire dogs, are an undemanding alternative.

Certainly, the biggest single impact of H&J was the sheer amount of time required to exercise them properly; for them, every walk was an adventure. They would transform a walk in the park or woods into something quite extraordinary. The mere putting on of a shoe, or grasping their leads would alert H&J to a walk in prospect, and raise their spirits. These outings, I am sure, were as essential for their mental health as for their physical well-being.

Although these regular outings resulted in a marked increase in my fitness - certainly, not to be scoffed at - their main value was the fitness and health they imbued in H&J. They always looked superbly fit, and never exceeded 34 kilos - with Hector usually a kilo or so heavier than his brother. They were lean, exceptionally fit and active boys. Their coats shone and, even when on their leads, they moved with an almost feline grace.

But time is a limited, one-off resource, and dogs demand that time. H&J enjoyed three walks a day, every day, come rain, shine, storms, cold, snow; irrespective of the seasons and circumstances - whether high-days or holidays, Christmas or domestic emergencies. This standard fare of three walks a day, amounting to two hours or more, is a big chunk of free time, and a sizeable, daily, commitment. One can achieve a great deal in two hours per day: read the whole of Shakespeare, Dickens and Austen, say, just in a year of that extra time. Or paint the house, and cultivate the garden. More likely, however, is that the majority of people will probably absorb more TV, internet or video games. I saw our two or three hours per day as an investment in fitness, and a rich diet of experiences and memories.

H&J would often decide which walk they preferred - a tug or two on the lead would express their preference. If they had visited the woods in the morning, their lunch-time or evening preference would be for the Park. If they had enjoyed a particular woodland walk yesterday, their preference this morning would be to approach the woods differently. They were always of the same mind on these points, and I was perfectly happy to accede to their requests; a happy Hector & Jason was a happy me.

But even if you are unwell, are hungover or tired, not in the mood or the weather is foul - that's where the inconvenience rears its head - your pet will still need - and want - his or her quota of walks and attention. And it is your responsibility to make these available, if your pet is to remain healthy and happy. Most writers on the subject recommend a minimum of 20 minutes exercise for dogs each day. But it really depends on the breed or type of dog. If you wish to acquire a medium-sized or large gun dog - say Retriever or Labrador Retriever - then between one and two hours exercise per day should be the adult norm.

In our own case, two hours would be the typical day's exercise - plus travelling time if, say, one of these walks required a short car journey. Not acknowledging these needs and responsibilities not only leads to unhappy, over-weight pets, but is the main reason behind a national disgrace - the many, many thousands of healthy, friendly dogs that, every year, suffer neglect, abuse and abandonment, and have to be rescued by animal and domestic pet charities. The appalling number of healthy animals that are destroyed each year is a damning indictment on our rose-tinted view of our nation as one of animal lovers.

Another characteristic that may have been unique to Hector & Jason was their desire to utilise the garden at least two or three times during the night. Every night. Though this desire may have lessened over the years, it did so slowly; I became used to getting out of bed, zombie-like, at two or three in the morning, then again at four or five - and six. It was like having a young child - but for an inordinate time. This pattern continued at home, in France, or on the camp-site; wherever we were.

In a strange way, I even quite enjoyed these punctuations to my nightly rest - certainly whenever we were in Normandy, or camping - since I would need to take the boys for a proper walk, on leads. There was a frisson of excitement in walking, by lamplight or moonlight, with the boys adding a dimension of experience to what might otherwise have been a pretty forlorn, even weird, exercise. Walking around a camp-site at 3.00am might arouse suspicion in other circumstances, but in tandem with two eager dogs is innocence itself. How many times has one heard on the TV News: "(victim)...*was discovered last night by a man walking his dog*". Fortunately, I never had this kind of unpleasant experience - but did come mighty close.

Travel itself entails a great deal of time and care, limitations and compromises. You may not always be able to stay in the hotel of your choice, or visit the best beaches, or even easily visit the shops when the dogs are with you - especially if the weather is hot. So all this requires meticulous planning, and an acceptance that one can't always enjoy complete freedom. But since the dogs are part of the family and you love them, you will do everything possible to keep them safe, comfortable and happy. The compromise, or sacrifice, is freely made, and generously given; you enjoy their company, and would do no other. But, inevitably, on occasions, you will wish that you could eat your cake and still have it.

Finally, it's a question of priorities. The greatest sacrifice - if we view it as such - is that of putting the dogs *first*. When you arrive home, tired after a hard day's work, the dogs will be delighted to see you - and they will want to be with you. So to leave them in the evenings, on anything like a regular basis, to get your fill of Mozart or Minogue, or Mumford, or Beethoven, Beatles, or Bond, is not to be endured. Your boy or girl has sorely missed you during the daytime, and the evening is for him, her, or them. My Mozart - even Minogue - has mostly been enjoyed in the relative comfort of our home. Almost every evening and every weekend has been with the boys; if we have visited relatives or friends, H&J have usually accompanied us, or we have ensured that our absence is as short as possible. And almost every holiday has been spent in their company: they have shared in our experience, and we in theirs, and to mutual benefit.

Strange, though, how our modern lives are constructed; so tight, managed, and constricted. Eight hours of sleep. Eight hours of work. Eight hours of - what? Domestic chores? Television? Internet? Washing, cleaning, cooking? In all this, what sparks our lives? What provides memory, value, purpose, meaning? Conversing, reading, TV, music? I did all this, and still do, but squeeze in two hours of dog-walking - and exercise, and socialising, and thinking - somehow in parallel.

And if you decide that you need a couple of weeks of 'me time', jetting off to the sun - or even a Caribbean cruise - what of your beloved pet? Will they not miss you? How are they to be cared for? On rare occasions, we did board H&J - but only in the most salubrious accommodation, and only for a few days. It simply made no sense to cause H&J the trauma of travelling to Normandy for a three or four day return trip. On our return from one of these rare H&J boarding experiences, I was waiting to pay our bill, anxious to be re-united with the boys at the earliest possible moment. At the reception desk, a lady in front of me - with mahogany-toned skin - was also keen to settle her dues. The proprietor, clearly salivating, muttered: "*Let me see, that's 65 days at....*". 65 days! Is it really fair and decent to have a dog, if one wants to go gallivanting around for this length of time?

On another, even more sobering, occasion, I bumped into a former colleague unexpectedly, in a little market town. I remembered her as extremely jolly and loquacious. It transpired that she and her husband had just returned from a year-long world tour. After expressing the usual envy, and knowing that she had an assortment of dogs and cats, I innocently enquired what arrangements she had made for them whilst away. In her familiar sing-song voice, she informed me: "*O, we had them put down before we left; they were quite old...*". I do hope she has no children.

To celebrate an important anniversary, June and I once planned a trip to Rome - the 'eternal City' that we'd long wanted to visit. We were excited and expectant as we planned the short but culture-rich break. Of course it entailed flying, and no place for H&J. On reflection, and with sad hearts, we didn't go. Hopefully, there will be time anon; but we had our priorities, and our responsibilities, and had learned to be happy with our chosen - and in truth quite amazing - life-style and lot.

That is really only a snapshot of the true costs and liabilities of dog ownership. Given these, it's remarkable how many people do actually choose to acquire and share their lives with a dog. To reiterate, however, it's pretty unremarkable how many unwanted dogs there are, in the care of Dogs Trust and other similarly splendid organisations. It's equally plain why cats - with their additional independence, general ability to look after themselves and ability to use a litter tray - are now more popular than dogs, in the UK.

So why make this momentous, life-changing choice? Again, this is a decision that should be made only after a great deal of thought and consideration. For, above all, a dog must be something - someone - that you - and your family - really, really want.

This is the good bit. If you've read the foregoing, shrugged your shoulders and muttered: '*so what?*' then here, in a nutshell, are the benefits of dog ownership - for you and your pet. But if you need much convincing, perhaps have a nap, or a cold shower, and move on...

A survey called 'Mappiness' has sought to find out what activities make us happy, or happier, and which make us unhappy. The main conclusion seems to be that 'doing stuff' makes us happier than 'buying stuff'. Not surprisingly, we are far happier spending time with friends, or immersed in nature, than we are when at work or merely acquiring new consumer merchandise. My own greatest joy has been in exploring with friends - my boys - whilst rambling through nature. So, my memories of H&J, in the woods, or in the French bocage, or at the beach, are almost entirely happy ones.

And for you, also, there's regular exercise, and increased fitness. There's also a case to be made for a variety of health benefits - lower blood pressure, lower cholesterol, and an improvement in overall health and well-being. Plus a marked improvement in your state of mind and state of being.

Exercise - walking - has undoubted physical and psychological benefits. One feels more alive, sees more, experiences more, feels the wind in one's face, the world at one's feet. And a good dog enhances the pleasure, through its sharp senses and different perspective, its sheer physical presence, its warmth and closeness, but also its otherness, as a separate but affiliated being. Interaction with dogs is a good stress-buster; the psychological benefits of companionship, and comradeship, were, for me, impossible to exaggerate.

Walking exercises the heart, engages the mind, energises the spirit. Take one dog, and the impact is doubled. Take two dogs...well. Amazingly, Hector, Jason and I discovered eight quite distinct walks starting at the front door of our (Midlands) home - with two separate woodlands, the local Park, and the streets and bye-ways radiating around our Estate. With a little bit of imagination, these eight walks could be varied almost infinitely. H&J - and I'm sure I, too - found this variety very satisfying. We walked in searing heat, and in sheering rain;

in snow, in frost, in storms, in every season and at all times of the day and night. We enjoyed being up, and out and about, at an early hour, to enjoy the breaking day at its most fresh and calm, with most of the world still asleep.

Regular exercise is a fundamental aspect of dog ownership. You will acquire your very own personal trainer - who will insist on the daily regime. Also, there's a sort of psychological balance; work and other concerns are put in their appropriate box. The ego-attrition that is a by-product of work will also be ameliorated by the pleasure of communing with your dog, and strolling with him through the countryside. And Dr Phil Hammond, in his book *Staying Alive* has suggested that *'for 90% of symptoms, dog is better than doctor'*.

The new bench-mark for daily exercise is the magic 10,000 steps a day. That said, how many people choose to, or can even concentrate to count, 10,000 steps? Why not just say four miles, since most of us can measure out a mile - and, if we can't, it's roughly a brisk 20-minute walk. So, an hour and a half should suffice. I have always found that what may become a slightly onerous chore, or routine, is so much more pleasurable in the company of one's dog, or dogs. In the company of H&J four miles flew by in no time at all. There we are: instant fitness, with no hassle or expense - save for the shoe-leather.

Yet more research, this time by St Andrew's University, published in *Preventive Medicine*, has confirmed that walking a dog has significant health benefits. This is true particularly for older people: walking a dog increases physical activity, and therefore fitness, and also helps overcome barriers such as lack of social support, and concerns over personal safety. Indeed, the study found that, on average, those pensioners with a dog 'achieved' exercise levels of people 10 years younger. The 547 people who participated in the study had an average age of 79 years; nine percent of them own dogs. In addition to the increased activity, it is well known that pet ownership helps to alleviate feelings of loneliness and depression in older people. Indeed, the study has led to calls for dog lending schemes. So there is hope for most of us, if we grasp, in this case, the lead!

A dog will also cause you to roam where you otherwise wouldn't: to local parks, woodlands and further afield. You will meet new people - some of them very nice - and interesting new dogs. You will encounter more memorable situations than is possible whilst lying on the sofa, watching brain-numbing TV, playing video games, surfing the net or collecting 'friends' on Facebook. Even if you are already a serial socialiser, you will meet more people, make more new acquaintances - and even a few, genuine friends - than you are ever likely to via social media.

Yet even these incidental benefits are not the main reason for acquiring a canine friend. Far, far more importantly, you will find a source of love and loyalty that is second to none: dogs give more than any other species of animal known to man. The companionship of a truly special dog is one of the greatest gifts that life can confer. You will have a companion who, over time, will become closer to you than practically anyone else in your life. And the more you give, the more tenderness you confer, the greater will be your reward.

H&J made extraordinary demands on our time, and our wallet (not their fault, in any sense). What they gave back, in commitment and devotion, was extraordinary, and life-changing. Though June and I lead very full and busy lives, they were true friends who transformed and enriched those lives immeasurably, making life more complete in every sense.

The boys gave me a sense of pride, an added zest, something extra to live for. Through H&J, I remained far more physically fit than otherwise, saw more of the country than otherwise, and experienced the magic of the changing seasons and the drama of the ever-changing weather. I even met more interesting people than an alternative life-style would have offered: (TV is a passive medium, and the internet an often sterile waster of time - both have their place, but no-one went to the grave muttering *'I wish I'd watched more telly'*).

Dogs can play many roles - they can multi-task. They can be companion; friend (sometimes fiend!); comforter; fitness trainer; draught excluder, social glue, or guru; guard; protector. The psychological, emotional and physical benefits of dog ownership have, for me, proved immense.

So that's you; what's in it for the dog? Well, in this scenario, your treasured pet will be welcomed into a loving family, enjoy a cosy home, good food, treats, enjoyable walks, exciting holidays...what's not to like? The quality of our lives in the second decade of the 21 Century would have astounded our grandparents, never mind our great grandparents. What we are now able to offer to a family pet - the deal - is quite remarkable. Hector & Jason enjoyed a fantastic life, and we were proud and privileged to take them with us on our shared journey. It is exactly this sense of mutual involvement in a life-long adventure, of sharing our daily experience and accumulated memory, that binds us so closely together.

I remember returning home from work in my car one lunchtime, and passed H&J being exercised by our friends and neighbours. I had a sharp intake of breath at their striking elegance, their supreme confidence. They looked magnificent, and quite superb, in this unusual (for me) perspective.

We received many kind compliments over the years on their so-handsome appearance. Many of these encounters were in France, where total strangers would approach us, asking about the boys: what breed were they? What relationship had they? How old were they? Could they be stroked? The answer to the last question was always *"yes!"* The boys - particularly Hector - always enjoyed attention, and were happy to oblige. French people really seem to love their dogs, and were often fascinated by H&J: one does not encounter too many Golden Retrievers in France, and the boys stood out from the crowd - any crowd.

One thing I have learned from life is not to be surprised when others are quite under-whelmed by one's good fortune. Dogs are different. Hector & Jason were delighted by everything we did, everywhere we went - practically every breath we took. For me, this took 'content with life' to a new and unexpected level. More than anything, H&J made me content, kept me balanced, and played a major part in my well-being; my happiness. It's hard to put a price on that. It just doesn't get any better. In response to this boundless largesse, I loved them, and will continue to love them forever. The trust of a special dog is a truly humbling privilege. A canine friendship provides companionship, re-assurance, and a warm, sentient presence; a deep, heart-felt friendship and, above all, unconditional love.

Finally, the company of a dog helps to root us in the natural world, our almost-forgotten domain, and keenly enhances our appreciation of an absorbing dimension that unfolds before us, awaiting our sensory exploration. It may be objected that there are better things in life than a good walk with a good dog. I would concur, but add: *"Maybe, but not many".*

"Lord, if I must walk, let it be with my friend, my dog..."

In the last analysis, this book must remain a memoir of two supreme dogs. My intention is not to offer a hymn to dog ownership, but to set out the facts, fairly and squarely. The decision to share your life with another - to give your life to another - must remain a personal choice: a choice that reflects your circumstances, aspirations, and needs. You need to make this choice with your eyes wide open.

2. Choices and Compromises

The choice is clear: to eat one's cake, and eat one's hog,
Or compromise; eat half - the other's for the dog.

Colin Hill

The decision, making the choice, to share your life with a dog, or dogs - and to share *their* lives - is a life-changing one. Such a decision involves commitment, and obligation, and a realisation that this is a lifetime commitment - for the duration of your life, or the dog(s) - whichever ends sooner.

With 14 years dog ownership 'under their belts', many people may have thought that they had more than sufficient experience to take on a further dog, or dogs. Even given this experience, and though the basics may not change too much, good practice in terms of dog ownership - feeding, behaviour, care, health - continues to evolve.

Shortly before we took the momentous decision of life-long commitment to Hector & Jason, I bought a slim tome entitled, appropriately enough, *The Golden Retriever*, by an American author, James E Walsh Junior. It was an invaluable purchase - full of practical advice, based on long experience. The American 'way' may be a little different to British convention, in dog-caring terms, (contrasting in many ways with Lucille Sawtrell's earlier *All about the Golden Retriever*) but in many ways the book was ahead of its (British) time - for instance in its emphasis on cleaning up dog poo, and its caution on managing one's canine friend.

Therefore, one strong piece of advice given by James Walsh is to keep one's charge - or charges - on a leash at all times, when in a public place. There is a good case for adhering to this injunction. An out of sight, and/or out of control dog can get into all sorts of trouble. There are so many risks and dangers, even in our sanitised, modern world - indeed, perhaps more so. The animal might frighten another human being, perhaps a child, even if not intentionally. It may attack, or be attacked, by another dog. It may ingest something disgusting, or even poisonous. It might be involved in a collision with a motor vehicle (injuring or killing the dog - and risking the the possibility of human injury, and consequent legal action). Or the dog may be stolen, or injured, by a human being with which it comes into contact. All of these possibilities - and more - are real, and serious.

Yet, in my experience, most dog owners allow their charges to be off their leads, most of the time, and in most environments. Clearly, they take a calculated risk, based on the circumstances, the specific environment they're in, and their knowledge of their dog. However, this fortuitous set of circumstances applies principally to the UK - and of course France. In America, (you guessed) it is not unknown for dog walkers who dare to allow their charges to run free in public parks to be... tasered.

H&J proved to be an unusual and difficult case. When walking along the streets, or anywhere near a road, they were on their leads; no question. In new, strange or unusual places - they were also on their leads. Where I thought there were particular dangers - they were on their leads. Certainly, on our Normandy walks, even near to the cottage, H&J would be on their leads. We had heard scary stories, of dogs - out hunting with their owners - chasing after wild animals and never coming back. All my instincts, then, particularly given my intimate knowledge of these super boys, was to ensure their safety, by keeping them close to me.

Allowing H&J freedom involved daily anxieties, real risks narrowly averted, a large slice of luck, and a few nasty incidents. The boys, however, for all their exuberance and speed, were imbued with sound heads: much as I often doubted it, they had a good dose of common sense, that helped keep them safe. My main fear - which sadly turned out to be only too true - was of the risks posed, in various forms, by my fellow human beings.

And yet...and yet. More than any other dogs that I had ever known, seen, or even heard of, Hector & Jason needed to run. Truly, madly, gladly - they were born to run. More precisely, Hector was born to seek, and to hunt. Jason was born to run...and run. These were their deepest instincts, their greatest desires. Despite a myriad of anxieties, I delighted in their joy, in their exercise of their power; I revelled in their pursuit of life. I sensed their need, and, whenever I could, allowed them freedom to express their most vital desires.

I am so proud that, throughout their gloriously full lives, H&J were (hackneyed terms) 'empowered' to achieve their 'potential'. This was the best of them, their deepest yearning; their peak of life. They experienced their best, their true natures; their very life force.

Clearly, prosaically, I assessed the risks and judged these to be acceptable - though these were never non-existent. I also knew that H&J would never, ever, threaten a human being, or another dog. I could not magic away the risks; all I could do was to manage them, in prescribed environments - our local woodlands, where we were well known, and where roads ran outside a kind of field-based buffer zone - and our local Park where, despite the proximity of roads, I could actually see the boys, charging around the perimeter.

And I experienced them at the zenith of their being. There was something magnificent, something almost spiritual, in this. Think Muhammed Ali. Think Roger Federer. Think Pelé. Think Bolt. Sublimity must have a chance to flourish, to flower. And, in the mind of Hector, and in the miracle of Jason, flower it most certainly did.

3. Vets need Pets

As pets need vets, it's true to say,
That pets need vets just once, in May;
Though vet needs pet, nay, every day.

Colin Hill

Yes; that's right. Never forget that you are the customer, and that Colin the cat is the consumer.

Hector & Jason's attitude to vets was identical; they viewed the experience as we might a visit to the dentist. As soon as the surgery door opened, both boys rose to their feet - and headed for the exit. I had the unenviable job of 'guiding' them through the appropriate aperture.

Given their anxiety and reticence, we always ensured that, during the veterinary experience, H&J were treated with the utmost sensitivity and care. On one occasion, in France, we felt that a vet had been a little cavalier in his treatment of them. We found a new vet, and never returned.

Even so, H&J benefited from regular access to two veterinary practices - in the UK, and in Normandy. Not that they saw it in this light: they kind of accepted it, with grim resolution, but were very keen to leave the premises, and resume their lives, at the earliest possible opportunity. But this dual arrangement meant that they were examined at least every other month, and this definitely contributed towards maintaining their long-term health.

Make no mistake, you - and your pet - will need a vet: a vet that you can trust; your pet's health and very life are at stake. We are indeed fortunate today in having *access* to professional, expert and caring veterinary practices. But how to choose?

All modern vets are of course qualified, and all veterinary practices accredited; but this should be a starting point in the search for your family vet. Not all vets are great. Indeed, in my view, not every vet can be described as good. However, I do believe that the great majority of vets are competent (as well as qualified) and are caring and compassionate.

But you cannot take excellence, or even quality of care, for granted. There exists no tome of comparative qualitative data that will provide you with evidence of outcomes, or client - or patient - satisfaction. In any case, such qualitative - and comparative - data would probably be impossible to compile.

That means - as you care passionately about your pet, and its health - that the responsibility for engaging a high quality vet lies entirely with you. You can go about this research in a variety of ways. You can ask the views of fellow pet-owners: which veterinary practice do they use, and why? You can read the marketing 'blurb' on local services on veterinary practices' own websites, or literature. What does their 'mission statement' say about their values and service? What services do they offer? What facilities do they provide? For example, can they provide actual surgery, in cases of accident or various types of illness? Do they provide overnight care facilities, for when pets need around-the-clock professional care? Do they provide emergency and out-of-hours facilities? What diagnostic facilities are available - for example, for blood tests, x-rays and MRI scans?

The next, obvious, step, when you have done all of the above, is to visit practices in your area (by arrangement) and talk to staff, and look around the premises. Be open about your motives and intentions; be honest and sensitive. Preferably, such visits should be out of hours - but at times convenient for staff and their actual patients.

I would suggest that, if a brief visit is not feasible - that is, if the practice is unwilling to discuss its services with you - then you may wish to look elsewhere. You are, after all, the customer, and your interest should be encouraged, welcomed even, rather than deflected. Reflect on your visit: what was the attitude of the staff to your questions? Were they friendly and open, or evasive? Were they helpful, or defensive? Were the premises clean and well-managed? If there was a photograph on the vet's desk, does it depict his dog, or his wife and kids?

Quality care comes at a cost. Veterinary practices are not part of the National Health Service. The regular trip to the vets in France cost 130 euros a go: multiply this by five and we have a neat little number of 750 euros per year. Like it or lump it, as our friends in DEFRA might say.

In my view, cost itself should not be a factor in choosing a vet, though you should expect value for money. And veterinary treatment in the UK cannot be inexpensive, given the highly qualified staff, the cost of medication, and expense of premises, modern equipment and skilled care required. And the pretty obvious but often over-looked fact that the expensive facility needs to actually exist - in readiness, 24/7, primed and ready for your call.

Pet insurance is of course available, but is arguably expensive in itself; there is normally an excess, and you often have to make a claim *after* paying the veterinary bill. And there is generally a maximum that you can claim per treatment, which may be well below the actual cost incurred. Added to this is the fact that many policies become prohibitively expensive when your pet becomes elderly, and more likely to develop a serious (and expensive) condition. And, if your pet develops a long-term chronic illness, well, good luck.

It's true that, these days, anything that can be done, medically, for a human being can be done for a dog or cat. Available treatments may include complex surgery, chemotherapy, and radiotherapy. However, the fact that such treatments are possible, and available, does not mean that they are necessarily appropriate. What may be suitable, and advisable, for a four-year-old pet, may not be suitable for a 14-year-old pet. Circumstances, and context, are as significant in assessing treatment as the diagnosis itself. A key consideration is whether you are aiding your beloved pet to recovery, or merely delaying the inevitable for a few weeks. Your friend's quality of life, and the utmost consideration for their welfare, must be your guide.

We always relied on the Bank of June and Colin to meet H&J's veterinary costs. We don't have to seek permission; we just do it. But we may have been lucky, and the past is not necessarily a guide to the future. If you are in any doubt, and for your peace of mind, it is almost certainly best to insure your pet: a difficult, complex or prolonged treatment could end up costing you hundreds - or even thousands - of pounds. If this makes you blench - don't think *"it can't happen to us"* - get the best insurance cover you can afford, and cut out something unnecessary - like eating or drinking.

If you choose the self-fund route, my view is that, at 2019 prices, (if not insured) you will need to set aside at least £1,000 per year for your pet's vet bills; if you have more than one pet, a further £500 per pet might be in order. These figures are greater than what you would pay for pet insurance but, remember, it's (your) money in the bank unless it's needed, whereas money spent on insurance is not in itself recoverable. If, at the end of Year 1, you're 'quids in', (as, hopefully, you will be with a young dog or cat) then roll it forward, along with your allocation for the following year - inevitably, you're bound to need it at some stage. In fact, a separate bank or building society account for this specific purpose is to be recommended - perhaps funded by monthly direct debit. Most people don't do this of course - often, because they don't want to know how much Ben is really likely to cost them, or because they have more urgent calls on their money. But it is a price worth paying for peace of mind, and to ensure that your pet can receive the best possible treatment, as and when the need arises.

The point of all this is that, if you love your pets, you must love your (chosen) vet. And you must be in a financial position so as not to stint or delay access to treatment, if you feel that your friend requires attention. So you must be sure that you are in a position to afford appropriate treatment before making the fateful decision to share your life with a dog, or dogs. Again, if in doubt, take out one of the many pet insurance policies available. If we had not taken the young Hector to our vet when he had swallowed a stone, or not taken Jason when (as it happened) he had a grain of corn in his eye, the consequences would have been tragic, certainly in Hector's case. Strangely enough, the general cost of caring for two dogs is not that much more expensive than the cost of caring for one; but this happy equation breaks down in the face of veterinary costs.

In practice, this means that you must be your pet's best friend, always looking out for him or her, always careful to ensure that they do not suffer in silence, always ready to ensure access to the highest possible quality of care. Your vet should be your trusted, caring, right-hand-man, or woman, in ensuring the long-term health of your best friend.

Choose a good one - and stick with them.

4. In the very Beginning – Origin of a Species

When the Man waked up he said,
"What is Wild Dog doing here?"
And the Woman said,
"His name is not Wild Dog any more,
but the First Friend,
because he will be our friend
for always and always and always."

Rudyard Kipling

According to the fossil record - *'in the deep backward and abysm of time'* - canids first evolved around six million years ago, in North America. Around a million years ago, wolves, foxes, jackals and coyotes emerged as separate species. Modern research has revealed that today's domestic dog is descended from the Eurasian wolf, specifically, and that this domestication process began at least 25,000 years ago. Much later, perhaps, the selective breeding of the animal began, to adapt its natural instincts for specific needs: hunter, protector, retriever, herder.

Archaeological evidence suggests that the association of man and dog may stretch as far back as 100,000 years. However, the dog fossil record is more recent, dating to around 20,000 years ago.

The lack of fossil or burial evidence before this period suggests that the dog-human relationship began to become more meaningful around this time. In addition, burial of dogs with humans also seems to have started at this stage in our evolution - indicating a close emotional bond between the two species. The oldest such finding dates from Germany - and is more than 14,000 years old. Another fossil from this time, found in Israel, rather poignantly reveals a man and his dog - the man's hand resting on the head of his dog. And, in the Chauvet cave in the Ardeche region of France, a short trail of a boy's footprints, alongside those of a large canid - dated to around 22,000 years ago - hints at a close relationship between the two. The historian Rodney Castledon has noted, in *Stonehenge People,* from the evidence of dog bones found at Stonehenge, that *'some dogs lived to be old, beyond their useful working lives, so their owners kept them out of affection'*.

It remains unclear whether, in the mists of time, man adopted dog, or dog adopted man. Most likely, there was a strong element of mutual self-interest. The things that matter most - food, shelter, protection - could all occur more readily, be more available, if man and dog worked in partnership, complementing each other's strengths and skills. John Bradshaw points out that the special ability of dogs to respond to humans may have been a key factor in the evolving relationship: *'This capacity for the dog to adopt a dual identity - part human and part wolf - is essential in accounting for the transition from primitive pet to truly domestic animal'*. In addition, dogs have proved adaptable for all kinds of valuable roles for their human partners. Bradshaw concludes: *'such flexibility must lie at the heart of the enduring power of the human-canine relationship'*.

Dogs are represented in art, and literature, from the earliest times - for example, in Stone Age cave art, and in Egyptian paintings inside the pyramids. And in literature: Odysseus's dog, Argus, waited patiently for ten long years for his master's return from the Trojan wars.

The ancient Greeks and Romans developed a number of breeds, including the greyhound, mastiff and bloodhound (called such because of its noble blood). The greyhound is the only dog to be mentioned in the Bible; the fastest specimens can reach 45mph, so they would have proved invaluable in the field.

Of course, as with all his partnerships, it would be man who would establish, almost literally, the 'whip hand', and who would increasingly dictate the terms of the relationship. Yet, for the most part, and as they became bred for specific roles, dogs would have fitted, fairly submissively but gamely, into the roles intended for them: pointing, retrieving, hunting, chasing, protecting. In return, they would be provided with food, shelter, and protection by their new 'tribe'. And we know that dogs have been used as allies in warfare - from rotweilers employed by Roman legions, to message dogs that provided service to the armies of World War 1.

Over time, the canine-human partnership would become almost ideal, such was the practical usefulness of these animals, their adaptability, and the strong bond they established with their human counterparts. As we moved into modern times, certainly in modern western countries, dogs became valued in and for themselves, as social and family companions. Walk round any ancestral home and there are the proud family portraits - made complete by the family dog: Gainsborough's *Mr and Mrs Andrews* is a wonderful example. However, of course many breeds - including the Golden Retriever - continue to be employed as working dogs.

John Bradshaw's insightful *In Defence of Dogs* has enriched my own knowledge, and given me opportunity to reflect on my own experience. In the context of this book it is important to highlight some of the key findings and insights revealed in Bradshaw's work. The fact that the modern dog is descended from the wolf has, sadly, been responsible for a great deal of misunderstanding of the species. This is partly the result of the study of today's Eurasian wolves, which differ significantly in behaviour from dogs; not only have dogs undergone perhaps 25,000 years of domestication and cross-breeding, considerably altering their nature in the process, but it is likely that the wolves from whom they are descended were themselves quite different (mutations) from the independent, mistrustful (of humans) pack animals that are now studied so avidly. This is not to deny that dogs - especially when in packs - can be difficult, dangerous, even deadly - just as we would not deny that capacity in some human beings.

In particular, the belief that dogs are descended from, and very similar in character to, wolves has led to an almost scientifically respectable view that they are inherently dangerous, and with an innate desire to dominate their human companions. Certainly, modern dogs share 99.6% of their DNA with the Eurasian wolf. However, John Bradshaw explains that the character of the modern dog is different in so many respects to wolves as to make comparison - for purposes of training and developing relationships - virtually meaningless: and that dogs (unlike modern wolves) have an outgoing, sociable nature, and a genuine capacity for friendship and affection with their human friends.

My - most - experience of dogs holds these findings to be irrefutable; so that the only true study of the dog...is the dog. Though not published until 2011 - long after I began caring for H&J - I am indebted to *In Defence of Dogs* for giving me further opportunity to reflect on my lifetime of experience and interaction with my two super-boys.

There are around 4,000 species of mammal on the planet and, at first sight, it seems remarkable that we have chosen the dog as our special, singular, companion. After all, we share 99% of our DNA with chimpanzees. Maybe this species is rather too close for comfort; rather uncomfortably on our own peculiar human level. And cats are far less dependent, and absorb far less of our precious time. Perhaps chimpanzees would hold up a mirror to ourselves, whilst cats are just too independent, even scary, for many people.

Certainly, for mankind down the ages, dogs have been the most loyal and useful companions - providing complementary aptitudes and skills: able to hunt, retrieve, guard, and provide friendship, loyalty, and undemanding affection. And demanding very little in return.

At the same time, the practical usefulness of dogs may be in retreat, given our increasingly urbanised, atomised, 'wired' lives. And few of us hunt game these days, since Sainsbury's is so much more convenient. Fortunate, too, that, in 2019, few of us actually need to be guarded.

The man-dog journey that began perhaps 100,000 years ago is a very long evolutionary road. That road has led, ultimately, to modern pedigree dogs. Today, The Kennel Club recognises over 150 separate breeds, with 800 breeds being recognised worldwide.

The breed now known as the Golden Retriever first emerged in the 1860s. The breed was developed by Lord Tweedsmuir (sometimes referred to as Sir Dudley Majoribanks) in the 1860s, allegedly, and fancifully, from a troupe of Russian circus dogs. More prosaically, however, the story goes that, in 1865, the said Lord Tweedsmuir bought a yellow wavy-coated Retriever as a puppy from a cobbler in Brighton (but bred by Lord Chichester). The yellow dog was called Nous, the only yellow dog from a litter of black Retrievers. Nous was mated with Belle, from the now-extinct Tweed Water Spaniel breed. Other crosses were made with, again, Tweed Water Spaniels, black Retrievers, an Irish Setter, and a Bloodhound. By 1913 the Kennel Club was able to recognise the resulting dog as a separate breed. The whole process - from inception to formal recognition - had taken less than 50 years.

The Golden Retriever is now the seventh most popular breed in the UK and the second most popular breed in the United States. Golden Retrievers are nothing if not versatile. They can be working dogs, family and companion dogs, search and rescue dogs, sniffer dogs, guide dogs, or therapy dogs. Whilst Retrievers can perform any of these roles, they are quintessentially a companion and friend; the family pet: handsome in appearance, with a gentle character, and a loyal and affectionate nature.

A Mrs W M Charlesworth was a notable champion of the Golden Retriever, being for many years the Honorary Secretary of the Golden Retriever Club. In 1932 she published her pioneering *Book of the Golden Retriever*. My own favourite reference book on the breed is Lucille Sawtrell's seminal *All about the Golden Retriever*, first published in 1971. June and I first read this so-useful work in preparation for the arrival of Victor; by good fortune, I recently purchased a second-hand copy, from a National Trust bookshop. Mrs Sawtrell has some amusing anecdotes about Mrs Charlesworth - many of them relating to the lady's being often mistaken for a man by reason of her no-nonsense manner and style of dressing. I imagine her to be like my own Mrs Henslow - but at heart caring deeply for this breed, and their continued development as active, working dogs.

Victor, and Hector & Jason, are therefore part of a long genetic line, bred over generations to develop and capture certain key characteristics: the ability to retrieve game from woodland, moor and water; to be receptive to commands; to protect their master's family and home. The breed's chief characteristics are given as '*symmetrical, active and powerful...sound and well put together*'. (*Encyclopaedia of the Dog*).

So our Retrievers are large dogs - typically around 35 kilos - with strong, flexible frames, softened by thick, soft but sturdy coats. They are built for stamina, and long days in the field. These dogs enjoy, and need, lots of exercise each day. They are intelligent, adaptable, devoted. Golden Retrievers are, certainly, markedly handsome, with open, happy faces. They are positive dogs, who respond best to positive and active people.

There is no mention here (and why should there be?) - unlike the Greyhound, Borzoi, or Saluki - of any notion of speed, grace or even beauty; though 'handsome' is a commonly used epithet. Indeed, it will be clear from the above that, whatever Lord Tweedsmuir's aims in selecting dogs to create the new breed, speed of movement was not his primary consideration. To put it bluntly, the 'game' they were meant to retrieve had already been immobilised by a gunshot. (I can only conjecture, then, what Lord Tweedsmuir, or indeed Mrs Charlesworth, would have made of Jason).

Each specimen of the breed will of course differ, in the extent to which they possess the required and ideal breed characteristics - in terms of both physique and temperament. But I must end with further reference to *In Defence of Dogs,* which expresses deep concerns as to the in-breeding of pedigree dogs based on 'show' criteria - i.e. bred for their appearance, rather than for their health and personality. Thus, there are around 100,000 Golden Retrievers resident in the UK - with about 8,000 new dogs being registered each year. John Bradshaw states that, since the breed's inception six generations ago, in-breeding has removed more than 90% of the variation that once characterised the breed. That should give pause and reflection - and some distress - to all who love the Golden Retriever.

So, while I can again give thanks for Hector & Jason, and their sheer, remarkable difference, I must be saddened to think that such difference may be smoothed and eroded from the breed as the in-breeding process continues its remorseless progression.

The patient reader will note, however, how Hector & Jason shaped up to their breed's standard; and can hope with me that genetics may still prove a cunning genie to tame.

5. THE GLOBAL CELEBRITIES

*That small world, like the great one out of doors, had the capacity
of easily forgetting its dead; and when the cook had said she was
a quiet-tempered lady, and the housekeeper had said it was the
common lot, and the butler had said who'd have thought it, and
the housemaid had said she couldn't hardly believe it, and the
footman had said it seemed exactly like a dream, they had quite
worn the subject out, and began to think their mourning was
wearing rusty too.*

Dombey and Son - Charles Dickens

*'Celebrity' - the word that all the world admires;
Salute the meek, the brave, for charging at the fires.*

Colin Hill

Most dogs do not achieve celebrity status. They wave a final paw, and are gone forever into the eternal forest. And how should it be otherwise? Their lives are relatively brief; they are not able to create their own fanfare, or to write a carefully crafted account of a life well-spent.

Hector & Jason achieved a little fame, but in their own neck of their own little woods. Over the years, they must have touched and, hopefully, brightened the lives of some thousands of people. But, in the lexicon of canine history, Hector and Jason's place is - like my own - no doubt relatively modest.

But echoes persist, for example in literature. Take, for instance, Jerome K Jerome's *Three Men in a Boat*. The company includes a dog, Montmorency. A classic comedy set-piece takes place in Chapter 14, with the Irish stew, made by mixing most of the leftovers in the party's food hamper:

'I forget the other ingredients, but I know nothing was wasted; and I remember that, towards the end, Montmorency, who had evinced great

interest in the proceedings throughout, strolled away with an earnest and thoughtful air, reappearing, a few minutes afterwards, with a dead water-rat in his mouth, which he evidently wished to present as his contribution to the dinner; whether in a sarcastic spirit, or with a genuine desire to assist, I cannot say.'

When I read that, I think: *"How very Hector!"*.

When set beside others of their kin - heroes who save lives, or perform amazing feats - H&J's contribution to history is - as mine - written in a different key. As with most dogs, their own fame rests on their impact on the lives that they touched, their unerring affection, and some exceptional characteristics. But by way of comparison, and to inspire a little thought on the significance of the canine species, a sideways glance at the exploits of the most distinguished of their kind may not be amiss.

There are some canines who have become global celebrities - some in their lifetimes, some following their demise; or even through the nature of their demise. I think it is useful to examine a few of these great lives, since it is from these that we may draw an idea of the true capacity of the canine species - for affection, for heroism, for endurance, for intelligence; a capacity that has shaped the reputation of the entire race.

If, in order to show the glory that is humankind, a sealed vessel is launched into outer space - in the hope of its being intercepted by intelligent extra-terrestrials - it would not contain your or my stories, but those of Bach, Einstein, Leonardo, Shakespeare. And so with these celebrated canines - exemplars of their kind.

There are of course many, many, famous dogs in history - 'real', such as Greyfriars Bobby; fictitious, such as Lassie, or Bullseye; and legendary, such as King Arthur's Cayfall, or Argus, Odysseus's dog - immortal in the memory. These dogs represent many breeds, and often dogs that are mixtures of breeds: it is of course humans who place importance on breed purity, not dogs themselves.

I reviewed the literature on famous dogs with curiosity - to see how H&J compared to these noble exemplars of their kind; what, exactly, they may have had in common, and what sets particular dogs apart from their race. But all dogs can reflect in the glories of the 'best' (by our light), of their species. A handful of these dogs' stories are sketched out below, as representative of the qualities - bravery, loyalty, devotion - inherent in the family of dogs.

In this respect, Hector & Jason were true to their race - in striving to be, as dog as dog can be. In achieving their potential. In seizing the day.

Argus

Argus belonged to Odysseus. According to Homer's *Iliad,* Odysseus played a notable, and noble, part in the Trojan Wars. Following his exciting and dangerous adventures, chronicled in *The Odyssey,* he returned 20 years later to his kingdom of Ithaca, in disguise, dressed as a beggar.

Argus, too, has fallen on hard times. An old, worn dog, he lay abandoned on the heaps of dung that lay outside the palace gates. Odysseus's companion - Eumaeus - who does not know the beggar's identity - informs him that, in his prime, Argus was peerless for his looks, and speed and power in the forest. Despite his age and his master's disguise, it is Argus alone who recognises his master, and wags his tail: *'Now, at the moment he perceived that Odysseus had come close to him, he thumped his tail, nuzzling low, and his ears dropped'.* Odysseus - the most hardened of men - brushes away a tear.

Alexander Pope memorably described the scene as follows:

'When wise Ulysses, from his native coast
Long kept by wars, and long by tempests toss'd,
Arrived at last, poor, disguised, alone,
To all his friends, and ev'n his Queen unknown...

Forgot of all his own domestic crew,
The faithful Dog alone his rightful master knew!
Unfed, unhous'd, neglected, on the clay
Like an old servant now cashier'd, he lay;

Touch'd with resentment of ungrateful man,
And longing to behold his ancient lord again.
Him when he saw he rose, and crawl'd to meet,
(T'was all he could) and fawn'd and kiss'd his feet,

Seiz'd with dumb joy; then falling by his side,
Own'd his returning lord, look'd up, and died!'

Argus had been waiting for that supreme moment of reunion, and promptly succumbed - happily - upon the event. This is a touching tale of undying devotion, of never giving up hope, and of canine selflessness.

The Dog of Montargis

In 1371, the knight Aubrey de Montdidier, courtier of King Charles V of France, was murdered in a forest near Montargis.

When the knight failed to show up for a tournament his friend DeNarsac went to search for him. He could not find his friend but, later, de Montdidier's greyhound turned up at his door, in great distress. The dog led him to his master's body, lying deep in the forest.

The greyhound was a gentle animal but, later, at court, began to behave aggressively towards a certain knight, Richard Macaire. This Macaire was known as an enemy of de Montdidier, and suspicions were aroused.

The issue came before the King. Macaire denied his guilt. However, it was decreed that Macaire should meet the greyhound in a trial by combat. Despite Macaire's being armed with a cudgel, the determined dog soon got the better of him. Macaire begged for mercy, and confessed his guilt.

A statue depicting the fight now stands in front of the Girodet Museum in the town of Montargis.

Owney

Some dogs fetch the newspaper, but Owney helped escort buckets of mail all over the United States. When postal workers in Albany, New York found a stray mutt in their office, they decided to let him sleep on a pile of mailbags. Apparently, the dog was attracted to the scent of the bags, since he followed them right onto a train and rode with them all over the state and eventually the country.

The workers at the Albany office had named the dog Owney, and became worried that he would be lost during his travels. So they gave him a collar with a tag that read 'Owney, Post Office, Albany, New York'. Owney became the unofficial mascot of the railway mail service, and postal clerks saw him as a good luck charm, since none of the trains he rode on ever crashed.

Other post offices began to give him tags for each place he visited, until the Postmaster General even gave him a jacket to hold them all. Owney even made an around-the-world trip through Asia and Europe before arriving back in Albany.

Unfortunately, Owney's life ended after a postal worker in Toledo, Ohio mistreated him and was bitten. Fearing the dog was rabid, a local police officer shot him. Owney's preserved body and medals are now on display at the US Postal Museum in Washington, DC.

Stubby

Stubby is the only dog ever to have been promoted to the rank of sergeant.

A young stray was found on the Yale campus by John Robert Conroy, who named him Stubby. Conroy was undergoing military training, and when it came time for him to ship out for World War I, he smuggled Stubby along with him. For the next 18 months, Stubby became one of many war dogs living in the trenches of France. He soon distinguished himself enough to earn the official rank of sergeant.

How? By doing things most human soldiers never even get a chance to do. Stubby's acute sense of smell and hearing allowed him to warn his unit of poison gas attacks and incoming artillery. He managed to locate and rescue wounded soldiers on the battlefield, and even single-handedly captured a German spy.

Overall, Stubby participated in 17 battles, and was awarded several patches and medals - which he wore on a coat made for him by the women of a liberated French town. After the war, Conroy smuggled Stubby back home, where he went on to meet several Presidents and act as Georgetown's football mascot, before passing away in Conroy's arms.

Barry

Barry, a 'barihund' or 'bear-dog' (later known as St Bernards) worked as a rescue dog in the mountains of Switzerland near a monastary in Great St. Bernard pass, where he also lived.

During the 12 years of Barry's career (1800-1812), he is credited with rescuing at least 40 people who were lost in the Alps during heavy snow. One famous tale says Barry discovered a small child on top of an icy ledge and began licking his face to keep him warm and awake, while barking loudly for the monks to find them (as he was trained to do). When the snow began to fall even harder and the monks couldn't climb the steep cliff to reach them, the young boy wrapped his arms around Barry's neck and the dog carried him all the way down the mountain.

Barry was eventually retired in 1812, following wounding by a man he was trying to rescue. He lived out the rest of his days under the care of a monk.

Togo and Balto

Both Togo and Balto were sled dogs assigned to lead a team through Alaska carrying serum for the town of Nome. In January 1925, doctors in the area feared that a diphtheria epidemic could hit the whole town, but the only available serum was in Anchorage, almost 1,000 miles away. With their only aircraft's engines frozen, officials in Anchorage decided the serum would be relayed by several teams of sled dogs.

Togo's team was chosen to carry the serum through the most treacherous part of the route, and ended up travelling almost twice the distance of any of the other teams. Balto's team took the cargo for the last leg of the journey, and ultimately delivered the serum ahead of schedule. Because he was the one who finished the run, Balto received almost all of the glory for it - even having some of Togo's achievements attributed to him.

Sadly, following their achievements, Balto and his pals were sold to a vaudeville show. When businessman George Kimble came across them in Los Angeles, they were in a sorry state. Mr Kimble promptly offered to buy the dogs for $2,000: the nation rose to the occasion, and Balto and six other dogs were re-homed in Cleveland Zoo. It is said that 15,000 people visited Balto and co. on their first day in their new home.

Balto died in 1933. His body is displayed at the Cleveland Museum of Natural History. A statue, erected in his honour, stands proudly in New York's Central Park.

Hachiko

In 1924, a Professor Hidesaburo Ueno from the University of Tokyo brought his dog, Hachiko, to live with him. The two developed a routine, where the dog would see the professor off at his home and then meet him at the Shibuya train station later. Then one day, the Professor didn't show up at the train station. Sadly, he'd suffered a stroke at the university, and died.

Hachiko was given away to another owner, but he would often escape and turn up at his old home. Hachiko eventually realized that Professor Ueno wasn't coming home, and so he went to look for him at the train station. For ten years, Hachiko would arrive at the train station exactly when the evening train showed up and would wait patiently for his owner.

Other commuters noticed the loyal dog and began to bring him food and snacks. He even gained national attention when a former student of Ueno's published several articles about him. One artist even built and erected a bronze statue of the dog while he was still alive. Hachiko died in 1935, but his legend continues to live on in Japan.

His story has been made into a film, with Richard Gere playing Professor Ueno.

Chips

Chips was a famous War Dog, whose exploits have been commemorated by a Disney film of the same name.

During World War II, the German Shepherd cross was donated to the war effort and was soon on the front lines acting as a tank guard dog in Africa, Italy, France, and Germany. At one point, he dragged a 'phone cable across a raging battlefield, so that his platoon could call for backup.

The signal event Chips is most famous for happened on a beach in Sicily: when he and his handler came under fire from a hidden pillbox, Chips sprang from his handler and drove straight into the enemy emplacement. The soldiers inside came out moments later and surrendered - with Chips standing behind them.

Later that night, Chips also alerted his squad to some approaching Italians, who were promptly captured. Chips received a Silver Star and a Purple Heart for his adventures. These awards were unavailable, later, when dogs were reclassified in the military as 'equipment', making Chips the last canine to be officially decorated.

Old Shep

In the USA, in 1936, a sheep herder became unwell and travelled to Fort Benton, Montana, to seek treatment. He took his loyal dog, Shep, with him. Sadly, the herder died a few days later: his body was boxed up, and sent by train to his relatives.

Shep followed his master's coffin to the Fort Benton railway station, and watched anxiously as the train carrying it pulled away. And that is where Shep stayed for the next five and a half years. Shep kept vigil at the station, greeting the four trains that arrived each day; watching and waiting for his master's return.

Shep's loyalty touched the nation, and he received fan mail from far and wide. Sadly, having grown somewhat deaf, Shep's long watch came to an end in January 1942 when he slipped on an icy rail when trying to avoid the 10.17 train.

Hundreds of people attended Shep's funeral, which had a guard of honour and pall-bearers.

Shep's grave remains open to visitors, and his collar and dog bowl are displayed in the Museum of Upper Missouri. In 1994, he was honoured with a bronze sculpture.

Greyfriars Bobby

Greyfriars Bobby was a famous Skye Terrier, his life celebrated in the Disney movie of the same name.

John Gray, a night-watchman with the Edinburgh police force, adopted Bobby, to keep him company on his vigils. Watchman and Watchdog became a celebrated sight on the streets of the City. In 1858, Gray (Old Jock) died of tuberculosis, and was buried in old Greyfriars Churchyard, in Edinburgh. The distraught Bobby refused to leave his master's grave, whatever the weather (and believe me, Edinburgh has weather!).

The kirkyard gardener kindly built Bobby a shelter near to the grave. The loyal dog kept vigil near to his master for the next 14 years, until his own death in 1872.

Baroness Burdett-Coutts, President of the Ladies Committee of the RSPCA, was instrumental in the erection of a granite fountain in Bobby's memory. The fountain is crowned by a sculpture of this hero, created from life by William Brody. The fountain was unveiled in 1873. The memorial stands, proudly, to this day.

The headstone reads: *'Greyfriars Bobby - died 14 January 1872 - aged 16 years - Let his loyalty and devotion be a lesson to us all....'*

Indeed. And pause for thought.

ACKNOWLEDGEMENTS

The author is grateful for the following sources that are referenced in *Born to Run: The Story of Hector & Jason:*

Chapter 1
On the Origin of Species - Charles Darwin
A Rough Guide to the Future - Professor James Lovelock

Chapter 2
Memoirs - Lorenzo da Ponte
Mozart - the Golden Years - H C Robbins Landon

Chapter 5
The Voyage of the Beagle - Charles Darwin

Chapter 7
In Defence of Dogs - John Bradshaw
All about the Golden Retriever - Lucille Sawtrell
Running My Life - Sebastian Coe

Chapter 8
Barking Man - Madison Smartt Bell
Her Dog - Tobias Wolff

Chapter 12
Wolf Hall - Hilary Mantel

Chapter 13
I Bought a Mountain - Thomas Furbank

Chapter 16
How do we Fix this Mess? - Robert Peston
A History of the World - Andrew Marr

Chapter 18
Landscapes in France - A N Wilson
Normandy - Arthur Eperon

Chapter 19
The 59ᵗʰ Division - Peter Knight
D-Day - The Battle for Normandy - Antony Beevor
The Blue Guide to Normandy - John McNeill
British War Dogs - Lt.-Colonel E.H. Richardson

Chapter 22
French Provincial Cooking - Elizabeth David

Chapter 28
The Story of Music - Howard Goodall

Chapter 29
The Republic - Plato

Chapter 30
Thomas Hardy - Claire Tomalin

Part 4 - Pause for Thought:
The Golden Retriever - James E Walsh
Stonehenge People - Rodney Castleton
A Dogs' Miscellany - J A Wines
The Diary of Virginia Woolf, Volume 5
Encyclopaedia of the Dog
Three Men in a Boat - Jerome K Jerome

BV - #0036 - 110520 - C18 - 229/152/23 - PB - 9781913425098